SEPARABILITY AND AGGREGATION

SEPARABILITY AND AGGREGATION

Collected Works of W. M. Gorman
Volume I

Edited by

C. BLACKORBY and A. F. SHORROCKS

CLARENDON PRESS · OXFORD
1995

This book has been printed digitally and produced in a standard specification in order to ensure its continuing availability

OXFORD
UNIVERSITY PRESS

Great Clarendon Street, Oxford OX2 6DP

Oxford University Press is a department of the University of Oxford. It furthers the University's objective of excellence in research, scholarship, and education by publishing worldwide in

Oxford New York

Auckland Cape Town Dar es Salaam Hong Kong Karachi Kuala Lumpur Madrid Melbourne Mexico City Nairobi New Delhi Shanghai Taipei Toronto

With offices in

Argentina Austria Brazil Chile Czech Republic France Greece Guatemala Hungary Italy Japan South Korea Poland Portugal Singapore Switzerland Thailand Turkey Ukraine Vietnam

Oxford is a registered trade mark of Oxford University Press in the UK and in certain other countries

Published in the United States by Oxford University Press Inc., New York

Reprinted 2010

ISBN 978-0-19-828521-2

PREFACE

Terence Gorman has been a major figure in the development of economics during the past forty years. His publications on separability, aggregation, duality, and demand are recognized as fundamental contributions to economic theory. Many of his unpublished papers have achieved similar status as underground classics, eagerly sought by the *cognoscenti.* This volume brings together for the first time all of Gorman's important work on aggregation across commodities and agents, including separability, budgeting, representative agents, and the construction of capital and labour aggregates. A second volume, entitled *Modelling and Methodology* will cover topics on duality, demand, trade, and welfare.

About half of the material in this volume has not been published previously. In deciding which papers to include, and their order of appearance, we have attempted to indicate how the choice of topics, and the treatment of those topics, has evolved. This leads to a certain degree of duplication as some of the earlier ideas are developed more fully in later work. Nevertheless, readers should find something of interest in all the papers reproduced here. By way of assistance, each chapter except the first is preceded by an editorial introduction which describes its origin and place in the literature, as well as the main results themselves. These introductions are intended to serve as a reader's guide, but inevitably reflect the somewhat idiosyncratic views of the editors. The first chapter is Gorman's contribution to *The New Palgrave: A Dictionary of Economics* and represents his own summary of many of these issues.

In preparing this material for publication, we have had to make more than the usual number of editorial decisions. Many of the unpublished papers were never intended for publication, and are not fully polished products. Furthermore, some no longer exist in their original form: footnotes, diagrams and, on occasion, whole pages of text are missing. In other cases, the chapters are based on extracts from handwritten notes. We have tried to piece these together in a coherent fashion, sometimes making use of versions written, or amended, at different times. Some degree of consistency has been imposed in the way that sections, equations, and footnotes are numbered in the different chapters, even where this differs from the original publication. We have also taken the opportunity to correct typographical errors and inconsistencies in notation that came to our attention. However, apart from these cosmetic changes, the papers are just as written. No attempt has been made to adopt a single notation throughout; as a consequence, the notation used in the introductions also varies from one chapter to the next. Nor have we tried to fill gaps in the arguments, or to correct those arguments that are just plain wrong. Instead, editorial notes are used to draw attention to the problems, and to suggest how they might be overcome. This seems appropriate, since Terence Gorman has often argued that the process by which knowledge is accumulated is often as important as the knowledge itself. It is possible to proceed in this way because, to the best of our knowledge, all of the main theorems are correct, even when the arguments are faulty.

We are indebted to Terence for helping to identify errors, some of our making, in the draft chapters, and to Dan Primont for his help with a number of the typescripts that have survived in less than perfect shape. The introduction to Chapter 13 is due to Peter Simmons, and that of Chapter 16 to Bill Schworm. We have also been ably served by secretarial assistance from Julie Lord, Linda Day, and Tina Corsi. Much of the proof reading was done by Vassilios Kolliniatis, whose familiarity with the Greek alphabet was tested to the full. Finally, we owe thanks to the University of British Columbia, GREQE (EHESS), the University of Essex, and Southern Methodist University for the liberal use of their facilities.

Chuck Blackorby
Tony Shorrocks

August 1993

CONTENTS

PART I
Separability and Budgeting

PART I

SEPARABILITY AND BUDGETING

1

Separability

Suppose you were interested in the demand for tomatoes in Ireland. A few words with traders, producers, agricultural scientists, official statisticians, and anthropologists would provide a mass of 'facts' about that particular market, the data available, and the role of tomatoes in Irish culture, which would never occur to pure-minded economists. We commonly neglect such matters, assembling our models from stock components which may be incapable of catching what may, after all, be the essence of the problem we believe ourselves to be investigating.

To proceed differently we would need to be able to tailor models for particular problems and particular data. That is where separability, duality, and the idea of characteristics common to different phenomena, for instance, come in.

Separability is about the structure we are to impose on our model: what to investigate in detail, what can be sketched in with broad strokes without violence to the facts. Perfect competition and the absence of external economies, which allow us to examine the behaviour of individual firms in isolation; constant returns, permitting us to discuss the structure of a firm's production plans without knowing its size; Samuelson's independence axiom which says that how we use our resources when it shines is independent of how we would have had it rained; and Bergson's Social Welfare Function, based on the sovereignty of self-regarding households; all embodying separability assumptions, whose function is to allow us to examine one aspect of a problem in at least relative isolation from the others, given that we have posed it in terms of appropriate independent variables.

However, the classical locus of the data is in the theory of demand and the classical treatment in Leontief's two papers (1947*a*, 1947*b*) on functional structure; the first including a proof that addition is, in essence, the only really well-behaved associative operation; the second, a diagram showing that he realized the full implications of that fact, as spelled out below, in 1947.

Say that the vector x is *separable* in the utility function $f(\cdot)$ if $u = f(x, y) = F(\phi(x), y)$, say, where all the functions are *well behaved*; that is to say scalar valued, strictly increasing in their functional arguments, and continuous. Such an assumption might be appropriate were the goods X—in an obvious notation—closely related. In that case the Y might be broad aggregates, whose effect on the X needed to be sketched in.

Suppose that each of the vectors x_t, or better, of the *sectors* $t \in T$, is separable in $f(\cdot)$. Then and only then

$$u = f(x, y) = F(v, y), \tag{1}$$

either locally or globally according to the nature of the domain, where

$$x = (x_t)_{t \in T}, \quad v = (v_t)_{t \in T}, \quad v_t = f^t(x_t), \tag{2}$$

and the functions are well behaved, so that the sectors are jointly separable. Say that the function $f(\cdot)$ is *weakly separable*, whenever (1)–(2) hold, and *separable* when y is the null vector so that $u = f(x) = F(v)$.

One reason for postulating separability, first advanced by Strotz (1957), is that households may budget in two stages, first deciding how much, m_t, to allocate to each of the broad groups, leaving the final choice

$$x_i = \psi^i(p_t, m_t), \qquad \text{each } i \in t, \tag{3}$$

of how to spend it until the 'appropriate' prices $p_t = (p_i)_{i \in t}$, are known. Given that the right m_t were chosen at the first stage, a separable utility function would clearly lead to demands like (3), which in turn effectively implies separability. Everything therefore turns on the likelihood of the m_t being chosen well, and hence on the information needed to do so.

Strotz was formally wrong in assuming that we only need to know a single set of price indices, but essentially right. Should a household have converged on the correct m_t at some stage, perhaps in a period of stable prices, it would be able to update its budget continuously from then on, using two sets of differential indices of the form $\mathrm{d}P_t/P_t = \sum_{i \in t} w_i \mathrm{d}p_i/p_i$, one, a Divisia index with the weights $w_i = p_i x_i/m_t$, to deflate the money expenditures m_t, the other, using the corresponding marginal expenditure pattern $w_i = p_i \partial x_i/\partial m_t$, to allow for substitution between goods. To budget in real terms, then, only the second set is needed. This is because (3), coupled with their symmetry, implies that the substitution effects

$$\begin{aligned} \sigma_{ij} = \delta x_i/\delta p_j &= \lambda_{rs} \partial x_i/\partial m_r \cdot \partial x_j/\partial m_s \\ &= \mu_{rs} \partial x_i/\partial m \cdot \partial x_j/\partial m, \text{ say,} \end{aligned} \tag{4}$$

each $i \in r$, $j \in s \neq r$, where the δ's denote compensated derivatives as Pearce (1961) showed. The λ's and μ's are symmetrical, the former being intergroup substitution effects.

If households do budget in two stages, it is probably to save hassle, even at the cost of mistakes—so that (4) would hold only approximately. Given the quantity and quality of our data it would be well worth imposing nevertheless, to save degrees of freedom. Unfortunately it does not save enough in practice, so that Stone, Theil, and their colleagues in Cambridge and Rotterdam followed Frisch and his in Oslo in assuming *additive* utility[1]

$$u = f(x) = \sum f^t(x_t), \tag{5}$$

where $f(\cdot)$, and each $f^t(\cdot)$, is well behaved, in an appropriate normalization, as had the early utilitarians Bentham and Paley in their really rather sophisticated discussions, not to speak of Bernouilli, Ramsey, von Neumann, and Savage.[2] Indeed they commonly imposed *complete additivity*, with the x_t scalars, not just *groupwise additivity*. In either case, each set of sectors is clearly separable, so that

$$\mu_{rs} = \mu_{r,-r} = \mu_{-s,s} = \mu, \text{ say,} \tag{6}$$

where $-r = \{t \in T \mid t \neq r\}$, in (4).

The substitution effects as measured in these early studies were commonly very small—so small indeed that gross complementarity was the norm. If correct this would have had important implications for economic policy. Suspecting that this might reflect the approximate proportionality between own prices and income elasticities, pointed out in Pigou (1910), and commonly implied by (6), Deaton (1974) ran unrestricted regressions, finding no such tendency towards proportionality and much more substitition. Since then demand analysts, following Deaton and Muellbauer (1980*b*), have tended to forgo additivity, except over time, and use composite commodities, a generalization of quasi-homothetic separability as defined below, instead.

Slutsky had shown in his classic article that the marginal utility of at most one good increases near a chosen point in the case of complete additivity. If one does, all the other goods are inferior, which is frequently unacceptable, so that we can commonly assume each $f^t(\cdot)$ concave, implying that all the goods are normal and substitutes for each other, points of importance in both theoretical and empirical work.

Since additivity plays such a large role in the theoretical analyses of choice over time, under uncertainty, and by benevolent governments, it is worth discussing further. Equation (6) suggests that it will hold if each set of sectors is separable, as Debreu (1960) proved for rather general product spaces, beyond which it can readily be extended. Indeed it looks as if it should be enough that each set $-t$ were separable, a particular case of a general result that we need only a few sets to be separable for all to be if they overlap enough. This follows from the fact that addition is, in effect, the only strictly increasing continuous associative operation, so that $f(x, y, z) = G(g(x, y), z) = H(x, h(y, z))$, implies that it can be written as

[1] See e.g. Stone (1954), Theil (1975, 1976), and Frisch (1959).
[2] See Bernouilli (1738), Ramsey (1931), and Savage (1954).

$F(a(x) + b(y) + c(z))$, where each function is well behaved. Because of this it is frequently easy to dream up plausible, easily understood assumptions to justify additivity in an appropriate normalization.

Consider, for example, a benevolent government, facing uncertainty, interested only in the welfare of its self-centred citizens. Let x_{is} be the consumption vector for individual i in state s. The rows of the corresponding grid are separable, and so are the columns if it satisfies a weak form of Samuelson's independence axiom, which many would say is a minimal condition for rationality. These overlap a great deal more than needed to imply

$$W = f(x) = \sum_{is} f^{is}(x_{is}) = \sum_i v_i = \sum_s w_s, \text{ say,} \tag{7}$$

in an appropriate normalization, where $v_i = \sum_s f^{is}(x_{is})$, is i's welfare, *ex ante*, and $w_s = \sum_i f^{is}(x_{is})$, society's, *ex post* in state s: Savage and Bentham at a blow, if you like, with state-dependent preferences, too.

This does not say that individual utility functions are additive, but that the government cannot act rationally—in the sense of the weak independence axiom—on the basis of a Bergson Social Welfare Function, if they are not. Even if we applied that axiom to the individuals, it would imply only separability, not additivity. This paradox is not unduly worrying here, because a stronger form of Samuelson's axiom which is also widely accepted would imply additivity if applied to individual utility functions.

Look therefore at another case. The future is separable in a utility function iff it can be written $u_t = f_t(x_t, u_{t+1})$, $t = 0, 1, \ldots$. Apply this to the social welfare function instead, and we get (7) once again, though there is no obvious justification for additivity over time in the case of individuals.

That a set of axioms implies additivity is as likely to be evidence against them as for it.

Separability is often used in the analysis of market choices, for which prices are the natural independent variables. It is therefore useful that additivity is readily specified in the dual. Appropriately generalized, Slutsky's result implies that any reasonable additive quasi-concave utility $f(\cdot)$ is concave, so that its component functions $f^t(\cdot)$ are too. It can therefore be represented by its profit function

$$g(p, q) = \sup\{qf(x) - p \cdot x\} = \sum_t g^t(p_t, q),$$

where $g^t(\cdot)$ is that corresponding to $f^t(\cdot)$, and q, the shadow price of utility, is the inverse of the marginal utility of expenditure. Moreover

$$x_i = -g_i(p, q) = -g_i^t(p_t, q), \qquad \text{each } i \notin t,$$

$$u = g_0(p, q) = \sum_t g_0^t(p_t, q), \tag{8}$$

under strict quasi-concavity, where subscripts stand for derivatives, and 0 corresponds to q.

The only disadvantage with completely additive utility, then, is that it does not fit the facts. Can it be adapted to do so?

Under it

$$f'^{i}(x_i) = \lambda p_i = \mu r_i; \tag{9i}$$

$$x_i = -g_i^i(p_i, q) = -h'^{i}(\mu r_i), \tag{9ii}$$

by (5), (8), and homogeneity, where λ is the marginal utility of expenditure, $\mu = \lambda m = \mu(r)$, $r_i = p_i/m$, $h^i(z) = g^i(z, 1)$, and the prime denotes differentiation.

Pollak (1972) defined *generalized additive separability* as yielding demand curves of the form

$$x_i = \alpha^i(r_i, \rho(r)); \qquad \text{that is,} \qquad r_i = \beta^i(x_i, \xi(x)), \text{ say.} \tag{10}$$

The Slutsky conditions yield a complicated set of partial differential equations here, because the compensating change in m alters each of the r's. Not surprisingly, therefore, it yields several distinct classes of solution. However the largest and most interesting has utility functions

$$u = \sum f^i(\xi x_i) - \phi(\xi) = \sum h^i(\rho r_i) - \theta(\rho). \tag{11}$$

ξ, then, is costly to produce, in terms of utility, but increases the *effective quantity* of each good from x_i to $x_i^* = \xi x_i = \xi(x)x_i$ while its *effective price* becomes $r_i^* = \rho r_i = \rho(r)r_i$. One might expect that $\rho\xi = 1$, were it not for (9ii) which suggests $\rho\xi = \mu$, instead. This is correct; utility, not money income, is the appropriate numeraire here. The corresponding quantities demanded and 'prices' offered are $x_i^* = \xi(x)x_i = -h'^{i}(\rho(r)r_i) = -h'^{i}(r_i^*)$; $r_i^* = \rho(r)r_i = f'^{i}\xi(x)x_i) = f'^{i}(x_i^*)$, which is satisfying and is paralleled by $\xi = -\theta'(\rho)$, $\rho = -\phi'(\xi)$ in a trivial normalization.

I have not seen this system tried, which is a pity, since it is easily understood, is related to a leading theoretical model, and would be very useful should it fit. μ, too, is dimension free, given the utility function, as is $r_j x_j$—a further advantage of this formulation.

Pollak suggests corresponding generalizations of groupwise additivity and straightforward separability, which can also be interpreted in terms of decentralization, reminiscent of two-stage budgeting.

We have already seen that additive utility does not stand up in empirical demand analysis, and it is easily shown that separable utility cannot in general be simply represented in the dual, unless the *component functions* $f^t(\cdot)$ are *quasi-homothetic*, that is to say have cost functions which may be written

$$m_t = g^t(p_t, v_t) = a^t(p_t)v_t + b^t(p_t), \text{ say,} \tag{12}$$

in an appropriate normalization. Say that $(\cdot)$ is *quasi-homothetically separable* in such cases. Its cost function $g(p, u) = G(a(p), u) + b(p)$, say, where $G(\cdot, u)$ is that corresponding to $F(\cdot)$, $a(p) = (a^t(p_t))_{t \in T}$, because $a^t(p_t)$ is the marginal cost, or shadow price, of V_t, and $b(p) = \sum_{t \in T} b^t(p_t)$.

This is a useful result for three reasons. First, given strict quasi-concavity, it implies that

$$x_i = G_t a_i^t(p_t) + b_i^t(p_t) = v_t a_i^t(p_t) + b_i^t(p_t),$$

each $i \in t$, where $G_t = \partial G / \partial a^t$, by which (12) yields

$$x_i = (m_t - b^t(p_t))a_i^t(p_t) + b_i^t(p_t), \tag{13}$$

so that both stages in the decision process are easily carried out, and analysed; secondly because (12) may be taken as a Taylor approximation around a 'typical' value of v_t to a general cost function; and thirdly because it not only implies that the Engel curves are straight lines as in (13) but is implied by it, so that separable quasi-homothetic functions are quasi-homothetically separable.

Turn now to production theory, and let u be the firm's output. Businessmen, accountants, operations research workers, and statisticians who work in the field all talk of overhead, and variable costs, fixed per unit of output up to near capacity; that is, quasi-homothetic production functions; if these are separable, then they are quasi-homothetically separable.

Return again to utility theory. Long ago Hicks interpreted the $f^t(\cdot)$ in (1)–(2) as production functions for intermediate goods V_t, 'produced' in the household, or human body, from the physical goods we buy, and themselves yielding utility. If these are anything like the businessman's production functions, the utility function will be quasi-homothetically separable or nearly so.

Quasi-homotheticity is at once empirically plausible, at least as an approximation, analytically tractable, at least for those who can handle the dual, and apt to turn up in the solution of puzzles. Here accordingly is a little more about its interpretation.

Clearly $b^r(p_t) = g^t(p_t, 0)$ in (12), and so may be regarded as representing overhead costs, just as $a^t(p_t)$ does variable or prime costs per unit of 'output'. As a cost function $b^t(\cdot)$ is closed concave *conical*; that is, positively homogeneous of degree one. Suppose v_t is unbounded above; then $a^t(\cdot)$ is closed concave conical too. It may therefore be interpreted as a unit cost function corresponding to an *activity* yielding constant returns and running at the level v_t. Call the conical production functions corresponding to these unit costs functions $\alpha^t(\cdot)$, $\beta^t(\cdot)$. Then $v_t = f^t(x_t) = \sup\{\alpha^t(y_t) \mid \beta^t(z_t) \geqslant 1, y_t + z_t \leqslant x_t\}$, so that it is in itself separable in a slightly generalized sense. Moreover $\alpha^t(\cdot)$, $\beta^t(\cdot)$, being conical, may certainly be regarded as the quantitites of composite goods, A_t, B_t, an interpretation which I will often use below, and one which underlies much modern demand analysis. Strictly, of course, it is available only when $a^t(\cdot)$ is concave. Equally well, it is only needed because most of us continue to think more naturally in the primal. The important thing about $\alpha^t(\cdot)$ is that it generates an expenditure pattern $a'^t(p) = (a_i^t(p))$ each i at the margin, whether or not $\alpha^t(\cdot)$ is concave.

So far I have only discussed the extreme cases of separability—that in which none of the separable sets overlaps or even intersects, and that in which they overlap as much as possible. What if we are given a general collection of separable sets $A \subseteq T$?

It yields a utility tree, each node being either weakly separable, as in (1)–(2), or additive, as in (5), so that a knowledge of these two polar cases is in fact all that we need. Note that, since a quasi-homothetic separable function is quasi-homothetically separable, quasi-homotheticity is inherited from any function in this tree to its component functions and hence to their components and so on. If, therefore, the top node is quasi-homothetically separable, so is every node, and the dual representation follows immediately from the primal.

Businessmen talk of overheads and variable costs, economists of constant returns. That is, we neglect the overheads. This is partly because overheads raise difficulties for perfect competition, and partly because they cannot easily be represented in the primal. Despite apparent unreality, constant returns are historically important; they also emerge as the solution to various theoretical puzzles. The corresponding concept here is *homothetic separability*—the special case of quasi-homothetic separability in which we can take each $b^t(p_t) = 0$, or, equivalently, each $f^t(\cdot)$ conical. Everything I said about quasi-homothetic separability holds for homothetic separability. The Engel curves in question are, of course linear—straight lines through the origin—rather than merely affine, so that the income elasticity of demand for each good in the same sector is the same. If we think of these as being closely related goods, that is commonly unacceptable in utility theory, where different models of the 'same' good correspond roughly to different income levels.

If some postulates turn out to imply homothetically separable utility, check carefully before accepting them.

Another way of bringing duality and separability to bear on the same problem is to work with the distance function $h(x, u) = k$ if $u = f(x/k)$, introduced into economics by Malmquist (1953) as a measure of the standard of living compared with a norm u, but also underlying Debreu's (1951) coefficient of resource utilization. It is clearly conical, and so may be called the *conical representation* of preferences. It is concave iff $f(\cdot)$ is quasi-concave, and is then easily shown to be the full dual of the cost function $g(p, u)$, so that

$$g(p, u) = \inf\{p \cdot x \mid h(x, u) \geqslant 1\},$$

$$h(x, u) = \inf\{x \cdot p \mid g(p, u) \geq 1\}, \tag{14}$$

for instance. The corresponding separability concept is *quasi-separability* which holds when

$$h(x, u) = H(v, u); \qquad v = (v_t)_{t \in T}; \qquad v_t = h^t(x_t, u), \tag{15}$$

are well behaved, in which case the cost function $g(p, u) = G(w, u)$, where $w = (w_t)_{t \in T}$, $w_t = g^t(p_t, u)$, and $G(\cdot)$, $H(\cdot)$, and each pair $g^t(\cdot)$, $h^t(\cdot)$, are duals, so that

$$x_i = g_i(p, u) = G_t g_i^t(p_t, u) = v_t g_i^t(p_t, u), \tag{16}$$

each $i \in t$, in the obvious notation, and a compensated change in the price of a good causes the demand for each good in any other group to change in the same proportion, as with homothetic separability, and for the same reason, but less objectionably because real income u has remained constant, so that there is no immediate difficulty about luxuries, conventional necessities, and inferior goods being in the same group. Nevertheless, quasi-separable tastes seem to me somewhat unlikely. They do however emerge as the solution of various technical problems. I stumbled upon them myself, for instance, when discussing a problem in decentralization.

Note that (16) yields an analogue of (4): the substitution effect

$$\sigma_{ij} = \delta x_i/\delta p_j = \mu_{rs} x_i x_j \qquad \text{when } i \in r, j \in s \neq r, \tag{17}$$

where

$$\mu_{rs} v_r v_s = G_{rs} = \delta v_r/\delta w_s = \delta v_s/\delta w_r, \qquad r \neq s, \tag{18}$$

is the intergroup substitution effect. Note that (4) and (17) are equivalent iff tastes are homothetically separable.

So far u has been a scalar. This is quite unnecessary. Consider, for example, a short-run technology $S(u)$, where $u \geq 0$ is a vector of fixed inputs. Its *conical representation* $h(x, u) = \inf\{k \mid x \in kS(u)\}$, is indeed conical in x, defines $S(u)$ exactly if it is closed, and is concave in x iff $S(u)$ is convex, under normal assumptions. Equations (14)–(18) go through just as before. Indeed u might contain a complete description of the firm and its endowment, or, in the case of a household, of all its relevant characteristics—including for instance its composition—as well as the utility level, or the levels for the different individuals in it.

So far we have considered concepts of separability of preferences related to two modes of specification: the utility and distance functions. Many others of the form $k(x, u) = 1$, are possible, to each such there corresponds a separability concept

$$k(x, u) = K(v, u); \qquad v = (v_t)_{t \in T}; \qquad v_t = k^t(x_t, u), \tag{19}$$

where the functions are well behaved. Most are uninteresting, largely because they do not relate easily to the dual, except in a special case which bears much the same relation to quasi-homothetic separability as quasi-separability does to homotheticity. Another relates to the representation, $y = -k(x, u)$, which is sometimes convenient, particularly if Y is in some sense a natural numeraire and we have reduced the economy to two sectors, its advantage being that the price $p_i = k_i(x, u)$, each i. The separability concept (19) with this $k(\cdot)$ sometimes turns up in theoretical investigations, for instance in the theory of taxation.

Another possibility is to start from the indirect utility function, considered either as a function of $r = p/m$, as by Pollak above, or of (p, m).

Separability, then, is an organizing idea, to be deployed in a form appropriate to the problem under discussion. To do that effectively, one has to have played about with it enough to be able to guess where a particular concept may lead when combined with other assumptions, and how to get there. Now most economic series deal with aggregates, commonly taken to be over independent agents acting competitively. It is to separability in that context that I will now turn.

Here the classical problem is the measurement of the quantity, $v = k(u)$, of Capital in an economy, where $u = (u_f)_{f\in F}$, $x = \sum_{f\in F} x_f$, give the *endowments of fixed inputs*, and *net outputs of current goods* in the economy, F, as a whole; u_f, x_f, in firm f.

I will sketch the basic arguments in this context, and in the remarkably similar problem of measuring the quantity of Labour, though they can be deployed much more widely to yield similar results, suggesting natural generalizations of *classical separability* as used above, until it effectively becomes equivalent to the use of composite goods, as in modern demand analysis.

To state the problem of measuring Capital formally in terms of classical separability, say that v is a *perfect measure* of it if the equation of the production frontier may be written

$$\Phi(x, v) = 1, \qquad \text{where} \quad v = k(u), \tag{20}$$

where $\Phi(\cdot)$ and $k(\cdot)$ are well behaved, and $k(\cdot)$ is strictly increasing, though this last is unnecessarily strong.

Now bring to bear the fact that F is made up of perfectly competing firms. I will require that there are no external effects, though that can be weakened to allow, for example, for public fixed inputs. Hence the *short-run technology* for the economy F as a whole $S(u) = \sum S^f(u_f)$, where $S^f(u_f)$ is that for f. This simple additive structure is best exploited here by using the *gross profit functions* $h(p, v) = g(p, u) = \sum g^f(p, u_f)$, which have the advantage of being scalar rather than set valued. Sometimes it is better to use the *net supply functions* which add up in the same way. That they are vector valued leads to difficulties with the inversion below, which sometimes implies that the results are only local in p, but it does allow us to deal with more complicated problems.

The crucial point in each case is that current goods are represented by their prices rather than their quantities. That is what is to be expected: it is by having common shadow prices that the individual firms are kept in line, and total output kept on the production frontier; and, by holding prices constant we can observe the effects of changing the endowments of one firm in isolation. This suggests that some sort of separability in a dual may emerge as the basic notion, as indeed it will.

I will now show that there exist perfect Capital measures $v_f = k^f(u_f)$, such that $v = \sum v_f$, in an appropriate normalization, in terms of which the gross profit functions may be written

$$g^f(p, u_f) = a(p)v_f + b^f(p), \quad g(p, u) = a(p)v + b(p) \tag{21}$$

where $b(p) = \sum b^f(p)$. If we take v_f as a measure of the *scale* at which f operates, and $-b^f(p)$ of its overheads, this is reminiscent of what businessmen say. That is agreeable, as is the fact that the quantities, v_f, of Capital in the individual firms, add up to that, v, in the economy as a whole. At first glance the fact that the shadow price $a(p)$ of Capital is automatically the same in each firm is also agreeable. At the second, not so. Give any firm enough extra equipment to raise its profits by \$M, and it will produce exactly $a_i(p)/a(p)$ more of good i, so that each has the same marginal production plan: about as unrealistic an assumption as one could imagine for a natural economy.

'What would you expect', Mrs Robinson would have asked, 'if you attempt anything so absurd as measuring Capital?' Unfortunately, precisely the same problem arises if one tries to measure Labour, or for that matter, the production of Food, or Plastic goods. This is less surprising when we realize that (20) can be solved for $v = \phi(x)$, say, and the corresponding equation for firm f for $v_f = \phi^f(x_f)$, so that

$$k^f(u_f) = v_f = \phi^f(x_f), \quad k(u) = v = \phi(x), \tag{22}$$

and v_f, v may just as well be taken as a measures of Production as of Capital. Indeed it is in that role that (21) is equivalent to quasi-homothetic separability. Think of V as an intermediate good, produced from fixed inputs and itself defining the scale of current production. Given appropriate convexity, indeed, $a(\cdot)$ is the unit profit function of an activity which runs at level v_t in t.

Next for the 'proof'. It consists of four stages, of which only the third leads to problems in more complicated cases.

(*a*) Take a *base endowment vector* $\bar{u} = (\bar{u}_f)_{f \in F}$, define *base profits* $b^f(p) = g^f(p, \bar{u}_f)$, $b(p) = \sum b^f(p) = g(p, \bar{u})$, and the *quasi-rents*

$$r^f(p, u_f) = g^f(p, u_f) - b^f(p); \qquad s(p, v) = h(p, v) - b(p), \tag{23}$$

to get

$$s(p, v) = \sum r^f(p, u_f) = r^f(p, u_f) \qquad \text{when } u_{-f} = \bar{u}_{-f}, \tag{24}$$

so that this trick has allowed us to bring the existence of an economy-wide measure of Capital to bear on the individual firms.

(*b*) Define the quasi-rents,

$$v^* := s(\bar{p}, v) = \sum r^f(\bar{p}, u^f) =: \sum v_f^*, \tag{25}$$

earned at standard prices $\bar{p}$, as tentative measures of the quantities of Capital.

(*c*) Invert (25) to get $v = \theta(v^*) = \theta(\sum v_f^*)$, say, and substitute into (24) to get

$$s(p, v) = s^*\left(p, \sum v_f^*\right) = \sum r^f(p, u_f) = \sum s^*(p, v_f^*), \text{ say}, \tag{26}$$

by (25).

(*d*) Equation (26) is Cauchy's equation. $s^*(p, \cdot)$ is both continuous and strictly increasing. Either would imply that its solution is $s^*(p, v^*) = a(p)v^*$, say. Substituting this into (23), using (24), and dropping the asterisks we get (21) as required.

Now Cauchy's functional equation yields linearity when v is a vector, too. It is therefore unsurprising that there exist perfect measures, $v_{ft} = k^{ft}(u_{ft})$, such that $v_t = \sum_f v_{ft}$, in an appropriate normalization, for each firm, if $v = (v_t)_{t \in T}$ is a vector of perfect measures of Land, Structures, and Equipment, for instance, so that (20) holds with $v_t = k^t(u_t)$, all in an obvious notation, and that this happens iff $g^f(p, u_f) = \sum_t a^t(p)v_{ft} + b^f(p)$, which lends itself to the same interpretation as (22), and is just as unrealistic, for the same reasons, unless we choose separate classes for fixed inputs for every industry, or process, which defeats the purpose of such aggregates in most cases.

Turn now to aggregates $v_f = k^t(x_t)$, for classes $t \in T$ of current goods: say Labour, Plastic goods, Services, . . . Here one works with the supply functions instead of the gross profit functions. Since I will deal with labour, I will use the input demand function instead. Hold prices constant throughout the argument as before. First give a particular firm f enough additional fixed inputs to persuade it to spend an extra \$M on labour, called t. It will increase its demand for the various types of labour by a vector Δx_{ft}. Now go back to square one. Give firm $g \neq f$ fixed inputs leading to it spending an extra \$M on labour instead. It would change its demand by Δx_{gt}. The economy-wide demand for labour, x_t, has changed by the same amount, Δx_t in each case. Hence $\Delta x_{gt} = \Delta x_t = \Delta x_{ft}$—exactly what worried us earlier.

However we can go further. Keeping all the other firms in their original positions, but leaving g with its gift, give it a further such, leading to a further increase $\Delta' x_{gt}$, say, in its demand vector for labour. This is the same increase as would have occurred if f had had a corresponding gift. But f is in the same position as it was initially, hence its change would once again be Δx_{ft}. Hence, $\Delta' x_{gt} = \Delta x_{ft} = \Delta x_{gt}$, so that the Engel curves for labour, for instance, are straight lines. Measuring quantities as net supplies again, we get

$$g_i^f(p, u_f) = a_i^t(p_t)v_{ft} + b_i^f(p), \qquad \text{each } i \in t, \tag{27}$$

easily, as one would expect. Integrating yields

$$g^f(p, u_f) = R^f(a(p), u_f) + b^f(p), \text{ say,}$$

where $a(p) = (a^t(p_t))_{t\in T}$. We can clearly normalize so that $b^f(p) = g^f(p, \bar{u}_f)$, the gross profits available at the base endowments $\bar{u}_f$, as in the case of Capital, so that $R^f(a(p), u_f) = r^f(p, u_f)$, the quasi-rents due to having u_f instead of $\bar{u}_f$. Multiplying (27) by p_i, adding and using the fact that the a's and b's are conical, we get $R^f(a(p), u_f) = \sum_t a^t(p_t)\, v_{ft}$, so that $v_{ft} = R_t^f(a(p), u_f) = \partial R^f/\partial a^t = 0$ when $u_f = \bar{u}_f$, which is highly agreeable, a^t being the common shadow price of V_t. However, we do not have $v_{ft} = k^{ft}(x_{ft})$, in the obvious notation, in general, though we do if returns are constant in the long run, or if $g^f(p, u_f) = 0$ for some u_f in its domain.

Two points emerge: that measuring Labour is quite as unrealistic as measuring Capital under these assumptions; and that the appropriate separability concept may be that of the quasi-rent function, as, indeed, it often is.

Household behaviour can be analysed in the same way, where u_h will commonly be a vector of h's characteristics, and the conclusion, that each behaves in the same way at the relevant margin, is comparably unreasonable.

Separability as we have defined it so far, then, is not well adapted to the aggregative data with which we commonly have to work. What if each variable were allowed to enter into the basic model through several channels, rather than just one?

Once again, I will begin with Capital theory and suppose that the endowment u of fixed inputs effects the short-run production possibilities $S(u)$ through a vector $v = (v_t)_{t\in T}$ of intermediate variables. There are two main cases

$$v_t = k^t(u); \tag{28i}$$

$$v_t = k^t(u, p). \tag{28ii}$$

Think of v as not just intermediate variables, but quantities of intermediate goods. In each case then $v \in S^*(u)$, say, the *upstream technology*. In (28i),

v is determined once u is known—a case of generalized fixed coefficients if you like. In (28ii), it may be chosen from $S^*(u)$ in the light of the prices p of the ultimate products. In each case we deal with an appropriate set of $\#T$ net supply equations. Commonly those can only be inverted locally, but the rest of the argument (*a*)–(*d*) above goes though as before since Cauchy's equation yields linearity for vector-valued functions too. We therefore get that corresponding intermediate variables v_{ft} exist for each firm, with corresponding shadow prices $a^t(p)$, $\sum_f v_{ft} = v_t$ in an appropriate normalization, and the quasi-rent functions

$$r^f(p, u_f) = \sum_t a^t(p)v_{ft}; \qquad v_{ft} = k^{ft}(u_f), \text{ say,} \tag{29i}$$

$$r^f(p, u_f) = R^f(a(p), u_f) = \sum_t a^t(p)v_{ft}, \tag{29ii}$$

since $v_{ft} = R^f_t(a(p), u_f)$. Note now that the vector $v_f = (v_{ft})_{t \in T}$ can be interpreted either as giving several measures of Capital; or as the levels at which the corresponding activities $a^t(\cdot)$ are run: measures either for Capital or Current Goods, as in the initial scalar case (22).

Equations (29) look very like our previous results. Nevertheless they are, on the face of it, far less obviously unrealistic, because a gift of a piece of equipment will lead to a change $\sum_t \Delta v_{ft} a'^t(p)$ in f's net output vector x_f, which depends on how it affects the individual v_{ft}, and so may be quite different in different firms.

Equation (28i) was applied to Sri Lankan households by Deaton in 1980 with considerable success. Since we cannot observe utility levels, household income, m_h, is one of the components of its characteristic vector u_h. Since it is the only characteristic which interests us at the moment, incorporate the others into the label h. Then there exist functions $v_{ht} = k^{ht}(m_h)$ for each household for which the household demand functions are of the form $x_{hi} = \sum_t v_{ht} a^{hti}(p) + b^{hi}(p)$. That these should be homogeneous of degree zero in (p, m_h) already implies a lot; Slutsky a lot more. Indeed it almost turns out that the indirect utility function is of the form

$$\alpha(p) + \beta(p)/[1 - (m/\gamma(p))^\theta], \tag{30}$$

where θ is either real or a pure imaginary number, $\alpha(\cdot)$, $\beta(\cdot)$ are homogeneous of degree zero, and $\gamma(\cdot)$ of degree one, with log z replacing z^θ when $\theta = 0$, as in Deaton's application, where the budget shares are quadratic in log m. The surprising point is that it was on survey data—i.e. micro-data—that it proved itself, not on the macro-data for which it was designed, though it would obviously permit the use of both in investigating the same demand system.

Equation (30) makes no mention of the households' other characteristics. θ might even differ from one block of households to another. However, the natural case is that in which it does not, and we take $\alpha^h(p) = \alpha(p)$,

$\beta^h(p) = b_h\beta(p)$, $\gamma^h(p) = c_h\gamma(p)$, where b_h, c_h are the effective characteristics of h. These enter into the households' weighting system. That said, the corresponding aggregates v_t are appropriate averages of m_h, $m_h^{1-\theta}$, and $m_h^{1+\theta}$, or m_h, $m_h \log m_h$ and $m_h(\log m_h)^2$, respectively. $\theta = 1$ corresponds to demand functions quadratic in income, and appropriate averages of m_h and m_h^2. In other words, we are dealing in appropriate moments of the income distribution.

Equation (28ii) finds its obvious application in organization theory, where we may imagine a businessman building up an empire which he can rule by setting a relatively small number, $\#T$, of targets, and then letting the serfs get on with it. He would presumably do so by buying up this, and selling off that, until he had a viable organization. If so, the prices would have quasi-rent functions $R^f(a(p), u_f)$; his effective controls would not be the targets $v = (v_t)$, but a knowledge of the likely marginal profitabilities, or shadow prices, $a^t(p)$ of the various activities. These he, in the central office, would pass on to the factory managers, who would calculate the $v_{ft} = R_t^f(a(p), u_f)$, in the light of their detailed knowledge of their factory's plant, u_f. The specialist activity managers would be told these levels v_{ft} at which they should run their activities, and choose the net supply vectors $v_{ft}a'^t(p)$ in the light of their up-to-date knowledge of the appropriate prices in p. Given appropriate convexity, each stage would be a profit centre. Given time, the businessman would learn a good deal about the $R^f(\cdot, u_f)$, and hence where to direct his investment. Note the similarity with two-stage budgeting.

Many of these arguments were driven by varying the fixed inputs parametrically. In the long run there is none. As long as we confine ourselves to classical separability—scalar aggregates corresponding to different classes of goods—we can vary appropriate prices instead to get the same results as before, except in one anomalous case, from only slightly stronger assumptions. They are quite as unacceptable here, as you might argue, as is the assumption of perfect competition, or something very like it, which underlies much of this analysis, and which sits badly with the stress I put on overheads—hence my concentration on demand analysis, and the efficient organization of a firm.[3]

Another weakness in this résumé is the requirement of strict monotonicity. The maximum, or the minimum, of a pair of elements, is a continuous, increasing function of them. Each is a limiting case of additivity, but not additivity itself. Bliss (1975) in his book on Capital, and, more recently, Mak (1984) have done valuable work here.

Yet another is that I have confined myself to functional separability, though some of the functions are vector valued. If you reread my third paragraph, you will see that this is a distinctly special case. Even here, I have

[3] In terms of *shadow prices, p*.

neglected homogeneity in the main, and uniformity over time entirely, as well as Barten's work on nearly additive utility, Diewert's on flexible functional forms, Jorgenson's on translog functions, and, above all, that of Nataf, e.g. Fourgéaud and Nataf (1959), on demand and aggregation. More importantly still, I have had nothing to say about separability in complete models, where, incidentally, the aggregates appropriate to one sector very rarely are to others; or, like Fisher and more recently, Mak, about approximate separability. Nor have I taken account of possible statistical regularities, as Theil did admirably in the 1950s, and Stoker in the 1980s.

Should you want to go into functional separability more deeply, Blackorby, *et al.* (1978*a*) and, on the demand side, Deaton and Muellbauer (1980*a*) have full bibliographies as well as being well worth reading for their own sakes.

2

Two-Stage Budgeting

Editorial Remarks

This is the first of a series of papers on the general subject of budgeting. In general, budgeting refers to the rather vague notion that households, organizations, or governments first allocate a given total expenditure to various subsets of commodities, such as 'food', 'recreation', or 'saving'. Only after the allocations to these broad sectors have been specified, does the agent or organization decide how to split each sectoral expenditure among its component parts, such as the particular food commodities. This set of papers assumes that the agent or organization has a well-defined preference ordering over all relevant commodities, and hence the problems are cast in the context of consumer theory. It is worth noting, however, that this is done purely for expositional purposes. Reinterpreting the results in terms of a firm presents no special difficulties, and allows a variety of problems to be discussed.

'Two-Stage Budgeting' supposes that the correct intersector allocations have been made, and then shows that separability of that sector is necessary and sufficient for the resulting intrasector allocations to be optimal. The next paper—'Separable Utility and Aggregation'—assumes that each sector is separable, so that correct intrasector allocations can be made, and investigates the circumstances in which optimal intersector allocations depend only upon total expenditure and a price index for each sector. These indices are not assumed to be homogeneous or even homothetic. 'Consumer Budgets and Price Indices' poses the same question, but drops the separability assumption. These three papers complete this particular set of questions.

Another common budgeting rule assumes that the consumer allocates a fixed proportion of its expenditures to each sector, where that proportion may or may not depend upon prices. 'Professor Friedman's Consumption Function and the Theory of Choice' provides necessary and sufficient conditions for the optimality of this procedure. Finally, in 'Conditions for Generalized Additive Separability' Gorman determines the circumstances in which it would be optimal to make intrasector allocations that depend only upon sector-specific normalized prices and some function of all normalized prices.

Each of these papers makes precise a principle of budgeting frequently invoked without full recognition of its implications. Three of them have never been published before. The techniques employed remain novel even today, and the ideas in 'Consumer Budgets and Price Indices' have not appeared anywhere else in the literature.

The first version of this paper was presented during a series of lectures at LSE in 1967. This version was written for a workshop which Gorman and Sydney Afriat conducted at the University of North Carolina in 1970. It is clear, however, that most of the results were known fifteen years earlier, for much of its content was used in his 1959 paper 'Separable Utility and Aggregation'.

Editorial Summary

Suppose that a consumer has a well-behaved utility function with R separable groups or sectors of commodities; it can be written therefore as

$$U(x) = F(v^1(x_1), v^2(x_2), \ldots, v^R(x_R)), \tag{0.1}$$

where $x = (x_1, x_2, \ldots, x_R)$ and F is increasing in each argument. Facing prices p with income m, the consumer maximizes (0.1) subject to the budget constraint $p \cdot x \leqslant m$, obtaining demand functions

$$x_i = \phi^i(p, m) \tag{0.2}$$

which depend on all prices and income. It is easy to show that the separable structure in (0.1) implies, without loss of generality, that these demands can be written as functions of the prices in their own group, p_r, and expenditure on all commodities in that group, m_r; that is, (0.1) implies that the demand functions in (0.2) can be written as

$$x_i = f^i(p, m_r), \tag{0.3}$$

for all i in group r, for each group r. Therefore, separability rationalizes the idea of two-stage budgeting in the sense that if the agent knows the amount of money to be spent on a group and the prices in that group, then optimal demands can also be calculated. In this case, the consumer can first allocate money to each group without thinking about the detailed expenditure within that group. Then, using only information about prices in that group in addition to the group's income allocation, the consumer can correctly calculate the specific demands within the group. What is less obvious, but true, is that (0.3) implies (0.1). That is, separability is both necessary and sufficient for two-stage budgeting. This is the content of Section 2 of the paper.

Section 3 presents differential conditions on the demand functions that are necessary and sufficient for (0.1). These conditions had already been published by Pearce (1961) and by Goldman and Uzawa (1964); the proof given here is rather more straightforward.[1] These conditions are given by

$$\delta x_i/\delta p_j = \mu_{rs}(\partial x_i/\partial m)(\partial x_j/\partial m) \tag{0.4}$$

for i in group r, j in group s, and for $f \neq s$, where δ refers to a compensated derivative and ∂ to an uncompensated derivative. In this case it is easiest to think of μ_{rs}, x_i, and x_j as function of all prices and incomes.[2]

[1] Gorman clearly knew the results of Goldman and Uzawa because his files contain a referee's report on their paper along with a response by Uzawa in which he claims to be certain that Gorman is the referee. There are also several letters from Pearce on the subject.

[2] One may of course substitute (0.3) in if one wishes, for each m_r is a function of all prices and incomes.

The negative semi-definite property of the Hessian in prices of the expenditure function contains all the comparative static information in the demand functions. Section 4 demonstrates that this quadratic form can be broken down into within-group quadratic forms which are negative semi-definite and a between-group quadratic form which has the same property. This is equivalent to showing that if the utility function is quasi-concave and can be written as in (0.1), then each v^r, as well as F, can be chosen to be quasi-concave.

One of the problems with this type of two-stage budgeting is that the expenditure on each group, m_r, $r = 1, 2, \ldots, R$, is, in general, a function of all prices and income. However, it is clear that the rationale for this budgeting scheme is one of informational economy. If one has to solve the entire maximization problem in order to compute these group expenditure functions then there has been no saving at all. Gorman's solution to this problem is to suppose that prices are not changing too much from period to period, and hence that the consumer can update the intergroup allocations from the previous period without making excessively large errors. This is what he demonstrates in Section 5 using Divisia indices—the subject of a later paper.

Two Stage Budgeting

1. SUMMARY

Suppose that goods fall into R classes and that the demands for goods in group r may be written

$$x_i = f_i(p_r, m_r), \qquad i \in r,\ r = 1, 2, \ldots, R, \tag{1.1}$$

where $p_r = (p_r)_{i \in r}$ is a vector of the prices in that group, and m_r the total expenditure allocated to it. Then I will say that there is two-stage budgeting. I will show that two-stage budgeting is justified iff the utility function is separable, that is may be written

$$U(x) = F(v^1(x_1), v^2(x_2), \ldots, v^R(x_R)), \qquad x = (x_1, x_2, \ldots, x_R),^1 \tag{1.2}$$

will show that each is true iff the between-group Slutsky effects[2]

$$\delta x_i/\delta p_j = \mu_{rs}(\partial x_i/\partial m)(\partial x_j/\partial m), \qquad i \in r,\ j \in s,\ r \neq s, \tag{1.3}$$

will derive between and within-group Slutsky inequalities, and will show how changes in the first stage allocations $m_1, m_2, \ldots, m_R$ are determined.

2. TWO-STAGE BUDGETING AND SEPARABLE UTILITY

Let us assume that the utility function is *well behaved*—that is strictly increasing and quasi-concave. If it is separable, then we may take $F(\cdot)$ in (1.2) to be strictly increasing, and each of the specific satisfaction functions $v^1(\cdot), v^2(\cdot), \ldots, v^R(\cdot)$ well behaved, without loss of generality. Do so.

I will now prove

THEOREM: *If the utility function is well behaved, it is separable iff two-stage budgeting is justified.*[3]

PROOF: That separability justifies two-stage budgeting is obvious: given the allocations $m_1, m_2, \ldots, m_R$ to the groups, one obviously maximizes $v^r(x_r)$ subject to $p_r \cdot x_r \leq m_r$, each r, and this yields (1.1).

The converse is a little more difficult to prove.

[1] [eds.] Each x_r will commonly be a vector, conformable with p_r.
[2] I use δ to denote derivatives calculated with u held constant, i.e. compensated derivatives.
[3] i.e. if the optimal decision can be taken in this way.

The fundamental idea is to show that the demand functions (1.1) correspond to 'utility' functions $v^1(x_1), v^2(x_2), \ldots, v^R(x_R)$, which they therefore reveal. To do so it would have to satisfy, e.g., the weak axiom of revealed preference which is not easily verified. Instead, therefore, we proceed as follows.

Consider consumption vectors of the form $x = (\bar{x}_{-r}, x_r)$, where $\bar{x}_{-r}$ stands for fixed consumption off sector r. It will be chosen at some prices $p = (p_{-r}, p_r)$ and income $m = p \cdot x$, because $U(\cdot)$ is quasi-concave. Given $m_r = p_r \cdot x_r$, x_r will be chosen to maximize $v^r(x_r) = u(\bar{x}_{-r}, x_r)$ subject to $p_r \cdot x_r \leqslant m_r$. This maximization will yield

$$x_i = g^i(p, m_r \mid \bar{x}_{-r}), \qquad i \in r,\ r = 1, 2, \ldots, R. \tag{2.1}$$

This must agree with (1.1) at all (p_r, m_r) at which $g^i(\cdot \mid \bar{x}_{-r})$ is defined. If the conditions were such that it is defined at all $(p_r, m_r) > 0$, $g^i(p_r, m_r \mid \bar{x}_{-r}) \equiv f^i(p_i, m_r)$. Hence (1.1) would be derived from the 'utility' function $v^r(\cdot)$, which it would therefore reveal.[4] Since the conditional orderings on r given what happens off it are certainly representable by 'utility' functions, this would show that all of them are defined by the same 'utility' function $v_r(\cdot)$; that is, that sector r would be separable. Each sector being separable, so would be the utility function.

It remains to show that (2.1) is defined for each $(p_r, m_r) > 0$. We proceed as follows. Fix $\bar{x}_{-r}$. For any $(p_r, m_r) > 0$ maximize $v^r(x^r) = u(\bar{x}_{-r}, x_r)$ subject to $p_r \cdot x_r \leqslant m_r$. Using this Hicks aggregate for group r, set $u(x) = U^r(x_{-r}, m_r)$. $U^r(\cdot)$ is well behaved. Hence there are prices $(p_{-r}, 1)$ and income $m = p_{-r} \cdot \bar{x}_{-r} + m_r$ at which $(\bar{x}_{-r}, m_r)$ is chosen. In this arbitrary budgetary situation, x_i satisfies (2.1), which therefore holds for all $(p, m_r) > 0$ as required. This completes the proof.

COROLLARY: *Let* $x = (x_0, x_1, \ldots, x_R)$, *then* (1.1) *holds for each* $r = 1, 2, \ldots, R$ *iff*[5]

$$u(x) = F(x_0, v^1(x_1), \ldots, v^R(x_R)). \tag{2.2}$$

3. THE SLUTSKY CONDITIONS

Suppose that (1.1) holds. Then the effect of any change from outside group r on the demand for goods in it will be channelled through m_r. In particular this will be true of a compensated price change in another group. Hence[6]

[4] If the income elasticity of demand is unbounded, an extension of the usual method of revealed preference may be needed. See Gorman (1971).

[5] $F(\cdot)$ is continuous, $F(x_0, \cdot)$ strictly increasing, each $v^r(\cdot)$ well behaved.

[6] [eds.] Remember that ∂ represents the derivative of an uncompensated demand function while δ indicates the derivative of a compensated demand function.

$$\delta x_i/\delta p_j = (\partial x_i/\partial m_r)(\delta m_r/\delta p_j), \qquad i \in r, j \in s, r \neq s,$$
$$= (\partial x_j/\partial m_s)(\delta m_s/\delta p_i), \tag{3.1}$$

by symmetry. Dividing across by $(\partial m_i/\partial m_r)(\partial x_j/\partial m_s)$, we get

$$\frac{\delta m_r/\delta p_j}{\partial x_j/\partial m_s} = \frac{\delta m_s/\delta p_i}{\partial x_i/\partial m_r}, \qquad i \in r, j \in s, r \neq s,$$
$$= \lambda_{rs}, \text{ say}, \tag{3.2}$$

since the left-hand side is independent of i and the right-hand side is independent of j. Hence

$$\delta m_r/\delta p_j = \lambda_{rs}\partial x_j/\partial m_s, \qquad j \in s \neq r, \tag{3.3}$$

and

$$\delta x_i/\delta p_j = \lambda_{rs}(\partial x_i/\partial m_r)(\partial x_j/\partial m_s), \qquad i \in r, j \in s, r \neq s, \tag{3.4}$$

yielding

$$\delta x_i/\delta p_j = \mu_{rs}(\partial x_i/\partial m)(\partial x_j/\partial m), \qquad i \in r, j \in s, r \neq s, \tag{3.5}$$

where $\lambda_{rs} = \mu_{rs}(\partial m_r/\partial m)(\partial m_s/\partial m)$, $r \neq s$.

Clearly

$$\lambda_{rs} = \lambda_{sr}, \tag{3.6}$$

hence

$$\mu_{rs} = \mu_{sr}. \tag{3.7}$$

I will interpret (3.6) and (3.7) later. Meanwhile I will prove

THEOREM: *Condition* (3.5) *is necessary and sufficient for two-stage budgeting to be justified.*

PROOF: We have already seen that (1.1) implies (3.5). It remains to prove the converse. Now[7]

$$\partial x_i/\partial p_j = (\mu_{rs}\partial x_j/\partial m - x_j)\partial x_i/\partial m, \qquad i \in r, j \in s, r \neq s. \tag{3.8}$$

Multiply this by p_i and add over $i \in r$ to get

$$\partial m_r/\partial p_j = (\mu_{rs}\partial x_j/\partial m - x_j)\partial m_r/\partial m, \qquad j \in s \neq r. \tag{3.9}$$

Hence[8]

$$\partial x_i/\partial m = a^i \partial m_r/\partial m, \qquad \partial x_i/\partial p_j = a^i \partial m_r/\partial p_j, \text{ say}, \qquad i \in r, j \notin r, \tag{3.10}$$

[7] [eds.] To derive (3.8) substitute (3.5) into the Slutsky equation.
[8] [eds.] Divide (3.9) by (3.8) and cross-multiply.

so that[9]

$$\mathrm{d}x_i = \sum_{j\in r} (\partial x_i/\partial p_j - a^i \partial m_r/\partial p_j)\mathrm{d}p_j + a^i \mathrm{d}m_r \tag{3.11}$$

and, integrating[10]

$$x_i = f^i(p_r, m_r), \text{ say.} \tag{3.12}$$

COROLLARY 1: *Condition* (3.5) *is necessary and sufficient for separability.*

Suppose next that $x = (x_0, x_1, \ldots, x_R)$. Then we have

COROLLARY 2: *Condition* (3.5) *holds for* $r, s = 1, 2, \ldots, R$ *iff* (1.1) *holds for* $r = 1, 2, \ldots, R$ *iff* (2.2) *holds.*

Return now to (3.6). To interpret it we need to know the 'meaning' of λ_{rs}. To find this, multiply (3.3) by p_j and add over $j \in s$ to get

$$\lambda_{rs} = \sum_{j\in s} p_j \delta m_r/\delta p_j, \qquad r \neq s. \tag{3.13}$$

It is therefore the effect on m_r of an equi-proportional increase in the price of each good in group s, $s \neq r$. Let us define Hicks aggregates for each group. Then λ_{rs} is the compensated, or Slutsky, effect of a sth Hicks aggregate on the demand for the rth.[11] In other words (3.6), and equivalently (3.7), is the 'between-group Slutsky relation'.

So far we have not defined λ_{rr}. The corresponding definition would be the substitution effect of a compensated change in the price of the rth Hicks aggregate on the demand for itself. To find this, write $p_r = P_r q_r$, $X_r = q_r \cdot x_r = m_r/P_r$ yielding the compensated effect $\delta(m_r/P_r)/\delta P_r = (\delta m_r/\delta p_r)/P_r - m_r/P_r^2$. Now $\delta m_r/\delta P_r = \sum_{j\in r} p_j \delta m_r/\delta p_j$. Normalizing, therefore, so that $P_r = 1$ as before, we have

$$\lambda_{rr} = \sum_{j\in r} p_j \delta m_r/\delta p_j - m_r. \tag{3.14}$$

[9] [eds.] To derive (3.11), note that

$$\mathrm{d}x_i = \sum_{j\in r} \frac{\partial x_i}{\partial p_j} \mathrm{d}p_j + \sum_{j\notin r} \frac{\partial x_i}{\partial p_j} \mathrm{d}p_j + \frac{\partial x_i}{\partial m} \mathrm{d}m,$$

and hence, using (3.10),

$$\mathrm{d}x_i - \sum_{j\in r} \frac{\partial x_i}{\partial p_j} \mathrm{d}p_j = a^i \left[\sum_{j\notin r} \frac{\partial m_r}{\partial p_j} \mathrm{d}p_j + \frac{\partial m_r}{\partial p} \mathrm{d}m \right] = a^i \left[\mathrm{d}m_r - \sum_{j\in r} \frac{\partial m_r}{\partial p_j} \mathrm{d}p_j \right].$$

[10] For this to hold globally, the regions in which p_r, m_r are constant have to be arc-connected. Otherwise the result is only local.

[11] Their prices being normalized to be one at the point in question.

The m_r term arises from the fact that $m_r = p_r \cdot x_r$ will change by an amount $(P_r - 1)m_r$ when p_r changes to $P_r p_r$, even if there is no substitution.

With this definition

$$\sum_s \lambda_{rs} = \sum_j p_j \delta m_r / \delta p_j - m_r = 0, \tag{3.15}$$

since $m_r = h^r(p, u)$ is clearly homogeneous of degree one in p.[12]

4. THE SLUTSKY INEQUALITIES

Define the cost function

$$g(p, u) = \inf\{p \cdot x \mid u(x) \geqslant u\}, \tag{4.1}$$

so that the compensated demand functions are

$$x_i = g_i(p, u) = \partial g / \partial p_i, \tag{4.2}$$

and the Slutsky, or compensated, effects are

$$\delta x_i / \delta p_j = g_{ij} = \partial^2 g / \partial p_i \partial p_j. \tag{4.3}$$

Now the cost function can easily be shown to be concave, so that

$$\sum g_{ij} \theta_i \theta_j \leqslant 0, \qquad \text{each } \theta, \tag{4.4}$$

while

$$\sum g_{ij} p_i p_j = 0, \tag{4.5}$$

since $g(\cdot, u)$ is homogeneous of degree one. The former is the Slutsky inequality.

Let us now define cost functions.

$$g^r(p_r, v^r) = \inf\{p_r \cdot x_r \mid v^r(x_r) \geqslant v^r\}, \qquad r = 1, 2, \ldots, R, \tag{4.6}$$

for the specific satisfaction functions $v^1(\cdot), \ldots, v^R(\cdot)$. They, too, are concave and homogeneous, so that

$$\sum_{ij \in r} g^r_{ij} \theta_i \theta_j \leqslant 0, \qquad \text{each } r, \tag{4.7}$$

[12] [eds.] As $m = g(p, u)$, the expenditure function is homogeneous of degree one in prices, it follows that h^r, defined by

$$m_r = h^r(p, u) := m^r(p, g(p, u)),$$

is clearly homogeneous of degree one in prices as claimed.

$$\sum_{ij \in r} g^r_{ij} p_i p_j = 0, \qquad \text{each } r, \tag{4.8}$$

of which the former are the within-group Slutsky inequalities.

Finally we may define Hicks aggregates for each group. The concavity of the cost function for them[13] yields the between-group Slutsky inequality

$$\sum \lambda_{rs} \phi_r \phi_s \leqslant 0. \tag{4.9}$$

I will now prove the following theorem tying these results together.

THEOREM:

$$\sum g_{ij} \theta_i \theta_j = \sum_r \sum_{ij \in r} g^r_{ij} \theta_i \theta_j + \sum_r \sum_s \lambda_{rs} \left(\sum_{i \in r} \theta_i \partial x_i / \partial m_r \right) \left(\sum_{j \in s} \theta_j \partial x_j / \partial m_s \right) \tag{4.10}$$

PROOF:

$$g_{ij} = f^i_j + f^i_0 \delta m_r / \delta p_j, \qquad i, j \in r, \tag{4.11}$$

$$g^r_{ij} = f^i_j + f^i_0 x_j, \qquad i, j \in r, \tag{4.12}$$

where $f^i_j = \partial f^i / \partial p_j$, $f^i_0 = \partial f^i / \partial m_r$ in (1.1). Hence

$$g_{ij} = g^r_{ij} + f^i_0 (\delta m_r / \delta p_j - x_j). \tag{4.13}$$

Now

$$\begin{aligned} \delta m_r / \delta p_j &= \delta \left(m - \sum_{s \neq r} m_s \right) \Big/ \delta p_j, \\ &= x_j - \left(\sum_{s \neq r} \lambda_{rs} \right) \partial x_j / \partial m_r \\ &= x_j + \lambda_{rr} \partial x_j / \partial m_r, \qquad j \in r, \end{aligned} \tag{4.14}$$

by (3.3) and (3.15). Since $\partial x_i / \partial m_r = f^i_0$, (4.13) and (4.14) imply that

$$g_{ij} = g^r_{ij} + \lambda_{rr} (\partial x_i / \partial m_r)(\partial x_j / \partial m_r), \qquad i, j \in r, \tag{4.15}$$

which immediately yields (4.10).

COROLLARY: *Each of the* $R+1$ *quadratic forms in* (4.10) *is negative semi-definite.*

Note that we can derive (4.9) from (4.4) by setting $\theta_i = \lambda \phi_r p_i$, $i \in r$, each r.

[13] Corresponding to the utility function $U(X_1, \ldots, X_R)$ in the obvious notation.

5. ALLOCATION AT THE FIRST STAGE

Assume that the correct allocation is known at last period's prices p and income m. How can this be updated, assuming that p and m change smoothly?

THEOREM:

$$\mathrm{d}\log m_r/Q_r = \sum\nolimits_s \nu_{rs}\,\mathrm{d}\log P_s + \eta_r\,\mathrm{d}\log m/Q,\ \textit{say}, \tag{5.1}$$

where

$$\nu_{rs} = \lambda_{rs}/m_r, \quad \eta_r = (\partial m_r/\partial m)(m_r/m) \tag{5.2}$$

$$\mathrm{d}\log P_s = \mathrm{d}P_s/P_s = \sum_{j\in s} (\partial m_j/\partial m_s)(\mathrm{d}p_j/p_j) \tag{5.3}$$

$$\mathrm{d}\log Q_s = \mathrm{d}Q_s/Q_s = \sum_{j\in s} (m_j/m_s)(\mathrm{d}p_j/p_j) \tag{5.4}$$

$$\mathrm{d}\log Q = \mathrm{d}Q/Q = \sum (m_j/m)(\mathrm{d}p_j/p_j) = \sum (m_s/m)\mathrm{d}Q_s/Q_s \tag{5.5}$$

and

$$m_j = p_j x_j = \textit{expenditure on good } j. \tag{5.6}$$

PROOF:

$$\delta m_r/\delta p_j = \delta_{rs}x_j + \lambda_{rs}\partial x_j/\partial m_s, \qquad j\in s, \tag{5.7}$$

where δ_{rs} is Kronecker δ, by (3.3) and (4.14). Hence

$$\delta\log m_r/\delta\log p_j = \delta_{rs}m_j/m_s + \nu_{rs}\partial m_j/\partial m_s \qquad j\in s, \tag{5.8}$$

where $\nu_{rs} = \lambda_{rs}/m_r$ is the compensated elasticity of demand for the rth Hicks aggregate with respect to the price of the sth. Hence

$$\begin{aligned}\mathrm{d}\log m_r &= \sum(\delta\log m_r/\delta\log p_j)\mathrm{d}\log p_j + (\partial\log m_r/\partial m)\left(\mathrm{d}m - \sum x_j\mathrm{d}p_j\right)\\ &= \sum\nolimits_s \nu_{rs}\mathrm{d}\log P_s + \mathrm{d}\log Q_r + (\partial\log m_r/\partial\log m)(\mathrm{d}\log m - \mathrm{d}\log Q)\end{aligned} \tag{5.9}$$

yielding (5.1) immediately.[14]

[14] [eds.] Letting a sum with no running indices be over all prices yields

$$\mathrm{d}m_r = \sum \frac{\partial m_r}{\partial p_j}\mathrm{d}p_j + \frac{\partial m_r}{\partial m}\mathrm{d}m.$$

Remembering that

As long as the coefficients in (5.1) do not vary too greatly in the region observed, we may treat them as constant, and regard (5.1) as an equation to be fitted. Of the variables in it m_r/Q^r are directly observable, while the P's depend on the marginal propensities to spend on the various goods, which must be estimated by fitting (1.1). In fitting these we can use the within-group Slutsky conditions. Of course the estimated P's will be subject to a measurement error; with luck, small, since it is only a matter of the weights being wrong. The obvious solution is to use the Q's as instrumental variables. In doing so we should, of course, make use of the between-groups Slutsky conditions.

$$m_r \nu_{rs} = \lambda_{rs} = \lambda_{sr} = m_s \nu_{sr}. \tag{5.10}$$

Note the Q_r and Q are Divisia price indices. Appropriately weighted the corresponding quantity indices X_r, X equal m_r/Q_r, m/Q in an appropriate normalization. We may therefore write (5.1) in the form

$$\mathrm{d} \log X_r = \sum \nu_{rs} \mathrm{d} \log P_s + \eta_r \mathrm{d} \log X \tag{5.11}$$

should we wish to do so.

$$m_r = m_r(p, m) = m_r(p, g(p, u)) = m_r(p, u),$$

in a slight abuse of notation, and differentiating with respect to p_j yields

$$\frac{\partial m_r}{\partial p_j} + \frac{\partial m_r}{\partial m} g_j = \frac{\delta m_r}{\delta p_j}.$$

Using the fact that $g_r(p, u) = x_i$ in the above expression and substituting the result in the definition of $\mathrm{d}m_r$ above yields

$$\mathrm{d}m_r = \sum \frac{\delta m_r}{\delta p_j} \mathrm{d}p_j - \sum x_j \frac{\partial m_r}{\partial m} \mathrm{d}p_j + \frac{\partial m_r}{\partial m} \mathrm{d}m.$$

Converting this to logs yields (5.9), and substituting (5.8) into the result finishes the task.

3

Separable Utility and Aggregation

Editorial Remarks

This article has an amusing history. When Gorman was visiting MIT, he was asked by Robert Solow to referee an article by R. H. Strotz which had been submitted to *Econometrica*. He wrote the report the same evening and gave it to Solow the next day. Unfortunately it was handwritten, probably not as clear as one might have wished, and, to make matters worse, covered with strawberry jam from his breakfast. Any one of these factors may have caused Solow to ignore the report. In any case, the Strotz paper was published in more or less the same form as submitted, and hence with all the errors indicated in Gorman's report.[1] The paper which follows is an elaboration of this referee's report.

Editorial Summary

Separability is a maintained hypothesis throughout this paper; hence, the results of the previous paper are applicable. That is, we begin with the assumption that *two-stage budgeting* is possible; however, no restrictions are imposed on the information used to discover the optimal expenditure on each group. This paper considers the implications of reducing the information available to make the *intergroup* allocation decision.

It begins by investigating the conditions in which a consumer with a well-behaved separable utility function can find the optimal income allocation for group r, y_r, given only the price indices for each group, P_r, $r = 1, 2, \ldots, n$, and total income Y: in other words,

$$y_r = \phi_r(P_1, P_2, \ldots, P_n, Y) \tag{0.1}$$

for $r = 1, 2, \ldots, n$. The answer to this question clearly depends upon what is meant by a price index and the two parts of the paper reflect alternative interpretations.

In Section 1 Gorman posits the existence of differential prices indices for which (0.1) holds locally. These are given by his equations (5) and (6) and repeated here as

[1] Although Strotz (1957) is normally credited with having formalized the idea of budgeting, as a matter of historical record, the problem was quite clearly set out in Arrow *et al.* (1951). This paper was never published but circulated widely.

$$\delta_r = \sum_i w_{ri} \mathrm{d}p_{ri}, \qquad w_{ri} = w_{ri}(p, Y) \tag{0.2}$$

and

$$\mathrm{d}y_r = \sum_{s=1}^{n} a_{rs}\delta_s + a_{ro}\mathrm{d}Y, \qquad a_{rt} = a_{rt}(p, Y). \tag{0.3}$$

Proposition I provides necessary and sufficient conditions for this 'local price aggregation', maintaining separability of the direct utility function. There are three possible solutions each of which involves essentially two groups:

(i) there are only two groups,

$$u(x) = F(v_1(x_1), v_2(x_2)); \tag{0.4}$$

(ii) $n - 1$ groups are separable from the remaining group, and each of these $n - 1$ groups is itself homothetically separable,

$$u(x) = F(v_1, f(v_2(x_2), \ldots, v_n(x_n))), \tag{0.5}$$

where v_r for $r = 2, \ldots, n$ is homogeneous of degree one; and

(iii) the function has $d + 1$ additive terms, of which d are sector-specific functions and the last is a function of the remaining groups, each of which is homothetically separable,

$$u(x) = v_1(x_1) + \ldots + v_d(x_d) + f(v_{d+1}(x_{d+1}), \ldots, v_n(x_n)) \tag{0.6}$$

where v_r for $r = 2\ d + 1\ , \ldots, n$ is homogeneous of degree one.

Roughly speaking, when there are only two groups, one can define a local price index for one group almost arbitrarily and the budget constraint then provides an index for the other group.

The proof itself must have been rather difficult to follow as it relies heavily upon duality (the indirect utility function) and separability arguments not widely understood at the time.

Section 2 considers the case of perfect price aggregates. This is the case where each P_r in (0.1) is a function of prices in its own group alone. The sector-specific income allocation functions are then written as

$$y_r = \phi_r(P_1(p_1), P_2(p_2), \ldots, P_n(p_n), Y) \tag{0.7}$$

for all r. It is clear that perfect price aggregation implies local price aggregation, and an example is presented to show that the converse is not true. Proposition II provides necessary and sufficient conditions for perfect price aggregation when cases (i) and (ii) of the first proposition are excluded. He also show that these conditions are sufficient for these two excluded cases.[2] Each element of the first d additive sectors must satisfy an additional restriction, namely, that the sector-specific indirect utility functions,

$$g_r(y_r, p_r) = \max\{v_r(x_r) \mid p_r x_r \leqslant y_r\}, \tag{0.8}$$

[2] It was later shown that these conditions were also necessary in the first two cases; see Blackorby *et al.* (1978*b*) or Section 5.4.3 of Blackorby *et al.* (1978*a*).

can be written as

$$g_r(y_r, p_r) = G_r\left(\frac{y_r}{P_r(p_r)}\right) + Q_r(p_r), \tag{0.9}$$

where the P_r are homogeneous of degree one and the Q_r are homogeneous of degree zero. Note, in particular, that the price indices are not assumed to be homogeneous, or even homothetic. That they are so is an implication of perfect price aggregation.

The easiest way to begin to understand this solution is to demonstrate sufficiency. The first-order necessary conditions for

$$\max_{\{y_r\}}\left\{\sum_{r=1}^{d}\left[G_r\left(\frac{y_r}{P_r(p_r)}\right) + Q_r(p_r)\right] + f\left(\frac{y_{d+1}}{P_{d+1}(p_{d+1})}, \ldots, \frac{y_n}{P_n(p_n)}\right) \middle| \sum y_r = Y\right\} \tag{0.10}$$

are given by

$$G_r'\left(\frac{y_r}{P_r(p_r)}\right) = \lambda P_r(p_r) \tag{0.11}$$

for $r = 1, \ldots, d$ and

$$f_r\left(\frac{y_{d+1}}{P_{d+1}(p_{d+1})}, \ldots, \frac{y_n}{P_n(p_n)}\right) = \lambda P_r(p_r) \tag{0.12}$$

for $r = d + 1, \ldots, n$, plus, of course, the budget constraint. One sees immediately that the solution is of the required form, namely (0.7).

The paper concludes with several ways of interpreting these index numbers[3] and some specific remarks about Strotz's claims.

[3] In particular, that they can be interpreted as Divisia indices.

Separable Utility and Aggregation

SUMMARY

The first step in budgeting is commonly to allocate expenditure among broad groups of commodities. Professor R. H. Strotz (1957) has recently discussed this procedure and concluded that it is justified if the consumer's utility function is separable. In the present paper, I shall argue that one has to go further and assume, broadly, that the utility function falls into two parts, the first of which is *additively* separable, while the specific satisfaction functions in the second are homogeneous.[1] Even when this condition is satisfied, the consumer will usually find that he has made mistakes, though these will be small ones.[2] A set of conditions under which he would make no mistakes at all is discussed in Section 2 and summarized in Proposition II.

1. LOCAL AGGREGATION

Consider the separable utility function

$$u = u[v_1(x_1), v_2(x_2), \ldots, v_n(x_n)], \tag{1}$$

where $x_r = (x_{r1}, x_{r2}, \ldots)$, $r = 1, 2, \ldots, n$,[3] is the *consumption vector for the* r^{th} *group of commodities*, and v_r is the corresponding *specific satisfaction* function.

Throughout this paper, we shall be dealing with utility functions of this type, and this must be assumed even when it is not explicity mentioned.

For obvious reasons we shall also assume throughout the paper that

$$u_r = \partial u/\partial v_r > 0; \qquad v_{ri} = \partial v_r/\partial x_{ri} > 0, \qquad \text{for all } r, i, \tag{2}$$

that the indifference manifolds are strictly convex,[4] that $x_{ri} > 0$ for all r and i, and that all the functions which appear in the analysis are sufficiently continuous to allow us to use differential equations in analysing them.[5]

[1] See the opening paragraph of Sect. 1 for a definition of the specific satisfaction functions. We use the word 'homogeneous' in the economist's sense; it might be better to write 'are functions of a function which is homogeneous of degree one'. We will use 'homogeneous' in this extended sense throughout the paper.

[2] If the price changes in particular commodities from one period to the next are small, his errors will be of the second order of smalls.

[3] We will not always give the precise domain of a suffix, but will sometimes leave it to be understood from the context.

[4] This implies, with (2), that the constant specific satisfaction manifolds are also strictly convex.

[5] And to use the particular methods we do use! This is all we will say about continuity!

Let $p_r = (p_{r1}, \ldots, p_{rn})$[6] be the price vector for the rth group, and $y_r = \sum_i p_{ri} x_{ri}$ be the consumer's expenditure on the goods in group r when his income $Y = \sum y_r$.

The question we are about to analyse is: under what conditions can we define a set of price indices $P = (P_1, P_2, \ldots, P_n)$ for the different groups of commodities, such that

$$y_r = \phi_r(P_1, P_2, \ldots, P_n, Y), \qquad r = 1, 2, \ldots, n? \tag{3}$$

that is, such that the consumer does not need to know the actual prices of the individual goods in order to carry out his preliminary allocation, as long as he knows the values of the price indices, and, of course, his own income.

Unfortunately, it is not too clear just what class of price indices should be taken as admissible. In Section 2 of this paper we shall require that price indices be of the form

$$P_r = P_r(p_r); \qquad r = 1, 2, \ldots, n. \tag{4}$$

Aggregates such as these we shall call 'perfect aggregates'. Unfortunately, the conditions for perfect aggregation turn out to be rather stringent. In the present section, we shall accordingly concentrate our attention on a somewhat weaker formulation of the problem:

Under what conditions do there exist differential price indices

$$\delta_r = \sum_i w_{ri} \mathrm{d}p_{ri}, \qquad w_{ri} = w_{ri}(p_1, p_2, p_3, \ldots, p_n; Y)^7 \tag{5}$$

such that

$$\mathrm{d}y_r = \sum_{s=1}^{n} a_{rs}\delta_s + a_{r0}\mathrm{d}Y; \qquad a_{rt} = a_{rt}(p_1, \ldots, p_n; Y)? \tag{6}$$

The idea underlying this new approach is that the consumer budgets at the beginning of each period in full knowledge of what happened in the previous period. His problem is how to adjust his previous period's allocations in order to take account of the changes he expects in his income and in prices. (6) tells him how to do so even if he does not know exactly what prices he expects as long as he knows the price indices $\delta_1, \ldots, \delta_n$. This preliminary allocation is likely to prove wrong, but the mistakes will be of the second order only, as long as the changes which occur between the two periods are themselves small. He should be able to correct them easily if he leaves himself a little flexibility.[8]

[6] Each $p_{ri} > 0$.

[7] See n. 1.

[8] In fact he will either have to make the adjustment or at least compute what it should be, for (5) only gives the further adjustment needed from the old optimum position.

We shall call $\delta_1, \delta_2, \ldots, \delta_n$, *local aggregates*, and, if they exist we will say that *local aggregation is possible*. The remainder of this section will be devoted to the discussion and proof of the following proposition:

PROPOSITION I: *Local aggregates exist if and only if the utility function can be written in one or other of the following forms*:

$$\text{(i)} \quad u = F(v_1, v_2), \tag{7}$$

$$\text{(ii)} \quad u = F[v_1, f(v_2, \ldots, v_n)], \tag{8}$$

$$\text{(iii)} \quad u = v_1 + \ldots + v_d + f(v_{d+1}, \ldots, v_n), \qquad 0 \leq d \leq n, \tag{9}$$

where F and f are general functions, but all the arguments of f are homogeneous of degree one.[9]

Broadly speaking, what this means is that all the groups—if any—whose specific satisfaction functions are homogeneous can be thrown together to form a new large group, with what might be called a lower-order specific satisfaction function f, which is, of course, itself separable. If, when we count this large group as a single unit, there are more than two groups, F is *additively* separable, but this need not be so if there are only two groups.

We shall divide the proof into numbered sections.

1.1. Preliminary discussion

(5) and (6) together imply that

$$\frac{\partial y_r / \partial p_{si}}{\partial y_r / \partial p_{sj}} \text{ is independent of } r, \tag{10}$$

since it equals w_{si}/w_{sj}.[10] Moreover, if (10) is true, one can obviously construct local aggregates to satisfy (5) and (6). (10) is therefore both a necessary and sufficient condition for local aggregation, so that we need only discuss the conditions for (10) to hold.

If there are only two groups of goods, $y_1 + y_2 = Y$. Hence $\partial y_1/\partial p_{si} = -\partial y_2/\partial p_{si}$ and (10) holds. This proves the sufficiency of (7). We can assume from here on that there are least three groups.

In passing, it is worth noting that (4) and (5) imply that

$$\frac{\partial y_r/\partial p_{si}}{\partial y_r/\partial p_{sj}} = \frac{\partial P_s/\partial p_{si}}{\partial P_s/\partial p_{sj}},$$

[9] *After* normalization, of course. Remember that we said that it is required only that u can be put in this form. Of course, F, f, and the v's have to be monotonically increasing and have to yield strictly convex indifference manifolds. These conditions were stated once and for all at the beginning of the section. (i) is really a special case of (ii).

[10] Of course, it is indeterminate if $a_{rs} = 0$, but this need not detain us.

which is independent of r. *Perfect aggregation therefore implies local aggregation.*

1.2. The equations for $\partial y_r/\partial p_{si}$

Following Professor Strotz, we shall write

$$u = F[g_1(y_1, p_1), g_2(y_2, p_2), \ldots, g_n(y_n, p_n)] \tag{11}$$

where $g_r(y_r, p_r)$ is the maximum value of v_r subject to the constraint that $\sum_i p_{ri}x_{ri} = y_r =$ constant; that is, subject to a given preliminary allocation. For an optimal allocation, we must maximize (11) subject to the constraint

$$\sum y_r = Y. \tag{12}$$

The maximizing conditions are

$$u_1g_1' - u_sg_s' = u_2g_2' - u_sg_s' = \ldots = u_ng_n' - u_sg_n' = 0,^{11} \tag{13}$$

where $g_r' = \partial g_r/\partial y_r$.[12] Differentiate (12) and (13) with respect to p_{si},[13] we find:

$$A[\partial y_1/\partial p_{si}, \ldots, \partial y_n/\partial p_{si}] = g_{si}\rho_s + u_sg_{si}'\sigma, \tag{14}$$

where

$$\rho_s' = [u_{ss}g_s' - u_{1s}g_1', u_{ss}g_s' - u_{2s}g_2', \ldots, u_{ss}g_s' - u_{ns}g_n', 0], \tag{15}$$

$$\sigma' = [1, 1, \ldots, 1, 0], \tag{16}$$

$g_{ri} = \partial g_r/\partial p_{ri}$, $g_{ri}' = \partial^2 g_r/\partial p_{ri}\partial y_r$ and A is a non-degenerate square matrix, and *is independent of i.*

(10) is clearly equivalent to the statement that the direction of the solution vector of (14) should be independent of i. This in turn will be true if and only if *either*

(A) g_{si}'/g_{si} is independent if i, *or*
(B) ρ_s and σ are collinear.[14]

1.3. The case (A)

Throughout this subsection we shall be concerned with the sth group only. For simplicity, we shall therefore drop the suffix s which refers to it. (A) is then equivalent to:

[11] Giving $n - 1$ equations in all, since $u_sg_s^s - u_sg_s' \equiv 0$. (11) is, of course, the nth equation. This means, of course, that ρ_s and σ below have no component corresponding to g_s. They have n components in all.

[12] [eds.] Equation (13) might be easier to read if u_r were replaced with F_r, the derivative of F with respect to its r_{th} argument.

[13] s is held fixed in the succeeding discussion, until we explicitly begin to discuss other groups.

[14] Subject to the conditions (12) and (13), of course.

$$\frac{\partial(g_i/g_j)}{\partial y} = 0. \tag{17}$$

Hence by Theorem 1 of Klein (1946*a*), g is a separable function of p and y, that is,

$$g = G(y, K), \text{ say;} \qquad K = K(p). \tag{18}$$

A consumer is not affected if his income is doubled at the same time as all the prices facing him are doubled.[15] g is therefore homogeneous of degree zero in p and y. That is

$$(\partial G/\partial K)\sum K_i p_i + y\,\partial G/\partial y = 0.$$

Hence by the first part of (18), $\sum K_i p_i$ depends only on K and y. By the second part, it is independent of y. We may therefore write

$$\sum K_i p_i = \phi(K) \quad \text{and} \quad P(K) = \exp\left\{\int dK/\phi\right\} \tag{19}$$

to get

$$\sum p_i \partial P/\partial p_i = P' \sum K_i p_i = P \tag{20}$$

in an obvious notation.

P is therefore homogeneous of degree one in the prices. Changing our notation slightly we can therefore write $g = G(y, P)$ and $P = P(p)$ which is homogeneous of degree one in the prices.

Clearly g is now homogeneous of degree zero in y and P[16] so that we can write finally

$$g = h(y/P). \tag{21}$$

Now g is the polar form of the specific satisfaction function v, and (21) is therefore a necessary and sufficient condition for v to be homogeneous in x.[17] By an appropriate normalization we can make v homogeneous of the first degree in x. If we do so, (21) becomes

$$g = y/P; \quad P = P(p), \text{ homogeneous of degree one.} \tag{22}$$

1.4. Intermediate discussion

As we examine each group in turn in this manner, we can see which fall into (A), i.e. have homogeneous specific satisfaction functions, and which do not.

[15] g is strictly a specific satisfaction function rather than a utility function, but this does not affect the point at issue.

[16] This is pretty obvious. It is also easily proved.

[17] This is, of course, well known. It is easily shown that $x_i/x_j = g_i/g_j = P_i/P_j$ is independent of y—which really proves the matter. See n. 1.

For simplicity, we shall renumber the groups so that the latter, i.e. those which come under (B), are numbered 1, 2, ..., d, and the homogeneous ones $d+1, d+2, \ldots, n$. We shall use the suffixes a, b to denote members of the first set, m, t for those of the second, and r, s for elements which may belong to either.

1.5. The case (B) if there is only one non-homogeneous specific satisfaction function

Since $d = 1$, we must take $s = 1$ in (15).[18] (B) therefore implies that $u_{m1} g'_m$ is independent of m, $m > 1$. Since $u_m g'_m$ is also independent of m by (13), this implies that u_{m1}/u_m is independent too. Hence

$$\frac{\partial(u_m/u_t)}{\partial g_1} = 0, \qquad m, t \neq 1. \tag{23}$$

This is Leontief's (1947*a*) condition that u should be separable in the fashion

$$u = F[g_1, f(g_2, \ldots, g_n)] \tag{24}$$

and it is easily seen that if u is of this form (B) is satisfied. Returning to the direct form of the function, (24) becomes

$$u = F[v_1, f(v_2, \ldots, v_n)], \tag{25}$$

where $v_2, \ldots, v_n$ are homogeneous of degree one. This is case (ii) of Proposition I.

1.6. The case (B) if there is more than one non-homogeneous specific satisfaction function

By an argument similar to that used in Subsection 1.5 we soon see that

$$u_{ra}/u_r = u_{sa}/u_s, \qquad r, s \neq a, \; a \leqslant d. \tag{26}$$

Applying this result repeatedly, we find that

$$u_{ra}/u_r u_a = u_{sb}/u_s u_b, \qquad r \neq a, \; s \neq b, \; a, b \leqslant d. \tag{27}$$

Setting $r = s$ in (27), we find that

$$\frac{\partial(u_a/u_b)}{\partial g_r} = 0, \qquad a, b \leqslant d, \tag{28}$$

and setting $a = b$ in (27)

$$\frac{\partial(u_r/u_s)}{\partial g_a} = 0, \qquad a \leqslant d. \tag{29}$$

[18] This, of course, means that the first component of p_s is $u_{11}g'_1 - u_{21}g'_2$.

Hence by Theorem 2 of Leontief (1947*a*) we can write the utility function u in the form

$$u = F\left[\sum_{a=1}^{d} k_a(g_a) + f(g_{d+1}, \ldots, g_n)\right], \text{ say.} \tag{30}$$

By a slight change of notation—equivalent to a normalization of the specific satisfaction functions and of the utility function itself—(30) can be rewritten as

$$u = g_1 + \ldots + g_d + f(g_{d+1}, \ldots, g_n) \tag{31}$$

or, returning to the direct forms of the function,

$$u = v_1 + \ldots + v_d + f(v_{d+1}, \ldots, v_n), \tag{32}$$

where $v_{d+1}, \ldots, v_n$ are homogeneous of degree one.

This completes the proof of the necessity of the conditions. The reader will have no difficulty in establishing their sufficiency.

What is their meaning?

Broadly speaking, they imply that the utility function falls into two parts, either of which may be empty. The first is *additively* separable, the second is a function of homogeneous specific satisfaction functions.

Let us first consider the meaning of homogeneity. If the specific satisfaction for clothes is homogeneous, and the consumer's income rises sufficiently for him to double his expenditure on clothes, he will buy twice as many blue jeans as before, and twice as many evening suits.[19] In fact the income elasticity of demand for all types of clothes would be the same. If the specific satisfaction functions are to be homogeneous, we must never group luxuries, near-luxuries, and necessities together, and yet it is my impression that many groups used in household budgeting do just this.[20]

Additivity seems to me to be a less drastic assumption than homogeneity. If a utility function is to be separable at all, the marginal rates of substitution between any two items in the same group must be independent of the consumption of goods in the other groups, e.g. the marginal rate of substitution between blue jeans and evening dress must be independent of the type of holidays we take. Additivity merely extends this postulate to items from a pair of different groups, e.g. the marginal rate of substitution between blue jeans and steak should be independent of the consumption of tents.[21]

[19] The same would be true, of course, if a change in the price of butter were to lead him to double his expenditure on clothes. It is implicitly assumed, of course, that clothes form a 'group'.

[20] Though it must be admitted that some people have separate categories for luxuries and for 'basic necessities'.

[21] In practice, of course, we require that the marginal rate of substitution between, e.g. blue jeans and steak should be 'much less' dependent on the consumption of tents than it is on goods within the groups in question, e.g. shirts.

Whichever is the more so, there is no doubt that they are both fairly drastic, and the conditions laid down in Proposition I correspondingly stringent.

On the whole, I think, this is a good thing. The point of Professor Strotz's article is that people budget in a certain manner, and that one way of explaining this is to assume that their utility functions are separable. That this is not enough, and that we have to go further and assume something like *additive* separability is in a sense a good thing, for it implies more stringent constraints on the utility function; constraints moreover which considerably simplify demand analysis and may form the basis for useful advances in that field.[22] On the other hand, it must be admitted that it seems possible to explain the observed budgetary behaviour without assuming separability at all. In particular, it is easy to construction non-separable utility functions which imply that the consumer will spend a constant proportion of his income on each group of goods.[23] The question therefore is: Is additive separability such a stringent condition that one should look elsewhere for one's explanation of our budgetary behaviour? I do not think so; indeed it seems to me a natural working hypothesis.

2. PERFECT AGGREGATION

We have already seen that perfect aggregation implies local aggregation, so that we can confine our attention to the cases displayed in Proposition I. On the other hand, local aggregation does not imply perfect aggregation, for

$$u = \sum_{r=1}^{n} v_r, \qquad v_r = -e^{-x_{r1}} x_{r2}^{-1}, \qquad r = 1, 2, \ldots, n,^{24}$$

is a well-behaved utility function[25] for which no perfect aggregates exist, though local aggregates do. There is therefore a problem to be discussed.

The basic result in this field is:

PROPOSITION II: *If there are more than two groups, and if not precisely* $(n-1)$ *of the specific satisfaction functions are homogeneous, perfect*

[22] I am myself using it in the analysis of the demand for related goods. I understand that Professor Frisch is also using it.

[23] If the utility function is homogeneous of degree a_r in x_r, $r = 1, 2, \ldots, n$, $\sum a_r = 1$, then $y_r = a_r Y$, $r = 1, 2, \ldots, n$. This is, of course, quite a wide class of functions.

[24] [eds.] Do not be misled by the fact that utility is negative; it has all the properties of a well-behaved utility function. Note that the marginal rate of substitution between goods one and two in group r is equal to x_{r2}. Hence all of the indifference curves are horizontal translates of each other.

[25] i.e. it has the qualities enumerated in the opening paragraphs of Sect. 1.

aggregation is possible if and only if the utility function can be written in the form:

$$u = v_1 + \ldots + v_d + f(v_{d+1}, \ldots, v_n), \qquad 0 \leqslant d \leqslant n, \tag{33}$$

where

$$\text{(i) } v_m = v_m(x_m), \qquad m = d+1, \ldots, n, \textit{ is homogeneous of degree one}; \tag{34}$$

and

$$\text{(ii) } v_s = G_s(y_s/P_s) + Q_s(p_s) \textit{ in polar form}, \qquad s = 1, \ldots, n,^{26} \tag{35}$$

where

$$P_s = P_s(p_s) \textit{ is homogeneous of degree one}, \tag{36}$$

and

$$Q_s = Q_s(p_s) \textit{ is homogeneous of degree zero}. \tag{37}$$

2.1. Preliminary discussion

If perfect aggregates exist

$$\frac{\partial y_r/\partial p_{si}}{\partial y_r/\partial p_{sj}} \text{ depends only on } p_s,\ s,\ i, \text{ and } j, \tag{38}$$

since it equals P_{si}/P_{sj},[27] so that (38) is necessary for perfect aggregation. The reader will have little difficulty in proving that it is also sufficient.

2.2. The marginal satisfaction of expenditure

$$\partial v_s/\partial y_s = y_s^{-1} H_s(y_s/P_s), \text{ say}, \qquad s = 1, 2, \ldots, n. \tag{39}$$

The preliminary conditions clearly rule out cases (i) and (ii) of Proposition I, so that we can confine our attention to case (iii). This already implies (33) and (34).

Moreover, in the polar form (33) becomes:

$$u = g_1(y_1, p_1) + \ldots + g_d(y_d, p_d) + f(g_{d+1}, \ldots, g_n), \tag{40}$$

where

$$g_m = y_m/P_m \text{ and } P_m = P_m(p_m) \text{ is homogeneous of degree one}, \\ m = d+1, \ldots, n, \text{ by (22)}. \tag{41}$$

Maximizing u with respect to the y's, subject to $\sum y_r = Y$ and differentiating the result with respect to p_{si} as in the proof of Proposition I, we find that

[26] (34) implies that (35) is automatically satisfied for $s > d$.

[27] Unless, of course, y_r is independent of p_s, in which case the ratio is indeterminate. This difficulty need not detain us.

$$\frac{\partial y_r/\partial p_{si}}{\partial y_r/\partial p_{sj}} = \frac{g'_{si}}{g'_{sj}} \tag{42}$$

(38) is automatically satisfied if $s > d$, since (42) then becomes P_{si}/P_{sj}. In general, however, (41) implies that

$$\frac{\partial(g'_{si}/g'_{sj})}{\partial y_s} = 0, \tag{43}$$

which is very similar to (17). Since g_s is homogeneous of degree zero in y_s and p_s, g'_s is homogeneous of degree minus one. If the reader remembers this, he will have little difficulty in proving that

$$g'_s = y_s^{-1} H_s(y_s/P_s), \text{ say,}^{28} \qquad s = 1, 2, \ldots, n, \tag{44}$$

where $P_s = P_s(p_s)$ is homogeneous of degree one, $s = 1, \ldots, n$, as required for (36). The argument parallels that in Subsection 1.3 of the proof of Proposition I.

2.3. *Final step*

(39) may be written in the form

$$\partial g_s/\partial \log y_s = H_s(e^{\log y_s - \log P_s}).^{29} \tag{45}$$

Integrating with respect to y_s and making some obvious transformations, we find that

$$g_s = G_s(y_s/P_s) + Q_s(p_s),^{30} \qquad s = 1, 2, \ldots, n,$$

as required for (35). Moreover, a doubling of all prices and of y_s leaves g_s and G_s unchanged.

Here it also leaves Q_s unchanged, which proves (37).

(35)–(37) are of course automatically satisfied if

$$s > d, \qquad \text{with} \quad Q_s \equiv 0 \quad \text{and} \quad G_s = y_s/P_s. \tag{46}$$

This proves the necessity of (33)–(37). The reader will have no difficulty in proving their sufficiency.

2.4. *The two special cases*

If there are only two groups, or if *precisely* $(n - 1)$ of the specific satisfaction functions are homogeneous,

[28] This is automatically satisfied, with $H_s \equiv y_s/P_s$, if $s > d$.

[29] [eds.] Note that throughout this section Gorman uses v_s and g_s interchangeably.

[30] Automatically satisfied with $Q_s \equiv 0$ and $G_s \equiv y_s/P_s$ if $s > d$.

$$\frac{\partial y_r/\partial p_{si}}{\partial y_r/\partial p_{sj}} = \frac{Ag_{si} + g'_{si}}{Ag_{sj} + g'_{sj}}, \tag{47}$$

where A is a complicated function of all the variables in the system. If v_s is homogeneous, it can be normalized to be homogeneous of degree one, in which case $v_s = y_s/P_s$ as in (41), and (47) becomes P_{si}/P_{sj} so that (38) is automatically satisfied.

If we can write $u = v_1 + v_2$, or $u = v_1 + f(v_2, \ldots, v_n)$[31] according to which of the special cases we are in, $A = 0$, so that (47) reduces to (42) which implies (35)–(37).

We therefore have the corollary

COROLLARY: (33)–(37) *are a set of sufficient conditions for perfect aggregates, though they may not be necessary in the two special cases cited.*[32]

Each of the points made in the following discussion should be qualified by the phrase 'except, possibly in those two special cases'.

The most interesting implications of Proposition II are

(*a*) *If perfect aggregates exist at all they may be taken to be homogeneous in the relevant prices.*

PROOF: This follows from (36).

(*b*) $y_r = \phi_r(P_1, \ldots, P_n, Y) = P_r D_r(P_1/Y, \ldots, P_n/Y)$, *say.*

PROOF: y_r is homogeneous of degree one in $p_1, p_2, \ldots, p_n, Y$. Hence $\phi_r = \sum_{si} \phi_{rs} P_{si} p_{si} + \phi_{r0} Y = \sum_s \phi_{rs} P_s + \phi_{r0} Y$ by (36).[33] Hence ϕ_r is homogeneous of degree one in $P_1, \ldots, P_n, Y$ which proves (*b*).

(*b*) suggests that it might be fruitful to define

$$X_r = y_r/P_r, \qquad r = 1, 2, \ldots, n, \tag{48}$$

to find the conventional demand functions

$$X_r = D_r(P_1/Y, P_2/Y, \ldots, P_n/Y). \tag{49}$$

On the other hand, we clearly cannot go behind these demand equations to a utility function defined in terms of the X's except when all the specific satisfaction functions are homogeneous. Of course, if they are homogeneous, we can normalize them to be homogeneous of degree one, so that

[31] In general, of course, u might be a function of these values.

[32] I have not been able to find any example of a utility function yielding perfect aggregates which has not satisfied (33)–(37).

[33] $\partial \phi_r/\partial P_s = \phi_{rs}$, $\partial \phi_r/\partial Y = \phi_{r0}$.

$$X_r = y_r/P_r = g_r = v_r(x_r). \tag{50}$$

If the special satisfaction functions are all homogeneous, our aggregates have the following further qualities.

(*c*) *$X_r = v_r(x_r)$ is homogeneous of degree one.*

(*d*) *$X_{ri} = v_{ri} = p_{ri}/P_r$ and $P_{ri} = x_{ri}/X_r$ are positive.*[34]

PROOF: $F_r g_{ri} = \lambda p_{ri}$ in equilibrium where λ is the marginal utility of income. Hence $F_r X_r = F_r \sum_i X_{ri} x_{ri}$ by (*c*) which equals $\lambda \sum_i p_{ri} x_{ri} = \lambda y_r$, and $X_{ri} = X_r p_{ri}/y_r = p_{ri}/P_r$. This proves the first formula, a similar argument applied to the polar form proves the second. Incidentally, this proves that P_r is necessarily positive.

(*e*) $\mathrm{d}X_r/X_r = \sum_i p_{ri}\mathrm{d}x_{ri}/\sum_i p_{ri}x_{ri}; \qquad \mathrm{d}P_r/P_r = \sum_i x_{ri}\mathrm{d}p_{ri}/\sum_i p_{ri}x_{ri},$

so that the *X*'s and *P*'s are Divisia indices (Divisia, 1928).

PROOF: This follows immediately from (50) and (*d*).

(*f*) *Since v_r is constant if and only if y_r/P_r is constant for each r, we can call the P's Geary indices* (Geary, 1951).

(*g*) *The allocation problem reduces to the maximization of the utility function $u = u(X_1, \ldots, X_n)$ subject to the constraint $\sum P_r X_r = Y$.*

PROOF: Follows immediately from (48) and (50).

This implies that

$$\partial u/\partial X_r = \lambda P_r, \qquad r = 1, 2, \ldots, n, \tag{51}$$

in equilibrium. The *P*'s and *X*'s are therefore Klein aggregates (Klein, 1946*a*).

It can easily be shown that (*g*) holds if and only if each of the specific satisfaction functions is homogeneous. However, (*c*)–(*f*) and (51) hold for any particular group which happens to have a homogeneous specific satisfaction function whether or not the other groups have them.

The obvious generalization of a homogeneous function is one in which the Engel curves are linear, for it shares with the former the property that the proportion of an extra £ spent on a group as a whole which is spent on each particular good in it depends only on the prices of the goods in the group.[35] The question which presents itself is: Is this the class of functions

[34] Given our continuity assumption, we can always take v_r to be zero at the origin and positive throughout the positive orthant.

[35] However, such functions appear in other branches of aggregation theory.

defined by (35)–(37), and, if not, how are the two classes related to each other?

It is easily shown that (35)–(37) imply that

$$x_{si} = y_s P_{si}/P_s - P_s Q_{si}/G'_s. \tag{52}$$

Therefore,

$$dx_{si}/\partial y_s = P_{si}/P_s + P_s Q_{si} G''_s / G'^2_s.$$

For this to be independent of y_s, G''_s/G'^2_s would have to be independent of y_s. Since it is a function of y_s/P_s, this implies that G''_s/G'^2_s is a constant. Integrating this differential equation we find that

$$G_s = a_s \log(y_s/P_s - b_s) + C_s, \text{ say.}^{36} \tag{53}$$

Since G_s is a general function in (35),[37] it clearly need not be of this form, so that the functions defined by (35) do not necessarily have linear Engel curves.

It can be shown quite easily that if the Engel curves are linear, then perfect aggregation is possible if and only if we can write *either*

$$v_s = A_s e^{B_s W_s} + C_s \quad \text{or} \quad v_s = A_s W_s + B_s, \tag{54}$$

where A_s, B_s, and C_s are arbitrary constants, and W_s is a normalized form of the specific satisfaction function in which the marginal utility of expenditure is[38] independent of income (see Gorman (1961)).

May I finish with a comment on Section 4 of Strotz (1957)? There seem to me to be two points at issue here. On the one hand the second last paragraph on p. 278 states quite clearly that 'the determination of the *values* of the index numbers'[39] is approximate because it depends on the weights being known and constant, though, of course, the *formulae* which define them are *precise*. On the other hand the discussion on p. 277 seems to me to imply that indices satisfying (29) *exist*, however difficult they may be to *estimate*. If they do it is clear that they will normally be neither perfect aggregates nor the indices defined in Section 3 of Strotz (1957) even if utility is additively separable.

If we add '+ terms of the second order' to (29) in Strotz (1957) we get an approximation which holds in the neighbourhood of a defined equilibrium point, though, of course, the function *f varies from point to point*. Here, of course, the indices are relatively easily estimated, it is the allocation which may be wrong. If we follow Strotz (1959) and assume that the utility

[36] Unless the constant is zero, but the utility function in (33) then turns out to be ill-behaved, unless there are precisely $n - 1$ homogeneous specific satisfaction functions.

[37] Subject to the usual convexity etc., properties, of course.

[38] $v_s = A_s W_s + B_s$ in the case discussed in n. 13.

[39] The italics are mine.

functions are additively separable,[40] we can easily show that $(\partial y_t/\partial p_{si})/(\partial y_t/\partial Y)$ is independent of $t \neq s$. Writing w_{si} for it and setting $\lambda_r = \partial y_r/\partial Y$ and $\delta_s = \sum_i w_{si} \mathrm{d}p_{si}$, (6) in Section 1 becomes

$$\mathrm{d}y_r = -\,\delta_r + \lambda_r\left(\sum_i \delta_s + \mathrm{d}\,Y\right). \tag{55}$$

Alternatively, we can set $P_s = \sum_i w_{si} p_{si}$ and get the approximation discussed above which corresponds to (29): $y_r = \mu_r - P_r + \lambda_r(\sum P_s + Y) +$ second-order terms. λ_r and μ_r depend on the equilibrium point in question. These are the equations which tell the consumer approximately how to allocate his expenditure.[41]

[40] It is enough to assume that they satisfy the conditions for Proposition I. The discussion is very similar to that in sect. 3 of Strotz (1957).

[41] If perfect aggregates exist, of course, he will do better to use them.

4

Notes on Divisia Indices

Editorial Remarks

This paper was written for a workshop at the University of North Carolina in 1970 run by Gorman and Sydney Afriat. All of the notes from this period were written 'on demand', so it is clear that most of the results were known much earlier. For example, Proposition II(*e*) of the previous paper demonstrates that the perfect price and quantity indices found there are Divisia indices. In fact, these notes probably date from January 1949 when Gorman went to the University of Birmingham as a research fellow and was promptly informed that he would have to give the lectures in statistics. The material delivered in those lectures was based on Dresch (1938, 1949).

This paper is a good summary of what was known at the time about these indices plus some illuminating sidelights. Although somewhat terse, it remains a good summary of the subject even today.

Notes on Divisia Indices

1. INTRODUCTION[1]

In their important article in which they introduced Divisia indices to economists in general, Jorgenson and Griliches (1967) listed their main properties, pointing out how desirable a set of indices these made them. Richter (1966) had already shown that they provided the only generally acceptable measure of technical progress, at least if there are constant returns, and perfect competition.

The main disadvantages of these indices is that they depend for some of their properties on these two perhaps unrealistic assumptions, and that their value at any point in general depends on the whole past history of the economy. Despite this I believe that they are the best set of indices available.

In the present note, I list again these properties, noting the assumptions needed for each, and then go on to discuss the conditions under which the Divisia indices are independent of the path followed from the base to the current position. The conclusion: that, given constant returns and perfect competition, the Divisia indices corresponding to a set of goods are independent of the path if a 'true' aggregate exists for these goods, in a reasonable sense of the word, and that the Divisia indices then give the value of that aggregate, and of a corresponding price aggregate, should strengthen our acceptance of these indices, at least given these assumptions.

In the final section I discuss a generalization of the idea of a Divisia index, arising from the work of Professor Solow and Mr Hulten.

I will assume throughout that there is enough smoothness and connectivity and monotonicity to permit the use of simple calculus methods.

I suggest that those already reasonably well acquainted with Divisia indices should skip Section 2.

2. KNOWN RESULTS

Let $x = (x_1, \ldots, x_n)$ be a vector of quantities and $p = (p_1, \ldots, p_n)$ of the corresponding prices and $v = (v_1, \ldots, v_n)$ of expenditures $v_i = p_i x_i$, each i, $V = \sum v_i = p \cdot x$. The Divisia quantity and price indices are defined in differential form as

$$\mathrm{d}X/X = p \cdot \mathrm{d}x/p \cdot x, \qquad \mathrm{d}P/P = x \cdot \mathrm{d}p/x \cdot p. \tag{2.1}$$

[1] [eds.] The original of this paper contains references to footnotes, but the text of these notes has been lost.

Alternatively we may write (2.1) in the form

$$\mathrm{d}\log X = \sum_i v_i \,\mathrm{d}\log x_i/V, \qquad \mathrm{d}\log P = \sum_i v_i \,\mathrm{d}\log p_i/V, \tag{2.2}$$

where

$$v_i = p_i x_i, \qquad V = \sum_i v_i = \sum_i p_i x_i = p \cdot x, \tag{2.3}$$

the integration being carried out along the actual time-path.

Various results follow immediately.

A. *These are continuously chained Laspeyre indices*

$$\begin{aligned} X(t+\mathrm{d}t)/X(t) &= (X(t) + \mathrm{d}X(t))/X(t) \\ &= p(t) \cdot (x(t) + \mathrm{d}x(t))/p(t) \cdot x(t) \\ &= p(t) \cdot x(t+\mathrm{d}t)/p(t) \cdot x(t). \end{aligned} \tag{2.4}$$

B. *They are continuously chained Paasche and Fisher indices*

Replacing $p(t)$ by $p(t + \mathrm{d}t)$ introduces only second-order terms into (2.2).

C. *They satisfy the factor reversal test*

$$\begin{aligned} \mathrm{d}PX/PX &= \mathrm{d}P/P + \mathrm{d}X/X = (p \cdot \mathrm{d}x + x \cdot \mathrm{d}p)/p \cdot x \\ &= \mathrm{d}(p \cdot x)/p \cdot x = \mathrm{d}V/V. \end{aligned} \tag{2.5}$$

Note that if we normalize so that $P_0 X_0 = V_0$ initially,

$$PX = V \tag{2.6}$$

throughout. *Do so from now on.*

D. *They satisfy the time-reversal test*

$$\log X(T)/X(0) = \int_0^T p \cdot \mathrm{d}x/p \cdot x. \tag{2.7}$$

$$\log X(0)/X(T) = -\log X(T)/X(0) = \int_T^0 p \cdot \mathrm{d}x/p \cdot x. \tag{2.8}$$

E. *Sectional indices aggregate conformably*

Let $x = (x_1, \ldots, x_R)$, $p = (p_1, \ldots, p_R)$ be conformable partitions of x, p. Then

$$\begin{aligned} \mathrm{d}X/X &= p \cdot \mathrm{d}x/p \cdot x = \sum p_r \cdot \mathrm{d}x_r \Big/ \sum p_r \cdot x_r \\ &= \sum p_r \cdot x_r (p_r \cdot \mathrm{d}x_r/p_r \cdot x_r) \Big/ \sum p_r \cdot x_r \\ &= \sum P_r X_r (\mathrm{d}X_r/X_r) \Big/ \sum P_r \cdot X_r \\ &= \sum P_r \mathrm{d}X_r \Big/ \sum P_r X_r. \end{aligned} \tag{2.9}$$

None of these very satisfactory results depends on any assumptions about the economy. Those that follow do.

F. *If x is an individual consumption vector and p is a vector of efficiency prices, X = constant as we move along an indifferent surface*

$$\begin{aligned} \mathrm{d}X/X &= \sum p_i \mathrm{d}x_i \Big/ \sum p_i x_i = \sum u_i \mathrm{d}x_i \Big/ \sum u_i x_i \\ &= \mathrm{d}u \Big/ \sum u_i x_i \\ &= 0 \qquad \text{when } \mathrm{d}u = 0. \end{aligned} \tag{2.10}$$

G. *Similar results hold for movements along a community indifference surface, or a production frontier*

Note that it is not claimed that X returns to its old value if one leaves and then returns to a given indifference surface. Indeed it will normally be different even if one returns to the same consumption vector. This is the point discussed in Section 3.

I now turn to the measurement of productive efficiency. Let x, y be vectors of inputs and outputs, and p, q the corresponding price vectors. *Let there be perfect competition and constant returns to scale.* Then

H. $PX = p \cdot x = q \cdot y = QY$, *so that*

$$Y/X = P/Q = E, \text{ say.} \tag{2.11}$$

Y/X is an obvious candidate for a measure of efficiency. We will see that it is a good one under these assumptions. (2.11) says that a given increase in productive efficiency will show itself in a similar decrease in the price of outputs in comparison with that of inputs.

I. *Given perfect competition and constant returns, E = constant on a fixed production frontier*

Let the production frontier be

$$F(x, y) = 1, \tag{2.12}$$

where $F(\cdot)$ is homogeneous of degree zero, reflecting constant returns, so that

$$F_i = \partial F/\partial x_i = -\lambda p_i, \quad F_j = \partial F/\partial y_j = \lambda q_j, \text{ say,} \tag{2.13}$$

and, using the homogeneity property $\sum F_j y_j + \sum F_i x_i = 0$,

$$\mathrm{d}E/E = \mathrm{d}Y/Y - \mathrm{d}X/X = q \cdot \mathrm{d}y/q \cdot y - p \cdot \mathrm{d}x/p \cdot x \tag{2.14}$$

$$= \sum_j F_j \mathrm{d}y_j \Big/ \sum_j F_j y_j - \sum_i F_i \mathrm{d}x_i \Big/ \sum_i F_i x_i \tag{2.15}$$

$$= \left(\sum_j F_j \mathrm{d}y_j + \sum_i F_i \mathrm{d}x_i \right) \Big/ \sum_j F_j y_j$$

$$= \mathrm{d}F \Big/ \sum_j F_j y_j = 0, \tag{2.16}$$

since $\mathrm{d}F = 0$.

J. *If there is perfect competition and constant returns, but the production frontier is moving*

$$\dot{E}/E = (\mathrm{d}E/\mathrm{d}t)/E = \rho(x, y, t), \textit{ say,}$$

$$= \textit{the proportional rate at which all outputs can grow, inputs remaining constant} \qquad (2.17)$$

$$= \textit{the proportional rate at which all inputs can decline, outputs remaining constant.} \qquad (2.18)$$

Let the equation of the production frontier be

$$\log F(x, y) = \sigma(t), \qquad (2.19)$$

where $F(\cdot)$ is conical. Then, using (2.15),

$$\frac{\sum_j F_j \dot{y}_j}{\sum_j F_j y_j} - \frac{\sum_i F_i \dot{x}_i}{\sum_i F_i x_i} = \dot{\sigma}(t). \qquad (2.20)$$

Setting each $\dot{x}_i = 0$, $\dot{y}_j = \mu y_j$, we find that $\mu = \dot{\sigma}$, while a trivially similar argument yields $\lambda = \dot{\sigma}$, when each $\dot{x}_i = -\lambda x_i$, $\dot{y}_j = 0$, so that $\lambda = \mu = \dot{\sigma} = \dot{E}/E = \rho(x, y, t)$. These are two very special cases. I leave the proof of the general case to the reader.

K. I *and* J *hold in the absence of perfect competition, as long as the markets for inputs share a common degree of monopoly, and those for outputs a, possibly different, common degree of monopoly*

Perfect competition was used only in moving from (2.14) to (2.15), where only the ratio of different input, or different output, prices occur.

Richter (1966) discussed the measurement of productivity from an axiomatic point of view and concluded that, given perfect competition and constant returns, only the Divisia index E would do. I will now look at this problem in a less rigorous manner.

Let us say that an index, I, of efficiency is acceptable if

(α) Along any time path

$$\mathrm{d}I/I = \sum_j b_j \mathrm{d}y_j - \sum_i a_i \mathrm{d}x_i,$$

so that small changes in the structure of production cannot lead to a finite change in measured efficiency.

(β) Along a production frontier, $F(x, y) = 1$, say,

$$\mathrm{d}I = 0,$$

so that there can be no increase in efficiency without a change in technology.

(γ) If all outputs grow at the same proportional rate $\dot{y}_j/y_j=\sigma$ while all inputs remain fixed,

$$\dot{I}/I=+\sigma.$$

(δ) If all inputs grow at the same proportional rate $\dot{x}_i/x_i=\rho$, while all outputs remain fixed,

$$\dot{I}/I=-\rho.$$

Then

L. *Under perfect competition $I=E$ is the only acceptable index of efficiency and it is acceptable only if there are constant returns.*

(α) and (β) immediately imply

$$a_i=-\mu F_i, \quad b_j=\mu F_j, \quad \mathrm{d}I/I=\mu \mathrm{d}F, \text{ say.} \tag{2.21}$$

(γ) and (δ) then yield

$$\sigma=\mu\sigma\sum F_j y_j, \quad \rho=-\mu\rho\sum F_i x_i, \tag{2.22}$$

so that

$$\sum F_i x_i=-\sum F_j y_j. \tag{2.23}$$

That is, there are constant returns, and

$$\frac{\mathrm{d}I}{I}=\mu\mathrm{d}F=\frac{\sum F_j \mathrm{d}y_j}{\sum F_j y_j}-\frac{\sum F_i \mathrm{d}x_i}{\sum F_i x_i}, \tag{2.24}$$

which is the Divisia formula with efficiency prices. It therefore holds under perfect competition.

M. L *is true if the degree of monopoly is the same in all product markets, and the degree of monopsony is the same in all input markets.*

3. INDEPENDENCE OF PATH

According to (2.1)

$$\log X_T/X_0=\int_C p\cdot \mathrm{d}x/p\cdot x, \tag{3.1}$$

the integral being calculated along the actual time-path followed by the economy from x_0 to x_T. Unless the integrand is a perfect differential, the integral, hence x_T/x_0, will depend on the entire path and not just on its end points x_0, x_T.

Now suppose the integral along one C joining a, b is T and along another D, joining them is S. Then the integral around the entire circuit $C^* = C$ followed by $-D$, from a back to a again is $T - S = \alpha$, say. Indeed it does not matter when we break into the circuit, the integral around it will still be α, so that X will be e^{α} times as great when it comes back to any given point on the circuit as when it last visited it and, after t circuits, $e^{\alpha t}$ times as great. In other words, X will follow a cycle about a strict exponential trend while the actual economy is cycling about a stagnant level, which would obviously be pretty misleading, though how misleading would of course depend on how big $|\alpha|$ is.

For this not to occur it is necessary and sufficient for the integrand in (3.1) to be a perfect differential, in which case we have

$$X_t = X(x_t), \text{ say.} \tag{3.2}$$

What does this imply about the economy?

Consider first the case where x is an individual's consumption vector, so that $p_i = \lambda u_i = \lambda \partial u/\partial x_i$, u being the utility function, and

$$\mathrm{d}X/X = \sum u_i \mathrm{d}x_i \Big/ \sum u_i x_i = \mathrm{d}u \Big/ \sum u_i x_i, \tag{3.3}$$

so that

$$\mathrm{d}X = \mu \mathrm{d}u, \text{ say,} \tag{3.4}$$

and

$$X = \phi(u), \text{ say,} \qquad \phi' = \mu > 0. \tag{3.5}$$

Alternative:

$$X = \phi(u),$$

$$\frac{\phi'(u)\mathrm{d}u}{\phi(u)} = \frac{\mathrm{d}u}{\sum u_i x_i},$$

$$\sum u_i x_i = \frac{\phi(u)}{\phi'(u)},$$

$$\sum \phi'(u) u_i x_i = \phi(u),$$

$$\sum \frac{\partial \phi}{\partial x_i} x_i = \phi.$$

We may therefore normalize to get

$$u(x) = X(x), \tag{3.6}$$

without loss of generality, in which case (3.3) implies

$$\sum u_i x_i = u, \tag{3.7}$$

so that $u(x)$ and $X(x)$ are homogeneous of degree one.

In other words X is independent of the path followed if the utility function is homothetic. In that case $X(\cdot)$ is positively homogeneous of degree one and is itself an acceptable utility function.

Turn now to the corresponding price index.

Note that the cost of reaching a given level of utility u at prices p

$$g(p, u) = uk(p), \text{ say,} \tag{3.8}$$

in this normalization, where $k(p)$ is the cost of reaching $u = 1$. Hence

$$x_i = g_i = uk_i, \tag{3.9}$$

the subscripts denoting differentiation, and

$$\begin{aligned} \mathrm{d}P/P &= \sum k_i \mathrm{d}p_i \Big/ \sum k_i p_i \\ &= \mathrm{d}k/k, \end{aligned} \tag{3.10}$$

since k obviously doubles when p does.

Hence

$$P = k(p) \tag{3.11}$$

after trivial normalization. Hence P is also independent of the path if X is, it too is then possibly homogeneous of degree one and is, in fact, the average cost of producing the aggregate $X(\cdot)$ from the micro-variables x.

Had we begun by requiring that P be independent of the path of integration we would have written $x_i = g_i(p, u)$ to get

$$P_i/P_j = x_i/x_j = g_i/g_j \tag{3.12}$$

by (3.1) and (3.11), so that

$$g = G(P(p), u) \tag{3.13}$$

by Leontief's theorem on separability and

$$\mathrm{d}P/P = \sum P_i \mathrm{d}p_i \Big/ \sum P_i p_i = \mathrm{d}P \Big/ \sum P_i p_i, \tag{3.14}$$

so that

$$P = \sum P_i p_i, \tag{3.15}$$

and is therefore positively homogeneous of degree one. Since $g(u, \cdot)$ is also positively homogeneous of degree one this implies that $g(u, p) = \phi(u)P(p)$, or, after the obvious normalization

$$g(u, p) = uP(p), \tag{3.16}$$

so that utility is produced under constant costs; that is the utility function,

$$u = u(x) \tag{3.17}$$

is positively homogeneous of degree one, so that, once again,

$$X = u(x). \tag{3.18}$$

In other words, if either X or P is independent of the path of integration, so is the other; each is positively homogeneous of degree one, X yields the level of utility in an appropriate normalization, and PX is the income needed to earn it.

If $u(\cdot)$ is a production function instead of a utility function, the indices are independent of the path if $u(\cdot)$ is homogeneous. In particular they are so if production is under constant returns. In that case the input index X gives the level of output and the input prices index P is average or unit cost.

One impressive thing about all this is that one does not have to know the formula for the production function to calculate the amount produced, or its average cost. The Divisia calculations grind these values out automatically.

Consider now the case of sectional indices, say on the production side. Let $x = (x^1, x^2, \ldots, x^R)$ where x^r is a vector of net inputs of goods in class r—negative net outputs being inputs, of course. Write $x^1 = (y^1, z^1)$ where y^1 is a scalar, and solve the production relation for

$$y^1 = F(z^1, x^2, \ldots, x^R). \tag{3.19}$$

Let us now suppose that the Divisia indices $X^1, \ldots, X^R$ are independent of the path of integration. Then

$$X_i^r / X^r = F_i \Big/ \sum_{j \in r} x_j F_j, \qquad i \in r > 1, \tag{3.20}$$

where suffixes still denote differentiation. Hence $F_i/F_j = X_i^r(x^r)/X_j^r(x^r)$, $r > 1$ so that

$$y^1 = F = G(z^1, X^2(x^2), \ldots, X^R(x^R)), \qquad \text{where } X^1 = (y^1, z^1), \tag{3.21}$$

by Leontief's theorem on separability. Solving next for X^R in terms of $(x^1, X^2, \ldots, X^{R-1})$ and applying a similar analysis, we ultimately find that the production relation can be written

$$H(X^1(x^1), \ldots, X^R(x^R)) = 0. \tag{3.22}$$

Using once again the fact that $p_i = \lambda F_i$, we have

$$\begin{aligned} \mathrm{d}X^r / X^r &= \sum_{i \in r} X_i^r \mathrm{d}x_i \Big/ \sum_{i \in r} X_i^r x_i \\ &= \mathrm{d}X^r \Big/ \sum_{i \in r} X_i^r x_i, \end{aligned} \tag{3.23}$$

$$X^r = \sum_{i \in r} X_i^r x_i, \tag{3.24}$$

and each X^r is positively homogeneous of degree one.

It is easy to show that, in this case too, the corresponding price indices are independent of the path of integration, and that, after trivial normalization,

$$P^r(p^r) = \min \{p^r \cdot x^r / X^r(x^r) \geqslant 1\} \tag{3.25}$$

and is therefore the cost of producing a unit of the aggregate X^r from the corresponding micro-goods x^r.

Finally, requiring that P^r be independent of the path of integration has exactly the same implications.

One final word. Suppose that aggregates $(X^1(x^1), \ldots, X^R(x^R))$ exist such that the production relation can be written in the form (3.22). Then it can be shown rather easily, and under rather weak regularity conditions, that each $X^r(\cdot)$ may be taken to be positively homogeneous of degree one without loss of generality. In other words, the conditions for the Divisia indices to be independent of the path of integration are satisfied; the indices in question reproduce the values of the aggregates and their corresponding prices, or unit costs, without our needing to know the formulae for either, or anything more than their mere existence.

4. ALTERNATIVE DEFLATORS

Suppose that there is a single output y and that

$$y = f(x, z)$$

when x, z are vectors of two different types of input. Following an idea of Solow (1957), Charles R. Hulten has shown that

$$\mathrm{d}X^*/X^* = p \cdot \mathrm{d}x/qy = \sum f_i \mathrm{d}x_i/f \tag{4.1}$$

is independent of the path if functions $X(x)$, $Z(z)$ of x, z exist such that

$$y = X(x)Z(z), \tag{4.2}$$

which is quite different from homogeneity—at least at first sight.

Let us now explore these ideas more generally. First let there be a vector y of outputs so that

$$F(x, y, z) \equiv y_1 - f(x, z, w) = 0, \qquad w = (y_2, \ldots, y_n), \tag{4.3}$$

and let

$$\mathrm{d}X^*/X^* = p \cdot \mathrm{d}x/q \cdot y = -\sum F_i \mathrm{d}x_i/F_j y_j \tag{4.4}$$

be independent of the path, so that it is the differential of a function $\log X^*(x)$. Hence $F_i/F_j = X_i^*/X_j^* = f_i/f_j$, and

$$F(x, y, z) \equiv y_1 - f^*(X^*(x), z, w) = 0. \tag{4.5}$$

Solve this for X^* to get

$$X^*(x) = g(y, z) \tag{4.6}$$

and

$$\mathrm{d}X^*/X^* = \sum X_i^* \mathrm{d}x_i \Big/ \sum g_j y_j = \mathrm{d}X^* \Big/ \sum g_j y_j, \tag{4.7}$$

implying that

$$\sum g_j y_j = g, \tag{4.8}$$

so that $(\cdot, z)$ is homogeneous of degree one and equation (4.6) can be written

$$F(X^*(x), y, z) = 0 \tag{4.9}$$

when F is homogeneous of degree zero in X^*, y, or, alternatively, as

$$g(y/X^*(x), z) = 1 \tag{4.10}$$

in general.

Suppose now that the output vector y also has some Divisia-type index—either with itself or some other group providing the deflator. Then it is trivial that y is separable in $g(y, z)$. Since $g(\cdot, z)$ is homogeneous of degree one, this implies that its component $\bar{Y}(y)$ may be taken to be homogeneous of degree one. Then $g(y, z) = G(\bar{Y}(y), z)$ will be homogeneous of degree one in $\bar{Y}$, so that

$$X^*(x) = \bar{Y}(y)h(z), \tag{4.11}$$

a generalization of (4.2), with $\bar{Y}(\cdot)$ *homogeneous*.

Suppose now that there are several groups with vectors $x^1, \ldots, x^n$, $y^1, \ldots, y^N$, the latter being the deflator groups. Suppose y^R is used to deflate its own index Y^R, and also the indices

$$\mathrm{d}X_r^*/X_r^* = p_r \cdot \mathrm{d}x_r/q_r \cdot y_r, \qquad r \in R, \tag{4.12}$$

in an obvious notation. Arguments similar to the above then imply readily that the production equation may be written in the form

$$F(z) = 0, \quad z = (z_1, \ldots, z_N), \qquad z_R = \prod_{r \in R} X_r^*(x_r) \Big/ \prod_{r \in R} Y^r(y_r), \tag{4.13}$$

when each $Y^r(\cdot)$ is homogeneous of degree one. The generalization of (4.2) is obvious: its interest less so.

5

Consumer Budgets and Price Indices

Editorial Summary

This is the most ambitious of the papers that are explicitly concerned with budgeting. Here Gorman discards the previously maintained hypothesis of separability and attempts to discover the implications of perfect price aggregation itself.[1] Specifically, in the notation of this paper, he looks for the conditions under which a consumer with a well-behaved utility function can determine the optimal intersector allocations, M_r, as a function of sector-specific price indices, $\{P^r\}$, and total income, M; i.e.

$$M_r = F^r(M, P^1(p^1), P^2(p^2), \ldots, P^n(p^n)) \tag{0.1}$$

for $r = 1, \ldots, n$.

Section 2 of the paper—up to equation (2.19)—solves this problem by deriving necessary and sufficient conditions on the indirect utility function for (0.1) to hold, while (2.24)–(2.26) express these conditions in term of the cost, or expenditure, function. The results show that the indirect utility function can be written as

$$\phi(M, p) = H(h(M, P^1(p^1), \ldots, P^n(p^n)), p), \tag{0.2}$$

where H is homogeneous of degree zero in the prices of each sector, p^r, $r = 1, \ldots, n$. Solving $u = \phi(M, p)$ for M yields the cost function

$$M = L(u, p) = K(k(u, p), P^1(p^1), P^2(p^2), \ldots, P^n(p^n)), \tag{0.3}$$

where k is homogeneous of degree zero in each p^r, $r = 1, \ldots, n$. The special cases of perfect price aggregation derived earlier in 'Separable Utility and Aggregation' are, of course, of this form.

Using Roy's identity in (0.2) or Shephard's lemma in (0.3), it is easy to see that these conditions are sufficient. From (0.3) the compensated demand for commodity i in group r is given by

$$\begin{aligned} x_i^r = {} & K_0(k(u, p), P^1(p^1), P^2(p^2), \ldots, P^n(p^n))k_i(u, p) \\ & + K_r(k(u, p), P^1(p^1), P^2(p^2), \ldots, P^n(p^n))P_i^r(p^r). \end{aligned} \tag{0.4}$$

[1] The version of the paper that appears here is dated 1965, so the work was clearly done somewhat earlier.

Multiplying (0.4) by p_i and summing over $i \in r$ yields (0.1), because k is homogeneous of degree zero in p^r.

To establish necessity, he employs a transformation of variables which is particularly useful in the present context. Noticing in (0.1) that we are given an index of the prices in sector r that can be normalized to be homogeneous of degree one, he constructs a one-to-one mapping from sector r prices to a vector consisting of the price index P^r and a vector of functions, $\{q_i^r\}$, of dimension one less than the dimension of sector r, each of which is homogeneous of degree zero in p^r. His equation (2.10) redefines the indirect utility function in terms of these new variables. The original formulation of the problem then becomes a simple separability issue, and leads to the solution given in (2.17).

The rest of Section 2 attempts to find the direct utility functions that are dual to (0.2) and (0.3). There are several technical innovations in this part of the paper which are worth studying for their own sake. However, it is all somewhat ironic because Gorman frequently chastised his students and colleagues for spending (not necessarily wasting) time searching for a direct representation when a representation in a dual space was already available. Clearly, this is a temptation that even Gorman finds difficult to avoid.

One problem that arises frequently in this sort of work first reveals itself here: the price indices cannot be shown to be concave, even though they are linearly homogeneous. When they are not concave, standard duality procedures for recovering the direct utility function will not suffice. Furthermore, it is difficult to know exactly how to interpret these functions when they are not concave. In a different context, this question is answered in appendix B of 'More Measures for Fixed Factors'.

To return to the task at hand, from (2.27) to (2.33) he takes k in (0.3) to be independent of prices, and assumes sufficient concavity to show that the corresponding direct utility function is homothetically separable; that is,

$$u(x) = U(X^1(x^1), \ldots, X^n(x^n)) \tag{0.5}$$

where each X^r is linearly homogeneous. This dual structure is already evident in the remarks at the end of the 1959 paper 'Separable Utility and Aggregation'.

When k is not independent of prices, retrieving the direct utility function is more difficult. He proceeds by deriving the demands from (0.3) to obtain

$$\begin{aligned} x_i &= K_r(k(u, p), P^1(p^1), \ldots, P^n(p^n))P_i^r(p^r) \\ &\quad + K_0(k(u, p), P^1(p^1), \ldots, P^n(p^n))k_i(u, p) \\ &=: y_i + z_i, \end{aligned} \tag{0.6}$$

for all i in group r, where y_i and z_i are defined implicitly. Furthermore, using the stated homogeneity properties of the cost function k, it is clear that $\sum_{i \in r} p_i y_i = M_r$ and that $\sum_{i \in r} p_i z_i = 0$. Hence one can divide the demand for x_i into two parts, one of which accounts for the total group expenditure, and the other involves intragroup corrections that net out to zero. He then demonstrates that y_i and z_i cannot represent different uses of the same good for different purposes.

The rest of Section 2 comprises a final attempt to find a direct utility function with the above interpretation, so that each unit of a commodity can be divided into two different uses or sources of utility. Most of the discussion is framed in terms of a rather different situation in which this interpretation is possible. It is interesting for a variety of reasons. First, in order to proceed he defines what is now called the distance function and shows that it is an indirect cost function and that it is the perfect dual to the ordinary (direct) cost function.[2] (2.42)–(2.45) are regularity assumptions imposed to avoid the above-mentioned concavity problem. (2.46)–(2.51) establish the duality between cost and distance functions. In passing, one sees that the direct distance function is in fact an indirect cost function and that the cost function is an indirect distance function. It is, we believe, the first statement of this duality,[3] although, as usual, it only arises here because it is needed to solve the subsequent problem.

In any case, he begins anew in (2.52) by positing a cost function L that is dual to a utility function u and is given by

$$M = L(\psi(u, p), P^1(p^1), \ldots, P^n(p^n)), \tag{0.7}$$

where L is linearly homogeneous in its arguments. The assumption that ψ is a cost function which yields the budgeting result (2.45) suffices to establish that this expenditure function pair (L, ψ) is also a solution to this budgeting problem.

The balance of this section derives the direct utility function that is dual to this pair. For this reason the distance function is employed both as a direct representation and also as an indirect cost function. The final outcome is given in (2.63) if one ignores the homogeneity of v, or by (2.63*a*) if one imposes it. In any case, this interpretation as a utility function in which there is more that one source of utility, and in which each good can contribute to both sources and the division can be done optimally, has since appeared in many different applications, both by Gorman and others.[4]

Section 3 adds a new assumption. Given perfect price aggregation (which yields the expenditure function given by (0.3)), suppose that the intragroup allocation is

$$\begin{aligned} x_i &= f^i(M^r, p^r, P^1(p^1), \ldots, P^{r-1}(p^{r-1})), P^{r+1}(p^{r+1}), \ldots, P^n(p^n)) \\ &:= f^i(M^r, p^r, P^{-r}), \end{aligned} \tag{0.8}$$

for all i in group r where P^{-r} refers to the vector of price indices other than r. Remember that, for each r, k in (0.3) is homogeneous of degree zero in the prices of group r. Note that if f^i in (0.8) is independent of P^{-r} then the theorem in 'Two-Stage Budgeting' implies that the direct utility function is separable. This, in combination with perfect price aggregation, yields the results in 'Separable Utility and Aggregation'.

In the remainder of Section 3, he shows that (0.8) implies that k in (0.3) can be written in either of two ways. In the first case, k depends only upon the prices of one group, for example group 1, and can be written as

$$k(u, p) = \tilde{k}(u, p^1), \tag{0.9}$$

[2] A later paper, 'Quasi-Separable Preferences, Costs, and Technologies' is a detailed examination of this indirect cost function, its properties, and its uses.

[3] This duality appears clearly in Shephard (1970).

[4] Unfortunately, because it was unpublished, many of us have had to rediscover this result from first principles.

or in an additively separable form as in

$$k(u, p) = \tilde{k}(u) + \sum_r k^r(p^r), \tag{0.10}$$

where each k^r is homogeneous of degree zero.

The last section imposes a further requirement, namely, that the demand functions given by (0.8) are derived from conditional subutility functions of the form $v(x^r, P^r(p^r))$. First he shows that this requirement eliminates (0.9) as a possible solution, leaving only (0.10). Then we see that one obtains the homothetically separable and additively separable cases of 'Separable Utility and Aggregation' and, in addition, one structure that is not separable at all.

Consumer Budgets and Price Indices

1. INTRODUCTION

A good deal of recent work on demand has turned on the notion that consumers typically budget in two stages, first deciding how much to spend on food, clothing, etc., and then how to spread these amounts over the individual goods. To the best of my knowledge nobody has tried to find how widely such a procedure is used; those who do use it presumably do so because they find it simple to apply and efficient. These criteria seem to lead directly to the assumption of separable utility,

$$u(x) = F(v^1(x^1), \ldots, v^n(x^n)), \tag{1.1}$$

where $x^r = (x_i)_{i \in r}$ is the consumption vector in the rth group, and $x = (x^1, \ldots, x^n)$ the overall consumption vector. Given an allocation $M^1, \ldots, M^n$ of expenditure to the various groups, u is maximized by maximizing each $v^r(x^r)$ subject to $p^r \cdot x^r = M^r$ in the obvious notation, so that the second stage, or *conditional demand functions* may be written

$$x_i = f^i(M^r, p^r), \qquad i \in r, \tag{1.2}$$

which may reasonably be called simple, and which is certainly fully efficient if the allocation between the groups is correct. This preliminary allocation, too, is reasonably simple if the utility function is separable, at least in the sense that the change in the optimal allocation depends, to the first order, on the change in income and on two price indices for each group—one corresponding to the income effects, and the other to the substitution effects, of the price changes in it. All the same, the notion of two separate price levels for each category would not perhaps appeal greatly to most housewives. Recent work by Dr Ray Byron has also suggested that separable utility, at least using the reasonable groups which he examined, and under static assumptions, does not fit the facts at all well. Assuming that people do indeed budget in two stages, perhaps we should seek an alternative justification.

Since (1.2) is in fact equivalent to (1.1), it will clearly have to be dropped as the definition of 'simplicity'. Instead, let us first require that the optimal allocation between groups can be written

$$M^r = F^r(M, P), \qquad r = 1, 2, \ldots, n \tag{1.3}$$

$$P = P(p) = (P^1(p^1), \ldots, P^n(p^n)), \qquad p^r = (p_i)_{i \in r}, \qquad r = 1, 2, \ldots, n, \tag{1.4}$$

where the P's are group price indices, the notion being that *at this stage*, the consumer knows what the price level is likely to be in each group, but does not know the individual prices.

In the present paper I first explore the consequences of (1.3). Later I enquire what further conditions are required in order that the second-stage demand functions may be written in the form

$$x_i = f^i(M^r, p^r, P^{-r}), \qquad \text{each } i \in r, \qquad P^{-r} = (P^t)_{t \neq r}, \qquad r = 1, 2, \ldots, n, \tag{1.5}$$

and, later still, that these may be derivable from conditional criteria

$$v^r = v^r(x^r, P^{-r}), \qquad r = 1, 2, \ldots, n. \tag{1.6}$$

While I think that some readers will find the conditions required for these properties conformable to their intuition and even mildly informative, I cannot believe that they are wildly exciting or suggest interesting new lines of research. However, the methods I use may be interesting. Moreover, this sort of analysis has recently become fashionable again, and it seems worth while marking the spot 'here he deserts'. The reason for this aridity may be that it is unreasonable to require that the price aggregate should depend only on the prices in the corresponding groups.

There will be no attempt at rigour in this paper. In particular I will always assume, usually implicitly, that the functions I use are sufficiently smooth to justify the calculus methods I will employ.

2. THE ALLOCATION BETWEEN GROUPS

Suppose the consumer's preferences to be such that the optimal expenditure on goods in group r may be written

$$M^r = F^r(M, P) > 0, \qquad r = 1, 2, \ldots, n, \tag{2.1}$$

where

$$P = P(p) = (P^1(p^1), P^2(p^2), \ldots, P^n(p^n)) \tag{2.2}$$

is a vector of price aggregates, none of which decreases when the corresponding prices increase, and all of which actually increase when those prices all increase in the same proportion; that is,

$$P_i^r = \partial P^r/\partial p_i \geqslant 0, \qquad \text{each } i \in r, \qquad r = 1, 2, \ldots, n, \tag{2.3a}$$

$$\sum_{i \in r} p_i P_i^r > 0, \qquad r = 1, 2, \ldots, n, \tag{2.3b}$$

where suffixes on functions denote derivatives both here and throughout this paper.

What can we deduce? In the first place, that each of the $P^r(\cdot)$ are homothetic and may be normalized to be homogeneous of degree one without loss of generality.

To show this it will be convenient to introduce the quantitites

$$X^r = M^r/P^r = G^r(M, P), \text{ say}, \qquad r = 1, 2, \ldots, n, \tag{2.4}$$

demanded of the fictitious macro-goods $r = 1, 2, \ldots, n$. Since $P^r X^r = M^r$, at least one $G^r_s = \partial G^r/\partial P^s \neq 0$ for any given (M, P). Moreover $G^r(\cdot)$ is clearly homogeneous of degree zero in $p = (p^1, \ldots, p^n)$.[1] Hence

$$\sum_{j\in s} p_j P^s_j = -\left(\sum_{t\neq s} G^r_t \sum_{k\in t} p_k P^t_k\right) \Big/ G^r_s$$

$$= \phi^s(P^s(p^s)), \text{ say}, \qquad > 0 \text{ by (2.3}b\text{)}, \tag{2.5}$$

since the left-hand side depends only on p^s, which enters into the right-hand side only via $P^s(p^s)$. Hence we may define

$$\bar{P}^s = \psi^s(P^s) = \exp\left(\int \mathrm{d}P^s/\phi^s\right) > 0, \tag{2.6}$$

so that

$$\mathrm{d}\bar{P}^s/\mathrm{d}P^s = \bar{P}^s/\phi^s, \tag{2.7}$$

and

$$\sum_{j\in s} p_j \bar{P}^s_j = \left(\sum_{j\in s} p_j P^s_j\right) \mathrm{d}\bar{P}^s/\mathrm{d}P^s = \bar{P}^s, \tag{2.8}$$

by (2.5) and (2.7). Since $\bar{P}^s$ is a strictly increasing function of P^s by (2.5)–(2.7), we can solve (2.6) for P^s in terms of $\bar{P}^s$, substitute into (2.1) and (2.4), drop the bars, and thus ensure that all the P's are positively homogeneous of degree one, that is, in Sydney Afriat's simple and suggestive terminology, *conical*. Because of (2.7), (2.1)–(2.3) remain true. Say that such indices, conical and satisfying (2.3), are admissible.

Turn now to the preference field behind (2.1)–(2.4). Since we are interested in demand equations it may appropriately be represented by the indirect or polar utility function

$$u = \phi(M, p), \tag{2.9}$$

which is, of course, homogeneous of degree zero in (M, p).

[1] [eds.] This argument is incomplete, if not wrong. In any case, he offers a correct argument of this proposition in Gorman (1959). What one wants to show is that (2.3) implies that each function P^r can be chosen to be homogeneous of degree one even though no such assumption has been made about them. Noticing that M^r is homogeneous of degree one in all prices and income yields

$$F^r(M, P^1(p^1), \ldots, P^n(p^n)) = \lambda^{-1} F^r(M, P^1(\lambda p^1), \ldots, P^n(\lambda p^n))$$

for all positive λ. From this it is clear that the level sets of P^r are the same at p^r and at λp^r, implying that P^r is homothetic. Given that each price index is homothetic, Gorman's argument demonstrating that it can be chosen to be homogeneous of degree one is, of course, correct.

Before analysing its relation with (2.1), it will clearly be convenient to introduce the P's into (2.9) as explanatory variables. I will do this in a way which is frequently convenient in such cases.

Let $p^r \leftrightarrow (P^r, q^r)$ be a smooth (1, 1) mapping, where the components of $q^r = (q_j)_{j\in r}$ are homogeneous of degree zero in p^r. Use it to transform (2.9) to get

$$u = \phi(M, p) = \psi(M, P(p), q(p)), \text{ say.} \tag{2.10}$$

The demand for good i, is therefore

$$x_i = -\phi_i/\phi_0,$$

$$= -\left(\psi_r P_i^r + \sum_{j\in r} \psi_j q_{ji}^r\right)\Big/\psi_0, \tag{2.11}$$

where $\phi_i = \partial\phi/\partial p_i$, $\phi_0 = \partial\phi/\partial M$, $\psi_r = \partial\psi/\partial P^r$, $\psi_j = \partial\psi/\partial q_j$, $\psi_0 = \partial\psi/\partial M$, and $q_{ji}^r = \partial q_j^r/\partial p_i$.

Hence

$$M^r = \sum_{i\in r} p_i x_i = -\psi_r P^r/\psi_0, \tag{2.12}$$

by homogeneity. Looking at (2.4) we immediately see that

$$-\psi_r/\psi_0 = G^r(M, P), \tag{2.13}$$

implying that M, P are separable from q in (2.10) which may therefore be written

$$u = \psi(M, P, q) = \theta(h(M,P), q), \text{ say.} \tag{2.14}$$

Substitute $q = q(p)$ in this to get

$$\theta(h, q(p)) = H(h, p), \tag{2.15}$$

where

$$\sum_{i\in r} H_i p_i = \sum_{j\in r} \theta_j \sum_{i\in r} q_{ji} p_i = 0, \tag{2.16}$$

that is, H is homogeneous of degree zero in each p^r. Conversely, if this is so, it can be thrown into the form $\theta(h, q(p))$.

Substituting from (2.15) into (2.14) and then into (2.10), we have

$$u = H(h(M, P(p)), p), \tag{2.17}$$

subject to (2.16). This in turn implies

$$x_i = -(H_0 h_r P_i^r + H_i)/H_0 h_0, \qquad \text{each } i\in r, \tag{2.18}$$

in the obvious notation, so that

$$M^r = -h_r P^r/h_0, \tag{2.19}$$

which is of the required form (2.1) by (2.14). In terms of the fictional macro-variables X this reads

$$X^r = G^r(M, P) = -h_r/h_0, \tag{2.20}$$

which is, of course, the direct analogue of (2.11). In other words, the demand for these fictitious goods is that which would have been predicted by an indirect utility function $h(M, P)$.

Does $h(\cdot)$ have the formal properties required of an indirect utility function? It is easily verified that it is indeed homogeneous of degree zero as required, but there are also the convexity conditions which are more easily discussed in its alias as a cost function. This I will do in a moment, but first let me remark that (2.20) is in fact equivalent to the usual Slutsky conditions on the aggregate demands $X^r = G^r(M, P)$. In fact, (2.20) implies that $\mathrm{d}M - \sum G^r \mathrm{d}P^r$ has an integrating factor h_0 so that

$$1 \cdot (G_s^r - G_r^s) - G^r(G_0^s - 0) - G^s(0 - G_0^r) = 0 \tag{2.21}$$

or

$$G_s^r + G^s G_0^r = G_r^s + G^r G_0^s, \tag{2.22}$$

where the $G_0^r = \partial G^r/\partial M$. Conversely (2.22) implies the existence of a function $h^*(M, P)$ such that $G^r = \lambda h_r^* = \lambda \partial h^*/\partial P^r$, $1 = -\lambda h_0^* = -\lambda \partial h/\partial M$, so that $G^r = -h_r^*/h_0^*$. Since $\sum P^r G^r = M$, h^* is homogeneous of degree zero as required. This strongly suggests that a proposed set of fictitious aggregate demand functions $X^r = G^r(M, P)$ may correspond to some genuine preferences iff they can be derived from some fictitious aggregate utility function

$$U = U(X), \qquad X = (X^1, \ldots, X^n). \tag{2.23}$$

I will now discuss this idea with the aid of the cost function, whose precise mathematical properties are more simply stated than those of the indirect or direct utility functions.[2]

In (2.17), u is strictly increasing in M. We may therefore normalize so that h is strictly increasing in M and H in h. Do so, invert to get

$$h(M, P(p)) = k(u, p), \text{ say,} \tag{2.24}$$

where

$$\sum_{i \in r} k_i p_i = 0, \qquad r = 1, 2, \ldots, n, \tag{2.25}$$

and then invert once more to get

[2] The cost function is increasing closed concave conical in p, the indirect utility functions decreasing, closed quasi-concave in p/M, so that there is not much in it. However, the cost function is easier to use.

$$M = L(u, p) = K(k(u, p), P(p)), \text{ say.} \tag{2.26}$$

Call $k(u, p)$ an *admissible pseudo-utility* if it satisfies (2.25).

As a cost function, K is positively homogeneous and closed concave in p. I will now show that this implies that it is also positively homogeneous and closed concave in P—in other words that $K(U, P)$ is the cost function corresponding to an aggregate utility function $U(X)$ as in (2.23) which yields the aggregate 'demand functions' $X^r = G^r(M, P) = -h_r/h_0$ when maximized subject to $\sum P^r X^r = M$.

First, it is conical. Replace p by λp. This transforms M into λM, K into λK, and P into λP, while k is unaffected. QED.

Secondly, it is concave. Choose p such that each $P^r(p^r) = 1$, $\bar{q}^r = \bar{Q}^r p^r$, $\bar{\bar{q}}^r = \bar{\bar{Q}}^r p^r$. Then $K = \bar{K}(k, Q)$ where $Q = \bar{Q}$, $\bar{\bar{Q}}$ or $(\bar{Q} + \bar{\bar{Q}})/2$, where $k = k(u, p)$ throughout. Concavity in P immediately follows from that in p.

Finally, closure follows immediately from the assumed continuity of $P(\cdot)$.

$K(U, P)$ is therefore closed concave conical in P, that is, is an *admissible cost function*. Call it the *aggregate cost function*. It corresponds to the *aggregate utility function* $U(X)$ of (2.23); that is, $K(U, P) = \inf\{P \cdot X \mid U(X) \geq u\}$. Maximizing U subject to $\sum P^r X^r = M$ naturally gives

$$X^r = G^r(M, P), \text{ say,} \tag{2.27}$$

as required, where X^r is defined to be M^r/P^r, as in (2.4).

It would seem, then, that we are right in saying that (2.1) can hold iff it can be derived from a fictitious aggregate utility function. However, this is so only in rather a special sense.

In saying that the aggregate demand functions $X^r = G^r(M, P)$ are derivable from a well-behaved cost function $K(U, P)$, we say nothing about the price indices. It is at least conceivable that there exist price indices $P(p)$ which are conical and increasing, for which there exists no admissible pseudo-utility $k(u, p)$ such that $K(k(u, p), P(p))$ is an admissible cost function in p. If that were so, there would exist no true, or micro-, tastes which were consistent with the fictitious aggregate demand functions $X^r = G^r(M, P)$ even though these arise from a fictitious aggregate utility function $U = U(X)$. What is true is that only aggregate demand functions so derived can be consistent with the maximization of a true micro-utility function and that, given such a set of aggregate demand functions, we can easily construct admissible price indices $P(p)$ and an admissible pseudo-utility $k(u, p)$ such that $K(k(u, p), P(p))$ is an admissible cost function in p; that is, it corresponds to a true micro-utility function $u(x)$.

Let us then be given an aggregate cost function $K(U, P)$ corresponding to the demand functions $G^r(M, P)$, and seek admissible $k(u, p)$, $P(p)$, such that $K(k(u, p), P(p))$ is an admissible cost function in p. In fact let us try $k(u, p) = u$, so that the micro- and macro-utilities u and U are equal, and seek admissible $P(p)$ such that $K(u, P(p))$ is positively homogeneous of degree one and closed concave in p.

Since $K(k, P)$ is positively homogeneous of degree one in P, and $P(p)$ in p, K is in p, given (2.25).

Choose now p^r, q^r such that $P^r(p^r) = P^r(q^r) = P^r$, and hold p^s constant, $s \neq r$. Since K is quasi-concave in p^r, and increasing in P^r, $P^r(p^r + q^r)/2 \geqslant P^r$. That is, $P^r(\cdot)$ is quasi-concave. Being positively homogeneous of degree one, it is therefore concave.

Conversely, it is trivial that if $K(u, P(p))$ is closed concave conical in $P(p)$, and $P(p)$ in p, so is $K(u, P(p))$ in p, so that it corresponds to a micro-utility function $u(x)$.

This proves our result.

What do we know about $u(x)$ in this case?

According to the general theory of support functions, the utility function $u(x)$ corresponding to the cost function $g(p, u)$ is given by

$$u = u(x) \quad \text{iff} \quad \sup_{p}\{g(p, u) - p \cdot x\} = 0. \tag{2.28}$$

In the present case, therefore,

$$u = u(x) \quad \text{iff} \quad \inf_{p}\{p \cdot x - K(u, P(p))\} = 0,$$

$$U = U(X) \quad \text{iff} \quad \inf_{P}\{P \cdot X - K(U, P))\} = 0. \tag{2.29}$$

Define now

$$X^r(x^r) = \inf_{p^r}\{p^r \cdot x^r \mid P^r(p^r) = 1\}, \tag{2.30}$$

which is clearly conical. Then

$$\begin{aligned} \inf_{p}\{p \cdot x - K(u, P(p))\} &= \inf_{P}\left\{\inf_{p}\{p \cdot x - K(u, P) \mid P(p) = P\}\right\}. \\ &= \inf_{P}\left\{\sum\nolimits_r \inf_{p^r}\{p^r \cdot x^r \mid P^r(p^r) = P^r\} - K(u, P)\right\} \\ &= \inf_{P}\left\{\sum P^r X^r(x^r) - K(u, P)\right\}. \end{aligned} \tag{2.31}$$

According to (2.29), therefore,

$$u = u(x) \quad \text{iff} \quad U = U(X(x)). \tag{2.32}$$

However, $u = U$ by construction, hence

$$u = u(x) = U(X(x)). \tag{2.33}$$

In this case, therefore, the utility function is homothetically separable. The specific satisfaction functions $X(x)$ are the duals of the price indices $P(p)$ and hence closed concave conical.

Note that the quantitites $X^1, \ldots, X^n$ of the fictional macro-goods are here the rather acceptable quantity aggregates $X^1(x^1), \ldots, X^n(x^n)$.

For each admissible macro-cost function $K(U, P)$ and admissible indices $P^1(p^1), \ldots, P^r(p^r)$, we may define the set $S(K(\cdot), P(\cdot))$ of admissible pseudo-utilities $k(u, p)$ for which $K(k(u, p), P(p))$ is an admissible micro-cost function.

Apparently, then, it may be empty, but if each $P^r(\cdot)$ is closed concave, it contains the element u and, presumably, some at least of its neighbouring elements.

What do I mean by this?

In elucidating this it will be convenient to use calculus arguments. In particular, I will have to assume various functions to be continuously twice differentiable. This I will do without further warning. The argument I use will be even less rigorous than normal in this paper.

In general let us be given an admissible pseudo-utility $k(u, p)$ such that

$$\psi(u, p) = K(k(u, p), P(p)), \tag{2.34}$$

is *highly concave* in p, that is to say such that $\sum \psi_{ij}\theta_i\theta_j > 0$ unless $\theta = \lambda p$, all p, u. Take now an admissible pseudo-utility $k^*(u, p)$ and consider

$$\psi^\rho(u, p) = K(k(u, p) + \rho k^*(u, p), P(p)). \tag{2.35}$$

Then

$$\sum \psi^\rho_{ij}\theta_i\theta_j = \sum \psi_{ij}\theta_i\theta_j + \rho \sum \alpha_{ij}\theta_i\theta_j, \text{ say,} \tag{2.36}$$

plus higher-order terms in ρ. For any particular (u, p), let $\mu > 0$ be the second smallest root of $[\psi_{ij}]$, and let the largest modulus of any root of $[\alpha_{ij}]$ be ν. Taking $\rho > \mu/\nu = \sigma$ guarantees that the quadratic form on the right be positive unless $\theta = \lambda p$; taking ρ sufficiently small to guarantee that the higher-order terms in (2.36) may be neglected, renders $\psi^\rho(u, p)$ highly concave at this point.

Can we guarantee that it is highly concave everywhere? Only by the argument if $\inf \rho > 0$. Is it?

In the first place, note that all the terms in (2.36) are homogeneous of the degree minus one in p. Their relative size is therefore independent of the level of prices. We may therefore normalize p so that $\sum p_i = 1$, each $p_i \geqslant 0$. Do so, and confine u to a closed interval; (u, p) therefore belongs to a compact set V. By our continuity assumptions $\sigma = \nu/\mu$ is continuous in u, p. Hence it attains its infimum σ^* at Q^* in V. Since $\sigma > 0$ everywhere, $\sigma^* > 0$, and by uniform continuity, taking ρ small enough allows us to neglect the higher-order terms in (2.36) everywhere. Hence there is a ρ^* such that $|\rho| \leqslant \rho^*$ implies that ψ^ρ is highly concave, and therefore concave. Note that this means that both $k^\rho = k + \rho k^*$ and $k^{-\rho} = k - \rho k^*$ belong to $S(K(\cdot), P(\cdot))$ so that we may reasonably say that $k(u, p)$ is an interior point of $S(K(\cdot), P(\cdot))$ if it is highly concave.

If some latent roots of $[\psi_{ij}]$ vanish at some points, it would appear to be enough to have $k^*(u, p) = 0$ in their neighbourhoods.

In the particular case where $k(u, p) = u$, $\psi(u, p)$ is highly concave in p iff $K(u, P)$ is highly concave in P, and each $P^r(p^r)$ is highly concave in p^r. In this case, therefore, it is reasonable to say that all $k(u, p)$ neighbouring u belong to $S(K(\cdot), P(\cdot))$; otherwise only some may.

Returning now to (2.26) we see that

$$x_i = K_r P_i^r + K_0 k_i, \qquad i \in r, \tag{2.37}$$

where $K_r = \partial K / \partial P^r$, $K_0 = \partial K / \partial k$, $k_i = \partial k / \partial p_i$. Hence

$$M^r = K_r P^r \quad \text{and} \quad X^r = K_r, \tag{2.38}$$

which is, of course, the aggregate demand predicted by the fictitious aggregate cost function $K(U, P)$ introduced above. Substituting into (2.37) we get

$$\begin{aligned} x_i &= X^r P_i^r + K_0 k_i, \qquad i \in r, \\ &= y_i + z_i, \quad \text{say}, \end{aligned} \tag{2.39}$$

where

$$p^r \cdot y^r = X^r P^r(p^r) = M^r, \quad p^r \cdot z^r = 0, \qquad \text{each } r. \tag{2.40}$$

Where the $P^r(\cdot)$ are concave, $X^r P^r(p^r)$ is the cost function corresponding to the specific satisfaction function $X^r(x^r)$, so that y^r is exactly the demand for goods in group r, and is predicted by the macro-utility function $U(X(y))$.

z^r, on the other hand, is the vector of 'departmental' corrections which just happen to pay for each other within each group, so that their net cost within each group is precisely nothing.

Even if $P^r(\cdot)$ is not concave, it seems reasonable to regard $X^r P^r(p^r)$ as a 'source of demand' or potential function and the $X^r P_i^r = y_i$ as the demands for individual goods corresponding to the fictitious macro-demand X^r.

It is tempting to regard the y_i and z_i of (2.39) as representing two different uses of the same good for distinct purposes, some units being used for one, some for another, and each having the same efficiency price. This is an interpretation which frequently works well in such cases but not, I think, here.

The idea would be that the micro-utility function would be of the form $\phi(y, z)$, which would become $\psi(X(y), z)$ when the price indices are concave. The utility function $u(x)$ would be derived by maximizing this subject to $x = y + z$, that is

$$u(x) = \max\{\psi(X(y), z) \mid y + z \leqslant x\}, \tag{2.41}$$

and the cost function $K(k(u, q), P(p))$ by minimizing $p \cdot y + q \cdot z$ given $u \leqslant \psi(X(y),z)$. However there would also be a cost function $C(u, p, q)$ derived by minimizing $p \cdot y + q \cdot z$ given $u \leqslant \phi(y, z)$. What would this be? We would like it to be $K(k(u, q), P(p))$ because of the association of y with the argument of P and z with that of k in $y_i = K_r P_i^r$, $z_i = K_0 k_i$, in (2.39). Now K is homogeneous of degree zero in q, because k is. Being such, it cannot be concave in q as it would have to be in a cost function.[3]

Looking at the utility function $\phi(y, z)$ instead, we note that it would have to be such that expenditure on z^r vanishes identically whenever the shadow prices of the y and z are equal, but this does not seem to lead any further.

At one time I thought that $\phi(y, z)$ might possibly be homogeneous of degree zero in each z^r. The calculus conditions for an optimum would of course yield $\partial\phi/\partial z_i = \lambda p_i$, so that $\lambda p^r \cdot z^r = \sum z_i \partial\phi/\partial z_i \equiv 0$ as we would like. Unfortunately these calculus conditions seem quite inappropriate in this case, basically because of the singularity at $z^r = 0$.

This can be seen in Figure 5.1, which gives the indifference curves in the z^1 plane given $z^2, \ldots, z^n$ and y, a set of straight lines radiating from the origin, and a set of parallel budget lines according to the amount allocated to buy z^1. Clearly the only possible calculus solution occurs when the budget line passes through the origin and accordingly coincides with an indifference curve. However, the indifference curves converge on the origin so that, near it, a penny becomes indefinitely valuable, so that it would certainly be worth diverting funds to buying z^1. The calculus solution is meaningless, and the

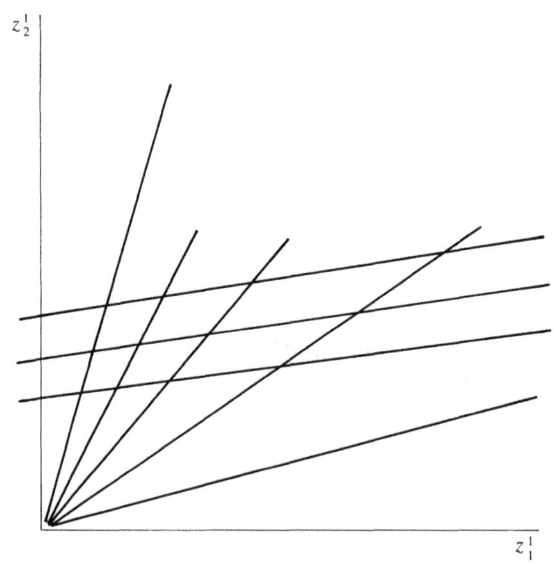

FIG. 5.1.

[3] Unless it depends only on u, of course.

idea of a utility function $\phi(y, z)$ homogeneous of degree zero in each z^r must be dismissed.

Let us look for another moment at z nevertheless. Since $p_i z_i = K_0 p_i k_i$, $i \in r$, we note that the relative expenditure on the corrections for different goods, depending only on the $p_i k_i$, are independent of the levels of prices in the various groups, depending only on the relative prices within them.

An interpretation of the utility function along the lines of (2.41) seems impossible, then, with the division (2.39) of x between y and z. However, it frequently does work with a closely related division. To this I now turn.

In the first place, note that we must have

$$P^r(\cdot) \text{ closed concave conical, and strictly increasing, each } r, \tag{2.42}$$

if they are to be unit cost functions corresponding to the 'production functions' $X^r(\cdot)$. Assume this. Then, as we have already seen

$$M = K(u, P(p)) \tag{2.43}$$

will be the cost function corresponding to a utility function

$$u(x) = U(X(x)), \tag{2.44}$$

yielding

$$M^r = F^r(M, P(p)), \qquad \text{each } r, \tag{2.45}$$

iff $K(u, \cdot)$ is closed concave conical. Now consider any utility function

$$v(x) > 0 \tag{2.46}$$

yielding (2.45) and define

$$\phi(v, x) = a \quad \text{if} \quad v(x/a) = 1, \tag{2.47}$$

so that the corresponding cost function

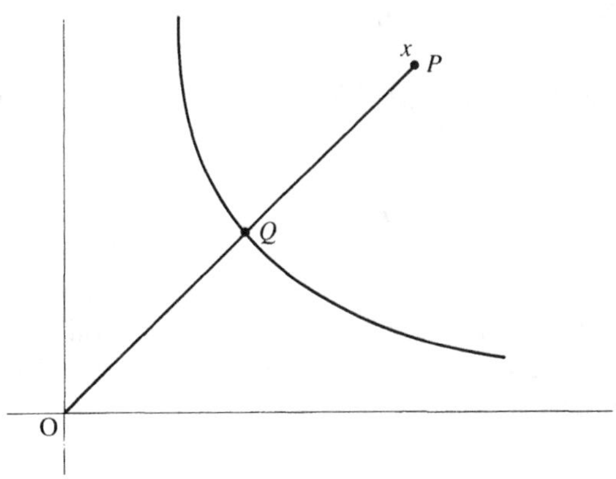

FIG. 5.2. $OP/OQ = a = \phi(v, x)$

$$\begin{aligned}\psi(v,p) &= \inf\{p\cdot x \mid v(x)\geqslant v\}\\ &= \inf\{p\cdot x \mid \phi(v,x)\geqslant 1\}\\ &= \inf\{p\cdot x/\phi(v,x)\},\end{aligned} \tag{2.48}$$

since $\phi(v, \cdot)$ is clearly conical. Hence

$$\phi(v,x)\psi(v,p)\leqslant p\cdot x, \tag{2.49}$$

in general, with

$$\phi(v,x)\psi(v,p) = p\cdot x \tag{2.50}$$

iff x is chosen at prices p and real income or utility v, that is, is the cheapest way of securing that level of real income at those prices.[4] From the symmetry of (2.49) and (2.50) it should be clear that, dually,

$$\phi(v,x) = \inf\{p\cdot x \mid \psi(v,p)\geqslant 1\}, \tag{2.51}$$

so that $\phi(v, x)$, $\psi(v, p)$ are dual representations of the consumer's preferences.

Now take any closed concave conical function $L(\cdot)$ in R^{n+1}.

$$M = L(\psi(u,p), P(p)) \tag{2.52}$$

is then the cost function corresponding to a utility function $u = u(x)$. Moreover

$$x_i = L_0\psi_i + L_r P_i^r, \qquad i\in r, \tag{2.53}$$

$$M^r = L_0 \sum_{i\in r} p_i\psi_i + L_r P^r, \tag{2.54}$$

$$\begin{aligned}M &= L_0\textstyle\sum_i p_i\psi_i + \sum_r L_r P^r\\ &= L_0\psi + \textstyle\sum_r L_r P^r = L(\psi, P),\end{aligned} \tag{2.55}$$

of course. Now set $\bar{M} = L_0\psi$, $\bar{\bar{M}} = \sum L_r P^r$, the amount 'spent on ψ' and 'P' respectively, and let $\psi(\cdot)$ be a cost function yielding (2.45) itself. Since we can solve (2.52) for $\psi = \theta(M, P(p))$,[5] this division depends only on M, $P(p)$. So do the proportions $L_r P^r/\sum L_s P^s$, $\sum_{i\in r} p_i\psi_i/\psi$ of these sums spent on goods in group r. Hence so does the total expenditure in group r. Hence (2.52), too, yields (2.45).

What is the corresponding utility function $u = u(x)$ like?

Since $L(\cdot)$ is a strictly increasing closed concave conical function, there is a 'quasi-utility function' $\lambda(w) = \lambda(w^0, w^1, \ldots, w^n)$, say, such that

[4] The uniqueness of the minimum is ensured by the presumed differentiability of the cost function.

[5] $M(\cdot)$ is strictly increasing.

$$L(\psi, P) = \inf\left\{\psi w^0 + \sum P^r w^r | \lambda(w) \geq 1\right\}. \tag{2.56}$$

In terms of this, the direct utility function is

$$u(x) = \sup\{u \mid \lambda(\phi(u, z), X(y)) \leq 1, y + z \leq x\}. \tag{2.57}$$

To prove this, we introduce prices q, r for the quasi-goods y, z, respectively,[6] and show that $L(\psi(u, r), P(q))$ is indeed the cost function corresponding to the quasi-utility function $\lambda(\phi(u, z), X(y))$ in the homogeneous representation in (2.56). The latter cost function is

$$\begin{aligned} C(u, q, r) &= \inf\{q \cdot y + r \cdot z \mid \lambda(\phi(u, z), X(y)) \geq 1\}, \\ &= \inf\left\{\sum_{t>0} \inf\{q^t \cdot y^t \mid X^t(y^t) \geq w^t\} + \inf\{r \cdot z \mid \phi(u, z) \geq w^0\} \mid \lambda(w) \geq 1\right\} \\ &= \inf\left\{\sum_{t>0} w^t \inf\{q^t \cdot \bar{y}^t \mid X^t(\bar{y}^t) \geq 1\} + w^0 \inf\{r \cdot \bar{z} \mid \phi(u, \bar{z}) \geq 1\} \mid \lambda(w) \geq 1\right\}, \end{aligned} \tag{2.58}$$

where $\bar{y}^t = y^t/w^t$, $\bar{z} = z/w^0$ because each $X(\cdot)$ and $\phi(u, \cdot)$ is conical. Hence

$$\begin{aligned} C(u, q, r) &= \inf\left\{\sum_{t>0} w^t P^t(q^t) + w^0 \psi(u, r) \mid \lambda(w) \geq 1\right\} \\ &= L(\psi(u, r), P(q)) \end{aligned} \tag{2.59}$$

by the definition (2.56). Hence $L(\phi(u, p), P(p))$ is the cost function corresponding to the utility function (2.57) as required.

Revert for a moment to $\lambda(\phi(u, z), X(y)) = 1$. It yields

$$\phi(u, z) = F(X(y)), \text{ say,} \tag{2.60}$$

on solution. Because $\phi(u, \cdot)$ is conical, this means that $\phi(u, z/F) = 1$, or, equivalently,

$$u = v(z/F(X(y))), \tag{2.61}$$

where $v(\cdot)$ is the utility function (2.45). At first this looks peculiar, as if increasing y reduced utility. However, this is wrong. A glance at Figure 5.2 or the definition (2.47) shows that $\phi(u, z)$ decreases in u. Hence $F(\cdot)$ is, if you like, a quasi-disutility function, not a quasi-utility function. Since it is certainly positive, this means that its inverse $U(X) = 1/F(X)$ is the quasi-utility function, and (2.61) may be better written

$$u = v(z\,U(X(y))), \tag{2.62}$$

and the true utility function

[6] Later we will set $p = q = r$, to denote the fact that they are actually quantitites of the same goods. For the moment, think of them as French Salt under the State Monopoly, with possibly vastly different prices according to the destined use. Then relax this discrimination.

$$u(x) = \sup\{v(zU(X(y)))\,|\,y + z \leqslant x\}. \tag{2.63}$$

In the particular case discussed at the outset, $v(z)$ is homogeneous of degree α^r, each r, and $\sum\alpha^r = 1$. Hence it is homogeneous of degree one in z and (2.62)–(2.63) become

$$u = U(X(y))v(z), \tag{2.62a}$$

$$u(x) = \sup\{U(X(y))v(z)\,|\,y + z \leqslant x\}. \tag{2.63a}$$

In other words, we can here think of each good having two alternative uses, one in producing X^r, the other in producing v, which, in the special case just mentioned, is a sort of generalized Cobb–Douglas utility. The consumer's problem is to divide x approximately between the two uses.

It does not of course follow that such an interpretation is always possible, because it is possible that no nearly concave function $L(\cdot)$ may exist for particular utility functions yielding (2.47). However, it is certainly true that we can always write in (2.26)

$$\begin{aligned} M &= K(k(u, p), P(p)) = L(k(u, p)\textstyle\prod(P^r)^{\alpha^r}, P(p)), \quad \sum\alpha^r = 1, \\ &= L(\psi(u, p), P(p)), \end{aligned} \tag{2.64}$$

where $\psi(u, \cdot)$ is of the appropriate generalized Cobb–Douglas type. That this function is conical is clear, but it need not be concave, though it is conceivable that it could always be made so by an appropriate choice of $\alpha^1, \ldots, \alpha^n$. Indeed we have more freedom of choice than this, since we may write

$$M = K(k(u, p), P(p)) = L(\theta(k(u, p)\textstyle\prod(P^r)^{\alpha^r}, P(p)), \tag{2.65}$$

so that we have a general increasing function θ as well as $\alpha^1 \ldots, \alpha^n$ at our disposal in our search for a concave $L(\cdot)$.[7]

I have not explored this point further.

3. ALLOCATION WITHIN THE GROUPS

According to (2.37) and (2.38) the conditional demand at the second stage can depend in rather a general and complicated manner on *all* the prices, both inside and outside the group in question. Now the great appeal of the two-stage procedure lies in its presumed simplicity. We have ensured that of the first stage by (2.1). The obvious way to ensure that the second stage should be equally simple would be to require that $x_i = f^i(M^r, p^r)$, $i \in r$, so

[7] This is indeed the greatest choice at our disposal. If $\psi(u, p) = \bar{K}(k, P)$ is homogeneous of degree α^r in p^r, each r, $\sum\alpha^r = 1$ and $\bar{K}_r P^r = \alpha^r \bar{K}$, each r, so that $\mathrm{d}\log\bar{K} = \sum\alpha^r\,\mathrm{d}\log P^r + \phi(k)$ and $\psi = \bar{K} = \theta(k(u, p)\Pi(P^r)^{\alpha^r}$ as used above.

that, in deciding how to spend the funds available for food, for instance, the consumer would only have to look at food prices. However, this would lead us straight to separability, a hypothesis which has already been explored rather fully. Let us therefore require instead that

$$x_i = f^i(M, p^r, P^{-r}), \quad i \in r, \quad P^{-r} = (P^s)_{s \neq r}, \tag{3.1}$$

so that the price indices for the other groups, which have already been used in making the allocation between groups, enter as parameters into the conditional demand functions.

According to (2.38)

$$M^r = K_r(k, P)P^r, \tag{3.2}$$

so that (3.1) implies

$$x_i = g^i(k, p^r, P^{-r}), \text{ say,} \qquad i \in r. \tag{3.3}$$

This will in turn imply (3.1) iff $K^r(k, P)$ is strictly monotonic in k. Since $M^r = 0$ when $M = 0$ this means, iff M^r is a strictly increasing function of M; that is to say iff each group taken as a whole is normal, which seems rather acceptable.

In any case I will now analyse the implications of (3.3), which will of course also be implications of (3.1).

According to (2.37)

$$x_i = K_r(k, P)P_i^r(p^r) + K_0(k, P)k_i(u, p), \qquad i \in r, \tag{3.4}$$

so that (3.3) is equivalent to

$$k_i(u, p) = \sigma^i(k(u, p), p^r, P^{-r}(p)), \text{ say,} \qquad i \in r, \text{ each } r. \tag{3.5}$$

Define now $q^r = p^r$, $q^s = p^s/P^s(p^s)$, $s \neq r$, to get

$$\begin{aligned} \sigma^i(k, p^r, P^{-r}) = k_i(u, p) = k_i(u, q) = \sigma^i(k, p^r, e) \\ = \psi^i(k, p^r), \text{ say,} \qquad i \in r, \end{aligned} \tag{3.6}$$

by the homogeneity properties of the P's and k, where $P^s = P^s(p^s)$, $k = k(u, p) = k(u, q)$ and e is a vector of ones. Hence (3.3) is equivalent to

$$k_i(u, p) = \psi^i(k(u, p), p^r), \qquad i \in r, \text{ each } r. \tag{3.7}$$

If k is independent of p, then each $k_i = 0$, so that (3.1) certainly holds. In this case, of course, we can take $k = u$, and, doing so, see that it is the one discussed at length in Section 2.

If k depends only on u and p^1, for instance, we may write

$$k = k(u, p^1) \tag{3.8}$$

with a trivial change in notation. Since k is strictly increasing in u we may solve for

$$u = \theta(k, p^1), \text{ say,} \tag{3.9}$$

to get

$$\begin{aligned} k_i &= k_i(\theta(k, p^1), p^1), \qquad i \in 1,^8 \\ &= 0, \qquad\qquad\qquad i \notin 1, \end{aligned} \tag{3.10}$$

satisfying (3.7) and hence (3.3) in either case.

There remains the case in which k depends on the prices in at least two groups. Choosing i and j from two *distinct* groups of this sort, (3.7) yields

$$k_{ij}/k_i k_j = k_{i0}/k_i k_0, \tag{3.11}$$

since $k_{ij} = \psi_{i0} \cdot k_j$ and $k_{i0} = \psi_{i0} \cdot k_0$, that is, u and each p^r are additively separable in $k(\cdot)$. In an appropriate normalization, therefore,

$$k(u, p) = u + \sum k^r(p^r), \tag{3.12}$$

where

$$\sum_{i \in r} p_i k_i^r = 0, \qquad \text{each } r. \tag{3.13}$$

This in turn yields $k_i = k_i^r(p^r)$ which certainly satisfies (3.7) and hence (3.3).

To summarize, therefore, for (3.3) it is necessary and sufficient that either

(A) $k = k(u, p^1)$, say,

or

(B) $k = u + \sum k^r(p^r), \quad \sum_{i \in r} p_i k_i^r = 0.$

If each group, taken as a whole, is normal, these are necessary and sufficient for (3.1), too. In any case they are necessary for it.

4. A CONDITIONAL CRITERION?

In this section I will ask: under what conditions can the conditional demand functions

$$\begin{aligned} x_i = f^i(M^r, p^r, P^{-r}) &= K_r P_i^r + K_0 k_i, \qquad i \in r \\ &= y_i + z_i, \end{aligned} \tag{4.1}$$

[8] [eds.] By this, he means for i in group one.

where

(A) $k = k(u, p^1)$, say,

or

(B) $k = u + \sum k^r(p^r)$,

be derived from a *conditional criterion*

$$v^r = v^r(x^r, P^{-r}), \qquad \text{each } r? \tag{4.2}$$

Should each v^r be independent of P^{-r} they would of course be specific satisfaction functions, that is to say, the overall utility function would be separable, with the v^r as components.

In case (B), at least, the entire effect of the P^{-r} is canalized through K_0, which merely changes the z_i in a common proportion. This is a limited role. It does not give much flexibility to adapt to new, integrability conditions for each group. We are therefore bound to ask ourselves: can the price indices P^{-r} enter into the conditional criteria in (4.2), or does the requirement that such criteria should exist imply separability?

First a preliminary: $k(\cdot)$ is additively separable in case (A), too, if (4.2) holds, so that this possibility may be subsumed under (B).

It will be convenient in proving this to write

$$K(k, P) = R(k, Q), \quad Q^r = \log P^r, \text{ say}, \qquad \text{each } r, \tag{4.3}$$

and to neglect at the outset the fact that $k(\cdot)$ must satisfy either (A) or (B).

In (4.3) we have

$$x_i = R_r Q_i^r + R_0 k_i = R_r(P_i^r/P^r) + R_0 k_i, \qquad i \in r, \tag{4.4}$$

$$M^r = R_r, \tag{4.5}$$

in the obvious notation.

The Slutsky conditions for (4.1) are

$$\sigma_{ij} = f_j^i + f^j f_0^i = \sigma_{ji}, \qquad i, j \in r, \tag{4.6}$$

where $f_j^i = \partial f^i/\partial p^j$, $f_0^i = \partial f^i/\partial M^r$.

After a fair number of elementary operations, (4.4)–(4.6) yield

$$\begin{aligned}[R_{0r}(R_0 - R_{r0}) - R_{00}(R_r - R_{rr})]\,(Q_i^r k_j - Q_j^r k_i)k_0 \\ = R_0[(R_r Q_j^r + R_0 k_j)k_{i0} - (R_r Q_i^r + R_0 k_i)k_{j0}]\end{aligned} \tag{4.7}$$

for all $i, j \in r$. Multiplying by p_j, adding over all $j \in r$, and using the homogeneity of k, k_i and e^{Q^r}, we get

$$k_{i0}/k_i k_0 = [R_{0r}(R_0 - R_{r0}) - R_{00}(R_r - R_{rr})]/R_0 R_r. \tag{4.8}$$

Replacing p^s by $q^s = p^s/P^s(p^s)$ does not affect the left-hand side of this. Hence it does not affect the right either. Since the right depends, at most, on k and Q, this means that it is a function of k alone. Hence

$$k_{i0}/k_i k_0 = \phi^r(k), \text{ say,} \qquad i \in r, \tag{4.9}$$

for all r in which k depends on p^r.

In (A), (4.9) is satisfied with $\phi^r(k) = 0$. In (B) it is required to hold only for $r = 1$. Let us write $\phi^1 = \phi$ in this case to get

$$k_{i0}/k_i k_0 = \phi(k). \tag{4.10}$$

Write now

$$k^* = \theta(k) \tag{4.11}$$

to get

$$k^*_{i0}/k^*_i k^*_j = (\theta'' + \phi\theta')/\theta'^2. \tag{4.12}$$

Taking

$$\theta = \int^k \exp\left(-\int^b \phi(a)\mathrm{d}a\right)\mathrm{d}b, \tag{4.13}$$

we get $k^*_{i0} = 0$, each $i \in 1$. Replace k by k^* and drop the *, to see (B) as a special case of (A) here.

We may therefore take

$$k_{i0} = 0, \qquad \text{each } i, \tag{4.14}$$

without loss of generality. Doing so, substituting into (4.7), multiplying by p_j as before and adding over all $j \in r$, we get

$$R_{0r}(R_0 - R_{r0}) = R_{00}(R_r - R_{rr}), \qquad \text{each } r \in T, \tag{4.15}$$

where

$$T \text{ is the set of groups whose prices enter into } k. \tag{4.16}$$

For the remaining groups

$$v^r = X^r(x^r), \qquad r \notin T \tag{4.17}$$

is, of course, a conditional criterion which is also a specific satisfaction function. It is homogeneous of degree one.

Now it is shown in Gorman (1959) that, if a separable utility function permits allocation by means of price indices at the first stage as in (2.1), it is either homothetically separable—i.e. has all its component specific satisfaction functions conical—or additively separable, or a mixture of the two in which one of the additive components is made up of the homogeneous specific satisfaction functions. Therefore, if the existence of conditional criteria as in (4.2) implies separability, we might expect (4.15) to imply additive separability. Indeed, with luck, actual additive separability in the normalization which yields (B). This being so, should we not specify tastes in a manner such that such separability would be easily recognized if present?

The definition of additive separability is that in the normalization in question

$$u = \sum w^r(x^r), \text{ say,} \tag{4.18}$$

so that one possible procedure would be to work in terms of the direct utility function.[9] To do so I would have to translate our previous results into the direct form, which I would have done already if I could. Luckily another form is available. Think of $w^1(x^1), \ldots, w^n(x^n)$ as the production functions of a firm made up of n plants, each making the same product u out of distinct groups of inputs $x^1, \ldots, x^n$. The profits made in the group as a whole would be the sum of those made in the individual plants. Actually it is slightly more convenient to work in terms of the, if lucky, negative losses. The loss function, then, for the firm as whole

$$\begin{aligned} \lambda(p_0, p) &= \inf\{p \cdot x - p_0 u(x)\}, \text{ say,} \\ &= \sum \lambda^r(p_0, p^r), \end{aligned} \tag{4.19}$$

where

$$\lambda^r(p_0, p^r) = \inf\{p^r \cdot x^r - p_0 w^r(x^r)\} \tag{4.20}$$

is the loss function for the rth plant.

In our case, neglecting (4.20),

$$\begin{aligned} \lambda(p_0, p) &= \inf\{p \cdot x - p_0 u(x)\} \\ &= \inf_u\{\inf\{p \cdot x \mid u(x) \geqslant u\} - p_0 u\}, \qquad \text{using (A),} \\ &= \inf_u\{K(u + \textstyle\sum k^r(p^r), P(p)) - p_0 u\} \\ &= \inf_U\{K(U, P(p)) - p_0 U\} + p_0 \textstyle\sum k^r(p^r) \\ &= \mu(p_0, P(p)) + p_0 \textstyle\sum k^r(p^r), \end{aligned} \tag{4.21}$$

where

$$\mu(p_0, P) = \inf\{P \cdot X - p_0 U(X)\} = \inf_U\{K(U, P) - p_0 U\} \tag{4.22}$$

is the *macro-loss function* corresponding to the macro-utility function $U(X)$ or, equivalently, to the macro-cost function $K(U, P)$.

[9] I have implicitly assumed the utility function concave in the additive normalization. As it happens most peculiar phenomena occur if it is not, so that we may, and will, assume it concave with a clear conscience. See Gorman (1970).

As at the beginning of this section, it will be convenient to write

$$\mu(p_0, P) = L(p_0, Q), \quad Q^r = \log P^r, \qquad \text{each } r. \tag{4.23}$$

We now have

$$\lambda(p_0, p) = L(p_0, Q) + p_0 \sum_{r \in T} k^r(p^r), \tag{4.24}$$

a form which certainly suggests that, if we are searching for additive separability, we have chosen the right normalization for u. Nevertheless it is better to be reasonably sure, especially since it is not clear from Gorman (1959) whether additive separability follows if there are only two groups or if all but one of them are homothetically separable.[10]

(4.24) gives

$$x_i = \lambda_i = L_r Q_i^r + p_0 k_i^r, \qquad i \in r \in T; \qquad x_i = h_r Q_i^r, \quad r \notin T, \tag{4.25}$$

$$M^r = L_r, \tag{4.26}$$

so that the criterion function $v^r(x^r, P^{-r})$ in (4.2) is independent of P^{-r}, and group $r \in T$ separable, iff

$$p_0 = \theta^r(L_r, p^r), \tag{4.27}$$

in which case $r \in S$, say, and is additively separable; or $r \notin T$, so that it is homothetically separable.

Now profit functions use the closed convex hull of the utility function, hence the marginal utility of income is decreasing and p_0 is therefore an increasing function of M. If it is strictly increasing, so that marginal utility in our normalization is strictly decreasing, and if M^r is too, so that the group as a whole is normal, we can invert (4.27) to get

$$L_r = \phi^r(p_0, p^r) = \bar{\phi}^r(p_0, Q^r), \text{ say,} \qquad \text{when } r \in S, \tag{4.28}$$

since the second expression remains unaffected when p^r is changed, holding $Q^r(p^r)$ constant.

This immediately gives

$$L = \sum_{r \in S} \psi^r(p_0, Q^r) + \psi^S(p_0, Q^S), \tag{4.29}$$

where $Q^S = (Q^r)_{r \in S}$, and where we can arrange to have each ψ^r concave conical in (p_0, P^r), and ψ^S in (p_0, P^S).

Hence

$$\lambda = \sum_{r \in S} (\psi^r(p_0, Q^r(p^r)) + p_0 k^r(p^r)) + \psi^S(p_0, Q^S). \tag{4.30}$$

[10] [eds.] It is clear from Blackorby *et al.* (1978*a*, 1978*b*).

Clearly, therefore, we have chosen the correct normalization to find separability if it exists. Clearly too, this separability is additive or homothetic even in the moot cases of Gorman (1959) where there are only two groups or all but one is homothetically separable.

We may therefore continue with this normalization.

The Slutsky condition (4.7) then yields

$$(Q_j^r k_i^r - Q_i^r k_j^r)(L_r - L_{rr} - p_0 L_{r0}) = 0, \qquad i, j \in r.^{11} \tag{4.31}$$

Multiplying this by p_j, adding for all $j \in r$ and using the homotheticity of Q^r and k^r, we find

$$k_i^r(L_r - L_{rr} - p_0 L_{r0}) = 0, \qquad i \in r, \tag{4.32}$$

so that

$$L_r = L_{rr} + p_0 L_{r0}, \qquad \text{each } r \notin T, \tag{4.33}$$

or, equivalently,

$$P^r \mu_{rr} + p_0 \mu_{r0} = 0, \qquad \text{each } r \notin T. \tag{4.34}$$

Now μ_r is homogeneous of degree zero in p_0, P. (4.34) is therefore equivalent to

$$\sum_{s \neq r,0} P^s \mu_{rs} = 0, \qquad \text{each } r \notin T. \tag{4.35}$$

In the language of production used above, these say that no input aggregate outside T is affected if its price and that of the product change in the same proportion, the prices of the other inputs remaining constant, or if the latter change in the same proportion, the price of the given input and the product remaining fixed. If we do not wish to talk in terms of these fictitious macro-goods, we can instead say that expenditure on any given group of inputs outside T—say the rth—is unaffected if the prices of all others increase in the same proportion.

This is easily seen to be true in the additively separable case. Is it only here that it is?

At this stage it will simplify our argument somewhat if we write

$$\mu(p_0, P) = L(p_0, Q) = p_0 \phi(V), \quad V^r = Q^r - \log p_0, \tag{4.36}$$

as we can because the homogeneity of (4.33) is equivalent to

$$\sum_{s \neq r} \phi_{rs} = 0, \qquad \text{each } r \notin T, \tag{4.37}$$

[11] [eds.] k^r is homogeneous of degree zero. Q^r is not homogeneous at all, but inherits a translatability property from the homogeneity of P^r.

while additive separability implies

$$\phi(V) = \sum \psi_r(V^r), \tag{4.38}$$

that is,

$$\phi_{rs} = 0, \qquad r \neq s. \tag{4.39}$$

Clearly (4.39) implies (4.37). What about the converse?

In discussing this I will confine myself to the case where no groups belong to T, that is, each p^r enters into k.

If $n = 2$, (4.37) reads $\phi_{12} = 0$ which is (4.38). If $n = 3$ we have $\phi_{12} + \phi_{13} = \phi_{23} + \phi_{21} = \phi_{31} + \phi_{21} = 0$. Because of the symmetry of ϕ_{rs} these are three linear equations in three unknowns. Since they cannot degenerate, each $\phi_{rs} = 0$, $r \neq s$. If $n = 4$, however,

$$\phi = \sum V^r + \left(\sum V^r\right)^2 - 6(V^1 V^2 - V^3 V^4) \tag{4.40}$$

satisfies (4.37) even though no single $\phi_{rs} = 0$.

(4.37) does nevertheless limit the amount of interaction between the groups. I will limit my discussion of this point to the case where T is empty, so that each p^r enters into $k(\cdot)$ and therefore,

$$\sum_{s \neq r} \phi_{rs} = 0, \qquad \text{each } r, \tag{4.41}$$

and assume ϕ to be indefinitely differentiable about the origin. I will then show that we can write $\phi = \sum \psi_r(R_r) + \theta(R)$ where $\theta(R)$ is a polynomial form of at most degree n.

Suppose that ϕ has the Taylor expansion, about the origin.

$$\phi = \sum a_i R_i^{i(1)} \ldots, R_n^{i(n)}, \quad i = (i(1), \ldots, i(n)). \tag{4.42}$$

If θ is a solution of (4.41), so is $\theta + \sum \psi_r(R_r)$, any $\psi_1(R_1), \ldots, \psi_n(R_r)$. Hence we may assume without loss of generality that

$$a_i = 0 \quad \text{if } N(i) \geqslant n - 1, \tag{4.43}$$

where

$$N(i) = \text{number of zero components of } i = (i(1), \ldots, i(n)). \tag{4.44}$$

Define also

$$Z(i) = \text{set of zero components of } i, \tag{4.45}$$

$$S(i) = \sum\nolimits_r i(r), \tag{4.46}$$

$$\delta(r) = \text{unit vector in the direction } r. \tag{4.47}$$

What I wish to prove then is that

$$a_j = 0 \text{ if } S(j) > n. \tag{4.48}$$

$$\begin{aligned}(i(r)+1)_{a+\delta(r)} &= \textstyle\sum_s (i(s)+1)a_{i+\delta(s)} \\ &= b_i, \text{ say,} \qquad r \notin Z(i),\end{aligned} \tag{4.49}$$

which is equivalent to (4.39).

Adding this over the $r \in Z(i)$ we have

$$(n - N(i) - 1)b_i = \sum_{r \in Z(i)} a_{i+\delta(r)}. \tag{4.50}$$

If $N(i) = 0$, so that $Z(i) = 0$, we therefore have $b_i = 0$, and hence

$$a_{i+\delta(r)} = 0, \quad \text{if} \quad N(i) = 0 \tag{4.51}$$

which immediately implies

$$a_j = 0 \quad \text{if} \quad \delta(j) > n \quad \text{and} \quad N(j) = 0. \tag{4.52}$$

Erect now the inductive hypothesis

$$a_j = 0 \quad \text{if} \quad \delta(j) > n \quad \text{and} \quad N(j) \leqslant m \leqslant n - 2. \tag{4.53}$$

Take now $a \in j$ with $S(j) > n$ and $N(j) = m + 1$. At least one $j(r) > 1$. Take such an r and define

$$i = j - \delta(r), \tag{4.54}$$

so that $r \notin Z(i) = Z(j)$, $N(i) = N(j)$, and $S(i) = S(j) - 1$. If $s \in Z(i) = Z(j)$, then $N(i + \delta(s)) = N(i) - 1 = m$, while $S(i + \delta(s)) = S(j) > n$. Hence $a_{i+\delta(r)} = 0$, $s \in Z(i)$ by the inductive hypothesis (4.51), so that $b_i = 0$ in (4.50) and $a_j = a_{i+\delta(r)} = 0$ in (4.48). Hence, if the inductive hypothesis holds for $m = m^* < n - 2$, it also holds for $m = m^* + 1$. It holds for $m = 0$, hence for $m = 0, 1, 2, \ldots, n - 2$. In our normalization it holds for $m = n - 1$ or n by (4.43), and hence for all m.

This proves (4.41) so that

$$\phi = \sum \psi_r(R_r) + \theta(R) \tag{4.55}$$

in general, where θ is a mixed polynomial of order at most n.

6

Professor Friedman's Consumption Function and the Theory of Choice

Editorial Summary

Although this paper can be read as a straightforward budgeting argument, it was inspired by a claim of Sargan's about the necessary and sufficient conditions for Friedman's permanent income hypothesis to be valid. The question is simple: suppose that a consumer maximizes a utility function $F(x_0, x_1, \ldots, x_T)$, where $x_t = (x_{t0}, \ldots, x_{tn})$, subject to $\sum_t \sum_i p_{ti} x_{ti} \leqslant y$; in what circumstances can the amount spent on period (or group) t, $y_t = \sum_i p_{ti} x_{ti}$, be written as

$$y_t = \rho_t(p) y \tag{0.1}$$

for all t? This is a version of Friedman's permanent income hypothesis; a 10 per cent increase in permanent income leads to a 10 per cent increase in expenditure in every period.

Sargan (1957) claimed that this would lead to a 10 per cent increase in expenditure on every commodity. Section 2 disposes of the Sargan claim by means of a counter-example, and Section 3 presents the restrictions on the cost function that are both necessary and sufficient for (0.1) to hold. The appropriate expenditure function is given by

$$y = G(u, p) = P(p) h(u, p), \tag{0.2}$$

where $h(u, \cdot)$ is homogeneous of degree zero in p_t, for $t = 0, 1, \ldots, T$. Using Shephard's lemma it is easy to verify that this is sufficient for Friedman's hypothesis: the demand for commodity i in period t is given by

$$x_{ti} = G_{\{ti\}}(u, p) = P_{\{ti\}}(p) h(u, p) + P(p) h_{\{ti\}}(u, p) \tag{0.3}$$

where, for example, $G_{\{ti\}} = \partial G / \partial p_{ti}$. Expenditure on period t is

$$y_t = \sum_{i \in t} p_{ti} x_{ti} = h(u, p) \sum_{i \in t} p_{ti} P_{\{ti\}}(p) + P(p) \sum_{i \in t} p_{ti} h_{\{ti\}}(u, p)$$

$$= h(u, p) \sum_{i \in t} p_{ti} P_{\{ti\}}(p)$$

$$= \frac{\sum_{i \in t} p_{ti} P_{\{ti\}}(p)}{P(p)} y, \tag{0.4}$$

where the second line follows from the fact that h is homogeneous of degree zero in p_t, and the third line follows from (0.2).

To show that (0.2) is necessary is another matter. To do this Gorman uses a clever transformation of variables actually suggested by the problem. Using the expenditure function, the proportional budgeting requirement (0.1) can be rewritten as

$$\frac{\sum_i p_{ti} G_{\{ti\}}(u, p)}{G(u, p)} = \rho_t(p). \tag{0.5}$$

This suggests that the problem could be more naturally written in shares. To do that explicitly, let $q_{ti} := \ln p_{ti}$, $g(u, q) := \ln G(u, p)$, and $\sigma_t(q) := \rho_t(p)$. Using the log cost function, (0.5) becomes

$$\sum_i g_{\{ti\}}(u, q) = \sigma_t(q). \tag{0.6}$$

As the right side of (0.6) is independent of utility, take the derivative with respect to u to obtain

$$\sum_i g'_{\{ti\}}(u, q) = 0 \tag{0.7}$$

where $g'_{\{ti\}} = \partial^2 g(u, q)/\partial u \partial q_{ti}$. (0.7) can be expressed as

$$\sum_{i=1}^{n} g'_{\{ti\}}(u, q) = -g'_{\{t0\}}(u, q). \tag{0.8}$$

Using (0.8), the total differential of g' in terms of q is given by

$$\begin{aligned} d_q g'(u, q) &= \sum_t \sum_i g'_{\{ti\}}(u, q) dq_{ti} \\ &= \sum_t \sum_{i \neq 0} g'_{\{ti\}}(u, q)[dq_{ti} - dq_{t0}]. \end{aligned} \tag{0.9}$$

The identity (0.9) shows that g' is constant for price changes that keep $q_{ti} - q_{t0}$ constant. However, this is the same as keeping the price ratios r_{ti}/p_{t0} constant. This is his equation (17) and yields, in an abuse of notation,

$$g' = g'(u, r_0, r_1, \ldots, r_T). \tag{0.10}$$

Integrating (0.10), and undoing the transformations of variables, yields (0.2) as a necessary, as well as sufficient, condition for (0.1).

The rest of this article applies this solution and its special cases to problems of decentralized decision-making suggested by Strotz and Samuelson, and to a problem discussed by Drèze.

Professor Friedman's Consumption Function and the Theory of Choice

1. INTRODUCTION AND SUMMARY[1]

In his contribution to an Oxford symposium on savings, Mr J. D. Sargan (1957) wrote:

> Turning now to the Friedman theory of consumption, there is a basic assumption which is fundamental to this theory which must be challenged. This is that the utility function can be assumed to be homogeneous in the value of consumption at different dates. For this to be true for all possible sets of prices for the different commodities it would be necessary for the utility function to be completely homogeneous in the quantities of all the goods consumed. And, if this were true, then a change in the level of income would produce proportionate changes in the consumption of all commodities. This is so contrary to common sense and the results of empirical research that the assumption of complete homogeneity must be dismissed. It follows that Friedman's basic assumption of the homogeneity of the utility function considered as a function of the total value of consumption at different periods could only hold true for certain special sets of prices. And it seems *a priori* rather unlikely that one of these special sets of prices should happen to coincide with the actual and expected market prices.

Sargan claims, then, that Friedman's (1957) postulate that a 10 per cent increase in permanent income would lead to a 10 per cent increase in the expenditure in each period implies that it would lead to a 10 per cent increase in the expenditure on each individual good in each period.

If correct this would be a very damaging attack, for it is quite clear that some goods are luxuries, some necessities, and yet others luxuries for some and necessities for others.

It will be shown below that the statement is incorrect, that a very wide class of utility functions satisfies Friedman's hypothesis, and in particular, that the latter has no bearing at all on the division of goods into luxuries, necessities, and the like.

These results can be applied when purchases are classified by quite different criteria—say by the member of the family who makes them, rather than the period in which they are made. If we do so we can cast some light on some of the recent discussions of decentralized decisions, notably by Professor Strotz (1957, 1959) and Professor Samuelson (1956). This is done in Section 5.

[1] My thanks are due to Mr Esra Bennathan for his comments on an earlier verion of this paper, and to M. Edmond Malinvaud and M. Jacques Drèze who expressed disbelief when I quoted Mr Sargan's results to them during the Amsterdam meeting of the Econometric Society.

J. Drèze (1960) has pointed out that we do not just make a once-and-for-all mistake about the level of our permanent income. Each year we find we have been rather mistaken. This being so, the utility function has to obey the types of rules laid down in Sections 3 and 4 of this paper beginning at any fixed point we care to mention. The implications of this are briefly discussed in Section 6.

2. PRELIMINARIES

Consider a consumer whose net worth, including the discounted value of his future income stream, is y, and who plans to consume x_{ti} units of the ith good, $i = 0, 1, \ldots, n$, in the tth period, $t = 0, 1, \ldots, T$. The present discounted value of one unit of this good bought in that period is p_{ti}.[2]

We write

$$p_t = (p_{t0}, p_{t1}, \ldots, p_{tn}); \qquad x_t = (x_{t0}, \ldots, x_{tn}) \tag{1}$$

$$p = (p_0, p_1, \ldots, p_T); \qquad x = (x_0, \ldots, x_T); \tag{2}$$

$$y_t = \sum_i p_{ti} x_{ti}; \qquad z_i = \sum_t p_{ti} x_{ti}. \tag{3}$$

y_t and z_i stand respectively for the total expenditure in the tth period, and on the ith good, suitably discounted in each case.

The consumer maximizes his utility function $u = F(x)$, subject to the budget constraint $y = \sum_{ti} p_{ti} x_{ti}$. Uncertainty is neglected, or at least assumed to be taken care of in the discount factor. His choices agree with Friedman's (1957) theory if

$$y_t = \rho_t y; \qquad \sum \rho_t = 1, \quad t = 0, 1, \ldots, T, \tag{4}$$

where

$$\rho_t = \rho_t(p) \text{ in general.} \tag{5}$$

3. A COUNTER-EXAMPLE

Take *any* well-behaved utility function[3]

$$u = F(x_0, X_1, \ldots, X_n) \tag{6}$$

and substitute into it

[2] We use this particular formulation so that the results will also be directly applicable to other principles of application, e.g. where the index t refers to the individual in an organization making a particular purchase.

[3] We shall use subscripts to denote differentiation throughout this paper, except at one point in Section 4 where differentiation with respect to u is denoted by a prime.

$$X_i = \prod_t x_{ti}^{\rho_t}, \qquad i = 0, 1, \ldots, n, \tag{7}$$

where

$$\text{the } \rho\text{'s are constants and } \sum \rho_t = 1. \tag{8}$$

Maximizing (6) subject to (7) and the budget constraint we find that

$$\lambda p_{ti} x_{ti} = \rho_t F_i X_i; \qquad F_i = \partial F / \partial X_i, \tag{9}$$

in the usual notation.[4] This immediately implies that $y_t = \rho_t y$, so that Friedman's hypothesis is satisfied.

Since (6) is a perfectly general utility function it seems clear that the constraint $y_t = \rho_t y$ does not affect the allocation of funds between the different goods, but merely their distribution over time.

This may be worth a glance. Suppose that the ratio $q_{ti} = p_{ti}/p_{0i}$ of the 'price' of the ith good in period t, to its initial price is known for each good and period. We may then introduce the composite commodities

$$x_i^* = \sum_t q_{ti} x_{ti}, \qquad i = 0, 1, \ldots, n. \tag{10}$$

Setting $p_i = p_{0i}$, we will have $p_{ti} = p_i q_{ti}$ so that $p_i x_i^* = \sum_t p_{ti} x_{ti} = z_i$. x_i^* may therefore be taken to represent the 'aggregate consumption' of the ith good, and p_i its price.

Substituting from (9) and (10) into (7) we soon find that

$$X_i = Q_i x_i^*; \qquad Q_i = \prod_t (\rho_t / q_{ti})^{\rho_t},$$

so that the consumer chooses x_i^* to maximize

$$u = F(Q_1 x_1^*, Q_2 x_2^*, \ldots, Q_n x_n^*) \tag{11}$$

subject to $\sum p_i x_i^* = y$. The Q's merely represent a change in the units of measurement; u is still a perfectly general utility function—to all intents the same one as before. Even in this very special case, where the distribution of expenditure over time is independent of the prices as well as of the funds available, nothing whatever is implied about the allocation of the funds among the different goods. These may include close substitutes, complements, high luxuries, and basic necessities.

(3) and (9) immediately imply that

$$p_{ti} x_{ti} = \rho_t z_i, \tag{12}$$

[4] Perhaps not absolutely the most general, because we assume sufficient continuity to allow us to use differential equations in the analysis, and it is possible, though possibly not very likely, that preference fields of quite a different form which did not satisfy this condition, do satisfy Friedman's hypothesis.

so that the time-pattern of expenditure is the same for each good. This is merely a quirk in our particular example, however. It is not true in general, even when the ρ's are constant.

4. THE GENERAL FRIEDMAN PREFERENCE FIELD

In this section we shall seek the most general preference field satisfying Friedman's hypothesis.[5] It will be convenient to represent it in the form

$$y = G(u, p), \tag{13}$$

which tells us the funds needed to achieve a utility level u at prices p. Since these double when prices double, G is homogeneous of degree one in the prices, so that

$$\textstyle\sum_{ti} p_{ti} G_{ti} = G = y; \qquad G_{ti} = \partial G/\partial p_{ti}. \tag{14}$$

In equilibrium

$$x_{ti} = \delta y/\delta p_{ti} = G_{ti}, \tag{15}$$

since this is the change in income needed to compensate the original price change. Hence

$$y_t = \textstyle\sum_i p_{ti} G_{ti}. \tag{16}$$

If $y_t = \rho_t(p)y$, we immediately find that

$$\textstyle\sum_i \partial g/\partial \log p_{ti} = \rho_t(p), \qquad \text{where } g = \log G.$$

Using a prime to denote differentiation with respect to u, this yields

$$\textstyle\sum_i \partial g'/\partial \log p_{ti} = 0, \qquad t = 0, 1, \ldots, T.$$

Therefore,

$$\mathrm{d}g' = g''\mathrm{d}u + \sum_t \sum_{i>0} (\partial g'/\partial \log p_{ti})\mathrm{d} \log p_{ti}/p_{t0},$$

so that g' is constant when y and each of the

$$r_{ti} = p_{ti}/p_{t0}, \qquad t = 0, 1, \ldots, T; \qquad i = 0, 1, \ldots, n, \tag{17}$$

[5] By well behaved we mean that u is an increasing function of the consumption of each good and that the indifference surfaces are convex. It is easily shown that

$$U(x) = F\left(\prod_t x_{t0}^{\rho_t}, \prod_t x_{t1}^{\rho_t}, \ldots\right)$$

will also be well behaved if $F(X_0, \ldots, X_T)$ is.

is constant. That is

$$g' = g'(u, r_0\, r_1, \ldots, r_T),$$

where $r_t = (r_{t1}, \ldots, r_{tn})$ gives the prices in the tth period of each of the other goods in terms of the 0-good as a numeraire.

Integrating with respect to u, writing $y = G = e^g$, and noting that y is homogeneous of degree one in the prices, we find that

$$y = P(p)H(u, r_0, r_1, \ldots, r_T), \tag{18}$$

where the price index $P(p)$ is homogeneous of degree one, so that

$$P(p) = \sum\nolimits_{ti} P_{ti} p_{ti}. \tag{19}$$

(18) can of course be written in the more familiar polar form if required. It is then

$$u = K(y/P, r_0, r_1, \ldots, r_T). \tag{20}$$

We shall verify in a moment that this preference field really does satisfy Friedman's hypothesis. First let us note its extreme generality: P is an arbitrary homogeneous function of $(n + 1)(T + 1)$ variables, K another arbitrary function of $n(T + 1) + 1$.

In actual fact (20) though normally more useful than the ordinary direct form of the utility function—as in (6)—is not nearly so easy to work with in general as is the form (13) or (18). This is because the demand functions (15) can be derived from it. Before deriving them in this case we shall rewrite (18) in the equivalent form:

$$y = Ph(u, p), \tag{21}$$

for symmetry, where

$$\sum\nolimits_i h_{ti} p_{ti} = 0, \quad h_{ti} = \partial h / \partial p_{ti}; \qquad \text{each } t. \tag{22}$$

This yields

$$x_{ti} = Ph_{ti} + hP_{ti} \tag{23}$$

and

$$y_t = h \sum\nolimits_i p_{ti} P_{ti} = y \rho_t(p) \tag{24}$$

by (19) and (22), where

$$\rho_t = \sum\nolimits_i P_{ti} p_{ti} / P. \tag{25}$$

(18) and (19) therefore define the most general preference field satisfying Friedman's hypothesis.

One way to realize the generality of (18) is to use it to derive the class of preference fields in which the ρ's are constants. This is clearly a drastic specialization of (18) yet it yields a much more general class of fields than we found in Section 3, general though that was. We shall not go through the integration; the method is in any case similar to that just used. The resulting preference field is

$$y = P_0 H(u, r_0, r_1, \ldots, r_T); \qquad P_0 = \prod_t p_{t0}^{\rho_t}, \tag{26}$$

and is quite interesting in its own right. We use it in our discussion of Samuelsonian 'shibboleths' in Section 5.

If we finally require that the time-pattern of expenditure should be the same for each particular good, as in our original example, we get

$$y = P_0 H(u, R_1, \ldots, R_n); \qquad R_i = \prod_i r_{ti}^{\rho_t}, \tag{27}$$

which can easily be shown to be equivalent to (6) and (7), so that that is the most general preference field with that particular quality. Before this last specialization H was an arbitrary function of $n(T+1)+1$ variables. Now it contains only $n+1$. Yet even now the choice between the different goods remains perfectly general, as we saw in Section 3.

5. DECENTRALIZED DECISIONS

We have grouped purchases according to the period in which they were made. Other groupings are clearly possible, e.g. according to the person making a purchase or the 'need' being satisfied. To bring these under our analysis we need merely refer to the 't^{th} group' instead of the 't^{th} period'. This may seem peculiar, since we have assumed so far that the same goods are consumed in each period, so that, in particular, there are the same number of goods in each group. The reader will easily verify, however, that neither assumption plays any part in our main discussion. In particular all the results in Section 4 up to and including (26) carry over to the case where different goods—and different numbers of them—appear in the different groups. Indeed the only difficulty which does arise is when, for instance, the several members of a family buy the same goods, and *at the same prices*. In such cases more general preference fields than those discovered in Section 4 may imply a proportional allocation $y_t = \rho_t(p)y$ of expenditure. This merely strengthens our main argument, however, which is once again that such fields are extremely numerous.

Let us first consider Professor Strotz's 'utility tree'. In his recent articles in *Econometrica*, Strotz (1957, 1959) set out from the observed fact that we frequently plan our expenditure in sectors, allocating so much to each sector and deciding exactly how to spend the money so allocated when one learned, among other things, just what the prices were. His idea was that one had a rough idea of these prices beforehand sufficiently accurate to determine an index number

$$P_t = \sum_i w_{ti} p_{ti}, \qquad t = 0, 1, \ldots, T, \tag{28}$$

of the prices in each of the groups. The preliminary allocation was then to be determined by a 'demand equation'

$$y_t = \phi_t(y, P_0, \ldots, P_T). \tag{29}$$

It transpired that one could do something like this if the utility function was additively separable, so that it could be written in the form

$$u = \sum_t v_t(x_t), \tag{30}$$

and he argued strongly that this was evidence in favour of that form.

If we now put

$$w_{ti} = P_{ti}/P, \tag{31}$$

(25) implies that Strotz's price index $P_t = \rho_t$ for each group. Moreover, these weights have a good deal to recommend them, for they are those which are used in (19) in computing the general price index P. It is as if we had defined the real price of food as the ratio of the food component in the cost-of-living index to the total. Of course the weights themselves depend on all the prices; but this is true of Strotz's own indices.

If we use indices, we get

$$y_t = yP_t, \tag{32}$$

which is a special case of (29). Professor Strotz's budgetary procedure is therefore consistent with a very wide range of preference fields including all those defined in (18). Equation (32) is not itself very realistic because it implies that one's expenditure on each particular group of commodities goes up in proportion to one's income, which does not seem to be consistent with the sorts of classification which one has in mind, since these tend to allocate luxuries and necessities to different groups. Nevertheless the fact that an extremely wide class of preference fields is consistent with even this very special case of the budgetary procedure observed by Strotz, suggests that an even wider class must satisfy the general formulation (31) and (32). That (30) is one very special member of that class would seem to yield rather weak empirical evidence in its favour.

Proportional budgeting of the form $y_t = \rho_t(p)y$ may not be very common in some branches of consumer demand; but it is common in many fields. Universities, for instance, may hand over the control of fixed proportions of their income to particular departments, University Grants Committees to particular universities, families to particular members. Professor Samuelson (1956) calls such a procedure a 'shibboleth' and points that it is inconsistent with the maximization of a social welfare function. This is certainly true in general if we assume that there are no interactions between the different groups, so that the 'objective function' to be maximized is in the form

$$u = F(v_0(x_0), \ldots, v_T(x_T)), \tag{33}$$

for such a function is consistent with a shibboleth $y_t = \rho_t y$ with constant ρ's only if it can be written in the very special form $u = \sum \rho_t \log v_t$, where the v's are homogeneous of degree zero in the prices.[6] This general form of the social welfare or 'objective' function u may be acceptable—it may be called the Bernouilli–Bentham version—but the implication that the expenditure on each good increases in the same proportion as income changes is scarcely acceptable.

One might think that the assumption (33) was most appropriate for decentralization, for it implies that everyone looks after his own concerns. Yet we now see that the very opposite is true. If there are external economies, so that the behaviour of one department affects the plans of another, a wide class of 'shibboleth-type' preference fields are available—those defined by (18) if the proportion of the organization's income put at each member's disposal is allowed to depend on the prices which have to be paid; those defined by (26) otherwise. This may have some importance for the theory of organization.

6. MISTAKES

Actually the discussion so far is better adapted to decentralized decisions in general than to decisions over time. This is because, as M. Drèze has pointed out, expectations are rarely satisfied, so that the consumer has to draw up a new plan at the beginning of each period. Assuming that his expectations are single-valued,[7] the problem which faces him is:

1. Substitute past consumption into your utility function $u(x)$.
2. Maximize u subject to the new (expected) budget constraint.

The results will be consistent with Friedman's theory if and only if the utility function $u(x) = u(x_0, x_1, \ldots, x_T)$, $u_1(x) = u(x_0^*, x_1, \ldots, x_T)$, $u_2(x) = u(x_0^*, x_1^*, x_2, \ldots, x_T), \ldots$ can each be written in the polar form (21),

[6] At least if it is to be true at all prices—which implies among other things that each member of the family, and each department, buys in a different market.

[7] Since we are discussing the *permanent* component this seems the most sensible assumption, even if it does imply that the consumer continues to be sure of himself despite continued disappointments. It is a case of 'divide and rule'.

(22).[8] Here $x_0^* x_1^*, \ldots$ represent the actual pattern of consumption in the successive periods. Since the conditions (21), (22) relate to the polar form, while the problem itself is most naturally discussed in direct form, it is a difficult one to analyse, and I have not succeeded in discovering the general class of utility functions which satisfies the new more stringent conditions. Indeed it is not even completely clear how these conditions should be stated, that is, what sort of mistakes the consumer be allowed to have made.

It is possible, however, to construct quite a wide class of utility functions which do satisfy them, even if stringently stated, and hence to disprove Sargan's conjecture in this case too.

The counter-example discussed in Section 3 clearly provides such a class of utility functions. Whatever the past pattern of consumption, the consumer will spend in period t a proportion $\rho_t/(\rho_t + \rho_{t+1} + \ldots)$ of his (expected) net worth at the beginning of that period. Rather a more general class is found if we replace (7) by

$$X_i = \prod_t x_{ti_t}^{\rho_t}, \qquad i = 0, 1, \ldots, n,$$

where $(0_0, 1_0, \ldots, n_0)$, $(0_1, 1_1, \ldots, n_1)$, $\ldots$, $(0_T, 1_T, \ldots, n_T)$ are each permutations of $(0, 1, \ldots, n)$, that is to say, where different goods may enter into a given aggregate in different periods.

These counter-examples were easily discovered because they arise from the direct form of the utility function. How to analyse the general case is another matter.

[8] With '1' replacing '0' in u_1, '2' replacing it in u_2, etc.

7

Quasi-Separable Preferences, Costs, and Technologies

Editorial Remarks

While at the University of North Carolina in 1970, Gorman went on a seminar tour. This paper was among those prepared for the tour, and was presented at Harvard in November 1970.

The paper itself is a thorough analysis of the distance function which Gorman first discovered in 'Consumer Budgets and Prices Indices', where it was used to recover the form of the direct preferences from a dual representation. In this paper it stands on its own and is shown to be the natural dual of the cost or expenditure function. Natural in this context means that the distance function has the same properties in quantities as the cost function does in prices. His interest in the distance function reflects his concern for choosing the right mathematics for the economic problem at hand, just as his use of duality reflects the fact that prices are frequently the natural variables to take as primitive because, in a competitive world at least, it is the prices of private commodities that agents have in common. On the other hand, to analyse public goods, it is quantities that agents have in common. In order to construct price indices, the cost function is the natural representation of preferences, because it is homogeneous of degree one in prices. It follows that if one is interested in constructing quantity or standard-of-living indices then one should search for an implicit representation of the preference ordering that is homogeneous of degree one in quantities. The distance function turns out to be just the right representation of preferences for this task.

Editorial Summary

In Section 2 the technical properties of the distance function are set out in more detail than in 'Budgeting and Price Indices'. Suppose the utility function is given by

$$u = \phi(x), \tag{0.1}$$

where ϕ is continuous and increasing. The distance function is then defined by

$$f(u, x) = c \leftrightarrow u = \phi(x/c) \tag{0.2}$$

for $c > 0$. f is continuous, decreasing in u, and increasing, concave, and linearly homogeneous in x. From (0.2) it is clear that

$$f(u, x) \gtreqless 1 \leftrightarrow \phi(x) \gtreqless u. \tag{0.3}$$

Next, he demonstrates that the distance function is the natural dual to the cost function. That is, the cost function g can be written as

$$g(u, p) = \inf_x \{p \cdot x \,|\, \phi(x) \geqslant u\} \tag{0.4}$$

or, equivalently, as

$$g(u, p) = \inf_x \{p \cdot x \,|\, f(u, x) \geqslant 1\}, \tag{0.5}$$

while the distance function f operates as an indirect cost function, and satisfies

$$f(u, x) = \inf_p \{p \cdot x \,|\, g(u, p) \geqslant 1\}. \tag{0.6}$$

Section 3 defines the notion of *quasi-separability*.[1] It imposes the same structure on the distance function as on the cost function. Preferences are said to be *quasi-separable* if the distance function can be written in the form

$$f(u, x) = F(u, f^1(u, x^1), \dots, f^T(u, x^T)), \tag{0.7}$$

where $x = (x^1 \dots, x^T)$. Equivalently, the cost function can be expressed as

$$g(u, p) = G(u, g^1(u, p^1), \dots, g^T(u, p^T)), \tag{0.8}$$

where g^t is dual to f^t and F is dual to G, as in (0.5) and (0.6) above. Hence, one can choose f^t to be homogeneous of degree one in x^t and F to be homogeneous of degree one in $\{f^t\}$, while g^t is homogeneous of degree one in p^t and G in $\{g^t\}$.

The relationship of budgeting to quasi-separability is seen by applying Shephard's lemma to (0.8) to obtain

$$x_i = G_t(u, g^1(u, p^1), \dots, g^T(u, p^T))g_i^t(u, p^t) \tag{0.9}$$

for all i in group t. Multiplying by p_i and summing over all i in group t yields the expenditure on group t, m^t. Using the fact that g^t is linearly homogeneous in p^t (as f^t is in x^t) yields

$$m^t = G_t(u, g^1(u, p^1), \dots, g^T(u, p^T))g^T(u, p^t) \tag{0.10}$$

by Euler's theorem. Solving (0.10) for G_t and substituting this into (0.9) gives

$$x_i = m^t \times \frac{g_i^t(u, p^t)}{g^t(u, p^t)}, \tag{0.11}$$

for all i in group t. This is an intragroup budgeting rule which is quite different from those which we have examined to date: one needs to know the level of real income in order to proceed.

[1] A more informative name would be homogeneous implicit separability, as f is an implicit representation of preferences that has also been chosen to be homogeneous in quantities.

Section 4 analyses the additive analogue of (0.7) (or equivalently (0.8)) and obtains implicit CES solutions. These result from the fact that homogeneity and additivity in general yield the CES/Cobb–Douglas family of functions. This sort of interaction between homotheticity and separability appears often in this sort of work. The following paper entitled 'Separability and Linear Engel Curves' further exploits this interrelationship.

Quasi-Separable Preferences, Costs, and Technologies

1. INTRODUCTION

The natural independent variables in a piece of economic analysis are frequently prices rather than quantities. Other things being equal, it is convenient to have them as such from the outset. This is why we use cost, profit, and related functions to specify tastes and technologies.

Recently economists have tended to simplify difficult problems by assuming some sort of separability, so that different aspects can be studied in relative isolation. Unfortunately, this simple structure, e.g. in a direct utility function, is typically not reflected in its various indirect, or dual, formulations. Equally, should one of them turn out to be separable, it does not normally mean that the utility function is.

There are several exceptions, whose usefulness is made greater by the fact that we can frequently choose one of several dual specifications for purely mathematical convenience. Thus it may not greatly matter whether we move a consumer along his Engel curve by varying his income, utility, or even marginal utility of income. In such cases he can choose between the indirect utility function, the cost function, and sometimes, the profit function, according to which is mathematically the more tractable.

If the utility function is additive, so is the profit function. Of course we should only use it if the utility function is concave: but we will frequently have reason to believe that it is in this normalization.

If the utility function is homogeneously separable, we can choose its component functions to be positively homogeneous of degree one. They are, if you like, produced under constant returns, or, equivalently, under constant average costs, which are of course, positively homogeneous of degree one in the corresponding prices. They themselves may be regarded as the macro-prices of the corresponding quantity aggregates. The cost and profit functions turn out to be separable with the same structure as the utility functions, and with them as arguments.

This will be true, in particular, if the original utility function, as well as being separable, is homothetic; that is, if its Engel curves are straight lines through the origin in which case it too may conveniently be normalized to be positively homogeneous of degree one i.e. to be 'produced' under constant average costs.

If instead it has linear Engel curves which do not pass through the origin, and is separable, so will all its components, and so on all down the utility tree. Each can be normalized to be produced under constant marginal costs, with some sort of 'overhead' costs in addition if you like. The marginal or variable costs are of course positively homogeneous of degree one in the corresponding prices, and once more act very like macro-prices of the corresponding aggregates. In particular the marginal cost function corresponding to the utility function has the same structure as it, with them as its components. The 'overheads', of course, just add up.

In the present paper I develop a concept of separability in which the direct and indirect specifications always have the same structure. This runs in terms of a function $f(u, x)$ which is positively homogeneous of degree one in x, and takes the value one when $u = \phi(x)$, where $\phi(\cdot)$ is the utility function. It turns out to be a perfect dual of the cost function $g(u, p)$, so that we can frequently move backwards and forwards between them rather easily. Because of this duality, too, $f(u, \cdot)$ and $g(u, \cdot)$ have precisely the same structure, and corresponding components are closely related to each other. When either—and therefore each—is separable, I say that tastes are quasi-separable. The implications of quasi-separability turn out to be easy to understand, though not necessarily realistic.

Similar analyses can be applied in production theory, where, for instance, u might be a vector of outputs.

Professor Afriat tells me that $f(u, \cdot)$ is a distance function and that its duality with the cost, or support, function $g(u, \cdot)$ is proved in Chapter 3.5 of Eggleston (1958), which is actually entitled 'Distance and Support Functions of a Convex Set'. For myself, I came upon it in attempting to interpret some old results of mine about two-stage budgeting, which I had thought of presenting to you today: so that it came to some extent at least out of economics rather than mathematics.

Like Heinz ketchup, this paper was picked, cooked, and bottled, all in a day: two to be precise. There are loose ends, inconsistencies, and errors. I have pointed out those which have occurred to me in the footnotes.

2. HOMOGENEOUS SPECIFICATION OF PREFERENCES AND TECHNOLOGIES

Consider a continuous and strictly increasing utility function

$$u = \phi(x), \tag{2.1}$$

defined on a closed convex cone K in the positive orthant.[1] Set

[1] In my terminology, the positive orthant is $x \geqslant 0$. It therefore excludes the origin. K is closed relative to this—a punctured, or vertexless cone. To require that K be the entire positive orthant would be to rule out utility functions, such as the Cobb–Douglas, which are not strictly increasing on the co-ordinate flats, unless we were to drop the assumption that $\phi(\cdot)$ be strictly increasing, which is a considerable convenience in discussing separability. Note that the range of $\phi(\cdot)$ is open at its lower end.

$$f(u, x) = c \quad \text{when} \quad u = \phi(x/c); \quad c > 0,\ x \geqslant 0, \tag{2.2}$$

and[2]

$$f(u, 0) = 0. \tag{2.3}$$

Then

$$f(u, ax) = af(u, x), \qquad a \geqslant 0 \tag{2.4}$$

$$f(u, x) > 0, \qquad x \geqslant 0, \tag{2.5}$$

and

$$f(u, x) \gtreqless 1 \quad \text{iff} \quad \phi(x) \gtreqless u, \tag{2.6}$$

so that $f(u, \cdot)$ is strictly increasing, and $f(\cdot, x)$ strictly decreasing, if $\phi(\cdot)$ is strictly increasing, as we have assumed it to be.

Since $\phi(\cdot)$ is also continuous, so is $f(\cdot)$. To see this we let $(u^n, x^n) \to (u, x)$, $x \neq 0$ and let

$$u^n = \phi(x^n/c^n), \quad u = \phi(x/c), \tag{2.7}$$

$\{c^n\}$ is bounded. Let $\bar{c}$ be a limit point. Then

$$u = \phi(x/\bar{c}), \tag{2.8}$$

by the continuity of $\phi(\cdot)$, and $c = \bar{c}$ in (2.7) and (2.8) by its strict monotonicity. Now (2.7) means

$$F(u^n, x^n) = c^n, \qquad f(u, x) = c. \tag{2.9}$$

Hence $f(u^n, x^n) \to f(u, x)$ as required, $x \neq 0$. Continuity at $(u, 0)$ is obvious.

The converse is also true. If $u^n = \phi(x^n)$ and $x^n \to x \neq 0$, then $u^n \to u = \phi(x)$. This is because $f(u^n, x^n) = 1$, so that if $\bar{u}$ is a limit point of $\{u^n\}$, $f(\bar{u}, x) = 1$ and $\bar{u} = \phi(x) = u$.

$\phi(\cdot)$ is therefore continuous and strictly increasing iff $f(\cdot)$ is continuous, $f(u, \cdot)$ strictly increasing, and $f(\cdot, x)$ strictly decreasing.

It is frequently assumed that utility functions are quasi-concave. $\phi(\cdot)$ is iff $f(u, \cdot)$ is concave.

Suppose first that $\phi(\cdot)$ is quasi-concave, or, equivalently, that

$$\phi(cx + dy) \geqslant u, \qquad \text{when} \qquad \phi(x), \phi(y) \geqslant u, \tag{2.10}$$

and

$$c, d \geqslant 0, \qquad c + d = 1, \tag{2.11}$$

that is, if

$$f(u, cx + dy) \geqslant 1 \qquad \text{when} \qquad f(u, x), f(u, y) \geqslant 1, \tag{2.12}$$

[2] Had we defined $\phi(0)$, we would have had $f(\phi(0), 0) = 1$, leading to a discontinuity.

given (2.10). Let now

$$f(u, x) = A, \quad f(u, y) = B, \tag{2.13}$$

in general. Then

$$f(u, x/A) = f(u, y/B) = 1, \tag{2.14}$$

so that

$$f(u, (ax + by)/(aA + bB)) \geqslant 1, \tag{2.15}$$

when

$$a, b \geqslant 0, \tag{2.16}$$

by (2.10), with $c = aA/(aA + bB)$, $d = bB/(aA + bB)$. Hence

$$f(u, ax + by) \geqslant aA + bB = af(u, x) + bf(u, y), \tag{2.17}$$

by (2.4) and (2.13), a and b satisfying (2.16). Setting $a + b = 1$, we show that $f(u, \cdot)$ is concave. (2.16)–(2.17) are equivalent to this and (2.4).

Hence $f(u, \cdot)$ is concave if $\phi(\cdot)$ is quasi-concave. To prove the converse we set $a + b = 1$, $f(u, x) = f(u, y) = 1$ in (2.17), to get (2.12) and, therefore, (2.10).

The utility function $\phi(\cdot)$ is therefore continuous, strictly increasing, and quasi-concave iff $f(\cdot)$ is continuous,[3] $f(\cdot, x)$ strictly decreasing, and $f(u, \cdot)$ strictly increasing, concave, and positively homogeneous of degree one. Let us call such a function *well behaved.* I will assume $f(\cdot)$ well behaved from now on except where I specifically state the contrary.

These conditions are so similar to those commonly required of cost functions that one is led to expect some close relationship between the two, as, indeed there is.

The cost function is of course

$$g(u, p) = \inf\{p \cdot x \mid \phi(x) \geqslant u\} = \inf\{p \cdot x \mid f(u, x) \geqslant 1\} \tag{2.18}$$

which turns out to imply that

$$f(u, x) = \inf\{p \cdot x \mid g(u, p) \geqslant 1\}. \tag{2.19}$$

Because of the homogeneity of $f(u, \cdot)$, $g(u, \cdot)$, (2.18) and (2.19) become[4]

$$g(u, p) = \inf\{p \cdot x/f(u, x)\}, \tag{2.20}$$

$$f(u, x) = \inf\{p \cdot x/g(u, p)\}. \tag{2.21}$$

[3] Being strictly increasing and positively homogeneous of degree one in $x \in K$, $f(u, \cdot)$ is also positive.

[4] Since $p \cdot x/f(u, x)$, given p, and $p \cdot x/g(u, p)$, given x, are each constant along rays, we can isolate the origin in calculating their infima, and therefore need not be bothered by their singularity there.

Because of the concavity of $f(u, \cdot)$, each $\bar{x}$ in K yields the infimum in (2.18) at some prices $\bar{p} \geqslant 0$, in the sense that

$$\bar{p} \cdot \bar{x} = f(u, \bar{x}) g(u, \bar{p}), \tag{2.22}$$

while, of course,

$$p \cdot \bar{x} \geqslant f(u, \bar{x}) g(u, p), \tag{2.23}$$

in general, since the infimum may or may not be attained at $\bar{x}$ when the prices are p. (2.22) and (2.23) immediately imply (2.21) and hence (2.19).

If $p \cdot \bar{x}/f(u, \bar{x})$ attains its minimum at $\bar{p}$, then $\bar{p} \cdot x/g(u, \bar{p})$ does at $\bar{x}$ and vice versa. Using a terminology introduced by Professor S. N. Afriat in a closely related field, let us say that $\bar{p}$, $\bar{x}$ are then *conjugates*. Then we have

$$p \cdot x \geqslant f(u, x) g(u, p), \qquad \text{each } p \geqslant 0, x \in K, \tag{2.24}$$

$$p \cdot x = f(u, x) g(u, p) \quad \text{iff} \quad p, x \text{ are conjugates}. \tag{2.25}$$

Production may be analysed in a similar manner. Suppose for instance that u is a *vector* of outputs, x of inputs, and that the technology is defined by

$$\phi(u, x) \geqslant 0, \tag{2.26}$$

where $\phi(\cdot)$ is continuous, $\phi(u, \cdot)$ strictly increasing, and $\phi(\cdot, x)$ strictly decreasing, and where, for any given u, the set of x's determined by (2.26) is convex.[5] Then define

$$f(u, x) = c \quad \text{if} \quad \phi(u, x/c) = 1, \qquad c > 0, x \geqslant 0, \tag{2.27}$$

and

$$f(u, 0) = 0, \tag{2.28}$$

by analogy with (2.27) and (2.3). The previous analysis then carries over unchanged despite the fact that u is now a vector.

Alternatively u might be a vector of fixed inputs, x of outputs and variable inputs.[6] Then we would have to use the gross profit function instead of the cost function, but this would lead to no essential differences.[7]

If the technology yields constant returns,

$$\phi(au, ax) = 0 \quad \text{iff} \quad \phi(u, x) = 0, \qquad \text{each } a \geqslant 0, \tag{2.29}$$

so that

$$f(au, ax) = 1 \quad \text{iff} \quad f(u, x) = 1. \tag{2.30}$$

[5] All normal and rather acceptable assumptions.

[6] The outputs and variable inputs are assumed to adapt perfectly to the market, the fixed inputs to be fixed.

[7] I have not thought out this case in any detail: profit functions are more difficult to handle than cost functions because of the possibility that receipts and costs may both tend to infinity.

Suppose now that

$$f(u, x) = c. \tag{2.31}$$

Then $f(u, x/c) = 1$, so that $f(au, ax/c) = 1$, each $a \geqslant 0$, by (2.30) and

$$f(au, ax) = c = f(u, x), \qquad \text{each } a \geqslant 0, \tag{2.32}$$

by (2.4), or, equivalently given (2.4),

$$f(au, x) = a^{-1}f(au, ax) = a^{-1}f(u, x), \tag{2.33}$$

so that $f(\cdot, x)$ is positively homogeneous of degree -1.

In the case of a consumer whose utility function is positively homogeneous of degree one this implies

$$f(u, x) = h(x)/u, \text{ say,} \tag{2.34}$$

where

$$h(x) = f(1, x) \tag{2.35}$$

is positively homogeneous of degree one. If $\phi(\cdot)$ is merely homothetic, there exists a $\theta(\phi(x))$ which is positively homogeneous of degree one, and

$$f(u, x) = h(x)/\theta(u), \tag{2.36}$$

where (2.35) still holds if we normalize so that

$$\theta(1) = 1. \tag{2.37}$$

As one might expect, the corresponding results for the cost functions are

$$g(au, p) = ag(u, p), \qquad a \geqslant 0, \tag{2.34a}$$

$$g(u, p) = uk(p), \text{ say,} \tag{2.35a}$$

$$g(u, p) = \theta(u)k(p), \tag{2.36a}$$

where

$$k(p) = g(1, p) = \inf\{p \cdot x \,|\, h(x) \geqslant 1\}. \tag{2.38}$$

in the normalization (2.37).

I leave the proofs to the reader.

3. QUASI-SEPARABILITY

Let us now say that the preference order or technology specified by $f(\cdot)$ is *quasi-separable*, or alternatively that $f(\cdot)$ itself is *quasi-separable*, iff $f(u, \cdot)$ is separable, that is, iff

$$f(u, x) = F(u, f^1(u, x^1), \ldots, f^T(u, x^T)), \tag{3.1}$$

where

$$x = (x^1, \ldots, x^T), \quad x^t = (x_i)_{i \in t} \in K^t, \text{ each } t, \qquad K = \prod_{t=1}^{T} K^t, \text{ say.} \tag{3.2}$$

If so we can normalize so that[8]

$$f(u, 0, \ldots, 0, x^t, 0, \ldots, 0) = F(u, 0, \ldots, 0, f^t(u, x^t), 0, \ldots, 0) = f^t(u, x^t), \tag{3.3}$$

implying in particular that each $f^t(\cdot)$ is well behaved when $f(\cdot)$ is. I leave it to the reader to verify that $F(\cdot)$ is also well behaved in this normalization, which I will use throughout.

Consider now the cost function

$$\begin{aligned} g(u, p) &= \inf\{p \cdot x \,|\, f(u, x) \geq 1\} \\ &= \inf\left\{\sum p^t \cdot x^t \,|\, F(u, f^1(u, x^1), \ldots, f^t(u, x^t)) \geq 1\right\} \\ &= \inf\left\{\sum \inf\{p^t \cdot x^t \,|\, f^t(u, x^t) \geq v^t\} \,|\, F(u, v) \geq 1\right\} \\ &= \inf\left\{\sum v^t \inf\{p^t \cdot y^t \,|\, f^t(u, y^t) \geq 1\} \,|\, F(u, v) \geq 1\right\} \end{aligned} \tag{3.4}$$

where

$$y^t = x^t / v^t, \qquad \text{each } t, \quad v = (v^t, \ldots, v^T). \tag{3.5}$$

Hence

$$\begin{aligned} g(u, p) &= \inf\left\{\sum v^t g^t(u, p^t) \,|\, F(u, v) \geq 1\right\}, \\ &= G(u, g^1(u, p^1), \ldots, g^T(u, P^T)), \end{aligned} \tag{3.6}$$

where

$$\begin{aligned} g(u, p^t) &= \inf\{p^t \cdot x^t \,|\, f^t(u, x^t) \geq 1\} \\ &= \inf\{p^t \cdot x^t \,|\, \phi(x^t) \geq u\} \end{aligned} \tag{3.7}$$

$$\begin{aligned} G(u, w) &= \inf\{v \cdot x \,|\, F(u, v) \geq 1\} \\ &= \inf\{v \cdot w \,|\, \Phi(v) \geq u\} \end{aligned} \tag{3.8}$$

[8] This is legitimate only when K is the positive orthant. Cobb–Douglas-type functions are then ruled out, which is a real cost. We can use $a \in K$ as a reference vector instead of 0. This yields $f^t(\cdot)$ which have all the desirable properties except homogeneity of degree one. They can be transformed to be that too, but conceivably at the cost of losing their continuity and strictly decreasing properties in u. They remain continuous in x.

Since we can multiply each by any function of u we wish, it is quite likely that they can be rendered strictly decreasing in u, possibly under some further assumptions. I have not looked into the continuity of $f^t(\cdot)$ as distinct from $f^t(u, \cdot)$.

Since the $f^t(u, \cdot)$ will now have all the desirable properties, the analysis below goes through whether or not $f^t(\cdot)$ is continuous and $f^t(\cdot, x)$ strictly decreasing, but the interpretation in terms of the 'utilities' $\phi(\cdot)$, $\Phi(\cdot)$, breaks down.

are cost functions themselves, corresponding to the group, and macro-, 'utility' functions.[9]

$$u^t = \phi^t(x^t) \text{ iff } f^t(u^t, x^t) = 1, \quad \text{each } t, \tag{3.9}$$

$$U = \Phi(v) \text{ iff } F(U, v) = 1 \tag{3.10}$$

or, if you like, to their obvious correlates $f^t(\cdot)$ and $F(\cdot)$ in (3.1).

Note too that they are normalized along the same lines as the f's in (3.3).

The cost function $g(\cdot)$, then, is quasi-separable if $f(\cdot)$ is. Because of the duality spelled out in (2.18) and (2.19), $g(\cdot)$ is therefore quasi-separable iff $f(\cdot)$ is.

The implications of quasi-separability flow directly from the cost function (3.6). For simplicity of exposition I will assume that it is differentiable. Being concave it is differentiable almost everywhere in its domain, in any case. To assume it so everywhere is to assume $\phi(\cdot)$ in (2.1) or $\phi(u, \cdot)$ in (2.26) strictly concave, or equivalently $f(u, \cdot)$ strictly quasi-concave as well as concave.

Consider the case of consumer preferences, for example. As might be expected the implications relate to the compensated demand functions

$$x_i = g_i(u, p) = G_t(u, g^1, \ldots, g^T)g_i^t(u, p^t), \quad i \in t, \tag{3.11}$$

where subscripts denote derivatives. Hence the total expenditure on group t

$$m^t = G_t(u, g^1, \ldots, g^T)g^t(u, p^t), \quad \text{each } t, \tag{3.12}$$

since $g^t(u, \cdot)$ is positively homogeneous of degree one, and therefore depends only on real income u and the group price indices $g^1(u, p^1), \ldots, g^T(u, p^T)$.[10] That these should depend on the consumer's standard of living seems acceptable. Viewed from the standpoint of two-stage budgeting, however, the noticeable thing about (3.12) is that the procedure will work reasonably well only if the consumer has a reasonably good idea beforehand of what his real income is going to be. In an age of sectional bargaining based to a considerable extent on the cost of living, and of inflation hedging investment, it may be at least as reasonable to assume this, as that he has a good idea of his prospective money income, particularly if he thinks in terms of some sort of permanent income concept.

(3.9) and (3.10) imply that

$$x_i = m^t g_i^t(u, p^t)/g^t(u, p^t), \quad i \in t, \tag{3.13}$$

at the second stage. Given one's real income therefore, the second-stage decisions depend only on the prices p^t in the group. The proportional

[9] $\phi^t(x^t) = \phi(0, \ldots, 0, x^t, 0, \ldots, 0)$, each t, in the normalization (3.3), which is highly acceptable.

[10] Each $g^t(u, \cdot)$ is positively homogeneous of degree one, and strictly increasing in the prices of goods which are actually consumed, which is acceptable.

breakdown of m^t between the goods in the group therefore remains the same if m^t changes because of price changes elsewhere, though not necessarily so if it changes because u does. This is a limited form of homogeneity, but it may be too great for some purposes.

$g^t(u, p^t)$ is the cost function corresponding to the utility function $\phi^t(x^t)$ of (3.9). Now, knowing $u, g^1, \ldots, g^T$ beforehand, one knows G_t in (3.11). Hence one can tell oneself at the first stage to maximize

$$\phi^t(x^t/G_t), \tag{3.14}$$

subject to

$$p^t \cdot x^t \leqslant m^t, \tag{3.15}$$

at the second. This is, I suppose, a fairly decent pattern of decentralization.

Suppose instead that u is a vector of outputs and x of inputs. Having decided on these outputs, and knowing the price indices $g^t(u, p^t)$ for the different groups of inputs, the central controller allocates expenditures m^t to each of the buying departments. He tells them G_t and they maximize (3.14) subject to (3.15). Again a fairly simple pattern of decentralization to carry out and understand. About its realism I say nothing.

4. TWO SPECIAL CASES

Because $f(u, \cdot)$, $F(u, \cdot)$ each $f^t(u, \cdot)$, $g(u, \cdot)$, $G(u, \cdot)$ and each $g^t(u, \cdot)$ are continuous and strictly increasing, the analysis used for utility trees can be carried over to $f(u, \cdot)$ and $g(u, \cdot)$. Because (2.1) and (3.6) are equivalent, each has the same structure. In particular, therefore, $f(u, \cdot)$ is additively separable iff $g(u, \cdot)$ is.

What are they like in that case?

By definition

$$f(u, x) = H\left(u, \sum h^t(u, x^t)\right), \text{ say.} \tag{4.1}$$

Taking $h^t(u, 0) = 0$ without loss of generality,[11] we see that

$$f^t(u, x^t) = H(u, h^t(u, x^t)), \tag{4.2}$$

so that

$$h^t(u, x^t) = \theta(u, f^t(u, x^t)), \text{ say.} \tag{4.3}$$

and

[11] Actually there is a loss of generality here. We might have $h^t(u, 0) = -\infty$. It is this which rules out the Cobb–Douglas case of the CES solution. I do not see any difficulty in dropping the normalization.

$$h^t(u, ax^t) = \theta(u, af^t). \tag{4.4}$$

Hence

$$F(u, f^1, \ldots, f^T) = H\left(u, \sum \theta(u, f^t)\right). \tag{4.5}$$

and, since $F(u, \cdot)$ is homogeneous,

$$aF(u, f^1, \ldots, f^T) = H\left(u, \sum \theta(u, af^t)\right) = aH\left(u, \sum \theta(u, f^t)\right) \tag{4.6}$$

a functional equation whose solutions, as one might expect, are

$$\theta(u, f) = A(u) f^{a(u)} \quad \text{or} \quad A(u) \log f \tag{4.7}$$

$$H(u, v) = (v/A(u))^{1/a(u)} \quad \text{or} \quad e^{v/A(u)}. \tag{4.8}$$

Hence

$$f(u, x)^{a(u)} = \sum f^t(u, x^t)^{a(u)} \quad \text{or} \quad f(u, x) = \prod f^t(u, x^t). \tag{4.9}$$

Since the latter is not strictly increasing in x when some $x^t = 0$, it is not well behaved. We therefore drop it.[12] The utility function is therefore implicitly defined by

$$\sum f^t(u, x^t)^{a(u)} = 1. \tag{4.10}$$

It is straightforward to derive the corresponding cost function. It is given by

$$g(u, p)^{b(u)} = \sum g^t(u, p^t)^{b(u)} \tag{4.11}$$

where[13]

$$(a(u) - 1)(b(u) - 1) = 1. \tag{4.12}$$

The analogy of all this with the CES technology is an obvious one. In fact the elasticity of substitution between real expenditure in different groups is $1 - b(u)$ in this case, and is therefore constant along any given indifference surface, and the same between different groups.[14] Indeed it may be defined as a quasi-separable technology with this property.

A more interesting special case is that in which some or all of the group utility functions are themselves homothetic. In that case we may write

$$f^t(u, x^t) = h^t(x^t)/\sum \theta^t(u), \text{ say,} \tag{4.13}$$

[12] The true reason for dropping it is that it is inconsistent with the normalization rule $h^t(u, 0) = 0$ on which the analysis depends. See n. 11.

[13] This is the usual CES formula.

[14] As for the CES. One holds relative prices constant within the groups, changing their levels, and using Hicks aggregates for 'real expenditure'.

when $h^t(ax^t) = ah^t(x^t)$ according to (2.29). The $\theta^t(u)$ terms can be integrated into the first argument of $F(\cdot)$ to get

$$f(u, x) = H(u, f^R, h^S), \tag{4.14}$$

where S is composed of the separable groups, R of the remainder, and

$$f^R = (f^r(u, x^t))_{r \in R}, \quad h^S = (h^s(x^s))_{s \in S}. \tag{4.15}$$

Setting $f(u, x) = 1$ we get

$$u = \phi(x) = \psi(x^R, h^S), \text{ say,} \tag{4.16}$$

where

$$x^R = (x^r)_{r \in R}, \tag{4.17}$$

so that the groups are homothetically separable in $\phi(\cdot)$. Conversely, if this is so, define

$$H(u, x^R, h^S) = c \quad \text{iff} \quad \psi(x^R/c, h^S/c) = 1, \tag{4.18}$$

that is, iff $\phi(x^R/c, x^S/c) = 1$ because of the homogeneity of the h's. Hence

$$f(u, x) = H(u, x^R, h^S), \tag{4.19}$$

which, if it is quasi-separable with these groups, implies (4.14).

I leave it to the reader to prove that the cost function is

$$g(u, p) = K(u, g^R, k^S) \tag{4.20}$$

where

$$g^R = (g^r(u, p^r))_{r \in R}, \quad k^S = (k^s(u, p^s))_{s \in S}, \tag{4.21}$$

and

$$k^s(u, p^s) = \inf\{p^s \cdot x^s \mid h^s(x^s) \geqslant 1\}. \tag{4.22}$$

If all the groups are homothetic,

$$u = \phi(x) = \psi(h^1(x^1), \ldots, h^T(x^T)), \tag{4.23}$$

is homothetically separable, and, as is well known, the $h^t(x^t)$ can be treated as quantities of macro-goods whose prices are $k^t(p^t)$ in all analyses in which the groups appear as units. The corresponding cost function is

$$g(u, p) = K(u, k_1(p_1), \ldots, k^T(p^T)). \tag{4.24}$$

(4.23) and (4.24) are, in fact, equivalent.

8

Separability and Linear Engel Curves

Editorial Remarks

The following article comprises three notes on the relationship between separability and the linearity of Engel curves which we have put together into one paper with three sections. They were apparently all written about the same time: one of them is dated March 1971. Preferences with linear Engel curves are a natural generalization of homotheticity, which yields straight-line Engel curves passing through the origin. It has appeared tangentially in some of the budgeting papers and reappears in the discussion of representative consumers and firms in Part II of this volume.

Editorial Summary

The first section characterizes utility or production functions that are separable in some partition of the variables, and have linear Engel curves. The following section repeats the exercise for additive separability, while the final section adds the requirement of constant average and constant marginal propensities to spend on each group.

Section 1 teases out the implications of assuming that the direct utility function is separable,

$$U(x) = F(u_1(x_1), \ldots, u_T(x_T)), \tag{0.1}$$

and that the Engel curves are straight lines. Linear Engel curves imply that the cost function can be written as

$$g(U, p) = R(p)U + S(p). \tag{0.2}$$

By simple manipulation Gorman shows that this implies

$$g(U, p) = K(P_1(p_1), \ldots, P_T(p_T))U + L(P_1(p_1), \ldots, P_T(p_T)) + \textstyle\sum_t Q_t(p_t). \tag{0.3}$$

In this case, there are two kinds of overheads or fixed costs: those associated with the macro-utility function, F, which are given by L and depend upon the vector of price indices $\{P_t(p_t)\}$; and those associated with each group, t, which are given by $Q_t(p_t)$ for all t.

This is slightly misleading because there is a normalization issue here which haunts all this type of work. Although both types of overheads are possible, it appears that only one type of overhead can occur at any given time. To see this, assume that $L \neq 0$, for otherwise there are only micro-overheads. Rewrite Gorman's equation (1.4) using his condition (1.5) to obtain

$$R(p)U - \sum_t P_t(p_t)u_t^* = R(p)U - G(P_1(p_1), \ldots, P_T(p_T), U)$$

$$= \sum_t Q_t(p_t) - S(p) \tag{0.4}$$

where the star refers to the optimizers in his (1.4) or (1.5). The right side of this equation is independent of utility, and so the left side must be also. From (0.4) and from his (1.7), one obtains

$$S(p) - L(P_1(p_1), \ldots, P_T(p_T)) = \sum_t Q_t(p_t). \tag{0.5}$$

Now, if $S = 0$, then

$$-L(P_1(p_1), \ldots, P_T(p_T)) = \sum_t Q_t(p_t), \tag{0.6}$$

and hence

$$\sum_t Q_t(p_t) = \sum_t \tilde{Q}_t(P_t(p_t)) \tag{0.7}$$

for some function $\tilde{Q}$. As each Q_t is homogeneous of degree one, this can be rewritten as

$$\sum_t Q_t(p_t) = \sum_t \alpha_t P_t(p_t), \tag{0.8}$$

which demonstrates that there are only macro-overheads. Next, suppose that $S \neq 0$. Differentiating (0.5) with respect to $i \in r$, and then k, $l \in s$, yields

$$\frac{S_{ik}}{S_{il}} = \frac{\dfrac{\partial}{\partial p_k} P_s(p_s)}{\dfrac{\partial}{\partial p_l} P_s(p_s)}. \tag{0.9}$$

Integrating (0.9) twice one obtains

$$S(p) = \hat{S}(\{P_s(p_s)\}_{s \neq r}, p_r) + \tilde{S}(\{P_s(p_s)\}_{s \neq r}). \tag{0.10}$$

However, (0.10) must hold for all r and hence

$$S(p) = S(P_1(p_1), \ldots, P_T(p_T)). \tag{0.11}$$

Substituting (0.11) into (0.5) yields (0.8), as before, demonstrating that there cannot be both macro- and micro-overheads.

These normalization problems can be vexatious and Gorman manipulates them with more rapidity than makes for easy reading, as is evident in the next section.

Section 2 asks essentially the same question, but with respect to additive separability rather than just separability. Hence (0.1) above is replaced by

$$F(U(x)) = \sum_t f_t(u_t(x_t)). \tag{0.12}$$

In general, the original utility function U is only ordinally equivalent to an additive function. In addition, he assumes that each term on the right side of (0.12) is strictly concave. The latter assumption permits him to use the profit function representation of preferences. That is, letting the price of transformed utility be p_0, the profit function is given by

$$\begin{aligned} H(p_0, p) &= \max_{x_{it}} \left\{ p_0 F(u(x)) + \sum_t \sum_i p_{it} x_{it} \right\} \\ &= \max \{ p_0 F(U(x)) - G(p, U) \}, \end{aligned} \tag{0.13}$$

where G is the cost or expenditure function given by his (2.1). The reason for using the profit function here and the cost function in the previous section is that the profit function inherits the assumed additivity of the utility function, whereas the cost function does not.

He finds in (2.26) that the resulting utility function must be CES/Cobb–Douglas, that is,

$$[U(x)]^\delta = \sum_t [u_t(x_t)]^\delta \tag{0.14}$$

for $0 \neq \delta < 1$. (The limits as δ goes to zero is the Cobb–Douglas case as usual.) This is, of course, a special case of the result found in Section 4 of 'Quasi-Separable Preferences, Costs, and Technologies' where implicit additivity was analysed. He also notes that this is similar to a utility function that has a constant marginal propensity to save in each period, and hence wonders if this is the most general case of this phenomenon. This leads to the next section.

In Section 3 he addresses a slightly different question: in what circumstances do utility functions that are additively separable yield either constant average or marginal propensities to consume? This section was written after Gorman had seen a paper by Pollak (1971) which posed this question about functions that are additive in the coordinate partition of their variables. Gorman's results are more general, for the functions may be additive in groups and not just scalars. It is also a testament to the simplicity of working with dual variables.

He begins with a new normalization of the utility function given, in a slight abuse of notation, as

$$U(x) = \sum_t u_t(x_t) \tag{0.15}$$

with a profit function given by

$$\sum_t h^t(p_0, p) := \max \left\{ p_0 \sum_t u_t(x_t) - \sum_t p_t x_t \right\}. \tag{0.16}$$

He first investigates the circumstances in which this yields a constant average propensity to consume goods in each group. The answer, not surprisingly perhaps, is

$$U(x) = \sum_t a_t \log v_t(x_t), \tag{0.17}$$

where v_t is homogeneous of degree one. Sufficiency is easily verified.

Next, he asks when the marginal propensity to consume on each group is a constant. The answer is given by (0.17), but in this case the function v_t is quasi-homogeneous rather than homogeneous (linear Engel curves which do not necessarily go through the origin). Hence the cost function dual to each v_t is given by

$$m_t = P^t(p^t)v^t + Q^t(p^t) \tag{0.18}$$

for all t. This also demonstrates that the overall utility function must be homothetic.

Separability and Linear Engel Curves

1. SEPARABLE UTILITY AND LINEAR ENGEL CURVES

Write the utility function

$$U(x) = F(u_1(x_1), \ldots, u_T(x_T)). \tag{1.1}$$

Since the utility function has linear Engel curves, so do the component-specific satisfaction functions. Normalize so that the corresponding cost functions may be written

$$m = R(p)U + S(p), \tag{1.2}$$

$$m_t = P_t(p_t)u_t + Q_t(p_t), \tag{1.3}$$

so that

$$\begin{aligned} R(p)U + S(p) &= \min\left\{\sum (P_t(p_t)u_t + Q_t(p_t)) \,\middle|\, F(u) \geqslant U\right\} \\ &= \min\left\{\sum P_t(p_t)u_t \,\middle|\, F(u) \geqslant U\right\} + \sum Q_t(p_t) \\ &= G(P(p), U) + \sum Q_t(p_t) \end{aligned} \tag{1.4}$$

in an obvious notation, where

$$G(P, U) = \min\left\{\sum P_t u_t \,\middle|\, F(u) \geqslant U\right\} \tag{1.5}$$

is the cost function associated with the 'production function' $F(\cdot)$.

Differentiate (1.4) with respect to U to get

$$R(p) = G_0(P(p), U) = K(P(p)), \text{ say,} \tag{1.6}$$

so that

$$G(P(p),U) = K(P(p))U + L(P(p)), \text{ say.} \tag{1.7}$$

Since $G(\cdot)$ is the cost function associated with the 'production function' $F(\cdot)$, this means that the latter has linear Engel curves in its arguments. The total cost function is

$$K(P(p))U + L(p)) + \sum Q_t(p_t), \qquad P(p) = (P_1(p_1), \ldots, P_T(p_T)), \tag{1.8}$$

that is, the marginal cost function $K(P(p))$ is a function of the marginal cost of the components, while the overheads $L(P(p)) + \sum Q_t(p_t)$ comprise the overheads *specific* to the overall utility function as a function of the components, plus the overheads for the component-specific satisfaction functions.

Consider now a utility tree. Apply (1.8) to each node in turn. Call the actual goods the bottom nodes, and their prices the marginal costs, so that their overheads are zero. Then the marginal cost function at each node depends only on the marginal costs at the set of nodes immediately below it in the tree. Hence the overall marginal cost function has the same structure as the utility function itself, and is, of course, homothetically separable.

Turning next to the overheads at each node we note that they are the sum of those specific to it and to all lower modes—those specific to any particular node being specific to it as a function of its component functions and therefore depending only on their marginal costs, that is, only on the marginal costs at the next lower nodes.

What happens at an additively separable node is discussed in the next section. It is shown that the component at that node may be taken to be CES in *its* components: in that normalization there are no overheads associated with it.

2. ADDITIVELY SEPARABLE UTILITY AND LINEAR ENGEL CURVES

Since the utility function $U(x) = \sum_t u_t(x_t)$ has linear Engel curves, so also does each felicity function $u_t(\cdot)$. Normalize so that the corresponding cost curves may be written

$$G(p, U) = R(p)U + S(p), \tag{2.1}$$

$$g_t(p, u_t) = P_t(p_t)u_t + Q_t(p_t), \qquad \text{each } t, \tag{2.2}$$

in the obvious notation. Note that we can still renormalize to set each $\tilde{u}_t = a_t u_t + b_t$, $\tilde{U} = AU + B$, when the a's and b's, A and B are all constants, without affecting (2.1) and (2.2).

In this normalization, additive separability implies that we can write

$$F(U) = \sum f_t(u_t). \tag{2.3}$$

We may assume $F(U(\cdot))$ strictly concave by the arguments in Gorman (1970). Hence so is $f_t(u_t(\cdot))$, each t. Since $u_t(\cdot)$ and $U(\cdot)$ are only just concave because of the linear relations $x_{ti} = P_{ti}u_t + a_{ti}$, each t_i, and $x_t = R_i U + S_i$ in total, this implies that $F(\cdot)$ and each $f_t(\cdot)$, are strictly concave.

To exploit the additive separability in (2.3) we need to use profit rather cost functions. That associated with the utility function $F(U(\cdot))$ is

$$\begin{aligned}\max\{p_0F(U) - R(p)U - S(p)\} &= \max\{p_0F(U) - R(p)U)\} - S(p)\\ &= H(p_0, R(p)) - S(p), \text{ say,}\end{aligned} \tag{2.4}$$

where $H(p_0, R) = \max\{p_0F(U) - RU\}$ is the profit function corresponding to the 'production function' $F(\cdot)$. Using the additive separability of (2.3), it is also

$$\max\left\{p_0\sum f_t(u_t) - \sum P_t(p_t)u_t - \sum Q_t(p_t)\right\}$$
$$= \sum \max\{p_0 f_t(u_t) - P_t(p_t)u_t\} - \sum Q_t(p_t)$$
$$= \sum h_t(p_0, P_t(p_t)) - \sum Q_t(p_t), \tag{2.5}$$

where $h_t(p_0, p_t) = \max\{p_0 f_t(u_t) - P_t u_t\}$ is the profit function corresponding to the production function $f_t(\cdot)$. (2.4) and (2.5) imply

$$H(p_0, R(p)) = \sum h_t(p_0, P_t(p_t)) + Q(p), \text{ say.} \tag{2.6}$$

Differentiating this with respect to p_0 we get

$$\dot{H}(p_0, R(p)) = \sum \dot{h}_t(p_0, P_t(p_t)) \tag{2.7}$$

in the obvious notation, so that

$$R(p) = \phi\left(\sum \dot{h}_t(p_0, P_t(p_t)), p_0\right), \text{ say}$$
$$= V(P(p)), \quad P(p) = (P_1(p_1), \ldots, P_T(p_T)), \text{ say.} \tag{2.8}$$

Substituting into (2.7) and differentiating with respect to P_t we get

$$\dot{H}' V_t(P) = \dot{h}_t'(p_0, P_t), \tag{2.9}$$

so that

$$V_s(P)/V_t(P) = \dot{h}_s'(p_0, P_s)/\dot{h}_t'(p_0, P_t)$$
$$= \phi_s(P_s)/\phi_t(P_t)$$
$$= a_s P_s^{\alpha-1}/a_t P_t^{\alpha-1}, \text{ say,} \tag{2.10}$$

by homogeneity. Hence

$$V = \phi\left(\sum a_t P_t^{\alpha}\right) = \left(\sum a_t P_t^{\alpha}\right)^{\beta}, \quad \alpha\beta = 1, \tag{2.11}$$

in an appropriate normalization, by homogeneity. By homogeneity, too,

$$\dot{h}_t'(p_0, P_t) = c a_t p_0^{-\alpha} P_t^{\alpha-1}, \text{ say,} \tag{2.12}$$

$$h_t'(p_0, P_t) = d a_t p_0^{1-\alpha} P_t^{\alpha-1} + b_t, \text{ say,} \tag{2.13}$$

$$h_t(p_0, P_t) = e a_t p_0^{1-\alpha} P_t^{\alpha} + b_t P_t + c_t p_0, \text{say,} \tag{2.14}$$

in succession. Write now

$$u_t = e a_t \tilde{u}_t - b_t, \qquad \text{each } t, \tag{2.15}$$

$$F(U) = \tilde{F}(U) + \sum R_t, \tag{2.16}$$

to get, after dropping the ~'s,

$$h_t(p_0, P_t) = p_0^{1-\alpha} P_t^\alpha, \quad V = \left(\sum P_t^\alpha\right)^\beta, \tag{2.17}$$

and

$$\dot{H}' P_t^{\alpha-1} V^{1-\alpha} = \alpha(1-\alpha) p_0^{-\alpha} P_t^{\alpha-1} \tag{2.18}$$

or, equivalently,

$$\dot{H}' = \alpha(1-\alpha) p_0^{-\alpha} V^{\alpha-1}. \tag{2.19}$$

(2.19) yields

$$H = p_0^{1-\alpha} V^\alpha + BV + Cp_0. \tag{2.20}$$

Differentiating with respect to p_0 and using (2.7) we see that $C = 0$, and writing $U = \tilde{U} + B$, we get

$$H = p_0^{1-\alpha} V^\alpha \tag{2.21}$$

after dropping the ~'s. Thus

$$p_0^{1-\alpha}\left(\sum P_t^\alpha\right) = \sum p_0^{1-\alpha} P_t^\alpha \tag{2.22}$$

and $Q(p) = 0$ in (2.6). Now the profit function associated with a production function cy^γ is

$$\max\{p_0 cy^\gamma - Py\} \tag{2.23}$$

yielding

$$y = P^{\delta-1}(p_0 c\gamma)^{1-\delta}, \quad (\delta-1)(\gamma-1) = 1, \tag{2.24}$$

and thus

$$p_0 c\gamma y^\gamma = Py = \text{constant} \times P^\delta p_0^{1-\delta}. \tag{2.25}$$

Hence $f_t(y) = F(y) = ky^\delta$, say, each t, where $(\alpha - 1)(\delta - 1) = 1$. Dividing across k we get

$$U^\delta = \sum u_t^\delta, \tag{2.26}$$

as the final CES form of the utility function. The convexity condition yields $\delta < 1$. We get a Cobb–Douglas special case corresponding to $\delta = 0$.

Now the cost function (2.2) yields $u_t = (m_t - Q_t)/P_t$ so that (2.26) becomes

$$U^\delta = \sum((m_t - Q_t)/P_t)^\delta, \tag{2.27}$$

which is reminiscent of $U = \sum a_t(x_t - b_t)^\alpha$. This is a very common form of felicity function, corresponding to a constant marginal propensity to save in each individual period, which may however vary from period to period according to the weighting factors a_t. Is then (2.27) the most general utility function yielding constant marginal propensities to save in each period? Apparently not.

Write the utility function as

$$U(x) = \sum u_t(x_t); \qquad x = (x_1, \ldots, x_T), \tag{2.28}$$

so that the corresponding profit function

$$H(p_0, p) = \sum h_t(p_0, p_t), \qquad p = (p_1, \ldots, p_T), \tag{2.29}$$

where x and p are partitioned vectors. Then

$$m_t = \sum_{i \in t} p_i x_i = -\sum_{i \in t} p_i H_i = -\sum_{i \in t} p_i h_i \tag{2.30}$$

and

$$\partial m_t / \partial p_0 = -\sum_{i \in t} p_i \dot{H}_i = -\sum_{i \in t} p_i \dot{h}_{ti}, \tag{2.31}$$

in an obvious notation. Hence

$$\frac{\sum_{i \in s} p_i \dot{h}_{si}}{\sum_{i \in t} p_i \dot{h}_{ti}} = \frac{\phi_s(p_s)}{\phi_t(p_t)} = \frac{P_s(p_s)^{\alpha - 1}}{P_t(p_t)^{\alpha - 1}}, \text{ say,} \tag{2.32}$$

where each $P_t(\cdot)$ is positively homogeneous of degree one, by homogeneity, when the marginal propensity to save is independent of net worth. Transform to

$$p_t \to (P_t, q_t), \tag{2.33}$$

where q_t is homogeneous of degree zero in p_t, and has one less co-ordinate. Then write $h_t = k_t(P_t, q_t)$ to get $\sum_{i \in t} p_i h_{ti} = k_t' = \partial k_t / \partial P_t$ and

$$\dot{h}_0' / h_t' = p_0^{\alpha - 1} / P_t^{\alpha - 1} \tag{2.34}$$

just as before. This yields in the present case

$$\begin{aligned} h_t &= e p_0^{1-\alpha} P_t^{\alpha} + b_t(q_t) P_t + c_t(q_t) p_0 \\ &= e p_0^{1-\alpha} P_t^{\alpha} - Q_t(p_t) + c_t(q_t) p_0. \end{aligned} \tag{2.35}$$

The first two terms correspond to (2.27), the third to a distribution of expenditure over the goods which cancels out over all the goods in group t.

3. ADDITIVELY SEPARABLE UTILITY FUNCTIONS YIELDING CONSTANT AVERAGE AND CONSTANT MARGINAL PROPENSITIES TO SPEND ON EACH GROUP

It will be convenient to use the profit function

$$\sum h_t(p_0, p_t), \tag{3.1}$$

where p_0 is the 'price of utility', to introduce a price aggregate $P_t(p_t)$, homogeneous of degree one, and to write

$$h_t(p_0, p_t) = k_t(p_0, P_t, q_t), \tag{3.2}$$

when q_t is a vector of relative prices in group t. Then expenditure in group t is

$$-\partial k_t/\partial \log P_t. \tag{3.3}$$

If the average propensity to spend on goods in group t is a_t, a constant, then

$$-\frac{\partial k_t/\partial \log P_t}{a_t} \text{ is independent of } t. \tag{3.4}$$

It therefore depends only on p_0, and, being homogeneous of degree one is cp_0, say. Writing $ca_t = c_t$ we have

$$\partial k_t/\partial \log P_t = -c_t p_0, \tag{3.5}$$

so that

$$k_t = -c_t p_0(\log P_t + Q_t(p_0, q_t)). \tag{3.6}$$

Since this is homogeneous of degree one in p_0, P_t, the term in brackets is homogeneous of degree zero. Hence $1 + p_0 \partial Q_t/\partial p_0 = 0$ and $Q_t = -\log p_0 + \log \psi_t(q_t)$. Writing $\bar{P}_t = P_t \psi_t(q_t)$, still homogeneous of degree one in p_t, and dropping the bar, we have

$$h_t = k_t = c_t p_0(\log p_0 - \log P_t(p_t)), \tag{3.7}$$

so that the felicity function u_t is given by

$$u_t = \partial h_t/\partial p_0 = c_t(\log p_0 - \log P_t(p_t) + 1) \tag{3.8}$$

and expenditure in period t by

$$m_t = -\partial h_t/\partial \log P_t = c_t p_0. \tag{3.9}$$

Substituting from (3.9) into (3.8) we get

$$u_t = c_t \log(em_t/c_t P_t). \tag{3.10}$$

Write now $\bar{P}_t = c_t P_t/e$ and drop the bar to get

$$u_t = c_t \log v_t; \qquad v_t = m_t/P_t. \tag{3.11}$$

Hence

$$u = \sum a_t \log v_t \tag{3.12}$$

after renormalization, when $v_t(\cdot)$ is defined by its cost function

$$m_t = v_t P_t(p_t); \tag{3.13}$$

that is, v_t is positively homogeneous of degree one. I leave it to the reader to show that the average propensity to spend on group t is indeed the constant a_t.

If the marginal propensity to spend on group t is a_t, (3.2) yields

$$\frac{\partial^2 k_t/\partial p_0 \partial \log P_t}{a_t}, \tag{3.14}$$

independent of t and therefore depending only on p_0. Being homogeneous of degree zero it is a constant c. Writing $ca_t = -c_t$ here, we have

$$\partial^2 k_t/\partial p_0 \partial \log P_t = -c_t, \tag{3.15}$$

so that

$$\partial k_t/\partial p_0 = -c_t(\log P_t + Q_t(p_0, q_t)). \tag{3.16}$$

This being homogeneous of degree zero in P_t, p_0 we have that $1 + p_0 \partial Q_t/\partial p_0 = 0$ once more and $Q_t = -\log p_0 + \log \psi_t(q_t)$, say. Defining again $\bar{P}_t(p_t) = P_t(p_t)\psi_t(q_t)$, which is still homogeneous of degree one in p_t, and dropping the bar, we have

$$\partial h_t/\partial p_0 = \partial k_t/\partial p_0 = c_t(\log p_0 - \log P_t(p_t)), \tag{3.17}$$

so that

$$h_t = c_t p_0(\log p_0 - \log P_t(p_t) - 1) + R_t(p_t), \text{ say,} \tag{3.18}$$

where $R_t(p_t)$ is homogeneous of degree one since h_t is. Here $u_t = \partial h_t/\partial p_0$ is given by (3.17) while expenditure in period t is

$$m_t = c_t p_0 + R_t. \tag{3.19}$$

Substituting from (3.19) into u_t as given by (3.17) we get

$$u_t = c_t \log (m_t - R_t)/c_t P_t. \tag{3.20}$$

Setting now $\bar{P}_t = c_t P_t$, dropping the bar, and renormalizing u trivially, we have

$$u = \sum a_t \log v_t \tag{3.21}$$

again, when v_t is now given by its cost function

$$m_t = P_t(p_t)v_t + R_t(p_t); \tag{3.22}$$

in other words v_t is quasi-homogeneous of degree one.

Note that (3.18) implies that

$$x_i = c_t p_0 P_{ti}/P_t + R_{ti}, \qquad i \in t, \tag{3.23}$$

so that the Engel paths are straight lines and the overall utility function quasi-homothetic. I leave it to the reader to prove it is homothetic in the case defined by (3.7).

9

The Concavity of Additive Utility Functions

Editorial Summary

This paper also dates from 1970, the year Gorman spent at the University of North Carolina. It seems likely, however, that most of the results had been known for some time; the first footnote states that Theorem 1 stems from a discussion in the mid-1950s.

When confronted with additivity, it is far more convenient to use profit functions than cost functions or indirect utility functions. The reason for this is clear. If the objective function is additive then the resulting profit function is also additive, so one does not lose all of the explicit original structure in moving to the dual. To be able to do this, however, each of the functions in question must be concave. But concavity is typically not an easy assumption to accept in utility theory. The question addressed in this paper is whether concavity is more plausible in the case of additive separability.

More specifically, suppose that the utility function can be written in the additive form

$$u(x) = F\left[\sum_{t=1}^{T} f^t(x^t)\right], \tag{0.1}$$

where u is quasi-concave. It follows that each f^t is also quasi-concave. To see this, fix x^s for all $s \neq t$ at $\bar{x}^s$. Then u is a function of x^t only, and is still quasi-concave. Hence f^t must also be quasi-concave. But will it be concave also?

This question can be posed two different ways: how many of the $\{f^t\}$, $t = 1, \ldots, T$, can fail to be concave?; or, how many of the $\{f^t\}$, $t = 1, \ldots, T$, are concave? The answer to the first question is 'at most one', and hence the answer to the second is 'at least $T - 1$'. This is the content of Theorem 1.[1] Gorman goes on to show that even the one which is not concave is likely to be nearly concave. For he shows that in any region of non-concavity all the other $T - 1$ groups must be inferior goods. This seems implausible. The assumption that all f^t, $t = 1, \ldots, T$, are concave therefore appears to be rather weak.

[1] According to n. 1 Green (1961) worked this out for addivity in the co-ordinate partition of the variables.

The Concavity of Additive Utility Functions

1. INTRODUCTION AND SUMMARY[1]

Utility functions of the type

$$u(x) = \sum_{t=1}^{T} f^t(x^t), \tag{1.1}$$

where

$$x = (x^1, \ldots, x^T) \tag{1.2}$$

is a partitioned vector, are frequently used in discussing decisions over time and/or under uncertainty as well as in practical demand analysis.

Typically, in such cases, one is interested in the demand functions which are implied, so that prices $p = (p^1, \ldots, p^T)$, rather than quantities $x = (x^1, \ldots, x^T)$ emerge as the independent variables. Frequently, therefore, it is convenient to specify the tastes (1.1) in terms of the prices from the outset, and, in such cases it is convenient to maintain the simple additive structure of (1.1) when we can do so without incurring heavy costs elsewhere. This suggests the use of the profit function

$$g(p^0, p) = \sup\{p^0 u - p \cdot x \mid u \leqslant u(x)\} \tag{1.3}$$

$$= \sup\left\{\sum (p^0 f^t - p^t \cdot x^t) \mid f^t \leqslant f^t(x^t) \text{ each } t\right\}$$

$$= \sum \sup\{p^0 f^t - p^t \cdot x^t \mid f^t \leqslant f^t(x^t)\}$$

$$= \sum g^t(p^0, p^t), \tag{1.4}$$

where

$$g^t(p^0, p^t) = \{p^0 f^t - p^t \cdot x^t \mid f^t \leqslant f^t(x^t)\} \tag{1.5}$$

is the profit function for the tth group. It is as if we imagined utility as being produced in T independent factories in such a way as to maximize the profits from its sale. The efficiency price p^0 of utility is, of course, the inverse of the marginal utility λ of income, which, in equilibrium is the same on whichever group the marginal \$ is spent.

[1] Professor H. A. John Green (1961) derived the main result of this paper for the case of a completely additively separable utility function e.g. where there is just one good in each group. The extension to the vector case is fairly obvious; but has recently become of some importance because of the interest in duality. Theorem 1 arose out of the discussion of a paper which Dr Sten Thore read in Birmingham in the mid-1950s.

Knowledge of the profit function is equivalent to that of the production or utility function if the latter is concave. Otherwise it merely permits us to recreate its concave closure

$$v(x) = \sup\left\{\sum a_m u(x_m) \mid \sum a_m x_m = x, \quad \sum a_m = 1, \quad \text{each } a_m \geqslant 0\right\}.^2 \tag{1.6}$$

This does not greatly matter if there is a true competitive market, because the supply, or demand, functions corresponding to $u(x)$ and $v(x)$ are so similar.[3] However, there is no actual market for utility so that the justification for (1.3) would have to be that it was equivalent to (1.1)—which it will only be if $u(x)$ is concave—or that it permits us to reconstruct the actual demand functions for goods pretty accurately.

Let us look into this point about there being no market for utility.

Forget about the special structure in (1.1) for the moment and assume merely that $u(\cdot)$ is strictly increasing and quasi-concave, so that each x is chosen in some budgeting situation. Since, however, utility is only ordinal we may assume without loss of generality that the marginal utility of income increases over a considerable region, u or, if you like, that utility is produced under conditions of decreasing marginal costs there. Were it being produced for sale in a competitive market, x's in the region in question would never be used. Accordingly, the demand functions yielded by (1.3) can never predict them.

Return now to (1.1). It yields a natural normalization for u, which renders it cardinal.[4] Hence concavity is at least a meaningful concept for $u(\cdot)$ here. Is it possible that (1.1), together with some other acceptable assumptions actually implies that it is concave?

Pretty well so.

First suppose that we are willing to assume that $u(\cdot)$ is at least quasi-concave. Then, under fairly normal continuity assumptions, it turns out that at least $T - 1$ of the *felicity functions* $f^t(\cdot)$ are actually concave. Now there are quite often constant multiples of each other, the weights being discount factors or probabilities, or combinations of the two. In such cases the concavity of one, let alone $T - 1$, of them implies the concavity of each, and hence of $u(\cdot)$, too.

Suppose however that the $f^t(\cdot)$ are independent functions. Then one of them might not be concave. If so, however, there will be considerable regions over which each of the other groups taken as a whole is inferior, that is, where the expenditure on each falls as income increases.[5]

[2] That is, the set bounded above by the graph of $v(\cdot)$ is the convex closure of these bounded above by that of $u(\cdot)$.

[3] Though they do differ in the important respect that v predicts that every point will be optimal at some 'prices', which u denies unless it is concave.

[4] i.e., defined up to a change of origin and scale.

[5] I think 'considerable regions' is a fair comment, but it is not a very precise term, of course.

Such almost universal inferiority will frequently seem unlikely, so that we will feel free to assume that each $f^t(\cdot)$, and therefore $u(\cdot)$, is actually concave.

In such cases, therefore, we can use the profit function (1.3) with a clear conscience.

Before cheering too loudly, however, we must remember that all this depends on the assumption that the utility function $u(\cdot)$ is quasi-concave.

Why are we normally willing to assume that?

One reason is that the demand functions are relatively little affected if we replace the actual utility function $u(\cdot)$ by its quasi-concave closure,

$$w(x) = \sup\left\{w \mid x = \sum a_m x_m,\ \ \sum a_m = 1,\ \ \text{each } a_m \geqslant 0,\ \ \text{each } u(x_m) \geqslant w\right\}.^6 \quad (1.7)$$

The quasi-concave $w(\cdot)$ being more convenient to use than $u(\cdot)$, we accordingly do so. If $u(\cdot)$ is quasi-concave, they coincide, of course. Unfortunately, there seems to be no reason why the quasi-convex closure of an additively separable utility function should be additively separable, so that there is no justification for this argument here.

The next most obvious justification for quasi-concavity lies in averaging. For instance it may be assumed that our aim is to raise the average level of current satisfaction $f^t(x^t)$, determined by the current consumption vector x^t, as high as possible, subject to the average flow of goods for a given consumption vector x. The resulting utility function is concave in this normalization and therefore quasi-concave in general. In general there is no reason why this normalization and that in (1.1) should agree; however, joint axiomatizations implying that they do in particular cases can be constructed.[7] In such cases one does not have to justify the concavity of $u(\cdot)$ by the sort of arguments used below.

What if one is unwilling to assume quasi-concavity?

It will still be true that each chosen point[8] is a point of local quasi-concavity. The arguments below then imply that at least $T-1$ of the f's are locally concave at all chosen points and that the curious inferiority discussed above arises when one of them is not locally concave.[9] This means that, given reasonable continuity, we can represent the utility function by a profit function locally. By this I do not mean to an approximation (e.g. first order) in the neighbourhood of a point, but perfectly over a finite region.

[6] i.e. the region bounded below by $w(x) = w$ is the convex closure of that bounded below by $u(x) = w$.

[7] e.g. (1.1) might refer to choices under uncertainty, while the averaging is over time. One can give a joint axiomatization of the two which gives additive separability over both.

[8] i.e., each point which maximizes utility in some budgetary situation.

[9] Of course one has to make the appropriate continuity assumptions locally.

2. THE PROOFS

THEOREM 1: *If*

$$u(x) = \sum f^t(x^t), \qquad x = (x^1, \ldots, x^T), \tag{2.1}$$

is quasi-concave and twice continuously differentiable, at least $T - 1$ *of the* f*'s are concave.*

PROOF: Since $u(\cdot)$ is quasi-concave

$$\sum u_{ij}\theta_i\theta_j \leqslant 0 \qquad \text{when} \quad \sum u_i\theta_i = 0, \tag{2.2}$$

where subscripts on functions denote derivatives so that $u_i = \partial u/\partial x_i$, $u_{ij} = \partial^2 u/\partial x_i \partial x_j$.

Setting $\theta_i = 0$, $i \notin t$, we have

$$\sum f^t_{ij}\theta_i\theta_j = 0 \quad \text{if} \quad \sum f^t_i\theta_i = 0, \tag{2.3}$$

the summation being over i, $j \in t$, so that each $f^t(\cdot)$ is quasi-concave, as is indeed obvious.

Suppose now that both $f^r(\cdot)$ and $f^s(\cdot)$ have points of local non-concavity. Take these. Thus there exists ϕ^r, ϕ^s such that

$$\sum f^t_{ij}\phi^t_i\phi^t_j > 0, \qquad t = r, s, \tag{2.4}$$

so that

$$\sum f^t_i\phi^t_i = \alpha_r \neq 0, \qquad t = r, s. \tag{2.5}$$

Define now

$$\theta_i = \alpha_r\phi^s_i, \ i \in s; \qquad \theta_i = \alpha_s\phi^r_i, \qquad i \in r; \qquad \theta_i = 0, \qquad i \notin r, s, \tag{2.6}$$

to get

$$\sum u_{ij}\theta_i\theta_j = \alpha_r^2 \sum f^s_{ij}\phi^s_i\phi^s_j + \alpha_s^2 \sum f^r_{ij}\phi^r_i\phi^r_j > 0, \tag{2.7}$$

by (2.4), while

$$\sum u_i\theta_i = \alpha_r \sum f^s_i\phi^s_i - \alpha_s \sum f^r_i\phi^r_i = 0 \tag{2.8}$$

by (2.5), contradicting (2.2).

Hence at most one $f^t(\cdot)$ has points of local non-concavity, and at least $T - 1$ are concave.

Remark: This argument, being local, can be applied to points of local quasi-concavity even if $u(\cdot)$ is not concave overall. *These include all the 'chosen points'*, that is, those which maximize utility in some budgetary situation. It then implies

COROLLARY: *If $u(\cdot)$ is twice continuously differentiable in* (2.1), *on at least* $(T-1)$ *of the f's, points of local quasi-concavity are points of local concavity.*

THEOREM 2: *If $u(\cdot)$ is increasing quasi-concave and twice continuously differentiable, and if its demand functions are continuously differentiable in income, the marginal utility of expenditures on group s is increasing at points where $f^s(\cdot)$ is not locally concave.*

PROOF: Suppose $\bar{x}$ is chosen at prices $\bar{p}$ and income $\bar{m} = \bar{p} \cdot \bar{x}$. Define

$$\bar{m}^s = \bar{p}^s \cdot \bar{x}^s, \tag{2.9}$$

the expenditure on group s. Then

$$\bar{x}^s \text{ maximizes } f^s(x^s) \text{ subject to } \bar{p}^s \cdot \bar{x}^s \leqslant \bar{m}^s. \tag{2.10}$$

Knowing the expenditure $\bar{m}^s$ on group s, we can always work out the detailed consumption pattern in this way. Equally, we can calculate the advantage of an extra dollar allocated to group s.

Let us apply a classical Hicksian analysis to this problem, dropping the suffix s for the moment, since the entire argument will relate to that group.

(2.10) implies

$$f^i = \lambda p_j, \qquad \sum p_j x_j = m, \tag{2.11}$$

when λ is the marginal utility of expenditure on this group. Hence

$$\sum f_{ij}\dot{x}_j = \dot{\lambda} p_j, \qquad \sum p_j \dot{x}_j = 1, \tag{2.12}$$

when a dot over a symbol implies differentiation with respect to m. Hence

$$\lambda F\dot{x} = \dot{\lambda}\phi, \qquad \phi'\dot{x} = \lambda, \tag{2.13}$$

where

$$F = [f_{ij}], \qquad \phi' = (f_i), \tag{2.14}$$

and primes denote transposition, so that

$$\lambda\dot{x} = \dot{\lambda}F^{-1}\phi, \qquad \dot{\lambda}\phi' F^{-1}\phi = \lambda^2. \tag{2.15}$$

Now let $f(\cdot)$ not be locally concave at $\bar{x}$, so that there is a θ such that

$$\sum f_{ij}\theta_i\theta_j = \theta' F\theta > 0. \tag{2.16}$$

Now project θ parallel to x on to the plane $p \cdot x = 0$ to get

$$\theta = \psi + \alpha\dot{x} = \psi + \beta F^{-1}\phi, \text{ say}, \tag{2.17}$$

by (2.15), where

$$\phi'\psi = \sum f_i \psi_i = 0. \tag{2.18}$$

Then

$$\theta' F\theta = (\psi' - \beta\phi' F^{-1})F(\psi + \beta F^{-1}\phi)$$
$$= \psi' F\psi + \beta^2 \phi' F^{-1}\phi, \tag{2.19}$$

since $\beta\phi' F^{-1} F\psi = \beta\phi'\psi = 0$. Since $f(\cdot)$ is quasi-concave, (2.3) and (2.18) imply that $\psi' F\psi \leqslant 0$. (2.16) and (2.19) therefore yield $\phi' F^{-1}\phi > 0$, and (2.15) yields

$$\dot{\lambda} > 0. \tag{2.20}$$

The marginal utility of expenditure on group s is therefore increasing at $(\bar{p}^s, \bar{m}^s)$.

Remarks: (i) Once again, the argument is local, so that it can be applied to any chosen point even if $u(\cdot)$ is not concave overall. The continuity assumptions need only apply locally, too.

(ii) Setting $\psi = 0$ in (2.19) we see that $\dot{\lambda} \leqslant 0$ at a point of local concavity, and therefore everywhere in the other groups, or at least at all chosen points in them.

(iii) Consider again the budgetary situation $(\bar{p}, \bar{m})$ in which the consumer chooses $\bar{x}^s$ at which $f^s(\cdot)$ is not locally concave. The marginal utility $\bar{\lambda}^t$[10] of expenditure on group t will be the same, λ, for each group. Now suppose another dollar to become available. It will be spent in such a manner as to keep the λ^t equal. Now extra expenditures on the group lowers λ^t, $t \neq s$, and increases λ^s. Hence he will either increase expenditure on group s and reduce expenditure on each of the others or vice versa. In the former case the marginal utilities increase, in the latter decrease. Hence the former will yield the greater increase in utility and will accordingly be chosen. That is, he will actually decrease his expenditure on each group other than s as he gets richer. They are all inferior, if you like.

That is fairly startling, but we might feel that it could only happen at a few isolated sets of prices, and therefore not be too important. This is not so.[11] In the first place, if $f^s(\cdot)$ is not locally concave at $\bar{x}^s$, it will not be in its neighbourhood either. In the second, suppose $\bar{x}^s$ chosen as in (2.10) once more, and consider *any* prices.

$$p^{-s} = (p^t)_{t \neq s} \tag{2.21}$$

for the other groups. Write

[10] The $\bar{\lambda}^t$ because defined at $(\bar{p}, \bar{m})$.

[11] I think this is a reasonable claim.

$$p^s = \rho \bar{p}^s \tag{2.22}$$

where ρ is still to be determined. Now from the Hicksian aggregates

$$X = \bar{p}^s \cdot x^s, \qquad Y = p^{\sim s} \cdot x^{\sim s}, \tag{2.23}$$

for group s and all the other groups combined. The price of the former in terms of the latter is ρ. The chances are that for any ρ there is an income at which $X = \bar{m}^s$ and therefore $x^s = \bar{x}^s$. In any case the quasi-concavity of the utility function is retained under Hicksian aggregation, so that there will at least be a pair (ρ, m) at which $X = \bar{m}^s$ and $x^s = \bar{x}^s$. Choosing $\bar{x}^s$ once again to be a point at which $f^s(\cdot)$ is not locally concave, we see that, *whatever the prices in the other groups*, there are ranges of prices in group s, and incomes, for which the expenditure on each of the other groups falls as the consumer gets richer.

If we are willing to rule this out we can neglect the possibility of $u(\cdot)$ failing to be locally concave at a chosen point, or failing to be concave if we are willing to assume it quasi-concave.

(iv) If each $f^t(\cdot)$ is concave, remark (i) implies that the marginal utility of expenditure decreases in each group as income increases, so that expenditure on each group increases as income does. Similar results hold for local concavity.

3. THE NORMAL CASE

Let us say that we are in the normal case when each $f^t(\cdot)$, and hence $u(\cdot)$, too, is concave and in the abnormal case if one is not. In the normal case we can derive some well-known results from the profit function (1.4).

$$g(p^0, p) = \sum g^t(p^0, p^t). \tag{3.1}$$

Use subscripts for derivatives. Then

$$u = g_0, \quad x_i = -g_i = -g_i^t, \qquad i \in t, \tag{3.2}$$

while the Slutsky term

$$\delta x_t / \delta p_j = -g_{ij} - g_{i0}\,\delta p^0 / \delta p_j,^{12} \tag{3.3}$$

where $u = g_0$ is held constant while differentiating. Hence

$$\delta p^0 / \delta p_j = -g_{j0}/g_{00} \tag{3.4}$$

and

$$\delta x_i / \delta p_j = g_{i0} g_{j0} / g_{00} = g_{i0}^s g_{j0}^t / g_{00}, \qquad i \in s,\ j \in t,\ s \neq t. \tag{3.5}$$

[12] δ denotes compensated derivatives.

Now $g = p^0 u - p \cdot x = p^0 g_0 - m$, so that

$$\partial m/\partial p^0 = p^0 g_{00}, \tag{3.6}$$

and (3.5) yields

$$\frac{\delta x_i}{\delta p_j} = \frac{\partial x_i/\partial m \cdot \partial x_j/\partial m \cdot (\partial m/\partial p^0)^2 p^0}{\partial m/\partial p^0} = -\frac{m}{\varepsilon}\frac{\partial x_i}{\partial m}\frac{\partial x_j}{\partial m}, \qquad i \in s,\ j \in t,\ s \neq t, \tag{3.7}$$

where

$$\varepsilon = \partial \log \lambda/\partial \log m = -\partial \log p^0/\partial \log m \tag{3.8}$$

is the normal elasticity of the marginal utility of income with respect to income, and as such is negative when $u(\cdot)$ is concave as here.

Let us now say that goods are normal if we spend more on them as we get richer and inferior otherwise. Then (3.7) states that, a pair of goods in different groups are substitutes if both are normal, or both inferior, and complements if there is one of each.

If we form Hicksian aggregates for each group, each is normal by Remark (iv) at the end of Section 2. Hence the different groups are substitutes for each other.

10

Pseudo-Separability

Editorial Remarks

This brief note was extracted from handwritten notes. It is included because it is the culmination of one line of thought about the budgeting problem, and because pseudo-separability, or 'implict separability' as it is sometimes called, has now cropped up in a number of different problems. The notes themselves were written in August 1975 to facilitate a project on 'Hedonic Housing' with Richard Blundell which, in the event, did not proceed.

Pseudo-Separability

If a preference field can be written

$$F(u, f^1(u, x_1), \ldots, f^R(u, x_R)) = 1, \tag{1}$$

or equivalently,

$$u = \phi(v), \quad v_r = f^r(u, x_r), \quad v = (v_r), \tag{2}$$

each r, we will say it is *pseudo-separable*, where $F(u, \cdot)$ and $f^r(u, \cdot)$ are not *necessarily conical*. If they are conical, then preferences are quasi-separable.

Let $g^r(v_r, p^r; u)$ be the cost function corresponding to $v_r = f^r(u, x_r)$. Then the problem is to minimize

$$M = \sum m_r = \sum g^r(v_r, p^r; u), \qquad \text{given } u = \phi(v), \tag{3}$$

yielding

$$\dot{g}^r(v_r, p^r; u) = \lambda\phi_r(v), \qquad r = 1, 2, \ldots, R, \tag{4}$$

where $\dot{g}^r = \partial g^r/\partial v$. This determines v given u and/or $m = (m_r)$ given M. Given v_r and u,

$$x_i = g_i^r(v^r, p^r; u), \qquad i \in r, \tag{5}$$

and given m,

$$x_i = -\frac{h_i^r(m_r, p^r; u)}{\dot{h}^r(m_r, p^r; u)}, \qquad i \in r, \tag{6}$$

where h^r is the dual to g^r, and where u is, of course implied by m; indeed

$$u = \phi(h^1(m_1, p^1; u), \ldots, h^R(m_R, p^R; u)). \tag{7}$$

To apply this, suppose that y is a vector of housing characteristics and x a vector of other goods so that preferences can be written as

$$u = f(x, y), \tag{8}$$

and suppose in addition y is pseudo-separable from x so that

$$F(u, x, \theta(u, y)) = 0 \quad \text{iff} \quad u = f(x, y). \tag{9}$$

This means that the cost function can be written as in (3) above with the obvious change of notation. Letting the cost function dual to θ be given by γ, we see that the demand for a characteristic of housing is given by

$$y_i = \gamma_i(v_h, q, u), \text{ say,}^1 \tag{10}$$

for all i in the housing sector, where v_h is chosen at its optimal level and the subscript h refers to housing. Using Euler's theorem this means that total expenditure on housing is given by $\gamma(v_h, p_h, u)$. This means that the housing budget depends only upon the level of real income, the prices of housing characteristics, and an aggregate measure of the amount of housing which at the optimum depends upon everything.

[1] q is a vector of shadow prices for housing characteristics y, implicitly normalized to add up—itself a large assumption.

11

Conditions for Additive Separability

Editorial Remarks

Suppose that an agent has preferences over a finite time-horizon, and that in addition marginal rates of substitution between adjacent time-periods are independent of the level of consumption in other time-periods. This means, for example, that marginal rates of substitution between commodities in periods 1 and 2 are independent of consumption in period 3, and that marginal rates of substitution between commodities in periods 2 and 3 are independent of consumption in period 1. Then, by the overlapping theorem, the utility function must be additive in the consumption of the three periods. A proof along these lines is presented in Section 4 of 'The Structure of Utility Functions'. This paper presents an alternative proof of the same theorem.

The problem was posed by John Whitaker at the Oxford Mathematical Economics Seminar in 1964. Gorman submitted the paper to *Econometrica* in July 1965, but it took three years to be published.

Conditions for Additive Separability

That the marginal rates of substitution between consumption in widely separated periods should be independent of what happens in the meantime seems unlikely; yet this is necessarily so in the conventional *additively separable* savings model $u(x) = f^1(x^1) + \ldots + f^T(x^T)$, $T > 2$, where the x^t are in general vectors. What can we prove if we require only that the marginal rates of substitution between adjacent periods be independent of what happens in the others? It is shown that this apparently more acceptable assumption is already strong enough to imply additive separability; and, in general, that the information that the marginal rates of substitution between consumption of goods in group s and t should depend only on (x^s, x^t) when $a_{st} \neq 0$ implies additive separability if and only if the symmetric matrix $A = [a_{st}]$ is indecomposable. The implications of a decomposable A are given in a corollary.

Let us say that a utility function $u(x)$ is *well behaved* if it is defined, strictly monotonic, and twice continuously differentiable on the non-negative orthant $x \geqslant 0$. It is well known that a well-behaved utility function is additively separable; that is, it can be written in the form

$$u(x) = u(x^1, \ldots, x^T) = \sum f^t(x^t), \qquad T > 2, \tag{1}$$

in an appropriate normalization, after an appropriate strictly increasing, twice continuously differentiable transformation, where $x^t = (x_i)_{i \in t}$[1] is a vector giving the quantities of the goods in group t, iff the marginal rate of substitution

$$\frac{u_i}{u_j} \text{ depends only on } i, j, x^s, x^t, \qquad \text{each } i \in s, j \in t, s, t\text{[2]} \tag{2}$$

where subscripts denote differentiation.

One well-known application of this result is in savings theory, where t refers to a time-period. According to (2), the Ramsey-type model (1) holds only if the marginal rate of substitution between planned consumption next year and twenty years hence, for instance, is independent of one's plans for

[1] $(x_i)_{i \in t}$ means the vector we get by listing the x_i, $i \in t$. It is convenient to call the tth group 't', rather than '$\Theta(t)$', for instance, and it really causes no problems. I assume $T > 2$ throughout this paper.

[2] Leontief (1947*a*) shows that $du = \lambda \sum_t \sum_{i \in t} f_i^t dx_i$, the subscripts denoting differentiation, which implies that (1) holds locally. In our case it is easily shown that if $\sum f^t(x^t)/\sum f^t(y^t) = a$, for instance, x and y are connected by a smooth curve C at each point z of which $\sum f^t(z^t) = a$—implying that $\sum_t \sum_{i \in t} f_i^t(z^t) dz_i = 0$ along C. Hence, $u(y) - u(x) = \int_C du = \int_C \lambda \sum_t \sum_{i \in t} f_i^t dz_i = 0$, so that $\sum f^t(x^t) = \sum f^t(y^t)$ implies $u(x) = u(y)$. Hence $u(x) = F(\sum f^t(x^t))$. It is easily shown that $F(\cdot)$ and $f^t(\cdot)$ can be taken to be well behaved. Hence $u^*(x) = F^{-1}(u(x))$ is well behaved and (1) holds in this normalization.

the interim. This seems unlikely. An apparently more reasonable requirement suggested recently by Professor John Whitaker[3] would be that (2) should hold merely for adjacent periods; that is, for $s = t + 1$, $t = 1, 2, \ldots, T - 1$. We will see, however, that this apparently more acceptable requirement is equivalent to (2) and hence to (1), so that any search for a more acceptable generalization of Ramsey's model will have to proceed in another way.[4]

While this problem presented the motivation for the analysis below,[5] it will be convenient to proceed somewhat more generally.

Suppose that we are given a symmetric matrix A and told

$$\frac{u_i}{u_j} \text{ depends only on } i, j, x^s, x^t, \qquad \text{each } i \in s,\ j \in t,\ a_{st} \neq 0.^6 \tag{3}$$

I will demonstrate the following theorem.

THEOREM: *If* $u(\cdot)$ *is well behaved,* (3) *implies that it is additively separable iff* A *is indecomposable.*

Remark: In the savings example, A has zeros everywhere except on the super- and sub-diagonals, where all its elements differ from zero. It is therefore indecomposable, so that the result quoted in the text is a particular case of this theorem.

PROOF: Let us first assume that A is indecomposable. Say that s is *joined* to t if $a_{st} \neq 0$ and *connected* to it if there is a chain $s = r_0, r_1, \ldots, r_m = t$, each element of which, other than the last, is joined to its successor. Since A is indecomposable, each pair of groups is connected. Since $T > 2$, therefore, each group is joined to at least one other, and some to at least two others.[7] Let R be the set of the latter. Any pair $r, s \in R$ is connected by a chain, all of whose elements are in R. Each element of R's complement S is joined to just one other group and it belongs to R. S may therefore be partitioned

[3] The suggestion was made in a paper on 'Optimal Savings' which he read to the Oxford Mathematical Economics Seminar in Michaelmas Term, 1964.

[4] Professor Kenneth Arrow has suggested to me that one might require u_i/u_j to depend only on $(x_{s-\theta}, x_{s-\theta+1}, \ldots, x_{t+\tau})$ when $i \in t$, $j \in t$, $s \leqslant t$.

[5] As it happens, I have known the answer to this particular problem since the mid-1950s. Probably others have too. It does not seem to have been published, though I have seen an unpublished paper by Professor Koopmans (1966) discussing this point in a more general model since my submission of this paper to *Econometrica* in July 1965. The general result below arose out of a talk with Professor Whitaker after his paper.

[6] I say this, rather than e.g. 'when $(s, t) \in \Omega$' where $(s, t) \in \Omega \Rightarrow (t, s) \in \Omega$, because it permits the theorem to be stated immediately in generally recognizable terms. This is only a matter of phraseology, of course.

[7] In relation to 'others', we note that we might have some $a_{tt} \neq 0$. It transpires from the analysis below that such information is redundant when A is indecomposable. It is not used explicitly.

into sets $S(r)$, $r \in R$, where $S(r)$ is composed of just those elements of S that are joined to r.

Take now any group $r \in R$ and any pair of groups s, t which are joined to it. The marginal rate of substitution between any two goods in group r depends only on x^r, x^s by (3), and only on x^r, x^t. It therefore depends only on x^r. Hence

$$u(x) = F(h^R, x^S), \quad h^R = (h^r(x^r))_{r \in R}, \quad x^S = (x^s)_{s \in S},^{8} \tag{4}$$

say, by Leontief's separability theorem.[9]

If S is empty, then

$$u(x) = G(h), \text{ say}, \qquad h = (h^1(x^1), \ldots, h^T(x^T)). \tag{5}$$

If S is not empty, take $s \in S(r)$, say, to get

$$\frac{F_j}{F_r} = u_j \frac{h_i^r}{u_i} = \phi^j(h^r, x^s),^{10} \tag{6}$$

say, where $i \in r$, $j \in s \in S(r)$, and subscripts once more denote differentiation, since the first depends only on j, h^R, x^S, and the second only on i, j, x^r, x^s.[11]

Since $r \in R$ it is also joined to a second group $t \neq s$. If $t \in R$, a similar argument shows

$$\frac{F_t}{F_r} = \phi^{rt}(h^r, h^t). \tag{7}$$

Now $\mathrm{d}F/F_r$ has an integrating factor F_r. Applying the ordinary integrability condition for this differential form to the trio $r, j \in s, k \in t$ if $t \in S(r)$, or to $r, j \in s, t$ if $t \in R$, we get

$$\begin{aligned} \frac{\partial \log \phi^j}{\partial h^r} &= \frac{\partial \log \phi^k}{\partial h^r} \quad \text{if } t \in S(r), \\ &= \frac{\partial \log \phi^{rt}}{\partial h^r} \quad \text{if } t \in R, \\ &= \frac{\mathrm{d} \log \alpha^r(h^r)}{\mathrm{d}h^r}, \end{aligned} \tag{8}$$

say, in either case, since the first term depends only on j, h^r, x^s, the second only on k, h^r, x^t,[12] and the third only on r, t, h^r, h^t. Hence,

[8] We can easily normalize so that $F(\cdot)$, $G(\cdot)$, and the $h(\cdot)$'s, in (4) and (5), are all well behaved.

[9] See Leontief (1947*a*). This theorem is local but holds globally here by an argument similar to that sketched in n. 2. This fact is used in several places below.

[10] All the derivatives of F and G are positive in an appropriate normalization. This fact is used in several places below.

[11] Since $j \in s \in S(r)$, and the s's and $S(r)$'s are disjoint, we need not mention s, r explicitly.

[12] Replace j, s in n. 10 by k, t.

$$\frac{F_j}{F_r} = \phi^j(h^r, x^s) = \alpha^r(h^r)\beta^j(x^s), \qquad j \in s \in S(r), \tag{9}$$

say, so that

$$\frac{F_j}{F_k} = \frac{\beta^j(x^s)}{\beta^k(x^s)}, \qquad \text{each } j, k \in s \in S, \tag{10}$$

which immediately implies (5) by Leontief's separability theorem, when S is not empty, too.

Suppose once more that s is joined to $r \in R$.[13] Then

$$\frac{G_s}{G_r} = \theta^{rs}(h^r, h^s), \tag{11}$$

say, as in (6) and (7), subscripts once more denoting differentiation. Let t be joined to r also and apply the integrability condition for $\mathrm{d}G/G_s$ to the trio r, s, t to get

$$\frac{\partial \log \theta^{rs}}{\partial h^r} = \frac{\partial \log \theta^{rt}}{\partial h^r} = \frac{\mathrm{d} \log \alpha(h^r)}{\mathrm{d}h^r}, \tag{12}$$

as in (8), yielding, with (11),

$$\frac{G_s}{G_r} = \theta^{rs} = \frac{\alpha^r(x^r)}{\beta^{sr}(x^s)}, \qquad \text{when } a_{rs} \neq 0,\ r \in R, \tag{13}$$

say. If $s \in S(r)$, we can define $\beta^{sr}(x^s) = \alpha^s(x^s)$ without loss of generality[14] so that

$$\frac{G_s}{G_r} = \frac{\alpha^r(x^r)}{\alpha^s(x^s)} \quad \text{if } s \in S(r). \tag{14}$$

If $s \in R$, (13) implies

$$\frac{\beta^{rs}(x^r)}{\alpha^r(x^r)} = \frac{\alpha^s(x^s)}{\beta^{rs}(x^s)} = c^{rs}, \tag{15}$$

say.[15] Equations (14) and (15) imply that

$$\frac{G_s}{G_r} = c^{rs}\frac{\alpha^r(x)}{\alpha^s(x)}, \tag{16}$$

with appropriate constants c^{rs}, when $a_{rs} \neq 0$. Because of the indecomposability of A this immediately implies that (16) holds for all r, s. Leontief's

[13] At least one $r, s \in R$ because of the indecomposability of A.

[14] The expression $\alpha^s(x^s)$ has not yet been defined for $s \notin R$. Since any such s is in just one $S(r)$, there is only one $S(r)$, so that the definition in the test is unique.

[15] Actually, we can take each $c^{rs} = 1$ without loss of generality.

additive separability theorem therefore yields (1) with $f^t(x^t) = k(h^t(x^t))$, say,[16] in an appropriate normalization.

Hence, (3) implies additive separability if A is indecomposable.

On the other hand, if A is decomposable, it can be put in block diagonal form, the P blocks $A^1, \ldots, A^P$ being symmetric and indecomposable, because of the symmetry of A. Let $\{\Omega(1), \ldots, \Omega(P)\}$ be the corresponding partition of $\{1, 2, \ldots, T\}$ and $(y^1, \ldots, y^P)$ of x, so that $y^p = (x^t)_{t \in \Omega(p)}$, each p. Then any function of the form

$$u(x) = \Phi(\phi^1(y^1), \ldots, \phi^P(y^P)), \tag{17}$$

where

$$\Phi(\cdot) \text{ and each } \phi^p(\cdot) \text{ are well behaved,}^{17} \tag{18}$$

and

$$\phi^p(y^p) = \sum_{t \in \Omega(p)} \psi^t(x^t), \tag{19}$$

when $\Omega(p)$ has more than two elements, is clearly well behaved and satisfies (3).

This completes the proof.

COROLLARY: *Equation* (3) *is equivalent to* (17)–(19) *if* $u(\cdot)$ *is well behaved.*

We have seen that (3) follows from (17)–(19). Equations (17) and (19) follow from Leontief's separability theorems and the indecomposability of the A^p by the arguments leading up to (5) and (16), respectively, and (18) from the good behaviour of $u(\cdot)$.[18]

[16] See Leontief (1947*a*) and nn. 2 and 9 above.
[17] In an appropriate normalization, $u(0) = 0$, $\phi^p(x^p) = u(0, \ldots, 0, x^p, 0, \ldots, 0)$.
[18] See nn. 2, 9, and 17.

12

The Structure of Utility Functions

Editorial Summary

The central result of this paper is amazing, useful, and fortunately easy to understand. It is often called the *overlapping theorem.* To give the flavour of the theorem we describe a useful special case.

Suppose that U is a continuous, increasing (utility) function defined on Euclidean n-space. Let $\Omega = \{1, 2, \ldots, n\}$ be the index set. If $A \subset \Omega$ and $\bar{A} = \Omega - A$, then A is separable if the conditional ordering determined by $U(x_A, x_{\bar{A}})$ is the same for all $x_{\bar{A}}$.

Now suppose that A and B are separable subsets of Ω, that they have a non-empty intersection, and that neither is a subset of the other (A and B are said to *overlap* in this case). Then the sets

$$A \cup B,\ A \cap B,\ A - B,\ B - A, \text{ and } A - B \cup B - A \tag{0.1}$$

are all separable. Letting x stand for x_{A-B}, y for $x_{A \cap B}$, z for x_{B-A}, and θ for the rest, that is for $x_{\bar{A} \cap \bar{B}}$, the utility function can be written as

$$U(x, y, z, \theta) = F(u(x) + v(y) + w(x), \theta). \tag{0.2}$$

In other words, the overlapping of two separable sets implies that the function is additive in the intersection and two set differences, conditional on the rest of the variables in the function. Not only is this a surprising result, but it is difficult to prove.

The easiest way to demonstrate the usefulness of the *overlapping* theorem is to use it in some examples. Suppose that there is a social welfare function which is defined on the incomes of everyone in society, $W(y_1, \ldots, y_n)$, and that it is continuous, increasing, and symmetric. Symmetry is a natural assumption to make for welfare functions. In addition, suppose that one pair of incomes, say $\{1,2\}$, is separable. There might be a variety of reasons for such separability; the pair may be within a family unit whose preferences are respected by the social welfare function, or the pair may live in a different geographic region so that it makes sense to analyse what happens between the pair without paying a great deal of attention to what is going on in the rest of society. Whatever the reason, the separability of this pair implies that $W(\cdot)$ is an additive function, that is,

$$W(y_1, \ldots, y_n) = W^*(\phi(y_1) + \phi(y_2) + \ldots + \phi(y_n)). \tag{0.3}$$

The proof is easy enough using the overlapping theorem. By symmetry

$$W(y_1, y_2, y_3, \ldots, y_n) = W(y_1, y_3, y_2, \ldots, y_n). \quad (0.4)$$

The separability of $\{1,2\}$ implies that W can be written as

$$W(y_1, y_2, \ldots, y_n) = \bar{W}(f(y_1, y_2), y_3, \ldots, y_n). \quad (0.5)$$

However, (0.4) implies that

$$W(y_1, y_2, \ldots, y_n) = \bar{W}(f(y_1, y_3), y_2, \ldots, y_n). \quad (0.6)$$

Now let $A = \{1, 2\}$ and $B = \{2, 3\}$ so that $A - B = \{3\}$, $B - A = \{1\}$, and $A \cap B = \{2\}$. The overlapping theorem says that we can write W as

$$W(y_1, y_2, \ldots, y_n) = F(\phi(y_1) + \phi(y_2) + \phi(y_3), y_4, \ldots, y_n), \quad (0.7)$$

where symmetry ensures that ϕ is not indexed. Continuing by induction immediately yields (0.3) above.[1]

Another straightforward application is the expected utility hypothesis. Suppose that the utility function $U(x_1, \ldots, x_S)$ is defined over alternative states of nature and is continuous, increasing, and quasi-concave. The independence axiom asserts that anything which takes place in a subset of states must be independent of what happens in all other states. That is, the conditional orderings are independent of those things which do not happen. However, this means that every proper subset of $\{1, 2, \ldots, S\}$ is separable and hence that the utility function can be written as

$$U(x_1, \ldots, x_S) = U^*(u_1(x_1) + u_2(x_2) + \ldots + u_S(x_S)). \quad (0.8)$$

By the main theorem in 'The Concavity of Additive Utility Functions' at least $S - 1$ of these aggregator functions must be concave. However, the ordering of states of nature in assumed not to matter so that

$$U(x_1, \ldots, x_S) = U^*(u(x_1) + u(x_2) + \ldots + u(x_S)), \quad (0.9)$$

where u is concave. An assumption about an equal probability decomposition then completes the expected utility argument.[2]

These examples suffice to demonstrate the power of the overlapping theorem. Section 4 of the paper contains two more applications, one regarding intertemporal preferences[3] and the other a very nice proof of the Klein–Nataf theorem. Sections 3 and 5 contain alternatives procedures for uncovering the structure of any utility function, while Section 6 relaxes one of the maintained hypotheses, strict essentiality. The appendix contains two lemmas which prove separable representation theorems due to Debreu (1954).

Finally, just to show that no one is perfect, the reader should be warned that the corollary following the statement of the main theorem is false. The following is a counter-example to the statement that (iii) certainly implies (i) and (ii)' on which the corollary is based:

[1] The example is taken from Blackorby *et al.* (1981).
[2] This argument is taken from Blackorby *et al.* (1977)
[3] This is an alternative proof of the main result in 'Conditions for Additive Separability'.

$$U(x) = \hat{U}(U^2(x^2) + U^1(x^1) \cdot U^3(x^3), \theta). \tag{0.10}$$

The reader should also note that nothing of consequence need be changed; simply erase the corollary.[4] A somewhat different version of the paper appeared in 1967 as Technical Report No. 151 of the Institute for Mathematical Studies in the Social Sciences at Stanford. Although it does not contain this flaw, it is not sufficiently different in content to warrant republishing it as well.

[4] This example is taken from page 127 of Blackorby *et al.* (1978*a*).

The Structure of Utility Functions

1. INTRODUCTION AND SUMMARY[1]

Suppose that we are given

(P1) a continuous complete preference ordering $\succcurlyeq$ on a product space $S = S_1 \times S_2 \ldots \times S_n$,[2]

where

(P2) each S_i is topologically separable and are connected,[3]

implying that S is so too. A well-known result of Debreu (1954) then yields

LEMMA 0: *There exists a continuous utility function* $U(\cdot)$ *defined on* S *such that* $U(x) \geqslant U(x')$ *iff*[4] $x \succcurlyeq x'$, *each* $x, x' \in S$.

Let us write

$$x = (x_1, \ldots, x_n) = (x_i)_{i \in \Omega}, \quad x_i \in S_i, \qquad \text{each } i \in \Omega, \tag{1.1}$$

where

$$\Omega = (1, 2, \ldots, n) \tag{1.2}$$

is the set of *sectors*. These may be thought of as groups of goods or periods of time, for instance. In the latter case the S_i might be function spaces, the x_i being vectors whose components are time-series giving the consumption of the individual goods at each moment in the period in question.

Consider any set $A \subseteq \Omega$ of sectors and define

$$x_A = (x_i)_{i \in A}, \quad S_A = \prod_{i \in A} S_i, \quad \bar{A} = \Omega - A. \tag{1.3}$$

[1] Most of the work for this paper was done while the author was visiting Stanford on a grant from the National Science Foundation. Earlier versions were read to seminars at Stanford itself and at Chicago, Yale, Cambridge, Essex, and the London School of Economics. I am grateful to the members of these seminars and in particular to Kenneth Arrow, Frank Hahn, Mordecai Kurz, Tjalling Koopmans, James Mirrlees, T. N. Srinivasan, and David Starrett.

[2] *Complete ordering*: $\succcurlyeq$ is transitive and reflexive, and, if $x, y \in S$, either $x \succcurlyeq y$ or $y \succcurlyeq x$, or both. Debreu, for instance, calls this a preordering, because indifference is allowed.

Continuous: $\{y \in S : x \succcurlyeq y\}$ and $\{y \in S : y \succcurlyeq x\}$ are both closed, each $x \in S$.

[3] *Topologically separable*: S_i has a countably dense subset, such as the rationals among the reals or points with rational coordinates in R^n. Many rather rich spaces are topologically separable. Note that this has nothing to do with separability in Leontief's sense, which I use below.

Arc connected: If $x_i, y_i \in S_i$ they are joined by an arc in S_i. Debreu assumes 'connectivity' rather than 'arc connectivity'. However I need the stronger postulate to provide the proof of (1.6), which Debreu leaves to the reader. See the Appendix.

[4] 'iff' = 'if and only if'.

$\succcurlyeq$ clearly defines a conditional ordering on S_A, given what happens off it, whose utility functions may be written $U_A(x_A\colon x_{\bar{A}}) = U(x_A, x_{\bar{A}})$. If, given some $x_{\bar{A}}$, not all elements of S_A are indifferent, say that A is *essential*, if, given any, *strictly essential*. If the conditional ordering on A is the same for all $x_{\bar{A}}$, say that A is *separable*. This is Leontief's (1947*a*, 1947*b*) concept of separability, somewhat generalized. I will use the word in this sense throughout the remainder of this paper. It has nothing to do with the topological separability of (P2).

Take a *reference vector* $0 \in S$ and call its components on any S_B, $B \subseteq \Omega$, 0 also. It need not, of course, represent zero consumption. If A is separable, any conditional ordering on it may be represented by a continuous *subutility function*:

$$u_A(x_A) = U(x_A, 0). \tag{1.4}$$

Throughout this paper I will use the same reference vector $0 \in S$ for all separable sets, will write 0 for 0_A, its component in S_A, each $A \subseteq \Omega$, and will normalize so that

$$U(0) = 0. \tag{1.5}$$

Since inessential sets affect nothing, they may be neglected.[5] I will accordingly assume throughout the paper that

(P3) Each sector is essential

For simplicity of argument I will frequently make the stronger assumption

(P4) Each sector is strictly essential.

which I will however show in Section 6 can be replaced by the harmless (P3), except in one rather special case.

Debreu (1960) has also shown[6] that the utility function may be written

$$U(x) = F(U_1(x_1), \ldots, U_n(x_n)) \tag{1.6}$$

iff each sector is separable, and that, if at least three sectors are essential,

$$U(x) = U_1(x_1) + U_2(x_2) + \ldots + U_n(x_n) \tag{1.7}$$

in an appropriate normalization iff each set of sectors is separable, where the U_i's are the subutility functions just defined, and $F(\cdot)$ is continuous and strictly increasing. These correspond to Leontief's theorems on separability and additive separability, but are global while Leontief's are local,[7] and depend on weaker assumptions.

[5] This presumes that we know which sectors are inessential—surely not a strong requirement. (P3) might be further weakened, but it would complicate the exposition, so that it hardly seems worth while.

[6] Actually he leaves the proof of (1.6) to the reader.

[7] Though Leontief's theorems can frequently be proved to hold generally. See Gorman (1968*b*).

There are extreme cases: what do we know about the structure of $U(\cdot)$, if we are given a general collection $\mathscr{B}$ of separable sets? Call it a *separable* collection.

Even without (P4), it is clear that 0 and Ω are separable and that, if A and B are separable, so is their intersection. We will see in Section 2 that, if they *overlap*, that is intersect and neither contains the other, then (P4) implies that their union $A \cup B$, two differences $A - B$, $B - A$ and symmetric difference $A \Delta B = (A - B) \cup (B - A)$ are also separable. Let us say that a *collection* $\mathscr{A}$ of subsets of Ω is *complete* if

$$\text{If } A, B \in \mathscr{A} \text{ overlap, then } A \cap B,\ A - B,\ B - A, \text{ and } A \Delta B \text{ all belong to } \mathscr{A}; \tag{1.8a}$$

$$0, \Omega \in \mathscr{A}, \tag{1.8b}$$

and define the *completion* $\mathscr{A}(\mathscr{B})$ of $\mathscr{B}$ to be the intersection of all the complete collections containing $\mathscr{B}$: that is, the smallest such collection. Clearly all its elements are separable if (P4) holds. We will see in Section 3 that these are the only sets whose separability is implied by that of the elements of $\mathscr{B}$, even given (P4), and in Section 6 that their separability follows from (P3) except in one rather special case.

(P4) implies then, that we can assume without loss of generality that we are given a complete separable collection $\mathscr{A}$: if the original separable collection $\mathscr{B}$ is incomplete, we merely take $\mathscr{A} = \mathscr{A}(\mathscr{B})$. Of course if $\mathscr{B}$ is complete, we have no need of (P4), though (P3) is needed even then.

Now $\mathscr{A}$ is partially ordered under the relation $\supseteq$, with unique maximal and minimal elements Ω and 0. Call these the *trival elements* of $\mathscr{A}$, the others the *proper elements*, and the maximal proper elements—that is, those which are not contained in any other proper elements—the *top elements* of $\mathscr{A}$.

If no two top elements intersect, there is a partition $\{\Omega_0, \Omega_1, \ldots, \Omega_m\}$ of Ω in which $\Omega_1, \ldots, \Omega_m$ are top elements of $\mathscr{A}$, and Ω_0, the *free set*, is made up of those sectors which belong to no proper element of $\mathscr{A}$, since each proper element is contained in a top element. Let $(y_0, y_1, \ldots, y_m)$ be the corresponding partition of x. Since $\Omega_1, \ldots, \Omega_m$ are separable, an immediate generalization of (1.6), proved in the Appendix to this paper, shows that we can write

$$U(x) = F(y_0, U_1(y_1), \ldots, U_m(y_m)), \tag{1.9}$$

where $F(\cdot)$ is continuous, and strictly increasing in the subutilities $U_1, \ldots, U_m$.

If two of the top elements intersect, it is shown in Section 3 that there is a partition $\{\Omega_1, \Omega_2, \ldots, \Omega_m\}$ of Ω, the union of every subset[8] of which belongs to $\mathscr{A}$. Let $(y_1, y_2, \ldots, y_m)$ be the corresponding partition of x. An

[8] i.e. the union of each set of Ω's.

obvious extension of (1.7), proved in the Appendix, therefore implies that we can write

$$U(x) = U_1(y_1) + \ldots + U_m(y_m) \tag{1.10}$$

in an appropriate normalization.

It is shown in Section 3 that $\mathscr{A}$ may be broken down into $\mathscr{A}^*$, which is composed of Ω, 0 with $\Omega_1, \Omega_2, \ldots, \Omega_m$ in the first case discussed above, and with the union of each set of the Ω's in the second, and $\mathscr{A}_1, \mathscr{A}_2, \ldots, \mathscr{A}_m$ which bear the same relationship[9] to $\Omega_1, \Omega_2, \ldots, \Omega_m$ as $\mathscr{A}$ to Ω. The information in $\mathscr{A}^*$ yields (1.9) or (1.10) as the case may be; that in $\mathscr{A}_i$ permits a similar analysis of Ω_i, each i, and so down the utility tree. This permits a complete characterization of the form of the utility function in terms of $\mathscr{A}$.

Some applications are discussed in Section 4, an alternative approach sketched in Section 5, and (P4) replaced by (P3) in Section 6. This weaker postulate is also used in the proof of Theorem 1 in Section 2.

2. THE BASIC THEOREM

Let $\{\Omega_0, \Omega_1, \ldots, \Omega_m\}$ be a partition of Ω and $(y_0, y_1, \ldots, y_m)$ be the corresponding partition of x. It is shown in the Appendix that

LEMMA 1: *If $\Omega_1, \Omega_2, \ldots, \Omega_m$ are separable,* (P1)–(P2) *imply that we can write*

$$U(x) = F(y_0, U_1(y_1), \ldots, U_m(y_m)), \tag{2.1}$$

where $U_1(\cdot), \ldots, U_m(\cdot)$ are the continuous subutilities defined in (1.4) *and* (1.5), *and $F(\cdot)$ is* well behaved: *that is, is continuous in all its arguments and strictly increasing in the subutilities.*

COROLLARY: *F can be normalized to mirror the subutilities,* i.e.

$$U_i = F(0, \ldots, 0, U_i, 0, \ldots, 0), \qquad \text{each } i. \tag{2.2}$$

Lemma 1 then permits us to prove:

THEOREM 1: *If*

(0) *$A, B \subseteq \Omega$ overlap,*
(i) *$A, B \subseteq \Omega$ are separable,*
(ii) *$B - A$ is strictly essential,*[10]

[9] i.e. $\mathscr{A}_i$ satisfies the definition of completeness in (1.8) with Ω_i in the place of Ω, each i.
[10] Or, of course, $A - B$.

then (P1)–(P3) *imply that*

(iii) $A \cup B$, $A \cap B$, $A - B$, $B - A$ *and* $A \Delta B = (A - B) \cup (B - A)$ *are all separable and strictly essential.*

Remark: It will be convenient to change notation slightly and write x for x_{A-B}, y for $x_{A \cap B}$, z for x_{B-A}, θ for $x_{\bar{A} \cap \bar{B}}$, and therefore (x, y, z, θ) for x, in this section.

I will show that (i) and (ii) imply, with (0) and (P1)–(P3), that

(iv) $U(x, y, z, \theta) = F(u(x) + v(y) + w(z), \theta))$, say,

where $F(\cdot, \theta)$ is strictly increasing, which in turn clearly implies (iii): since (iii) certainly implies (i) and (ii) we have

COROLLARY: '(i) *and* (ii)', '(iii)', *and* '(iv)' *are equivalent, given* (P1)–(P3) *and* (0).

PROOF: Since A and B are both separable, the conditional preference ordering on $S_{A \cap B}$ is independent both of (z, θ) and of (y, θ), and is therefore independent of (y, z, θ). Hence their intersection is separable, too. Lemma 1 therefore implies that we can write:

$$U(x, y, z, \theta) = G(g(x, v(y)), z, \theta) = H(x, h(v(y), z), \theta), \tag{2.3}$$

where $v(y)$ is the subutility function for $A \cap B$, $g(x, v(y))$ for A, $h(v(y), z)$ for B, and all the functions are well behaved and mirror the subutility functions.[11] Since each is continuous on a connected domain, the range of each is an interval. $(x, y, z, \theta) \succ (x, y', z, \theta)$, some x, z, θ, y, y', since $A \cap B$ is essential, and hence for all x, z, θ, since it is separable. Hence this interval is non-degenerate. In particular, the range of

$$v(y) = U(0, y, 0, 0) = g(0, v(y)) = h(v(y), 0) \tag{2.4}$$

is a non-degenerate interval J containing 0.

Define analogously

$$u(x) = U(x, 0, 0, 0) = g(x, 0); \quad w(z) = U(0, 0, z, \theta) = h(0, z). \tag{2.5}$$

According to (2.3),

$$U(x, y, z, \theta) \geqslant U(x', y, z, \theta) \tag{2.6}$$

iff

$$g(x, v(y)) \geqslant g(x', v(y)), \tag{2.7}$$

[11] Since e.g. $h(v(y), 0) = U(0, y, 0, 0) = v(y)$. To say that $h(v(y), z)$ is well behaved is to say that it is continuous, and strictly increasing in v.

and also iff

$$H(x, h(v(y), z), \theta) \geqslant H(x', h(v(y), z), \theta), \tag{2.8}$$

so that (2.7) and (2.8) are equivalent. I will use this to show that (2.6) holds iff $u(x) \geqslant u(x')$, so that $A - B$ is separable.

Say that $v \in J$ is *joined* to $v' \in J$ if there are $z, z' \in S_{B-A}$ such that

$$h(v, z) = h(v', z'). \tag{2.9}$$

If so

$$g(x, v) \geqslant g(x', v) \quad \text{iff} \quad g(x, v') \geqslant g(x', v'), \tag{2.10}$$

because each is equivalent to $H(x, h, \theta) \geqslant H(x', h, \theta)$, where $h = h(v, z) = h(v', z')$.

Say that v is *connected* to v' if there exists a chain $v = v_0, v_1, \ldots, v_t = v'$, each element of which, except the last, is joined to its successor. Clearly (2.10) holds in this case, too.

'Being connected to' is an equivalence relation, and so partitions J into equivalence classes.

These equivalence classes are intervals. To see this, let $v, v', v < v'$, belong to the same equivalence class K, and take $\bar{v}$ such that $v > \bar{v} > v'$. In the chain connecting v, v' there are a pair v_i, v_{i+1} such that $v_i \geqslant \bar{v} \geqslant v_{i+1}$. In an obvious notation, therefore: $h(v_i, z_i) = h(v_{i+1}, z_{i+1}) \leqslant h(\bar{v}, z_{i+1}) \leqslant h(v_i, z_{i+1})$ because $h(\cdot, z_{i+1})$ is increasing. Since $h(v_i, \cdot)$ is continuous on the connected space S_{B-A}, this implies that there is a $\bar{z} \in S_{B-A}$ such that $h(v_i, \bar{z}) = h(\bar{v}, z_{i+1})$. $\bar{v}$ is therefore joined to $v_i \in K$, and hence belongs to K too. K is therefore an interval.

I will show that there is only one equivalence class, so that each $v \in J$ is connected to 0 in particular, implying, by (2.5)–(2.7) and (2.10), that $U(x, y, z, \theta) \geqslant U(x', y, z, \theta)$ iff $u(x) \geqslant u(x')$, so that $A - B$ is separable with subutility function $u(x) = U(x, 0, 0, 0)$.

Suppose the contrary and let v^* be a common frontier point of two equivalence classes J_1, J_2. Since J, being an interval, is connected, such a point exists. If either J_1 or J_2 is degenerate, it may be the end-point of J; otherwise it is an interior point, since both are intervals. In either case it belongs to J, and not merely to its closure. Should v^* be the upper bound of J, for instance, I_+ below is empty, but this does not affect the validity of the argument.

Since $B - A$ is strictly essential, there are $z, z' \in S_{B-A}$ such that

$$h(v^*, z) > h(v^*, z'). \tag{2.11}$$

Since h is well behaved by (2.3), there is a $\delta > 0$ such that

$$h(v^*, z) \geqslant h(v, z') \geqslant h(v^*, z'), \qquad v \in J \cap [v^*, v^* + \delta] = I_+, \text{ say}, \tag{2.12}$$

and since $h(v^*, \cdot)$ is continuous in z on the connected space S_{B-A}, there exists a $z^* \in S_{B-A}$ such that $h(v^*, z^*) = h(v, z')$. Hence v^* is connected to each $v \in I_+$. Similarly there exists an $\varepsilon > 0$ such that v^* is connected to each $v \in J \cap [v^* - \varepsilon, v^*] = I_-$, say. Since it is a common frontier point of $J_1, J_2 \subseteq J$, this implies that it belongs to both equivalence classes, which is impossible. There is therefore only one equivalence class, and $A - B$ is separable with subutility function $u(x)$. Being separable and essential, it is strictly essential. Hence $B - A$ is separable with subutility function $w(z)$ by a similar argument.

Lemma 1 now implies that we can write

$$U = G(h(u, v), w, \theta) = H(u, h(v, w), \theta) \tag{2.13}$$

in a slightly new notation, where all the functions are well behaved.

I will now show that this implies that we can write[12]

$$U(x, y, z, \theta) = F(a(u(x)) + b(v(y)) + c(w(z)), \theta), \tag{2.14}$$

where all functions are well behaved. Since this is just (iv) in a different notation, it proves both the theorem and the corollary.

According to a theorem of Aczel[13] on associative functions,

$$U = G(g(u, v), w) = H(u, h(v, w)), \tag{2.15}$$

where all functions are well behaved, and

$$u, v, w, g, h, G, H \text{ all range over the same interval } \langle\alpha, \beta\rangle, \tag{2.16}$$

would imply that we could write

$$g(u, v) = \phi(a(u) + b(v)), \quad h(u, w) = \psi(b((v) + c(w)),$$

$$G(g, w) = F(\phi^{-1}(g) + c(w)), \quad H(u, h) = F(a(u) + \psi^{-1}(h)), \tag{2.17}$$

so that

$$U = F(a(u) + b(v) + c(w)), \tag{2.18}$$

where

$$\text{all functions are well behaved.} \tag{2.19}$$

(2.18)–(2.19) is the sort of thing we want. There are two obstacles in the way of finding it: θ and the fact that (2.16) is not normally satisfied.

Consider the latter first. Since $u(\cdot)$ . . . are continuous on arc-connected domains S_{A-B}, . . . , and $A - B$, . . . are essential, the domains of u, v, w are all non-degenerate intervals. To make them all of the same type, restrict u, v, w to the interior of their domains until further notice. The domains of u, v, w are now all open intervals. So, by their continuity on connected spaces,

[12] If so, we can clearly normalize so that $F(\lambda, 0) = \lambda$, and $a(u(0)) = \ldots = 0$. Do so. Then $a + b + c$, b, a, c, $a + c$ are the subutility functions for $A \cup B$, $A \cap B$, $B - A$, $A - B$, $A \Delta B$, respectively. Since each of these sets is separable and essential, it is strictly essential.

[13] Aczel (1966), p. 321, Corollary 1 to Theorem 1 of p. 320.

are those of $g(\cdot)$ and $h(\cdot)$. We can map each of these intervals on to (0, 1) by well-behaved transformations which are independent of θ. Do so, and denote the transformed concepts by the same symbols as the old, thus retaining (2.13).

(2.13) also implies that the common range of $U(\cdot, \theta)$, $G(\cdot, \theta)$, and $H(\cdot, \theta)$ is an open interval. There is a well-behaved transformation L_θ which makes (0, 1) the common range of

$$L_\theta(U) = G_\theta(g(u, v), w) = H_\theta(u, h(v, w)), \tag{2.20}$$

where

$$G_\theta(g, w) = L_\theta(G(g, w, \theta)), \quad H_\theta(u, h) = L_\theta(H(u, h, \theta)). \tag{2.21}$$

All these functions are still well behaved, and (2.16) is now satisfied with G_θ, H_θ replacing G, H. By the argument proceding (2.20), we have (2.17)–(2.19), except that the new functions also require a subscript θ.

In particular, therefore

$$g(u, v) = \phi_\theta(a_\theta(u) + b_\theta(v)), \tag{2.22}$$

and we can clearly normalize so that

$$a_\theta(0.5) = b_\theta(0.5) = c_\theta(0.5) = 0, \qquad \text{each } \theta. \tag{2.23}$$

Do so, and drop the subscript 0 in the case $\theta = 0$ to get

$$\phi_\theta(a_\theta(u) + b_\theta(v)) = \phi(a(u) + b(v)). \tag{2.24}$$

Taking $v = 0.5$ first and then $u = 0.5$, we have

$$a_\theta = \phi^*_\theta(a), \quad b_\theta = \phi^*_\theta(b), \tag{2.25}$$

so that, by (2.24),

$$\phi^*_\theta(a + b) = \phi^*_\theta(a) + \phi^*_\theta(b), \tag{2.26}$$

where

$$\phi^*_\theta = \phi_\theta^{-1} \tag{2.27}$$

is well behaved by (2.19) on its interval domain I, say, which contains the origin. The domains of a and b being non-degenerate intervals, this implies

$$\phi^*_\theta(\lambda) = k_\theta \lambda, \text{ say}, \qquad \lambda \in I;\ k_\theta > 0, \text{ a constant}, \tag{2.28}$$

so that[14]

$$k_\theta = a_\theta/a = b_\theta/b \tag{2.29}$$

$$= c_\theta/c,$$

[14] a_θ, b_θ, c_θ, a, b, c all vanish together, so this creates no problems.

by a similar argument applied to $h(\cdot)$.

The θ-version of (2.18) is

$$L_\theta(U) = F_\theta(a_\theta(u) + b_\theta(v) + c_\theta(w))$$
$$= F_\theta(k_\theta(a(u) + b(v) + c(w))), \tag{2.30}$$

by (2.29), so that

$$U = F(a(u) + b(v) + c(w), \theta), \text{ say,} \tag{2.31}$$

as we wanted in (2.14), where all the functions are well behaved.[15]

All this so far only when u, v, w are restricted to the interior of their interval domains. It holds throughout these domains by the good behaviour of all the functions in (2.31).

This completes the proof of both theorem and corollary.

Given (P1), (P2), and (P4) we may therefore assume without loss of generality that we are given a complete collection $\mathscr{A}$ of subsets of Ω which are known to be separable, that is, a complete separable collection. Of course, the original separable collection $\mathscr{B}$ may already be complete. If so, we will not need (P4), though a certain amount of essentiality will be needed in applying the results.

The intersection of two complete collections, each containing a given collection $\mathscr{B}$, is clearly complete and contains $\mathscr{B}$. Hence there exists a smallest collection $\mathscr{A}(\mathscr{B})$ with these properties. To know that the elements of $\mathscr{B}$ are separable is to know that those of $\mathscr{A}(\mathscr{B})$ are, given (P1), (P2), and (P4).

3. THE UTILITY TREE

In this section I will show how the partial ordering of the complete collection $\mathscr{A}$ and under $\succcurlyeq$ determines the structure of $U(\cdot)$.

Consider first the partial ordering itself. For this we need no postulates at all other than the existence of the complete collection $\mathscr{A}$.

The definitions in Section 1 of a *top element* A of $\mathscr{A}$, as a maximal proper element, and the *free set* Ω_0, as composed of those sectors which belong to no proper element, may be rephrased as

$$A \in \mathscr{A} \text{ is a top element of } \mathscr{A} \quad \text{iff} \quad A \subset B \subset \Omega \Rightarrow B \notin \mathscr{A}, \tag{3.1}$$

$$\Omega_0 = \{i \in \Omega : i \in B \subset \Omega \Rightarrow B \notin \mathscr{A}\}, \tag{3.2}$$

where $\subset$ denotes strict inclusion, denying the possibility of equality.

Top elements may or may not intersect. Say that $\mathscr{A}$ is *top disjoint* if no pair of its top elements intersect, *top overlapping*, if at least one pair do. We

[15] We normalize so that $F(\lambda, 0) = \lambda$ once more, so that the argument of n. 12 works.

will see below that there are at least three top elements in the latter case, and that each pair overlap.

3.1. $\mathscr{A}$ top disjoint

Let $\Omega_1, \Omega_2, \ldots, \Omega_m$ be the top elements. Then

$$\{\Omega_0, \Omega_1, \ldots, \Omega_m\} \text{ is a partition of } \Omega, \tag{3.3}$$

where Ω_0 is the free set defined in (3.2). Let $(y_0, y_1, \ldots, y_m)$ be the corresponding partition of x. Lemma 1 implies

$$U(x) = F(y_0, U_1(y_1), \ldots, U_m(y_m)), \tag{3.4}$$

where the $U_i(\cdot)$ are continuous subutility functions, and $F(\cdot)$ is well behaved.

Suppose that a proper element C of $\mathscr{A}$ intersects one of the top elements. It is contained in it if $\mathscr{A}$ is top disjoint. This is obvious if $m = 1$, since C cannot contain free sectors. If $m \geqslant 2$, let C intersect Ω_i, Ω_j. Since (3.1) implies that it contains neither, it overlaps each. Hence $B = C \cup \Omega_i$ is a proper element of $\mathscr{A}$, contradicting (3.1). Hence $\mathscr{A}$ may be listed, with trivial double counting, as the union of

$$\mathscr{A}^* = \{\Omega, \Omega_1, \ldots, \Omega_m, 0\}$$

$$\mathscr{A}_i = \{C \in \mathscr{A} : C \subseteq \Omega_i\}, \qquad i = 1, 2, \ldots, m. \tag{3.5}$$

3.2. $\mathscr{A}$ top overlapping

Call the top elements $A_1, \ldots, A_m$. At least one pair intersect. Since neither contains the other by (3.1), they overlap. Suppose

$$A_i \text{ and } A_j \text{ overlap.} \tag{3.6}$$

Then $A_i \cup A_j \in \mathscr{A}$ by Theorem 1, so that

$$A_i \cup A_j = \Omega, \tag{3.7}$$

by (3.1). Hence

$$\Omega_0 = 0, \text{ by (3.2).} \tag{3.8}$$

Since no other top element contains either A_i or A_j by (3.1), (3.7) implies that any other overlaps both. Hence[16]

$$\text{(3.6) and (3.7) hold for each } i, j, \ i \neq j, \tag{3.9}$$

$$A_j - A_i = \bar{A}_i = \Omega_i, \text{ say,} \qquad \text{each } i, j, \ i \neq j, \tag{3.10}$$

[16] We see that each A_k overlaps A_i if A_i overlaps any A_j. Hence each A_l overlaps A_k.

and

$$\Omega_i \cap \Omega_j = \bar{A}_i \cap \bar{A}_j = \overline{A_i \cup A_j} = \bar{\Omega} = 0 \tag{3.11}$$

while, by Theorem 1,

$$\Omega_i = A_j - A_i \in \mathscr{A}, \quad \Omega_i \cup \Omega_j = A_i \,\Delta\, A_j \in \mathscr{A}, \tag{3.12}$$

because of (3.6).

Now

$$C_I = \bigcup_{i \in I} \Omega_i \in \mathscr{A}, \qquad \text{each } I \subseteq \{1, 2, \ldots, m\}, \tag{3.13}$$

by (3.12) and Theorem 1. This is most easily seen when $I = \{1, 2, \ldots, t\}$, say. Define in that case $D_j = \Omega_i \cup \Omega_j \in \mathscr{A}$ by (3.12). Hence $E_2 = D_2 \in \mathscr{A}$ and by repeated application of Theorem 1 so does each $E_j = E_{j-1} \cup D_j = \bigcup_{i=1}^{j} \Omega_i$. Since $C_I = E_t$ when $I = \{1, 2, \ldots, t\}$ this proves (3.13) in this particular case. The argument is clearly valid in general with trivial alterations. In particular, therefore $\bigcup_{i=1}^{m} \Omega_i \in \mathscr{A}$. It is contained in none of the top elements $A_1, A_2, \ldots, A_m$. Hence $\bigcup_{i=1}^{m} \Omega_i = \Omega$ (3.1), so that (3.11) implies that

$$\{\Omega_1, \Omega_2, \ldots, \Omega_m\} \text{ is a partition of } \Omega, \tag{3.14}$$

and

$$m \geqslant 3, \tag{3.15}$$

since otherwise $A_1 = \Omega_2$ and $A_2 = \Omega_1$ cannot intersect, contradicting (3.6). Notice too that

$$A_i = \bar{\Omega}_i = \bigcup_{j \neq i} \Omega_j, \tag{3.16}$$

$$\bigcap_{i \in I} A_i = \bigcap_{i \in I} \bar{\Omega}_i = \overline{\bigcup_{i \in I} \Omega_i} = \bigcup_{j \notin I} \Omega_j \in \mathscr{A}. \tag{3.17}$$

If $(y_1, y_2, \ldots, y_m)$ is the corresponding partition of x, (3.13)–(3.15) imply that

$$U(x) = U_1(y_1) + U_2(y_2) + \ldots + U_m(y_m), \tag{3.18}$$

in an appropriate normalization, where the $U_1(\cdot)$ are continuous subutility functions, by Lemma 2 in the Appendix.

Moreover no element $C \in \mathscr{A}$ overlaps an Ω_i: if it were to, it would be a proper element, and would therefore overlap $A_i = \bar{\Omega}_i$, too, by (3.1), so that $B = C \cup A_i$ would be a proper element of $\mathscr{A}$ by Theorem 1, contradicting (3.1). We can therefore once more list $\mathscr{A}$, with only trivial double counting, as the union of

$$\mathscr{A}^* = \{\bigcup_{i \in I} \Omega_i : I \subseteq \{1, 2, \ldots, m\}\},$$

$$\mathscr{A}_i = \{C \in \mathscr{A} : C \subseteq \Omega_i\}, \qquad i = 1, 2, \ldots, m. \tag{3.19}$$

3.3. *The main theorem*

Let us define a *complete collection relative to C* by replacing Ω by C in the definition of a complete collection (1.8). We may then summarize the main results of Sections 3.1 and 3.2 in the following theorem:

THEOREM 2: *Any complete collection $\mathscr{A}$ may be written*

$$\mathscr{A} = \mathscr{A}^* \cup \left(\bigcup_{i=1}^{m} \mathscr{A}_i \right), \tag{3.20}$$

where

$$\mathscr{A}_i = \{A \in \mathscr{A} : A \subseteq \Omega_i\} \text{ is complete relative to } \Omega_i, \quad i = 1, 2, \ldots, m, \tag{3.21}$$

and where the top collection

$$\mathscr{A}^* = \{0, \Omega, \Omega_1, \ldots, \Omega_m\}, \qquad m \geqslant 0, \tag{3.22}$$

if $\mathscr{A}$ is top disjoint, in which case

$$\{\Omega_0, \Omega_1, \ldots, \Omega_m\} \text{ is a partition of } \Omega, \text{ in which } \Omega_0 \text{ is the free set and } \Omega_1, \ldots, \Omega_m \text{ the top elements of } \mathscr{A}, \tag{3.23}$$

or

$$\mathscr{A}^* = \{C_I = \bigcup_{i \in I} \Omega_i : I \subseteq \Phi = \{1, 2, \ldots, \}\}, \qquad m \geqslant 3, \tag{3.24}$$

if $\mathscr{A}$ is top overlapping, in which case

$$\{\Omega_1, \Omega_2, \ldots, \Omega_m\} \text{ is a partition of } \Omega, \text{ so that } \Omega_0 \text{ is empty and the top elements of } \mathscr{A} \text{ are } \bar{\Omega}_1, \ldots, \bar{\Omega}_m, \qquad m \geqslant 3. \tag{3.25}$$

It is now clear how to find the structure of $U(\cdot)$, given the separable complete collection $\mathscr{A}$, and (P1)–(P3).

Determine the top elements of $\mathscr{A}$. Do they intersect? Determine the Ω_i, $\mathscr{A}^*$, $\mathscr{A}_i$. If $\mathscr{A}$ is top disjoint

$$U(x) = F(y_0, U_1(y_1), \ldots, U_m(y_m)), \tag{3.26}$$

as in (3.4), where $F(\cdot)$ is well behaved by Lemma 1. If top overlapping

$$U(x) = U_1(y_1) + U_2(y_2) + \ldots + U_m(y_m) \tag{3.27}$$

as in (3.18), in an appropriate normalization. This exhausts the information in $\mathscr{A}^*$.

In either case $U_i(\cdot)$ is a continuous subutility function defined on

$$S_{\Omega_i} = \prod_{j \in \Omega_i} S_j,$$

and $\mathscr{A}_i$ is complete relative to Ω_i by (3.21).

Look at each $\mathscr{A}_i$ in turn. Discover its top elements. Do they intersect? Find the Ω_{ij}, $\mathscr{A}_i^*$, $\mathscr{A}_{ij}$, in an obvious notation. If $\mathscr{A}_i$ is top disjoint, we can write

$$U_i(y_i) = F_i(y_{i0}, U_{i1}(y_{i1}), U_{i2}(y_{i2}), \ldots), \tag{3.26$'$}$$

where $F_i(\cdot)$ is well behaved; if top overlapping

$$U_i(y_i) = F_i\left(\sum_j U_{ij}(y_{ij})\right), \tag{3.27$'$}$$

in an appropriate normalization, where $F_i(\cdot)$ is continuous and strictly increasing. The presence of this latter $F_i(\cdot)$ may be surprising. It is needed because when $\mathscr{A}$ is top intersecting, the $U_i(y_i)$ will already have been normalized to secure (3.27), and so cannot now be renormalized to get rid of the $F_i(\cdot)$ in (3.27′).[17] This means, too, that the $U_{ij}(\cdot)$ in (3.27′) do not generally satisfy (3.26).[18] However, continuous strictly increasing transforms of them do, which is all that is required for us to be able to turn next to the $\mathscr{A}_{ij}$, legitimately, applying the same procedure, and so down the utility tree.

At each stage (3.26), or (3.27), or one of their analogues, is equivalent to the separability of the elements of the top collection. Since $\mathscr{A}$ is finite, each of its proper elements is contained in some top collection. Hence the structure discovered by this procedure is equivalent to the separability of each element of $\mathscr{A}$. If $\mathscr{A} = \mathscr{A}(\mathscr{B})$, as defined in Section 1, and (P4) holds, it is equivalent to the separability of the elements of $\mathscr{B}$.

This procedure can be represented graphically. Represent a top collection by  or 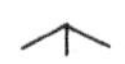 in the top disjoint case, according to whether or not there are free sectors, and by 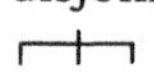 in the top overlapping case, when $m = 3$. If $m = 4$, for instance, use , , 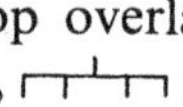 instead. The entire collection $\mathscr{A}$ can then be represented as in Figure 12.1. The sectors corresponding to each ray may be listed at its end, or separately as here:

$$\begin{array}{lll}
\Omega_0 = \{1, 2\}, & \Omega_1 = \{3, 4, 5\}, & \Omega_2 = \{6, \ldots, 13\}, \\
\Omega_{11} = \{3\}, & \Omega_{12} = \{4, 5\}, & \\
\Omega_{21} = \{6, 7, 8\}, & \Omega_{22} = \{9\}, & \Omega_{23} = \{10, \ldots, 13\}, \\
\Omega_{210} = \{6, 7\}, & \Omega_{211} = \{8\}, & \\
\Omega_{231} = \{10\}, & \Omega_{232} = \{11\} & \Omega_{233} = \{12, 13\}.
\end{array}$$

$U(\cdot)$ can be read straight off this information. Here it is[19]

[17] If $\mathscr{A}$ is top disjoint no such problem exists, nor does it in general if the next higher collection is.

[18] And so are not strictly subutility functions in the narrow sense in which I have used this term so far. Of course this does not matter at all since they reflect preference perfectly and are continuous.

[19] Where the F's are well behaved; that is, continuous in all their arguments, and strictly increasing in the F's among them. Having a choice between, for instance, $F_{231}(x_{10})$ and $U_{231}(x_{10})$, in the case of bottom sets, I chose the F notation for apparent consistency.

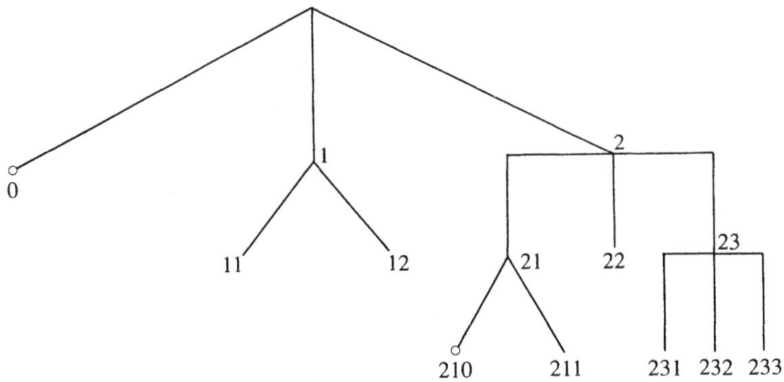

FIG. 12.1:

$$U(x) = F(x_1, x_2, F_1(F_{11}(x_3), F_{12}(x_4, x_5)), F_{21}(x_6, x_7, F_{211}(x_8)) + F_{22}(x_9) + F_{23}(F_{231}(x_{10}) + F_{232}(x_{11}) + F_{233}(x_{12}, x_{13}))). \quad (3.28)$$

Clearly it is sufficient to list the *bottom elements* of $\mathscr{A}$ here, that is, those of its proper elements of which no proper subset belongs to $\mathscr{A}$.

I will call the partial ordering of $\mathscr{A}$ under $\supseteq$, as represented in these diagrams, the *structure* of $\mathscr{A}$.

4. SOME APPLICATIONS

In this section I will apply these results to the theory of decisions over time and to the aggregation of production relations. The latter topic is a large one; accordingly I will merely sketch its treatment. I will assume essentiality throughout but not strict essentiality: to be precise, I use (P1)–(P3), but not (P4).

4.1. *Intertemporal preferences*

Consider first a person who expects to live n years and whose preferences among prospects from year i forward are independent of his plans for the interim. Formally

$$\mathscr{B} = \{B_i : B_i = \{i, i+1, \ldots, n\}, i = 1, \ldots, n, B_0 = 0\}. \quad (4.1)$$

This is a nested set of intervals, no two of which overlap, so that $\mathscr{A}(\mathscr{B}) = \mathscr{B}$. In particular, it is top disjoint at each stage. Its graph is given in Figure 12.2, and its utility function is

$$U(x) = F(x_1, F_{(1)}(x_2, F_{(2)}(x_3, \ldots, F_{(n-2)}(x_{n-1}, F_{(n-1)}(x_n)) \ldots,))) \quad (4.2)$$

in the notation (3.26) and (3.26′), where (i) stands for i 1's in a row.

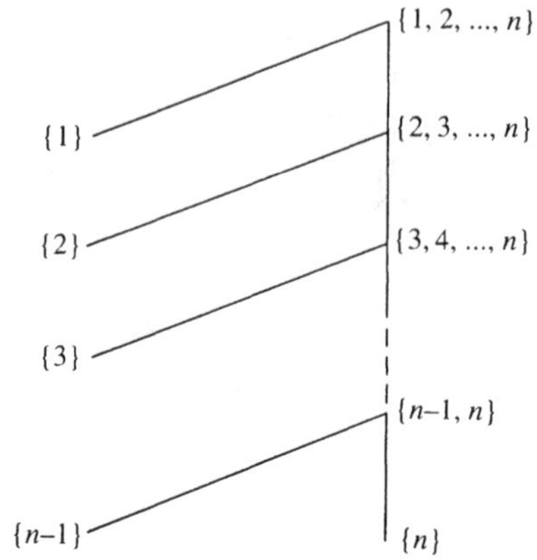

FIG. 12.2:

Suppose that his preferences in each of the initial periods

$$C_i = \{1, 2, \ldots, i\}, \qquad i = 1, 2, \ldots, n-1, \tag{4.3}$$

are also independent of what he means to do later, so that

$$\mathscr{B} = \{B_0, B_1, \ldots, B_n, C_1, C_2, \ldots, C_{n-1}\}. \tag{4.4}$$

Then

$$\{i\} \text{ and } A_i = \{\bar{i}\} \text{ are separable}, \qquad i = 1, 2, \ldots, n. \tag{4.5}$$

$\{1\} = C_1$, $\{n\} = B_n$, $\{i\} = B_i \cap C_i$, $i = 2, 3, \ldots, n-1$ are separable, and being essential therefore strictly essential. Hence each element of $\mathscr{A}(\mathscr{B})$ is separable. Moreover $A_1 = B_2$, $A_n = C_{n-1}$ and $A_i = B_i \Delta C_i$, $i = 2, \ldots, n-1$ are the top elements of $\mathscr{A}(\mathscr{B})$ so that, if $n \geqslant 3$,

$$U(x) = \sum U_i(x_i), \tag{4.6}$$

in an appropriate normalization.

Consider next a person who expects to live $n \geqslant 3$ years, whose preferences within each pair of adjacent years is independent of what he intends to do in the others. Formally

$$\mathscr{B} = \{D_1, D_2, \ldots, D_{n-1}\}, \quad D_i = \{i, i+1\}, \qquad i = 1, \ldots, n-1. \tag{4.7}$$

Hence $\{i\} = D_{i-1} \cap D_i$ is separable and hence strictly essential, $i = 2, 3, \ldots, n-1$. Thus $\{1\} = D_1 - D_2$ and $\{n\} = D_{n-1} - D_n$ are too, so that (P3) holds again, and each element of $\mathscr{A}(\mathscr{B})$ is once more separable. Hence

$$A_1 = \bigcup_{j=2}^{n-1} D_j, \quad A_n = \bigcup_{j=1}^{n-2} D_j, \quad A_i = \bigcup_{j=1}^{i-1} D_j \,\Delta \bigcup_{k=i}^{n-1} D_k \tag{4.8}$$

are the top elements of $\mathscr{A}(\mathscr{B})$. Since $\{i\} = A_i$, we have (4.6) once more.
This case was discussed in Gorman (1968*b*) and Koopmans (1960).

4.2. Klein–Nataf aggregation[20]

Suppose that we are given an economy of n firms with production frontiers

$$\phi_j(x_j) = 0, \qquad j = 1, 2, \ldots, n, \tag{4.9}$$

where

$$x_j = (x_j^0, x_j^1, \ldots, x_j^m), \tag{4.10}$$

gives the net output of each good and service[21] in firm j, and each x_j^i, that of those in the ith class. The classes may, for instance, be 'outputs', 'labour inputs', and 'capital inputs' as in Gorman (1967*b*) and Leontief (1947*a*). If so the labour and capital inputs will appear as negative net outputs.

Let us require that an aggregate production relation

$$X^0 = F(X^1, X^2, \ldots, X^m), \tag{4.11}$$

where

$$F(\cdot) \text{ is } \textit{well behaved}, \tag{4.12}$$

that is, continuous and strictly increasing,[22] should hold for the economy as a whole, given only that the individual firms lie on their own production frontiers, whether or not the allocation between them is efficient, where

$$X^i = X^i(x^i) = X^i(x_1^i, x_2^i, \ldots, x_n^i), \qquad i = 0, 1, \ldots, m, \tag{4.13}$$

and

$$X^i(\cdot) \text{ is continuous and strongly increasing}^{23} \text{ in each } x_j^i, \; i = 0, 1, \ldots, m, \tag{4.14}$$

is an aggregate measuring the net output of the ith class of good in the economy as a whole. Notice that it depends on how the total output $\sum_j x_j^i$ of goods in this class is divided among the firms.[24]

Choose a reference vector a_j for the jth firm, which is on its production frontier. Write $x_j = \bar{x}_j + a_j$ in the equations to date, $\bar{\phi}_j(\bar{x}_j) = \phi_j(\bar{x}_j + a_j)$,

[20] A full discussion of this topic would require a separate paper. Hence the rather sketchy analysis and *ad hoc* assumptions below.

[21] From now on I will use 'goods' to cover services too.

[22] This terminology is sufficiently consistent with that of Sections 2 and 3 not to be confusing, I hope.

[23] *Strongly increasing in each* x_j^i:

$$X^i(x^i) \geqslant X^i(y^i) \text{ if } x^i \geqslant y^i, \text{ and } X^i(x^i) > X^i(y^i) \text{ if } x^i \geqslant y^i,\ x_j^i > y_j^i, \text{ some } j.$$

[24] There is nothing, for instance, to ensure that different firms make equally efficient use of the same inputs = negative net outputs.

$\bar{X}^i(\bar{x}^i) = X^i(\bar{x}^i + a^i) - X^i(a^i)$, $\bar{F}(\bar{X}^1, \ldots, \bar{X}^m) = F(\bar{X}^1 + X^1(a^1), \ldots, \bar{X}^m + X^m(a^m)) - F(X^1(a^1), \ldots, X^m(a^m))$ and drop the bars to get (4.9)–(4.14) with

$$\phi_j(0) = x^i(0) = F(0) = 0, \qquad \text{each } i, j. \tag{4.15}$$

Define subaggregates

$$X_j^i(x_j^i) = X^i(0, \ldots, x_j^i, 0, \ldots), \text{ so that } X_j^i(0) = 0. \tag{4.16}$$

Setting $x_k = 0$, $k \neq j$, in (4.11), we have

$$X_j^0 = F(X_j^1, X_j^2, \ldots, X_j^m), \qquad X_j^i = X_j^i(x_j^i), \tag{4.17}$$

whenever the ith firm is on its production frontier. Let us require that the aggregate production relation (4.11) reflect the technologies of the individual firms in the sense that, if all but one of them are on their production frontiers, it holds only if the remaining one is too. Then (4.17) is the equation of this frontier.

Choose now a vector x_j on the jth firm's production frontier, each j. Vary x_j^0, holding $X_j^0(x_j^0)$ and each x_j^i, $i \neq 0$, constant. Each firm remains on its production frontier (4.17) and X^i remains unchanged, $i > 0$. (4.11) therefore implies that $X^0(x^0)$ remains unchanged also. Hence

$$X^0(x^0) = G^0(X_1^0(x_1^0), \ldots, X_n^0(x_n^0)), \text{ say,} \tag{4.18}$$

at least when x^0 is efficiently producible, that is, when each x_j^0 lies on its firm's production frontier for some (x_j^i), $i \neq 0$. Let us call the set of such x_j^0, S_j^0, and restrict each x_j^0 to S_j^0. Then (4.18) holds everywhere. Solving (4.11) for each X^i in turn, as we can by (4.12), restricting each x_j^i to S_j^i defined in a similar manner, and applying a similar argument, we get

$$X^i = G^i(X_1^i, X_2^i, \ldots, X_n^i), \qquad i = 0, 1, 2, \ldots, m, \tag{4.19}$$

where each

$$G^i(\cdot) \text{ is well behaved,} \qquad G^i(0) = 0, \quad G^i(0, \ldots, X_j^i, \ldots, 0) = X_j^i, \tag{4.20}$$

if each

$$S_j^i \text{ is tube connected,}^{25} \tag{4.21}$$

a reasonable assumption which I will make.

Substituting from (4.17) and (4.19) into (4.11), we get

$$X^0 = G^0(X_1^0, \ldots, X_n^0) = G^0(F(Y_1), \ldots, F(Y_n))$$

[25] S_j^i is *tube connected*: if $x_j^i, y_j^i \in S_j^i$, they are connected by an arc all of whose other points belong to the interior of S_j^i. Continuity follows as in Lemma 1, the strictly increasing property as in *n*. 10 to section IV of Gorman (1968*a*).

$$= F(X^1, \ldots, X^m)$$
$$= F(G^1(Y^1), G^2(Y^2), \ldots, G^m(Y^m))$$
$$= -U(X), \text{ say}, \tag{4.22}$$

where

$$X = (X_1^1, \ldots, X_n^m), \quad Y^i = (X_1^i, \ldots, X_n^i), \quad Y_j = (X_j^1, \ldots, X_j^m), \tag{4.23}$$

and

$$U(\cdot), \; -F(\cdot), \text{ each } G^i(\cdot), \text{ well behaved.} \tag{4.24}$$

This would seem to be just the sort of problem to which our results should be applied, $U(\cdot)$ ranking as an honorary utility function. Nevertheless two difficulties remain—we need to have (i, j) essential, each $i, j > 0$, and the space S of X must be a product space. The former can, as it happens, be considerably relaxed, but the latter is really needed.

Now it might be thought that we could just take

$$S = \prod_{i=1}^{m} \prod_{j=1}^{n} S_j^i, \tag{4.25}$$

which is certainly a product space. Unfortunately this is not so. Suppose for instance that firm j neither produces nor uses any good in class 0. Then the equation (4.17) of its production frontier is

$$F(X_j^1, X_j^2, \ldots, X_j^m) = X_j^0 = 0. \tag{4.26}$$

In other words, it is a constraint on $X_j^1, \ldots, X_j^m$. Since the aggregate production relation (4.22) is only required to hold when each firm is on its production frontier, it only holds for X constrained as in (4.26), and therefore not over the entire product space S. I will arbitrarily assume that this does not happen, and that (4.22) holds for all $X \in S$.

For essentiality it is sufficient to assume that each S_j^i contains a pair x_j^i, y_j^i with $x_j^i > y_j^i$. I do so.[26] Since (i, j) in the obvious notation is certainly separable, it is strictly essential.

I am now in a position to apply the analysis of Section 3 with

$$\Omega = \{(1, 1), \ldots, (m, n)\}, \text{ each } (i, j) \text{ strictly essential,}$$

and

$$\mathcal{B} = \{B^1, \ldots, B^m, C_1, \ldots, C_n\}, \tag{4.27}$$

[26] This assumption can be greatly weakened. Set $a_{ij} = 1$ if S_j^i contains such a pair and 0 if it does not, $i, j > 0$. Then (4.22) holds if A is *connected*; that is, if its rows and columns cannot be independently permuted to put A in block diagonal form, the blocks in general being rectangular.

where

$$B^i = \{(i, 1), \ldots, (i, n)\}, \quad C_j = \{(1, j), \ldots, (m, j)\}, \qquad \text{each } i, j > 0. \tag{4.28}$$

Now

$$\overline{\{(i, j)\}} = A^i_j = (B^i \,\Delta\, C_j) \cup \left(\bigcup_{k \neq j} C^k \right) \in \mathcal{A}(\mathcal{B}) \tag{4.29}$$

and is clearly a top element, each $i, j > 0$. Hence

$$U(X) = \sum U^i_j(X^i_j), \tag{4.30}$$

in an appropriate normalization, which merely comes to the application of a well-behaved transformation to X^0, which is certainly legitimate, and leaves (4.9)–(4.30) unchanged after trivial change in notation. Apply it. Of course

$$U(\cdot), \text{ and each } U^i_j(\cdot), \text{ are well behaved,} \tag{4.31}$$

$$U^i_j(0) = U(0) = 0, \qquad \text{each } i, j > 0. \tag{4.32}$$

Define now

$$f^i(X^i) = -F(0, \ldots, 0, X^i, 0, \ldots). \tag{4.33}$$

It is well behaved and $f^i(0) = 0$, so that we can apply this transformation to X^i without affecting any of (4.9)–(4.33) or the interpretation of the aggregates. Do so. Setting $X^k_j = 0$, $k \neq i$ in (4.22) yields

$$X^i = \sum_j U^i_j(X^i_j) \tag{4.34}$$

because of (4.20) and (4.32). Setting $X^i_k = 0$, $k \neq j$ in this yields

$$X^i_j = U^i_j(X^i_j), \tag{4.35}$$

so that

$$X^i = \sum_j X^i_j. \tag{4.36}$$

(4.22) and (4.30) now yield

$$\sum_{i=0}^{m} X^i(x^i) = 0 \tag{4.37}$$

and, when we put $x^i_k = 0$, $k \neq j$,

$$\sum_{i=0}^{m} X^i_j(x^i_j) = 0. \tag{4.38}$$

Since (4.38) clearly implies (4.37) which is of the form (4.11), with the definitions (4.36), such aggregation is possible iff well-behaved subaggregates $X_j^i(x_j^i)$ exist for each firm j and class of goods i, such that the equations of the production frontiers for the individual firms can be written in the form (4.38), and then the aggregates for the economy are the sum (4.36) of the corresponding subaggregates from the individual firms—as Nataf (1948) discovered.[27]

There is one apparent paradox. (4.38) implies that

$$\sum \bar{X}^i = 0 \tag{4.39}$$

too, where

$$\bar{X}^i(x^i) = \sum_j a_j X_j^i(x_j^i), \tag{4.40}$$

which is well behaved if each $a_j > 0$. Yet these $\bar{X}^i$ are not mere transforms of the X^i, and (4.39) represents quite a different locus in the space of the x_j^i than does (4.37). This is certainly true and an obvious source of worry for statisticians fitting aggregate production functions, but it does not upset our analysis. We looked for a particular relation and found it—it was never required that there should not be others.[28]

5. AN ALTERNATIVE APPROACH

In this section I will discuss briefly an alternative approach which is sometimes easier to apply than that in Section 3, at least in the case of complete additive separability.[29]

Say that $C \subseteq \Omega$ is a *component* of $\mathscr{B}$ if no element of $\mathscr{B}$ overlaps it. 0, Ω are the *trivial components*, the others *proper components*. The *component collection* $\mathscr{C}(\mathscr{B})$ of $\mathscr{B}$ is made up of the components of $\mathscr{B}$. It satisfies the following lemma.

LEMMA 3:

(i) *If* $\mathscr{B}^* \supseteq \mathscr{B}$, *then* $\mathscr{C}(\mathscr{B}^*) \subseteq \mathscr{C}(\mathscr{B})$,
(ii) *Component collections are complete*,
(iii) $\mathscr{C}(\mathscr{B}) = \mathscr{C}(\mathscr{A}(\mathscr{B}))$.

[27] Though his results were local while these are global, and depend on weaker assumptions. In particular he needed $n \geqslant 3$, while we only need $m, n \geqslant 2$ here.

[28] This point is discussed in Gorman (1953*b*) and touched on in Gorman (1968*a*).

[29] *Complete additive separability*: the case in which we can write $U(x) = \sum U_i(x_i)$ in an appropriate normalization.

PROOF OF (i): The components of $\mathcal{B}^*$ satisfy the conditions required of those of $\mathcal{B}$.

PROOF OF (ii): Take a pair A, B of overlapping elements of $\mathcal{C}(\mathcal{B})$ and a $D \in \mathcal{B}$. I will show that

$$D \text{ does not overlap any of } A \cup B,\ A \cap B,\ A - B,\ B - A \text{ or } A \Delta B. \tag{5.1}$$

Since $(0, \Omega) \in \mathcal{C}(\mathcal{B})$, this will prove (ii).

A, for instance, does not overlap D. Hence

$$\text{at least one of } D \supseteq A,\ A \supseteq D,\ D \cap A = 0, \text{ holds.} \tag{5.2}$$

Considering B, too, we have the following possibilities.

$D \supseteq B$, say: If $A \supseteq D$, $A \supseteq B$; if $D \cap A = 0$, $D \cap B = 0$. Neither is consistent with A and B overlapping. Hence $D \supseteq A$, implying that $D \supseteq A \cup B$.

$D \subseteq A, B$: implying that $D \subseteq A \cup B$.

$D \subseteq A$, $B \cap D = 0$, say: implying that $D \subseteq A - B$.

$A \cap D = B \cap D = 0$: implying that $(A \cup B) \cap D = 0$.

In none of these cases can D overlap any of $A \cup B$, $A \cap B$, $A - B$, $B - A$, $A \Delta B$. Hence (5.1) and therefore (ii) holds.

PROOF OF (iii): Since $\mathcal{A}(\mathcal{B}) \supseteq B$, $\mathcal{C}(\mathcal{A}(\mathcal{B})) \subseteq \mathcal{C}(\mathcal{B})$ by (i), so that we need only show that

$$\mathcal{C}(\mathcal{A}(\mathcal{B})) \supseteq \mathcal{C}(\mathcal{B}). \tag{5.3}$$

Take $\mathcal{C} \in \mathcal{C}(\mathcal{B})$ and define

$$\mathcal{B}_1 = \{B \in \mathcal{B} : B \subseteq C\}, \quad \mathcal{B}_2 = \{B \in \mathcal{B} : B \supseteq C \text{ or } B \cap C = 0\} = \mathcal{B} - \mathcal{B}_1, \tag{5.4}$$

since C does not overlap any element of $\mathcal{B}$. All the proper elements of $\mathcal{A}_1 = \mathcal{A}(\mathcal{B}_1)$ are contained in C, and each element of $\mathcal{A}_2 = \mathcal{A}(\mathcal{B}_2)$ either contains C or does not intersect it, as is obvious when one remembers that we could treat C as a single sector in constructing $\mathcal{A}(\mathcal{B}_2)$. Hence C is a component of $\mathcal{A} = \mathcal{A}_1 \cup \mathcal{A}_2$. Moreover $\mathcal{A}_1$ and $\mathcal{A}_2$ are each complete and no element of either overlaps the other. Hence $\mathcal{A}$ is complete. Since it certainly contains $\mathcal{B}$, $\mathcal{A} \supseteq \mathcal{A}(\mathcal{B})$. Hence C is a component of $\mathcal{A}(\mathcal{B})$; which immediately yields (5.3) and therefore (iii).

(ii) implies that we can define the top elements of $\mathcal{C}(\mathcal{B})$ in the same manner as we did those of $\mathcal{A}(\mathcal{B})$ in Section 3. Call them *top components* of $\mathcal{B}$—or of $\mathcal{A}(\mathcal{B})$. In particular, therefore, $\mathcal{C}(\mathcal{B})$ is either top disjoint or top overlapping. Indeed, it is top disjoint if $\mathcal{A}(\mathcal{B})$ is top overlapping and, except in one highly special case, top overlapping if $\mathcal{A}(\mathcal{B})$ is top disjoint.

If $\mathscr{A}(\mathscr{B})$ is top disjoint, the discussion in Section 3.1 implies that the union of any collection of the Ω_i, $i > 0$ and any of the free sectors, is a component of $\mathscr{B}$. The top components are therefore found by dropping from Ω any one free sector or any one top element Ω_i, $i > 0$, of $\mathscr{A}(\mathscr{B})$. If $m + p > 2$, where m is the number of top elements, and p of free sectors, $\mathscr{C}(\mathscr{B})$ is therefore top overlapping. If $m + p \leq 2$ it is clearly top disjoint.

If, on the other hand, $\mathscr{A}(\mathscr{B})$ is top overlapping, (3.18) implies that $\Omega_1, \Omega_2, \ldots, \Omega_m$ as defined in (3.10) are the top components, so that $\mathscr{C}(\mathscr{B})$ is top disjoint. Hence we have:

THEOREM 3: *If* $\{\Omega_1, \Omega_2, \ldots, \Omega_m\}$, $\{y_1, y_2, \ldots, y_m\}$ *are corresponding partitions of* Ω *and* x, *and* $m \geq 3$, (P1), (P2) *and* (P4) *imply that we can write*

$$U(x) = \sum U_i(y_i) \tag{5.5}$$

in an appropriate normalization, iff

$$\textit{each } \Omega_i \textit{ is a top component.} \tag{5.6}$$

Each $U_i(\cdot)$ *is continuous in this case.*

COROLLARY: (P1), (P2) *and* (P4) *imply that we can write*

$$U(x) = \sum U_i(x_i) \tag{5.7}$$

in an appropriate normalization, iff

$$\{1\}, \{2\}, \ldots, \{n\} \textit{ are the only proper components of } \mathscr{B}, \textit{ when } n \geq 3. \tag{5.8}$$

This is much the most useful result to be derived from this approach. Given (P1), (P2), and (P4), it would have yielded $U(x) = \sum U_i(x_i)$ in (4.6) immediately. Combined with the results of Section 6, it would have yielded the same results immediately, given (P1)–(P3). It is possible to give a complete analysis of the structure of $U(\cdot)$ using these methods, paralleling that in Section 3, but the existence of free sectors in the top overlapping case, and the possibility that $m + p \leq 2$, makes it relatively clumsy. I will therefore forbear to give it here.

However, one relation between the two approaches is worth bringing out. Let $r = ij \ldots k$, $k > 0$, in $(n + 1)$-ary notation, or a blank, and say $r \in R$ if $ij \ldots k$ is the label of a node or terminus in a diagram such as Figure 12.1 or 12.2. Then

$$\tilde{\mathscr{A}} = \{\Omega_r : r \in R\} \cup \{0\} \tag{5.9}$$

is complete and is composed of just those elements of $\mathscr{A}$ which are also components of it.[30]

[30] 0, $\Omega \in \tilde{\mathscr{A}}$ clearly. Since each Ω_r is a component of $\mathscr{A}$ and an element of it, no two overlap.

6. STRICT ESSENTIALITY RELAXED

In none of the examples discussed in Section 4 did I have to use strict essentiality. The reason was that in each case at least one pair of overlapping separable sets A, B had $A - B$ strictly essential because it was, or contained, the intersection of a number of separable sets, which, itself separable and essential, was strictly essential. Theorem 1 therefore implied that $B - A$, too, was strictly essential, which in turn implied that various other sets were, until I had enough strict essentiality to prove all I needed, without explicitly assuming any at all. Since ordinary essentiality is rather nugatory—inessential sets affect nothing and so may be neglected if known—it would be interesting to know whether this were commonly the case. In this section I will show that it is. Since a full and rigorous analysis would take up rather a lot of space, and this article is already too long, I will merely sketch the analysis at some points.

$\mathcal{B} = \{A, B\}$, where A overlap, is the simplest non-trivial, or *proper*, example of a *connected collection*; that is, one for which each pair of distinct elements A, B are *linked* in $\mathcal{B}$ by a *chain*,

$$A = B_1, B_2, \ldots, B_n = B, \tag{6.1}$$

of its elements, each of which, except the last, overlaps its successor.[31] In this case the proper elements of $\mathcal{A}(\mathcal{B})$ are clearly $\{A \cap B, A - B, B - A\}$ and their various combinations, in fact just those sets whose separability is implied by (P1)–(P3) iff $\mathcal{B}$ is separable and $A - B$ strictly essential. In fact this result is true in general as we will see in Theorem 4 below.

Call the elements $P_1, \ldots, P_s$ of the partition $\mathcal{P}(\mathcal{B})$ of the *overset*

$$\Omega(\mathcal{B}) = \bigcup_{B \in \mathcal{B}} B \tag{6.2}$$

of a proper connected collection $\mathcal{B}$, found by superimposing the partitions $\{B, \Omega(\mathcal{B}) - B\}$, $B \in \mathcal{B}$, the *parts* of $\mathcal{B}$, and

$$\mathcal{R}(\mathcal{B}) = \{C : C = \bigcup_{p \in S} P_p, \text{ some } S \subseteq \{1, \ldots, s\}\} \tag{6.3}$$

the *power collection* of $\mathcal{B}$.[32] We then have

THEOREM 4: *If a separable connected collection $\mathcal{B}$ contains an overlapping pair of elements A, B whose difference $A - B$ is strictly essential,* (P1)–(P3) *imply that $\mathcal{A}(\mathcal{B})$ is separable.*

PROOF OF THEOREM 4: I will proceed by proving a sequence of Lemmas.

[31] Let us ban empty connected collections. The *trivial* connected collections are then those containing only one element.

[32] In normal terminology, $\mathcal{R}(\mathcal{B})$ is the power collection of $\mathcal{P}(\mathcal{B})$. If $\mathcal{B}$ is trivial, $\mathcal{R}(\mathcal{B}) = \mathcal{B} \cup \{0\}$.

LEMMA 4: *If* $\mathcal{B}$ *is connected and* $0 \subset \mathcal{C} \subset \mathcal{B}$, *there are an overlapping pair* $A \in \mathcal{C}$, $B \in \mathcal{B} - \mathcal{C}$

PROOF: A chain linking $C \in \mathcal{C}$ with $D \in \mathcal{B} - \mathcal{C}$ has a first element in $\mathcal{B} - \mathcal{C}$. Call it B and its predecessor A.

LEMMA 5: *If* $\mathcal{B}$ *is connected and* $A, B \in \mathcal{B}$ *overlap, we can write* $\mathcal{B} = \{B_1, \ldots, B_k\}$, *say, where* $B_1 = A$, $B_2 = B$ *and each* $\mathcal{B}_j = \{B_1, B_2, B_{j-1}\}$ *is connected.*

PROOF: $\mathcal{B}_1$ and $\mathcal{B}_2$ are clearly connected. Suppose $\mathcal{B}_j$ is, some $2 \leqslant j < k$. According to Lemma 4, $\mathcal{B} - \mathcal{B}_j$ contains an element which overlaps an element of $\mathcal{B}_j$, and is therefore linked to all of them. Call it $\mathcal{B}_{j+1}$. $\mathcal{B}_{j+1}$ is connected.

LEMMA 6: *Theorem* 4 *holds if* $\mathcal{A}(\mathcal{B})$ *is replaced by* $\mathcal{R}(\mathcal{B})$.

PROOF: I will proceed by an induction on the number n of elements of $\mathcal{B}$.

Lemma 6 follows immediately from Theorem 1 when $n = 2$. I will assume it for $n = k - 1$ and prove it for $n = k$.

Define $\mathcal{C} = \mathcal{B}_{k-1}$ in the notation of Lemma 5. The inductive hypothesis implies that $\mathcal{C}$ satisfies Lemma 6, and we wish to prove that $\mathcal{B}$ does too.

Set

$$\mathcal{P}(\mathcal{C}) = \{Q_1, \ldots, Q_t\}, \tag{6.4}$$

so that the elements of $\mathcal{P}(\mathcal{B})$ are the non-empty ones among

$$\Omega(\mathcal{B}) - \Omega(\mathcal{C}) = B_k - \Omega(\mathcal{C}), \tag{6.5a}$$

$$Q_p - B_k, \text{ each } p, \tag{6.5b}$$

$$Q_p \cap B_k, \text{ each } p. \tag{6.5c}$$

I will first show that each of these and

$$\Omega(\mathcal{B}) \tag{6.6}$$

are separable and so strictly essential.

(6.6) implies, of course, that we can talk of components relative to $\Omega(\mathcal{B})$, while their definition implies that parts $P_1, \ldots, P_s$ of $\mathcal{B}$ may be taken as sectors and that they are the only components of $\mathcal{B}$ relative to $\Omega(\mathcal{B})$. Because of Lemma 2, the separability of the elements in (6.5*a*), (6.5*b*), and (6.6) is therefore all that is required to prove the lemma.

I will now prove that these elements are all separable.

Note first that $Q_p - B_k$ is certainly separable unless Q_p and B_k overlap, and $B_k - \Omega(\mathscr{C})$ if $B_k \subseteq \Omega(\mathscr{C})$. Since

$$\Omega(\mathscr{C}) \nsubseteq B_k, \tag{6.7}$$

because B_k overlaps some $B_j \in \mathscr{C}$ by Lemma 4, it remains to show that

$$Q_q - B_k \text{ is separable when it is not empty,} \tag{6.8}$$

$$B_k - \Omega(\mathscr{C}) \text{ is separable when it is not empty.} \tag{6.9}$$

This I will now do.

Suppose first that B_k intersects each of the parts Q_p of $\mathscr{C}$. Since it overlaps some $B_j \in \mathscr{C}$, it overlaps at least one Q_p. Suppose it overlaps Q_q. Then $B_k - Q_q$ contains each other $B_k \cap Q_q$ which, being the intersection of separable sets by the inductive hypothesis, is separable and hence strictly essential. Hence $B_k - Q_q$ is strictly essential and so, by Theorem 1, $Q_q - B_k$ is separable, proving (6.8) in this case. Moreover $\Omega(\mathscr{C}) - B_k \supseteq Q_q - B_k$, which, being separable is strictly essential. Since $\Omega(\mathscr{C})$ is separable by the inductive hypothesis this immediately implies (6.9) too. This completes the proof of Lemma 6 in this case.

Suppose next that B_k does not intersect each Q_p, so that some

$$Q_r \subseteq \Omega(\mathscr{C}) - B_k. \tag{6.10}$$

$\Omega(\mathscr{C}) - B_k$ is therefore strictly essential, implying (6.9) by Theorem 1. When B_k overlaps some Q_q, two cases arise. If $B_k - \Omega(\mathscr{C}) \neq 0$, it is strictly essential by (6.9), so that $B_k - Q_q \subseteq B_k - \Omega(\mathscr{C})$ is strictly essential too, and $Q_q - B_k$ therefore separable. If

$$B_k - \Omega(\mathscr{C}) = 0,$$

B_k must intersect another part Q_r of $\mathscr{C}$, since it overlaps a $B_j \in \mathscr{C}$. Hence $B_k - Q_q \supseteq B_k \cap Q_r$ which is separable and therefore strictly essential. Hence Theorem 1 implies once more that $Q_q - B_k$ is separable, completing the proof of the lemma.

LEMMA 7: *$\mathscr{A}(\mathscr{B}) = \mathscr{R}(\mathscr{B}) \cup \{\Omega\} = \mathscr{D}(\mathscr{B})$, say.*

PROOF: Lemma 6 immediately implies

$$\mathscr{A}(\mathscr{B}) \supseteq \mathscr{D}(\mathscr{B}). \tag{6.11}$$

If now C, $D \in \mathscr{D}(\mathscr{B})$ and overlap, they are the unions of parts of $\mathscr{B}$. So therefore are their differences, union, etc., which therefore belong to $\mathscr{D}(\mathscr{B})$ also. Since 0, $\Omega \in \mathscr{D}(\mathscr{B})$, it is complete. It clearly contains $\mathscr{B}$. Hence

$$\mathscr{A}(\mathscr{B}) \subseteq \mathscr{D}(\mathscr{B}). \tag{6.12}$$

(6.11) and (6.12) prove Lemma 7. Substituting into Lemma 6, we prove Theorem 4.

Define now the *nucleus* and *periphery*

$$N(\mathcal{B}) = \bigcap_{B \in \mathcal{B}} B, \quad P(\mathcal{B}) = \Omega(\mathcal{B}) - N(\mathcal{B}) \tag{6.13}$$

of a collection $\mathcal{B}$, and say that a proper connected collection is a *tangle*, or *tangled collection*, if its nucleus is empty, and a *star*, or *star collection*, if it is not. There are then three distinct types of connected collection: trivial—with one or no elements—star, and tangled. We have

COROLLARY TO THEOREM 4: *If* $\mathcal{B}$ *is a tangled collection*, (P1)–(P3) *imply that* $\mathcal{A}(\mathcal{B})$ *is separable.*

PROOF: Clearly $N(\mathcal{C}) = \bigcap_{B \in \mathcal{C}} \mathcal{B}$ is separable, each $0 \subset \mathcal{C} \subseteq \mathcal{B}$. Since $N(\mathcal{B}) = 0$ there is at least one collection $\mathcal{C}$ for which $N(\mathcal{C}) \neq 0$, $N(\mathcal{D}) = 0$, each $\mathcal{D} \supset \mathcal{C}$. According to Lemma 4 there is an overlapping pair $A \in \mathcal{C}$, $B \in \mathcal{B} - \mathcal{C}$. $A - B \supseteq N(\mathcal{C})$ which being separable, is strictly essential. Hence $A - B$ is strictly essential; proving the corollary.

To apply this analysis to a general separable collection $\mathcal{B}$, one breaks it down into connected pieces.

Say of two elements A, B of $\mathcal{B}$, that they are *joined in* $\mathcal{B}$ if $A = B$, or they are linked in $\mathcal{B}$. 'Being joined in $\mathcal{B}$' is an equivalence relation and so partitions $\mathcal{B}$ into equivalence classes or *pieces*,

$$\mathcal{B}^t, \; t \in T, \text{ say,} \tag{6.14}$$

with the property that elements in the same piece are joined while those in different pieces are not. Pieces are connected collections, indeed maximal connected collections in the obvious sense of the word. They may, of course, be trivial connected collections, containing only one element, but as elements of a partition, they cannot be empty.

THEOREM 5: *If* $\mathcal{B}^t$, $t \in T$, *are the pieces of* $\mathcal{B}$,

$$\mathcal{A}(\mathcal{B}) = \bigcup_{t \in T} \mathcal{A}(\mathcal{B}_t). \tag{6.15}$$

PROOF: Since $\mathcal{A}(\mathcal{B}) \supseteq \mathcal{A}(\mathcal{B}^t)$,

$$\mathcal{A}(\mathcal{B}) \supseteq \bigcup_{t \in T} \mathcal{A}(\mathcal{B}^t) = \mathcal{D}, \text{ say.} \tag{6.16}$$

I will now show that

$$\mathscr{D} \supseteq \mathscr{A}(\mathscr{B}), \tag{6.17}$$

also, thus proving (6.15). To do so, note that $\mathscr{D} \supseteq$ each $\mathscr{B}^t$. Hence $\mathscr{D} \supseteq \mathscr{B}$. It is also complete: it certainly contains 0, Ω, and if C, $D \in \mathscr{D}$ overlap, they both belong to the same $\mathscr{A}(\mathscr{B}^t)$, so that their union, differences, etc., do so too. Since $\mathscr{A}(\mathscr{B})$ is the intersection of the complete collections containing $\mathscr{B}$, this implies (6.17). With (6.16) this proves the theorem.

COROLLARY:

$$\mathscr{A}(\mathscr{B}) = \{\Omega\} \cup \left(\bigcup_{t \in T} \mathscr{R}(\mathscr{B}^t) \right). \tag{6.18}$$

(6.18) is a simple recipe for calculating $\mathscr{A}(\mathscr{B})$.

First one finds the pieces $\mathscr{B}^t$, $t \in T$ of $\mathscr{B}$. Since it is easy to see whether sets overlap, this is easily done. Then one finds the parts of the proper pieces. This is again easily done.

Consider now the collection $\mathscr{F}(\mathscr{B})$ composed of the oversets $\Omega(\mathscr{B}^t)$, $t \in T$, and the parts of the proper pieces, together with Ω and 0. Since none of its elements overlap, it is complete, and its structure, as defined in Section 3, is easily discovered.

So far there are no overlapping subcollections. However this is easily corrected. If an overset corresponds to a proper piece $\mathscr{B}^t$, $\mathscr{R}(\mathscr{B}^t)$ is overlapping. Mark $\Omega(\mathscr{B}^t)$ with a a +. All other nodes are disjoint.[33]

Clearly such a diagram exhausts all the information in $\mathscr{A}(\mathscr{B})$. Figure 12.3 is the analogue of Figure 12.1 in Section 3.[34] How to transform one into the other is obvious.

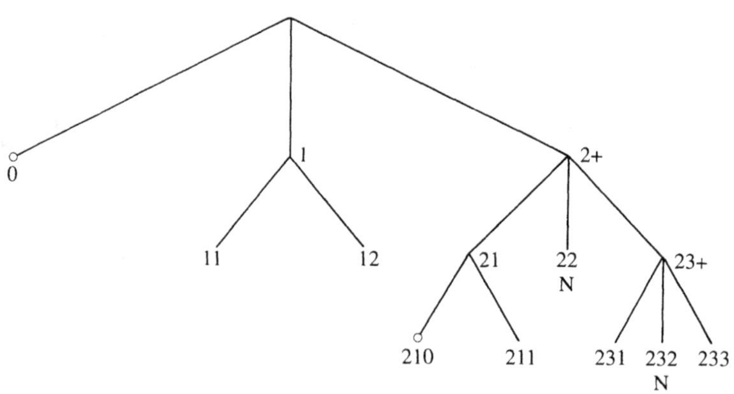

FIG. 12.3:

[33] The only element of a trivial complete collection intersects no other, nor does a part of a proper complete collection.

[34] Except for the N's which I will explain below.

There remains the difficulty that we have not assumed strict essentiality. As we have already seen, it is implied except possibly in the case of star pieces[35] of $\mathcal{B}$. For such, mark the nucleus with an N as in Figure 12.3.[36] We then have merely to see whether any peripheral part of the star piece in question is strictly essential by virtue of having a separable subset, as has Ω^{21} in Figure 12.3. Clearly we need only worry about *bottom star pieces*, that is, those such as $\mathcal{B}^{23}$ in Figure 12.3, none of whose peripheral elements contains an element of $\mathcal{B}$, or, equivalently of $\mathcal{A}(\mathcal{B})$.

What happens in such cases is discussed somewhat cursorily in Gorman (1967*b*). To discuss it fully would require several new concepts, quite a lot of space, and more of the reader's time than I feel justified in asking for at this stage.

[35] A star piece is a piece which is a star.

[36] I am assuming that $\mathcal{B}^2$ and $\mathcal{B}^{23}$ in the obvious notation are both stars rather than tangles.

Appendix

Debreu's results quoted in (1.6) and (1.7) of Section 1 underlie all my analysis in the slightly more general forms given below. He states but does not prove (1.6) in Debreu (1960), and his proof of (1.7), which follows almost immediately from Theorem 1, is difficult. Hence this Appendix.

LEMMA 1:[37] *If* $\{\Omega_0, \Omega_1, \ldots, \Omega_m\}$, $(y_0, y_1, \ldots, y_m)$ *are corresponding partitions of* Ω, x, (P1)–(P2) *imply that we can write*

$$U(x) = F(y_0, U_1(y_1), \ldots, U_m(y_m)), \tag{A.1}$$

where

$$F(y_0, \cdot) \text{ is strictly increasing,}^{38} \tag{A.2}$$

iff

$$\Omega_i \text{ is separable,} \qquad i = 1, 2, \ldots, m. \tag{A.3}$$

If so, we can take

$$U_i(y_i) = U(0, \ldots, 0, y_i, 0, \ldots); \quad U_i(0) = U(0) = 0, \qquad i = 1, \ldots, m, \tag{A.4}$$

without loss of generality, in which case

$$F(\cdot) \text{ is continuous.} \tag{A.5}$$

PROOF: (A.1)–(A.2) $\Rightarrow$ (A.3): obvious.

(A.3) $\Rightarrow$ (A.1)–(A.2). Take a continuous utility function $U(\cdot)$, normalize trivially to get $U(0) = 0$, and define the subutility functions as in (A.4).[39] Take $x', x'' \in S$. Move each y_i in turn from y_i' to y_i'', holding y_j, $j \neq i$ constant while doing so. The definition of separability in Section 1 implies that

$$y_0' = y_0'', \; U_i(y_i), \; U_i(y_i''), \; i = 1, \ldots, m \Rightarrow U(x') = U(x''). \tag{A.6}$$

$$y_0' = y_0'', \; U_i(y_i') \geqslant U_i(y_i''), \; i = 1, \ldots, m, \text{ with at least one strict inequality}$$
$$\Rightarrow U(x') > U(x''). \tag{A.7}$$

(A.6) is equivalent to (A.1), and hence (A.7) to (A.2).

[37] I am grateful to Kenneth Arrow for showing me how to streamline my original clumsy proof.
[38] $F(y_0, \cdot)$ *strictly increasing*: $F(y_0, U_1, \ldots, U_m)$ strictly increasing in $(U_1, U_2, \ldots, U_m)$.
[39] As in (1.4) and (1.5).

(A.1)–(A.4) ⇒ (A.5). Define

$$z = (y_0, U_1, \ldots, U_m) = (y_0, u), \quad Z = T_0 \times J = T_0 \times \prod_{i=1}^{m} J_i, \tag{A.8}$$

where

$$T_i = S_{\Omega_i},^{40} \quad i = 0, \ldots, m; \quad J_i = \text{range of } U_i(y_i), \qquad i = 1, \ldots, m. \tag{A.9}$$

I will prove $F(\cdot)$ continuous at $z \in \text{Int } z$. Only trivial modifications are required at the frontier.[41]

Let then

$$z^t \to z \in \text{Int } Z, \qquad \text{each } z^t \in Z, \tag{A.10}$$

and choose

$$y_i', y_i'' \in T_i, \text{ such that } U_i(y_i') < U_i < U_i(y_i''), \qquad i = 1, \ldots, m, \tag{A.11}$$

$$C_i \text{ an arc in } T_i \text{ connecting } y_i' \text{ to } y_i'', \quad i = 1, \ldots, m. \tag{A.12}$$

Ultimately

$$U_i(y_i') < U_i^t < U_i(y_i''), \qquad i = 1, \ldots, m, \quad t \geqslant T, \text{ say.} \tag{A.13}$$

Since the $U_i(\cdot)$ are continuous, we can find

$$y_i^t \in C_i \text{ such that } U_i(y_i^t) = U_i^t, \qquad i = 1, \ldots, m, \; t \geqslant T, \tag{A.14}$$

so that

$$(y_1^t, \ldots, y_m^t) \in \prod_{i=1}^{m} C_i = C, \text{ say,} \tag{A.15}$$

which is compact since each C_i is a homeomorphism of [0, 1]. Since $y_0^t \to y_0$ this implies that $\{x^t\}$[42] has a convergent subsequence. On any convergent subsequence of $\{x^t\}$,

$$F(z^t) = U(x^t) \to U(x) = F(z), \tag{A.16}$$

by the continuity of $U(\cdot)$, $U_1(\cdot), \ldots, U_m(\cdot)$, x being the limit point of the particular subsequence. Suppose now that $F(z^t) \nrightarrow F(z)$ in the full sequence $\{z^t\}$. Then there is an $\varepsilon > 0$ and a subsequence such that

$$|F(z^t) - F(z)| > \varepsilon, \tag{A.17}$$

40 i.e. $T_i = \bigcup_{j \in \Omega_i} S_j$. See (1.3).

41 If U_i is at the upper limit of J_i for instance, take $y_i'' \in T_i$ such that $U_i(y_i'') = U_i$. If J_i is degenerate—that is, Ω_i is inessential—take $y_i' = y_i'$ such that $U_i(y_i'))$, in which case each $y_i^t = y_i'$.

42 $x^t = (y_0^t, y_1^t, \ldots, y_m^t)$, of course.

on the subsequence in question. The corresponding subsequence of $\{x^t\}$ itself has a convergent subsequence. Hence $F(z^t) \to (F(z)$ for the subsequence of $\{z^t\}$ corresponding to this last, contradicting (A.17). Hence

$$F(z^t) \to F(z) \text{ on the full sequence.} \tag{A.18}$$

LEMMA 2: *If* $\{\Omega_1, \ldots, \Omega_m\}$, $(y_1, \ldots, y_m)$ *are corresponding partitions of* Ω, x, *and* $m \geqslant 3$, (P1), (P2) *and* (P4) *imply that we can write*

$$U(x) = \sum U_i(y_i) \tag{A.19}$$

in an appropriate normalization, iff

$$C_I = \bigcup_{i \in I} \Omega_i \text{ is separable, each } I \subseteq \Phi = \{1, 2, \ldots, m\}. \tag{A.20}$$

PROOF: (A.19) $\Rightarrow$ (A.20): obvious.

(A.20) $\Rightarrow$ (A.10): Let

$$\{I, J\}; \quad \{I', I''\}; \quad \{J', J''\} \text{ be partitions of } \Phi;\ I;\ J. \tag{A.21}$$

Then Theorem 1 and (A.4) imply that we can represent the preference ordering by either of the continuous utility functions[43]

$$U(x) = U_{I'}(y_{I'}) + U_{I''}(y_{I''}) + U_J(y_J) = U_I(y_I) + U_J(y_J), \tag{A.22}$$

$$V(x) = V_I(y_I) + V_{J'}(y_{J'}) + V_{J''}(y_{J''}) + V_I(y_I) + V_J(y_J), \tag{A.23}$$

in possibly different normalizations,[44] each consistent with (A.4). Now

$$V = F(U); \quad F(\cdot) \text{ continuous and strictly increasing.}^{45} \tag{A.24}$$

Hence, by (A.4)

$$F(U_I + U_J) = V_I + V_J = F(U_I) + F(U_J). \tag{A.25}$$

Since U_I, U_J range over non-degenerate intervals containing the origin, (A.24)–(A.25) imply

$$F(U) = \lambda U, \qquad \lambda > 0, \tag{A.26}$$

on the entire range of U. It is trivial[46] to normalize V so that $\lambda = 1$ and

$$U_J = U_{J'} + U_{J''}. \tag{A.27}$$

[43] Take $A = C_I$, $B = C_{I'' \cup J}$ as defined in (A.20) for (A.22), $A = C_{I \cup J'}$, $B = C_J$ for (A.23).

[44] Theorem 1 implies that the utility function can be put in the form $F_{I', I'', J}(u(y_{I'}) + v(y_{I''}) + w(y_J))$ for instance, where $F(\cdot)$ is continuous and strictly increasing.

[45] The proof that (A.1) – (A.4) $\Rightarrow$ (A.5) in Lemma 1 implies that $F(\cdot)$ is continuous and strictly increasing here.

[46] And unnecessary as it happens.

This really completes the proof, since it obviously permits us to split Φ into smaller and smaller pieces, until, ultimately, we get down to the individual Ω_i. For formal completeness however, let us make the inductive hypothesis

$$U = U_1 + U_2 + \ldots + U_k + U_J, \qquad J = \{k+1, \ldots, m\}, \tag{A.28}$$

which holds for $k = 2$ by (A.22) with $I' = \{1\}$, $I'' = \{2\}$ and implies

$$U = U_1 + U_2 + \ldots + U_{k+1} + U_{J''}, \qquad J'' = \{k+2, \ldots, m\}, \tag{A.29}$$

by (A.27) with $I' = \{1, 2, \ldots, k-1\}$, $I'' = \{k\}$, $J' = \{k+1\}$. Hence (A.28) holds for all $k \geqslant 2$, and hence for $k = m$, which is (A.19).

13

Conditions for Generalized Additive Separability

Editorial Remarks

This paper is a straightforward elaboration of a referee report on a paper by Robert Pollak which was eventually published in *Econometrica* (Pollak 1972). Gorman wrote the paper in a hurry because Pollak's paper could not be published until there was a paper to which Pollak could refer; Pollak used many results from the referee report. Pollak refers to this paper as forthcoming in *Econometrica*, but there is no evidence in the files that it was ever submitted.

The following summary was kindly provided by Peter Simmons, who published an extension of this paper in Simmons (1978).

Editorial Summary

In this paper Gorman explores the restrictions on preferences arising from Pollak's notion of generalized additive separability. Pollak essentially defines a generalization of separability as a restriction on the form of the demand curves; shows that it is a true generalization; and in some special cases finds the corresponding restrictions on direct and indirect utility. This leaves open the question of the general form of preferences implied by the demand-function restrictions, and it this question that Gorman addresses.

In many ways this paper needs no reader's guide because Gorman already provides this in the first section of the paper. Generalized additive separability holds if the demand function for each good can be written in the form

$$x_i = f^i(y_i, R(y)), \tag{0.1}$$

where $y_i = p_i/m$ is the income normalized price of good i. Gorman transforms this to the equivalent budget share restriction

$$y_i x_i = \frac{p_i x_i}{m} = g^i(z_i, T(z)) \tag{0.2}$$

where $z_i = \log y_i$.

In Section 1 he introduces the idea of the abnormal case of (0.2) in which, for all goods,

$$y_i x_i = \bar{g}^i(T(z)). \tag{0.3}$$

He then builds up special cases of utility functions which satisfy this, terminating in the general result given in equations (1.15)–(1.17), where the indirect utility function depends only on two linear homogeneous functions of the z's.

In the rest of Section 1, he considers the normal case in which at least one budget share depends on both z_i and $T(\cdot)$. He starts by showing that indirect additivity is a special case of the main case stated in Pollak's paper, in which the indirect utility has the form

$$v = \sum F^i(z_i + \phi(T)) - G(T). \tag{0.4}$$

He then shows that three other cases work:

$$v = G(z_1, z_2) + \sum a_i z_i; \tag{0.5}$$

$$v = G\left(z_i, \sum B_i e^{bz_i}\right); \tag{0.6}$$

and a kind of non-homothetic CES case defined by the indirect distance function

$$\sum \psi^i(v) e^{\phi(v) z_i} = 1. \tag{0.7}$$

Section 2 gives the general formal analysis of the normal case. The key result is equation (2.15). So long as there are more than three goods the solution of this equation requires discussion of five cases, differing mainly in the degree of dependence amongst the derivatives of the demands. For each of these the indirect utility function is derived. The general message is that either the Pollak case (0.4) holds, or else there are cases (0.5)–(0.7) based on Cobb–Douglas/CES generalizations.

Section 3 contains the formal analysis for the abnormal case. Again this is broken down into various cases depending on the degree of functional dependence between the demand functions. This section also contains a very interesting argument that the two direct utility functions

$$u = K\left(\sum a_i \log x_i, \sum b_i \log x_i\right) \tag{0.8}$$

and

$$u = \max\left\{L\left(\sum a_i \log \bar{x}_i, \sum b_i \log \hat{x}_i\right) \middle| \bar{x} + \hat{x} = x\right\} \tag{0.9}$$

are equivalent, in that they represent identical preferences.

Appendix A proves that if the budget shares depend only on a subset of the income-normalized prices then the indirect utility is the sum of a function of the logs of these normalized prices and a linear function of the logs of the remaining normalized prices. This follows because the Cobb–Douglas is the only case with constant budget shares.

Appendix B shows the connection between (0.8) and (0.9) and also derives the indirect utilities for these. This is of general interest, being used, for example, in Muellbauer's (1976) generalized linearity idea and Blackorby and Schworm's (1984*a*) aggregation results.

Conditions for Generalized Additive Separability

1. THE PROBLEM AND ITS SOLUTIONS

Professor Pollak (1972) introduces the consumption vector $X = (x_1, \ldots, x_n)$ and the vector $Y = (y_1, \ldots, y_n)$ of prices p_i/m, in the usual notation, quoted as proportions of income, so that

$$X \cdot Y = \sum x_i y_i = 1. \tag{1.1}$$

He says that a system of demand equations exhibits generalized additive separability if it can be thrown into the form

$$x_i = f^i(y_i, R(Y)), \qquad \text{each } i. \tag{1.2}$$

I address myself to the following questions: When is such a system of demand equations derivable from a consistent preference field? What is the corresponding utility function?

In the present section I will discuss some examples of generalized additive separability, in the next carry out the main analysis, and in Section 3 discuss the special case where the budget shares $g^i = y_i x_i = p_i x_i/m$ depend only on R. Two special topics are taken up in the appendices.

The analysis is considerably simpler when carried out in terms of the budget shares,

$$g^i = x_i y_i = y_i f^i = g^i(z_i, T(Z)), \qquad \text{each } i, \tag{1.3}$$

where

$$z_i = \log y_i, \quad Z = (z_1, \ldots, z_n), \quad T(Z) = R(Y). \tag{1.4}$$

In this notation, (1.1) becomes

$$\sum g^i(z_i, T) = 1. \tag{1.5}$$

This may be an equation in (Z, T), implicitly defining $T = T(Z)$, or an identity in (Z, T), in which case T must be defined as a function of Z already—in fact from the underlying preference ordering. In the latter case changing z_i would not change the left-hand side of the identity (1.5). Hence

$$g^i = \phi^i(T), \qquad \text{each } i, \tag{1.6}$$

where

$$\sum \phi^i(T) \equiv 1. \tag{1.7}$$

Let us call a good for which $g^i = \phi^i(T)$ *abnormal*. It is this special case in which all the goods are abnormal which I discuss in Section 3, having first cleared up that in which at least one good is normal in Section 2.

The simplest special case arises from the Cobb–Douglas utility function

$$u = \prod x_i^{a_i}, \quad \sum a_i = 1, \tag{1.8}$$

where the budget shares are, of course,

$$g^i = a_i. \tag{1.9}$$

The indirect utility function corresponding to (1.8) is of the form $u = A\prod y_i^{-a_i}$, yielding the indirect disutility function

$$v = \log A - \log u = \sum a_i z_i, \tag{1.10}$$

defined in terms of the logarithms of the normalized prices, which gives the usual equilibrium conditions

$$\begin{aligned} \lambda g^i &= v_i,^1 \\ &= a_i, \end{aligned} \tag{1.11}$$

where *suffixes denote differentiation, both here and below*, so that

$$\lambda = \lambda \sum g^i = \sum a_i = 1, \tag{1.12}$$

by (1.5), and hence (1.9) again.

I hope that this formal analysis of a well-known case will make the discussion below easier to understand.

(1.6) also holds automatically if there are only two goods. To see this, write

$$\begin{aligned} g^1 &= \psi(z_1, z_2), \text{ say,} \\ &= T(z_1, z_2), \end{aligned} \tag{1.13}$$

so that

$$g^2 = 1 - T(z_1, z_2) \tag{1.14}$$

and $g^1 + g^2 = 1$.

These two examples suggest a third, which contains both. Suppose that

$$u = \max\{F(\bar{w}, \bar{\bar{w}}) \mid \bar{x}_1 + \bar{\bar{x}} \leq x_i \text{ each } i\}, \tag{1.15}$$

where

[1] $v_i = \partial v/\partial z_i = \partial v/\partial \log y_i = \partial v/\partial \log p_i = p_i \partial v/\partial p_i = -\mu p_i x_i$, where μ is the marginal utility of income. $\mu = \lambda$ when income $m = 1$. Thus λ is the marginal utility of income in the normalization (1.1).

$$\bar{w} = \prod \bar{x}_i^{a_i}, \quad \bar{\bar{w}} = \prod \bar{\bar{x}}_i^{b_i}, \quad \sum a_i = \sum b_i = 1, \tag{1.16}$$

so that the same good may be used to minister to either of two needs, but the same unit of it cannot minister to both at once. Then, as is shown in Appendix B, the indirect disutility function may be written

$$v = H\left(\sum a_i z_i, \sum b_i z_i\right), \tag{1.17}$$

reflecting the fact that the shadow price of the same good will be the same in ministering to each need. Hence

$$\lambda g^i = v_i = H_1 a_i + H_2 b_i, \tag{1.18}$$

$$\lambda = \lambda \sum g^i = H_1 + H_2. \tag{1.19}$$

Define

$$T = H_2/(H_1 + H_2), \tag{1.20}$$

the proportion of the budget spent on satisfying the second need, i.e. $\bar{\bar{x}}$, to get

$$g^i = a_i(1 - T) + b_i T = \phi^i(T), \tag{1.21}$$

$$\sum \phi^i(T) \equiv 1. \tag{1.22}$$

We will see in Section 3 that this is the most general utility function satisfying (1.6) everywhere.

What happens in it, of course, is that the proportion of expenditure devoted to the two macro-goods $\bar{w}$, $\bar{\bar{w}}$ depends only on T, while the proportionate breakdown, within each, between the actual goods, is constant.

Turn now to the case in which there is at least one normal good. The most obvious example here is that of an indirectly additively separable disutility function

$$v = \sum f^i(z_i), \qquad z_i = \log p_i/w, \tag{1.23}$$

yielding

$$\lambda g^i = \dot{f}^i, \tag{1.24}$$

a point above a functional symbol denoting differentiation with respect to its sole argument both here and throughout this paper. Then, since $\sum g^i = 1$,

$$\lambda = \sum \dot{f}^i = T, \text{ say}, \tag{1.25}$$

so that

$$g^i = \dot{f}^i(z_i)/T, \tag{1.26}$$

T being determined by (1.5) as we should have expected.

It can reasonably be said that the main class of generalized additively separable demand equations is a generalization of indirect additivity.

Professor Pollak has shown that one of the solutions derived in Section 2 may be regarded as a generalization of indirect additivity. This is

$$g^i = \Psi^i(z_i + \phi(T))/\Theta(T), \qquad \text{each } i, \tag{1.27}$$

where T is implicitly defined by

$$\Theta(T) = \sum \Psi^i(z_i + \phi(T)). \tag{1.28}$$

As Professor Pollak has shown, this can be derived from an indirect disutility function

$$v = \sum F^i(z_i + \phi(T)) - G(T), \tag{1.29}$$

where

$$\dot{F}^i(z_i + \phi(T)) = \Psi^i(z_i + \phi(T)), \tag{1.30}$$

$$\dot{G}(T) = \Theta(T)\dot{\phi}(T). \tag{1.31}$$

This is because we certainly have

$$\begin{aligned} \lambda g^i &= \dot{F}^i + \left(\dot{\phi}\sum \dot{F}^j - \dot{G}\right) \\ &= \dot{F}^i = \Psi^i, \end{aligned} \tag{1.32}$$

by (1.3), (1.23), (1.24), (1.28), and (1.29). We get (1.26) immediately from (1.27).

The remaining cases can be constructed in the same general manner as those at the beginning of this section.

Suppose that

$$T = T(z_1, z_2), \tag{1.33}$$

for some reason. We can then solve to get

$$z_2 = \psi^2(z_1, T), \quad z_1 = \psi^1(z_2, T),^2 \tag{1.34}$$

and thus express any function $\theta(z_1, z_2)$ as

$$\begin{aligned} \theta(z_1, z_2) &= \theta(z_1, \psi^2(z_1, T)) = \theta^1(z_1, T), \text{ say,} \\ &= \theta^2(z_2, T), \text{ similarly.} \end{aligned} \tag{1.35}$$

Suppose now that we have three goods and that the division of the budget between them depends only on z_1, z_2. We can define one of these shares, say

[2] I assume that behaviour is good enough for local solvability to be all that is required.

g^3, as T, and get $g^1 = g^1(z_1, T)$, $g^2 = g^2(z_2, T)$ in this manner. In fact it is easily shown that the budget shares depend on z_1, z_2 iff the utility function can be written

$$u = F(x_1, x_2)x_3. \tag{1.36}$$

In general, this suggests we might replace x_3 by a Cobb–Douglas aggregate to get

$$u = F(x_1, x_2)\prod_{i>2} x_i^{a_i}, \quad \sum a_i = 1. \tag{1.37}$$

In the same construction as before, $T = T(z_1, z_2)$ will be the share of this aggregate in total expenditure, a_iT that of good i, $i > 2$.

To check this, we replace u by the indirect disutility function

$$v = -\log u = G(z_1, z_2) + \prod_{i>2} a_i z_i, \tag{1.38}$$

to get

$$\lambda g^1 = G_1, \quad \lambda g^2 = G_2, \quad \lambda g^i = a_i, \qquad \text{each } i > 2, \tag{1.39}$$

$$\lambda = G_1 + G_2 + 1 = 1/T, \text{ say}, \tag{1.40}$$

$$g^i = a_i T, \quad i > 2, \tag{1.41}$$

as required.

These examples depend on the Cobb–Douglas form. What of its immediate generalization, the CES? We will see that it generates a pair of interesting special cases.

Consider then a CES utility function

$$u = \sum A_i x_i^a, \tag{1.42}$$

to which there corresponds an indirect disutility function

$$v = \sum B_i e^{bz_i},[3] \tag{1.43}$$

yielding

$$\lambda g^i = bB_i e^{bz_i}, \tag{1.44}$$

$$\lambda = b\sum B_i e^{bz_i} = bv, \tag{1.45}$$

so that

$$g^i = B_i e^{bz_i}/v. \tag{1.46}$$

[3] $(a-1)(b-1) = 1$, $B_i = A_i^{1-b}$, $v = u^{1-b}$.

In this case, therefore, the utility function itself is the aggregate T.

Consider now a utility function of the form

$$u = F(U, x_n), \quad U = \sum_{i<n} A_i x_i^a, \tag{1.47}$$

with the corresponding indirect disutility function

$$v = G(V, z_n), \quad V = \sum_{i<n} B_i e^{bz_i}, \tag{1.48}$$

yielding

$$\lambda g^1 = G_1, \quad \lambda g^i = G_2 b B_i e^{bz_i}, \qquad i > 1, \tag{1.49}$$

$$\lambda = G_1 + bVG_2. \tag{1.50}$$

Define now

$$T = G_2(z_1, V)/(G_1(z_1, V) + VG_2(z_1, V)), \tag{1.51}$$

to get

$$g^1 = 1 - TV, \tag{1.52}$$

$$g^i = TB_i e^{bz_i}, \qquad i > 1. \tag{1.53}$$

Solving (1.51) for V in terms of T, z_1, and substituting into (1.52) and (1.53), we are home and dry.

One obvious generalization of the CES utility function is that defined implicitly by

$$\sum B^i(u) x_i^{\alpha(u)} = 1, \tag{1.54}$$

considered as a generalization of

$$\sum (A_i/u) x_i^a = 1. \tag{1.55}$$

The corresponding indirect disutility function is given by

$$\sum \Psi^i(v) e^{\phi(v) z_i} = 1, \text{ say,} \tag{1.56}$$

and the elasticity of substitution between a pair of goods is $1 - \phi(v)$, constant along an indifference curve, different on different curves.[4]

$$\mu g^i = \Psi^i(v) \exp(\phi(v) z_i), \tag{1.57}$$

where $\mu = \mu \sum g^i = 1$, by (1.56). Hence

$$g^i = \Psi^i(v) \exp(\phi(v) z_i), \tag{1.58}$$

and once again the utility function itself is our aggregate.

[4] It must be lower on higher indifference curves, of course.

We have already seen that generalized additive separability is automatic when there are only two goods. I will therefore assume throughout the remainder of the paper that the number of goods

$$n \geqslant 3. \tag{1.59}$$

In point of fact the exhaustiveness of the case discussed above is proved only for

$$n > 3, \tag{1.60}$$

but I will not assume this for the present.

2. THE NORMAL CASE

In this section and Section 3, I will apply Slutsky's symmetry condition

$$\sigma^{ij} = \sigma^{ji}, \tag{2.1}$$

to the budget shares

$$g^i = g^i(z_i, T(Z)), \qquad \text{each } i, \tag{2.2}$$

defined in (1.3).

σ^{ij} is determined by

$$y_i y_j \sigma^{ij} = g_T^i T_j - \left(g_i^i - g^i + g_T^i \sum T_k\right) g^j, \qquad i \neq j. \tag{2.3}$$

Now

$$\sum g^k(z_k, T(Z)) = 1, \tag{2.4}$$

being budget shares, hence

$$\rho T_j = - g_j^j, \qquad \text{each } j, \tag{2.5}$$

and

$$\sigma \sum T_k = - \sum g_k^k = - \sigma, \text{ say,} \tag{2.6}$$

where

$$\rho = \sum g_T^k, \tag{2.7}$$

subscripts denoting differentiation both here and throughout this paper.

In the present section I will assume

$$\rho \neq 0, \tag{2.8}$$

so that at least one good is normal.[5]

[5] If each $g_j^j = 0$ and $\rho \neq 0$, each $T_j = 0$. Isolated points should not matter. If T is constant over a region, and g^j is independent of z_j, it is constant and we are in the Cobb–Douglas case.

Multiply (2.3) across by $-\rho$ to get

$$-\rho y_i y_j \sigma^{ij} = g_T^i g_j^i + (\rho g_i^i - \rho g^i - \sigma g_T^i) g^j, \qquad i \neq j, \tag{2.9}$$

so that the Slutsky relation $\sigma^{ij} = \sigma^{ji}$ yields

$$(g_j^j - \sigma g^j) g_T^i + \rho g^j g_i^i = (g_i^i - \sigma g^i) g_T^j + \rho g^i g_j^i, \qquad \text{each } i, j,[6] \tag{2.10}$$

or equivalently,

$$(g_j^j - \sigma g^j) g_T^i + (\rho g^j - g_T^j) g_i^j + (\sigma g_T^j - \rho g_j^j) g^i = 0, \qquad \text{each } i, j, \tag{2.11}$$

which may be written

$$\alpha^j g_T^i + \beta^j g_i^i + \gamma^j g^i = 0, \qquad \text{each } i, j. \tag{2.12}$$

Introduce now

$$f^i(z_i, T) = \log g^i(z_i, T),[7] \tag{2.13}$$

so that each (f_T^i, f_i^i) solves the same set of linear equations

$$\alpha^j \xi + \beta^j \eta + \gamma^j = 0, \qquad \text{each } j, \tag{2.14}$$

implying that

$$f_T^i = f_T^1 = \delta^i (f_T^n - f_T^1), \quad f_i^i - f_1^1 = \delta^i (f_n^n - f_1^1), \text{ say}, \qquad \text{each } i, \tag{2.15}$$

where we may take any good as 1. This is the equation underlying the remainder of the analysis in this section.

When there are only three goods, (2.15) is equivalent to

$$\begin{vmatrix} f_T^1 & f_1^1 & 1 \\ f_T^2 & f_2^2 & 1 \\ f_T^3 & f_3^3 & 1 \end{vmatrix} = 0, \tag{2.16}$$

which is easily seen to be equivalent to (2.11).[8]

I have not been able to solve (2.16)—though all the solutions derived below for $n > 3$ certainly fit, there may be others—and hence will assume for the remainder of this section that

$$n > 3. \tag{2.17}$$

Define now

$$S = \{i \mid f_i^i = f_1^1\}, \tag{2.18}$$

and choose the good labelled 1 so that

[6] An identity for $i = j$, of course.

[7] I implicitly assume $g^i = 0$. We divide Z-space into regions according to the goods bought.

[8] Substitute $\rho = \sum g_T^i$, $\sigma = \sum g_i^i$ into $\sigma^{12} = \sigma^{21}$.

$$N(S) = \text{number of goods in } S, \tag{2.19}$$

is as great as possible.

It is now convenient to distinguish four cases, according to the size of $N(S)$.

Case (i): $N(S) = n$.
In this case

$$f_i^i(z_i, T) = f_j^j(z_j, T) = \phi, \text{ say,} \qquad \text{each } i, j, \tag{2.20}$$

so that either

$$\phi = \phi(T), \tag{2.21}$$

or $T = T(z_i, z_j)$, each $i, j, i \neq j$, which is clearly impossible when $n \geqslant 3$. Hence (2.21) holds, and

$$f^i = \phi(T) z_i + \psi^i(T), \text{ say,} \qquad \text{each } i, \tag{2.22}$$

yielding

$$g^i = \Psi^i(T) \exp(\phi(T) z_i), \tag{2.23}$$

where $\sum g^i = 1$ implies

$$\sum \Psi^i(T) \exp(\phi(T) z_i) = 1. \tag{2.24}$$

As we saw in (1.54)–(1.58) this is derivable from the indirect disutility function v yielded by

$$\sum \Psi^i(v) \exp(\phi(v) z_i) = 1, \tag{2.25}$$

so that $T = v$ here.

When $N(S) < n$, $n \notin S$,[9] so that $\delta^i = 0$, each $i \in S$, and $\delta^j \neq 0$, each $j \notin S$. Hence

$$f_i^i = \mu, \quad f_T^i = \nu, \text{ say,} \qquad \text{each } i \in S, \tag{2.26}$$

while

$$\frac{f_T^j - f_T^1}{f_j^j - f_1^1} = \lambda, \text{ say,} \qquad \text{each } j \notin S. \tag{2.27}$$

Within this, three further cases may be distinguished:

Case (ii): $N(S) = 1$, so that $S = \{1\}$.
(2.26) is nugatory while (2.27) becomes

[9] If $n \in S$, so does i by (2.15) and (2.18).

$$\frac{f^j_T - f^i_T}{f^j_j - f^i_i} = \lambda, \qquad \text{each } i, j, i \neq j.^{10} \tag{2.28}$$

Either, then

$$\lambda = \dot{\phi}(T), \text{ say,} \tag{2.29}$$

or $\lambda = \lambda^{ij}(T, z_i, z_j)$, each $i, j, i \neq j$, so that $T = T(z_i, z_j, z_k)$, each i, j, k, which is impossible when there are $n > 3$ goods. This is when we use (2.19).

Hence (2.29) holds. Clearing fractions in (2.28) and differentiating with respect to z_i we therefore have

$$f^i_{Ti} = \dot{\phi} f^i_{ii}, \tag{2.30}$$

so that

$$\mathrm{d}f^i_i = f^i_{ii}(\mathrm{d}z_i + \dot{\phi}\mathrm{d}T), \tag{2.31}$$

and

$$f^i_i = \dot{\psi}^i(z_i + \phi(T)), \text{ say,} \tag{2.32}$$

$$f^i = \psi^i(z_i + \phi(T)) - \theta^i(T), \text{ say,} \qquad \text{each } i. \tag{2.33}$$

Substituting from (2.33) into (2.28) we have $\dot{\theta}^i = \dot{\theta}^j$, so that, with a slight renormalization,

$$f^i = \psi^i(z_i + \phi(T)) - \theta(T), \text{ say,} \tag{2.34}$$

$$g^i = \Psi^i(z_i + \phi(T))/\Theta(T), \tag{2.35}$$

where $\sum g^i = 1$ yields

$$\Theta(T) = \sum \Psi^i(z_i + \phi(T)). \tag{2.36}$$

The indirect disutility function corresponding to (2.35)–(2.36) was discovered by Professor Pollak. It is given in (1.29).

Case (iii): $N(S) = 2$, $S = \{1, 2\}$, say.
(2.26) implies that either

$$f^i_T = \dot{\theta}(T), \quad f^i_i = \psi(T), \text{ say,} \qquad \text{each } i \in S, \tag{2.37}$$

or

$$T = T(z_1, z_2). \tag{2.38}$$

(2.37) will be discussed in case (iv). According to (2.2), (2.38) implies

[10] $f^i_i \neq f^j_j$, $i \neq j$, because good 1 was chosen to make S as large as possible, and S has only one element here.

$$g^j = \phi^j(T), \qquad j > 2. \tag{2.39}$$

As we will see in Appendix A, this implies

$$v = G(z_1, z_2) + \sum_{i>2} a_i z_i, \tag{2.40}$$

in an appropriate normalization. This is (1.38), which we showed to work there.

Case (iv): $n > N(S) \geqslant 3$.

(2.26) implies (2.37) by the sort of argument to which the reader should by now be accustomed. Moreover, for each $i \in S$, $\dot{\psi} = f^i_{iT} = f^i_{Ti} = 0$. Hence $\psi = b$, say, and (2.37) yields

$$f^i = bz_i + \theta(T) + b_i, \text{ say,} \qquad i \in S, \tag{2.41}$$

$$g^i = \Theta(T) B_i e^{bz_i}, \text{ say,} \qquad i \in S. \tag{2.42}$$

Now, if v is the disutility function,

$$\begin{aligned} dv &= \sum v_i dz_i = \lambda \sum g^i dz_i, \text{ say,} \\ &= \lambda(\Theta) b^{-1} \sum_{i \in S} B_i e^{bz_i} + \sum_{j \notin S} v_j dz_j, \end{aligned} \tag{2.43}$$

so that

$$v = G\left(\sum_{i \in S} B_i e^{bz_i}, Z_{\bar{S}}\right), \qquad Z_{\bar{S}} = (z_j)_{j \notin S}. \tag{2.44}$$

When $b = 0$, we get the analogous Cobb–Douglas formula.

Turn now to $\bar{S}$. (2.27) yields

$$h^j_T / h^j_j = h^n_T / h^n_n, \qquad \text{each } j \in S, \tag{2.45}$$

where

$$\begin{aligned} h^j &= f^j - (bz_j + \theta(T)), \qquad \text{each } j \in S, \\ &= h^j(z_j, T). \end{aligned} \tag{2.46}$$

If $N(S) = n - 1$ this is nugatory, $Z_{\bar{S}} = (z_n)$ and (2.44) becomes (1.48) which we have clearly seen to work.

If $N(S) = n - 2$, let $S = \{1, 2, \ldots, n - 2\}$. Then (2.45) yields either

$$T = T(z_n, z_{n-1}), \tag{2.47}$$

which leads straight back to (2.40), with z_n, z_{n-1} in the place of z_1, z_2, because $N(S) = n - 2$ there, as Professor Pollak has pointed out, or

$$h^j_T = \dot{\phi}(T) h^j_j, \qquad j = n - 1, n, \text{ say,} \tag{2.48}$$

so that

$$h^j = \psi^j(z_j + \phi(T)), \qquad j \in S, \tag{2.49}$$

$$\begin{aligned} f^j &= \psi^j(z_j + \phi(T)) + bz_j + \theta(T), \\ &= \psi^j(z_j + \phi(T)) - \tilde{\theta}(T), \qquad j \notin S, \end{aligned} \tag{2.50}$$

with a slight change of notation, where

$$\tilde{\theta}(T) = b\phi(T) - \theta(T), \tag{2.51}$$

so that

$$f^i = b(z_i + \Theta(T)) + \mathrm{d}_i - \tilde{\theta}(T), \qquad i \in S, \tag{2.52}$$

in (2.41), which is of course a special case of (2.50). Looking at (2.50) we see that all this is just a special case of (2.34) which we have already analysed.

We are finally left with $n - 2 > N(S) \geqslant 3$. In that case (2.26) yields (2.37) and hence (2.41), while (2.27) yields (2.49) and hence (2.52), which contains (2.49) as a special case once more, and is itself just (2.44) repeated. Hence we are reduced once more to (2.34), whose indirect disutility function is given in (1.29)–(1.31).

That covers all the possibilities.[11]

3. THE ABNORMAL CASE

When there are no normal goods we can write

$$g^i = \phi^i(T), \qquad \text{each } i, \tag{3.1}$$

with

$$\sum \phi^i(T) = 1. \tag{3.2}$$

Were (3.2) not an identity, it would determine T, and hence each g^i, as a constant.[12] This is the Cobb–Douglas case (1.8) where no T is needed.

From now on I will assume

$$\sum \phi^i(T) \equiv 1, \tag{3.3}$$

so that T has to be determined from outside: in fact from the preference ordering.

In this case $\rho = \sum g^i_T = \sum \dot{\phi}^i \equiv 0$, so that (2.10) becomes $0 \equiv 0$, and cannot form the basis of our analysis. However (2.3) yields

[11] Far from rigorously!

[12] The probability of multiple solutions does not seem worrying here.

$$y_i y_j \sigma^{ij} = \dot{\phi}^i T_j - (\dot{\phi}^i V - \phi^i)\phi^j, \qquad i \neq j, \tag{3.4}$$

where

$$V = \sum T_k, \tag{3.5}$$

so that the Slutsky relation $\sigma^{ij} = \sigma^{ji}$ becomes

$$\dot{\phi}^i (T_j - V\phi^j) = \dot{\phi}^j (T_i - V\phi^i), \qquad \text{each } i, j. \tag{3.6}$$

There are now three possibilities to be faced:

Case (i): Each $\dot{\phi}^k = 0$: the Cobb–Douglas case.
Case (ii): Some but not all $\dot{\phi}^k = 0$.
Let

$$K = \{k \mid \dot{\phi}^k = 0\}, \qquad J = \bar{K}. \tag{3.7}$$

(3.6) immediately yields

$$T_j = V\phi^j, \qquad \text{each } j \in J \tag{3.8}$$

so that

$$\mathrm{d}T = V \sum_{j \in J} \phi^j(T)\mathrm{d}z_j + \sum_{k \in K} T_k \mathrm{d}z_k, \tag{3.9}$$

and

$$\left(1 - V \sum_{j \in J} \dot{\phi}^j z_j\right) \mathrm{d}T = V\mathrm{d}\left(\sum_{j \in J} \phi^j(T) z_j\right) + \sum_{k \in K} T_k \mathrm{d}z_k, \tag{3.10}$$

implying that T is implicitly defined by[13]

$$T = F\left(\sum_{j \in J} \phi^j(T) z_j,\ Z_K\right), \tag{3.11}$$

where

$$Z_J = (z_j)_{j \in J}, \quad Z_K = (z_k)_{k \in K}. \tag{3.12}$$

Suppose now that

$$F(\alpha, \bar{Z}_K) = A, \quad F(\beta, \bar{Z}_K) = B \neq A. \tag{3.13}$$

If the planes

$$\sum_{j \in J} \phi^j(A) z_j = \alpha, \quad \sum_{j \in J} \phi^j(B) z_j = \beta, \tag{3.14}$$

[13] It might be more accurate to say $\psi(T, \sum_{j \in J} \theta^j(T) z_j, Z_k) = 0$. We could work with this instead.

intersect, let $\bar{Z}_J$ be on both. Then $T(\bar{Z}) = A$ and $T(\bar{Z}) = B \neq A$, which is not permitted. Hence the planes in (3.14) do not intersect. They are therefore parallel, *at least if we require (3.1) to hold throughout* R^n. Do so to get

$$\phi^j(T) = b_j\phi(T), \text{ say,} \tag{3.15}$$

so that (3.3) yields

$$\sum_{k\in K} a_k + \phi(T)\sum_{j\in J} b_j \equiv 1. \tag{3.16}$$

We can therefore take $\phi(T)$ = constant without loss of generality,[14] and so are back in the Cobb–Douglas case once more.

Case (iii): No $\dot{\phi}^i = 0$.

(3.6) yields

$$(T_j - V\phi^j)/\dot{\phi}^j = (T_i - V\phi^i)/\dot{\phi}^i = W, \text{ say,} \tag{3.17}$$

so that

$$T_j = V\phi^j + W\dot{\phi}^j, \qquad \text{each } j. \tag{3.18}$$

Considered as a set of linear equations for V, W, these may be either of rank one or rank two. If they are of rank one there exists a vector $\lambda(Z) = (\lambda^1, \ldots, \lambda^n)$ such that

$$T_j = \lambda^j T_1, \quad \phi^j = \lambda^j\phi^1, \quad \dot{\phi}^j = \lambda^j\dot{\phi}^1, \text{ say.} \tag{3.19}$$

The second of these yields $\lambda^j = \phi^j/\phi^1 = \lambda^j(T)$. Differentiating it with respect to T and subtracting the third we get $\dot{\lambda}^j\phi^1 = 0$, so that $\lambda^j = a_j$, say, implying that

$$\phi^j = a_j\phi^1, \tag{3.20}$$

so that we are once more back in the Cobb–Douglas case.

If (3.18) is of rank 2, and ϕ^1, ϕ^2 are independent in the sense that

$$\dot{\phi}^1\phi^2 \neq \dot{\phi}^2\phi^1,\text{[15]} \tag{3.21}$$

there exist

$$\lambda = (\lambda^1, \ldots, \lambda^n), \quad \mu = (\mu^1, \ldots, \mu^n), \tag{3.22}$$

such that

[14] If $\sum b_j \neq 0$, it has to be constant. If $\sum b_j = 0$ it does not matter.

[15] Isolated points should not matter, so (3.21) is more or less equivalent to $\phi^2 \neq k\phi^1$ over a 'solid' region. We might have to change the basis from one region to another. This is one of the things I have not looked into.

$$T_j = \lambda^j T_1 + \mu^j T_2, \tag{3.23}$$

$$\phi^j = \lambda^j \phi^1 + \mu^j \phi^2, \tag{3.24}$$

$$\dot{\phi}^j = \lambda^j \dot{\phi}^1 + \mu^j \dot{\phi}^2. \tag{3.25}$$

(3.24) and (3.25) may be solved for

$$\lambda = \lambda(T), \quad \mu = \mu(T). \tag{3.26}$$

Differentiating (3.24) with respect to T and subtracting (3.25) we get

$$\phi^1 \dot{\lambda}^1 = \phi^2 \dot{\mu}^i = 0, \tag{3.27}$$

while clearly

$$\lambda^1 = \mu^2 = 1, \quad \lambda^2 = \mu^1 = 0. \tag{3.28}$$

According to (3.24),

$$\mathrm{d}T = \sum T_j \mathrm{d}z_j = T_1 \sum \lambda^j(T)\mathrm{d}z_j + T_2 \sum \mu^j(T)\mathrm{d}z_j, \tag{3.29}$$

so that

$$\left(1 - T_1 \sum \dot{\lambda}^j z_j - T_2 \sum \dot{\mu}^j z_j\right)\mathrm{d}T = T_1 \mathrm{d}\left(\sum \lambda^j(T) z_j\right) + T_2 \mathrm{d}\left(\sum \mu^j(T) z_j\right), \tag{3.30}$$

implying that

$$T = F\left(\sum \lambda^j(T) z_j, \sum \mu^j(T) z_j\right).^{16} \tag{3.31}$$

Hence

$$\left(1 - F_1 \sum \dot{\lambda}^j z_j - F_2 \sum \dot{\mu}^j z_j\right)\mathrm{d}T = F_1 \mathrm{d}\left(\sum \lambda^j(T) z_j\right) + F_2 \mathrm{d}\left(\sum \mu^j(T) z_j\right) \tag{3.32}$$

or, using (3.27)

$$\left(1 - (F_1 - F_2 \phi^1/\phi^2) \sum \dot{\lambda}^j z_j\right) = F_1 \mathrm{d}\left(\sum \lambda^j(T) z_j\right) + F_2 \mathrm{d}\left(\sum \mu^j(T) z_j\right). \tag{3.33}$$

Now $\lambda = (1, 0, \ldots)$, $\mu = (0, 1, \ldots)$, $\dot{\lambda} = (0, 0, \ldots)$ so that $\dot{\lambda} = 0$ or is linearly independent of λ, μ.
If $\dot{\lambda} = 0$, $\dot{\mu} = 0$ too by (3.27), so that we may take

$$\lambda^i = a_i, \quad \mu^i = b_i, \qquad \text{each } i, \tag{3.34}$$

yielding

$$T = F\left(\sum a_i z_i, \sum b_i z_i\right), \tag{3.35}$$

$$\phi^i = a_i \phi^1 + b_i \phi^2. \tag{3.36}$$

[16] See n. 13.

Write the indirect disutility function in the form

$$v = G\left(\sum a_i z_i, \sum b_i z_i, z_3, \ldots, z_n\right), \tag{3.37}$$

to get, by (3.28) and (3.34),

$$\phi^1 = \lambda G_1, \quad \phi^2 = \lambda G_2, \tag{3.38}$$

$$\phi^i = \lambda G_1 a_i + \lambda G_2 b_i + \lambda G_i, \qquad i > 2,$$

$$= a_i \phi^1 + b_i \phi^2 + \lambda G_i, \qquad i > 2, \tag{3.39}$$

so that $G_i = 0$, $i > 2$, and

$$v = H\left(\sum a_i z_i, \sum b_i z_i\right), \text{ say,} \tag{3.40}$$

when we can easily normalize so that

$$\sum a_i = \sum b_i = 1.^{17} \tag{3.41}$$

We have already seen in (1.17)–(1.22) that this yields $g^i = \phi^i(T)$ as required with $T = H_2/(H_1 + H_2)$ for instance.

The alternative is that $\dot{\lambda}, \lambda, \mu$ should be linearly independent. In fact we will see, by *reductio ad absurdum*, that this is impossible, so that (3.40) is the complete solution for the abnormal case.[18]

Were $\dot{\lambda}, \lambda, \mu$ linearly independent, one could let $\sum \dot{\lambda}^k z^k$ in (3.33) take any value we liked while holding $\sum \lambda^k z^k$, $\sum \mu^k z^k$, T constant. If now

$$F_1 \neq F_2 \phi^1/\phi^2, \tag{3.42}$$

set

$$\sum \dot{\lambda}^j z^j = 1/(F_1 - F_2 \phi^1/\phi^2), \tag{3.43}$$

so that the coefficient of dT in (3.33) vanishes. Hence the right-hand side of (3.33) is zero. Since λ, μ are linearly independent this implies that $F_1 = F_2 = 0$, contradicting (3.42). Hence

$$F_1/F_2 = \phi^1(T)/\phi^2(T) = \psi(F), \text{ say,} \tag{3.44}$$

since $T = F$ by (3.31). Hence the constant $-F$ curves are straight lines. Since they cannot intersect, they are parallel. Hence $\psi(F) = k$, say, so that $\phi^1 = k\phi^2$ contradicting (3.21). That is, $\dot{\lambda}, \lambda, \mu$ cannot be linearly independent.

(3.40) is therefore the complete solution in the abnormal case.

[17] Were $\sum a_i = \sum b_i = 0$ we would have $1 = \sum g^i = 0$. Let $\sum a_i = a \neq 0$, $\sum b_i = b$, and define $a_i^* = a_i/a$, $b_i^* = (b+1)a_i^* - b_i$.

[18] Given that it is valid everywhere.

There is an apparent paradox here. (3.40) is of course

$$v = H\left(\sum a_i \log y_i, \sum b_i \log y_i\right), \tag{3.45}$$

so we would expect from the symmetry of $x_i y_i = \phi^i(T)$ that

$$u = K\left(\sum a_i \log x_i, \sum b_i \log x_i\right), \tag{3.46}$$

would also be a solution, indeed the general solution too,[19] as in fact it is. Yet, as is shown in Appendix B, (3.45) corresponds to the direct utility function of the form

$$u = \max\left\{L\left(\sum a_i \log \bar{x}_i, \sum b_i \log \bar{\bar{x}}_i\right) \mid \bar{X} + \bar{\bar{Y}} \leqslant X\right\}, \tag{3.47}$$

in the obvious notation, which looks very different from (3.46), and whose intuitive interpretation is certainly quite different: in (3.46) the same unit of each good ministers to both needs, in (3.47) each good can be used to minister to either, but each individual unit can only be used to meet one of them.

Yet (3.46) and (3.47) are in fact identical.[20] The proof is that each is the complete solution of the same problem, but the following corroboration may be pleasing. Remember that (3.45) and (3.47) are equivalent.

(3.45) yields

$$\begin{aligned} y_i x_i = g^i &= (a_i H_1 + b_i H_2)/(H_1 + H_2) \\ &= \psi^i\left(\sum a_i \log y_i, \sum b_i \log y_i\right), \quad \text{say.} \end{aligned} \tag{3.48}$$

$$\sum a_i \log x_i = \sum a_i \log \psi^i - \sum a_i \log y_i = \alpha\left(\sum a_i \log y_i, \sum b_i \log y_i\right). \tag{3.49}$$

$$\sum b_i \log x_i = \sum b_i \log \psi^i - \sum b_i \log y_i = \beta\left(\sum a_i \log y_i, \sum b_i \log y_i\right), \text{ say.} \tag{3.50}$$

Solving[21] (3.49) and (3.50) and substituting into (3.45) we have (3.46).

In this case, therefore, each of the apparently quite different interpretations of the consumers' tastes are equally acceptable: another identification problem.

4. A DISCLAIMER

Throughout this paper I have talked as if my claims were definitely proven. Of course this is not so: my arguments are far from rigorous. In particular I have used calculus arguments merely on the blanket assumption that all

[19] As a symmetric argument would show.

[20] Of course we must choose $L(\cdot)$ appropriately, given $K(\cdot)$.

[21] Question begging: but this is merely meant to corroborate something proved elsewhere.

the continuity and connectivity needed is there, and have assumed all sorts of equations solvable.

A word on connectivity. Suppose

$$y = f(X), \tag{4.1}$$

and

$$dy = \sum_{r=1}^{R} \phi^r(X) dg^r(X). \tag{4.2}$$

I have talked as if this immediately implied that

$$y = F(g^1(X), \ldots, g^R(X)). \tag{4.3}$$

How would one go about proving this?

Suppose

$$g^r(\bar{X}) = g^r(\bar{\bar{X}}), \qquad \text{each } r. \tag{4.4}$$

If there is a piecewise smooth curve connecting $\bar{X}$, $\bar{\bar{X}}$, at each point of which $g^r(X) = g^r(\bar{X})$, then $dg = 0$ along it, so that $\bar{y} = \bar{\bar{y}}$, so to speak. Say that $\bar{X}$, $\bar{\bar{X}}$ are level arc connected in that case. Then $y = F(g^1(X), \ldots, g^R(X))$ if each pair $\bar{X}$, $\bar{\bar{X}}$ satisfying (4.4) are level arc connected. This, then, I have implicitly assumed throughout wherever it has been needed.

Then again I have not distinguished between, e.g. $\rho \neq 0$ identically, and at particular points. As long as there is sufficient smoothness $\rho \neq 0$ at a point, implies that $\rho \neq 0$ in a 'solid' region,[22] to which we may consider our arguments in Section 2 to be limited. Actually we may go further. Behaviour of an integral on a set of measure zero does not affect the value of an integral, so that, as long as the paths of integration cut the region where $\rho = 0$ on a set of measure zero, all should be well. Given sufficient smoothness, then, we really need only worry when $\rho = 0$ on a solid region itself.

This particular example is of some importance, because the arguments I used in Section 3 explicitly assume that $\rho \neq 0$ throughout R^n. *Hence we do not know for sure what happens on a solid proper subset of R^n on which* $\rho = 0$.

Finally, I have said nothing at all about convexity.

These are, I hope, the most important gaps in my argument, but they are certainly not the only ones. My excuse for publishing a paper with such gaps is that I did not wish to delay Professor Pollak's article which uses these results.[23]

[22] The idea of a 'solid region' is fairly clear. Perhaps 'tube connected' is the best explication; i.e. each pair of points in it are connected by an arc, all of whose other points are interior.

[23] And which I regard as important.

Appendix A

THEOREM: *If the budget shares depend only on the normalized prices of goods in the set S, the indirect utility function may be written*

$$v = \sum_{i \notin S} a_i z_i + F(Z_S), \quad Z_S = (z_i)_{i \in S}. \tag{A.1}$$

PROOF: Write the budget share

$$g^i = \phi^i(Z_S), \qquad \text{each } i, \tag{A.2}$$

so that, v being the indirect utility function,

$$v_i/v_j = g^i/g^j = \phi^i(Z_S)/\phi^j(Z_S). \tag{A.3}$$

Taking $i, j \in S$, we see that S is separable so that

$$v = G(\theta(Z_S), Z_{\bar{S}}), \text{ say, } Z_{\bar{S}} = (z_j)_{j \notin S}. \tag{A.4}$$

Taking $i, j \notin S$ in (A.3) we now have

$$\phi^i(Z_S)/\phi^j(Z_S) = G_i(\theta(Z_S), Z_{\bar{S}})/G_j(\theta(Z_S), Z_{\bar{S}}) = \psi^i(\theta(Z_S))/\psi^j\theta(Z_S)), \text{ say,} \tag{A.5}$$

clearly. Hence

$$v_i = \lambda\psi^i(\theta), \qquad \text{each } i \notin S, \tag{A.6}$$

so that

$$dv = \lambda \sum_{i \notin S} \psi^i(\theta) dz_i + G_\theta d\theta = \lambda d\left(\sum \psi^i(\theta) z_i\right) + \left(G_\theta - \lambda \sum \psi^i(\theta) z_i\right) d\theta \tag{A.7}$$

and

$$v = H(\theta, \psi), \quad \theta = \theta(Z_S), \quad \psi = \sum_{i \notin S} \psi^i(\theta) z_i. \tag{A.8}$$

Now take $i \in S$, $j \notin S$. According to (A.8), (A.3) yields

$$\frac{(H_\theta + H_\psi \sum_{k \notin S} \dot{\psi}^k z_k)\theta_i}{H_\psi \psi^j} = \frac{\phi^i(Z_S)}{\phi^j(Z_S)}. \tag{A.9}$$

Since θ_j, ψ^j depend only on Z_S this is equivalent to

$$L + \sum \dot{\psi}^k z_k = \zeta(Z_S), \text{ say, } \qquad L = H_\theta/H_\psi \tag{A.10}$$

Differentiation with respect to z_j, $j \notin S$, yields

$$L_\psi \psi^j + \dot{\psi}^j = 0, \tag{A.11}$$

so that $\dot{\psi}^j/\psi^j = \dot{\psi}^1/\psi^1 = \dot{f}/f$, say, and

$$\psi^j = a_j f(\theta), \qquad \text{each } j \notin S, \tag{A.12}$$

so that

$$\psi = f(\theta) \sum_{j \notin S} a_j z_j. \tag{A.13}$$

Clearly the $f(\theta)$ can be embodied in the θ term in (A.9), to get

$$\psi = \sum_{j \notin S} a_j z_j = \psi(Z_{\bar{S}}). \tag{A.14}$$

(A.10) now becomes

$$H_\theta(\theta(Z_S), \psi(Z_{\bar{S}}))/H_\psi(\theta(Z_{\bar{S}}), \psi(Z_{\bar{S}})) = \zeta(Z_S) = \dot{\eta}(\theta), \tag{A.15}$$

say, clearly, so that

$$\mathrm{d}H = H_\psi(\mathrm{d}(\psi + \eta(\theta))) \tag{A.16}$$

and

$$v = H = K(\psi + \eta(\theta)), \tag{A.17}$$

which, on appropriate normalization, is (A.1).

COROLLARY 1: *Under normal assumptions, the a_i all have the same signs, so that we can normalize to get $\sum a_i = 1$. If so, a_i is the relative share of good i in the total expenditure on goods in $\bar{S}$.*

COROLLARY 2: *The corresponding direct utility function may be written*

$$u = G(X_S) \prod_{i \notin S} x_i^{a_i}, \quad X_S = (x_j)_{j \in S}.$$

Note the Cobb–Douglas aggregate for $\bar{S}$.

COROLLARY 3: *If there is generalized additive separability and S is the set of normal goods, $T = T(Z_S)$ so that each of the shares depends only on Z_S, (A.1) holds, and, in particular, a_i is the relative share of the abnormal good i in the total expenditure on abnormal goods and so*

$$g^i = a^i \phi(T), \qquad \text{say, } i \text{ abnormal}. \tag{A.18}$$

Appendix B

Suppose

$$u = F(\phi^1(X_1), \ldots, \phi^R(X_R)), \tag{B.1}$$

where each $\phi^R(\cdot)$ is homogeneous of degree one. Then we say that F is homothetically separable. Consider now

$$w_r = \phi^r(X_r), \qquad \text{each } r, \tag{B.2}$$

where the $\phi^r(\cdot)$ are considered as production functions, yielding macro-good r under constant returns. Clearly the cost

$$\Psi^r(P_r, w_r) = \min\{P_r \cdot X_r \mid \phi^r(X_r) \geqslant w_r\} = w_r \psi^r(P_r) \tag{B.3}$$

where

$$\psi^r(P_r) = \min\{P_r \cdot X_r \mid \phi^r(X_r) \geqslant 1\} = H^r(P_r, 1) \tag{B.4}$$

is the unit or average cost of producing the rth good. Hence the total cost of producing $W = (w_1, \ldots, w_R)$ is

$$\sum h^r(P_r) w_r, \tag{B.5}$$

and the cost of attaining a utility level u in (B.1) is

$$\min\left\{\sum P_r X_r \mid F(\phi^1(X_1), \ldots, \phi^R(X_R)) \geqslant u\right\} = \min\left\{\sum \psi^r(P_r) w_r \mid F(W) \geqslant u\right\}$$
$$= K(\psi^1(P_1), \ldots, \psi^R(P_R), u), \text{ say}, \tag{B.6}$$

where

$$K(Q, u) = \min\{Q \cdot W \mid F(W) \geqslant u\} \tag{B.7}$$

is the cost function associated with the macro-level utility function $F(\cdot)$, defined in terms of the quantities $W = (w_1, \ldots, w_R)$ of the macro-goods. Consider now the case where $X_1, \ldots, X_R$ are all vectors of the same goods, put to different uses, so that

$$\sum X_r = X \tag{B.8}$$

is the total consumption vector. Considered as a function of it

$$u = U(X) = \max\left\{F(\phi^1(X_1), \ldots, \phi^R(X_R)) \mid \sum X_r \leqslant X\right\}, \tag{B.9}$$

so that its cost function

$$\min\left\{P \cdot X \,|\, F(\phi^1(X_1), \ldots, \phi^R(X_R)) \geq u, \sum X_r \leq X\right\}$$
$$= \min\left\{\sum P \cdot X_r \,|\, F(\phi^1(X_1), \ldots, \phi^R(X_R)) \geq u\right\}$$
$$= K(h^1(P), \ldots, h^R(P), u), \tag{B.10}$$

where

$$K(Q, u) = \min\left\{\sum Q_r w_r \,|\, F(W) \geq u\right\} \tag{B.11}$$

is the cost function associated with the macro-utility function $F(\cdot)$.

Moreover, as long as $h^1(\cdot), \ldots, h^R(\cdot)$, $K(\cdot, u)$ are admissible cost functions—that is, are closed convex and positively homogeneous of degree one—we can associate with each of the former a unique homogeneous quasi-concave 'production' function $\phi^r(\cdot)$, whose unit cost function is b, and with the latter a unique quasi-concave utility function $F(\cdot)$ whose cost function it is, to get (B.9). That is, given the appropriate regularity conditions, (B.9) and (B.11) are equivalent.

Now (B.11) is

$$m = K(\psi^1(P), \ldots, \psi^R(P), u), \tag{B.12}$$

so that

$$K(\psi^1(Y), \ldots, \psi^R(Y), u) = 1, \tag{B.13}$$

in Professor Pollak's notation, whence

$$u = L(\psi^1(Y), \ldots, \psi^R(Y)), \text{ say.} \tag{B.14}$$

Moreover, as long as $\psi^1(\cdot), \ldots, \psi^R(\cdot)$ are admissible cost functions, we can reverse this argument to get (B.14) $\Rightarrow$ (B.11) $\Rightarrow$ (B.9). In other words (B.14) is the indirect form of a utility function of type (B.9).

Turn now to the text. The indirect utility function (3.40) may be written

$$v = F\left(\prod y_i^{a_i}, \prod y_i^{b_i}\right), \quad \sum a_i = \sum b_i = 1. \tag{B.15}$$

Now $\Pi p_i^{a_i}$, $\Pi p_i^{b_i}$ are admissible unit cost functions: those corresponding to production functions $A\Pi x_i^{a_i}$, $B\Pi x_i^{b_i}$, say. Hence (B.15) is the indirect form of a utility function

$$u = \max\left\{G\left(\prod \bar{x}_i^{a_i}, \prod \bar{\bar{x}}_i^{b_i}\right) \,|\, \bar{X} + \bar{\bar{X}} \leq X\right\} \tag{B.16}$$

as mentioned at the end of Section 3.

14

Facing an Uncertain Future

Editorial Remarks

This paper analyses uncertainty in an intertemporal context, and it is the only paper of its kind in the portfolio. It is different because Gorman begins with both the problem and the desired answer, and sets himself the task of finding the minimal assumptions that can generate it. It is also a paper designed to use to the fullest extent possible the overlapping theorem presented in 'The Structure of Utility Functions'. As such, this paper may be regarded as an exercise, but that does not mean that it is either easy or uninteresting. It is interesting that such a weak set of assumptions is capable of generating 'Benthan and Bernoulli at a stroke', and difficult to keep track of the overlaps.

At each point of time a set of states of the world is possible, presenting the agent with a utility tree. The agent has a complete set of preferences over all possible states of the world at all periods of time. One of these states occurs, and in the next period he or she faces some smaller portion of the tree; obviously, that part of the tree following events that do not take place are irrelevant. Assumption 2 requires the states that follow any branch of the tree to be separable from those events that can no longer happen—conditional on the actual history followed. He calls this the 'very weak independence axiom'. The only other assumption used is that the agent only examines the future closely for the next two periods, and for the rest of the future is content with a summary statistic. Hence Assumption 3 requires the future from $t+2$ to the horizon to be separable from its complement at each t. These two assumptions are enough to generate 'Bentham and Bernoulli at a stroke'.

In editing, we had the benefit of a very thorough set of comments on this paper that were very helpful. We do not know who is the author of these notes but give our thanks anonymously.

Facing an Uncertain Future

1. INTRODUCTION AND MOTIVATION[1]

Economists often assume that organizations use criteria of the form

$$\sum_{t=0}^{T} c^t E[f(y_t)], \tag{1.1}$$

in deciding on their actions, where $E(\cdot)$ is an expectations operator. If you like: that they seek to maximize the mathematical expectation of a discounted utility stream. This is a special case of an additive criterion

$$\sum_{s=0}^{S} \sum_{t=0} f^{st}(y_{st}) \tag{1.2}$$

where y_{st} is a vector of flows which occur in period t if state s obtains.

The convenience of assuming (1.1) or (1.2) is clear. Is either justified? They require, after all, that utility is additive over time, and over states, and *that the same normalization does for each.*

In many problems, all three of these results arise as the joint products of single argument. This is because addition is, effectively, the only strictly increasing associative operation. Suppose for instance, that

$$f(w, x, y, z) = \mathrm{d}(w, \delta(x, y), z) = e[w, x, \varepsilon(y, z)], \tag{1.3}$$

where all functions are continuous, and strictly increasing[2] in the subutilities δ and ε. We then say that $X \times Y$, $Y \times Z$ are both *separable*, where X is the space of x, ... This is possible iff

$$f(w, x, y, z) = g[w, (a(x) + b(y) + c(z)], \tag{1.4}$$

[1] Earlier versions of this paper were read at Johns Hopkins, Stanford, and the University of California at Berkeley in the Spring of 1980, and a later version at the London School of Economics in 1981. I am grateful to the auditors for their comments, particularly to Peter Hammond for his suggestion that assumption (A2) should be called 'consistency over time'. I had discussed the apparent coincidence that the same normalization should do for time and uncertainty with Kenneth Arrow, Martin Browning, Frank Hahn, Hugh Rose, Amartya Sen, and John Wise at various times, and the possible relationship between the structure of a criterion function and an information tree such as that depicted in Figure 14.3 with Bernt Stigum in 1967. I thank them all, especially Martin Browning who pointed out the importance of (A3) at the London School of Economics, and Bernt Stigum.

[2] monotonically increasing: $f(y) \geqslant f(x)$ if $y \geqslant x$,
strictly increasing: $f(y) > f(x)$ if $y > x$,
very strictly increasing: $f(y) > f(x)$ if $y \geqslant x$,
Here x and y are vectors. If they are scalars, strictly increasing and very strictly increasing coincide.

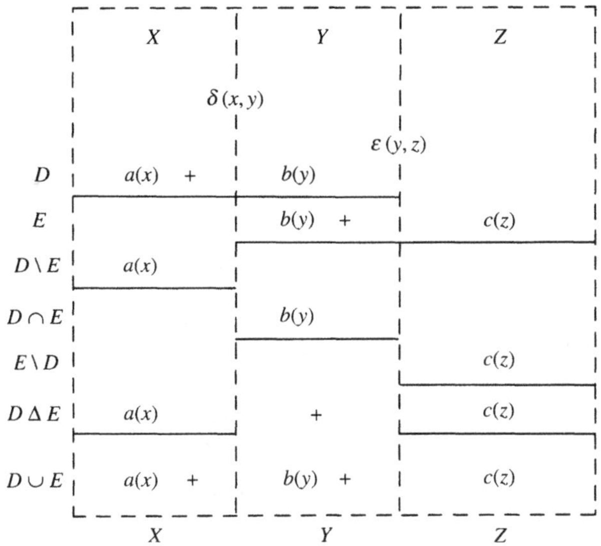

FIG. 14.1: *Illustrating overlapping separable spaces $X \times Y$, $Y \times Z$, or sets D, E, with their subutilities $\delta(x, y)$, $\varepsilon(y, z)$ and the associated separable spaces, or sets, with their normalized subutilities.*

where $g(\cdot)$ is continuous and $g(w, \cdot)$ is strictly increasing. The secret is the *overlap* between (x, y) and (y, z), or, better, between $X \times Y$ and $Y \times Z$. To be able to tear y out of its association with x in $\delta(x, y)$, and put it in with z in $\varepsilon(y, z)$ instead, one effectively needs addition, or at least a strictly increasing transformation $g(w, \cdot)$ of it.

What one wants to generate a criterion like (1.2) is a considerable number of overlaps roughly of this type.

Consider the following, related example, illustrated in Figure 14.2. A society contains a finite set H of self-regarding households, h, and faces a finite set S of possible state, s, of the world. h consumes y_{hs} in state s and is interested only in its own welfare.

$$\alpha^h(x_h); \quad x_h = (y_{hs})_{s \in S} = h\text{'s consumption vector,} \tag{1.5}$$

while society as a whole is only interested in the welfare of its members as judged by themselves and wishes them all well. It is accordingly guided by a strictly increasing social welfare function.

$$W = a[\alpha^h(x_h) \mid h \in H] = f(y_{hs} \mid h \in H, s \in S), \text{ say.} \tag{1.6}$$

Society also satisfies Samuelson's weak independence axiom in the form

$$f(y_{hs} \mid h \in H, s \in S) = b(\beta^s(z_s) \mid s \in S), \quad b(\cdot) \text{ very strictly increasing,} \tag{1.7}$$

Consumption vectors: $y_{hs} \in Y_{hs}$

STATES OF THE WORLD	1	2	...	s	...	
HOUSEHOLDS						Extended vector
1	y_{11}	y_{12}	...	y_{1s}	...	$x_1 \in X_1$
2	y_{21}	y_{22}	...	y_{2s}	...	$x_2 \in X_2$
...	...	...	...	...	...	
h	y_{h1}	y_{h2}	...	y_{hs}	...	$x_h \in X_h$
...	...	...	...	...	...	
Extended vector	z_1	z_2	...	z_s	...	
Space	Z_1	Z_2	...	Z_s	...	

Each space $X_h = \prod_{s \in S} Y_{hs}$ is separable by consumer sovereignty.

Each space $Y_s = \prod_{h \in H} Y_{hs}$ is separable by the weak independence axiom.

FIG. 14.2: *The social welfare function—Bentham & Bernoulli at a stroke*

where all functions are assumed continuous. Both continuity and the very strict monotonicity needed can be derived from the Debreu (1960) approach followed by Gorman (1968*c*), for instance.

In this case each $X_h = \prod_{s \in S} Y_{hs}$, and each $Z_s = \prod_{h \in H} Y_{hs}$ is separable. Each pair X_h, Z_s actually overlaps, in Y_{hs}, so that it is not surprising that (1.6) and (1.7), common assumptions in welfare economics and the theory of choice under uncertainty respectively, jointly imply that we can write

$$W = \sum_{\substack{h \in H \\ s \in S}} f^{hs}(y_{hs}) = \sum_{h \in H} \alpha^h(x_h) = \sum_{s \in S} \beta^s(z_s), \tag{1.8}$$

where

$$\alpha^h(x_h) = \sum_{s \in S} f^{hs}(y_{hs}), \tag{1.9}$$

$$\beta^s(z_s) = \sum_{h \in H} f^{hs}(y_{hs}), \tag{1.10}$$

are the overall welfare, or utility of household h, and of society as a whole in state s: Bentham and Bernoulli at a stroke—and with the same normalization holding for each.

Why not apply a similar analysis to time and uncertainty in the case of an organization as to households and uncertainty here? Once one assumes Samuelson's weak axiom for uncertainty in the form (1.7), one has a considerable choice of assumptions about time to replace (1.6). One can

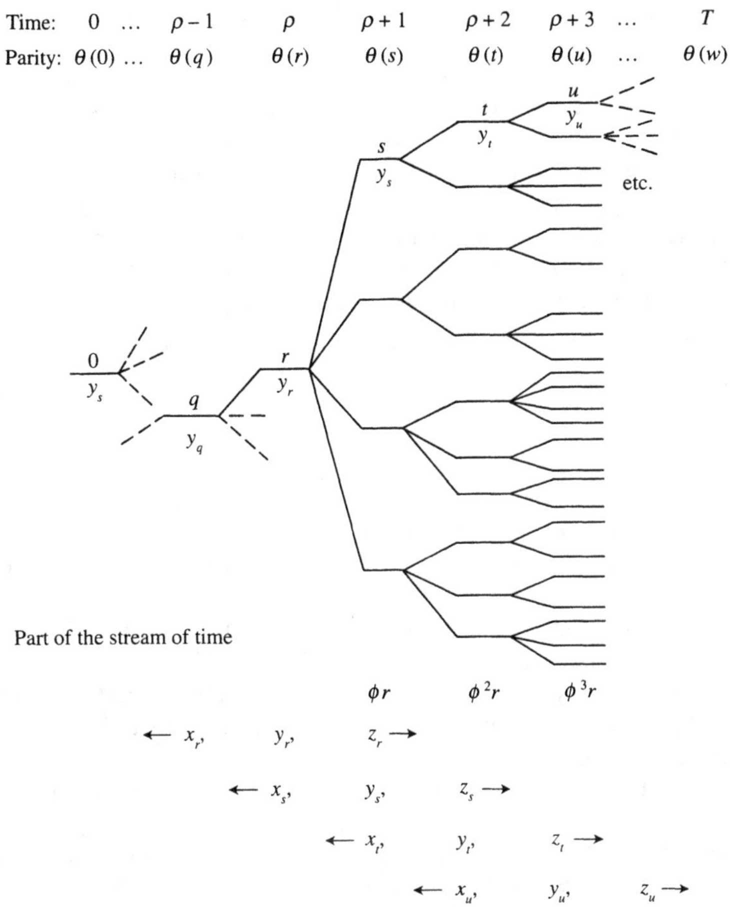

(a) $u \phi t \phi s \phi r \phi q$

(b) $t\phi^2 r$, $u\phi^3 r$, $u\phi^4 q$, etc.

(c) $x_s = (x_r, y_r)$, each $s \phi r$

(d) $z_r = (y_s, z_s)$, $s \phi r$

FIG. 14.3: *Illustrating* (A1) *and* (A2)

assume the exact analogue, that each period is separable from society's point of view, or that the future from each period forward is, to take two simple possibilities, either of which yields (1.8)–(1.10) with h now standing for time.

Unhappily, time and uncertainty are not orthogonal in this pleasant manner. Instead, the world unfolds before us as we meander through time. Contrast Figure 14.2 with Figure 14.3. Here I go to the other extreme and assume that the world unfolds itself in a predetermined manner. We do not know who will be elected President in November, but we do know that someone will be.[3] Broadly speaking, this is the model I will explore.

Before proceeding further with this model may I discuss the argument whereby Samuelson, in particular, derived additivity over states. He replaced his weak axiom (1.7) by a strong axiom which states that *each set of states* of the world is separable, not just the individual states themselves. The idea is, I suppose, that once one knows that one will be in some one of a particular set of states it would be absurd to allow one's calculations to be affected by what one might have done if in some quite different state. This yields innumerable separable spaces, which overlap most satisfactorily, and yield the required additively separable criterion

$$\sum_{s \in S} f^s(y_s) \tag{1.11}$$

as is proved by Debreu (1960).

The bother about that argument, as I see it, is that it assumes from the outset that we are all very bright, and especially so at computation. A similar approach involving time as well would be even more demanding.

The approach I take in this paper is based on the contrary idea, that we are pretty limited beings, only able to hold a few ideas in our minds at a time, and accordingly unwilling to attempt difficult calculations until we really need to, and that organizations are collectively quite as limited as their members. It is interesting that, in Britain at least, it is the politicians, representing the biggest organization, who take pride in not crossing bridges until they come to them![4]

To be precise, I assume that we look ahead two periods in detail, summarizing the impact of our choices on more distant prospects in a *single figure*—'capital', if you like. Should you believe organizations to be more far-sighted, use a k-period rolling horizon, with $k > 2$. The results will be much the same, though the end-effects will last longer.

The other notion underlying this discussion is that, dull though we are, we manage quite well. In particular, we do not spend much time bewailing missed opportunities. If so, this may be another piece of stupidity—we do not realize we missed them[5]—or a piece of benign sociobiological economy which saves us from wasting our limited mental resources on lost causes. In this paper I explore another alternative: that our tastes are adapted to our abilities, so that we *can* really satisfy them quite well—to

[3] We need to know the potential candidates, too, ahead of time. The path we follow from November depends on what happens at that election.

[4] Perhaps this is only a way of evading embarrassing questions from interviewers: if so, at least it works. See end of third last paragraph in Sec. 1.

[5] Often it is the ablest students who believe they did badly in an examination, because they realize what they failed to mention.

wit perfectly—by these limited procedures. Man grew as a social animal and his ability to organize developed as he did, so that I will use the same argument about organizations. I doubt myself whether we do look ahead as clear-headedly in organizations as we do as individuals—for one thing individual members of organizations may become politically committed to particular policies, and be unwilling to recognize unfavourable developments leading to inconsistencies. There may be self-regarding reasons for this, too. One reason why British politicians are unwilling to cross bridges until they come to them is probably that they realize the danger of precommitting themselves in public. Nevertheless, I will assume that we are.

Of course, this is all rather dishonest. The motivating idea of my analysis is the need to economize in computing. Yet computing costs are nowhere to be seen in it. I claim that my assumptions are made more realistic than Samuelson's: since they imply and are implied by virtually the same results, implicitly I assume pretty well what he does.[6]

Perhaps, I should repeat that, despite the absence of probabilities, this paper is about *unknown* futures. One can introduce probabilities into treatments of this type by, e.g., defining them as 'the proportion of equally likely alternatives' which are favourable to an event. Frequently, they seem to me to obscure, rather than enlighten.

2. MORE ABOUT SEPARABILITY

Consider the world as seen from an arbitrary initial point 0, from which paths into the future radiate, as they do from r in Figure 14.3. I will deal with the set R of such nodes r, including 0 itself, and assume a continuous preference ordering $\succcurlyeq$ defined on the connected, topologically separable,[7] product space $Y_R = \prod_{r \in R} Y_r$, where $y_r \in Y_r$ may be thought of as the output vector of the organization at node r.

I will assume that each sector Y_r is *strictly essential*: what happens on it matters, whatever is happening off it.

I will call *all this* Assumption (A1). It implies that the preference ordering may be represented by a continuous criterion function on Y_R

$$f^0(y_R) \tag{2.1}$$

Consider $Y_S = \prod_{r \in S} Y_r$, $S \subseteq R$. I hold production $y_{\sim S} = \bar{y}_{\sim S}$ *off* Y_S constant and define the conditional preference ordering $(\succcurlyeq_S | \bar{y}_{\sim S})$ on Y_S in the obvious manner. It can be represented by the continuous criterion

[6] Perhaps overstated: Samuelson introduces probabilities; I cover time as well as uncertainty and have annoying end-effects.

[7] 'Topologically separable': a completely different concept from 'separable' as it is used in this paper. It means that the space contains a countably dense subset—such as the rationals among the reals—which can be used in arguments from continuity, just assumed.

$$f^S(y_S|\bar{y}_{\sim S}) = f^0(y_S, \bar{y}_{\sim S}). \tag{2.2}$$

Iff this ordering is the same for each $\bar{y}_{\sim S} \in Y_{\sim S}$, we say that Y_S is *separable*. In that case the condition $\bar{y}_{\sim S}$ does not matter. Accordingly, let us take a bounded arbitrary vector in Y_R as basis, call it 0 by the simple procedure of measuring y_R as a deviation from it. Then

$$f^0(y_R) = g^S(f^S(y_S), y_{\sim S}), \quad g^S(\cdot) \text{ continuous}, g^S(\cdot, y_{\sim S}) \text{ strictly increasing}, \tag{2.3}$$

$$f^S(y_S) := f^0(y_S, 0_{\sim S}), \tag{2.4}$$

in a slightly changed notation.

I will make copious use of this normalizing device in Section 3. Note the strict monotonicity of the higher-order utility function, $g^S(\cdot)$, in the lower, $f^S(\cdot)$. This is always so, given (A1), as is the continuity of $g^S(\cdot)$. I will use these facts continually in Section 3 as well.

Given all this, the basic theorem in this field is that (1.3) implies (1.4). It allows us to determine functions for which given collections of spaces, $Y_s = \prod_{r \in S} Y_r$, $S \subseteq R$, are separable.

For the present let us talk of the sets $S \subseteq R$ as being separable, rather than the corresponding spaces Y_S.

Look at Figure 14.1 again.

To say that (1.3) implies (1.4) is equivalent to saying that, if D, E are separable and overlap, then $D \backslash E$, $D \cap E$, $E \backslash D$, $D \Delta E$, and $D \cup E$ are also separable. In (1.3) the spaces corresponding to D and E are $X \times Y$ and $Y \times Z$, and, to the other X, Y, Z, $X \times Z$ and $X \times Y \times Z$ in turn, with subutilities $a(x) + b(y)$, $b(y) + c(z)$, $a(x)$, $b(y)$, $c(z)$, $a(x) + c(z)$, and $a(x) + b(y) + c(z)$ respectively. Call a collection $\mathscr{A}$ of subsets $S \subseteq R$ *complete* if it contains R, the empty set ϕ, and, with overlapping D, E, the list associated with them above, and the *completion* $\mathscr{A}(\mathscr{B})$ of any collection $\mathscr{B}$ of $S \subseteq R$, the intersection of all complete collections containing it. To know that the elements of $\mathscr{B}$ are separable is to know that those of $\mathscr{A}(\mathscr{B})$ are under (A1).

As it happens, complete collections have a particularly simple ordering under set inclusion '$\supseteq$', and the structure of the utility function mirrors it. This is discussed at length in Gorman (1968*c*), continuing Debreu (1960) and Leontief (1947*a*). All we need to know here is the following: take a continuous function $h(x_1, x_2, \ldots, x_n)$ defined on $X_1 \times X_2 \times \ldots \times X_n$. It can be put in the form

$$\sum_{j=1}^{n} h^j(x_j), \tag{2.5}$$

by a continuous, strictly increasing transformation iff $V_i = \Pi_{j \neq i} x_j$ is separable for each $i = 1, 2, \ldots, n$. The corresponding subutilities as used in Debreu are, of course, $\sum_{j \neq i} h^j(x_j)$, each i.

This is the result which I will bring to bear in Section 3. Before reading it, may I remind you of the tree, in Figure 14.3, which we will study there, and the notation defined below it.

In particular, at node r: x_r is past output, y_r current output, and z_r a vector of possible future outputs, along all the paths directed from r into the future.

Let me remind you that I will use normalizations such as (2.4) very frequently, and that (A1) assures that all my functions will be continuous in all their arguments and very strictly increasing in the 'subutilities' among them, as in (2.3).

3. MAIN ANALYSIS

Look at Figure 14.3 again. It represents a particular type of unfolding future. At a given node r, one does not know what is about to happen, but does know the possibilities facing one; and, looking forward from r to some $v\psi r$, one knows what questions will be answered at v, should we ever reach it, though not what the answers will be.

Think of Figure 14.3 as representing the outward flow of blood from the heart 0, if you like. Major arteries divide into smaller and yet smaller ones, then into major capillaries, and so on. Think of the organization as a corpuscle carried along in the blood stream. Having reached r it does not know down which of the succeeding channels it will be carried, but it does know that it will be one of those leading directly to an $s\phi r$—that is to a *direct successor* of r—and that it will reach that s in the next period, if at all.

Now for some formal notation, spelled out under Figure 14.3. First *successors*:

$$t\phi^{\tau}r \quad \text{iff} \quad t\phi^{\tau-1}s, \quad \text{some } s\phi r,\ \tau = 2, 3, \ldots, \tag{3.1}$$

$$t\phi^{1}r \quad \text{iff} \quad t\phi r,\ r\phi^{0}r, \tag{3.2}$$

$$t\psi r \quad \text{iff} \quad t\phi^{\tau}r, \quad \text{some } \tau = 0, 1, 2, \ldots, T. \tag{3.3}$$

Next the *period*:

$$\theta(r) = \rho, \tag{3.4}$$

in which r occurs if it ever does. If $t\phi^{\tau}r$,

$$\theta(t) = \rho + \tau. \tag{3.5}$$

We choose

$$\theta(0) = 0, \quad \text{so that} \quad \theta(r) = \rho \quad \text{iff} \quad r\phi^{\rho}0. \tag{3.6}$$

Next *output*:

$$x_r,\ y_r,\ z_r, \tag{3.7}$$

stand respectively for past, present, and potential future output vectors at r. Hence

$$x_s = (x_r,\ y_r), \qquad \text{each } s\phi r, \tag{3.8}$$

$$z_r = (y_s,\ z_s)_{s\phi r}. \tag{3.9}$$

May I now remind you that the aim of this analysis is to derive the common form

$$f^r(x_r,\ y_r, z_r) = \sum_{v\psi r} a^v(y_v), \tag{3.10}$$

of the criterion function at $r \in R$, where

$$R = \psi 0 := \{r \mid r\psi 0\}, \tag{3.11}$$

by (3.3).

Remarks: (i) Note the assumption, implicit in the form $f^r(x_r,\ y_r,\ z_r)$, that, given that it has reached r, it does not matter what the organization might have chosen, had the world evolved differently. The form $\sum_{v\psi r} a^v(y_v)$, on the right-hand side, implies that the actual behaviour in the past, x_r, does not matter either. While this may be less repugnant for organizations than individuals, one would not like to assume it from the outset. Hence, the x_r in $f^r(x_r,\ y_r,\ z_r)$.

(ii) Note, too, that we do not have columns, representing states of the world, overlapping rows, representing time-periods, in the way which yielded additive separability in a related problem in Section 2. If overlaps are needed for additive separability, they will have to be introduced explicitly, as in the assumption (A3) below, about the existence of a two-period rolling horizon. This assumption does not give the necessary overlaps at the very beginning and the very end of the organization's life, so that we never quite get (3.10). Very similar results, with longer-lived end-effects, can be found with a k-period rolling horizon when $k > 2$.

If you think of T as at all large, and the distant future as not being of critical importance, these end-effects scarcely matter. In any case, I will assume

$$T > 3 \tag{3.12}$$

as a minimum. Include it in (A1). In addition to (A1), and the rolling horizon (A3) just mentioned, I will need

(A2) *Very Weak Independence Assumption*

$$f^r(x_r,\ y_r, z_r) = g^r(x_r,\ y_r;\ f^s(x_s,\ y_s,\ z_s) \mid s\phi r) \tag{3.13}$$

$$= g^r(x_s,\ f^s(x_s,\ y_s,\ z_s) \mid s\phi r) \tag{3.14}$$

where

$$g^r(x_r, y_r, \cdot) \text{ is very strictly increasing.} \tag{3.15}$$

Remarks: (i) $(x_r, y_r) = x_s$ is repeated in (3.14) for each $s \phi r$, so that $g^r(\cdot)$ is not strictly the same there as in (3.13), nor even uniquely specified. The values are the same, and the notation is convenient.

(ii) I use '$\cdot \mid s\phi r$' instead of '$(\cdot)_{s\phi r}$' where it seems simpler. Its domain extends back to the previous ';' if there is one. In either case '$\cdot$' is taken for each $s\phi r$. I have dropped the quantifier to preserve the analogy with the normal notation.

(iii) Why: very weak independence axiom?

Samuelson's weak axiom may be written in the form

$$f(z) = g(f^s(y_s) \mid s \in S), \text{ say,} \qquad g(\cdot) \text{ very strictly increasing,} \tag{3.16}$$

all functions being continuous, and S being defined so that it ignores both past and present output, x_r, y_r at the point of consideration r. (3.13) seems weak since $(x_r, y_r) = x_s$, appears through each of the future criteria $f^s(x_s, y_s, z_s)$, $s\phi r$, and also as an additional argument in $g^r(\cdot)$.

Next to show that (A2) implies consistency over time *in an obvious* sense.[8]

Remember that I warned you in Section 2 that I would make copious use of normalizations based on the arbitrary reference vector

$$\bar{y} = (\bar{y}_r)_{r \in R} = 0, \tag{3.17}$$

without loss of generality. In particular, I will set

$$f^r(0) = 0, \qquad \text{each } r \in R, \tag{3.18}$$

again without loss of generality.

Note now that

$$f^r(x_r, y_r, z_r) = f^r(x_s, y_s, z_s; (y_\sigma, z_\sigma) \mid \sigma\phi r, \sigma \neq s), \qquad \text{each } s\phi r, \tag{3.19}$$

and define

$$\tilde{f}^s(x_s, y_s, z_s) := f^r(x_s, y_s, x_s; (0_\sigma) \mid \sigma\phi r, \sigma \neq s), \tag{3.20}$$

$$=: f^r(x_s, y_s, z_s; X_s \times Y_s \times Z_s), \tag{3.21}$$

$$= g^r(x_s, f^s(x_s, y_s, z_s); f^\sigma(x_s, 0, 0) \mid \sigma\phi r, \sigma \neq s). \tag{3.22}$$

Remarks: (i) Since g^r is strictly increasing in f^s given x_s in (3.22), and x_s is already past history at s, $\tilde{f}^s(\cdot)$ is just as good a criterion at s as is $f^s(\cdot)$.

[8] When I read an earlier version of this paper in Stanford in May 1980, Peter Hammond suggested that (A2) should be called 'the consistency axiom' and a case can certainly be made for that. It certainly implies (3.27) which I had listed as a separate assumption.

(ii) Clearly (3.20)–(3.22) are calculated by ignoring irrelevant information, or, more precisely, setting it at its reference level 0. This is done explicitly in (3.20), and implicitly in (3.21) which list the relevant space $X_s \times Y_s \times Z_s$, where information should not be written over in this manner. It is sometimes convenient to write

$$f^s(x_s, y_s, z_s; X_s \times Y_s \times Z_s) =: \bar{f}^r(x_s, y_s, z_s), \tag{3.23}$$

where the ellipsis is understood. This exploits the symmetry about ';' in $f^r(\cdot; \cdot)$ while the bar in $\bar{f}^r(x_s, y_s, z_s)$ reminds one that it is not merely a matter of replacing (x_r, y_r, z_r) in $f^r(x_r, y_r, z_r)$ by (x_s, y_s, z_s), which would imply an infinite time-horizon, a great deal of extra structure, and essentially constant 'tastes' in the organization.

(iii) One must imagine the normalization carried out with $r = 0$ first, then with the r's with $\theta(r) = 1, 2, \ldots, T-1$ in turn.

(iv) Having done so we find

$$f^r(x_r, y_r, z_r) = g^r(x_s, f^s(x_s, y_s, z_s) \mid s\phi r), \tag{3.24}$$

$$= h^r(x_t, f^t(x_t, y_t, z_t) \mid t\phi^2 r), \tag{3.25}$$

$$= k^r(x_u, f^u(x_u, y_u, z_u) \mid u\phi^3 r) = \ldots, \tag{3.26}$$

say, from (3.14), and

$$f^s(x_s, y_s, z_s) = f^r(x_s, y_s, z_s; X_s \times Y_s \times Z_s) = \bar{f}^r(x_s, y_s, z_s), \qquad \text{each } s\phi r, \tag{3.27}$$

$$= f^q(x_s, y_s, z_s; X_s \times Y_s \times Z_s) = \bar{f}^q(x_s, y_s, z_s), \qquad \text{each } s\phi^2 q, \tag{3.28}$$

$$= f^0(x_s, y_s, z_s; X_s \times Y_s \times Z_s) = \bar{f}^0(x_s, y_s, z_s), \qquad \text{each } s \in R, \tag{3.29}$$

from (3.20) and (3.23).

Remarks: Because of (A1) we were able to choose $f^0(\cdot)$ to be continuous. So therefore is each $f^r(\cdot)$. Because Y_r is strictly essential, each $r \in R$:

> The functions in (3.24)–(3.29) are continuous; and very strictly increasing in their functional arguments. (3.30)

I now turn to my main assumption

(A3) *Two-Period Rolling Horizon*

$$f^r(x_r, y_r, z_r) = c^r(\, (x_t, y_t)_{t\phi^2 r}, \gamma^r(z_t \mid t\phi^2 r)\,), \tag{3.31}$$

which states that the organization looks into the next two periods in detail, but summarizes what may happen thereafter in the single number γ^r.

Since each period is strictly essential, (A1) implies that we can normalize to get

$$\gamma^r(z_t \mid t\phi^2 r) = f^r(\, (z_t)_{t\phi^2 r}; \prod_{t\phi^2 r} Z_t), \tag{3.32}$$

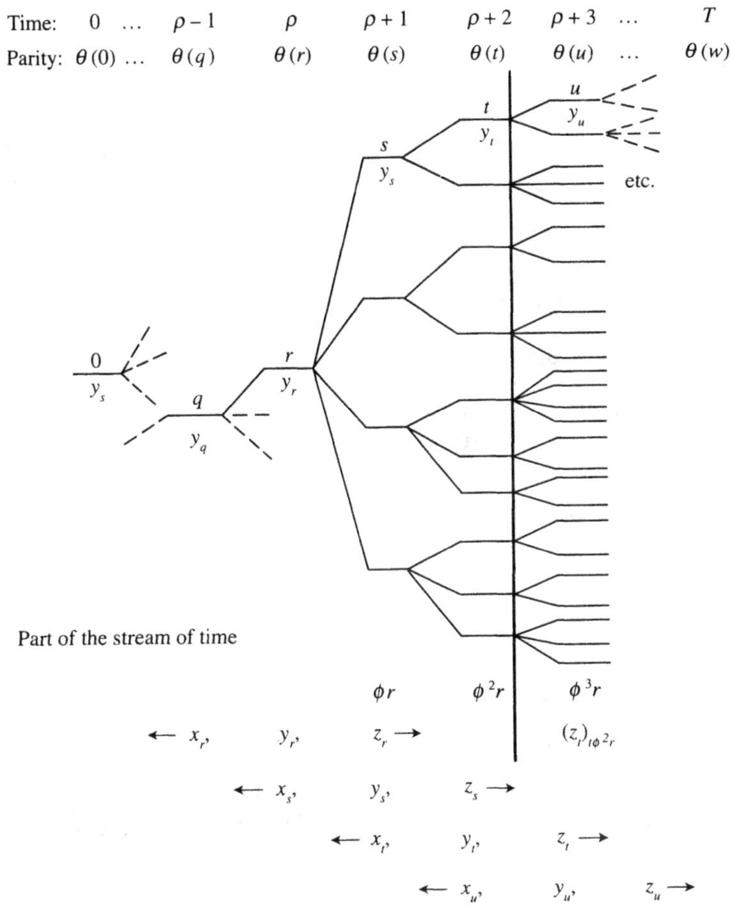

(a) $u\phi t\phi s\phi r\phi q$

(b) $t\phi^2 r$, $u\phi^3 r$, $u\phi^4 q$, etc.

(c) $x_s=(x_r, y_r)$, each $s\phi r$

(d) $z_r=(y_s, z_s)$, $s\phi r$

FIG. 14.4: *Illustrating* (A3)

and

$$c^r(\cdot) \text{ continuous,} \qquad c^r(\,(x_t, y_t)_{t\phi^2 r}, \cdot) \text{ strictly increasing.} \tag{3.33}$$

So far I have paid no attention to possible end-effects. From now on I will have to take them seriously. Let

$$\theta(R) = \{\theta(r)\,|\, r\in R\} = (0, 1, 2, \ldots, T), \tag{3.34}$$

as in Figure 14.4. When

$$\theta(r) \geqslant T-2, \tag{3.35}$$

$$\prod_{t\phi^2 r} Z_t \text{ is null,} \tag{3.36}$$

so that arguments based on (A3) are empty. Hence, the need for care.

(A1)–(A3) imply that we may take the future as separable at all nodes u such that

$$\theta(u) \geqslant 3, \tag{3.37}$$

and that this implies that we can write the criterion at u as

$$f^u(y_u, z_u) \qquad \text{when } \theta(u) \geqslant 3, \tag{3.38}$$

in an appropriate normalization.

Since $T \geqslant 3$, there is an r such that

$$u\phi^3 r, \tag{3.39}$$

and

$$f^u(x_u, y_u, z_u) = f^r(x_u, y_u, z_u; X_u \times Y_u, \times Z_u), \text{ by (3.27)}, \tag{3.40}$$

$$= c^r(x_u, \gamma^r(y_u, z_u; Y_u \times Z_u); X_u) \tag{3.41}$$

where $c^r(\cdot)$ is continuous and $c^r(x_r, \cdot)$ is strictly increasing. Hence,

$$\tilde{f}^u(y_u, z_u) := \gamma^r(y_u, z_u; Y_u \times Z_u), \quad u\phi^3 r, \tag{3.42}$$

is a perfectly good criterion at u, when $\theta(u) \geqslant 3$.

It is easily verified that the $\tilde{f}^r(\cdot)$ satisfy (3.13), (3.27), and (3.31) when $\theta(r) \geqslant 3$, so that we can drop the tildes, and get

$$f^r(x_r, y_r, z_r) = h^r(x_t, f^t(y_t, z_t) \mid t\phi^2 r), \tag{3.25*}$$

$$= c^r((x_t, y_t)_{t\phi^2 r}, \gamma^r(z_t \mid t\phi^2 r)), \tag{3.31*}$$

in particular, when

$$1 \leqslant \theta(r) \leqslant T-3, \tag{3.43}$$

the functions being continuous, and strictly increasing in their functional arguments. Hence,

$$\prod_{t\phi^2 r} X_t; \quad \text{and} \quad Y_t \times Z_t, \qquad \text{each } t\phi^2 r, \tag{3.44}$$

are separable in $f^r(\cdot)$, given (3.43), so that

$$f^r(x_r, y_r, z_r) = j^r((x_t)_{t\phi^2 r}, \sum_{t\phi^2 r} (\alpha^t(y_t) + \beta^t(z_t))), \tag{3.45}$$

say, where

Sets				
	1	3	5	7
	2	4	6	8

Spaces				
	Y_1	Y_2	Y_3	Y_4
	Z_1	Z_2	Z_3	Z_4

Given that $W_t = Y_t \times Z_t$ is separable, each t, i.e. that each of the sets $A_1 = \{1, 2\}$, $A_2 = \{3, 4\}$, $A_3 = \{5, 6\}$, $A_4 = \{7, 8\}$ is separable, and that $z = \prod_t Z_t$ is separable, i.e. that the set $B = (2, 4, 6, 8)$ is separable in $h(y_t, Z_t \mid t = 1, 2, 3, 4)$, I will show that the complementary spaces

$$R_1 = \prod_{t=2} Y_t \times \prod_{t=1} Z_t; \qquad S_1 = \prod_{t=1} Y_t \times \prod_{t=2} Z_t$$

of Y_1 and Z_1 respectively are separable. Since the ordering (1, 2, 3, 4) is immaterial, this will show that the complement of each cell above is separable and hence $h = \sum \alpha^t(y_t) + \sum \beta^t(z_t)$, say, in an appropriate normalization.

Proof: in terms of sets $R_1 \sim ((B \cup A_2) \cup A_3) \cup A_4$
$S_1 \sim (((B \cup A_1) \cup A_2) \cup A_3) \cup A_4$

FIG. 14.5: *Illustrating* (2.5) *and* (3.44)–(3.45)

$$j^r(\cdot) \text{ continuous, } j^r((x_t)_{t\phi^2 r}, \cdot) \text{ is strictly increasing,} \tag{3.46}$$

$$1 \leq \theta(r) \leq T - 3, \tag{3.47}$$

by the argument sketched in and below Figure 14.5.
Clearly we can normalize to get

$$\alpha^t(0) = \beta^t(0) = 0, \tag{3.48}$$

and therefore

$$f^t(y_t, z_t) = f^r(y_t, z_t; Y_t \times Z_t) = j^r(0; \alpha^t(y_t) + \beta^t(z_t)),$$

$$=: k^r(\alpha^t(y_t) + \beta^t(z_t)); \qquad t\phi^2 r, \qquad 3 \leq \theta(t) \leq T - 1, \tag{3.49}$$

where $k^r(\cdot)$ is continuous and strictly increasing.[9] Hence,

$$\ell^r(f^t(y_t, z_t)) = \alpha^t(y_t) + \beta^t(z_t), \tag{3.50}$$

is a perfectly good alternative criterion at t, where

$$\ell^r(k^r(\varepsilon)) = \varepsilon, \qquad 1 \leq \theta(r) \leq T - 3, \tag{3.51}$$

[9] [eds.] The function $k^r(\cdot)$ here is not the same as that defined in (3.26).

and

$$3 \leqslant \theta(t) \leqslant T - 1. \tag{3.52}$$

The next step towards (3.10) is to show that, in a trivial renormalization,

$$\beta^s(z_s) = \sum_{t\phi s} (\alpha^t(y_t) + \beta^t(z_t)), \qquad 3 \leqslant \theta(s) \leqslant T - 2. \tag{3.53}$$

Assume for the moment that (3.53) holds. Then (3.50) yields

$$\alpha^s(y_s) + \beta^s(z_s) = \alpha^s(y_s) + \sum_{t\psi s} (\alpha^t(y_t) + \beta^t(z_t)) = \ldots,$$

$$= \sum_{\substack{t\psi s \\ \theta(t) \leqslant T-1}} \alpha^t(y_t) + \sum_{\substack{t\psi s \\ \theta(t) = T-1}} \beta^t(z_t), \tag{3.54}$$

when

$$\theta(s) \geqslant 3. \tag{3.55}$$

The proof of (3.53) is illustrated in Figure 14.4, where

$$t\phi s\phi r\phi q, \tag{3.56}$$

to yield

$$k^q(\beta^s(z_s)) = f^s(0, z_s) = f^r(z_s; Z_s) = k^r\left(\sum_{t\phi s} (\alpha^t(y_t) + \beta^t(z_t))\right), \tag{3.57}$$

$$k^q\left(\sum_{s\phi r} \beta^s(z_s)\right) = f^r\left((z_s)_{s\phi r}; \prod_{s\phi r} Z_s\right) = k^r\left(\sum_{t\phi^2 r} (\alpha^t(y_t) + \beta^t(z_t))\right), \tag{3.58}$$

where

$$1 \leqslant \theta(q) \leqslant T - 4. \tag{3.59}$$

Define now

$$m^r(\varepsilon) = \ell^r(k^q(\varepsilon)), \qquad 2 \leqslant \theta(r) \leqslant T - 3, \tag{3.60}$$

to get

$$m^r\left(\sum_{s\phi r} \beta^s(z_s)\right) = \sum_{t\phi^2 r} (\alpha^t(y_t) + \beta^t(z_t)), \tag{3.61}$$

$$= \sum_{s\phi r} \sum_{t\phi s} (\alpha^t(y_t) + \beta^t(z_t)),$$

$$= \sum_{s\phi r} m^r(\beta^s(z_s)), \qquad 2 \leqslant \theta(r) \leqslant T - 3. \tag{3.62}$$

Since $m^r(\cdot)$ is continuous and strictly increasing this implies

$$m^r(\varepsilon) = a_r\varepsilon, \text{ say}, \qquad a_r \text{ constant}, \; 2 \leqslant \theta(r) \leqslant T - 3, \tag{3.63}$$

so that

$$a_r\beta^s(z_s) = \sum_{t\in s} (\alpha^t(y_t) + \beta^t(z_t)), \qquad 3 \leqslant \theta(s) \leqslant T - 2, \tag{3.64}$$

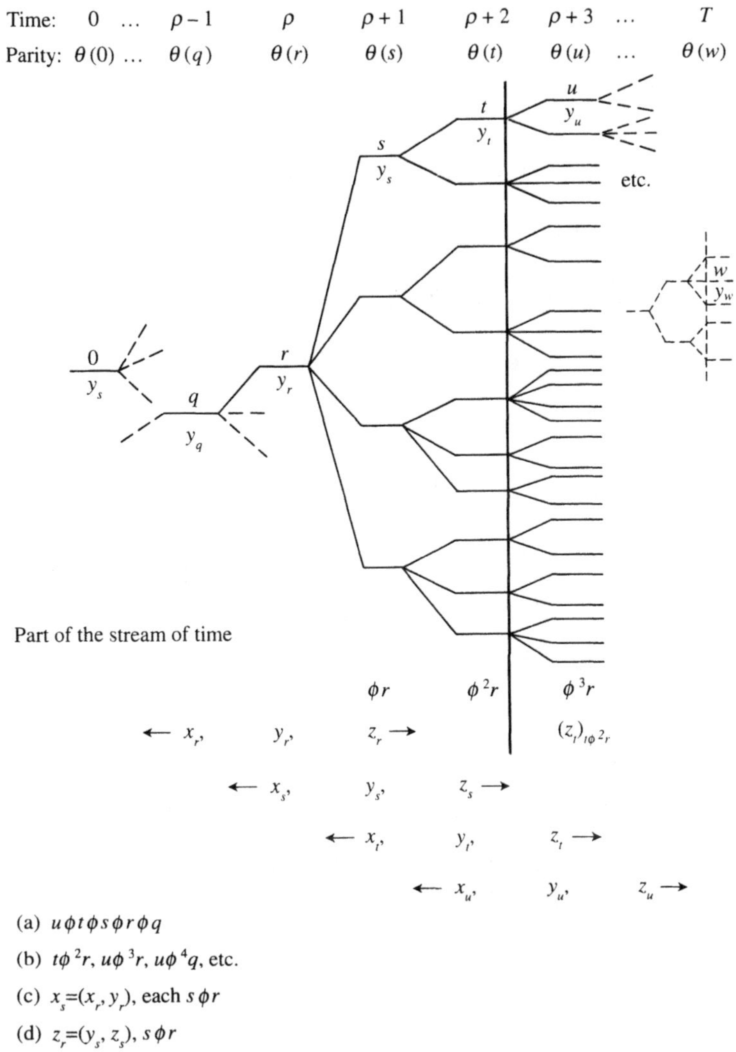

FIG. 14.6: *Illustrating* (3.71)

when we set $y_v = z_v = 0$, $v\phi^2 r$, $v\sim\phi s$, in (3.57).

Now introduce a set of positive constants b_t, one for each node with $3 \leqslant \theta(t) \leqslant T-1$ such that

$$a_r b_t = b_s \quad t\phi s\phi r, \tag{3.65}$$

as we clearly can, and define

$$\tilde{\alpha}^t(y_t) = b_t\alpha^t(y_t), \quad \tilde{\beta}^t(z_t) = b_t\beta^t(z_t), \qquad 3 \leqslant \theta(t) \leqslant T-1, \tag{3.66}$$

and hence

$$\tilde{\beta}^r(z_r) = \sum_{s\phi r} (\tilde{\alpha}^s(y_s) + \tilde{\beta}(y_s)), \qquad 3 \leqslant \theta(r) \leqslant T-2. \tag{3.67}$$

Drop the tildes to get (3.53) and (3.54)

COROLLARY 1: *In this normalization, when* $\theta(r) \geqslant 3$,

$$f^r(y_r, z_r) = \alpha^r(y_r) + \beta^r(z_r), \tag{3.68}$$

$$= \alpha^r(y_r) + \sum_{s\phi r} \alpha^s(y_s) + \sum_{s\phi r} \beta^s(z_s), \tag{3.69}$$

$$= \ldots = \sum_{\substack{v\phi r \\ \theta(v) \leqslant T-1}} \alpha^v(y_v) + \sum_{\substack{v\phi r \\ \theta(v) = T-1}} \beta^v(z_v), \tag{3.70}$$

$$= \sum_{\substack{v\psi r \\ \theta(v) \leqslant T-1}} \alpha^v(y_v) + \sum_{\substack{v\psi r \\ \theta(v) = T-1}} \delta^v(\varepsilon(y_w) \mid w\phi v). \tag{3.71}$$

(3.68)–(3.70) are trivial. To get (3.71) we note that the criterion function at a terminal point w, with $\theta(w) = T$, may be defined by

$$f^w(y_w) := f^v(y_w;\, Y_w) = \beta^v(y_w;\, Y_w), \quad w\phi v,$$

$$=: \varepsilon^w(y_w), \tag{3.72}$$

implying (3.71) by (3.24) and (3.31) where

$$\delta^v(\varepsilon) = g^v(0, \varepsilon). \tag{3.73}$$

In a sense (3.73) advances the terminal point for (3.70) by one more hesitant step. One can push back the opening value, $\theta(r)$, from 3 to 2 to get

$$f^r(x_r, y_r, z_r) = \alpha^r(x_r, y_r) + \beta^r(z_r), \text{ say}, \qquad \theta(r) = 2, \tag{3.74}$$

where

$$\beta^r(z_r) = \sum_{s\phi r} (\alpha^s(y_s) + \beta^s(z_s)), \tag{3.75}$$

now for $\theta(r) = 2$, as well as $3 \leqslant \theta(r) \leqslant T-2$ as in (3.67). I will not spell out the argument here. It is similar to that given above, and just as clumsy.

I suspect that such arguments are unnecessary, and that the results in this section can be derived directly from Theorem 1 in Gorman (1968*c*). I hope to have a shot at this later.[10]

[10] Actually, the results can be strengthened for $\theta(r) < 2$.

4. ADDITIVITY OVER STREAMS

Tastes are learned from experience; organizations presumably '*learn by doing*' and may 'improve' their criteria in consequence. Separability over time is doubtfully desirable.

What about additivity over streams, identified by their terminal nodes w, such that

$$\theta(w) = T? \tag{4.1}$$

First, consider a timeless model. By tomorrow we will know in which of $2k \geqslant 4$ states we are in. For the usual reasons, the weak independence axiom

$$f(z) = g(f^1(y_1), f^2(y_2), \ldots, f^{2k}(y_{2k})),$$

$$g(\cdot) \text{ continuous and strictly increasing,} \tag{4.2}$$

is acceptable. Now suppose that $1, 2, \ldots, 2k$ is a natural order—say by the rate of inflation, or the percentage of Democrats in the House. Assume that one will know ahead of time that the world will be in a particular '*broad set*'

$$S_1 = \{1, 2, \ldots, k\},\ S_2 = \{2, 3, \ldots, k+1\}, \ldots, S_{k+1} = \{k+1, k+2, \ldots, 2k\}. \tag{4.3}$$

These are the bridges, one of which the organization will soon be called upon to cross. Perhaps it is reasonable to assume each separable. Call this *broad separability*. Then

$$f(z) = h^j(v_{\sim j}, k^j(v_j)), \qquad \text{each } h^j(\cdot) \text{ continuous, } h^j(v_{\sim j}, \cdot) \text{ strictly increasing,} \tag{4.4}$$

where $v^j = (y_j, y_{j+1}, \ldots, y_{j+k-1})$, $v_{\sim j}$ its complement.

Call the complement of i

$$\sim i = \{1, 2, \ldots, i-1, i+1, \ldots, 2k\}, \tag{4.5}$$

and take $i \leqslant k$ without loss of generality. When $i = 1$,

$$\sim 1 = (((S_2 \cup S_3) \cup S_4) \ldots) \cup S_{k+1}. \tag{4.6}$$

When $1 < i \leqslant k$,

$$\sim i = (((S_1 \,\Delta\, S_i) \cup S_{i+1}) \cup S_{i+2} \ldots) \cup S_k. \tag{4.7}$$

Each $\sim i$ is therefore separable, and (4.4) yields

$$f(z) = \sum_{i=1}^{2k} f^i(y_i), \tag{4.8}$$

in an appropriate normalization.

A similar treatment yields the same result when there are $2k - 1 \geqslant 3$ states. Note that (4.2) is a result, not an assumption, in this case.

Can one get (4.8), or something like it when the world reveals itself as in Figure 14.3? One can, but only by applying broad separability, based on rough foresight, at least two periods ahead, rather as in (A3). In fact, the simplest assumptions which suggest themselves are (A1), (A2) and

(A3*) *Broad Separability within a Two-Period Rolling Plan*

$$f^r(x_r, y_r, z_r) = d^S((x_t)_{t\phi^2 r}, (y_t, z_t)_{t\in \sim S}, \delta^S(x_t, y_t, z_t \mid t\in S)), \tag{4.9}$$

say, for each of the broad sets S of $t\phi^2 r$ defined as in (4.3), $\sim S$ being its complement with respect to the set of $t\phi^2 r$. Given (A1), this immediately yields

$$f^r(x_r, y_r, z_r) = a^r\left((x_t)_{t\phi^2 r}, \sum_{t\phi^2 r} \alpha^t(x_t, y_t, z_t)\right), \text{ say,} \tag{4.10}$$

where

$$a^r((x_t)_{t\phi^2 r}, \cdot) \text{ is strictly increasing,} \tag{4.11}$$

and we can normalize to get

$$\alpha^t(x_t, 0, 0) = 0, \qquad \text{when } \theta(t) \geq 2, \tag{4.12}$$

by absorbing any such term into the blanket $(x_t)_{t\phi^2 r}$ argument in $a^r(\cdot)$. Do so.

Normalize the $f^r(\cdot)$ to satisfy (3.27)–(3.29) as in Section 3. (4.9) then yields

$$f^t(x_t, y_t, z_t) = f^r(x_t, y_t, z_t; X_t \times Y_t \times Z_t), \quad t\phi^2 r, \tag{4.13}$$

$$= c^t(x_t, \alpha^t(x_t, y_t, z_t)), \quad \text{say}, \quad t\phi^2 r, \tag{4.14}$$

$$f^s(x_s, y_s, z_s) = f^r(x_s, y_s, z_s; X_s \times Y_s \times Z_s), \quad \text{say}, \quad s\phi r, \tag{4.15}$$

$$= b^s\left(x_s, y_s, \sum_{t\phi s} \alpha^t(x_t, y_t, z_t)\right), \text{ say, } s\phi r, \tag{4.16}$$

where

$$a^r((x_t)_{t\phi^2 r}, \cdot), \quad b^s(x_s, y_s, \cdot), \quad c^t(x_t, \cdot) \text{ are strictly increasing,} \tag{4.17}$$

when

$$\theta(r) \geq 0, \quad \theta(s) \geq 1, \quad \theta(t) \geq 2. \tag{4.18}$$

Clearly

$$\alpha^t(x_t, y_t, z_t) \tag{4.19}$$

is a perfectly good criterion at t when

$$\theta(t) \geq 2. \tag{4.20}$$

I will now prove

THEOREM: *In a simple renormalization*

$$\alpha^r(x_r, y_r, z_r) = \sum_{s\phi r} \alpha^s(x_s, y_s, z_s) = \sum_{t\phi^2 r} \alpha^t(x_t, y_t, z_t)$$

$$= \ldots = \sum_{w\psi r}{}^{*} \alpha^w(x_w, y_w, z_w), \qquad \textit{when } \phi(r) \geqslant 2, \tag{4.21}$$

where $\sum^*$ *is taken over terminal nodes* w, *as foreshadowed in* (4.1).

Remarks: This is virtually what I set out to get. Once again, there is an end—or rather initial—effect. (4.21) does not apply when $\theta(r) = 0$ or 1. In these cases we have

$$f^0(y_0, z_0) = a^0\left((x_t)_{t\phi^2 0}, \sum_{w\psi 0}{}^{*} \alpha^w(x_w, y_w, z_w)\right), \tag{4.22}$$

$$f^r(x_r, y_r, z_r) = b^r\left(x_r, y_r, \sum_{w\psi r}{}^{*} \alpha^w(x_w, y_w, z_w)\right), \qquad \text{when } \theta(r) = 1, \tag{4.23}$$

by (4.10) and (4.16) respectively.

PROOF: The argument is similar to that in Section 3. Once again we set out to derive a linear relationship via the linearity equation $f(\sum x_i) = \sum f(x_i)$. First solve (4.14) for α^t and substitute s for t in the result to get

$$\alpha^s(x_s, y_s, z_s) = i^s(x_s, f^s(x_s, y_s, z_s)), \text{ say}, \qquad i^s(x_s, \cdot) \text{ strictly increasing}, \tag{4.24}$$

$$= j^s\left(x_s, y_s, \sum_{t\phi s} \alpha^t(x_t, y_t, z_t)\right), \text{ say}, \qquad j^s(x_s, y_s, \cdot) \text{ strictly increasing}, \tag{4.25}$$

by (4.16).[11] Then solve (4.16) for $\sum_{t\phi s} \alpha^t(x_t, y_t, z_t)$ and substitute s for t, and r for s, in the result to get

$$\sum_{s\phi r} \alpha^s(x_s, y_s, z_s) = k^r(x_r, y_r, f^r(x_r, y_r, z_r)), \text{ say},$$

$$k^r(x_r, y_r, \cdot) \text{ strictly increasing}, \tag{4.26}$$

$$= \ell^r\left((x_t)_{t\phi^2 r}, \sum_{t\phi^2 r} \alpha^t(x_t, y_t, z_t)\right), \text{ say}, \qquad \ell^r((x_t)_{t\phi^2 r}, \cdot) \text{ strictly increasing}, \tag{4.27}$$

when

$$\theta(s) \geqslant 2, \quad \theta(r) \geqslant 1, \text{ respectively}. \tag{4.28}$$

Hence,

$$\sum_{s\phi r} j^s\left(x_s, y_s, \sum_{t\phi s} \alpha^t(x_t, y_t, x_t)\right) = \ell^r\left((x_s, y_s)_{s\phi r}, \sum_{t\phi^2 r} \alpha^t(x_t, y_t, z_t)\right). \tag{4.29}$$

[11] [eds.] The functions $j^s(\cdot)$, $k^r(\cdot)$ and $\ell^r(\cdot)$ defined in (4.25)–(4.27) differ from those used in Sec. 3.

Notice the linearity equation beginning to emerge. Take now $s\phi r$ and set

$$y_t = z_t = 0, \quad t\phi^2 r, \quad t\sim\phi s, \tag{4.30}$$

to get

$$j^s\left(x_s, y_s, \sum_{t\phi s} \alpha^t(x_t, y_t, z_t)\right) = \ell^r\left((x_s, y_s)_{s\phi r}, \sum_{t\phi s} \alpha^t(x_t, y_t, z_t)\right), \tag{4.31}$$

by (4.12) and (4.25), so that

$$j^s(x_s, y_s, \varepsilon) = \ell^r((x_s, y_s)_{s\phi r}, \varepsilon) = m^r(x_r, y_r, \varepsilon), \text{ say,} \tag{4.32}$$

where, of course,

$$(x_r, y_r) = x_s, \qquad \text{each } s\phi r. \tag{4.33}$$

(4.29) therefore becomes

$$\sum_{s\phi r} m^r(x_r, y_r, \varepsilon_s) = m^r\left(x_r, y_r, \sum_{s\phi r} \varepsilon_s\right), \qquad \text{when } \theta(t) \geqslant 1, \tag{4.34}$$

where

$$\varepsilon_s = \sum_{t\phi s} \alpha^t(x_t, y_t, z_t). \tag{4.35}$$

Since $m^r(x_r, y_r, \cdot)$ is strictly increasing, these imply

$$m^r(x_r, y_r, \varepsilon) = e^r(x_r, y_r)\varepsilon, \text{ say,} \qquad e^r > 0, \tag{4.36}$$

and hence,

$$\alpha^s(x_s, y_s, z_s) = j^s\left(x_s, y_s, \sum_{t\phi s} \alpha^t(x_t, y_t, z_t)\right), \quad \text{by (4.25),} \tag{4.37}$$

$$= m^r\left(x_r, y_r \sum_{t\phi s} \alpha^t(x_t, y_t, z_t)\right), \quad \text{by (4.32),} \tag{4.38}$$

$$= e^r(x_r, y_r) \sum_{t\phi s} \alpha^t(x_t, y_t, z_t). \tag{4.39}$$

Now, choose multipliers

$$\lambda^r(x_r, y_r) > 0, \qquad \text{each } r \text{ such that } \theta(r) \leqslant T-2, \tag{4.40}$$

with $\lambda^0(y_0) = 1$, such that

$$\lambda^s(x_s, y_s) = e^s(x_s, y_s)\lambda^r(x_r, y_r), \qquad \text{each } s\phi r, \tag{4.41}$$

and define

$$\tilde{\alpha}^t(x_t, y_t, z_t) = \lambda^r(x_r, y_r)\alpha^t(x_t, y_t, z_t), \qquad \text{each } t\phi^2 r, \tag{4.42}$$

to get

$$\tilde{\alpha}^s(x_s, y_s, z_s) = \sum_{t\phi s} \tilde{\alpha}^t(x_t, y_t, z_t), \qquad 2 \leqslant \theta(s) \leqslant T-1. \tag{4.43}$$

The construction is clearly simple in a model such as that depicted in Figure 14.3, that is, given (A1). Moreover, (x_r, y_r) is past history at t, so that $\tilde{\alpha}^t(x_t, y_t, z_t)$ is just as good a criterion there as is $\alpha^t(x_t, y_t, z_t)$. We may, therefore, drop the tildes in (4.43) and replace s by r to get the first equation in (4.21). The others follow trivially. We have proved the Theorem.

Remark: 'Proved' is a big word. To justify it I would have to discuss the range of the ε's in (4.34). That might be tricky. I do not think it would affect the result.

PART II

AGGREGATION ACROSS AGENTS AND FIRMS

15

Community Preference Fields

Editorial Summary

This is Gorman's first published paper and it is an impressive piece of work. The question is both interesting and important. Under what conditions does there exist a community preference map? That is, when does an entire community behave as if it were as single person? This remains a common assumption in both applied and theoretical work.

Section 2 contains as clear a statement of classical welfare economics as one could want. First, however, the notation. There is an economy of N people and n goods. Person r consumes $x_r = (x_{r1}, \ldots, x_{rn})$ and the total consumption of society is $\sum x_r = x$. Individual utility depends only upon one's own consumption, so that the utility of individual r is given by $u_r(x_r)$.

The *community preference set* $P(u^*)$ is the set of all x that can provide at least the vector of utilities u^* (now called the Scitovsky set). Conversely, the *utility attainability set* $A(x^*)$ is the set of utilities attainable with the vector of commodities x^*. Their boundaries are called the *community indifference set* and the *utility possibility set*, $X(u^*)$ and $U(x^*)$, respectively; Theorem VII shows that $x^* \in X(u^*)$ if and only if $u^* \in U(x^*)$. He notes that this is an interesting result, in that community indifference maps and utility possibility maps have a common equation of the form

$$F(x, u) = 0, \tag{0.1}$$

which he calls the equation of the community preference field.

The question at hand is straightforward: under what conditions does there exist only one community indifference curve through each point of the domain (or, only one utility possibility frontier through each point). He first shows that there is only one community indifference curve through each point if and only if there is only one utility possibility curve through each point (Theorem VIII). To see this, observe that if there is just one community indifference curve through each point, then the level surfaces of F in x must be independent of u. In this case, F can be rewritten as

$$F(x, u) = \bar{F}(f(x), u), \text{ say,} \tag{0.2}$$

and hence, using (0.1) that

$$F(x, u) = 0 = f(x) + g(u), \text{ say.} \tag{0.3}$$

In Section 4 he proceeds to the main argument.

The regularity assumptions adopted show that he understood the structure of these aggregation problems in a way which escaped others for a long time. In particular, preferences are only defined on a closed convex set in the interior of the positive orthant. This is important because it excludes the origin from the domain of the problem. If the origin is left in the problem, then no matter what region of space is being considered, the solution has to hold if any subset of the variables are zero. This forces all possible solutions to hold globally. While in some circumstances this may be an interesting question in its own right, it is unreasonable to presume that it is the only question of interest. Hence excluding the origin is not merely a minor technical restriction in this case, but rather one which permits the analysis of a more general class of problems.

Theorems IX and X present the solutions, now well known, that the income–consumption curves of all agents must be straight lines and parallel to each other.[1] To generate the solution, pick, for each person, a base indifference curve indexed by zero utility, and let $x_r^*(p)$ be the compensated demands of individual r at prices p and zero utility. Then the system of compensated demands can be written as

$$x_r^*(p) + c(p)u_r \tag{0.4}$$

for each individual r and by

$$x^*(p) + c(p)\sum_r u_r \tag{0.5}$$

for society as a whole, where

$$x^*(p) = \sum_r x_r^*(p). \tag{0.6}$$

The balance of the paper discusses the implications of relaxing the assumptions and applications of this result. In passing, there is a nice statement of the composite commodity theorem in Section V.

The way in which Gorman solves these problems is in terms of normals and tangents and cries out for a dual approach. Between acceptance of the paper by *Econometrica* and the arrival of the page proofs, Gorman says that he discovered the cost function solution and representation of this problem. However he thought that this would entail more changes in the proofs than the journal would tolerate. A closed form dual solution was later published in 'On a Class of Preference Fields' in 1961. However, it does not hurt to foreshadow those results here.

Suppose that consumer r has an expenditure function given by

$$m_r = g_r(u_r, p) \tag{0.7}$$

Then there exists a community preference field if and only if the expenditure function of each consumer can be written as

$$m_r = g_r(u_r, p) = b_r(p) + u_r c(p). \tag{0.8}$$

Using Shephard's lemma, this yields parallel linear Engel curves

[1] Gorman uses the phrase 'income–consumption curve' to describe the ordinary (Marshallian) demand function and reserves the phrase 'Engel Curve' for its compensated analogue.

$$\frac{\partial x_{ri}}{\partial u_r} = \frac{\partial^2 g_r(u_r, p)}{\partial p_i \partial u_r} + c_i(p). \tag{0.9}$$

Furthermore, total expenditure, which is the support function of the community preference (or Scitovsky) set, is given by

$$\sum_r m_r = b(p) + c(p) \sum_r u_r. \tag{0.10}$$

Aggregate demand is given by taking the derivatives of this support function with respect to prices.[2]

[2] See the end of the editorial remarks on 'Measuring the Quantity of Fixed Factors' for further elaboration of this structure in the dual.

Community Preference Fields

A series of formal relationships between community indifference maps and utility possibility maps are stated and it is proved that a given system of personal indifference maps yields a unique community indifference map if, and only if, the personal Engel curves are parallel straight lines for *different* individuals at the *same* prices. The most general method of constructing such a set of indifference maps is discovered, and it appears that the utility possibility map can then be written in the form $\sum u = \text{constant}$. Various applications are discussed.

1. INTRODUCTION AND SYNOPSIS[1]

Community indifference and utility possibility loci are among the most useful concepts of welfare economics. Their great disadvantage is that they may intersect. Through each point in 'commodity space' there is normally an infinite family of community indifference surfaces; through each point in 'utility space', there is an infinite family of utility possibility surfaces. In analysing any particular problem one usually has to move from one such surface to another. Thus the analysis is made more difficult and frequently becomes inconclusive. This became clear following the discussion of Nicholas Kaldor's (1939) attempt to distinguish between problems of efficiency and problems of distribution, and to erect a separate criterion of efficiency using the compensation principle. If the utility possibility surfaces cut, this distinction breaks down. The criterion of efficiency comes to depend on the distribution. If they do not cut, the distinction can be maintained.

It will be shown below that no pair of utility possibility surfaces cut if, and only if, no pair of community indifference surfaces cut. It may therefore be asked: under what conditions is either of these statements true? In fact we will show that there is just one community indifference locus through each point if, and only if, the Engel curves for different individuals at the same prices are parallel straight lines. The slope of these lines may be different at different prices. In this case, we can write the equation of any utility possibility locus in the form $\sum_r u_r = \text{const.}$, where u_r is the utility index of the rth individual. Of course, this result depends on an appropriate choice

[1] This article arises partly from a discussion of a particular case with Mr H. G. Johnson of King's College, Cambridge. I also have had fruitful discussions of the subject with Dr F. H. Hahn of Birmingham University and Mr S. J. Prais of the Department of Applied Economics, Cambridge. In writing the article I have been torn between a desire for rigour and a desire for simplicity, and each has had to be sacrificed in part to the other.

of the index in question. Nevertheless, it has interesting consequences in various fields.

These conditions are rather restrictive. However, if we are only interested in the aggregate consumption of broad categories of goods, and if we can assume that the relative prices of goods in the same category are constant, we can select a separate numeraire for each category—say the first good in it. We can then construct indifference maps between these numeraires and apply the analysis below to these indifference loci.

The necessary and sufficient condition quoted above is intuitively reasonable. It says, in effect, that an extra unit of purchasing power should be spent in the same way no matter to whom it is given. Nevertheless, it does not seem to have been discovered before. In the central section of this article the construction of a set of personal indifference maps obeying this criterion is discussed. It is shown that the most general method of doing so is to choose one indifference locus for each person *freely*. To determine the slopes of the Engel lines we draw a further convex surface, again freely. Using these surfaces, we can always construct the required indifference maps. Clearly, a very wide family of such maps can be constructed. Clearly too, the tastes of different individuals may be different.[2]

In the final section of the paper, some applications of the results are briefly discussed.

2. DEFINITIONS

Consider an economy of N persons and n goods. The rth person consumes $x_{ri} \geqslant 0$ units of the ith good ($r = 1, 2, \ldots, N$; $i = 1, 2, \ldots, n$). Define the following: r^{th} *consumption vector*,

$$x_r = (x_{r1}, x_{r2}, \ldots, x_{rn});$$

total consumption of the ith *good*,

$$x_i = \sum\nolimits_r x_{ri};$$

and the *total consumption vector*,

$$x = (x_1, x_2, \ldots, x_n) = \sum\nolimits_r x_r.$$

Each individual is assumed to order situations solely on the basis of his own consumption, and, other things being equal, to prefer a greater to a smaller consumption of any good. His tastes may therefore be represented by a utility index[3] of the form: r^{th} *utility index*, $u_r = u_r(x_r)$, which is a strictly

[2] On this point, see the last paragraph of Sect. 5.

[3] It is well known that any increasing function of this index will represent his tastes equally well. I want to make it clear that my choice of one particular index in no way implies that I

increasing function of each x_{ri}. We will further introduce *the distribution of utility*, $u = (u_1, u_2, \ldots, u_N)$.

We will write $y > x$, and say that *the total consumption at y is greater than at x*, if $y_i \geqslant x_i$, for all $i = 1, \ldots, n$ and $y_i > x_i$ for at least one such i. The statements $x < y$ and $y > x$ are equivalent. We similarly define $u > v$ and $u < v$. We will say that x is a minimal member of a set S if there is no $y < x$ belonging to S. The minimal subset of S is the set of minimal elements of S. The maximal subset of a set of u's is similarly defined.

Consider now a distribution of utility u^*. If this can be attained with a total consumption x it can clearly be attained with any $y > x$.[4] We may define the *community preference set* $P(u^*)$ *associated with a distribution* u^* to be the set of all x at which u^* is attainable. The *community indifference set* is the minimal subset of this set. It is, therefore, the set $X(u^*)$ of x's such that (i) u^* is attainable at x, and (ii) u^* is not attainable at any $y < x$. Each such minimal supply vector x will be said to be 'associated' with u^*.

The *utility attainability set* $A(x^*)$ *associated with a supply vector* x^* may be similarly defined as the set of u's attainable at x^*. The *utility possibility set* $U(x^*)$ is its maximal subset. It is the set of u's such that (i) u is attainable at x^*, and (ii) no $v > u$ is attainable at x^*. Any such maximal distribution u will be said to be *associated* with the supply x^*.

Clearly x is in $P(u)$ if, and only if, u is in $A(x)$. Since the u_r are strictly increasing functions of the x_r we would also expect that u would belong to $U(x)$ if, and only if, x belonged to $X(u)$. It will be proved below that this is true as long as all the variables are continuous. It is not necessarily true if they are discrete. Consider a community of one individual who is faced with two possibilities: he may consume (*a*) an apple yielding him u units of utility; or (*b*) a banana, yielding him $v > u$ units.[5] Then b belongs to $X(u)$, since u is attainable in b while there is no $x < b$ at which it is attainable. On the other hand, u does not belong to $U(b)$, since $v > u$ can be attained there. This argument is perfectly general and does not depend on the fact that there is only one person in the community nor on the fact that he cannot consume some of each good at the same time.

regard utility as, in some sense, measurable. One cannot discuss utility possibility surfaces without choosing some particular utility indices. It is possible to imagine consistent preference systems which could not be represented by a utility indicator; e.g. a person might always prefer any situation with more butter to one with less, but for a given quantity of butter, prefer to have more jam. We have assumed implicitly that the preference system is not of a higher order than the continuum. This seems reasonable.

[4] We may define: u^* is *attainable* at x^* if there is a set of non-negative numbers y^*_{ri} such that for all $i = 1, \ldots, n$, (i) $\sum_r y^*_{ri} \leqslant x^*_i$, (ii) each $u_r(x_r)$ is defined at $x_r = y^*_r = (y_{r1}, \ldots, y^*_{rn})$, and (iii) $u_r(y^*_r) \geqslant u^*_r$ for each $r = 1, \ldots, N$.

[5] These statements refer to some particular set of utility indicators. We could equally well choose u_2 and v_2. The result is quite independent of the system of indicators that we use.

3. SOME GENERAL RESULTS

In this section we will prove some general relationships between the utility possibility and community indifference maps. Throughout the section we will confine our attention to certain regions of discourse. For the rth person's indifference map, this will be a region R_r defined by $u_r(x_r) \geqslant u_r^0$. We can make this region coincide with the positive orthant by taking $u_r^0 = u_r(0)$, but this will not normally be necessary, since one must eat to live. For the community indifference map the region of discourse will be the set $R = \sum_r R_r$; that is, the set of $x = \sum_r x_r$, where x_r is in R_r. For the utility possibility map, the region of discourse will be the set S of distributions attainable in R. Topological terms such as 'interior', 'frontier', and 'closed' are normally used relative to the appropriate region of discourse, except in Theorem V, where they are used relative to the entire Euclidean space in question. This makes Theorem III (below) formally incorrect for points on the boundary of the regions of discourse relative to a wider space.

We will assume the following:

ASSUMPTION I: The x_{ri} $(i = 1, \ldots, n)$ are continuously variable over R_r $(r = 1, \ldots, N)$.

ASSUMPTION II: $u_r(x_r)$ is defined and is a continuous and strictly increasing function of x_r throughout R_r $(r = 1, \ldots, N)$.

ASSUMPTION III: Each personal preference set $u_r(x_r) \geqslant u_r^*$ is strictly convex; that is, if y_r and z_r are in it, $(y_r + z_r)/2$ is in its interior.

The proofs of the following results will not be given.

THEOREM I: *The community preference sets $P(u)$ are closed and strictly convex.*

THEOREM II: *The utility attainability set $A(x)$ is closed.*

THEOREM III: *The community indifference set $X(u)$ is the frontier of the set $P(u)$, and the utility possibility set $U(x)$ is the frontier of $A(x)$.*

THEOREM IV: *Through each point of R there is at least one community indifference set. Through each point of S there is at least one utility possibility set.*

THEOREM V: *To each point x in the interior of R there is a utility possibility set $U(x)$ which is a continuous $N-1$ dimensional hyper-surface in S. To each point u in the interior of S there is a community indifference set $X(u)$ which is a continuous $n-1$ dimensional hyper-surface in R.*

THEOREM VI: *If X^* and X^{**} are a pair of non-identical community indifference sets, we can choose points y and z, one belonging to each, such that $y > z$. If U^* and U^{**} are a pair of non-identical utility possibility sets, we can choose points v and w, one belonging to each, such that $v > w$.*

These results have been given in the most convenient order, not in the order in which they were proven. On account of Theorem V we will henceforth speak of community indifference and utility possibility *surfaces*. From them we can deduce the following theorem.

THEOREM VII: *x is in $X(u)$ if and only if u is in $U(x)$.*

We will prove that, if x is in $X(u)$, u is in $U(x)$. Clearly u is attainable at x. If, then, u does not belong to $U(x)$, it must be because some $v > u$ is attainable there. Someone must be better off under v than u; suppose that it is the first person. Keeping everything else the same, reduce his holding of the first good, but not sufficiently to make him worse off than in u. This can be done because of the continuity of $u_1(x_1)$. We thus reach a distribution $w > u$ which is attainable with a supply less than x—call it y. Hence u is attainable with $y < x$, so that x does not belong to $X(u)$, which contradicts our assumption. Hence the first half of the theorem is proved; the other half is proved in the same manner.

This is a useful result. In conjunction with Theorem III, it implies that the community indifference and utility possibility maps have a common equation of the form $F(x, u) = 0$. This may be called the equation of the community preference field.

THEOREM VIII: *There is just one community indifference surface through each point of R, if and only if there is just one utility possibility surface through each point of S.*

We will first prove that there is just one community indifference surface through each point of R if there is just one utility possibility surface through each point of S. Assume, first, that a pair of non-identical community indifference surfaces $X(v)$ and $X(w)$ pass through a given point x. We can then choose a point y on one of these, say $X(v)$, and a point z on the other, such that $y > z$. This follows from Theorem VI. Hence, for each distribution v^* attainable at y there is a distribution $w^* > v^*$ attainable at z. Hence $U(y)$ and $U(z)$ have no point in common. By Theorem VII, v belongs to both

$U(x)$ and $U(y)$. But there is just one utility possibility surface through v. Hence $U(y)$ is identical with $U(x)$ and $U(z)$ is identical with $U(x)$; hence they are identical with each other. We proved above that they are distinct. This is a contradiction. Hence, there is not more than one community indifference set through any point. By Theorem IV, there is at least one through each point. Hence there is just one through each point.

The proof of the other half of the theorem is exactly similar. In this case there is a unique community indifference surface through each point in C, and a unique utility possibility surface through each point in S. We will express these facts by saying that there is a *unique community preference field.*

4. THE MAIN DISCUSSION

In this section we will deduce most of the main results mentioned in the introduction for the case in which the utility indices are differentiable. We will use Assumptions I–III as well as the following:

ASSUMPTION IV: The base indifference surfaces do not intersect the coordinate planes. This clearly implies that no higher indifference surface does so either.

ASSUMPTION V: $u_{ri}(x_r) = \partial u_r/\partial x_{ri}$ exists and is single-valued and positive at each point of R_r ($r = 1, \ldots, N$; $i = 1, \ldots, n$).

The two assumptions are needed as a basis for the differential methods used in this section. They will be relaxed in Section 5.

Let us now search for the community indifference surface associated with a given distribution u. To do so we first fix $x_2, \ldots, x_n$ and find the extremals of x_1 subject to the restriction that u be attainable. Later we show that the locus so defined is indeed the required community indifference surface. It will clearly include it.

Introducing Lagrange multipliers $p = (p_1, p_2, \ldots, p_n) = (1, p_2, \ldots, p_n)$ and $q = (q_1, q_2, \ldots, q_N)$, we seek the extremals of $\sum_i p_i x_i - \sum_r q_r u_r$, where

$$x_i = \sum_r x_{ri}; \quad u_r = u_r(x_r), \qquad r = 1, \ldots, N; \; i = 1, \ldots, n. \tag{1}$$

Differentiating with respect to x_{ri} and putting the result $= 0$, we find

$$q_r u_{ri} = p_i, \qquad r = 1, \ldots, N; \; i = 1, \ldots, n. \tag{2}$$

From (2), we have $u_{ri}/u_{r1} = p_i/p_1 = p_i$. Now, u_{ri} is always positive, since we have assumed u_r to be a strictly increasing function of x_r. Hence p_i is positive, and hence q_r is positive also, by (2). Moreover p_i is plainly the marginal rate of substitution between the ith and first good for each person. It may therefore be regarded as the price of the ith good in terms of the first. We will therefore call p a price vector. Similarly q_r may be visualized as the marginal utility of income to the rth person (or, more accurately, its inverse: the money price of utility).

We have here Nn equations (2) and $N + n$ equations (1), together with the single equation $p_1 = 1$. Unless the system is degenerate, which it cannot be,[6] we can use $N + n + nN$ of these to solve for the N q's, the n p's, and the nN x_{ri}'s in terms of the remaining variables, and u. Substituting these in the remaining equation we have

$$F(x, u) = 0. \tag{3}$$

From (2) we have

$$q_r \mathrm{d}u_r = \sum_i q_r u_{ri} \mathrm{d}x_{ri} = \sum_i p_i \mathrm{d}x_{ri}. \tag{4}$$

Hence, along a personal indifference surface, $\sum_i p_i \mathrm{d}x_{ri} = 0$, that is, p is normal to the surface u_r = constant = u_r^*, say. Moreover, adding:

$$\sum_r q_r \mathrm{d}u_r = \sum_{ri} p_i \mathrm{d}x_{ri} = \sum_i p_i \mathrm{d}x_i. \tag{5}$$

Hence, for a given $u = u^*$, say, $\sum_i p_i \mathrm{d}x_i = 0$; that is, p is normal to the surface $F(x, u^*) = 0$.

We will now show that this surface is the community indifference surface $X(u^*)$. Consider any point x^* on it, and let p^*, x_r^* be the corresponding normal direction and r^{th} consumption vector. Consider now a displacement from x_r^* to $x_r^* + \delta x_r$ in $u_r(x_r) \geqslant u_r^*$. Clearly $\sum_i p_i^* \delta x_{ri} = 0$ is a supporting hyperplane of this strictly convex region. Hence $\sum_i p_i^* \delta x_{ri}$ is either positive for all points of the region, or negative for all points of it. But it is equal to plus one at the point x_r^{**} where $x_{r1}^{**} = x_{r1}^* + 1$, $x_{ri}^{**} = x_{ri}^*$ $(i = 2, \ldots, n)$. Hence

$$\sum_i p_i^* \delta x_{ri} > 0. \tag{6}$$

In addition, we have that $\sum_i p_i^* \delta x_i$ is positive for any displacement which leaves everyone at least as well off as before. Now each p_i is positive, so that δx is not a negative vector. Hence $x^* + \delta x \nless x^*$. But the displacement δx

[6] Remembering that the locus defined by (1) and (2) must include, for a given u, the $n - 1$ dimensional surface $X(u)$, we can prove that the system cannot be degenerate. Two sorts of degeneracy are possible. In the first place the equations (1) and (2) might be inconsistent, so that the locus they define is null. This is clearly impossible. In the second place there might be several eliminant equations. This would happen, for instance, if the community fell into disjoint classes, the members of no two classes consuming a common good. In this case, the locus defined by (1) and (2) for a given u would be $n - e$ dimensional where $e \geqslant 2$ is the number of eliminants. This cannot include a $n - 1$ dimensional surface.

was perfectly general, subject to the restriction that nobody be made worse off. Hence x^* is indeed a minimal supply vector subject to this restriction. It therefore belongs to $X(u^*)$, whose equation is therefore $F(x, u^*) = 0$, which is what we set out to prove. Moreover, by Theorem VII the equation of the utility possibility locus $U(x^*)$ is $F(x^*, u) = 0$. This result could be proved directly by applying the argument of Theorem VII to the present case.

Consider now the case where there is a unique community indifference surface through each point in R. Let x be such a point, and let p be the direction normal to the community indifference locus through it.[7] Let u be *any* associated utility distribution, and x_r be the rth person's consumption vector. Then p is normal to u_r at x_r. As we pass through the various utility distributions associated with x, the x_r will trace out paths. At each point of these paths, the direction normal to the corresponding personal indifference locus will be parallel to the fixed direction p. I will follow tradition and call these curves Engel curves. To distinguish them from income–consumption curves, which are also frequently called Engel curves, I will refer to the latter as *classical* Engel curves. The two families of curves are closely related.

We will now show that a necessary condition for the existence of a unique preference field is that these Engel curves should be straight lines, which should be parallel for *different individuals* at the *same prices*. The Engel curves may be represented parametrically by $x_{ri} = f_{ri}(u_r; p)$. Consider now a supply vector x^* and an associated utility distribution u^*. Take any s in $2, 3, \ldots, N$. Fix x^* and $u_r = u_r^*$, $r \neq 1, s$. Vary u_1 slightly to $u_1^* + \mathrm{d}u_1$, and u_s to $u_s + \mathrm{d}u_s$ so that $F(x^*, u) = 0$ remains true.

Writing $f'_{ri} = \mathrm{d}f_{ri}/\mathrm{d}u_r$, we have that $\mathrm{d}x_{ri} = f'_{ri}\,\mathrm{d}u_r = 0$ if $f \neq 1, s$. Hence $\mathrm{d}x_i = \sum_r \mathrm{d}x_{ri} = f'_{1r}\,\mathrm{d}u_1 + f'_{si}\,\mathrm{d}u_s = 0$, since we held the total supply constant. Hence $-\mathrm{d}u_s/\mathrm{d}u_1 = f'_{si}/f'_{1i}$. Putting $i = 1$, $-\mathrm{d}u_s/\mathrm{d}u_1 = f'_{s1}/f'_{11}$. Therefore $f'_{si}/f'_{s1} = f'_{1i}/f'_{11}$. The left-hand side of this depends only on u_s and p, and the right on u_1 and p;[8] hence both depend on p alone. Let them equal $b_i(p)$; hence $f'_{si} = b_i(p)\,f'_{s1}$. Therefore, integrating, $x_{si} = f_{si} = a_{si}(p) + b_i(p)f_{s1}(u_s, p)$. Clearly $x_{1i} = a_{1i}(p) + b_i(p)f_{11}(p)$, where s was chosen freely from $2, \ldots, N$, and i from $1, 2, \ldots, n$. Hence, for all $r = 1, \ldots, N$ and $i = 1, \ldots, n$, $x_{ri} = a_{ri}(p) + b_i(p)f_{r1}(u_r; p)$. Hence the Engel curves for each individual are straight lines parallel to the vector $b_i(p) = (b_1, b_2, \ldots, b_n)$.

[7] It might be thought that the community indifference surface might have a 'corner' at x. This is, however, ruled out by (5).

[8] The argument is: if not, vary u_s holding u_1 constant. The left-hand side then varies while the right remains constant. It may be objected that, if we do vary u_s, we must vary u_1, because of $F(x^*, u) = 0$. It can, however, be shown that there is a unique point on each community indifference surface at which the normal direction is p. Hence, as we vary u_s, we can vary u and move from indifference surface to indifference surface to hold u_1 constant. Alternatively, if there are more than two people, we can hold u_1 constant by varying u_r, $r \neq 1, s$ when we change u_s. Hence, if there are more than two citizens, and if there is one community indifference curve which is not cut by any other, then no indifference curve below it is cut either. Other similar corollaries follow in this case.

It will be shown below that this necessary condition is also sufficient. In the meanwhile we will find the most general method of constructing a set of indifference maps having parallel straight Engel curves.

Choose now a surface u_r^* for each person to be his base indifference surface and let $x_r^* = x_r^*(p)$ be the point on it at which the normal is parallel to p.[9] Then $x_{ri}^* = a_{ri} + b_i f_{r1}$. Therefore we have

$$x_{ri} = x_{ri}^* + b_i g_r, \tag{7}$$

where $g_r = g_r(u_r, p) = f_{r1}(u_r, p) - f_{r1}(u_r^*, p)$.

If now we hold u_r fixed in this equation, and let p vary, we have $\mathrm{d}x_{ri} = \mathrm{d}x_{ri}^* + b_i\mathrm{d}g_r + g_r\mathrm{d}b_i$. Hence $\sum_i p_i\mathrm{d}x_{ri} = \sum_i p_i\mathrm{d}x_{ri}^* + \sum_i p_i b_i\mathrm{d}g_r + \sum_i p_i g_r\mathrm{d}b_i$. However, $\sum_i p_i\mathrm{d}x_{ri} = \sum_i p_i\mathrm{d}x_{ri}^* = 0$ by (4); hence $(\sum_i p_i b_i)\mathrm{d}g_r = -(\sum_i p_i\mathrm{d}b_i)g_r$. Putting $\ell_r = \log g_r$, this becomes $\mathrm{d}\ell_r = -\sum_i p_i\mathrm{d}b_i/\sum_i p_i b_i$. This equation is integrable since it has a solution $\ell_r = \log g_r(u_r^*, p)$. Moreover its left-hand side is independent of u_r and r.[10] Hence there is a function $\ell(p)$ such that $\mathrm{d}\ell = -\sum_i p_i\mathrm{d}b_i/\sum_i p_i b_i$. Subtracting, we have $\mathrm{d}\ell_r - \mathrm{d}\ell = 0$. Integrating this we find: $\ell_r = \ell(p) + m_r(u_r)$ since u_r has been held constant throughout. Hence $g_r = \exp \ell_r = g(p)h_r(u_r)$, where $g = \exp \ell$, $h_r = \exp m_r$. Putting $g(p)b_i(p) = c_i(p)$, we have

$$x_{ri} = x_{ri}^* + c_i h_r(u_r). \tag{7a}$$

Consider now a general small displacement $\mathrm{d}x_r$. Clearly $\mathrm{d}x_{ri} = \mathrm{d}x_{ri}^* + h_r\mathrm{d}c_i + c_i h_r'\mathrm{d}u_r$. Therefore $\sum_i p_i\mathrm{d}x_{ri} = \sum_i p_i\mathrm{d}x_{ri}^* + h_r\sum_i p_i\mathrm{d}c_i + h_r'\,\mathrm{d}u_r\sum_i p_i c_i = h_r\sum_i p_i\mathrm{d}c_i + h_r'\,\mathrm{d}u_r\sum_i p_i c_i$, since $\sum_i p_i\mathrm{d}x_{ri}^* = 0$ by (4). Therefore, we have: (i) if $\mathrm{d}u_r = 0$ is to imply $\sum_i p_i\mathrm{d}x_{ri} = 0$, we must have $h_r\sum_i p_i\mathrm{d}c_i = 0$. However, $h_r = 0$ implies that $x_r = x_r^* + c_i h_r(u_r)$ lies on the base locus u_r^* which is clearly illegitimate. Hence

$$\textstyle\sum_i p_i\mathrm{d}c_i = 0, \tag{8}$$

that is, either $\mathrm{d}c$ vanishes or is perpendicular to p. In the latter case c traces a locus to which p is the normal direction, in the former this locus can be regarded as degenerating to a single point. If $\mathrm{d}c = 0$ only for certain values of p, the locus has tangent discontinuities at these points.[11] In any case, it must be possible to construct the vectors $c(p)$ in (7a) by taking a locus C in n-space, and putting $c = c(p)$ = the vector to the point on this locus at which

[9] In order that u_r^* obey the Assumptions I–V, it must be a smooth $n - 1$ dimensional surface, such that the corresponding preference set is closed, strictly convex, and included in the interior of the positive orthant.

[10] This was pointed out to me by a referee, who also suggested the neat proof in the rest of the paragraph, which replaces a less elegant proof of my own. In an earlier draft I had given a proof almost identical with the present one, but wrongly decided that it was not rigorous.

[11] It might be objected that this would make some of the indifference surfaces have corners too. The reason why this is not so is that it is assumed chosen as a continuous, differential function of p throughout.

p is normal to the locus. (ii) If this condition holds, $\mathrm{d}u_r = 0$ does imply that $\sum_i p_i \mathrm{d}x_{ri} = 0$. (iii) If the condition holds and $\sum_i p_i \mathrm{d}x_{ri} = 0$, then $h'_r \,\mathrm{d}u_r \sum_i p_i c_i = 0$. If $h'_r = 0$, neighbouring indifference loci would pass through the same point. Hence this possibility must be excluded. If $\sum_i p_i c_i = 0$, either $c = 0$, which is clearly impossible, or it is perpendicular to p. This would imply that it lay in the surface u_r, which is clearly illegitimate. Therefore $\mathrm{d}u_r = 0$.

If therefore, $x^*_{ri} = x^*_{ri}(p)$ is the parametric equation of a hyper-surface in n-space, in terms of the normal vector as parameter, then (a) $x_{ri} = x^*_{ri}(p) + c_i(p)h_r(u_r)$ is the parametric equation of a non-intersecting system of such surfaces whose Engel curves are straight lines parallel to the direction $c(p)$ if, and only if, the conditions under (i) and (iii) are obeyed. (b) Under these conditions any such system of surfaces can be represented in this manner.

Let us now assume for the present that these systems of surfaces are acceptable as indifference maps; that is, they obey our Assumptions I–IV. Adding the equations (7*a*) and putting $x = \sum_r x_r$, $x^* = \sum_r x^*_r$, $h(u) = \sum_r h_r(u_r)$, we then have

$$x_i = x^*_i + c_i h = x^*_i(p) + c_i(p)h(u). \qquad (9).$$

This is clearly the parametric form of the relation $F(x, u) = 0$ between x and u. Taking differentials, we have $\mathrm{d}x_i = \mathrm{d}x^*_i + c_i \mathrm{d}h + h\mathrm{d}c_i$. Hence, $\sum_i p_i \mathrm{d}x_i = \sum_i p_i \mathrm{d}x^*_i + (\sum_i p_i c_i)\mathrm{d}h + (\sum_i p_i \mathrm{d}c_i)h$. But $\sum_i p_i \mathrm{d}x^*_i = 0$ by (5), and $\sum_i p_i \mathrm{d}c_i = 0$ by (8), while $\mathrm{d}h = \sum_i h'_r \,\mathrm{d}u_r$; hence $\sum_i p_i \mathrm{d}x_i = (\sum_i p_i c_i)(\sum_r h'_r \,\mathrm{d}u_r)$. But, by (5), $\sum_i p_i \mathrm{d}x_i = \sum_r q_r \mathrm{d}u_r$; hence $(\sum_i p_i c_i)h'_i = q_r$ which we know to be positive. Hence $\sum_i p_i c_i \neq 0$ and $h'_r \neq 0$. Clearly our assumptions require $\sum_i p_i c_i$ to be continuous. It has the same sign everywhere. Hence, if necessary, we can make it positive by a reflection of C in the origin. Assume this done, if necessary. Then each h'_r is positive, so that h_r is a strictly increasing function of $u_r (r = 1, \ldots, N)$. Hence we can take it as a new index of utility, and, with a slight change of notation write

$$x_{ri} = x^*_{ri} + c_i u_r = x^*_{ri}(p) + c_i(p)u_r, \qquad (7b)$$

$$x_i = x^*_i + c_i u = x^*_i(p) + c_i(p)u, \qquad (9a)$$

where $u = \sum_r u_r$.

We have not used the condition that the preference sets be strictly convex. The condition for this is that $\sum p_i \delta x_{ri}$ be positive for any displacement for which δu_r is non-negative. But $\sum_i p_i \delta x_{ri} = \sum_i p_i \delta x^*_{ri} + (\sum_i p_i c_i)\delta u_r + (\sum_i p_i \delta c_i)(u_r + \delta u_r)$. Now we must clearly choose the base indifference surface so that $\sum_i p_i \delta x^*_{ri}$ is positive. The second term of the right-hand side is certainly non-negative, since $\delta u_r \geqslant 0$. Everything therefore turns on the sign of the last term. Now $u_r = 0$ on the base indifference surface and tends to plus infinity with x_r. Hence we must have $\sum_i p_i \delta c_i$ non-negative if our indifference map is to cover the entire region R_r 'bounded below by the base indifference surface'. Moreover, if it is non-negative, $\sum_i p_i \delta x_{ri}$ is positive throughout R_r, as long as $\delta u_r \geq 0$.

We have now three conditions on C, that it be continuous, that $\sum_i p_i \delta c_i$ be non-negative, and that $\sum_i p_i c_i$ be positive. It can easily be shown that these, together with the condition that the base indifference surfaces should be chosen consistently with Assumptions I–V are sufficient to guarantee that the maps defined by (7*b*) both obey these assumptions and have parallel straight Engel curves. Are these conditions narrow? Clearly they are not. Any normal indifference surface could be taken as C, or almost any curve, or point on such a surface.

We can summarize our results to date in the following theorem:

THEOREM IX: *The class of indifference maps satisfying Assumptions* I–V *and permitting the construction of a unique community preference field is precisely the class of maps which can be constructed by the following process:*

(i) *For each person, choose as base indifference surface a smooth surface such that the corresponding preference set is closed, strictly convex, and contained within the interior of the positive orthant. Express the current point on the rth of these parametrically as $x_r^* = x_r^*(p)$ in terms of the normal direction p as parameter.*

(ii) *Choose also a continuous locus C which, when represented parametrically in terms of the normal direction p by $c = c(p)$, obeys the following conditions:* (a) *$\sum_i p_i \delta c_i$ is non-negative,* (b) *$\sum_i c_i p_i$ is positive, and* (c) *$\partial c_i / \partial p_j$ exists and is single-valued at all points of C, at which the normal direction p is strictly positive.*

(iii) *Then the equation of the rth person's indifference map is $x_r = x_r(p, u_r) = x_r^*(p) + c(p)u_r$.*

THEOREM X: *If there exists a unique community preference field it can be represented parametrically by the equation, $x(p, u) = x^*(p) + c(p)\sum_r u_r$ in the notation of Theorem* IX.

THEOREM XI: *If there is a unique community preference field its Cartesian equation can be written $G(x) = \sum_r u_r$.*

Consider x as fixed. Since there is a unique community indifference surface through each point, this fixes p. Hence it fixes x_i, x_i^*, c_i in equation (9*a*). It therefore fixes $\sum_r u_r$. Hence $\sum_r u_r$ is a function of x, say $G(x)$. There is only one relation between x and u, the equation of the community preference field, namely, $G(x) = \sum_r u_r$.

Therefore if the utility possibility surfaces do not cut, their equations can be written in the form $\sum_r u_r = \text{const}$. This fact sheds light on the choice of utility indicators in von Neumann and Morgenstern (1944) and on some aspects of welfare economics. The author hopes to publish some results in these fields later. Of course the equation only takes this simple form if the utility indices are chosen appropriately. On the other hand it should be remembered that they were not originally chosen for this reason, but to simplify the equations of the personal indifference maps.

Let us now consider the conditions (i) $\sum_i p_i \delta c_i > 0$ and (ii) $\sum_i p_i c_i$ on C. Our assumptions imply that each strictly positive direction p is normal to each indifference curve at some point. Hence these inequalities must hold for all such p. Now $\sum_i p_i x_i = \sum_i p_i c_i(p)$ is the equation of the tangent plane at $c(p)$. Hence this plane must not intersect the negative orthant, including the origin. We will show that each $c_i(p)$ is positive as long as each p_i is positive.

If not, let $c_1(p^*)$ be negative. Take $q_1 = \text{mod}[1/c_1(p^*)]$, $q_i = 1/2n \text{ mod } [1/c_i(p^*)]$ if $c_i(p^*) \neq 0$, and $q_i = 1$ if $c_i(p)^* = 0$ $(i = 2, \ldots, n)$. Then $\sum_i q_i c_i(p^*)$ is negative while $q_i > 0$ $(i = 1, \ldots, n)$. Consider now $c(q)$. $\sum_i q_i c_i(p) = \sum_i q_i c_i(p^*) - \sum_i q_i[c_i(p^*) - c_i(q)]$. But $\sum_i q_i c_i(p^*)$ is less than $-\frac{1}{2}$, and therefore negative, while $\sum_i q_i[c_i(p^*) - c_i(q)]$ is non-negative by (i); hence $\sum_i q_i c_i(q)$ is negative. This contradicts (ii); hence no c_i is negative and there are no inferior goods. We can avoid this difficulty by making the R_r finite. Since we are usually interested in finite regions, this does not matter. The matter will be discussed in Section 6.

5. RELAXATION OF THE ASSUMPTIONS[12]

The assumptions about the personal indifference maps may be summarized as follows:

(i) As consumption increases, so does the level of satisfaction (Assumptions II and V).
(ii) The personal preferences sets are strictly convex (Assumption III).
(iii) The personal indifference surfaces are smooth (Assumption V).
(iv) The personal indifference surfaces do not intersect the coordinate planes.

Assumptions (i) and (ii) are normal, and will not be discussed here. Assumptions (iii) and (iv) may be replaced by the following:

(v) The personal indifference surfaces are piecewise smooth;

that is, they are made up of smooth patches which may be surrounded by singularities such as 'corners' or 'edges'. We will only discuss the simpler case, in which (iii) is replaced by (v) while (iv) remains true. The complete discussion is very similar, but slightly more complex.

[12] The arguments in this section are far from rigorous. They can, however, be made rigorous.

Let us now seek the community indifference set corresponding to a given distribution u^*. From our assumptions and by Theorem I, we know that both the personal preference sets $u_r(x_r) \geqslant u_r^*$, and the community preference set $P(u^*)$ are closed strictly convex sets, such that, if a given supply belongs to any of them, so does any greater supply. Now, at any point x^* of the boundary of such a set there is a set of normals $p = (p_1, p_2, \ldots, p_n) = (1, p_2, \ldots, p_n)$ such that $\sum_i p_i x_i > \sum_i p_i x_i^*$ for all $x \neq x^*$ in the set. Moreover, if the boundary is smooth at x^*, there is only one such normal, and it is the conventional normal of Section 4. Under our assumptions it can be shown that (i) each normal direction p is strictly positive and (ii) each strictly positive p is normal at just one point on the frontier. We can regard p as a price vector. Remembering that the frontier of any preference set is the corresponding indifference surface, we have the following result: To any set of prices p and any preference set, there corresponds a uniquely cheapest basket of commodities and this basket lies on the corresponding indifference surface.

We can now find the community indifference surface $X(u^*)$, by taking each price vector p in turn and finding the cheapest supply at which u^* is attainable. Clearly this is done by finding the corresponding cheapest supply at which each consumer can reach the required level of satisfaction (u_r^*) and then adding these together. Clearly the vector p has in this process exactly the same function as it had in Section 4. Moreover the optimal character of 'perfect competition' appears much more obviously.

With the aid of this result we can put into terms of finite displacements the proof that the Engel curves for a given set of prices must be parallel stright lines if there is to be a unique community preference field and so carry it over. Moreover, if it is true, and if the direction of u_r increasing is the same for each individual, there is a unique community indifference map. The proof of these results is rather long and will not be given here.

Let us now consider a singular point x_r^* on the indifference surface u_r^*. At such a point there will be a cone P of normals p. The Engel lines corresponding to each such normal must pass through x_r^*. They may therefore either coincide completely or some two of them may intersect there. Let the Engel lines $c(p)$ and $c(q)$ intersect and let Figure 15.1 represent the section of the indifference map by the plane of $c(p)$ and $c(q)$. Then the tangents to the 'indifference curves' must be parallel where they cut $c(p)$. Hence, if the 'indifference curves' below are convex, with a 'diminishing marginal rate of substitution', those above it must show an 'increasing marginal rate of substitution', and be concave.[13] Hence, unless x_r^* is on the boundary of the region R_r, all the Engel lines through it must coincide and no two Engel lines can intersect in the interior of R_r. Hence, if there is a corner or edge on one indifference surface in the interior of R_r there will be a similar one on all of them.

[13] This argument is rather clumsy, but it can be made rigorous.

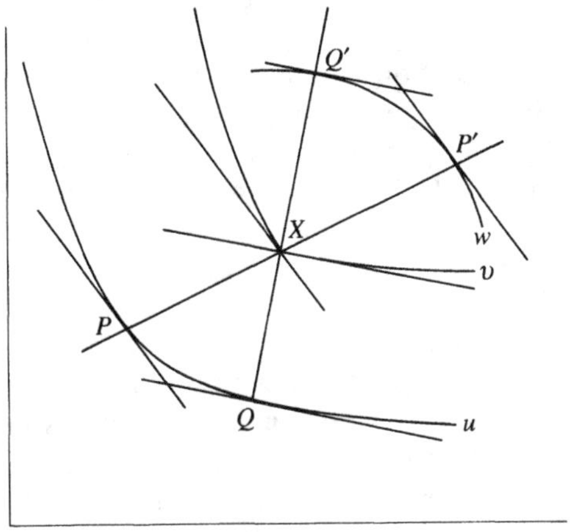

PXP', QXQ' are the Engle Lines corresponding to the prices *p*, *q*. *u*, *v*, *w* are the intersections of the plane *PXQ* with three different surfaces. The other lines are the intersections of this plane with the various tangent planes. They may be interpreted as price lines at prices *p* and *q*.

FIG. 15.1

We have assumed that the indifference surfaces are piecewise smooth. This allows us to divide the R_r into regions, bounded by the surfaces generated by Engel lines. Inside each of these Assumption V holds. We can apply the argument of Section 4 to each of these regions to find $x_r = x_r^* + c(p)u_r$ within them. By splicing at the singularities this formula can be made to apply everywhere. Theorem IX can now be carried over to the present case.

Suppose now that the indifference surfaces do cut the coordinate planes; that is, at some prices and some standards of living, somebody does not consume some of the goods. The argument above can be restated to cover this case also. Let us neglect the trivial case in which only the base surfaces cut the coordinate planes, and suppose that, at prices p and a standard of living above the minimum, the rth person does not consume any of the ith good. In the notation of Section 4, $x_{ri}(u_r; p) = 0$ for some $u_r \geqslant 0$. Now, by (7*b*), $x_{ri}(u_r; p) = x_{ri}^*(p) + c_i(p_i)u_r$, where neither x_{ri}, nor c_i can assume negative values. Hence they are both zero. Assuming perfect competition in consumption, we may interpret this result as follows: If Brown, whose income is sufficient to raise him above the minimum standard does not consume a certain good at certain prices, then each person's consumption of that good at those prices is independent of his income. In particular, Brown will not consume it, whatever his income, so long as the prices remain unchanged.

The condition that the Engel curves be parallel straight lines is in itself fairly restrictive. In conjunction with our choice of the regions R_r it implies that there are no inferior goods, as well as the result in the previous paragraph. These later implications are both due to the condition that $\sum_i p_i \delta c_i$ be non-negative. (Condition (ii-*a*) of Theorem IX—we will call it condition (*a*) below.) This condition was proved by taking each p in turn and letting $x_r(u_r; p)$ tend to infinity. It therefore made use of the fact that x_r would continue to lie in R_r under these conditions. Its function was to guarantee that no pair of Engel lines cut each other, and that neither of them cut an indifference surface twice within R_r. The obvious procedure is to exclude from R_r regions in which such intersections take place. We can cut out of R_r any regions bounded by portions of indifference surfaces, and by the ruled surfaces generated by Engel lines at their edges. By such methods we can generate a very wide class of regions. One particular case of interest would be the region between two indifference surfaces. Condition (*a*) does not apply to such a region for it does not matter if two Engel lines cut above the higher surface nor if they cut a higher surface twice. Hence inferior goods are possible in this case.

However the other disadvantage still applies. If at some set of prices one person does not consume a certain good, its income elasticity of consumption must be zero at those prices for everyone. To evade this difficulty, a much more drastic restriction on the R_r is needed. If we are interested merely in cases in which the relative prices of goods in certain selected groups remain unchanged we can treat each of these groups as a separate good so that it merely becomes necessary that each person should consume something from each set of goods.

Suppose now that the goods fall into m baskets $(B_1, \ldots, B_a, \ldots, B_m)$.[14] Let the total quantity of the ith good in the ath basket be x_{ai}. Let its price by $p_a q_{ai}$. We may regard q_{ai} as being the fixed price of the good in terms of a numeraire which can be used only to buy goods in that basket, while p_a is the price of the numeraire in terms of 'money'. Suppose that y_a is the value of the consumption of the ath basket in terms of the appropriate numeraire. Take now any non-negative vector y of these numeraires, and maximize $u(x)$ subject to the restrictions $y_a = \sum_i q_{ai} x_{ai}$.[15] This will give $x = (x(y; q), u(x) = u[x(y; q)] = v(y; q)$, say. For the given q we can draw up an indifference map between the y and apply the analysis above to it.

It is easily shown that the derivative map will satisfy Assumptions I–V if the original maps do so. We can therefore apply the arguments above to them.

[14] This is equivalent to taking the R_r to be m-dimensional ruled surfaces.
[15] We drop the r for convenience.

This allows us to speak of indifference maps between 'food' and 'clothing', etc., instead of maps between particular qualities of raspberries, socks, etc.

One final type of region is of some interest. If R_r includes the origin, the base indifference surface degenerates to a single point—the origin itself. Hence all the Engel lines must pass through this point and the indifference surfaces are projections of each other through the origin, that is, they are similar to each other. This is easily seen to imply that the C surface should be similar to any one of them. If each R_r includes the origin this will be true of all the maps. Hence each personal indifference surface will have to be similar to C and all the maps must be similar. Indeed they must all be contour maps of the same homogeneous function, that is, everybody's tastes must be the same. This does not, however, appear to be an economically significant special case. That a unique community preference field existed in this case has long been known. It is now shown that it is the only case where it does exist if each individual map includes the origin.

6. POSSIBLE APPLICATIONS

We will first show that our Engel lines are closely related to the classical Engel curves, or income–consumption curves, of the statisticians. Indeed the former are parallel straight lines if, and only if, the latter are. Later we will discuss the application of our results to some problems.

We have $x_{ri} = x^*_{ri} + u_r c_i$. Hence $\sum_i p_i x_{ri} = \sum_i p_i x^*_{ri} + u_r \sum_i p_i c_i$. Interpreting p_i as the price of the ith good in terms of the first good as numeraire, $\sum_i p_i x_{ri} = y_r$ (say) will be the total expenditure, and $\sum_i p_i x^*_{ri} = y_r$ total expenditure at these prices needed to reach the base indifference locus. Expenditure is in each case measured in terms of the first good. Put $\sum_i p_i c_i = t = t(p)$, then $y_r - y^*_r = u_r t$. Hence $\mathrm{d}u_r/\mathrm{d}t = 1/t$; that is to say, the marginal utility of expenditure at given prices is independent of income, and is the same for everybody. This is only so, of course, if we use our preferred index of utility. Solving for u_r, and substituting in (7*b*), we have $x_{ri} = x^*_{ri} + c_i(y_r - y^*_r)/t$. Now let $z_{ri} = p_i x_{ri}$ be the expenditure of the rth person on the ith good, and write $a_{ri} = p_i x^*_{ri} - b_i y^*_r$ and $b_i = p_i c_i/t$. Then $z_{ri} = a_{ri}(p) + b_i(p) y_r$. This is the equation of the classical Engel, or income–consumption, curve. They are seen to be straight lines, and to be parallel for different people at the same prices, as are the Engel curves. The converse result is also true; if the classical Engel curves are parallel straight lines at given prices, so are the Engel curves. Our condition really is that these classical Engel curves should be straight lines, parallel for different individuals at the same prices. A good deal of work has been done on these curves, particularly by Allen and Bowley (1935), and by Houthakker (1952). The older work of Allen and Bowley was based on the assumption that the classical Engel curves for different individuals at the same prices were parallel straight lines, but this has been rejected in the more recent work of Houthakker in favour of a doubly logarithmic form. However, the earlier assumption fits the data remarkably well. Of course, all this work runs in terms of 'baskets of commodities' such as food, clothing, shelter, etc. However, we have already shown that our analysis can be applied to such aggregates of goods as long as the relative prices of goods within the same basket can be assumed constant.[16]

Hence the conditions for the construction of a unique preference field are not unduly unrealistic. This is particularly true if we are not intending to analyse situations in which there will be considerable redistribution of income between different industrial groupings. It also suggests that even where a community indifference map for an entire nation may be thought to be unrealistic, individual class indifference maps may be used to analyse economic relationships between classes.

Granted the hypothesis that unique community indifference maps are in principle constructible is a reasonable one, and that they will then in practice be possible to construct, is there any advantage in using such unique curves? I think there is. Consider, for instance, the theory of international trade. On the basis of such curves we can construct unique offer curves and unique import–export indifference maps and hence define a unique optimum tariff which will therefore be independent of the distribution of income. On the basis of such results we can prove such theorems as that the optimum tariff can never be higher than that which maximizes government receipts.[17]

We have seen that it also implies that utility possibility loci for a given total supply can never cut. Hence under given production conditions there will be a unique optimum output. The utility possibility locus associated with such production conditions is just that associated with the optimum output. It is therefore the form $\sum_r u_r =$ constant and moreover cannot cut the locus appropriate to any other production conditions. This is where we assume that the optimum welfare conditions of production are consistent with the structure of competition and of taxation. However, for any realizable set of outputs there will still be a single optimum and hence a single utility possibility locus of the form $\sum_r u_r =$ constant. Any change in competitive conditions or taxation policy will therefore raise or lower this locus in a body. If the distribution of income can now be adjusted by lump-sum grants or some such method, we can say that one situation is definitely superior to the other. If lump-sum grants are ruled out, we may compare two situations on the basis of the total situation.

[16] The recent work on the variation of the quality of goods consumed at different income levels, and of the effect of varying family sizes might be discussed here, were there space.

[17] This would of course depend upon some other assumptions, namely, that there were no inferior goods and that there were no increasing returns industries, and that the government distributes its tariff revenue to its citizens. It also depends on the use of a two-industry model.

It is interesting to notice that since in any of these conditions the utility possibility locus will be $\sum_r u_r$ = constant, the modern welfare criteria reduce to those of the utilitarian as long as both contestants are willing to accept our 'preferred' utility indices. Similarly if our preferred indices are equivalent to von Neumann and Morgenstern's cardinal indices, based on probabilistic arguments, they justify their use of transferable utility. This is because they explicitly assume that all economic transactions will take place on the utility possibility locus. It may however be doubted if our index is equivalent to theirs, for if it were, gambling and insurance would be ruled out in so far as they are static phenomena.

One simplification which our assumption would not justify would be the neglect of changes in the distribution of income. If however these can be 'righted' by lump-sum grants and taxes in the manner of modern welfare economics, this need not discourage us. If on the other hand such grants and taxes are thought unrealistic, we can still consider as a whole the results of a given policy and will be able to use the same basic functions to analyse policies which lead to widely differing distributions of income. This will mean that it will frequently be possible to 'tamper' with one sector of the economy without changing policy everywhere else. For instance every time there is a slight change in the home distribution of income the optimum welfare tariff will not be altered.

The analysis of this section has not attempted to be rigorous, nor complete. It is merely a sketch of one part of the field and *it must be realized that the same analysis can be applied to problems outside welfare economics.* Moreover it has depended upon the assumption that the consumption sector is in equilibrium, which breaks down if leisure is included in the utility function. This is, of course, true of much the greater part of modern welfare economics.

16

Klein Aggregates and Conventional Index Numbers

Editorial Remarks

This paper was presented at the European Meeting of the Econometric Society in Innsbruck in 1953. It has never been published and survives in several drafts none of which is in great shape. It was, however, the first attempt to try to put together the issues raised by aggregation and equilibrium conditions. The following summary was kindly provided by Bill Schworm.

Editorial Summary

Klein (1946*a*, 1946*b*) posed the problem of aggregating inputs and outputs in an economy's production function when there are no equilibrium conditions restricting the allocation of commodities. This problem was solved by Nataf (1948) who derived the general forms of the aggregates and the economy technologies that are consistent with the Klein aggregation problem. Gorman, in this 1953 paper, analyses the usefulness of the aggregates that solve the Klein problem. Gorman argues that these Klein aggregates are not useful for many purposes in their general form and proposes additional requirements that useful Klein aggregates should satisfy. For several of these additional requirements, Gorman derives the circumstances in which such aggregates exist.

The problem posed by Klein (1946*a*) can be described as follows, where I use a modification of Gorman's notation. Suppose there are R firms in an economy and each firm's technology is described by the following production equation:

$$f^r(x^r, n^r, z^r) = 0, \tag{0.1}$$

where x^r, n^r, and z^r are vectors of arbitrary dimension and are interpreted as types of output, labour, and capital, respectively. The allocation of the commodities among firms is denoted by $x = (x^1, x^2, \ldots, x^R)$, $n = (n^1, n^2, \ldots, n^R)$, and $z = (z^1, z^2, \ldots, z^R)$. Then, a full description of the allocation of commodities in the production sector of the economy is given by the vector (x, n, z).

A key feature of the Klein problem, emphasized at the time by May (1946) and Pu (1946), is that no restrictions are imposed on the allocation (x, n, z). May and Pu argued that equilibrium conditions derived from the assumptions of competitive commodity markets and profit-maximizing behaviour could be used to restrict the admissible allocations and thereby weaken the force of the aggregation requirement. Klein (1946*b*) argued that the existence and construction of aggregates should not be made to depend on such untenable assumptions as competitive behaviour in competitive markets. The role of equilibrium restrictions in aggregation problems has maintained a central role in the research of Solow (1964), Fisher (1965, 1968*a*, 1968*b*, 1969, 1982, 1983), Gorman (1968*a*) and Blackorby and Schworm (1984*a*, 1988).

Aggregates are scalars, X, N, and Z, which are functions of the vectors, x, n, and z, respectively:

$$X = X(x), \quad N = N(n), \quad \text{and} \quad Z = Z(z), \tag{0.2}$$

The key feature here is that the aggregates are one-dimensional representations of vectors. Therefore, for general technologies some information is lost in constructing the aggregates that are relevant for the economy's production possibilities. The Klein aggregation requirement is that no *relevant* information be lost in constructing the aggregates. The formal requirement is that there exists an aggregate production equation, F, such that

$$F(X(x), N(n), Z(z)) = 0 \leftrightarrow f^r(x^r, n^r, z^r) = 0 \text{ for all } r = 1, \ldots, R. \tag{0.3}$$

If there exists such an aggregate production equation in aggregate commodity measures, then the production possibilities of the economy can be fully characterized by the three variables, X, N, and Z. An analysis of such a model would be vastly simpler than an analysis of the much more complex micro-model.

Nataf (1948) has shown that the Klein aggregates exist if and only if each firm's production equation can be written as

$$X^r + N^r + Z^r = 0, \tag{0.4}$$

where X^r, N^r and Z^r are firm-specific aggregates obtained by aggregating the corresponding firm variables:

$$X^r = X^r(x^r), \quad N^r = N^r(n^r), \quad \text{and} \quad Z^r = Z^r(z^r). \tag{0.5}$$

If each firm has a technology that can be expressed in this fashion, then the economy aggregates can be obtained by summing the firms' aggregates and production equations. That is, let $X = \sum_r X^r$, $N = \sum_r N^r$, and $Z = \sum_r Z^r$, and observe that

$$X + N + Z = 0, \tag{0.6}$$

if and only if (0.4) is satisfied for all $r = 1, \ldots, R$. Therefore, these aggregates satisfy the Klein aggregation criterion.

In this paper, however, Gorman's goal is to accept the existence of the Klein aggregates and to investigate the consequences of imposing some additional restrictions in order to render them more useful in economic analysis. The construction of the Klein aggregate X, for example, requires information on the allocation of the commodities to firms as described by the vector, x. Gorman begins by requiring that the Klein aggregates depend only on the total quantity of the commodities. Let $x^+ = \sum_r x^r$, $n^+ = \sum_r x^r$, and $z^+ = \sum_r z^r$. Then, Gorman's requirement is that the Klein aggregates can be written as

$$X = \bar{X}(x^+), \quad N = \bar{N}(n^+), \text{ and } Z = \bar{Z}(x^+). \tag{0.7}$$

The necessary and sufficient conditions for this problem are shown to be the following: every firm has a production equation given by

$$a \cdot x^r + b \cdot n^r + c \cdot z^r + d^r = 0, \tag{0.8}$$

where a, b, and c are appropriately dimensioned vectors that are the same for all firms, $r = 1, \ldots, R$. In this case, the economy production equation is the following:

$$a \cdot x^+ + b \cdot n^+ + c \cdot z^+ + d^+ = 0, \tag{0.9}$$

where $d^+ = \sum_r d^r$. In this case, the Klein aggregates are given by

$$X = \bar{X}(x^+) = a \cdot x^+, \tag{0.10}$$

$$N = \bar{N}(n^+) = b \cdot n^+, \tag{0.11}$$

and

$$Z = \bar{Z}(z^+) = c \cdot z^+. \tag{0.12}$$

Of course, these conditions are extremely restrictive and describe circumstances in which all firms have the same linear technology (up to a constant term).

In an effort to weaken these conditions, Gorman investigates the effect of approximate aggregation conditions. He continues to require the existence of exact Klein aggregates, but relaxes his requirement that the aggregates depend only on total quantities of the commodities. The new requirement is that the relations (0.7) hold approximately in a neighbourhood of a point (x, n, z) that is a competitive equilibrium allocation. There are two new aspects to this aggregation requirement. One is that the aggregates are only approximately related to the micro-variables. The other new aspect is that competitive equilibrium conditions are being exploited, although only at a point. Both of these aspects are important for the solution.

To use the competitive assumption, introduce prices (p, w, q) for the commodities (x^+, n^+, z^+). Introduce an arbitrary base commodity bundle denoted (x_0^+, n_0^+, z_0^+). Define aggregate prices and quantities as follows:

$$X = \frac{p \cdot x^+}{p \cdot x_0^+}, \quad N = \frac{w \cdot n^+}{w \cdot n_0^+}, \quad \text{and} \quad Z = \frac{q \cdot z^+}{q \cdot z_0^+} \tag{0.13}$$

and

$$P = p \cdot x_0^+, \quad W = w \cdot n_0^+, \quad \text{and} \quad Q = q \cdot z_0^+. \tag{0.14}$$

Then, define the aggregate production equation by

$$PX - WN - QZ - D = 0 \tag{0.15}$$

for an arbitrary constant D. Gorman shows that these aggregates provide a first-order approximation to any Klein aggregates in the neighbourhood of the competitive equilibrium supported by the prices (p, w, q).

There are several discussions in the paper concerning the way in which Klein aggregates may be incorporated into a general economic model with both a production side and a demand side. This alternative focus suggests additional requirements that useful aggregates should satisfy. In a full model it is useful if the linkages between different sectors of the model can be specified in terms of the aggregate variables. If they cannot, then much of the convenience associated with aggregates is lost. A related requirement is that equilibrium conditions in an economy be stated solely in terms of aggregates. It would be useful if the supply of X in the economy depended on aggregate prices (P, W, Q). Although these issues have received much attention since this discussion by Gorman, several of the problems remain unresolved.

The types of technological progress that can be modelled by Klein aggregates is quite restrictive. Gorman derives these restrictions and comments on their implications. A primary reason for interest in Klein aggregates is that they simplify the study of technological progress. Gorman's results show, however, that the existence of Klein aggregates is inconsistent with many interesting types of technological progress.

Klein Aggregates and Conventional Index Numbers

1. SUMMARY

The first section of the paper includes a discussion of the general problem of aggregation. A distinction is drawn between precise macro-models, whose equations are implied by those of an underlying micro-model, and approximate macro-models. In either case the most important characteristics of a good macro-model are that it should fall into autonomous sectors, and that its variables and equations should have intuitive significance.

In the remaining sections the construction of a precise autonomous model of the production sector to form part of a general model is discussed. This discussion follows Klein's (1946*a*, 1946*b*) approach. He suggested the construction of output, labour, and capital aggregates X, N, Z which respectively depend only upon the outputs, and labour and capital inputs of particular firms, and which obey an aggregative production equation given only that the individual firms make use of their technological opportunities. Nataf (1948) has found the conditions for this to be possible.

In this paper we seek the conditions under which the Klein aggregates depend only upon the aggregate production of the various goods, and use of particular inputs. This is in general only true under classical conditions of constant costs. However Klein aggregates can be constructed which can be closely approximated by functions of this nature in the neighbourhood of competitive equilibrium whenever Nataf's condition is met. Under certain conditions these obey a simple aggregative production equation, at least in the neighbourhood of long-run production equilibrium. Various attributes of these special Klein aggregates are mentioned, and their use in analysing particular types of structural change discussed. Their main disadvantage is that equilibrium equations in terms of them for the production sector have not been discovered, nor do conditions for such equations exist.

This, and similar discussion elsewhere, suggests that the search for precise, autonomous, sectoral models is unlikely to be successful.

2. INTRODUCTION

The economic world is very complex. It is therefore necessary to build simplified models of it running in terms of a few 'representative' variables. The choice of such variables constitutes the aggregation problem. The analogy with statistical decision functions is obvious; there the problem is the choice of a few representative variables to be observed. Malinvaud (1956) has worked out this analogy in some depth, and his approach clearly holds great promise.[1] Nevertheless we will use more conventional methods of analysis in this paper.

The most important reason for preferring a conventional approach to the aggregation problem is that Wald's (1947, 1950) techniques rely so heavily on the concept of the *cost* of making a wrong *terminal* decision. This clearly implies both that one has a well-defined end in view, and either that one's own work is final, or that its effect upon later development can be estimated rather precisely. Neither of these requirements seems to be met in economic analysis, though they may be in the building of policy models.

Secondly, the discussion of decision problems normally runs in probability terms while traditional economics does not; moreover in the case of aggregation the probabilities in question would be subjective.

Finally, the theory of statistical decisions is itself only incompletely developed, and has already run into considerable difficulties.

Consider a complete micro-model

$$F(x) = 0; \quad x = (x_1, \ldots, x_n), \tag{2.1}$$

and the (1, 1) transformation

$$X = K(x); \quad X = (X_1, \ldots, X_N), \qquad N < n, \tag{2.2a}$$

$$Y = L(x); \quad Y = (Y_1, \ldots, Y_{n-N}), \tag{2.2b}$$

and the inverse

$$x = k(X, Y). \tag{2.3}$$

After this transformation the micro-model becomes

$$\bar{f}(X, Y) \equiv F(k(X, Y)) = 0 \tag{2.4}$$

Solve now $(n - N)$ of these equations to find

$$Y = G(X), \tag{2.5}$$

and substitute in the remainder to find

$$F(X) = 0. \tag{2.6}$$

This equation (2.6) may be interpreted as a *precise* macro-model. Its solution $X = X^0$ yields precise information about the economy—that $K(x) = X^0$. $K(x)$ might be called the identifiable quality of the micro-model in the light of the macro-model. Clearly the solution x^0 of the micro-model depends upon a knowledge of Y as well as X^0, so that the complete micro-model will not be identifiable.

We will discuss only *precise* micro-models; that is, ones which give precise information about any identifiable quality of the macro-model. In practice

[1] See also Hurwicz (1952).

we would presumably prefer models which give appropriate information covering a somewhat wider field.[2]

The difficulty lies, of course, in the definition of 'approximate'. By evading this problem we are really side-stepping the more specifically 'decision function' aspect of the aggregation problem.

Now it is clear that there are many possible transformations (2.2) which we can apply to a given micro-model. What criteria should we use to choose between them?

In the first place it seems clear that the 'interesting' aspects of the micro-model should be identifiable. This might mean either that the variables X were interesting in their own right—as is the percentage employed, even if we do not know its effect on the demand for particular goods—or because they are pivotal variables in some sense. If, for instance, the demand for chocolate was known to depend upon the level of employment in a certain manner, and it was believed that this relation was unlikely to be affected by changes in the structure of the economy, then it might be sensible to set up a model to determine employment, if one were interested only in the demand for chocolate. If one follows this approach, one should choose a model such that the subsidiary equation $Y = G(X)$ would be little affected by the changes in structure which are considered likely.[3]

We see, then, that changes in the structure of the micro-model should, in some sense, be concentrated on the macro-model. The second requirement is that the effect of these changes on the structure of the macro-model should be calculable without detailed reference to the micro-model. In practice this would seem to imply that both the variables and the equations of the macro-model should have an obvious intuitive interpretation—at least for the trained economist—and that the equations should have a high degree of autonomy.[4]

This last requirement is the most interesting. An autonomous equation in a model is one which is, in a sense, independent of the others. Thus, for instance, the demand schedule for apples will depend largely upon consumer tastes, their supply upon cost factors. They are causally rather independent of one another. Largely because of this, one may reasonably hope to analyse the effects upon them of, say, the introduction of tomatoes, or ice-cream.[5]

[2] See Theil (1953).

[3] This raises two points: (i) We can always choose $Z = H(Y)$ such that small changes in Y imply large changes in Z, which plays the same role as Y in the model. The true condition is that the final effect on x should be small. Once again we are running into essentially decision problems. (ii) This depends on the assumption that the transformation (2.2) is functionally independent of the model (2.1), or, if this is not so, that it is invariant under 'likely' changes in that model.

[4] See Haavelmo (1944).

[5] *[eds.] The remainder of this section (one page of typescript) is lost.*

3. AGGREGATION OVER FIRMS

In this and the succeeding sections we will discuss aggregation in the production sector with special reference to Klein's work.

In a complete model the production sector normally contains two types of equations—the technical equations and the equilibrium conditions. If we are willing to assume that the sector is always in equilibrium we may integrate the two, otherwise there is a strong case for keeping them separate. This is what Klein sets out to do.

Consider an economy of $R \geqslant 3$ firms, of which the rth has the known production equation

$$F_r(x_r, n_r, z_r) = 0 \tag{3.1}$$

where

$x_r = (x_{1r}, \ldots, x_{mr})$: outputs of each type of good;

$n_r = (n_{1r}, \ldots, n_{sr})$: inputs of each type of labour;

$z_r = (z_{1r}, \ldots, z_{tr})$: inputs of each type of capital.

Put also $x = (x_1, \ldots, x_R) = (x_{11}, \ldots, x_{mR})$, etc. and $x^+ = (x_1^+, \ldots, x_m^+)$, etc. where $x_i^+ = \sum_r x_{ir}$, the total production of the ith good.

Klein wishes to set up aggregates

$$X = X(x); \quad N = N(n), \quad Z = Z(z), \tag{3.2}$$

which will obey some, as yet unknown, aggregate production equation:

$$F(X, N, Z) = 0, \tag{3.3}$$

whenever the technical conditions (3.1) hold.

Nataf (1948) has shown that this can be done if and only if there exist subaggregates

$$X_r = X_r(x_r); \quad N_r = N_r(n_r); \quad Z_r = Z_r(z_r), \tag{3.4}$$

such that the production equation (3.1) may be written

$$X_r = N_r + Z_r. \tag{3.1$'$}$$

This is Klein's (1946*a*, 1946*b*) model. We will not criticize it here.

If then k_r ($r = 1, \ldots, R$) is any series of parameters[6] independent of x, n, z, the most general form of the aggregate production equation is

$$X^+ = N^+ + Z^+, \tag{3.3$'$}$$

where $X^+ = \sum k_r K_r$; $N^+ = \sum k_r N_r$; $Z^+ = \sum k_r Z_r$.

[6] In particular they may depend on the prices, wage rates, etc. regarded as *parameters*.

The most general Klein aggregates are then:

$$X = X(X^+), \quad N = N(N^+), \quad Z = Z(Z^+), \tag{3.2$'$}$$

where $X(\cdot)$, $N(\cdot)$, $Z(\cdot)$ are any functions.

We note that Klein aggregates can only be constructed in rather special circumstances (3.1′). When they can be constructed, moreover, the presence of the k_r's in (3.3′) implies a real ambiguity in their definition.

4. APPROXIMATIONS ABOUT EQUILIBRIA

In the present paper we will assume that the production equations are of the form (3.1′), so that Klein aggregates exist. We will consider what further conditions are necessary before they are useful.

The obvious weakness of the aggregates is that their very existence, and their functional form, depends on production techniques. Hence they will be of limited use in analysing the effect of technical changes. This point will be discussed in Section 5. In this section we will discuss the requirement that the Klein production equation be capable of forming a part of a wider model. This seems to imply that $X = f(x_1^+, \ldots, x_m^+) = f(x^+)$[7] etc., since the inputs and outputs of particular factories are unlikely to enter the remainder of such a model except through the total input or output of the good in question. Of course we may not wish to analyse all conceivable situations, but only a subset of these. If so, X, N, Z need to be expressible in the form above only over that subset.

What then does it imply to require that $X = f(x_1^+, \ldots, x_m^+) = f(x^+)$, $N = g(n^+)$, $Z = h(z^+)$ everywhere?

Consider the aggregate $X = X(X^+)$, where $X^+ = \sum k_r X_r, \ldots,$ and $X_r = N_r + Z_r$ is the production equation of the rth firm. If $X(X^+) = X = f(x_1^+, \ldots, x_m^+)$ and the rth and s^{th} firms both produce the ith good, then

$$\frac{\partial X}{\partial x_{ir}} = \frac{\partial f}{\partial x_i} = \frac{\partial X}{\partial x_{is}}, \tag{4.1}$$

$$\frac{dX}{dX^+} \times k_r \frac{\partial X_r}{\partial x_{ir}} = \frac{dX}{dX^+} \times k_s \frac{\partial X_s}{\partial X_{is}}, \tag{4.2}$$

$$k_r \frac{\partial X_r}{\partial x_{ir}} = k_s \frac{\partial X_s}{\partial x_{is}}. \tag{4.3}$$

The left-hand side of this equation depends on x_r alone, the right on x_s alone. Hence they are both equal to a constant—call it a_i.

$$\frac{\partial X_r}{\partial x_{ir}} = \frac{a_i}{k_r}. \tag{4.4}$$

[7] I introduce functions $f(\cdot)$ at various points. Each is of purely local significance.

If each good is produced by at least two firms

$$k_r X_r = \sum_i a_i x_{ir} + A_r. \tag{4.5a}$$

Similarly, we find

$$k_r N_r = \sum_j b_j n_{jr} + B_r, \tag{4.5b}$$

$$k_r Z_r = \sum_k c_k z_{kr} + C_r, \tag{4.5c}$$

so that the production equation of the rth firm may be written

$$\sum_i a_i x_{ir} = \sum_j b_j n_{jr} + \sum_k c_k z_{kr} + D_r, \qquad D_r = B_r + C_r - A_r. \tag{4.6}$$

This yields an aggregate production equation

$$\sum_i a_i x_i = \sum_j b_j n_j + \sum_k c_k z_k + D; \qquad D = \sum_j D_r.\text{[8]} \tag{4.7}$$

These equations clearly represent the classical condition of constant costs. The existence of constant costs is therefore both a necessary and a sufficient condition for the Klein aggregates to depend only upon the total output of each good.[9]

Let us now relax our condition that $X = f(x^+)$ everywhere, and demand instead that this condition should hold to a sufficiently high order of approximation in the neighbourhood of equilibrium.

Let us assume perfect competition. Then, if the rth firm is in equilibrium at prices $p = (p_1, \ldots, p_m)$, wage rates $w = (w_1, \ldots, w_r)$, and unit capital costs $q = (q_1, \ldots, q_s)$, we have

$$\frac{\partial X_r}{\partial x_{ir}} = \frac{p_i}{m_r}, \quad \frac{\partial N_r}{\partial n_{jr}} = \frac{w_j}{m_r}, \quad \frac{\partial Z_r}{\partial z_{kr}} = \frac{q_k}{m_r} \tag{4.8}$$

over all its input and outputs. Here m_r is a proportionality factor. Solving for the equilibrium values x_r^*, n_r^*, z_r^* we get

$$x_r^* = x_r^*(p, w, q). \tag{4.9}$$

Hence $m_r = m_r(p, w, q)$ also.

Put now

$$\overline{X}_r = m_r X_r + a_r, \quad \overline{N}_r = m_r N_r + b_r, \quad \overline{Z}_r = m_r Z_r + c_r \tag{4.10}$$

[8] If the economy falls into disjoint sectors such that no firm of one sector has a common input or output with that of another, this aggregate production equation is not unique. The treatment of this case is obvious, as is that in which some inputs or outputs are specific to particular firms.

[9] If there are specific factors and products, constant costs need not apply to them. It is interesting to note that limber ratios analogous to those occurring in the theory of international trade under constant costs arise when the economy falls into disjoint sectors.

where a_r, b_r, c_r are as yet undetermined functions of p, w, and q, and m_r is also regarded as a function of p, w, and q.

Then, in the neighbourhood of the equilibrium point $x_r^*(p, w, q)$ associated with p, w, q,

$$\bar{X}_r = \bar{X}_r(x_r^*) + \sum_i \frac{\partial \bar{X}_r}{\partial x_{ir}}(x_{ir} - x_{ir}^*) + o(|x_r - x_r^*|) \tag{4.11}$$

$$= m_r X_r(x_r^*) + a_r + \sum_i p_i(x_{ir} + x_{ir}^*) + o(|x_r - x_r^*|). \tag{4.12}$$

Choosing now

$$a_r = a_r(p, w, q) = \sum_i p_i x_{ir}^* - m_r X_r(x_r^*), \tag{4.13}$$

$$\bar{X}_r = \sum_i p_i x_{ir} + o(|x_r - x_r^*|). \tag{4.14}$$

Similarly,

$$\bar{N}_r = \sum_j w_j n_{jr} + o(|n_r - n_r^*|), \text{ etc.} \tag{4.15}$$

Under the usual assumptions, these Klein aggregates can be approximated to the second order by functions of x^+ etc. in the neighbourhood of the equilibrium determined by (p, w, q). Moreover, if the economy does not split into disjoint sectors in the manner mentioned in note 8, and if there are no specific inputs or outputs, any other Klein output aggregate having this property is a function of $\bar{X}$, and similarly for labour and capital aggregates.

To prove the latter, let $X^+ = \sum k_r X_r$, $X = X(X^+) = f(x^+)$ to the second order about this equilibrium point. Hence

$$\frac{\partial X}{\partial x_{ir}} = \frac{\partial f}{\partial x_i} = \frac{\partial X}{\partial x_{is}} \tag{4.16}$$

at equilibrium. However,

$$\frac{\partial X}{\partial x_{ir}} = \frac{dX}{dX^+} \times k_r \frac{\partial X_r}{\partial x_{ir}} = \frac{dX}{dX^+} \times k_r \frac{p_i}{m_r}, \tag{4.17}$$

at equilibrium in the notation used above. Hence

$$k_r/m_r = k_s/m_s = \ldots = k, \text{ say.}$$

Hence $X^+ = k\bar{X}$, and $X = X(X^+) = H(\bar{X})$. The treatment of the special cases mentioned above is obvious.

We have now from (4.14):

$$\bar{X}_r = \sum_i p_i x_{ir} + o(|x_r - x_r^*|) \quad \text{and} \quad \bar{X} = \sum_i p_i x_i^+ + o(|x - x^*|) \tag{4.18}$$

about equilibrium, where $\bar{X} = \sum_r \bar{X}_r$, with similar results for the labour and capital aggregates. The disadvantage of these formulae is that $\bar{X}$, $\bar{N}$, $\bar{Z}$ will all double about the equilibrium point (p, w, q) if p, w, q all double. To avoid this difficulty we introduce 'base' baskets of commodities x^0, n^0, z^0 and set $P = \sum p_i x_i^0$, $W = \sum w_j n_j^0$, $Q = \sum q_k z_k^0$,

$$X = \bar{X}/P = \frac{\sum p_i x_i}{\sum p_i x_i^0} \tag{4.19}$$

about equilibrium, etc.[10] In terms of these the aggregate equation is $PX = WN + QZ + D$.

If, by analogy, we introduce the vectors $x_r^0, \ldots$, such that $\sum x_r^0 = x^0$, and 'prices' $P_r = \sum p_i x_{ir}^0, \ldots$, the production equation for the rth firm is then $P_r X_r = W_r N + Q_r Z_r + D_r$.

With this notation we will now prove that a set of necessary and sufficient conditions for equilibrium is that

$$X \sim \frac{\sum p_i x_i}{\sum p_i x_i^0}, \quad N \sim \frac{\sum w_j n_j}{\sum w_j n_j^0}, \quad Z \sim \frac{\sum q_k z_k}{\sum q_k z_k^0} \tag{4.20}$$

about equilibrium.

We have already shown that they are sufficient conditions. To prove their necessity we have:

$$\frac{\partial X}{\partial x_{ir}} = \frac{\partial X}{\partial x_i}\frac{\partial x_i}{\partial x_{ir}} = \frac{p_i}{P}, \tag{4.21}$$

$$\frac{P_r}{P}\frac{\partial X_r}{\partial x_{ir}} = \frac{p_i}{P}, \tag{4.22}$$

and

$$\frac{\partial X_r}{\partial x_{ir}} = \frac{p_i}{P_r}. \tag{4.23}$$

Similarly,

$$\frac{\partial N_r}{\partial n_{jr}} = \frac{w_j}{W_r}, \quad \frac{\partial Z_r}{\partial z_{kr}} = \frac{q_k}{Q_r}. \tag{4.24}$$

But $F_r(X, N, Z) \equiv P_r X_r - W_r N_r - Q_r Z_r - D_r = 0$ is the production equation for firm r. So

$$\frac{\partial F_r}{\partial x_{ir}} = p_i, \quad \frac{\partial F_r}{\partial n_{jr}} = w_j, \quad \frac{\partial F_r}{\partial z_{kr}} = q_k. \tag{4.25}$$

These imply the equilibrium of the rth firm.

[10] [eds.] Here (and elsewhere below) the superscript $^+$ has been omitted. Both x_i^0 and x_i refer to the aggregate output of good i.

Finally, we note that the Klein equation $PX = WN + QZ + D$ yields

$$\frac{\partial X}{\partial N} = \frac{W}{P}, \quad \frac{\partial X}{\partial Z} = \frac{Q}{P}, \tag{4.26}$$

equations analogous to the equilibrium condition for a firm. Unfortunately they are not equilibrium conditions here, but identities.

We see that the aggregates X, N, Z; P, W, Q have the following qualities.

(i) They always exist if Klein aggregates exist at all.

(ii) They are the only Klein aggregates which can be closely approximated by functions of total output etc. in the neighbourhood of an equilibrium point.

(iii) $X \sim \dfrac{\sum p_i x_i}{\sum p_i x_i^0}$, $X_r \sim \dfrac{\sum p_i x_{ir}}{\sum p_i x_{ir}^0}$ about equilibrium, have obvious meanings, and are closely related to the conventional Paasche index number.

(iv) $PX = \sum P_r X_r$ everywhere and equal $\sum p_i x_i$ about the appropriate equilibria.

(v) No necessary and sufficient conditions for equilibrium exist in terms of them.

(vi) $\dfrac{\partial X}{\partial N} = \dfrac{W}{P}, \dfrac{\partial X}{\partial Z} = \dfrac{Q}{P}, \dfrac{\partial X_r}{\partial N_r} = \dfrac{W_r}{P_r}, \dfrac{\partial X_r}{\partial Q_r} = \dfrac{Q_r}{P_r}$ (4.27)

(vii) $P = \sum_i p_i x_i^0$, $P_r = \sum_i p_i x_{ir}^0$ have the obvious interpretations, and satisfy $P = \sum_r P_r$.

These aggregates have three main disadvantages.

(i) Being Klein aggregates they depend upon the technical conditions.

(ii) They are functions of the prices etc. considered as parameters. This is all right as long as the prices are parameters, but the situation becomes more complex once they are variables determined in a complete model.

(iii) The equilibrium condition $\partial X/\partial x_{ir} = p_i$ etc. will normally depend on the micro-variables x, rather than the macro-variables X, N, Z, or even x^+, n^+, z^+.

Let us consider the last point first. Since these aggregates are only of interest in the neighbourhood of equilibrium, it seems reasonable to confine our attention to possible equilibrium values of x^+, n^+, z^+.

Suppose now $\partial X/\partial x_{ir} = f_{ir}(x_1, \ldots, x_m)$ everywhere. Then, at the production equilibrium x implied by prices p, w, q,

$$\frac{\partial X}{\partial x_{ir}} = p_i = \frac{\partial X}{\partial x_{is}} \tag{4.28}$$

if both the rth and s^{th} firm produce the ith good. Hence

$$\frac{\partial X}{\partial x_{ir}} = \frac{\partial X}{\partial x_{is}} \text{ at any equilibrium } x, \tag{4.29}$$

and also

$$f_{ir}(x_1, \ldots, x_m) = f_{is}(x_1, \ldots, x_m) \text{ at any equilibrium point } x, \tag{4.30}$$

so that over the set of such points we have $f_{ir}(x_1, \ldots, x_m) = f_i(x_1, \ldots, x_m)$, say. Moreover since

$$\frac{\partial^2 X}{\partial x_{ir} \partial x_{js}} = \frac{\partial^2 X}{\partial x_{js} \partial x_{ir}}, \tag{4.31}$$

it follows that

$$\frac{\partial f_I}{\partial x_j} = \frac{\partial f_j}{\partial x_i}. \tag{4.32}$$

Therefore, there exists a function $f(x_1, \ldots, x_m)$ such that

$$\frac{\partial f}{\partial x_i} = f_i = \frac{\partial X}{\partial x_{ir}}. \tag{4.33}$$

So

$$\mathrm{d}X = \sum \frac{\partial X}{\partial x_{ir}} \mathrm{d}x_{ir}, \quad \mathrm{d}f = \sum \frac{\partial f}{\partial x_i} \mathrm{d}x_i, \tag{4.34}$$

and

$$X(x) = f(x_1, \ldots, x_m) + \text{const} = g(x_1, \ldots, x_m), \text{ say}. \tag{4.35}$$

Now it is clear that many disequilibrium x's will yield equilibrium x^+'s. The analysis of the first part of this section applies and we are in the case of constant costs. The result holds, *a fortiori*, if $\partial X/\partial x_{ir} = f_{ir}(X)$.

At first sight this might seem to imply that Klein aggregates are only useful in the trivial case of constant costs.

Clearly if the production equilibrium sector of our model is merely intended to determine X, N, Z in conjunction with the aggregate transformation equation, it should normally contain only two equations. If it is to run in terms of x^+, n^+, and z^+, it should contain $m + s + t - 1$ equations. Above we have required that it should contain sufficient variables to determine the equilibrium of the *micro-model*. Since there are far fewer variables in the macro-model, this clearly implies considerable degeneracy, probably much more than would the requirement that there should be 2 (or $m + s + t - 1$) equilibrium equations capable of being expressed in terms of the aggregates.

The real problem is: under what conditions upon the micro-model is it possible to determine equilibrium conditions for the macro-model which, together with the transformation equation $PX = WN + QZ + D$, determine X, N, Z as functions of P, W, and Q? I have not been able to solve this problem.

This leads us immediately to a further difficulty. $D = D(p, w, q)$ and there is no obvious reason why it should be expressible as a function of (P, W, Q) above. However, we know that $D = \sum D_r$ and

$$D_r = P_r X_r - W_r N_r - Q_r Z_r = \sum_i p_i x_{ir} - \sum_j w_j n_{jr} - \sum_k q_k z_{kr}$$

at equilibrium. $D_r(p, w, q)$ therefore represents the equilibrium profits of the rth firm under perfect competition. If these vanish at all p, w, q which interest us, we can put each $D^r = 0$, and therefore $D = \sum D_r = 0$.

Now there are two cases in which pure profits vanish under perfect competition.

In the first place we may assume that all the transformation functions are homogeneous. The vanishing of profits at equilibrium then follows identically from Euler's theorem. In this case X_r, N_r, and Z_r will all be homogeneous of the same degree in x_r, n_r, z_r. The disadvantages of this approach are well known and are particularly important in the analysis of Klein's model where the behaviour of particular firms is of great importance.

In the second place we may assume freedom of entry and identical production functions within industries. As long as the new firms have production equations of the required form, our model can easily be adjusted to allow their entry. In this case, however, profits are made to vanish by *price changes*, and the result is only consistent with certain price structures. To see this we may consider a particular firm with the transformation equation $f(y) = 0$, $y = (y_1, \ldots, y_n)$. If profits are to vanish at all conceivable equilibria, these must also obey $\sum y_i (\partial f/\partial y_i) = 0$. Here the set of all admissible equilibria is $(N - 2)$ dimensional, while that of the price ratios is $(n - 1)$ dimensional. This implies that not all price ratios are admissible as long-run equilibrium price ratios. If $D = 0$ is to hold we must confine ourselves to these price ratios. As long as we are not interested in analysing changes in the production sector itself, this seems reasonable.

It is, of course, sufficient that $D = D(P, W, Q)$.

The objection that our aggregates depend upon the prices as parameters, and therefore break down where the prices are determined in the model, does not appear correct.

Suppose our model to be made up of an aggregate production equation $PX = WN + QZ + D(P, W, Q)$, two production equilibrium equations of the form $f(X, N, Z) = W/P$, $g(X, N, Z) = Q/P$, and a set of equations representing the demand etc. of the household sector as a function of (p, w, q).

Take a trial p, w, q and calculate the corresponding $X^h = \sum p_i x_i / \sum p_i x_{ir}^0$, . . . from the household sector, and $X^p = X(P, W, Q)$, from the production sector. If $X^h = X^p$, $N^h = N^p$, $Z^h = A^p$ regard the result as the equilibrium point for the macro-model. If not, try again. This procedure seems rather general. Indeed it would seem that the only difficulty about choosing aggregates which depend on the prices is that it is no longer literally true that the aggregates X, N, Z depend entirely upon the corresponding micro-variables.

5. TECHNICAL CHANGE

In this section we will consider the effect of technical change in Klein models. It was in the analysis of such changes that Klein saw the main advantages of his aggregates over those which are based on the assumption that the production sector is in equilibrium all the time. We will show that the only technical changes which can be analysed in this manner are those which send the transformation equations of the individual firms from $X_r = N_r + Z_r$ to $X_r = aN_r + bZ_r + c_r$, where a, b, and c_r are constants, of which a and b are the same for each firm.

In the first place we note that the transformation equations for the individual firms must remain in the form (3.1′) after the change as well as before it. Let us therefore suppose that the rth firm's transformation equation before the change was $X_r = N_r + Z_r$, and after the change $X_r^+ = N_r^+ + Z_r^+$. Suppose that the Klein output aggregate before the change was $X = X(X_0)$ where $X_0 = \sum_r k_r X_r$ with similar formulae for the other aggregates. If the aggregates have the same form after the change, we must have $X = X^+ = X^+(X_0^+)$ where there are some k_r^+'s independent of the x^+, n^+, z^+ such that $X_0^+ = \sum_r k_r^+ X_r^+$ etc. A necessary and sufficient condition for this is that $X_0^+ = f(X_0)$.

Differentiating we have:

$$k_r^+ \frac{\partial X_r^+}{\partial x_{ir}} = \frac{\partial X_0^+}{\partial x_{ir}} = \frac{\mathrm{d} X_0^+}{\mathrm{d} X_0} \frac{\partial X_0}{\partial x_{ir}} = \frac{\mathrm{d} X_0^+}{\mathrm{d} X_0} k_r \frac{\partial X_r}{\partial x_{ir}} \tag{5.1}$$

Hence:

$$\frac{\mathrm{d} X_0^+}{\mathrm{d} X_0} = \frac{k_r^+}{k_r} \times \frac{(\partial X_r^+ / \partial x_{ir})}{(\partial X_r / \partial x_{ir})} \tag{5.2}$$

depends upon x_r alone. Similarly, it depends upon x_s alone. Hence it is a constant. Call it a. Hence $X_0^+ = aX_0 + A$ where A is a constant. Similarly, $N_0^+ = bN_0 + B$ and $Z_0^+ = cZ_0 + C$.

From (5.1) we have

$$k_r^+ \frac{\partial X_r^+}{\partial x_{ir}} = ak_r \frac{\partial X_r}{\partial x_{ir}}. \tag{5.3}$$

Hence $k_r^+ \mathrm{d} X_r^+ = ak_r \mathrm{d} X_r$ and

$$k_r^+ X_r^+ = ak_r X_r + A_r. \tag{5.4}$$

Similarly,

$$k_r^+N_r^+ = bk_rN_r + B_r, \quad k_r^+Z_r^+ = ck_rZ_r + C_r, \tag{5.5}$$

where $A = \sum A_r$, $B = \sum B_r$, $C = \sum C_r$. The corresponding transformation equations are:

$$aX_r = bN_r + cZ_r + d_r; \quad d_r = B_r + C_r - A_r, \tag{5.6}$$

$$aX_0 = bN_0 + cZ_0 + d; \quad d = \sum d_r. \tag{5.7}$$

With a slight change of notation these may be written

$$X_r = aN_r + bZ_r + c_r; \quad X = aN + bZ + c. \tag{5.8}$$

It is clear from these equations that only a restricted class of technical changes can normally be investigated by Klein's method. If it is further demanded that the aggregates obey some other conditions—for instance that they should be Ideal Aggregates in the sense of the last section, or that they should obey equilibrium relations of the type $\partial X/\partial N = W/P$, $\partial X/\partial Z = Q/P$ as Klein further demands—then the class of technical changes which can be treated will clearly be more restricted.

The condition that the same indices should be 'ideal' before and after the change is that $m_r^+/m_r = \ldots = m_1^+/m_1$, where $\partial X_r/\partial x_{ir} = p_i/m_r, \ldots$ before the change and $\partial X_r/\partial x_{ir} = p_i/m_r^+$ after it. This condition is obeyed if X_r, N_r, Z_r are homogeneous of the first degree, but is not in general. We may note that the condition that the individual subaggregates should be homogeneous of degree one is more restrictive than the requirement that the transformation function should be homogeneous, as is frequently assumed in economics. To see this we note that $x = n^a n^{1-a} = 0$ has a homogeneous transformation function. Put in Klein form it becomes $\log x = a \log n + (1 - a) \log z$, which is not linear and homogeneous in x, n and z.

6. TWO SIMPLE MODELS

In this section we will consider two simple models using Klein aggregates.

First Model

Production Sector

$PX = WN + QZ$ Production Equation (6.1)

$f(X, N, Z) = W/P$ Production Equilibrium (6.2*a*)

$g(X, N, Z) = Q/P$ (6.2*b*)

Household Sector

$$X^+ = F(W/P,\ Q/P) \tag{6.3a}$$

$$N^+ = G(W/P,\ Q/P) \tag{6.3b}$$

$$Z^+ = H(W/P,\ Q/P) \tag{6.3c}$$

Here $X^+ = \sum p_i x_i / \sum p_i x_i^0$, where $x_i = x_i(p, w, q)$ is the quantity of x_i consumed at prices (p, w, q) etc., $P = \sum_i p_i x_i^0$ etc. From the Walras equation we have identically in P, W, Q in the zero-profit set: $PX^+ = WN^+ + QZ^+$. Hence we can neglect (6.3c). Finally we have the joint equilibrium conditions:

$$X = X^+, \quad N = N^+, \quad Z = Z^+. \tag{6.4}$$

This model can easily be solved to find the equilibrium X, N, Z. It can be used to find the effect of changes in the household sector, but not so easily in the production sector.

The difficulty in this model lies in our assumption that equilibrium conditions of the form (6.2) exist, and that the price aggregates used in them are also appropriate to the household sector.

This difficulty may be evaded by the use of a more complicated model for the household sector.

Second Model

Production Sector

$$PX = WN + QZ \quad \text{Production Equation} \tag{6.1}$$

$$f_i(x, n, z) = p_i/p_1 \quad \text{Production Equilibrium} \tag{6.5a}$$

$$g_i(x, n, z) = w_i/p_1 \tag{6.5b}$$

$$h_i(x, n, z) = q_i/p_1 \tag{6.5c}$$

$$PX = \sum p_i x_i; \quad WN = \sum w_i n_i; \quad QZ = \sum q_i z_i \tag{6.5d}$$

Household Sector

$$x_i^+ = F_i(P/p_1;\ W/p_1;\ Q/p_1) \tag{6.6a}$$

$$n_i^+ = G_i(P/p_1;\ W/p_1;\ Q/p_1) \tag{6.6b}$$

$$z_i^+ = H_i(P/p_1;\ w/p_1;\ Q/p_1). \tag{6.6c}$$

Here $x = (x^1, \ldots, x_m)$ is the total production vector, x_i being the total production of the ith good. x^+ is similarly the total consumption vector. In the household sector we have Walras's identity $\sum p_i x_i^+ = \sum_i w_i n_i^+ + \sum q_i z_i^+$.

We also have the joint equilibrium conditions:

$$x = x^+, \quad n = n^+, \quad z = z^+, \tag{6.7}$$

and the definitions

$$P = \sum p_i x_i^0, \quad W = \sum w_i n_i^0, \quad Q = \sum q_i z_i^0. \tag{6.8}$$

The disadvantages of this model are that it leaves the production equation 'up in the air', and that a great deal of the simplicity of the first model is lost. On the other hand it is easy to see that the equilibrium conditions (6.5) can be derived from the micro-model, for we can easily derive $x_{ir} = f_{ir}(p, w, q)$ etc. at equilibrium, and add to get $x_i = f_i(p, w, q)$ there. One of these equations must be dropped as following from the other and the production equation.

It seems clear that the first model is the type which is required, so that the main unsolved problem in this field is to derive the conditions under which equilibrium conditions of the form (6.2) exist. If these were satisfied the model would be useful in analysing the effect of changes in the household sector which allowed (6.3) to keep their form. It might also be useful in analysing small changes in competitive conditions. It is likely to be less useful in analysing technological change.

In the case of technological change, a paradox appears. Suppose we define $X =$ 'the ideal Klein aggregate for output' etc., rather than as a certain function of x, and suppose $D = 0$ in the aggregate production equation (Section 5).

Then this equation reads

$$PX = WN + QZ,$$

both before and after technological change, as long as the conditions for the existence of their aggregates are obeyed throughout. We seem to be in a paradox here—technological changes do not affect the production function. The resolution of the paradox is, of course, that the definition of the terms in the equation has changed. However, the interpretation in the neighbourhood of equilibrium remains unchanged, for we still have $X = \sum p_i x_i / \sum p_i x_i^0$ etc. As long, therefore, as we are only interested in behaviour close to production equilibria, it would seem that we can analyse fairly general technological changes—with the aid of a production function which does not change! It is, of course, the equilibrium conditions which change, and the probability is that they may become quite impossible to formulate as in (6.2).

7. CONCLUDING REMARKS

It seems clear that Klein aggregates are only of use in their 'ideal form', at least in quasi-equilibrium analysis. If this form is to be useful we must be able to write the aggregate production equation in the form $PX = WN + QZ + D$ where $D = D(P, W, Q)$, and to find equilibrium conditions of the form $f(X, N, Z) = W/P$, $g(X, N, Z) = Q/P$. It is not known what restrictions are required for equilibrium conditions of this type to exist.

We note that the main use of Klein aggregates would be in the analysis of change *outside the production sector*. It might therefore seem reasonable to amalgamate the two production subsectors—technical and equilibrium—to give a single set of equations. It might reasonably be hoped that this would allow Nataf's condition for the existence of Klein aggregates to be relaxed and give a wider choice of aggregates. Various attempts along these lines have suggested that this approach can only be fruitful in very special cases. In other words the attempt to discover production equations—including technical and equilibrium relationships—which are independent of structure of the remainder of the model seems doomed to failure. In terms of the micro-model, the autonomy of the production sector of the macro-model cannot be complete. This suggests that we can in general only hope to secure sector-models which are 'fairly stable' under changes in other sectors, and rather throws us back upon statistical and commonsensical considerations.

17

On a Class of Preference Fields

Editorial Summary

This short note begins with the assumption that the preferences of the consumer exhibit linear Engel curves, which were shown in 'Community Preference Fields' to be necessary for the existence of a community indifference map. Here, these preferences are characterized by closed form representations in terms of both the indirect utility function and the cost function.

Suppose that the compensated demand for good i is given by

$$x_i = f_i(p) + ug_i(p) \tag{0.1}$$

for all i. Then the expenditure function can be written as

$$r = f(p) + ug(p). \tag{0.2}$$

The term $f(p)$ denotes the expenditure needed to achieve zero utility and is dual to the base indifference curve constructed in 'Community Preference Fields'. Using this, the indirect utility function is given by

$$u = (r - f(p))/g(p), \tag{0.3}$$

and the ordinary demand functions can be derived using Roy's identity. He then shows that

$$g(p) = \prod_{i=1}^{n} p_i^{\rho} \tag{0.4}$$

if all marginal propensities to consume are constant. This is used to derive the preferences of a country with a constant marginal propensity to import a commodity whose elasticity of demand is constant.

On A Class of Preference Fields

Linear income–consumption curves crop up in several branches of economics.[1] In this note we will explore some of the properties of the preference fields in which they arise, and, in particular, of those in which the marginal propensity to consume each good is an absolute constant, and will discuss an application to international trade theory.

If the income consumption curves were linear throughout the closed positive orthant, they would all pass through the origin.[2] The underlying utility function would then be homogeneous.[3] Since the properties of homogeneous functions are well known to economists, we will confine our attention to a region in the interior of the positive orthant, and, for simplicity, we will take this to be the region R: $0 \leqslant u \leqslant U$ between two indifference surfaces.[4] By taking $U = \infty$ we will be able to consider the whole region above $u = 0$.

We will assume that all the functions appearing are twice continuously differentiable.[5]

1. QUASI-HOMOTHETICITY

Consider a consumer who purchases x_i units of the ith good, $i = 1, 2, \ldots, n$, when the prices of the goods are $p = (p_1, p_2, \ldots, p_n)$ and his income is

$$r = \sum p_i x_i. \tag{1.1}$$

It can be shown[6] that if his income–consumption curves are linear, then

$$x_i = f_i(p) + ug_i(p); \qquad i = 1, 2, \ldots, n, \tag{1.2}$$

where

$$\sum_i p_i \partial f_i / \partial p_j \equiv \sum_i p_i \partial g_i / \partial p_j \equiv 0; \qquad j = 1, 2, \ldots, n. \tag{1.3}$$

Define now

[1] e.g. welfare economics and market demand theory. Given an appropriate aggregation of the goods, they may be useful even for budget studies.

[2] If one often met the coordinate plane $x_i = 0$ at any other point, the marginal propensity to consume the ith good would be zero at one income and non-zero at another.

[3] More accurately, a function of a homogeneous function.

[4] The reader will have little difficulty in generalizing the argument to cover any region in the open positive orthant.

[5] So that we can use simple differential methods without fear of error.

[6] See e.g. Gorman (1953*a*).

$$f = \sum p_i f_i, \quad g = \sum p_i g_i. \tag{1.4}$$

Then

$$\partial f / \partial p_j = \sum p_i \partial f_i / \partial p_j + f_j = f_j, \qquad j = 1, \ldots, n, \tag{1.5}$$

by (1.3). Similarly

$$\partial g / \partial p_j = g_j, \qquad j = 1, 2, \ldots, n. \tag{1.6}$$

Hence, by (1.4)

$$f(p) \text{ and } g(p) \text{ are homogeneous of degree one,} \tag{1.7}$$

which is, indeed, intuitively obvious.

(1.5)–(1.7) clearly imply (1.3). Indeed, denoting differentiation with respect to p_i, u, and other prices being given, by the suffix i, we can say that (1.2) and (1.7) together imply (1.3)–(1.6), and therefore also imply the Slutsky relation $x_{ij} = x_{ji}$. (1.2) is therefore 'integrable' and represents a non-intersecting indifference map.[7]

Indeed

$$r = \sum p_i x_i = f(p) + ug(p), \tag{1.8}$$

by (1.1), (1.2), and (1.7), so that

$$u = (r - f)/g \tag{1.9}$$

is the polar form of the underlying utility function. Clearly, f is the income needed to reach the base indifference curve $u = 0$, and $r - f$ the excess needed to raise the consumer to the level u. This excess money income is deflated by the price index $g(p)$ to find the corresponding 'real income' u.

It is necessary and sufficient for 'strong', or Hicksian, concavity that $\sum x_{ij} t_i t_j$ should be negative semi-definite, taking the value zero only when $t_i = \lambda p_i$, $i = 1, 2, \ldots, n$. For this to hold throughout R, it is obviously necessary and sufficient that

$$\sum_{ij} f_{ij} t_i t_j < 0 \quad \text{unless} \quad t_i = \lambda p_i, \qquad i = 1, 2, \ldots, n,^8 \tag{1.10}$$

and

$$\sum_{ij} f_{ij} t_i t_j + u \sum_{ij} g_{ij} t_i t_j < 0, \quad \text{unless} \quad t_i = \lambda p_i, \qquad i = 1, 2, \ldots, n. \tag{1.11}$$

If R consists of the whole region $u \geqslant 0$, (1.11) becomes

[7] But see below for convexity, etc.

[8] Given our continuity assumption it is slightly stronger than strict convexity, which would be consistent with $\sum x_{ij} t_i t_j \geqslant 0$ for all t's if the higher-order derivatives behaved appropriately.

$$\textstyle\sum_{ij} g_{ij} t_i t_j \leq 0 \quad \text{everywhere.}^9 \tag{1.12}$$

For $x_i > 0$, $i = 1, 2, \ldots, n$ throughout R the corresponding conditions are

$$f_i > 0 \qquad i = 1, 2, \ldots, n; \tag{1.13}$$

$$f_i + ug_i > 0 \qquad i = 1, 2, \ldots, n; \tag{1.14}$$

$$g_i \geq 0 \qquad i = 1, 2, \ldots, n. \tag{1.15}$$

A given preference field will have linear income consumption curves throughout R and will be 'well behaved'[10] there if and only if it satisfies these conditions in addition to (1.2) and (1.7), which are in turn equivalent to (1.2) and (1.3).

Substituting from (1.9) and (1.2) we find the demand equations in this case:

$$x_i = (f_i - fg_i/g) + rg_i/g; \qquad i = 1, 2, \ldots, n, \tag{1.16}$$

so that the marginal propensity to consume the ith good is

$$\rho_i = p_i g_i/g = \partial \log g/\partial \log p_i, \qquad i = 1, 2, \ldots, n. \tag{1.17}$$

If these marginal propensities are all constant, we can integrate (1.17) to find

$$\log g = \textstyle\sum \rho_i \log p_i + \log A, \text{ say.} \tag{1.18}$$

Since the integration constant A can obviously be subsumed under the utility function u,[11] we can take $A = 1$ without loss of generality. It is therefore necessary and sufficient for the ρ's to be constant, that we can write

$$g = \textstyle\prod p_i^{\rho_i}. \tag{1.19}$$

Since $\sum \rho_i = 1$, g is a straightforward geometric mean of the prices.[12]

2. REPRESENTATIVE CONSUMER TRADE MODEL

In this section we will derive the preference field of a country A whose propensity to import, ρ,[13] and elasticity of demand for imports, j, are both

[9] Since u never actually equals ∞.

[10] 'Well behaved' means that the indifference surfaces should have the correct shape and should be 'strongly convex', and that each $x_i > 0$.

[11] Of course u becomes Au.

[12] The weight ρ_i will be negative if and only if i is an inferior good.

[13] More accurately, the marginal propensity to purchase imports. The valuation is at *domestic* prices.

constant. Since these are the parameters most frequently used in international trade theory, such a model will sometimes be useful for reference purposes.[14]

Suppose that X units of one good are exported in return for Y of another when the domestic price of the import good in terms of the export good is p. Its preference field is then of the form:[15]

$$X = F(p) - (1 - \rho)up^{\rho}, \tag{2.1}$$

$$Y = G(p) + \rho up^{\rho - 1}, \tag{2.2}$$

where

$$F' = pG'. \tag{2.3}$$

If A's foreign trade is balanced, and it levies a tariff of 100t per cent *ad valorem* on imports

$$pY = (1 + t)X. \tag{2.4}$$

Eliminating u from (2.2) by means of (2.1) and (2.4), differentiating with respect to p, and using (2.3) we find that

$$j = -\frac{p}{Y}\frac{\partial Y}{\partial p} = -\frac{F' - \rho F/p}{(1 - \rho)G + \rho F/p}. \tag{2.5}$$

Multiplying across by $(1 - \rho)G - \rho F/p$, differentiating again with respect to p, and using (2.3), we find that

$$p^2F'' + (j - \rho)pF' + \rho(1 - j)F = 0. \tag{2.6}$$

Trying the solution $F = CP^m$, we find that $m(m - 1) + (j - \rho)m + \rho(1 - j) = 0$, that is $m = 1 - j$ or ρ. Hence:

$$F = Ap^{1-j} + Bp^{\rho}; \qquad A,\ B, \text{ integration constants;}$$

and

$$G = A\frac{j - 1}{j}p^{-j} - B\frac{\rho}{1 - \rho}p^{\rho - 1},$$

by (2.5).

Setting $A = jC$, $Cu^* = u - B/(1 - \rho)$, and dropping the asterisk, (2.1) and (2.2) become

$$X = C(jp^{1-j} - (1 - \rho)up^{\rho}), \tag{2.7}$$

$$Y = C((j - 1)p^{-j} + \rho up^{\rho - 1}), \tag{2.8}$$

while (2.3) is automatically satisfied.

[14] e.g. in tariff theory.

[15] These correspond to (1.1) and (1.2) in Sect. 1. Remember that exporting causes a loss in utility, hence the negative sign in (2.1).

This is the equation of the required preference field. It is easily seen to be well behaved[16] throughout the positive orthant if $0 \leqslant \rho \leqslant 1$ and $j \geqslant 1$. The former of these conditions is merely that neither good should be inferior, and it can be relaxed somewhat if necessary. The latter states that the offer curve should not slope backwards, which is obviously economically necessary if its elasticity is to be constant.

[16] i.e. the indifference surfaces slope upwards and are strictly convex.

18

Capital Aggregation in Vintage Models

Editorial Remarks

In 1963–4 Gorman was asked to give a series of lectures at Oxford on problems related to capital aggregation and this paper is his first in this general area. Later, as editor of the *Review of Economic Studies*, Denis Sargan mentioned that Frank Fisher had submitted a paper on the existence of a capital aggregate in a vintage capital model. So Gorman tried to see what he could discover about the nature of this problem before reading Fisher's paper. This was, and is, a common habit of his.

The result of his investigations is the following paper, presented at the First World Congress of the Econometric Society in Rome, 1965. In the same session, André Nataf and Frank Fisher discussed their own work on aggregation, later published as Fisher (1965) and Nataf (1967).

To begin with, Gorman set out the problem in the primal with constant-returns-to-scale technologies. After some work he recognized that the solution is related to a concept that he had encounted in differential geometry, the 'edge of regression'. This then led him to reformulate the problem in the dual.

In fact, the Appendix contains a very detailed treatment of duality and the relationship between production functions and profit functions (in fact he uses the negative of the profit function which he calls the *loss* function). Theorem 1 (in the Appendix) is a general equivalence between production and profit functions, while Theorem 2 extends this to production functions with fixed factors and gross profit functions. This leaves, as is usual in these arguments, a certain asymmetry in the duality, as quantities are usually non-negative whereas prices are positive. Theorem 3 uses a boundedness assumption to establish a full duality. It is unfortunate that the paper was not more widely circulated, for most of the results took another decade to appear in the economics literature.[1]

Editorial Summary

The model itself is a straightforward vintage production structure. Total output is given by

[1] Of course, the generalization of this paper which appeared in the Hicks Festschrift in 1968, and is reproduced next, was available, but only rediscovered much later.

$$u = \sum_{t=1}^{T} u_t = \sum_{t=1}^{T} f_t(x_t, y_t) \tag{0.1}$$

where

$$u_t = f_t(x_t, y_t) \tag{0.2}$$

is the output generated using n_t machines of vintage t, the fixed inputs, $y_t = (y_{t1}, \ldots, y_{tn_t})$, and N variable inputs given by $x_t = (x_{t1}, \ldots, x_{Nt})$. As written, (0.1) above is not a production function as there is nothing to ensure that the variable inputs are being used efficiently. If the firm has a fixed amount of variable inputs to be distributed across the vintages, the production function can be written as

$$u = F(x, y) = \max \left\{ \sum_{t=1}^{T} f_t(x_t, y_t) \,\middle|\, \sum_{t=1}^{T} x_t, \leq x \right\}. \tag{0.3}$$

This is the same as assuming that the variable inputs have the same efficiency prices $p = (p_1, \ldots, P_N)$ everywhere in the firm.

The aggregation question posed here is under what conditions can the production function (0.3) be written as

$$u = F(x, y) = H(x, Y(y)), \tag{0.4}$$

where Y is a continuous aggregate of the capital stocks? To solve this problem, Gorman first characterizes it in the dual. Let the *net loss function* for each vintage be given by

$$g_t(p, y_t) = \min \left\{ \sum_{i=1}^{N} p_i x_i - f_t(x_t, y_t) \right\}, \tag{0.5}$$

and let the *net loss* function for the firm be given by

$$g(p, y) = \min \left\{ \sum_{i=1}^{T} p_i x_i - F(x, y) \right\} \tag{0.6}$$

which is obviously equal to the sum of the losses from each vintage,

$$g(p, y) = \sum_{t=1}^{T} g_t(p, y_t). \tag{0.7}$$

The *net loss* function for the firm with a capital aggregate Y is

$$K(p, Y(y)) = \min \left\{ \sum_{i=1}^{N} p_i x_i - H(x, Y(y)) \right\}, \tag{0.8}$$

so that the aggregation question posed in (0.4) may be written equivalently as

$$g(p, y) = K(p, Y(y)). \tag{0.9}$$

The answer, now well known, is given by

$$g_t(p, y_t) = c(p)\, Y_t(y_t) + d_t(p). \tag{0.10}$$

So the net loss function for the firm is given by

$$g(p, y) = c(p)\, Y(y) + d(p), \tag{0.11}$$

where

$$Y(y) = \sum_{i=1}^{T} Y_t(y_t) \tag{0.12}$$

and

$$d(p) = \sum_{t=1}^{T} d_t(p). \tag{0.13}$$

It is obvious that (0.10)–(0.13) are sufficient for (0.11) and hence (0.4).

The interpretation in this and the succeeding paper does not need to be repeated by us. However, one point is certainly worth making. Recall that if a commodity is efficiently (competitively) allocated, then there is always an aggregate, the simple sum of the optimal quantities allocated to each firm. The existence of a capital aggregate for the firm forces the existence of a capital aggregate in each vintage, $Y_t(y_t)$. Furthermore, this aggregate has the same shadow price in each vintage, $c(p)$. Of course, if the vector of aggregates, $(Y_1(y_1), \ldots, Y_T(y_T))$, are distributed efficiently, then they have the same efficiency price everywhere in the firm. Hence, a capital aggregate for the firm exists if and only if there is some aggregate measure of each vintage which is efficiently distributed within the firm. This interpretation was highlighted at the Rome conference by Negishi who asked if aggregation meant that there was no need for a capital market. Gorman remembers having answered 'yes' to this question, while Frank Fisher said 'no'.

Capital Aggregation in Vintage Models

1. GENERAL DISCUSSION[1]

Consider a firm producing a single good on machines of various vintages; in a simple model it might represent the entire productive sector. Assume that production is carried out independently on machinery of different vintages, so that there are, for instance, no common overheads; a strong assumption but usual. Total output can then be written

$$u = \sum_{t=1}^{T} u_t = \sum_{t=1}^{T} f_t(x_t, y_t), \tag{1}$$

where $y_t = (y_{t1}, y_{t2}, \ldots, y_{tn_t})$ is a vector of the *fixed* inputs of the n_t types of machine of vintage t, $x_t = (x_{t1}, \ldots, x_{tN})$ one of the *variable* inputs used with them, and u_t the resulting output. The same variable inputs are listed for each vintage, though it is not suggested that they are all used. Thus $x_{1i}, x_{2i}, \ldots, x_{Ti}$ all stand for quantities of the same variable input—say unskilled labour—but some, or indeed all, may be zero. On the other hand, the first type of machine of vintage 2, for instance may be completely different physically, and perform a completely different function, from the first of vintage 1. One innovation may pull together many operations, previously done on different machines, another split a process into its component parts.

(1) is not the production function. To find that one has to ensure that the variable inputs are efficiently deployed over the various vintages. That is, that they have the same *efficiency prices* $p = (p_1, p_2, \ldots, p_N)$ everywhere. For convenience these efficiency prices are measured in terms of the product as numeraire. When they are so deployed we get the production function

$$u = F(x, y), \tag{2}$$

where

$$x = \sum_{t=1}^{T} x_t; \quad y = (y_1, \ldots, y_T) = (y_{11}, y_{12}, \ldots, y_{Tn_T}). \tag{3}$$

The question we have to ask ourselves is: under what conditions can this production function be written in the form

$$F(x, y) = H(x, Y), \tag{4}$$

[1] I am grateful to F. H. Hahn, A. Nataf, F. M. Fisher, D. C. Rowan, J. D. Sargan, J. K. Whitaker, J. Wise, and the members of the class on Aggregation in Economics at Oxford for useful discussion.

where

$$Y = Y(y) \tag{5}$$

is a continuous[2] capital aggregate?

For convenience I will call Y the '*quantity of capital*', or, better, of the *quasi-factor capital*; $H(x, Y)$ the *quasi-production function*, to distinguish it from the true production function $F(x, y)$ which depends on the genuine inputs x, y; and will say that production is carried out under conditions of *quasi-constant returns to scale* when $H(x, Y)$ is homogeneous of the first degree in x, Y, so that doubling the 'quantity Y of capital' and of each of the variable inputs, doubles output.[3]

The production function is only one of many ways of characterizing a technology. In the present case each vintage sector has a given vector y_t of vintage t machinery and faces given efficiency prices p for its variable inputs. This being so, its technology can best be characterized by the quasi-rents, $-g_t(p, y_t)$, that these machines can earn in such circumstances.[4] $g_t(p, y_t)$ itself will be called the *net loss function*. Clearly it is $\min_{x_t}(\sum_i p_i x_{ti} - f_t(x_t, y_t))$.[5]

The relationship between these two methods of specifying a technology is examined in the Appendix. A more general discussion follows here.

Let us say that a production function $f(x, y)$ is *moderately well behaved in* R if, throughout R,

(A1) $0 \leqslant f(x, y) \leqslant \lambda(y)$, say, $< \infty$ if $y < \infty$

(A2) $f(x, y)$ is increasing in x and strictly increasing in y

(A3) $f(x, y)$ is continuous in (x, y)

(A4) $f(x, y)$ is concave in x.

Throughout the remainder of the paper I will assume that both the total and the vintage production functions are moderately well behaved throughout regions of the type

$$R = \{(x, y) \mid x \geqslant 0, a \leqslant y \leqslant b\}, \quad 0 \leqslant a < b \leqslant \infty. \tag{6}$$

This region can be generalized, for instance in much the same manner as in Gorman (1953*a*), and the assumptions considerably relaxed. Indeed, (A1) is

[2] Why continuous? A one to one mapping of y onto the real positive line exists. Call it $y \leftrightarrow Y$. Knowing Y, we know y. Hence any $F(x, y) = H(x, Y)$, say. Assuming continuity rules out such strange aggregates in monotonic functions, and is, in itself, quite sensible. Note that I do not assume differentiability, so that the various functions may have as many kinks as anyone might desire.

[3] Not a very interesting concept so far, since e.g. the square of the 'quantity of capital' is just as good an aggregate as Y itself. However the particular capital aggregate chosen later has the property that the 'total quantity of capital' is the sum of the 'quantities' of various vintages, which is an obviously acceptable normalization.

[4] i.e. receipts less variable costs, assuming the variable inputs to be paid their efficiency prices. 'Quasi-rents' seems a reasonable usage.

[5] That the minimum is attained is shown in the Appendix.

required only for convenience. The argument throughout will be confined to the region R, and aggregation will not be assumed possible elsewhere or even throughout the whole of R.[6]

As we have already seen, the corresponding net loss function is

$$g(p, y) = \min_{v \geq 0}\left(\sum p_i v_i - f(v, y)\right); \quad (p, y) \in R,^7$$

$$= \sum p_i x_i - f(x, y), \text{ say,} \tag{7}$$

where

$$x = \phi(p, y) \geq 0 \tag{8}$$

is an optimal variable input vector with the given equipment and shadow prices.

At any efficiency price q, then, $g(p, y) = \min_{v \geq 0} (\sum q_i v_i - f(v, y)) \leq \sum q_i x_i - f(x, y)$, so that

$$f(x, y) \leq \sum q_i x_i - g(q, y), \quad \text{all } q \geq 0. \tag{9}$$

If $x = \phi(p, y)$, so that x is optimal at these prices, (7) implies that

$$f(x, y) = \sum p_i x_i - g(p, y) = \min_{q \geq 0}\left(\sum q_i x_i - g(q, y)\right) \tag{10}$$

by (9). (A1)–(A4) imply that each x is optimal at some shadow prices

$$p = \psi(x, y) \geq 0, \tag{11}$$

so that (10) holds for all (x, y) in R.

Accordingly f and g are dual characterizations of the same technology, each yielding the other by a similar transformation (7), (10) and, in the process, yielding the optimal method of production at the efficiency prices p. Moreover it is shown in the Appendix that (A1)–(A4) both imply and are implied by

(B1) $0 \geq g(p, y) \geq -\lambda(y)$, say, $> -\infty$ if $y < \infty$,
(B2) $g(p, y)$ is increasing in p and strictly decreasing in y,
(B3) $g(p, y)$ is continuous in (p, y),
(B4) $g(p, y)$ is concave in p,

throughout R.

The duality is therefore rather strong.

Suppose for the moment that $g(p, y)$ is differentiable. (10) then yields

[6] It will not, of course, be assumed impossible elsewhere. These assumptions can, of course, be relaxed. In particular (A1) is for convenience only. The important results do not depend on boundedness.

[7] That the minimum is attained for all $(p, y) \in R$ is shown in the Appendix.

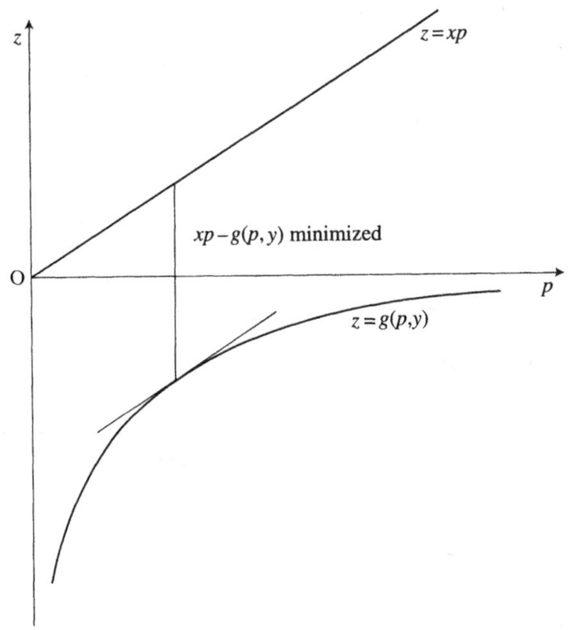

FIG: 18.1

$$x_i = g_i'(p, y), \quad \text{where } g_i' = \partial g/\partial p_i, \tag{12}$$

or, in vector form,

$$x = g'(p, y); \quad g' = (g_1', g_2', \ldots, g_N'), \tag{13}$$

so that g' is the *gradient* of g with respect to p, and the normal to $z = g(p, y)$ in the (p, z) space, i.e. for given equipment y, is parallel to $(g', -1)$. This is illustrated in Figure 18.1, for the case in which there is only one variable input.

In general $z = g(p, y)$ may have kinks and/or linear segments, so that there may be many tangent planes at any given point. If so the normals form a cone. If $(g'(p, y), -1)$ is parallel to any one of these at (p, y), we say that $g'(p, y)$ is a gradient there, and (13) remains true, the only difference being that g' may now be a multi-valued function.

Let us now return to our main problem (4)–(5). (7) and (10) clearly imply that $f(x, y) = h(x, Y(y))$, say, if and only if $g(p, y) = K(p, Y(y))$, say, and total net losses are clearly the sum of the net losses from the various vintages. Our problem therefore becomes: when is

$$g(p, y) = \sum g_t(p, y_t) = K(p, Y(y)), \text{ say,} \tag{14}$$

where $Y(y)$ is a continuous capital aggregate?

Take any fixed prices $p^* \geqslant 0$ and define

$$Y_t^*(y_t) = -g_t(p^*, y_t); \quad Y^*(y) = -K(p^*, Y(y)) = \sum Y_t^*(y_t). \tag{15}$$

According to (B1)–(B3) these aggregates are non-negative, continuous, and strictly increasing functions of their arguments y_t, y. This implies that $Y(y)$ is strictly monotonic also, since we could otherwise find y', $y'' \geqslant y'$, such that $Y^*(y') = Y^*(y'')$, contradicting the strict monotonicity of $Y^*(y)$. For simplicity assume that $Y(y)$ is strictly increasing. Then $Y^*(y)$ is a strictly increasing function of Y, and so, therefore, is Y of Y^*. Substituting into (14), dropping the asterisks, and changing notation in a trivial way, one gets

$$\sum g_t(p, y_t) = K\left(p, \sum Y_t\right); \quad Y_t = g_t(p^*, y_t). \tag{16}$$

Let us now vary y_t, holding y_s, $s \neq t$, and Y_t, constant. $g_t = K - \sum_{s \neq t} g_s$ is unchanged. This is, of course, true for all t. Hence

$$g_t(p, y_t) = k_t(p, Y_t), \text{ say.} \tag{17}$$

$$\sum k_t(p, Y_t) = K\left(p, \sum Y_t\right) \tag{18}$$

Adding θ to each Y_t in turn, one gets

$$\begin{aligned} K\left(p, \sum Y_t + \theta\right) - K\left(p, \sum Y_t\right) \\ &= k_1(p, Y_1 + \theta) - k_1(p, Y_1) = \ldots = k_T(p, Y_T + \theta) - k_T(p, Y_T) \\ &= \sum k_t(p, Y_t + \theta_t) - \sum k_t(p, Y_t) \quad \text{if} \quad \sum \theta_t = \theta, \end{aligned} \tag{19}$$

since the first term in the second line is independent of Y_T, for instance, so are they all, and, indeed of each Y_t. Hence all are of the form $\mu(p, \theta)$. According to the last line, therefore

$$\mu(p, \theta_1) + \mu(p, \theta_2) = \mu(p, \theta_1 + \theta_2), \text{ for instance.} \tag{20}$$

Since $g_t(p, y_t)$ and $Y_t(y_t)$ are both continuous in y_t, so is $k_t(p, Y_t)$ in Y_t. Hence so is $\mu(p, \theta)$ in θ. By a well-known argument,[8] therefore, (20) yields

$$\mu(p, \theta) = c(p)\theta, \text{ say,} \tag{21}$$

$$k_t(p, Y_t) - k_t(p, Y_t(a)) = c(p)(Y_t - Y_t(a)), \tag{22}$$

or alternatively

$$g_t(p, y_t) = k_t(p, Y_t) = c(p)\, Y_t + d_t(p), \text{ say,} \tag{23}$$

[8] Drop p for simplicity of notation. $\mu(r\phi) = r\mu(\phi)$ when r is a positive integer by mathematical induction, when r is a positive rational, $r = m/n$, m and n being integers. Hence $r\mu(\phi) = m\mu(\phi)/n = m\mu(\phi/n) = \mu(m\phi/n) = \mu(r\phi)$. Setting $\phi = 1$, $\mu(1) = c$, $r = \theta$ we see that $\mu(\theta) = c\theta$ when θ is a positive rational, and hence, by continuity, for positive reals too. Letting $\theta \to 0$, $\mu(0) = 0$. Finally $\mu(\theta) + \mu(-\theta) = \mu(0) = 0$, so that if $\theta < 0$, $\mu(\theta) = -\mu(-\theta) = -c(-\theta) = c\theta$ again.

and

$$g(p, y) = K(p, Y) = c(p)\,Y + d(p), \tag{24}$$

where

$$Y_t = Y_t(y_t), \quad Y = \sum Y_t, \quad d = \sum d_t. \tag{25}$$

Clearly (23) is sufficient as well as necessary for (14) and therefore for (4)–(5).

What does it 'mean'? First of all let us consider any particular technology satisfying

$$g(p, y) = c(p)\,Y(y) + d(p)^{9} \tag{26}$$

so that, in (13),

$$x = g' = c'(p)\,Y(y) + d'(p) \tag{27}$$

and

$$u = f = c_0(p)\,Y(y) + d_0(p), \tag{28}$$

say, by (10).

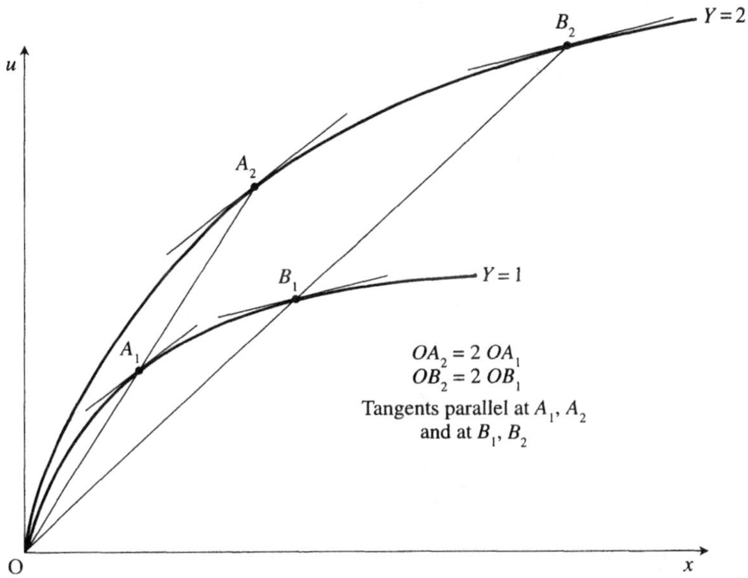

FIG. 18.2

[9] Got by dropping the subscript t in (23). I hope this notation will not be confusing. This result, specially in the form (28) or of (59) below reminds one of Nataf's (1948) classical result, which gave the first solution of the classical aggregation problem as posed by Klein (1946*a*, 1946*b*).

Fixing the equipment y, or alternatively the 'quantity of capital' Y, (27)–(28) is a parametric representation of the short-run production function.

Consider first the case of quasi-constant returns to scale. Doubling the 'quantity of capital' while the efficiency prices of the other inputs remain the same, doubles[10] those inputs, output, and net losses. Hence $d(p) = d'(p) = d_0(p) = 0$, so that

$$g = c(p)\,Y, \quad x = c'(p)\,Y, \quad u = c_0(p)\,Y. \tag{29}$$

Fixing p, now, and letting Y vary, we see that the curves joining points where the tangent planes to the short-run production functions are parallel—curves corresponding to the Engel curves of conventional consumer theory—are straight lines through the origin, as shown in Figure 18.2.

In the general case, the base short-run production curves can take any concave form, but the 'Engel curves' are still straight lines, though no longer, except by chance, through the origin (see Figure 18.3).

We have already seen in (15) that

$$Y_t(y_t) = -\,g_t(p^*, y_t) \geqslant 0 \tag{30}$$

and

$$Y_t(y_t) \text{ is continuous and strictly increasing when } a_t \leqslant y_t \leqslant b_t. \tag{31}$$

Define now

$$\begin{aligned} A_t(p) &= c(p)\,Y_t(a_t) + d_t(p) \\ B_t(p) &= c(p)\,Y_t(b_t) + d_t(p) \qquad \text{if } Y_t(b_t) < \infty \\ &= c(p) \qquad \text{otherwise,} \end{aligned} \tag{32}$$

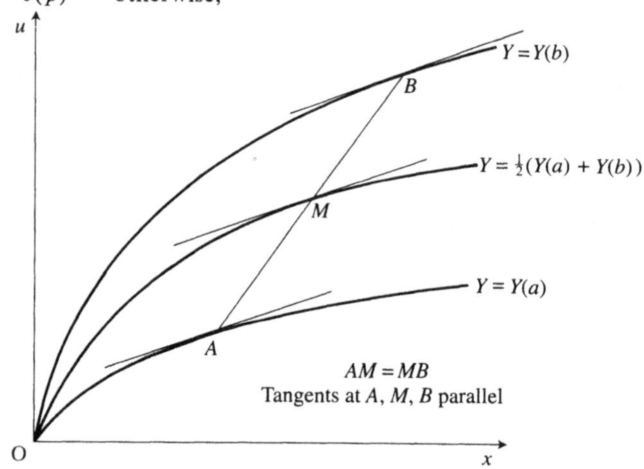

FIG. 18.3

[10] To be precise, the doubling still yields an optimal method of production. Of course, there may be many such.

where $\sum d_t(p) = 0$. It is shown in the Appendix that (B1)–(B4), or, equivalently, (A1)–(A4), hold iff, in addition to (31),

$A_t(p)$, $B_t(p)$ are continuous, increasing, concave, non-negative, and bounded, each t,[11] (33)

$c(p)$ is negative, (34)

and that $f(x, y)$ is concave in y, too, iff in addition

$Y_t(y_t)$ is concave, each t. (35)

(34) is required to ensure that output increases when more equipment is available and (33) to ensure that the top and bottom[12] short-run quasi-production functions—corresponding to $y_t = b_t$, a_t, respectively—should both be moderately well behaved,[13] which in turn ensures that the same is true of the intermediate ones.

Up to date we have been quoting prices in terms of the product. It is sometimes convenient to use *money prices* instead, setting

$$p = (p_0, p_1, \ldots, p_N), \qquad p_0 = \text{price of output}, \qquad p_i = \text{price of } i^{\text{th}} \text{ input};$$

$$x = (x_0, x_1, \ldots, x_N), \qquad x_0 = \text{amount of output}, \qquad x_i = \text{amount of } i^{\text{th}} \text{ input}. \tag{36}$$

In these terms the net loss function

$$\hat{g}(p, y), \text{ say}, \tag{37}$$

is homogeneous of degree one in p, which, by an analogue of Euler's theorem proved in the Appendix, implies that

$$x = \hat{g}'(p, y) \tag{38}$$

still, where now the output is on a par with the various inputs.

2. THE ECONOMIC 'MEANING' OF THE AGGREGATION CONDITIONS

In Section 1 we saw that capital aggregation was possible iff

$$g_t(p, y_t) = c(p)\,Y_t(y_t) + d_t(p) = k_t(p, Y_t(y_t)), \text{ say}, \tag{39}$$

[11] Of course, the assumption of boundedness in (A1), leading to that in (33), is for simplicity only.

[12] $f_t(x_t, b_t) = h_t(x_t, Y_t(b_t))$, $f_t(x_t, a_t) = h_t(x_t, Y_t(a_t))$ in fact. If $Y_t(b_t) = \infty$, $g_t(p, y_t) \to c(p)\,Y_t(y_t)$ as $y_t \to \infty$, so that we use $c(p)$ instead of $g_t(p, b_t)$ in (32), and the corresponding production function instead of $f_t(x_t, y_t)$ here.

[13] Of course, one should neglect the statements about y in the definitions (A1)–(A4), or (B1)–(B4), of 'moderately well behaved' since y_t is fixed.

where the $k_t(p, Y_t)$ are the quasi-net-loss functions corresponding to the quasi-production functions of Section 1,[14] each t, and the regularity conditions (31), (33), and (34) hold,[15] in which case

$$g(p, y) = c(p)\,Y(y) + d(p) = K(p, Y(y)), \text{ say,}$$
$$Y(y) = \sum Y_t(y_t), \quad d(p) = \sum d_t(p). \tag{40}$$

What do these conditions 'mean'?

Note first that they imply that the vintage and total production functions can be written in the forms

$$f_t(x_t, y_t) = h_t(x_t, Y_t), \quad F(x, y) = H\left(\sum x_t, \sum Y_t\right), \tag{41}$$

where each $Y_t = Y_t(y_t)$, and where the vintage functions—even considered as functions h_t of x_t and Y_t—normally differ, reflecting differences between the arbitrary functions $d_t(p)$ in (39). These are the quasi-production functions of Section 1, defined in terms of the 'quantity of capital' rather than the amounts of different sorts of equipment.

There are two obvious interpretations of the $Y_t(y_t)$.

In the first place we may regard them as indices of the quantities of machinery of the various vintages, and their sum Y as a corresponding index of the total quantity of machinery. The difficulty about this interpretation is that there is in general no reason why they should be homogeneous of the first degree in their arguments—that is, why these indices should double when all their components do so—though we will see below that that is necessarily so if production as a whole is carried out under constant returns to scale.

Another rather far-fetched but suggestive notion is that there is a separate 'capital producing industry', which produces $Y_t = Y_t(y_t)$ units of 'capital' on the machines of vintage t, *with the aid of no other inputs*, and a 'total quantity of capital' $Y = \sum Y_t$. In this interpretation each $h_t(x_t, Y_t)$ and $H(\sum x_t, \sum Y_t)$, is a production function in terms of a real 'quantity of capital' and of co-operant inputs. We have already seen that the quasi-production functions $h_1, h_2, \ldots, h_T$ normally differ because of differences between $d_1, d_2, \ldots, d_T$. One might therefore think that the 'capital' Y_t produced on vintage t machinery would in some sense have to be used in the specific vintage t production function, rather belying the homogeneity we have just been claiming for it. However (13) and (39) imply

$$x_t = c'(p)\,Y_t(y_t) + d_t'(p), \quad u_t = c_0(p)\,Y_t(y_t) + d_{t0}(p),^{16} \tag{42}$$

[14] i.e. the function defined in terms of x_t and the 'quantity of capital' Y_t, rather than x_t and the amounts y_t of fixed equipment used.

[15] These are equivalent to (A1)–(A4) which are, of course, themselves unnecessarily restrictive.

[16] If we had used money prices instead of 'own product prices' we would have had $x_t = c'(p)\,Y_t(y_t) + d_t'(p)$, covering both input and output, where p, x are as defined in (36) and c, d are defined similarly to g in (37).

$$c_0 = \sum p_i c_i - c,\quad d_{t0} = \sum p_i d_{ti} - d_t,\quad c' = (c_1, \ldots, c_N),\quad d_t' = (d_{t1}, \ldots, d_{tN}), \tag{43}$$

so that the x_{ti} and Y_t are linear functions of output u_t, and reducing the output of one sector[17] frees just enough capital and other inputs to increase the output of any other sector by the same amount—as long of course as one does not try so to reduce that of any one sector by so much that it would be forced to attempt to use a negative quantity of any input, so that we can shunt 'capital' backwards and forwards between the sectors pretty well as we like.

Let us assume for the moment that all our functions are differentiable. Denote differentiation with respect to p_i or x_{ti} by a suffix i, with respect to Y_t or Y by a point. In terms of the quasi-net-loss function

$$g_t(p, Y_t) = \sum p_i g_{ti} - h_t(g_{ti}, \ldots, g_{tN}, Y_t), \text{ say,} \tag{44}$$

since $x_{ti} = g_{ti} = k_{ti}$ by (13) and (39). Hence

$$\dot{k}_t = \dot{g}_t = \sum_t (p_i - h_{ti})\dot{g}_{ti} - \dot{h}_t = -\dot{h}_t \tag{45}$$

by (41), since the price p_i equals the marginal product h_{ti} in equilibrium. Similarly $\dot{K} = -\dot{H}$. Since each $\dot{k}_t = \dot{g} = c(p)$ by (39) and (40),

$$\dot{h}_1 = \dot{h}_2 = \ldots = \dot{h}_T = -\dot{K} = -c(p) = Q, \text{ say,} \tag{46}$$

where Q may be regarded as the efficiency price of 'capital'. In other words, capital is necessarily efficiently deployed over the various vintages if only the other inputs are in proper balance with it. This is because, as we have just seen, capital can be moved pretty well as we like from vintage to vintage, with its appropriate doses of co-operant factors, without affecting total output, so that it is always equally effectively used provided that they are correctly deployed in relation to it. However (46) does determine an efficiency price for this 'capital'. Moreover, the efficiency price q_{tr} of the rth type of vintage t is

$$q_{tr} = \dot{h}_t Y_{tr} = QY_{tr},\quad \text{where } Y_{tr} = \partial Y_t / \partial y_{tr}, \tag{47}$$

the ordinary marginal productivity condition for a 'capital producing' industry the price of whose product is Q. Finally, we will see below that, in so far as they affect y, the regularity conditions (A1)–(A4) are equivalent to the analogous conditions (31) on the 'capital-producing industry'.

In two leading special cases the quasi-production functions $h_1, h_2, \ldots, h_T, H$ are identical.

If there are constant returns to scale, doubling all the inputs doubles the outputs, leaving the efficiency prices unchanged. Assuming this is true of all vintages, each g_t is homogeneous of the first degree in y_t. It is then easily

[17] That is, reducing a u_t.

shown that the $Y_t(y_t)$ will be homogeneous of the first degree if we normalize so that

$$Y_t(0) = 0,^{18} \tag{48}$$

that is, that 'capital', so measured, is also produced under constant returns. In this case each $d_t = 0$, so that the quasi-production functions, $h_1, h_2, \ldots, h_T, H$ are identical. Since H is homogeneous of the first degree, u and each x_i doubles if Y does, given the prices, and hence so does net profit. Hence $g = c(p)\,Y(y)$. If, therefore, the different production functions differ only in the nature of the capital aggregate, all yield constant returns, (39), and therefore (40) and (41), always hold, and our type of aggregation is always possible.

The $Y_t(y_t)$ are more acceptable as indices of machinery input in this case, since they double when the amount of each sort of equipment does.

If there is only one type of machine of each vintage, y_t becomes a scalar, and $Y_t = \rho_t y_t$, where ρ_t is a measure of efficiency—one machine of efficiency ρ_t is precisely as good as ρ_t of unit efficiency. $Y = \sum \rho_t y_t$ just gives the equivalent number of such machines available for production and the various production functions are of the form $f_t = f(x_t, \rho_t y_t)$ and $F = f(\sum x_t, \sum \rho_t y_t)$. In the homogeneous case then, with only one type of machine of each vintage, aggregation is possible if and only if the only difference between the technologies lies in the efficiencies of their machines, thus narrowly defined.[19]

The second special case arises if production is impossible without equipment and capital aggregation is assumed possible however little equipment there is,[20] so that net profits all vanish when there is no equipment to earn them. Normalizing so that $Y_t(0) = 0$, so that there is no 'capital' if there is no equipment, we see that each $d_t(p) = 0$ in (39), so that

$$k_t = c(p)\,Y_t. \tag{49}$$

Hence

$$x_t = c'(p)\,Y_t, \quad u_t = c_0(p)\,Y_t, \tag{50}$$

in (42), and the quasi-production functions $h_1, h_2, \ldots, h_T, H$ are identical and homogeneous of the first degree in 'capital' and the co-operant inputs. That is, we have quasi-constant returns[21] in the sense introduced in Section 1. This clearly includes ordinary constant returns as a special case—that in which 'capital' itself is also 'produced' under conditions of constant returns, that is, that each $Y_t(y_t)$ is homogeneous of the first degree.

[18] $d_t(p) = g_t(p, 0) = 0$; $g_t(p, y_t)$ any y_t, by homogeneity, $= 0$.
[19] This can be proved directly by writing each $f_t(x_t, y_t) = y_t\phi(x_t/y_t)$.
[20] i.e. each $c_t = 0$.
[21] i.e. output doubled if the quantity of 'capital' and of each of the variable inputs doubles.

Suppose next that each vintage technology yields quasi-constant returns, so that, in (39)

$$g_t = c(p)\,Y_t(y_t) + d_t(p) = c_t^*(p)\,Y_t^*(y_t), \text{ say.} \tag{51}$$

Then $c_t^*(p)/c(p) = \{Y_t(y_t) - Y_t(a_t)\}/\{Y_t^*(y_t) - Y_t^*(a_t)\} = \rho_t$, say, a constant, so that $Y_t(y_t) - \rho_t Y_t^*(y_t) = Y_t(a_t) - \rho_t Y_t^*(a_t) = \sigma_t$, say, a constant. Setting $c_t^*(p) = \rho_t c(p)$ and $\bar{Y}_t(y_t) = Y_t - \sigma_t$, an acceptable normalization, we see that

$$g_t = c(p)\,\bar{Y}_t(y_t), \quad g = \sum g_t = c(p)\sum \bar{Y}_t(y_t), \tag{52}$$

so that, once again, $h_1, h_2, \ldots, h_T, H$ are identical.[22]

3. SEVERAL TYPES OF FIXED INPUT

The situation is almost completely unaffected if there are several classes of fixed factor, each with its own aggregate, instead of just one. Suppose, for instance, that there are two, 'land' and 'capital', though 'buildings' and 'machinery' might be a little more realistic. y's stand for machinery, z's for bits of land, and w for the output. Arguments almost identical with those above show that the net loss functions are of the form

$$g_t(p, y_t, z_t) = c(p)\,Y_t(y_t) + d(p)Z_t(z_t) + e_t(p) \tag{53}$$

as in (39), yielding quasi-production functions.

$$h_t(x_t, Y_t, Z_t),\ H\left(\sum x_t, \sum Y_t, \sum Z_t\right). \tag{54}$$

Once again the $Y_t(y_t)$, $Z_t(z_t)$ can be interpreted either as aggregates or as 'production functions'. Under constant returns, choosing $Y_t(0) = Z_t(0) = 0$ ensures that $e_t(p) = 0$, that $Y_t(y_t)$ and $Z_t(z_t)$ are homogeneous of the first degree in their arguments, and, if there are constant returns in each vintage, then all the quasi-production functions are identical. This is also true if aggregation is possible throughout the positive orthant, yielding quasi-constant returns as before. The smoothness and convexity conditions are effectively identical with those we have just found.

This result is of some interest in its own right. More important is the fact that it shows how to extend our original analysis to a set of T firms all, perhaps, producing different goods and perhaps several goods each.[23] Since

[22] In terms of the new aggregates $\bar{Y}_t(y_t)$ and $\bar{Y} = \sum \bar{Y}_t(y_t)$.

[23] I assume perfect competition in the market for variable inputs, or, more generally, that each firm enjoys the same degree of monopsony θ_t in all these markets. No such assumption is made about the market for products or fixed equipment. Even if two firms use the same type of equipment or produce the same good, it is not assumed that it will have the same 'price'.

there is really very little reason to believe that the marginal product of a given piece of fixed equipment is the same in different firms, this is quite an interesting problem.

For this purpose it is best to represent their technologies by the variable cost functions:

$$g_t(p, y_t, z_t) = \sum_i p_i x_{ti}(p, y_t, z_t), \tag{55}$$

where p is a vector of money prices[24] of the variable inputs, and z_t is here a vector of outputs. Since these costs are minimized for given p, y_t, z_t,

$$x_t = g_t'(p, y_t, z_t) \tag{56}$$

in the obvious notation. If output and capital aggregates $Z(z)$, $Y(y)$ exist for the whole economy, an argument similar to that in Section 1 shows that

$$g_t(p, y_t, z_t) = c(p)\, Y_t(y_t) + d(p) Z_t(z_t) + e_t(p) \tag{57}$$

yielding quasi-production functions

$$Z_t = h_t(x_t, Y_t), \quad \sum Z_t = H\left(\sum x_t, \sum Y_t\right), \tag{58}$$

which can be analysed just like (41) above. Since this would be a matter of almost word-for-word repetition, I will not bore the reader with it.

Return to the case in which there is a single product, but several types of fixed factor, each with its own aggregate. The general form of (53) is

$$g_t = \sum_{r=1}^{R} c_r(p)\, Y_{rt}(y_{rt}) + d_t(p), \tag{59}$$

where y_{rt} is a vector of the fixed inputs of type r. Set now

$$g_{rt} = c_r(p)\, Y_{rt}(y_{rt}), \quad r = 1, \ldots, R. \tag{60}$$

It is the net loss function of a quasi-homogeneous production function

$$\phi_r(x_{rt}, Y_{rt}(y_{rt})), \text{ say,} \tag{61}$$

while d_t is that of a production function

$$\psi_t(x_{0t}), \text{ say,} \quad t = 1, 2, \ldots, T. \tag{62}$$

Moreover these production functions are moderately well behaved if the c's and d's are and each $Y_{rt}(y_{rt})$ is continuous and increasing, and in particular, therefore, if this is so and

$$Y_{rt}(a_{rt}) = 0, \quad Y_{rt}(b_{rt}) = \infty, \qquad \text{each } r, t, \tag{63}$$

[24] I use a homogeneous formulation here, as in nn. 18–20 above. One directly analogous to that in the text could very easily be used, but would be less convenient.

so that Y_{rt} stands for the excess of the quantity of the rth factor over a certain basic amount, and there is no upper bound to the region in which aggregation is assumed possible.

In this notation

$$x_t = \sum_{r=0}^{R} x_{rt} \tag{64}$$

and total output is

$$u_t = \sum_{r=1}^{R} \phi_r(x_{rt}, Y_{rt}(y_{rt})) + \psi_t(x_{0t}). \tag{65}$$

Now let t stand for the tth firm in an industry rather than a vintage. It has a mixed bag of equipment which may or may not be similar to that owned by the other firms but which, in any case, is not transferable. We can regard it as having $R + 1$ plants. In its basic plant it has certain factors, specific to itself, which, in co-operation with $(a_{1t}, a_{2t}, \ldots, a_{Rt})$ units of the various prices of equipment and x_{0t} of the variable inputs, yields an input $\psi_t(x_{0t})$. Each of the others uses one type of equipment only, to produce, for instance, $\phi_r(x_{rt}, Y_{rt}(y_{rt}))$ units of output with the aid of x_{rt} of the variable inputs. Of course these various inputs have to be deployed efficiently over its various plants. Once it has done so, it is on its production function.

This suggests that the different fixed factors should be thought of as substitutes for each other, while each co-operates with the variable inputs in producing the final product.

Consider now a production function $w = \Phi(v)$. Let us say

v_i and v_j are *complements* if $\Phi_{ij} = \partial^2\Phi/\partial v_i \partial v_j \geqslant 0$

v_i and v_j are *substitutes* if $\Phi_{ij} \leqslant 0$.[25]

In this sense it turns out that, *if there is only one variable input*, it is indeed complementary with all the fixed factors, while they are substitutes for each other.

We have

$$g_t = \sum c_r(p)\, Y_{rt}(y_{rt}) + d_t(p), \tag{66}$$

where p is now a scalar, and the industry has only one variable input. Denote differentiation with respect to p by a prime. Then the quantity of the variable input

$$x_t = g_t' = \sum c_r'\, Y_{rt} + d_t', \tag{67}$$

[25] On reading the final version of Fisher (1965), I see that he uses much the same definition. Note that, if $\Phi_{ij} = 0$, v_i and v_j are both complements and substitutes. This scarcely matters and it simplifies the statements below.

while the marginal product $\partial h_t/\partial Y_{rt}$ of the rth fixed factor is $-c_r$ by the argument leading up to (46). Hence

$$h'_{tr} = -c'_r\,\partial p/\partial x_t = -c'_r h''_t \geqslant 0, \tag{68}$$

since h_t is concave and c_r increasing.[26] Similarly,

$$h_{trs} = -c'_r\,\partial p/\partial Y_{ts} = -c'_r c'_s h''_t \leqslant 0, \tag{69}$$

so that the fixed factors are substitutes for each other and complements of the variable factor.

Unfortunately this simple result does not carry over to the case in which there are several variable inputs. In that case (68), (69) become

$$h_{tri} = -\sum c_{rj} h_{tij},^{27} \tag{70}$$

$$h_{trs} = -\sum c_{ri} h_{tsi} = \sum h_{tij} c_{ri} c_{sj}. \tag{71}$$

Now h_t being concave in x_t, implies that $\sum h_{tij}\theta_i\theta_j \leqslant 0$. Hence

$$\sum h_{tri} c_{ri} \geqslant 0 \tag{72}$$

in (71), and since the c_{ri} are all positive[28] we may say that on the appropriate average—or, better, averages—the variable inputs are complements for each of the fixed 'factors'. Furthermore, should ϕ_r, ϕ_s use variable inputs in the same proportion, so that $c_{ri} = \rho c_{si}$, $\rho > 0$, then $h_{trs} = \rho \sum h_{tij} c_{si} c_{sj} \leqslant 0$, so that the rth and s^{th} fixed factors would be substitutes. This seems to be all we can say.

Since each $Y_{rt}(y_{rt})$ is an increasing function, all the statements made about a factor are also true of any fixed input in its group.[29]

4. COMPLETE MODELS

I assume all functions differentiable throughout this section.

The central difficulty about aggregation is that aggregates appropriate, for example, to the production sector, are normally meaningless in the consumption sector, and cannot, therefore, be used in complete models.

[26] Both are 'moderately well behaved'.

$$h'_{tr} = \partial^2 h_t/\partial x_t \partial Y_{tr}, \quad h''_t = \partial^2 h_t/\partial x_t^2, \quad h_{trs} = \partial^2 h_t/\partial Y_{tr}\partial Y_{ts}$$

[27] $h_{tri} = \partial^2 h_t/\partial Y_{tr}\partial x_{ti}$ etc.

[28] The c_r, being moderately well behaved, are increasing. This is needed to stop the demand for any inputs being negative.

[29] e.g. if there is only one variable input, fixed inputs in *different groups* are substitutes for each other, and all fixed inputs are complements of the variable input.

In our case the fundamental difficulty lies in the price Q of capital introduced in (46). The total expenditure on vintage t capital $\sum_r q_{tr}y_{tr} = Q\sum_r Y_{tr}$, by (47) equals QY_t, as it would have to in a complete model, if and only if $Y_t = \sum_r Y_{tr}y_{tr}$, that is, if and only if $Y_t(y_t)$ is homogeneous of the first degree.

Given that the $Y_t(y_t)$ are all homogeneous of the first degree, everything falls into place very nicely. Not only does a price index exist which works both for the supply and demand side, as we have just seen, but the $Y_t(y_t)$ are also relatively acceptable indices of the quality of capital themselves. Finally, the fact that quantities of capital of different vintages are added together in the aggregate production function is a great convenience when we consider changes over time, especially, of course, if there are constant returns to scale, so that the total quasi-production functions do not change over time.

What about depreciation? If the rate of depreciation on all pieces of equipment is the same, the aggregates, being homogeneous of the same degree, will also decay at the same rate. This would be one reason for considering, for example, buildings and equipment separately with separate aggregates and different rates of decay.

Broadly then, if there are constant returns to scale, so that the aggregates are necessarily homogeneous of the first degree, everything we could desire is true. Even in the absence of constant returns, we are in a pretty fortunate condition if the aggregates can be taken to be homogeneous of the first degree.

5. AN AGGREGATE FOR THE VARIABLE INPUTS?

Throughout this section I assume all functions differentiable and denote differentiation by subscripts.

It is well known that a sufficiently smooth production function $f(x, y)$, where x is a vector of variable inputs and y a vector of fixed inputs, can be written in the form $F(\phi(x), y)$ if and only if the marginal rates of substitution between any pair of variable inputs is independent of y. In the present case these marginal rates of substitution appear as ratios p_i/p_j of efficiency prices, so that the separability condition is that these prices shall all change in the same proportion if y changes while x is held constant:

$$\mathrm{d}p = p\,\mathrm{d}\theta, \text{ say.} \tag{73}$$

For the total production function (41) to be so separable, therefore, it is necessary and sufficient that

$$\left\{Y\sum_j c_{ij}p_j + \sum_j d_{ij}p_j\right\}\mathrm{d}\theta + c_i\mathrm{d}Y = 0 \tag{74}$$

for each i—a relation derived by differentiating (42), adding over t, and putting $\mathrm{d}x_i = 0$ using (73). That is, that

$$\sum_j c_{ij}p_j/c_i, \ \sum_j d_{ij}p_j/c_i, \tag{75}$$

should both be independent of i. Now $\sum_j c_{ij}p_j = \partial\{\sum c_j p_j - c\}/\partial p_i$ for instance. Hence (75) is equivalent to

$$\sum c_j p_j - c = A(c), \quad \sum d_j p_j - d = B(c), \text{ say.} \tag{76}$$

The former equation holds if and only if $c(p)$ is homothetic. Since it clearly is not homogeneous of degree zero, this implies that[30]

$$c(p) = C(\gamma), \text{ say,} \qquad \gamma = \gamma(p) \text{ homogeneous of the first degree.} \tag{77}$$

The second part of (75) has a particular solution $d = D(\gamma)$ where $\gamma D'(\gamma) - D(\gamma) = B(C(\gamma))$, say. Its general solution is

$$d(p) = D(\gamma) + \delta(p) \tag{78}$$

where $\sum \delta_i p_i = \delta$, so that δ also is homogeneous of the first degree.

Substituting from (77) and (78) into (75) we see that it is automatically satisfied. Hence, aggregates exist for both sets of factors if and only if each of the vintage net loss functions can be written in the form

$$g_t(p, y_t) = C(\gamma)\, Y_t(y_t) + d_t(p) \tag{79}$$

where

$$\sum_t d_t = D(\gamma) + \delta(p) \tag{80}$$

and

$$\gamma(p), \delta(p) \text{ are both homogeneous of the first degree.} \tag{81}$$

It is easy to give an acceptable partial explanation in the quasi-homogeneous case, which, you may remember, automatically holds if capital aggregation is possible however little equipment there is, but production impossible without any. In this case $d_t = 0$, so that the vintage quasi-production functions are all identical with each other and with the total quasi-production function. All these functions are then of the form $f(\phi(x_t), y_t)$, where ϕ is the dual of $\gamma(p)$—that is, the homogeneous production function corresponding to the 'constant average cost' function $\gamma(p)$—or, equivalently, $\phi(x) = \sum x_i \phi_i(x)$ where $\phi_i(x) = p_i$, $i = 1, \ldots, N$ is equivalent to $\gamma_i(p) = x_i$, $i = 1, \ldots, N$. f is, of course, homogeneous of the first degree in (ϕ, Y_t). I cannot interpret it in the general case. Since it is marginal to this paper, I hope that I may be forgiven.

[30] A homothetic function F is a function of a homogeneous function H. If the latter is homogeneous of degree zero, so is the former. If H is homogeneous of degree α, $h = H^{1/\alpha}$ is homogeneous of degree one. Hence a homothetic function is either homogeneous of degree zero, or a function of a function homogeneous of degree one. If c were homogeneous of degree zero, it would either be constant or some c_i would be positive and some negative, which we have already seen to be impossible on our assumptions.

Appendix: Production and Loss Functions

The following two lemmas will help us to examine the relation between production and loss functions.

By a *positively oriented* set I mean one which, if it contains x, contains all $y \geqslant x$. A single-valued scalar function $f(x)$ is *concave* if

$$f(\tfrac{1}{2}x + \tfrac{1}{2}y) \geqslant \tfrac{1}{2}f(x) + \tfrac{1}{2}f(y), \tag{A.1}$$

and is *finite* on X if it is bounded on every bounded subset of X.

All points are in $\mathbb{R}^n$, all sets subsets of $\mathbb{R}^n$.

LEMMA 1: *If $f(x)$ is concave on a convex set X, it is*

(i) *bounded below on each closed bounded subset of Int X,*[31]
(ii) *bounded above on each bounded subset of X,*
(iii) *continuous on Int X.*

Moreover there exists $f^*(x)$ such that

(iv) *$f^*(x)$ is concave on X,*
(v) *$f^*(x) \geqslant f(x)$ on X,*
(vi) *$f^*(x) = f(x)$ on Int X,*
(vii) *if $f(x)$ is finite on X, then $f^*(x)$ is finite and concave on any convex set X^* such that $X \subseteq X^* \subseteq$ closure of X,*
(viii) *$f^*(x)$ is continuous on X^* if $f(x)$ is finite on X, and X is a finite convex polyhedron or polyhedral cone.*

PROOF:[32] (i) If not, there would exist a sequence $x^N \to \bar{x} \in \operatorname{Int} X$, such that $f(x^N) \to -\infty$. Choose $\rho > 0$ such that

$$S(\rho, \bar{x}) = \{x \mid |x - \bar{x}| \leqslant \rho\} \subseteq \operatorname{Int} X, \tag{A.2}$$

and take $a^1, a^2, \ldots, a^n$ uniformly distributed on $|x - \bar{x}| = \rho$ so that

$$\bar{x} = \frac{1}{n}\sum a^r. \tag{A.3}$$

Ultimately

$$x^N = \sum k^{rN} a^r, \quad \text{each } k^{rN} > 0, \sum k^{rN} = 1, \tag{A.4}$$

so that, because of its concavity,

[31] Int X = interior of X.
[32] [eds.] There are several mistakes in the arguments which follow.

$$f(x^N) \geqslant \sum k^{rN} f(a^r), \tag{A.5}$$

and for some a^r, $f(a^r) \leqslant f(x^N)$, for all N. If $f(x^N) \to -\infty$ this is impossible, since each $f(a^r) > -\infty$, by (A.2).

(ii) If not, there would be a sequence of points $y^N \to \bar{y}$, each $y^N \in X$, such that $f(y^N) \to \infty$. Choose $\bar{x} \in \text{Int } X$ and define $\bar{z} = \tfrac{1}{2}\bar{x} + \tfrac{1}{2}\bar{y}$, $x^N = 2\bar{z} - y^N$. Then $x^N \to \bar{x}$ and since $f(\bar{z}) = f(\tfrac{1}{2}x^N + \tfrac{1}{2}y^N) \geqslant \tfrac{1}{2}f(x^N) + \tfrac{1}{2}f(y^N)$, by concavity, we have $f(x^N) \to -\infty$, even though $x^N \in S(\rho, \bar{x})$ which is closed bounded subset of Int X. This contradicts (i).

(iv)–(v) Unfortunately, for any X^* such that $X \subseteq X^* \subseteq$ closure of X, the set

$$R = \{(u, x) \mid x \in X^*, u \leqslant f(x)\} \tag{A.6}$$

though convex, is not necessarily closed. Introduce its closure

$$R^* = \{(u, x) \mid x \in X^*, u \leqslant f^*(x)\}, \text{ say,}^{33} \tag{A.7}$$

where

$$f^*(x^*) = \overline{\lim}\{f(x) \mid x \to x^*, x \in X, x^* \in X^*\}.$$

Both X^* and R^* are convex, by (A.1). Hence (iv). Furthermore, $R^* \supseteq R$. Hence (v).

(vi) If not, suppose $f^*(\bar{x}) > f(\bar{x})$ for some $\bar{x} \in \text{Int } X$. Choose $\rho, a^1, a^2, \ldots, a^n$ as in (A.2)–(A.3). Define $c = \min f(a^r) \leqslant f(\bar{x})$, by concavity, and let $d = \tfrac{1}{2}f(\bar{x}) + \tfrac{1}{2}f^*(\bar{x})$. Since (a^r, c) and $(\bar{x}, f^*(\bar{x})) \in R^*$, which is closed, the intersection (b^r, d) of the line joining them with $u = d < f^*(\bar{x})$ is too, and $\bar{x} = \sum b^r/n$.[34] Since $(b^r, c) \in R^*$, there is a sequence of points (b^{rN}, c^{rN}) in R converging on it, each r. Choosing N sufficiently large, we have each $c^{rN} \geqslant \tfrac{1}{4}f(\bar{x}) + \tfrac{3}{4}f(\bar{x})$, say, and $\bar{x} = \sum k^{rN} b^{rN}$, say, each $k^{rN} > 0$, $\sum k^{rN} = 1$. Since f is concave and $f(b^{rN}) \geqslant c^{rN}$ each r, $f(\bar{x}) \geqslant \tfrac{3}{4}f(\bar{x}) + \tfrac{1}{4}f^*(\bar{x})$, and $f(\bar{x}) \geqslant f^*(\bar{x})$. With (v), this implies (vi).

(iii) Take once more an $\bar{x} \in \text{Int } X$ and ρ to satisfy (A.2). Let $x \in S(\rho\varepsilon, \bar{x})$, $\varepsilon \leqslant 1$. Then $x = (1 - \varepsilon)\bar{x} + \varepsilon a$ for some $a \in \bar{S} = \{x \mid |x - \bar{x}| = \rho\}$, and hence $f(x) \geqslant (1 - \varepsilon)f(\bar{x}) + \varepsilon f(a)$, by concavity of f. But $c = \inf\{f(x) \mid x \in \bar{S}\}$ is finite, by (i). Hence

$$f(x) - f(\bar{x}) \geqslant -\varepsilon(f(\bar{x}) - c). \tag{A.8}$$

Consider now any sequence $x^N \to x^*$ in R^*. Since R^* is closed, $(\overline{\lim} f(x^N), x^*) \in R^*$. Hence

[33] X^* may not be closed since we might have a bounded sequence of $x^N \in X$ such that $f(x^N) \to -\infty$.

[34] $b^r = \alpha\bar{x} + (1 - \alpha)a^r$ where $\alpha = (d - c)/(f^*(\bar{x}) - c)$. Hence $\sum b^r = n\alpha\bar{x} + (1 - \alpha)\sum a^r = n\alpha\bar{x} + n(1 - \alpha)\bar{x} = n\bar{x}$.

$$\overline{\lim} f(x^N) \leqslant f(x^*) \tag{A.9}$$

while (A.8) implies

$$\underline{\lim}\, f(x^N) \geqslant f(x^*). \tag{A.10}$$

(A.9) and (A.10) together show that f is continuous at x^*, and hence throughout Int X.

(vii) Take any $x^* \in X^*$ and any $\rho > 0$. Any sequence $x^N \to x^*$ is ultimately contained in $S(\rho, x^*)$. Being finite, $f(x)$ is bounded on $S(\rho, x^*) \cap X$. Hence $f^*(x)$ is bounded on the latter's closure $S(\rho, x^*) > X^*$, and is therefore finite too. Since R^* is convex, this implies that $f^*(x)$ is concave in X^*.

(viii) Take any $x^* \in X^*$. If $x^* \in \text{Int}\, X^*$, choose $\rho > 0$ such that $S(\rho, x^*) \subseteq X^*$. If $x^* \in$ frontier of X^*, it lies on one or more facets. Choose $\rho > 0$ such that $S(\rho, x^*)$ does not intersect any facets not passing through x^*. Since the total number of facets is finite this is always possible. (A.9) and (A.10) now follow just as in the proof of (iii), with f^* replacing f. Hence f^* is continuous at x^*, and hence throughout X^*.

Finally, two counter-examples to prove that neither of the conditions of (ix) is sufficient for continuity on its own.

Example 1: $f(x)$ concave and finite on convex X does not imply $f^*(x)$ continuous, even if X is closed.

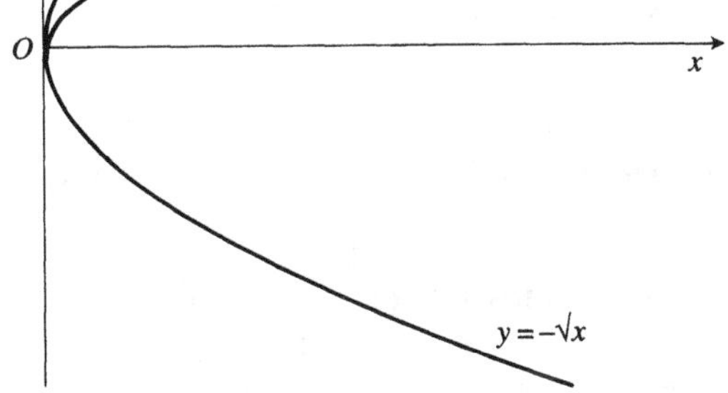

FIG. 18.4

Suppose $X = X^* = \{(x, y) \mid y^2 \leqslant x\}$, and define

$$f(x, y) = f^*(x, y) = -y^2/x, \quad x \neq 0,$$
$$f(0, 0) = 0,$$

so that $f(\cdot)$ is concave on X. Take $y = \sqrt{kx}$, $0 < k \leqslant 1$, so that $f^*(x, y) = -k$, and let $x \to 0$ to get $\lim f^*(x^N, y^N) = -k < f^*(0, 0) = 0$, which is not allowed.

Example 2: $f(x)$ concave on a convex polyhedron X does not imply $f^*(x)$ continuous.

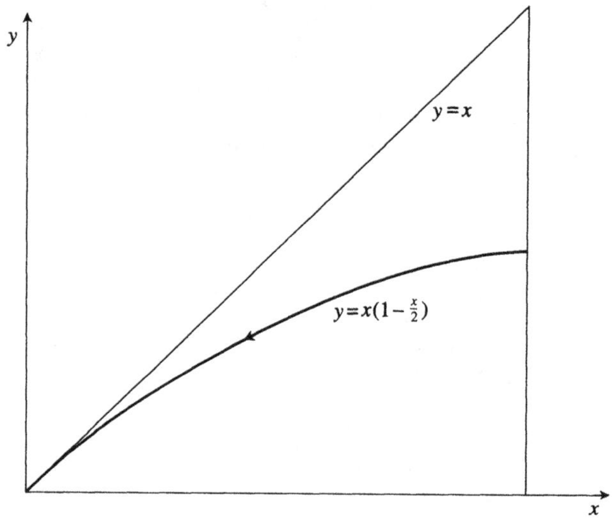

FIG. 18.5

Suppose $X = \{(x, y) \mid 0 \leqslant y < x \leqslant 1\} \cup (0, 0)$, and define

$$f(x, y) = y^2/(y - x), \quad (x, y) \in X, (x, y) \neq (0, 0),$$
$$f(0, 0) = 0.$$

Take $y = x(1 - x/k)$, $k > 0$, so that $f^*(x, y) = f(x, y) = -k(1 - x/k)^2$, and let $x \to 0$ to get $\lim f^*(x^N, y^N) = -k < f^*(0, 0) = 0$, although $(0, 0) \in X^*$.

Suppose now that I is a subset of $(1, 2, \ldots, n)$. Define x_I = the vector of x_i, $i \in I$,[35] and $X_I = \{x_I \mid x \in X\}$. Set $J = \bar{I}$, so that (I, J) is a partition of $(1, 2, \ldots, n)$. What happens to $f(x)$ if $x_J \to \infty$?[36]

[35] Taken, say, in their natural order.

[36] When I write things like this, I imply that elements not referred to—x_I in this case—remain constant.

LEMMA 2: *If $f(x)$ is non-decreasing, concave and bounded on a positively oriented convex set X, then*

(i) $f(x) \to f_I(x_I)$, *say, if* $x_J \to \infty$.
(ii) $f_I(x_I)$ *is non-decreasing, concave and bounded on* X_I, *which is convex and positively oriented.*
(iii) $f(x) \to f_I(x_I^*)$ *if* $x_I \to x_I^*$, $x_J \to \infty$, $x_I^* \in Int\ X_I$.

PROOF: (ii) is trivial, given (i), so that I will confine my attention to (i) and (iii). To prove (i), first consider the sequence

$$\{x^N\},\quad x_I^N = x_I,\quad x_J^N = Ne_J,\qquad \text{where } e_J = (1, 1, \ldots, 1).$$[37]

Since $f(x)$ is non-decreasing and bounded, $\{f(x^N)\}$ is a monotonically non-decreasing and bounded sequence, so that it converges. Call its limit $f_I(x_I)$. Clearly

$$f_I(x_I) \geqslant f(x),\quad \text{any } x_J < \infty, \tag{A.11}$$

since, ultimately, $x^N \geqslant x$.

Next consider any sequence $\{\bar{x}^N\}$, $\bar{x}_I^N \to x_I$, $\bar{x}_J^N \to \infty$. For any N, we can find N', N'' such that $\bar{x}_I^M \geqslant x_I^N$, when $M \geqslant N'$, and $x_J^M \geqslant \bar{x}_J^N$, when $M \geqslant N''$. Hence $f(\bar{x}^N) \to f_I(x_I)$, too, which proves (i). (ii) is trivial.

To prove (iii), consider a sequence $\{x^N\}$ such that $x_I^N \to x_I^* \in \text{Int } X_I$, $x_J^N \to \infty$. For any $\varepsilon > 0$, one can find $N(\varepsilon)$ such that

$$x_I^* + \varepsilon e_J \geqslant x_I^N \geqslant x_I^* - \varepsilon e_I,\quad \text{each } N \geqslant N(\varepsilon).$$

Consider the sequences $\{\bar{x}^N\}$, $\{\bar{\bar{x}}^N\}$ with

$$\bar{x}^N = x_I^* - \varepsilon e_I,\quad \bar{\bar{x}}_I^N = x_I^* + \varepsilon e_I,\quad \bar{x}_J^N = \bar{\bar{x}}_J^N = Ne_J.$$

For any N, we can find N', N'' such that $x^M \geqslant \bar{x}^N$, each $M \geqslant N'$, $\bar{\bar{x}}^M \geqslant x^N$, each $M \geqslant N''$. Since $f(x)$ is non-decreasing we have, in the limit as $N \to \infty$,

$$f_I(x_I^* - \varepsilon e_I) \leqslant \underline{\lim}\, f(x^N) \leqslant \overline{\lim}\, f(x^N) \leqslant f_I(x_I^* + \varepsilon e_I). \tag{A.12}$$

Now it is trivial that $f_I(x_I)$ is non-decreasing, concave, and bounded. Hence, by Lemma 1, it is continuous in the interior of X_I, and hence at x_I^*. Therefore the lower and upper limits in (A.12) coincide, and $f(x^N) \to f_I(x_I^*)$, which proves (iii).

Consider finally the case where J is partitioned into J', J'', $\ldots$, $J^{(m)}$, $x_{J'} \to \infty$ first, $x_{J''} \to \infty$ next and so on. Call this a *multi-stage process*. I will only discuss the two-stage case when $J = J' \cup J''$. The argument can easily be extended.

Define

$$I' = U \cup J'',\quad I'' = I \cup J', \tag{A.13}$$

[37] If $(x_I, x_J) \in X$, some x_J, then $x^N \in X$ ultimately, since X is positively oriented.

so that (I, J), (I', J'), (I'', J'') are all partitions of $(1, 2, \ldots, n)$. Let first $x_{J'}^N \to \infty$, $x_{I'}^N = x_{I'}$, and then $\bar{x}_{J''}^N \to \infty$, $\bar{x}_I^N = x_I$. The limit of the first stage is $f_{I'}(x_{I'})$. Since $f_{I'}(x_{I'})$ is non-decreasing, concave, and bounded, the second stage also has a limit $f_{I',I}(x_I)$, say.

I will now show that $f_{I',I}(x_I) = f_I(x_I)$. By definition

$$f_{I',I}(x_I) = \lim f_{I'}(\bar{x}_{I'}^N), \quad \bar{x}_I^N = x_I, \quad \bar{x}_{J''}^N \to \infty,$$

$$f_I(x_I) = \lim f(x^N), \quad x_I^N = x_I, \quad x_J^N \to \infty, \tag{A.14}$$

with a slight change of notation.

For each N we can find an N' such that $\bar{x}_I^M \geqslant x_I^N$ when $M \geqslant N'$. Applying (A.11) twice, to f and f_I, remembering that both are non-decreasing, and letting $N \to \infty$,

$$f_{I',I}(x_I) \geqslant f_I(x_I), \qquad \text{and similarly,} \qquad f_{I'',I}(x_I) \geqslant f_I(x_I) \tag{A.15}$$

where, by analogy with (A.14),

$$f_{I'',I}(x_I) = \lim f_{I''}(\bar{\bar{x}}_{I''}^N), \quad \bar{\bar{x}}_I^N = x_I, \quad \bar{\bar{x}}_{J'}^N = Ne_J \tag{A.16}$$

while

$$f_{I'}(\bar{x}_I^N) = \lim_{M \to \infty} f(x^{NM}), \quad x_{I'}^{NM} = x_{I'}^N, \quad \bar{x}_{I'}^{NM} = Me_{J'}.$$

$$f_{I''}(\bar{\bar{x}}_{I''}^N) = \lim_{M \to \infty} f(\bar{\bar{x}}^{NM}), \; x_{I''}^{MN} = x_{I''}^N, \; \bar{\bar{x}}_{J''}^{NM} = Me_{J''} \tag{A.17}$$

For each N, M in (A.17) there exists N' such that, in (A.14), $x^M \geqslant \frac{1}{2}(\bar{x}^{NM} + \bar{\bar{x}}^{NM})$ so that by (A.11), $f_I(x_I) \geqslant f(x^M) \geqslant \frac{1}{2}(f(\bar{x}^{NM}) + f(\bar{\bar{x}}^{NM}))$ since $f(x)$ is concave in $f_I(x_I) \geqslant \frac{1}{2}(f_{I',I}(x_I) + f_{I'',I}(x_I))$. Letting M, and then N, tend to ∞, (A.15) therefore implies

$$f_I(x_I) = f_{I',I}(x_I) = f_{I'',I}(x_I). \tag{A.18}$$

Analogous results can be proved where $x_{I'}^N \to x_{I'}^*$, $x_{J'}^N \to \infty$ followed by $\bar{x}_I^N \to x_I^{**}$, $\bar{x}_{J''}^N \to \infty$, $x_{I'}^* \in \operatorname{Int} X_{I'}$, $x_I^{**} \in \operatorname{Int} X_I$.

Hence we have

COROLLARY: (i), (ii), *and* (iii) *hold also for multi-stage processes under weak conditions.*

If we replace f by f^* as defined in Lemma 1, even these weak conditions can clearly be relaxed completely.

It is therefore convenient to define $f(x)$ 'at infinity' by

$$f(x_I, x_J) = f(x_I) \quad \text{if } x_I < \infty, \; x_J = \infty. \tag{A.19}$$

Assume, as in Lemma 1, that $f(x)$ is concave on the convex set X. Take $x^* \in \operatorname{Int} X$. There is a supporting half-space $p_0^*(z - f(x^*)) \leqslant \sum p_i^*(x_i - x_i^*)$

for the convex set R defined in (A.6). Clearly $p_0 \geqslant 0$. Since $x^* \in \text{Int } X$, $p_0 \neq 0$. We can therefore take $p_0 = 1$ without loss of generality to get, in particular

$$f(x) - f(x^*) \leqslant \sum p_i^*(x_i - x_i^*), \quad \text{all } x \in X. \tag{A.20}$$

If $f(x)$ is differentiable at x^*, p^* is unique and $p_i^* = f_i(x^*)$, where $f_i = \partial f / \partial x_i$. That is,

$$p^* = \text{grad} f(x^*) \tag{A.21}$$

is the gradient of $f(x)$ at x^*. In general there may be several such vectors. If so, they form a convex set. Call any element of it *a gradient of* $f(x)$ *at* x^* and write (A.21). We have:

LEMMA 3: *If $f(x)$ is concave and homogeneous of the first degree on a convex cone X, and $p^* = \text{grad } f(x^*)$ then*

(i) $p^* = \text{grad } f(\lambda x^*), \quad \text{all } \lambda > 0$
(ii) $f(x^*) = \sum p_i^* x_i^*$.

PROOF: (i)

$$f(x) - f(\lambda x^*) = \lambda(f(x/\lambda) - f(x^*)) \leqslant \lambda \sum p_i^* \left(\frac{1}{\lambda} x_i - x_i^* \right) = \sum p_i^* (x_i - \lambda x_i^*)$$

by homogeneity and (A.20).

(ii) Replacing x in (A.20) by λx, and letting $\lambda \to \infty$, one has

$$f(x) \leqslant \sum p_i^* x_i, \quad \text{all } x \in X, \tag{A.22}$$

and replacing x^* by λx^*, using (i), and letting $\lambda \to \infty$ again, one has

$$f(x^*) \geqslant \sum p_i^* x_i^*. \tag{A.23}$$

Since $x^* \in X$, (A.22) and (A.23) imply (ii).

THEOREM 1: *If $f(x)$ is non-decreasing continuous and concave on the closed positively oriented convex subset X of the positive orthant*

(i) $g(p) = \inf\limits_{x \in X} \left\{ \sum p_i x_i - f(x) \right\}$

is non-decreasing and concave on the positively oriented convex subset

$$P = \{ p \mid g(p) > -\infty \}$$

of the positive orthant and continuous in its interior.

(ii) $f(x) = \min\limits_{p \in P} \left\{ \sum p_i x_i - g(p) \right\}, \quad \textit{all } x \in \textit{Int } X$

(iii) $g(p) = \min\limits_{x \in X} \left\{ \sum p_i x_i - f(x) \right\}, \quad \textit{all } p \in \textit{Int } P$

PROOF: (ii) According to the definition in (i)

$$f(x) \leqslant \sum p_i x_i - g(p), \quad \text{all } p \in P. \tag{A.24}$$

Define the set

$$R = \{(u, x) \mid u \leqslant f(x), x \in X\}. \tag{A.25}$$

Take an $x^* \in \text{Int } X$. As in (A.21) there is a supporting half-space

$$u - f(x^*) \leqslant \sum p_i(x_i - x_i^*), \quad \text{all } (u, x) \in R^*, \tag{A.26}$$

where

$$p^* = \text{grad } f(x^*) \geqslant 0 \tag{A.27}$$

since, if $p_i^* < 0$, (A.26) implies that $f(x^* + \delta_i) < f(x^*)$ where $\delta_1 = (1, 0, 0, \ldots, 0)$, $\delta_2 = (0, 1, 0, \ldots, 0)$, etc. Hence

$$\sum p_i^* x_i^* - f(x^*) = \min_{x \in X} \left\{ \sum p_i^* x_i - f(x) \right\} = g(p^*) \tag{A.28}$$

which, with (A.24), implies

$$f(x^*) = \sum p_i^* x_i^* - g(p^*) = \min_{p \in P} \left\{ \sum p_i x_i^* - g(p) \right\} \tag{A.29}$$

if $x^* \in \text{Int } X$, $p^* = \text{grad } f(x^*)$, which in turn implies (ii).

(i) (A.28) implies that P is not empty since it is clearly positively oriented, its interior is not empty either. The set

$$H(x^*) = \{(v, p) \mid p \geqslant 0, v - g(p) \leqslant \sum x_i^*(p_i - p_i^*), p^* = \text{grad } f(x^*)\} \tag{A.30}$$

for $x^* \in \text{Int } X$ is closed, convex, and *productive*; that is, if $(v, p) \in H(x^*)$ and $v' \leqslant v$, $p' \geqslant p$, then $(v', p'') \in H(x^*)$.

So therefore is

$$S = \bigcap_{x \in \text{Int } X} H(x), \tag{A.31}$$

and

$$Q = \{p \mid (v, p) \in S, \text{ some } v\} \tag{A.32}$$

is convex and positively oriented. Take now any $p \in P$. According to (A.24), (A.27), and (A.29)

$$g(p) - g(p^*) \leqslant \sum x_i^*(p_i - p_i^*), \tag{A.33}$$

so that $(g(p), p) \in S$ and $p \in Q$. Hence $Q \geqslant P$. Moreover, if $p \in Q$, the maximum v[38] such that $(v, p) \in S$ is

$$\inf\left\{g(p^*) + \sum x_i^*(p_i - p_i^*)\right\} = \inf\left\{\sum p_i x_i^* - f(x^*)\right\} = g(p) \tag{A.34}$$

[38] Since S is closed, the maximum exists.

the infimum being taken over $x^* \in \text{Int}\, X$, with $p^* = \text{grad}\, f(x^*)$. Hence $g(p) > -\infty$ if $p \in Q$, so that $p \geqslant Q$. Since we have just seen that $Q \geqslant P$,

$$P = Q \tag{A.35}$$

so that, like Q, it is convex and positively oriented. (A.30), (A.31), (A.34), and (A.35) imply immediately that it is a subset of the non-negative orthant. Since S is closed, convex, and positively oriented, (A.34) and (A.35) imply that $g(p)$ is concave and non-decreasing on P by Lemma 1, continuous in its interior.

(iii) Take any $p \in \text{Int}\, P$. If

$$g(p) = \inf_{x \in X}\left\{\sum p_i x_i - f(x)\right\} \neq \min_{x \in X}\left\{\sum p_i x_i - f(x)\right\}$$

there is a sequence $\{x^N\}$ with $x_J^N \to \infty$, $x_I^N \to x_i^*$, say, $< \infty$, in the notation of Lemma 2, such that $h^N = \sum p_i x_i^N - f(x^N)$ is monotonically decreasing and therefore bounded above. Take now $\rho > 0$ sufficiently small to have $p - \rho e \in P$ where $e = (1, 1, \ldots, 1)$. Now $\sum (p_i - \rho) x_i^N - f(x^N) = h^N - \rho \sum x_i^N \to -\infty$. Hence $g(p - \rho e) = -\infty$ despite the fact that $p - \rho e \in P$, which is a contradiction proving (iii).

COROLLARIES TO THEOREM 1:[39]

(iv) $f(x) = \mathit{inf}_{p \in P}\left\{\sum p_i x_i - g(p)\right\}$, *all* $x \in X$.

PROOF: If $x \in \text{Int}\, X$, (ii) implies (iv). If x lies on the frontier of X, take a sequence $\{x^N\}$ with each $x^N \in \text{Int}\, X$ and $x^N \to x$. Let $p^N = \text{grad}\, f(x^N)$, so that $\sum p_i^N x_i^N - g(p^N) = f(x^N) \to f(x)$ by (A.28),[40] since f is continuous. Since $f(x) \leqslant \sum p_i x_i - g(p)$, all $p \in P$, this proves (iv).

Say that x^* is chosen at p^* if[41]

$$\begin{aligned}\sum p_i^* x_i^* - f(x^*) &\leqslant \sum p_i^* x_i^* - f(x), \quad \text{all } x \in X,\\ &= \min_{x \in X}\left\{\sum p_i^* x_i - f(x)\right\} = g(p^*),\end{aligned} \tag{A.36}$$

so that no basket x of inputs is chosen at prices p at which the infimum in (i) is not attained, and a basket x of inputs at which the infimum in (iv) is not attained is never chosen. Of course many different baskets may be chosen at given prices and one basket at many prices.[42]

[39] Numbered in sequence with the sections of the theorem.

[40] See (v) below.

[41] In our case $f(x)$ is of course the short-run production function for given y not referred to explicitly here, and $g(p)$ the corresponding net loss function, so that the 'chosen' inputs are those that maximize net profits.

[42] It is well known, and easily proven that the set of x chosen at Y^* and p at which x^* is chosen given Y^*, are both convex.

We have

(v) *The following three statements are equivalent*

(*a*) x^* *is chosen at* p^*;
(*b*) $p^* = grad\, f(x^*)$;
(*c*) $x^* = grad\, g(p^*)$.

PROOF: (*a*) implies (A.36) and

$$f(x) - f(x^*) \leqslant \sum p_i(x_i - x_i^*), \tag{A.37}$$

which implies (*b*). Since $g(p) \leqslant \sum p_i x_i^* - f(x^*)$, (*a*) also implies

$$g(p) - g(p^*) \leqslant \sum x_i^*(p_i - p_i^*), \quad \text{all } p \in P, \tag{A.38}$$

implying (*c*).

(*b*) implies (A.37) and (A.36) and, therefore (*a*).

Suppose (*c*) is true but not (*a*). Then there is a $\rho > 0$ such that $g(p^*) = \sum p_i^* x_i^* - f(x^*) - \rho$. Substituting into (A.38) we find that $f(x^*) \leqslant \sum p_i x_i^* - g(p) - \rho$, all $p \in P$, contradicting (iv). Hence (*c*) implies (*a*), completing the proof of (v).

(ii) and (iii) immediately imply

(vi) *Each* $x^* \in Int\, X$ *is chosen at some prices* $p^* \in P$, *and, at each* $p^* \in Int\ P$, *some* $x^* \in X$ *is chosen.*

So far we have been using the product as a numeraire. This is not always convenient.[43] Let us work in money prices $\bar{p} = (\bar{p}_0, \ldots, \bar{p}_n)$ instead for the moment, $\bar{p}_0$ is the price of the product and $\bar{p}_i$ of the ith input. Set also $\bar{x} = (x_0, x_1, \ldots, x_n)$ where $x_0 = u$ is the volume of production and x_i, as before, of the ith input. The net losses

$$\bar{g}(\bar{p}) = \bar{p}_0\, g(\bar{p}_1/\bar{p}_0, \ldots, \bar{p}_n/\bar{p}_0) \tag{A.39}$$

are homogeneous of degree one in $\bar{p}$. Theorem 1(iii) and Corollary (v), and Lemma 3 therefore imply

$$\bar{x} = \text{grad}\, \bar{g}(\bar{p}) \tag{A.40}$$

if $\bar{x}$ is chosen at money prices $\bar{p}$, putting output on a par with the inputs.

The difficulty in all this is, of course, that the frontier points of X may not be chosen at any finite prices, and no finite volume of inputs be chosen at prices on the frontier of P. The reasons are obvious: the marginal product of an input might be infinite when the minimum quantity of it is being used and, if the prices of the inputs are low enough in terms of the product, it might be worth using infinite quantities of them. Nevertheless, infinite prices

[43] e.g. if one has several products.

and infinite quantities are a bit unlikely, and the difficulties to which they give birth, perhaps a little unreal.

So far we have neglected the fixed inputs y. Once they are introduced, the frontiers of X and P may depend on y, introducing considerable difficulties of analysis and exposition.[44] In the following theorem, therefore, I take X to be the non-negative orthant, and by assuming that infinite profits cannot be derived from a given bundle of equipment when the prices of the variable inputs are positive, assume that Int P is the positive orthant.

THEOREM 2: *If $f(x, y)$ is concave and non-decreasing in x, increasing in y and continuous in (x, y) when $x \geqslant 0$, and*

$$y \in T = \{y \mid a \leqslant y \leqslant b\}, \quad 0 \leqslant a < b \leqslant \infty, \tag{A.41}$$

and if

$$g(p, y) = \inf_{x \geqslant 0}\left\{\sum p_i x_i - f(x, y)\right\} > -\infty \quad \text{when } p > 0,^{45} \tag{A.42}$$

then

(i) *$g(p, y)$ is concave and non-decreasing in p, decreasing in y and continuous in (p, y) when $p > 0$, $y \in T$.*

(ii) *$f(x, y) = \inf\limits_{p \geqslant 0} \{\sum p_i x_i - g(p, y)\}$, all $x \in X$.*

(iii) *the following three statements are equivalent*

(*a*) *x^* is chosen at p^*, y^**[46]

(*b*) $p^* = \underset{x}{\text{grad}}\, f(x^*, y^*)$[47]

(*c*) $x^* = \underset{p}{\text{grad}}\, g(p^*, y^*)$.[48]

(iv) *$g(p^*, y^*) = \min\limits_{x \geqslant 0} \{\sum p_i^* x_i - f(x, y^*)\}$ if $p^* > 0$, $y^* \in T$,*

$f(x^*, y^*) = \min\limits_{p \geqslant 0} \{\sum p_i x_i^* - g(p, y^*)\}$ if $x^* > 0$, $y^* \in T$,

so that each $x^* > 0$ is chosen at some prices[49] *and some x^* is bought at each (p, y^*)* if $p^* > 0$.

(A.42) implies that $P(y) = \{p \mid g(p, y) > -\infty\}$ contains the positive orthant, so that Int $P(y)$ is the positive orthant. Theorem 1(i) therefore implies that $g(p, y)$ is non-decreasing, concave—and of course continuous—in p

[44] Though by no means insuperable ones.

[45] The purpose of this assumption is to keep Int $P(y)$ independent of y where $P(y) = \{p \mid g(p, y) > -\infty\}$.

[46] i.e. $f(x^*, y) - \sum p_i^* x_i^* \geqslant f(x, y) - \sum p_i^* x_i$, all $x \geqslant 0$.

[47] i.e. $f(x, y) - f(x^*, y) \leqslant \sum p_i^* (x_i - x_i^*)$, all $x \geqslant 0$.

[48] i.e. $g(p, y) - g(p^*, y) \leqslant \sum x_i^* (p_i - p_i^*)$, all $p \geqslant 0$ including, perhaps, some points with some $p_i = 0$, which do not belong to $P(y)$. This does not matter since the corresponding $g(p, y) = -\infty$.

[49] Better 'at some prices, and the given y'.

when $p > 0$, $y \in T$. Corollary (iv) of Theorem 1 implies (ii), Corollary (v) implies (iii), and Corollary (vi), with Theorem 1 (ii) and (iii), implies (iv).

It remains to prove that $g(p, y)$ is decreasing in y and continuous in (p, y) when $p > 0$, $y \in T$.

To prove that it is decreasing in y, take $p^* > 0$, $y^* \leqslant b, \in T$, and $x^* = \operatorname{grad}_p g(p^*, y^*)$ to get $g(p^*, y^*) = \sum p_i^* x_i^* - f(x^*, y^*)$. Take now $y^{**} > y^*$ in T. Then

$$g(p^*, y^{**}) \leqslant \sum p_i^* x_i^* - f(x^*, y^{**}) < \sum p_i^* x_i^* - f(x^*, y^*) = g(p^*, y^*),$$

since $f(x, y)$ is increasing in y.

It is a little more complicated to show that $g(p, y)$ is continuous in (p, y), $p > 0$, $y \in T$.

Take $p^* > 0$, $y^* \in T$ and a moving point $(p, y) \to (p^*, y^*)$, with $p > 0$, $y \in T$ always. Define $p_i' = \min(p_i, p_i^*)$, $p_i'' = \max(p_i, p_i^*)$, $y_r' = \max(y_r, y_r^*)$, $y_r'' = \min(y_r, y_r^*)$, so that

$$0 < p' \leqslant p, \quad p^* \leqslant p'', \quad a \leqslant y'' \leqslant y, \quad y^* \leqslant y' \leqslant b. \tag{A.43}$$

Since $g(p, y)$ is non-decreasing in p and decreasing in y when $p > 0$, $a \leqslant y \leqslant b$,

$$g(p', y') \leqslant g(p, y), \quad g(p^*, y^*) \leqslant g(p'', y''). \tag{A.44}$$

If, therefore, we could prove

$$g(p', y') \to g(p^*, y^*) \text{ and } g(p'', y'') \to g(p^*, y^*)$$

we would have proved $g(p, y) \to g(p^*, y^*)$ and therefore continuity in (p, y). Clearly,

$$p' \leqslant p^* \leqslant p'', \quad y' \geqslant y^* \geqslant y'', \quad p', p'' \to p^*, \quad y', y'' \to y^*. \tag{A.45}$$

First consider p'', y''. Let $x^* = \operatorname{grad}_p g(p^*, y^*)$ so that

$$g(p^*, y^*) = \sum p_i^* x_i^* - f(x^*, y^*)$$

$$g(p'', y'') \leqslant \sum p_i'' x_i^* - f(x^*, y''). \tag{A.46}$$

Hence, by (A.43),

$$0 \leqslant g(p'', y'') - g(p^*, y^*) \leqslant \sum (p_i'' - p_i^*) x_i^* + f(x^*, y^*) - f(x^*, y'') \to 0 \tag{A.47}$$

by (A.45) and the continuity of f. Hence

$$g(p'', y'') \to g(p^*, y^*). \tag{A.48}$$

Turning now to (p', y'), let $x' = \operatorname{grad}_p g(p', y')$ to get, as in (A.47)

$$0 \leqslant g(p^*, y^*) - g(p', y') \leqslant \sum (p_i^* - p_i') x_i' + f(x', y') - f(x', y^*). \tag{A.49}$$

It does not follow immediately that the last term tends to zero as $(p', y') \to (p^*, y^*)$ since x' varies. If however, we can prove that x' is bounded, then (x', y') will be in a closed bounded set B. $f(x, y)$, being continuous, will be uniformly continuous on B,[50] so that $f(x', y') \to f(x', y^*)$ as $y' \to y^*$ since $\sum(p_i^* - p_i')x_i' \to 0$ as $p' \to p^*$ if x is bounded, the right-hand side of (A.49) will tend to zero, and $g(p', y') \to g(p^*, y^*)$.

It remains only to prove that x' is bounded.

Take $y^{**} \in T$ such that

$$y^{**} \geqslant y' \geqslant y^*, \text{ ultimately,} \tag{A.50}$$

and $\rho > 0$ such that $p^{**} = p^* - 2\rho e > 0$ and

$$p^{**} \leqslant p' - \rho e, \quad p' \leqslant p^*, \text{ ultimately.} \tag{A.51}$$

Since $x' = \operatorname{grad}_p g(p', y')$

$$g(p^{**}, y') - g(p', y') \leqslant \sum(p_i^{**} - p_i')x_i' \leqslant -\rho \sum x_i', \tag{A.52}$$

so that $g(p^{**}, y^{**}) \leqslant g(p^{**}, y')$, by (A.50), since g is a decreasing function of y; $g(p^{**}, y^{**}) \leqslant g(p', y') - \rho\sum x_i'$, by (A.52); $g(p', y') \leqslant g(p^*, y^*) - \rho\sum x_i'$, by (A.49). Hence $\sum x_i' \leqslant \{g(p^*, y^*) - g(p^{**}, y^{**})\}/\rho$. Since each $x_i' \geqslant 0$, this implies that x' is bounded, which completes the proof.

Theorem 2 is really sufficient for anything we might want. Nevertheless the slight asymmetry remaining between $f(x, y)$ and $g(p, y)$ is a little irksome—for instance, that we have to take $p > 0$ to ensure the continuity of the latter, while $x \geqslant 0$ does that of the former. This arises from the fact that, while the output $f(x, y)$ is certainly finite when very little is put in, it is worth while using an infinite amount of an input if its price vanishes, and, if $f(x, y) \to \infty$ as $x \to \infty$ in some manner, the resulting profit $-g(p, y)$ may be infinite when some of the $p_i = 0$. Since there is really no question of using an infinite quantity of any input, or producing an infinite quantity, the obvious thing to do is to 'cut off' $f(x, y)$ by taking $\tilde{f}(x, y) = f(x, y)$ if $f(x, y) \leqslant \lambda(y) < \infty$, and $\tilde{f}(x, y) = \lambda(y)$ if $f(x, y) > \lambda(y)$. Doing so, if necessary, one can satisfy the conditions of:

THEOREM 3: *If $f(x, y)$ is concave and non-decreasing in x, increasing in y, continuous in (x, y), and if*

$$0 \leqslant f(x, y) \leqslant \lambda(y)^{51} \tag{A.53}$$

when $x \geqslant 0$ and $y \in T$, and if we define $f(x, y)$ for 'infinite x' by $f(x_I, x_J, y) = f_I(x_I, y)$ in the notation of Lemma 2, when $x_J = \infty$, $x_I < \infty$, then

[50] i.e. $\sup_B f(x, y) - f(x^*, y^*) \to 0$.
[51] $\lambda(y) < \infty$ when $y < \infty$, of course.

(i) *$g(p, y)$ is concave and non-decreasing in p, decreasing in y and continuous in (p, y) when $p \geqslant 0$, $y \in T$ and*

$$0 \geqslant g(p, y) \geqslant -\lambda(y). \tag{A.54}$$

(iii) *of Theorem* 2, *of course, continues to hold, and* (ii) *and* (iv) *of Theorem* 2 *are replaced by*

$$\text{(ii)}\quad g(p^*, y^*) = \min_{x \geqslant 0} \{\textstyle\sum p_i^* x_i - f(x, y^*)\}, \quad \text{if } p^* \geqslant 0,\ y^* \in T,$$

$$f(x^*, y^*) = \min_{p \geqslant 0} \{\textstyle\sum p_i x_i^* - g(p, y^*)\}, \quad \text{if } x^* \geqslant 0,\ y^* \in T,$$

so that all $x^* \geqslant 0$ are chosen at appropriate prices if $y^* \in T$, and some bundle is chosen at each $p^* \geqslant 0$ if $y^* \in T$.

PROOF: (i) (A.54) follows immediately from (A.53) and the definition of $g(p, y)$ in (A.42). Theorem 1(i) therefore implies that $g(p, y)$ is concave, non-decreasing and continuous in p throughout $p \geqslant 0$, $y \in T$ and Theorem 2(i) that it is continuous in (p, y) throughout $p > 0$, $y \in T$. The argument used in Theorem 2(i) to prove that $g(p, y)$ is increasing in y throughout $p > 0$, $y \in T$, here proves this to be so throughout $p \geqslant 0$, $y \in T$.[52]

It remains to prove that $g(p, y)$ is continuous in (p, y) throughout $p \geqslant 0$, $y \in T$. An argument similar to that proving the analogous proposition in Theorem 2(i) will be used. Define first

$$S_I = \{(p, y): P_I > 0,\ P_J = 0,\ y \in T\}, \tag{A.55}$$

where I, J is a partition of $(1, 2, \ldots, n)$. Clearly

$$\begin{aligned} g(p_I^*, 0, y^*) &= \textstyle\sum_I p_i^* x_i^* - f_I(x_I^*, y^*), \text{ say} \\ &= \min\Big\{\textstyle\sum_I p_i^* x_i - f_I(x_I, y^*)\Big\} \end{aligned} \tag{A.56}$$

where f_I satisfies just the same condition as f. Hence

$$g(p, y) \to g(p^*, y^*) \quad \text{if } (p, y) \to (p^*, y^*), \text{ both in } S_I, \tag{A.57}$$

in just the same way as one proved the continuity of $g(p, y)$ when $p \geqslant 0$, $y \in T$.

Take now $(p^*, y^*) \in S_I$ and choose a sequence $(p^N, y^N) \to (p^*, y^*)$ where (p^N, y^N) need not be in S_I. Since $g(p^N, y^N)$ is bounded, it has convergent sub-sequences. Choose one such and remember it as the original sequence. Define as in the proof in Theorem 2(i), but with a slightly different notation

[52] We assume that $f(x, y)$ satisfies the conditions of the theorem even when 'x is infinite'.

$$\bar{p}_k^N = \min\{p_k^N, p_k^*\}, \quad \bar{\bar{p}}_k^N = \max\{p_k^N, p_k^*\}$$
$$\bar{y}_r^N = \max\{y_r^N, y_r^*\}, \quad \bar{\bar{y}}_r^N = \min\{y_r^N, y_r^*\}, \tag{A.58}$$

all k, r, to get

$$g(\bar{p}^N, \bar{y}^N) \leqslant g(p^N, y^N), \quad g(p^*, y^*) \leqslant g(\bar{\bar{p}}^N, \bar{\bar{y}}^N) \tag{A.59}$$

so that, as before, we only have to prove that $g(\bar{p}^N, \bar{y}^N)$, $g(\bar{\bar{p}}^N, \bar{\bar{y}}^N) \to g(p^*, y^*)$.

Notice first that

$$p_I^N, \quad \bar{p}_I^N, \quad \bar{\bar{p}}_I > 0, \qquad \text{ultimately, } \bar{p}_J^N = 0. \tag{A.60}$$

Hence (A.57) immediately implies that

$$g(\bar{p}^N, \bar{y}^N) \to g(p^*, y^*). \tag{A.61}$$

Now consider $(\bar{\bar{p}}^N, \bar{\bar{y}}^N)$. Choose a sub-sequence such that $\bar{\bar{p}}^N$ is monotonically decreasing and $\bar{\bar{y}}^N$ monotonically increasing,[53] and remember it as the original sequence. Take $\varepsilon > 0$ and M such that

$$0 \leqslant g(\bar{\bar{p}}_I^M, 0, \bar{\bar{y}}^M) - g(p^*, y^*) \leqslant \varepsilon/2, \tag{A.62}$$

as we can by (A.57) and the monotonic behaviour of $g(p, y)$, and R such that, when $N \geqslant R$,

$$0 \leqslant g(\bar{\bar{p}}_J^M, \bar{\bar{p}}_J^N, \bar{\bar{y}}^M) - g(\bar{\bar{p}}_I^M, 0, \bar{\bar{y}}^M) \leqslant \varepsilon/2 \tag{A.63}$$

as we can by the continuity of $g(p, y)$ in p throughout $p \geqslant 0$, $y \in T$. Hence

$$0 \leqslant g(\bar{\bar{p}}_J^M, \bar{\bar{p}}_J^N, \bar{\bar{y}}^M) - g(p^*, y^*) \leqslant \varepsilon. \tag{A.64}$$

Taking $N > M$, $\bar{\bar{p}}_I^N \leqslant \bar{\bar{p}}_I^M$. Hence, by the monotonic character of $g(p, y)$

$$0 \leqslant g(\bar{\bar{p}}^N, \bar{\bar{y}}^N) - g(p^*, y^*) \leqslant \varepsilon \tag{A.65}$$

so that

$$g(\bar{\bar{p}}^N, \bar{\bar{y}}^N) \to g(p^*, y^*) \tag{A.66}$$

which, with (A.59) and (A.61), proves the continuity of $g(p, y)$ in (p, y) at points where some $p_j = 0$. Since we have already seen that it is continuous when $p > 0$, we have proved it to be continuous in (p, y) throughout $p \geqslant 0$, $y \in T$.

This completes the proof of (i).

(ii) When $p > 0$, the first line follows from Theorem 2(iv). If $p_I^* > 0$, $p_J^* = 0$

[53] Not necessarily strictly decreasing, or strictly increasing, respectively.

$$g(p^*, y^*) = \inf_{x_I \geqslant 0} \left\{ \sum p_i^* x_i - f_I(x_I, y^*) \right\}, \tag{A.67}$$

where f_I has the same properties as f. Hence the minimum is attained, at x_i^* say, so that

$$\begin{aligned} g(p^*, y^*) &= \sum\nolimits_I p_i^* x_i^* - f_I(x_I^*, y^*) \\ &= \sum\nolimits_I p_i^* x_i^* - f(x^*, y^*), \end{aligned} \tag{A.68}$$

where $x_J^* = \infty$, so that the minimum in (ii) is attained.

$g(p, y)$ is now seen to satisfy the conditions of Lemma 2. We can therefore define $g_I(p_I, y)$ where $p_J = \infty$ as for $f_I(x_I, y)$ and redefine $g(p, y) = g_I(p_I, y)$ where $p_I < \infty$ to get the second line of (ii) by a similar argument.

The remainder follows immediately.

COROLLARIES:[54]

(iii) *If $g(p, y)$ is concave and non-decreasing in p, increasing in y, continuous in (p, y) and satisfies* (A.54) *in $p \geqslant 0$, $y \in T$ then $f(x, y)$ has the qualities listed at the beginning of Theorem* 3, *and* (ii) *still holds.*

A proof would parallel that of Theorem 3.

(iv) *If $f(x, y)$ satisfies the conditions of Theorem* 3 *and is concave in* (x, y), *throughout $x \geqslant 0$, $y \in T$ is convex in y throughout $p \geqslant 0$, $y \in T$.*

PROOF: Let $x' = \operatorname{grad}_p g(p, y')$, $x'' = \operatorname{grad}_p g(p, y'')$ and define

$$\bar{x} = \tfrac{1}{2}(x' + x''), \quad \bar{y} = \tfrac{1}{2}(y' + y'') \tag{A.69}$$

so that $g(p, y') = \sum p_i x_i' - f(x', y')$, $g(p, y'') = \sum p_i x_i'' - f(x'', y'')$, $g(p, \bar{y}) \leqslant \sum p_i \bar{x}_i - f(\bar{x}, \bar{y})$. Hence

$$g(p, \bar{y}) - \tfrac{1}{2}g(p, y') - \tfrac{1}{2}g(p, y'') \leqslant \tfrac{1}{2}f(x', y') + \tfrac{1}{2}f(x'', y'') - f(\bar{x}, \bar{y}) \leqslant 0 \tag{A.70}$$

by (A.69), since $f(x, y)$ is concave. Hence $g(p, y)$ is convex in y.

(v) *If $g(p, y)$ satisfies the conditions of Corollary* (iii) *and is convex in y, $f(x, y)$ is concave in (p, y).*

PROOF: Let $p = \operatorname{grad} f(\bar{x}, \bar{y})$ in the notation of (A.69). Then $f(x', y') \leqslant \sum p_i x_i' - g(p, y')$, $f(x'', y'') \leqslant \sum p_i x_i'' - g(p, y'')$, $f(\bar{x}, \bar{y}) = \sum p_i \bar{x}_i - g(\bar{p}, \bar{y})$. Hence

[54] Numbered in sequence with the sections of Theorem 3.

$$f(\bar{x}, \bar{y}) - \tfrac{1}{2}\{f(x'', y'')\} \geqslant \tfrac{1}{2}\{g(p, y'')\} - g(p, y) \geqslant 0 \qquad \text{(A.71)}$$

by (A.69) and the convexity of $g(p, y)$ in y. Hence $f(x, y)$ is concave in (x, y).

In the text I state that I will prove that (A.31)–(A.34) are necessary and sufficient for (B1)–(B4) and therefore for (A1)–(A4) given, of course, (A.39).[55] The proofs are both simple and obvious. Because of shortage of typing time I do not therefore give them here.

I claim in the text that

$$K(p, Y) = c(p)Y + d(p) \qquad \text{(A.72)}$$

implies that

$$K'(p, Y) = c'(p)Y + d'(p), \qquad \text{(A.73)}$$

where the prime denotes the gradient. Since I have only defined the gradient of a function which is either differentiable or concave, and c, d, may be neither, this cannot be true. This does not affect my results, since I have always assumed differentiability when I came to use (A.73) to prove anything.

In fact I have not been able to derive the correct form for (A.71) yet. Here are a few results given without proof for lack of typing time.

$$S(p) = \{(x, Y) \mid p = K'(p, Y)\} \qquad \text{(A.74)}$$

is convex, each t.

If the relative interior of $S(p)$ and $S(q)$ intersect, then $S(p) = S(q)$. (A.75)

In the notation of (A.72)

$$K(p, Y) = A(p)\frac{Y(b) - Y}{Y(b) - Y(a)} + B(p)\frac{Y - Y(a)}{Y(b) - Y(a)}. \qquad \text{(A.76)}$$

The obvious correction of (A.73) would be

$$K'(p, Y) = A'(p)\frac{Y(b) - Y}{Y(b) - Y(a)} + B'(p)\frac{Y - Y(a)}{Y(b) - Y(a)}. \qquad \text{(A.77)}$$

I have proved this when there is only one variable input but not in general, though (A.75) and (A.76) certainly suggest that it does hold in general.

If $c(p)$, $d(p)$ are concave, as would be the case if $y(a) = 0$, $y(b) = \infty$, we might expect (A.73) to hold. It does when there is only one variable input. Once again (A.74) and (A.75) would make one expect that it would hold however many variable inputs there were, but I have not yet proved this.

[55] Except, of course, that we would have $Y_t(y_t)$ strictly decreasing, each t, and $c(p) > 0$, instead of $Y_t(y_t)$ strictly increasing, each t, and $c(p) < 0$.

POSTSCRIPT

The following argument seems to prove (A.73) and (A.77).

First (A.73). Suppose that $c(p)$, $d(p)$ are moderately well-behaved net loss functions, as they will be if $Y(a) = 0$, $Y(b) = \infty$, for instance. Then $k_1(p, Y) = c(p)Y$ and $k_2(p) = d(p)$ are. A firm with two independent plants whose technologies are defined by these moderately well-behaved net loss functions will incur total net losses $K(p, Y) = k_1(p, Y) + k_2(p) = c(p)Y + d(p)$, at (p, Y). Moreover it will do so by producing $x_1 = k_1'(p, Y)$, $x_2 = k_2'(p)$ on them and only by doing so. Hence its total production $x = x_1 + x_2 = k_1'(p, Y) + k_2'(p) = c'(p)Y + d'(p)$. However $x = K'(p, Y)$ since $K(p, Y)$ is also a moderately well-behaved net loss function, thus proving (A.73).

(A.77) is proved in exactly the same way when $Y(b) < \infty$.

19

Measuring the Quantities of Fixed Factors

Editorial Remarks

This paper appeared in the Hicks Festschrift in 1968. It is a substantial generalization of 'Capital Aggregation in Vintage Models' and is mathematically somewhat more elegant. This time the problem is posed in terms of gross profit functions and technology sets. In addition, the problem is solved for arbitrary numbers of aggregates—a problem only touched upon in 'Capital Aggregation in Vintage Models'.

During the academic year 1966–7 Gorman gave a course at Stanford, part of which consisted of this paper and 'The Structure of Utility Functions'. Not surprisingly, only four students survived to the end of the course: Walt Heller jun., David Starrett, Ross Starr, and Kenneth Arrow. A version of this paper was presented in February 1967 to the joint Berkeley–Stanford Mathematical Economics Seminar, for which we have a set of typed notes. The structure of the argument presented in those notes is essentially the same as the published version reprinted here.

Editorial Summary

The economy consists of T firms each of which has a short-run technology set, $S_t(y_t)$, that depends upon a vector of fixed factors, y_t. A feasible *production plan* or *net output vector* is given by $x_t \in S_t(y_t)$. The vector of fixed factors in firm t is given by $y_t = (y_t^1, \dots, y_t^r, \dots, y_t^R)$, and the amount of the rth fixed factor in the economy is represented by $y^r = (y_1^r, \dots, y_t^r, \dots, y_T^r)$. $y = (y^1, \dots, y^r, \dots, y^R)$ is the vector of fixed factors in the economy. The short-run technology set of the economy, $S(y)$, is the set sum of the technology set of the firms in the economy,

$$S(y) = \sum_{t=1}^{T} S_t(y_t), \tag{0.1}$$

a formulation which assumes that there are no externalities in production.

This time, the aggregation question asks for the circumstances in which there exists a set of aggregates, $Y(y) = (Y^1(y^1), \dots, Y^r(y^r), \dots, Y^R(y^r))$ such that the short-run technology set of the economy can be written as

$$S(y) = \tilde{S}(Y^1(y^1), \ldots, Y^r(y^r), \ldots, Y^R(y^R)) = \tilde{S}(Y(y)). \tag{0.2}$$

The gross profit function for firm t is

$$g_t(p, y_t) = \max\left\{\sum_{i=1}^{n} p_i x_{ti} \mid x_t \in S_t(y_t)\right\}, \tag{0.3}$$

and for the economy it is

$$g(p, y) = \max\left\{\sum_{i=1}^{n} p_i x_i \mid x \in S(y)\right\}, \tag{0.4}$$

which of course is also

$$g(p, y) = \sum_{t=1}^{T} g_t(p, y_t). \tag{0.5}$$

The gross profit function dual to $\tilde{S}(Y(y))$ is

$$G(p, Y(y)) = \max\left\{\sum_{i=1}^{n} p_i x_{ti} \mid x_t \in \tilde{S}(Y(y))\right\}, \tag{0.6}$$

so that the aggregation question posed in (0.2) can be written equivalently as

$$g(p, y) = G(p, Y(y)). \tag{0.7}$$

The solution to this is an obvious generalization of the result in Gorman (1965*a*):

$$g_t(p, y_t) = \sum_{r=1}^{R} c^r(p)\, Y_t^r(y_t^r) + d_t(p),$$

$$g(p, y) = \sum_{r=1}^{R} c^r(p)\, Y^r(y^r) + d(p) \tag{0.8}$$

where

$$Y^r(y^r) = \sum_{t=1}^{T} Y_t^r(y_t^r) \tag{0.9}$$

for all aggregates $r = 1, \ldots, R$, and

$$d(p) = \sum_{t=1}^{T} d_t(p). \tag{0.10}$$

The interpretation of the subaggregates is very much as before and is carefully described in the paper. Note, however, that each of the aggregates is additive, an implication rather than an assumption of the problem. Section 2 is an extensive summary of the results, while Section 3 contains the needed duality arguments. They are presented somewhat more abstractly than in Gorman (1965*a*), which may account for the length of time it has taken the profession to absorb the material. Sections 4 and 5 present the main theorem summarized above, while the conclusion describes yet another interpretation of the results.

Before proceeding, it is of interest to note that, with a change in notation, this provides a complete dual proof of the first aggregation problem posed by Gorman, namely, the existence of a community preference map. To see this, let the 'no-worse-than' sets of each consumer be given by

$$S_t(u_t) = \{x_t \mid U(x_t) \geqslant u_t\}, \tag{0.11}$$

so that the *community preference* set (the Scitovsky set) is the set sum of these 'no-worse-than' sets, namely,

$$S(u) = \sum_{t=1}^{T} S_t(u_t), \tag{0.12}$$

where $u = (u_1, \ldots, u_T)$ is a distribution of utilities. The cost functions for consumer t and for the community as a whole are given by

$$g_t(p, u_t) = \min\left\{\sum_{i=1}^{n} p_i x_{ti} \,\middle|\, x_t \in S_t(u_t)\right\} \tag{0.13}$$

and

$$g(p, u) = \min\left\{\sum_{i=1}^{n} p_i x_i \,\middle|\, x \in S(u)\right\}, \tag{0.14}$$

respectively. From (0.12)–(0.14) it follows that

$$g(p, u) = \sum_{t=1}^{T} g_t(p, u_t). \tag{0.15}$$

Clearly there is a *community preference* fireld if and only if the *community preference* set only depends upon a scalar; that is, if and only if the Scitovsky set can be written as

$$S(u) = \tilde{S}(\phi(u)). \tag{0.16}$$

This is true if and only if

$$g(p, u) = G(p, \phi(u)). \tag{0.17}$$

From above, one sees immediately that a *community preference* field exists if and only if the cost functions of the consumers and the community can be written as

$$g_t(p, u_t) = c(p)\phi_t(u_t) + d_t(p) \tag{0.18}$$

and

$$g(p, u) = c(p)\phi(u) + d(p) \tag{0.19}$$

where

$$\phi(u) = \sum_{t=1}^{T} \phi_t(u_t) \tag{0.20}$$

and

$$d(p) = \sum_{t=1}^{T} d_t(p). \tag{0.21}$$

This yields the parallel linear Engel curves discovered as necessary and sufficient in Gorman (1953*a*), whose closed form dual representation was established in Gorman (1961). This further illustrates a lesson that Gorman tried hard to communicate, namely, that dual methods can be very powerful when appropriate.

Measuring the Quantities of Fixed Factors

1. INTRODUCTION[1]

Firms recruit and dismiss workers according to their needs. Similar workers are paid rather similar wages whoever employs them. Despite imperfections, therefore, it seems reasonable to measure labour in efficiency units, weighting each type by its wage rate, assumed to reflect its marginal productivity. Buildings and machinery are less easily shunted around. Once firms have them they are pretty well stuck with them, so they do not buy more just to meet a temporary demand. At any point of time, therefore, there is little reason to expect that the efficiency price of a certain sort of lathe, for instance, will be the same wherever it is used.

In measuring the 'quantity' of capital or any other fixed factor, then, it is dangerous to assume that it is optimally distributed; that is, to use equilibrium conditions.[2]

The central problem of aggregation outside equilibrium was raised by Klein (1946*a*) and solved by Nataf (1948).

Nataf considered T firms, with production equations, $f_t(x_t, n_t, z_t) = 0$, $t = 1, 2, \ldots, T$ where x_t, n_t, z_t are vectors of outputs, and labour and capital inputs, respectively. He showed that aggregates $X(x_1, \ldots, x_T)$, $Z(z_1, \ldots, z_T)$ exist which satisfy an aggregate production equation $F(X, N, Z) = 0$ iff[3] subaggregates $X_t(x_t)$, $N_t(n_t)$, $Z_t(z_t)$ exist for each firm, in terms of which its production relation can be written $X_t = N_t + Z_t$. Assuming this to be so, the aggregate production relation can be written $X = N + Z$ where $X = \sum a_t X_t$, $N = \sum a_t N_t$, $Z = \sum a_t Z_t$, the a's being arbitrary positive constants.

That the quantity of capital in an economy, for instance, should be the sum of the quantities in the individual firms, is very acceptable. But what are we to make of the arbitrary weights? Or of the fact that there are many

[1] Earlier versions of this paper were presented at Oxford in 1964 and at the Rome Econometric Conference in 1965. I am grateful to my colleagues at Oxford, the discussants at Rome: André Nataf and Takashi Negishi, and Frank Fisher, Frank Hahn, Leo Hurwicz, David Rowan, Paul Samuelson, John Whitaker, and John Wise, for useful comments.

Frank Fisher's paper, which was also presented at Rome, was written before mine. It has since been published (Fisher, 1965). André Nataf's contribution to the Rome discussion is also about to come out (Nataf, 1967). An explanation is in order for publishing a third essay in a limited field. This is it: the three papers differ markedly in method and consequently in structure. They seem to me to be complementary with each other and with John Whitaker's related paper (1966).

[2] Here, and throughout this paper, equilibria will be perfectly competitive, and the equilibrium conditions: that all goods, or at least all variable goods, have the same efficiency prices everywhere.

[3] 'iff' = 'if and only if' both here and throughout the paper.

equally acceptable versions of the aggregate relationship? When one thinks of it, this is quite a reasonable phenomenon: after all, the variables in the problem do satisfy T production relations, not one, and, with them, their various combinations. Nevertheless, it makes one rather chary of searching for the 'aggregate production function'.

More disturbing still is the fact that, except for the a's, the definition of these aggregates depends entirely on the existing technology. When the technology changes, so, normally, do the definitions of output, labour, and capital.[4] Indeed, if we keep to the canonical form $X = N + Z$, the aggregate production function is completely unaffected by technical change, whose only result is to change the *definition* of the aggregates which enter into it. Griliches (1963) and, more recently, Jorgenson and Griliches (1967) have argued that the fruits of technical change can be imputed largely to changes in the quality of the factors, so that more 'labour' can be extracted from a given work-force, for instance, but they would hardly say that the aggregate production function, however construed, has been completely invariant in a period of technical change.

For the same reason, these aggregates will normally have little meaning outside the production sector. The total volume of production, X, for instance, will normally change when Jones produces a hundred more Rhode Island Red eggs and Edwards a hundred fewer, and this even if they use the same techniques and their eggs are indistinguishable. Since the total quantity of individual goods is normally the only link between the demand and supply side in a complete model, this is a serious disadvantage.

These difficulties were discussed by Gorman (1953*b*), where it was shown that, if one allows the a's to depend on the prices as parameters, and if the technology is strictly convex, aggregates can be defined which depend only on the total quantities of the various goods and services produced or used, to the first order in the neighbourhood of equilibrium. To this order of approximation, indeed, they are Paasche indices—measures which are likely to have a meaning in other sectors.[5]

Despite this, Nataf's results are disturbing, not least because they show that aggregation is possible outside equilibrium only in rather special cases.

On the other hand Divisia (1928), Dresch (1938), and Richter (1966) have shown that chain base indices frequently work rather well if the productive sector is continuously in a state of instantaneous competitive equilibrium—normally a moving equilibrium of course.

Though this is unlikely for fixed inputs, it is not unreasonable for variable ones. This is the case discussed in the present paper where it is shown that

[4] Assuming, of course, that the new technology also satisfies Nataf's conditions.

[5] In terms of these aggregates the production relations become $\Pi = PX - WN - RZ$, where P, W and R are Laspeyres indices of prices, wage rates, and plant rentals, and Π is the equilibrium profits. The marginal productivity relations $\partial X/\partial N = W/P$, $\partial Z/\partial Z = R/P$ therefore hold *everywhere*.

the existence of variable goods and services, which earn, or are paid, their efficiency prices, makes the aggregation of fixed inputs even less likely to be possible, though the interpretation of the aggregates, when they exist, is more acceptable, since they represent the earning power of the corresponding inputs.

2. SUMMARY[6]

Consider a collection of T productive units: firms in an industry, industries in an economy, sectors in a vintage model. For simplicity call them firms in an economy. They may produce one or more commodities. Some may be intermediate goods, produced by some firms and used by others. The same firm may be a net producer of a good in some situations, a net user in others. They may or may not fall into industries each producing a common group of goods.

Goods are of two sorts: variable and fixed. The *n variable goods* are efficiently distributed, and so have the same *efficiency prices* $p = (p_1, \ldots, p_n)$ everywhere.[7] The *fixed goods* may or may not be—indeed the same type of fixed input may never be used by more than one firm. While the *variable goods are measured as outputs*, inputs negative, *the fixed goods are all inputs* and will be referred to, and measured as such. They fall into classes which I will call *fixed factors*: I will use 'capital', 'land', 'equipment', and 'buildings' as examples of fixed factors from time to time. I want to find *aggregates* for these fixed factors, which I will call the *quantity of capital, of land*, etc. The *quantity of equipment*, for instance, is required to depend only on the amounts of the various types of equipment used in the individual firms. It is not required to double, for instance, when all these components do so—larger quantities may be proportionately more or less productive—nor to remain constant when a given machine is moved from one firm to another—the new firm may use it more or less efficiently than the old, and, basically what we are looking for is a measure of the productive power of the equipment in the economy, fixed in its present locations.

We distinguish, then, between *fixed inputs*, which may, for example, be particular sorts of equipment or buildings, used by particular firms in given quantities, *fixed factors*, such as 'equipment', each a class of fixed inputs, and the *quantity*, e.g. *of equipment*, which may be altered if a particular machine is taken from one firm and given to another.

[6] The rest of the paper may be regarded as a mathematical appendix to this rather lengthy summary, to be read only by those technically interested. Sections 3–5 are the most mathematical.

[7] Of course these need not be uniquely determined: indeed kp will always do as well as p, where $k > 0$, since these are unnormalized accounting prices. What is required is that there be at least one vector of efficiency prices which is the same for all the firms.

Let $x_t = (x_{t1}, \ldots, x_{tn})$ be the *production plan* or *net output vector* of the tth firm, outputs positive, inputs negative. x_{ti} is its net output of the ith variable good. $x = \sum_t x_t$ is the *production plan* or *net output vector* for the economy as a whole.

y^r is the rth *fixed input vector for the tth firm*. If the rth fixed factor were equipment, for instance, it would give the amounts of different sorts of equipment owned by the firm. In the case of fixed goods, there is no necessary relationship between corresponding components for different firms, so that the rth *fixed input vector* $y_r = (y_1^r, \ldots, y_T^r)$ for the economy as a whole is just a list of the corresponding vectors for the individual firms. This is because a capstan lathe, for instance, is as good as its use, and there is nothing to ensure that different firms make equally good use of it. $y_t = (y_t^1, \ldots, y_r^R)$ and $y = (y^1, \ldots, y^R)$ are the *fixed goods vectors* for the tth firm and the economy.

We want to find aggregates $Y(y) = (Y^1(y^1), \ldots, Y^R(y^R))$ for the R fixed factors such that the *short-run production possibility set* $S(y)$, of production plans which are feasible for the economy as a whole with the fixed inputs y, can be written in the form $\tilde{S}(Y(y))$. The question is: what must the technologies of the individual firms be like for this to be possible? Now the information at the disposal of the individual firms is the prices p of the variable goods, and the quantities y_t of the fixed, available to them. It would seem a good idea, therefore, to specify their technologies in terms of these variables if possible.

Let us assume that the *short-run production possibility sets* $S_t(y_t)$, $t = 1, 2, \ldots, T$ for the individual firms, corresponding to $S(y)$ defined above for the economy as a whole, are convex: that is to say that the average of any pair of feasible production plans is also feasible. The short-run isoquants, then, are convex, and short-run returns decreasing or at least non-increasing. This seems reasonable when we remember that the fixed inputs are fixed in the short run. In Section 3 it is shown that a knowledge of the *gross profit function*[8]

$$g_t(p, y_t) = \max \sum p_i x_{ti},^{9}$$

given that x_t is a feasible production plan for the rth firm when it has the fixed inputs y_t, is equivalent to a knowledge of $S_t(y_t)$ itself in this case. The conditions which a function has to satisfy in order to be acceptable as a gross profit function are found,[10] and it is shown that $g_t(p, y_t)$ is homogene-

[8] This function is a direct analogue to the cost function $K(p, u)$ giving the minimum cost of producing an output u, or reaching a level u of utility, at prices p, whose use has been rather generally known for some time. The first systematic discussion of this class of functions was given in Samuelson (1965).

[9] 'sup' rather that 'max' really, because, in some limiting cases, it may theoretically be profitable to produce infinite quantities of some goods.

[10] They are: that it should be *positively homogeneous of degree one* and *closed convex* in the prices. The former merely means that gross profits increase k fold if each of the prices do, and

ous of degree one in y_t iff there is constant returns to scale in the long run, and concave in y_t iff the long-run production possibility set is convex.

It is also shown that the optimal production plan is $x_t = g_t'(p, y_t) = (g_{t1}, \ldots, g_{tn})$ when the differential coefficients $g_{ti} = \partial g_i / \partial p_i$ exist, and that the formula continues to hold with a slightly generalized definition of g_t' when they do not.

In Section 4 the regularity conditions required for the main analysis are introduced. On the whole these are rather weak: for instance the set over which aggregates are assumed to exist need not be a simple one like the positive orthant, some firms may never use some of the fixed factors, and differentiability is nowhere assumed. However, the aggregates do have to be assumed to be continuous. This is necessary in order to rule out certain trick aggregates which merely transcribe the entire vector y^r in a new code. Nevertheless one would prefer not to assume continuity in a field where lumpiness is so common, if it were avoidable.

The main result in the paper is proved in Section 5.

It is easily seen that $S(y) = \tilde{S}(Y(y))$—so that the short-run production possibilities for the economy as a whole depend only on the aggregates $Y(y) = (Y^1(y^1), \ldots, Y^R(y^R))$—iff the gross profit function for the economy as a whole

$$\sum g_t(p, y_t) = G(p, Y(y)), \text{ say.} \tag{1}$$

Let us now define the quantity $Y_t^r(y_t^r)$ of the rth fixed factor in the tth firm by its earning power there at certain base prices q,[11] that is,

$$Y_t^r(y_t^r) = g_t(q, 0, \ldots, 0, y_t^r, 0, \ldots, 0) - g_t(q, 0).^{12} \tag{2}$$

It is shown that we can take the corresponding aggregate for the economy as a whole in (1) to be

$$Y^r(y^r) = \sum_t Y_t^r(y_t^r) \tag{3}$$

$k \geqslant 0$. The latter is slightly stronger than ordinary convexity, which would assert that the gross profits at prices $(p+q)/2$ are not greater than the average of those at prices p and q separately. Together, they are equivalent to the statement that the set

$$U_t(y_t) = \{(p, u) \mid u \geqslant g_t(p, y_t)\}$$

is a closed convex cone.

[11] At which it was assumed ((G7) in Section 4) that the gross profit functions $g_t(q, y_t)$ were continuous in the y_t, and strongly increasing in each y_t^r, that is, having more of all the fixed inputs in any class actually increases each firm's gross profits *at these prices*. Hence the $Y_t^r(y_t^r)$ are also continuous and strongly increasing.

[12] Here it is implicitly assumed that 0 is admissible as a fixed input vector, while we might, for instance, wish to require aggregability only in a region in the interior of the positive orthant. Actually any vector b which is admissible as a fixed factor vector will do as a reference vector as well as 0. In Section 5, I chose a b which minimizes each $g_t(q, b_t)$, so that the minimum quantity of any fixed factor turns out to be zero.

the total earning power of the fixed inputs y^r in the economy, and that, in this notation, we can write the gross profit functions in the form

$$g_t(p, y_t) = G_t(p, Y_t(y_t)) = \sum c^r(p) Y_t^r(y_t^r) + d_t(p), \tag{4}$$

for each firm, and

$$\sum g_t(p, y_t) = G(p, Y(y)) = \sum c^r(p) Y^r(y^r) + d(p),^{13} \tag{5}$$

where $d = \sum d_t$, of course, for the economy as a whole. Since (4) clearly implies (5) which implies (1), it is both necessary and sufficient for it.

I will call the functions $G_t(p, Y_t)$ and $G(p, Y)$ *quasi-gross profit functions* because they are defined in terms of the fictional 'quantities' of the fixed factors instead of the actual fixed inputs. They have the same formal properties as ordinary gross profit functions. Similarly I will talk of *quasi-production possibility sets* $\tilde{S}_t(Y_t)$, $\tilde{S}(Y)$, and *quasi-technologies*, and will say that a firm, or the economy as a whole, produces under *quasi-constant returns* if doubling the quantities of the *fixed factors* at its disposal just permits it to double its net output of each of the variable goods. This does not imply, of course, that it produces under true constant returns, since doubling the fixed inputs need not double the quantities of the fixed factors.[14] According to (4) and (5) the tth firm produces under quasi-constant returns iff $d_t(p) = 0$, and the economy as a whole iff $d(p) = 0$.

These results are interpreted in Sections 6 and 7: the former dealing with the aggregates, the latter with the quasi-gross profit functions.

I will summarize the two sections as a unit.

We have already seen that (4) implies that the production possibilities facing the economy as a whole depend only on the total quantities $Y = \sum_t Y_t$ of the fixed *factors*. They are therefore the same however these are distributed over the firms, that is, the market for the variable goods guarantees that any given distribution of the fixed factors is just as productive as any other, that is, that it is efficient. In fact it is easily shown that $c^r(p)$ is the efficiency price of the rth fixed factor: it is automatically the same in all the firms. It is also the extra profit which an extra unit of the factor will earn in any of the firms. Since $c^r(q) = 1$ this confirms that the quantities of the factors are measured in terms of their earning power at these base prices.

Why is this so?

We have already seen that the optimal production plan of a firm is got by differentiating its gross profit function.[15] (4) and (5) therefore yield

[13] $Y_t = (Y_t^1, \ldots, Y_t^R)$; $Y = (Y^1, \ldots, Y^R) = \sum Y_t$ by (3).

[14] I sometimes renormalize the aggregates—measuring them from a new base point to make the a's vanish and get quasi-constant returns.

[15] If it is differentiable, which it is 'almost everywhere'. The conclusions below are valid even without differentiability.

$$x_t = \sum c'^r(p)\, Y_t^r + d_t'(p), \quad x = \sum c'^r(p)\, Y^r + d'(p), \tag{6}$$

where the primes represent vectors of derivatives. Hence the gift of an extra unit of the rth factor will cause whichever firm gets it to change its production plans in exactly the same way as it would any other[16] and will therefore earn it just the same increase in its profit.

This is serious. Suppose 'equipment' is one of the factors and that a heavy press represents just as much extra equipment to one firm as ten typewriters to another. The gift of the heavy press to it would induce it to change its production of all the variable goods—and use of all the variable inputs—by precisely the same amounts as that of the ten typewriters would the other.

The aggregation of fixed goods, of which capital aggregation is a particular example, is therefore very unlikely to be justified in an economy as a whole, at least with theoretically interesting definitions of the fixed factors. It is perhaps more acceptable for single industries, or for models of the economy in which the variable goods are themselves highly aggregated, as in vintage capital models, for instance.

Another interpretation of (4)–(6) is as follows: each firm has $(r + 1)$ plants, yielding profits $c^1(p)\, Y_t^1, \dots, c^R(p)\, Y_t^R$, $d_t(p)$, and producing outputs $c'^1(p)\, Y_t^1, \dots, c'^R(p)\, Y_t^R$, $d_t'(p)$. This interpretation is not always strictly justified, but it is shown in Section 7 that it frequently is. The rth plant in each firm, having the same quasi-gross profit function, has the same quasi-technology, which clearly yields quasi-constant returns. The base plants, corresponding to the $d_t(p)$, presumably use fixed factors, specific to the firm itself, and may differ as much as we like among themselves.

These plants are of course only theoretical constructs—normally fictions without physical analogues.

In terms of the quasi-technologies, defined in terms of the fixed factors rather than the fixed inputs, these are the only differences between the firms; even these disappear if all the firms[17] produce under quasi-constant returns, because each $d_t(p) \equiv 0$, then.

The other way in which firms can differ is, of course, in their aggregation functions

$$Y_t^r(\cdot).^{18} \tag{7}$$

We have already seen that the quantities of the fixed factors are *measured* in terms of their earning power. They may be *interpreted* either as indices of

[16] If $G_t(p, Y_t)$ is not differentiable, there will in general be many equally profitable production plans both before and after the gift. Any change which is optimal for any one firm is optimal for all.

[17] i.e. each firm can just produce twice as high a net output of each variable good if it has twice as much of each factor, or, equivalently, can earn just twice as large gross profits. In general this depends on the origin from which the quantity of equipment is measured. Throughout this section I assume each $Y_t^r(0) = 0$, as in (2).

[18] '$Y^r(\cdot)$'='the function Y_t^r'.

the quantities of the corresponding fixed inputs or as quantities of fictitious intermediate goods produced from the corresponding fixed inputs in the firms' *fixed factor-producing plants* with the production functions (7).

If so we may say that the firms differ only in these plants and in their basic plants, introduced above, their *fixed factor-using plants* being identical. I prefer this interpretation in general, because there is no reason why the Y_t^r should double when the corresponding inputs y_t^r do, and there goes my notion of what an acceptable index number should be like.

In one leading case, however, the $Y_t^r(\cdot)$ are homogeneous of the first degree—that in which each of the firms produces under genuine constant returns. In that case, therefore, either interpretation is equally acceptable: in the 'intermediate goods interpretation' we would say that the fixed factors were produced under constant returns. Incidentally the firms also produce under quasi-constant returns then, so that they all have the same quasi-technology, and so differ only in their factor-producing plants.

What about the substitutability relations among the inputs?

Suppose that there are only two variable goods—one an output, the other an input—and let us say that two inputs are complements if increasing the quantity of one increases the marginal product of the other, and substitutes if it decreases it. We see in Section 7 that the fixed factors can be divided into two groups according to whether they are substitutes for, or complements of, the variable input, and that factors in the same group are substitutes, in different groups, complements. The same is true of the corresponding inputs.

3. PRELIMINARIES: THE GROSS PROFIT FUNCTION

Each of the T firms introduced in Section 2 is assumed to maximize its gross profit $p \cdot x_t$ given the prices p of the variable goods and quantities y_t of the fixed. More precisely, it chooses a *production plan* x_t in its *short-run production possibility set* $S_t(y_t)$ to maximize $p \cdot x_t$.

Neglect t and y_t for the moment, since we will be holding them constant in any case, and define the *gross profit function*

$$g(p) = \sup\{p \cdot x \mid x \in S\}, \quad \text{each } p \in R^n, \tag{8}$$ [19]

so that $g(\cdot)$ is

(G1) *positively homogeneous of degree one*: $g(kp) = kg(p)$, each $k \geqslant 0$

(G2) *closed convex*: that is

$$U = \{(p, u) \mid u \geqslant g(p)\} \text{ is a closed convex set.} \tag{9}$$

[19] n is the number of variable goods. $g(p) = \infty$ if there is free disposal, for instance, and some of the prices are negative. This possibility does not create any real problems.

Clearly (G1)–(G2) are equivalent to

$$U \text{ is a closed convex cone.} \tag{10}$$

Clearly, too,

$$\begin{aligned} U &= \{(p, u) \mid u \geqslant p \cdot x, \text{ each } x \in S\} \\ &= \{(p, u) \mid -zp \cdot x + zu \geqslant 0, \text{ each } x \in S, z \geqslant 0\} \\ &= Z^+, \end{aligned} \tag{11}$$

the polar cone[20] of the cone

$$Z = \{(-zx, z) \mid x \in S, z \geqslant 0\}. \tag{12}$$

Whatever the price, no feasible plan can yield more than $g(p)$. Hence $S \subseteq S^*$, where

$$S^* = \{x \mid p \cdot x \leqslant g(p), \text{ each } p\} = \{x \mid p \cdot x \leqslant u, \text{ each } (p, u) \in U\}. \tag{13}$$

In fact

$$S^* \text{ is the convex closure of } S, \tag{14}$$

for

$$\{(-zx, z) \mid x \in S^*, z \geqslant 0\} = U^+ = Z^{++}, \tag{15}$$

which is the convex closure of the cone Z by a well-known theorem.

(14) implies that

$$S = S^* \tag{16}$$

iff

(S1) S is closed
(S2) S is convex.

In the case of *short-run* production possibility sets $S_t(y_t)$, (S1)–(S2) is a reasonable assumption.

The fixed inputs being taken as given, the possibility of increasing returns to scale need not worry us. From now on I will assume (S1)–(S2), as well as

(S0) S is not empty

for such sets for each individual firm, and hence for the economy as a whole, except where I specify the contrary.

[20] The polar cone V^+ of a set V is $\{w \mid v \cdot w \geqslant 0, \text{ each } v \in V\}$. It is a closed convex cone made up of those vectors which make acute, or right, angles, with all the vectors in V. V^{++} is the smallest closed convex cone containing V. $V^{++} = V$, therefore, iff V is itself a closed convex cone. If V is a cone, V^{++} is its convex closure. See e.g. Karlin (1959), Appendix B.3.

According to (13) and (16), therefore, knowledge of the gross profit function is equivalent to that of the production possibility set, both for the individual firms and the economy as a whole.[21]

Suppose now that we are given a function $g(\cdot)$ which may or may not satisfy (G1)–(G2), that is, which may or may not be an *admissible gross profit function*. Define U as in (9), S^* as in (13) $g^*(\cdot)$ from S^* and U^* from $g^*(\cdot)$ as in (8) and (9). Then, easily

$$U = U^{++} \tag{17}$$

the closure of the convex cone spanned by U, so that $U^* = U$ or equivalently

$$g^*(p) = g(p), \qquad \text{each } p, \tag{18}$$

iff (10), or, equivalently (G1)–(G2). That is, (18) holds only for admissible gross profit functions.

S^*, as the intersection of a collection of closed half spaces, is always closed and convex. Moreover, since $U^* = U^{++}$ is a closed convex cone, $g^*(\cdot)$ is always an admissible gross profit function.

Return now to the case where $g(\cdot)$ is an admissible gross profit function. The set

$$R = \{p \mid g(p) < \infty\} \tag{19}$$

is a convex cone by (G1)–(G2). Because $g(\cdot)$ is closed convex it can be shown that

$g(\cdot)$ is continuous, and has second-order partial derivatives almost everywhere, in Int R.[22] (20)

$$g(p) = \lim\inf\{g(q) \mid q \to p\} \text{ everywhere.} \tag{21}$$

We have not so far enquired whether the supremum in (8) is attained. If it is, however, there exists an *optimal production plan* $x \in S$ such that

$$x \cdot p = g(p). \tag{22}$$

(22) holds at all prices at which x is optimal, while

$$x \cdot q \leq g(q), \tag{23}$$

whether or not x is optimal at q. Hence

$$\phi(q, x) = g(q) - x \cdot q \tag{24}$$

is minimized with respect to q when $q = p$, and then takes the value zero. Because of (13) and (16), moreover, (22) and (23) imply that $x \in S$. They

[21] Even if S is neither closed nor convex, the gross profit functions effectively define the competitive market behaviour of firms, or, in general, the efficient behaviour of the economy.

[22] Int R = relative interior of R. The second-order partial derivatives are defined in a slightly unusual manner. The result is classical.

are therefore both necessary and sufficient for x to be an optimal plan at prices p.

In seeking to characterize these optimal plans explicitly—that is, to find the *supply function*—let us first assume that g is differentiable. Then

$$x = g'(p) = (g_1(p), \ldots, g_n(p)), \tag{25}$$

where $g_i = \partial g/\partial p_i$. $g'(p)$ is the *gradient* of g at p: that is $(-1, g'(p))$ is the unique normal to $u = g(p)$ there. Since $g(\cdot)$ is convex, this local extremum is a global minimum, and since it is positively homogeneous of the first degree, $g = p \cdot q' = \sum p_i g_i$ so that (22), and therefore (23), are indeed satisfied; and (25) is indeed both necessary and sufficient for x to be optimal at p.

In general $g(\cdot)$ may not be differentiable. Since $g(q)$ is convex, however, so is $\phi(q, x) = g(q) - x \cdot q$, so that its maximum is attained wherever it has a horizontal tangent plane. That is, where $u = g(q)$ has a tangent plane parallel to $u = x \cdot q$, or, equivalently, where it has a normal parallel to $(-1, x)$. At any such point p

$$g(q) - g(p) \geqslant x \cdot (1 - p) \tag{26}$$

because of the convexity of $g(\cdot)$. Setting $q + (k+1)p$ and remembering that $g(\cdot)$ is positively homogeneous of degree one by (G1), we see that $kg(p) \geqslant kx \cdot p$, $k \geqslant -1$, which implies (22), and, through (26), (23). If, therefore, we define a *gradient* $\psi'(q)$ at q *of any convex function* $\psi(q)$ as any vector such that $(-1, \psi'(q))$ is normal to $v = \psi(q)$ at q, we see that (25) remains a necessary and sufficient condition for x to be optimal at p in the non-differentiable case also.

The question of the existence of optimal plans, or equivalently of the attainment of the supremum in (8), is equivalent to that of the existence of a gradient $g'(p)$ of $g(\cdot)$ at p. There are three cases:

(i) $p \notin R$.

$g(p) = \infty$ and there exists an unbounded sequence $\{x^m\}$ in S, such that $p \cdot x^m \to \infty$.

(ii) $p \in \operatorname{Int} R$.

The supremum is attained at a finite point $x \in S$. Otherwise the continuity of $p \cdot x$ and x and the closedness of S would imply the existence of an unbounded sequence $\{x^m\}$ in S such that $p \cdot x^m$ is monotonically increasing. It has a sub-sequence such that $x_i^m \to +\infty$, $x = 1, \ldots, r$, $x_i^m \to -\infty$, $i = r+1, \ldots, r+s$, $r, s > 0$. Take δ as a vector whose first r components are $+\varepsilon$, next s, $-\varepsilon$, and remainder zero, $\varepsilon > 0$. Then $(p+\delta) \cdot x^m - p \cdot x^m = \delta \cdot x^m \to \infty$. However $p + \delta \in R$ for sufficiently small ε, so that $(p+\delta) \cdot x^m \leqslant g(p+\delta) < \infty$. Hence $p \cdot x^m \to -\infty$, and so is not monotonically increasing.

(iii) $p \in R \cap$ *frontier of* R.

If the supremum in (8) is attainable at a finite x, it can be shown that the optimal facet is unbounded.[23] 'Infinite' plans may not be necessary for maximum profits, therefore, but there is always one which is at least as good as any finite plan.

To summarize. Outside R no finite plan is optimal, inside R there is always an optimal finite plan and all infinite plans are 'infinitely bad', on the frontier of R, there may or may not be optimal finite plans; but, in any case, there are always 'infinite' plans at least as good as any of them.

Once we know R, then, we might as well confine our attention to it. If

(S3) *there is free disposal*: $x \in S$ if $x \leqslant x^* \in S$,

it would clearly be indefinitely profitable to buy indefinitely large quantities at negative prices. Hence

(G3) *R is contained in the positive orthant.*[24]

All these functions and sets should really have t and y_t as arguments, and have direct analogues for the economy as a whole. I wish now to discuss the long-run production possibilities and so will introduce the quantities of fixed goods y as an argument in the short-run concepts just discussed. I will continue to suppress t.

The *long run production possibility set* is

$$S = \{(x, y) \mid x \in S(y),\ y \in \Omega, \text{ say}\},^{25} \tag{27}$$

so that

$$S(y) = \{x \mid (x, y) \in S\}, \quad \text{each } y \in \Omega. \tag{28}$$

[23] I will sketch the proof for the case where $0 \in S$. It is slightly more complicated if $0 \notin S$.

Let $p \in R \cap$ frontier of R, and take a sequence $\{p + \delta^m\} \notin R$, $\delta^m \to 0$. Let $\{x^{mk}\}$, each m, be a sequence such that $(p + \delta^m) \cdot x^{mk} \to \infty$ each m, as $k \to \infty$. Choose a k for each m such that $(p + \delta^m) \cdot \bar{x}^m \to \infty$ where $\bar{x}^m = x^{mk(m)}$. Write $x^{*m} = \bar{x}^m/(\sum \bar{x}_i^m)$ so that $\{x^{*m}\}$ is in the fundamental simplex and therefore has a limit x^*. Choose a sub-sequence such that $x^{*m} \to x^*$ in the sub-sequence, and relabel its elements, and the corresponding elements of $\{\delta^m\}$, 1, 2, 3, ... Set $x^{*m} = x^* + \varepsilon^m$, $\bar{x}^m = \lambda^m x^{*m} = \lambda^m(x^* + \varepsilon^m)$ when $\varepsilon^m \to 0$. $\lambda^m \to \infty$, of course. Each μx^*, $\mu \geqslant 0$ belongs to S, since 0 does and S is closed and convex. Moreover $(p + \delta^m) \cdot \bar{x}^m \to \infty$. Hence $\lambda^m(p \cdot x^* + p \cdot \varepsilon^m + \delta^m \cdot x^* + \delta^m \cdot \varepsilon^m) \to \infty$. All but the first element in the bracket certainly tend to zero. Hence $(p + \delta^m) \cdot \bar{x}^m \sim \lambda^m p \cdot x^*$, unless $p \cdot x^* = 0$. This would imply $p \cdot \lambda^m x^* \to \infty$, where $\lambda^m x^* \in S$, so then $g(p) = \infty$, contradicting the fact that $p \in R$. Hence $p \cdot x^* = 0$. Let now $\{\tilde{x}^m\}$ be a sequence in S such that $p \cdot \tilde{x}^m \to g(p)$. Then $p \cdot \{(1 - \rho^m)\tilde{x}^m + \lambda^m x^*\} \to g(p)$ as $\rho^m \to 0$. Yet $\{(1 - \rho^m)\tilde{a}^m + \lambda^m a^*\}$ is unbounded. This seems the natural interpretation of the phrase 'the facet is unbounded'.

[24] i.e. if $p \in R$, $p \geqslant 0$. I will use 'strictly positive' to mean $p > 0$, but will not use 'non-negative' at all.

[25] Ω will be specified below.

(8), (13), and (16) immediately imply that there are *constant returns to scale* iff

(G4) *$g(p, \cdot)$ is positively homogeneous of degree one*[26]

$$g(p, ky) = kg(p, y), \qquad \text{each } k > 0,\ y,\ ky \in \Omega.$$

The long-run production possibility set is itself convex iff

(G5) *$g(p, \cdot)$ is concave on Ω,*

given of course that

(Ω4) *Ω is convex.*

To see this, observe first that, if $x \in S(y)$ and $x^* \in S(y^*)$, then $\tfrac{1}{2}(x + x^*) \in S(\tfrac{1}{2}(y + y^*))$ if S is convex. Hence

$$g(p, \tfrac{1}{2}(y + y^*)) \geqslant \tfrac{1}{2}(g(p, y) + g(p, y^*)). \tag{29}$$

If S is not convex, on the other hand, one can find $x \in S(y)$, $x^* \in S(y^*)$ such that $\tfrac{1}{2}(x + x^*) \notin S(\tfrac{1}{2}(y + y^*))$. Since $S(\tfrac{1}{2}(y + y^*))$ satisfies (S0)–(S2), (13) and (16) imply the existence of a p such that

$$g(p, \tfrac{1}{2}(y + y^*)) < \tfrac{1}{2}(x + x^*) \cdot p \leqslant \tfrac{1}{2}(g(p, y) + g(p, y^*)), \tag{30}$$

which completes the proof.

If

(G6) *$g(p, \cdot)$ is strictly concave on Ω,*

where Ω satisfies (Ω4), S is strictly convex by (13) and (16) applied to $S(\tfrac{1}{2}(y + y^*))$, because the weak inequality in (29) becomes strict.

Consider finally the *long-run profit function*

$$\begin{aligned} h(p, q) &= \sup\{p \cdot x - q \cdot y \mid (x, y) \in S\} \\ &= \sup\{g(p, y) - q \cdot y \mid y \in \Omega\}, \end{aligned} \tag{31}$$

where q is the vector of efficiency prices for the fixed goods. Under decreasing returns $g(p, \cdot)$ is concave. An argument similar to that leading up to (25) shows that

$$q = \dot{g}_2(p, y) = \text{gradient of } g(p, y) \text{ with respect to } y. \tag{32}$$

If $g(p, \cdot)$ is differentiable but not concave, (32) is the first-order condition for maximum profits, but some of the q it yields will correspond to other extrema and will not be true efficiency prices.

Being a profit function, $h(\cdot, \cdot)$ is of course positively homogeneous and closed concave.

[26] In using this result, I will frequently assume Ω to satisfy (Ω5). If $y \in \Omega$ and $k \geqslant 1$, then $ky \in \Omega$, but this is not necessary for its statement.

4. PRELIMINARIES: FORMAL STATEMENT OF THE PROBLEM

We want to be able to write the short-run production possibility set for the economy as a whole in the form

$$S(y) = \tilde{S}(Y(y)), \quad \text{each } y \in \Omega \tag{33}$$

say, where

(Y1) $\quad Y(y) = Y^1(y^1), \ldots, Y^R(y^R)), \text{ each } y \in \Omega,$

is a vector whose r^{th} component measures the '*quantity of the* r^{th} *factor*' in the economy as a whole.

I will consider the case where

(Ω1) $\quad \Omega = \Pi_t^r \Omega_t^r = \Pi^r \Omega^r = \Pi_t \Omega_t$

in the obvious notation,[27]

(Ω2) *each Ω^r is non-empty, closed and tube-connected and is bounded below*[28]

(Ω3) *for each factor r, the set $T(r) = \{t \mid \Omega_t^r$ has more than one element$\}$ contains more than one firm t.*[29]

The import of these rather weak restrictions is discussed in the footnotes.

In a sense (33) is always true![30] To see this: consider any strictly increasing mapping $y^r \to z^r$, where the $N(r)$ components of z^r are non-terminating decimals between zero and one.[31] Define Y^r to be another such decimal, having the first figure of z_1^r in its first place, the first of z_2^r in its second, . . . , the first of $z_{N(r)}^r$ in its $N(r)^{\text{th}}$, the second of z_1^r in its $N(r) + 1^{\text{th}}$, ... Clearly we can reconstruct z^r, and therefore y^r, from Y^r, so that we can write the short-run production possibility set $S(y)$ in the form $\tilde{S}(Y(y))$ whatever the technology. Trick aggregates such as these clearly should be excluded. It is

[27] i.e. Ω^r is the domain of y_t^r; $\Omega^r = \Pi_t \Omega_t^r$, $\Omega_t = \Pi^r \Omega_t^r$, each r, t.

[28] *Closure* is for convenience only. Dropping it would make the proof in Sect. 5 slightly more complicated.

Tube connectivity: if y_t^r, z_t^r are distinct points in Ω_t^r, they are joined by a continuous curve whose other points all lie in the interior of Ω_t^r. This is needed in the proof of (36), which is not given in this paper.

Bounded below: there exist $\beta^r > -\infty$ such that $y_t^r \geqslant \beta^r$ if $y^r \in \Omega_t^r$. This seems reasonable. Indeed it would seem reasonable to take $\beta_t^r = 0$. It simplifies the proof in Sect. 5 to have assumed boundedness below, but it is not necessary for the result.

[29] Required because we have to be able to shunt fixed inputs in each class backward and forward among the firms. (Ω2) implies that there are y_t^r, $z_t^r \in \Omega_t^r$ such that $y_t^r > z_t^r$ iff $t \in T(r)$. (Y2) therefore implies that Y^r can be changed just by changing y_t^r iff $t \in T(r)$.

[30] This construction, which replaces a much less elegant one of my own, was suggested to me by Professor L. Hurwicz in the course of a very valuable conversation—very valuable to me at least!

[31] $1/2 + 1/\pi$ arc tan y is a strictly increasing mapping of $(-\infty, \infty)$ on to $(0, 1)$ if we take the principal value of the arc tan.

not sufficient to require that admissible aggregates be increasing functions of their arguments, since the trick aggregates are actually strictly increasing. Continuity is the important thing. Accordingly I will require

(Y2) *each $Y^r(y^r)$ is continuous in y^r and strongly increasing in each y_t^r*,[32]

so that the range of each $Y^r(\cdot)$ is an interval I^r by (Ω1)–(Ω2).[33]

Finally I will need

(G7) *For some prices q, each $g_t(q, y_t)$ is continuous in y_t and strongly increasing in each y_t^r*,

The import of these requirements, too, is discussed in the footnotes. They are pretty weak.[34]

(8), (13), and (16) immediately imply that (33) holds iff

$$g(p, y) = \textstyle\sum_t g_t(p, y_t) = G(p, Y(y)), \quad \text{each } y \in \Omega, p. \tag{34}$$

Clearly (G7) implies that

$$g(p, y) \text{ is continuous in } y \text{ and strongly increasing in each } y_t^r, \text{ each } y \in \Omega. \tag{35}$$

With (Ω1)–(Ω3) and (Y1)–(Y2), it also implies

$$G(q, Y) \text{ is continuous and strictly increasing in } Y, \text{ each } Y \in I = \Pi^r I^r.^{35} \tag{36}$$

[32] *Strongly increasing in y_t^r*: if $y_t^r, z_t^r \in \Omega_t^r$ where $y_t^r > z_t^r$, and if $y_s^r \geqslant z_s^r \in \Omega_s^r$, each $s \neq t$, then $Y^r(y^r) > Y^r(z^r)$. Note that it is not necessary to state that $t \in T(r)$, even though the requirement is empty for $t \notin T(r)$. The slightly repugnant part of (Y2) is the requirement of continuity. One might like fixed equipment to be lumpy. I can only plead

(i) step functions can be indefinitely closely approximated by continuous functions.

(ii) age, etc. of equipment may be thought of as giving some sort of continous variability, even if the actual pieces are lumpy.

(iii) One might argue that the flow of services from equipment is continuously variable, and that it is this flow which determines production. This would soften the stark contrast between fixed and variable inputs which underlies my whole analysis.

The real defence is, however, that one cannot hope to get anywhere without continuity because of the trick aggregates mentioned in the text.

[33] I^r is bounded below and closed below, because Ω^r is. It can therefore be put in the form $[0, a_r\rangle$ by a trivial normalization. Here [,] denote closed ends, (,) open ends and ⟨ , ⟩ either.

[34] (Ω_2) and (Y2) can be considerably weakened, but the resulting form of (Y2), in particular, is difficult to understand. Without the order requirements, including (1), it implies the form (Y2) given in the text, with its distasteful demand for continuity.

[35] In Sect. 5, I will need $G(q, \cdot)$ strictly increasing. A brief sketch of the proof follows: Take $U, V \in I$ such that $U^r < V^r$, $r \leqslant m$, $U^r = V^r$, $r > m$, and $u, v \in \Omega$ such that $u^r = v^r$, $r > m$ and $Y(u) = U$, $Y(v) = V$.

Assume $u^r, v^r \in \text{Int } \Omega^r$, $r \leqslant m$. They are connected by a curve $C^r \subseteq \text{Int } \Omega^r$. There exists $\rho^r \geqslant 0$ such that $z^r + \rho^r e^r \in \Omega^r$. When $z^r \in C^r$, $e^r = (1, 1, \ldots, 1)$.

Define a finite sequence $z_r^0 = u^r, \ldots, z_r^j$ on C^r with z_r^{i+1}, $Y^r(z_r^{i+1}) = Y^r(z_i^r + \rho^r e^r) \geqslant V^r$. Define $z_r^{j+1} = z_r^j + \lambda^r e^r$ such that $Y^r(z_r^{j+1}) = V^r$. Let the earlier sequences to reach this final point mark time there until the others catch up. It is easily shown that $\{g(q, z_r^i)\}$ is a strictly increasing sequence. Hence, $G(q, U) = g(q, u) < g(q, v) = G(q, V)$.

Extend the result to the case when some u^r or $v^r \notin \text{Int } \Omega^r$ by the continuity of $g(q, y)$.

The proof of (36) is a little technical, and far from our main concerns, so that it is not given here. Those who doubt its validity may prefer to take (36) as a separate requirement—surely an acceptable one.

Our problem now is: given (Ω1)–(Ω3), (Y1)–(Y2), (G1)–(G2), and (G7), under what further conditions does (34) hold?

It will be discussed in the next section.

5. THE MAIN THEOREM

THEOREM: *Given* (Ω1)–Ω3), *and* (Y1)–(Y2) *and* (G7), *we can write*

$$g(p, y) = \sum g_t(p, y_t) = G(p, Y(y)), \quad \text{each } y \in \Omega, p \tag{37}$$

iff

there exist continuous and strongly increasing subaggregates $Y_t^r(y_t^r)$, *each* r, t[36] (38)

such that

$$g_t(p, y_t) = G_t(p, Y_t(y_t)) = H(p, Y_t(y_t)) + d_t(p), \tag{39}$$

say, all $y_t \in \Omega_t$, p *where* $Y_t = (Y_t^1, \ldots, Y_t^R)$ *and, under an appropriate normalization, which will be used throughout the remainder of this statement of the theorem,*

$$Y(y) = \sum_t Y_t(y_t) \tag{40}$$

$$H(p, Y + Z) = H(p, Y) + H(p, Z) \quad \text{when } Y, Z, Y + Z \in I \tag{41}$$

$$g(p, y) = G(p, Y(y)) = H(p, Y(y)) + d(p), \tag{42}$$

where

$$d(p) = \sum_t d_t(p). \tag{43}$$

PROOF: The sufficiency of (38)–(43) is obvious. I will prove their necessity.

$(Y1)$–$(Y2)$ and (Ω1)–(Ω2) imply that each $Y^r(y^r)$ attains its minimum value at some point $b^r \in \Omega^r$. Define

$$Y_t^r(y_t^r) = g_t(q, b_t^1, \ldots, y_t^r, \ldots, b_t^R) - g_t(q, b_t), \qquad \text{each } t, r \tag{44}$$

[36] *Strongly increasing in* y_t^r: if $y_t^r, z_t^r \in \Omega_t^r$, and $y_t^r > z_t^r$, then $Y_t^r(y_t^r) > Y_t^r(z_t^r)$. (38) is operative iff $t \in T(r)$.

in the obvious notation, where q is the price vector introduced in (G7). Because of (G7), these subaggregates, measuring the quantities of the various factors employed in the individual firms, satisfy (38). They have ranges

$$I_t^r = [0, a_t^r], \qquad \text{each } t, r, \text{ say.} \tag{45}$$

According to (37)

$$G(q, Y^1(b^1), \ldots, Y^r(y^r), \ldots, Y^R(b^R)) - G(q, Y^1(b^1), \ldots, Y^r(b^r), \ldots, Y^R(b^R))$$
$$= \sum\nolimits_t Y_t^r(y_t^r) = Y_r^*(y^r), \text{ say.} \tag{46}$$

Solve (46) for Y_r in terms of Y_r^* as we can by (36), to get $G(p, Y) = G^*(p, Y^*)$, say, where G^* and Y^* still satisfy (Y1)–(Y2) and (36). Drop the asterisks to get (37) and (40) in this normalization.

Now vary y_t, if possible, keeping $Y_t(y_t)$ and y_s, $s \neq t$, constant. $g_t = G - \sum_{s \neq t} g_s$ remains unchanged. Hence

$$g_t(p, y_t) = G_t(p, Y_t(y_t)), \tag{47}$$

say, so that, by (37),

$$G(p, Y(y)) = \sum\nolimits_t G_t(p, Y_t(y_t)) \tag{48}$$

and, therefore,

$$G_t(p, Y_t) - G_t(p, 0) = G(p, Y_t) - G(p, 0) = H(p, Y_t), \tag{49}$$

say. This immediately yields (39), (42), and (43), where

$$d_t(p) = G_t(p, 0) = g_t(p, b_t), \quad d(p) = G(p, 0) = g(p, b) \tag{50}$$

and, with (48),

$$H\left(p, \sum Y_t\right) = \sum H(p, Y_t), \qquad \text{each } Y_t \in I = \Pi^r I_t^r, \text{ each } t. \tag{51}$$

(51) does not imply (41) immediately since we only proved it when $Y_t^r \in I_t^r = [0, a_t^r\rangle$, each t, r.

Let us first prove (41) for a single firm. That is

$$H(p, Y_t + Z_t) - H(p, Y_t) = H(p, Z_t); \quad Y_t, Z_t, Y_t + Z_t \in I_t. \tag{52}$$

Since $H(0) = 0$ by (49), the two sides of (52) are certainly equal when $Y_t = 0$. I will show that they are for any $\tilde{Y}_t \in I_t$ such that $\tilde{Y}_t + Z_t \in I_t$ also. We can increase Y_t to $\tilde{Y}_t$ from 0 by increasing Y_t^1 to $\tilde{Y}_t^1$ first, then Y_t^2 to $\tilde{Y}_t^2, \ldots$, then Y_t^R to $\tilde{Y}_t^R$. I will do so, showing that $H(p, Y_t + Z_t) - H(p, Y_t)$ remains constant, and hence equal to $H(p, Z_t)$, throughout.

First notice that

$$H(p, Y_t + Z_t) - H(p, Y_t) = H(p, Y + Z_t) - H(p, Y), \tag{53}$$

where each $Y^r \in I^r = \sum_t I^r_t$. Begin with each $Y^r_t = 0$ and each $Y^r_s = d^r_s = \min(.9a^r_s, 1)$, $s \neq t$. ($\Omega3$) ensures the existence of at least one $d^r_s > 0$, each r. Increase Y^1_t from 0 to $\tilde{Y}^1_t$ or $\sum_{s \neq t} d^1_s$, whichever is the smaller, dropping Y^1_t, $s \neq t$, towards zero in such a way as to keep Y constant. The right-hand sides of (52) and (53) are unaffected by these changes: hence too, their common left-hand side. (52) therefore continues to hold. If $\tilde{Y}^1_t \leqslant \sum_{s \neq t} d^1_s$, we now move to the second factor $r = 2$. If not, we next change Y^1_s back to d^1_s, $s \neq 1$, keeping $Y^1_t = \sum_{s \neq t} d^1_s$. This affects neither side of (52), and we are now in a position to increase Y^1_t once more, reducing the other Y^1_s to keep Y constant.

Repeating such moves as often as necessary we finally bring Y^1_t to $\tilde{Y}^1_t$ without affecting either side of (52), which therefore continues to hold. Doing this for each factor r in turn, we finally get (52) with $Y_t = \tilde{Y}_t$. Since $\tilde{Y}_t$, Z_t are any pair of vectors satisfying the conditions of (52), this proves that equation in general. This proves (41) for each individual firm.

Now I will prove (41) for the economy as a whole. Take any Y, Z satisfying the conditions of (41). They can be written $Y = \sum Y_t$, $Z = \sum Z_t$ where the Y_t, Z_t satisfy those of (52). (51) therefore implies

$$\begin{aligned} &H(p, Y + Z) - H(p, Y) - H(p, Z) \\ &\qquad = \sum (H_t(p, Y_t + Z_t) - H(p, Y_t) - H(p, Z_t)) = 0, \quad \text{by (52)} \end{aligned}$$

(38)–(43) are therefore necessary for (37). Their sufficiency is obvious.

COROLLARY 1: (41) *is a well-known functional equation. Under any of many alternative assumptions, it is equivalent to*

$$H(p, Y) = \sum_r c^r(p) Y^r. \tag{54}$$

The one which seems most natural in our case is that,

(G8) $H(p, Y) = G(p, Y) - G(p, 0) \geqslant 0, \qquad \text{each } p,\ Y \in I.$

Given ($\Omega1$)–($\Omega3$), (Y1)–(Y2), (G7)–(G8), then (37) is equivalent to: (38), (40), (43) and

$$g_t(p, y_t) = G_t(p, Y_t(y_t)) = \sum_r c^r(p) Y^r_t(y^r_t) + d_t(p) \tag{55}$$

$$g(p, y) = G(p, Y(y)) = \sum_r c^r(p) Y^r(y^r) + d(p). \tag{56}$$

(44), (50), and (55) immediately imply that

$$c^r(q) = 1, \text{ each } r. \tag{57}$$

6. INTERPRETATION OF THE AGGREGATES

Looking first at the formal definition

$$Y_t^r(y_t^r) = g_t(q, b_t^1, \ldots, b_t^{r-1}, y_t^r, b_t^{r+1}, \ldots, b_t^R) - g_t(q, b_t) \tag{58}$$

in (44), we see that the quantities of the fixed factors are measured in terms of their earning power at the base prices q. In general, indeed, (55) shows that an extra unit of the rth factor earns the firm lucky enough to get it £$c^r(p)$ at prices p. At the base prices q it earns it £1 by (57).

This 'explains' why the quantities of the fixed factors held by different firms add up, so that

$$Y^r(y^r) = \textstyle\sum_t Y_t^r(y_t^r). \tag{59}$$

They represent profit-earning capacity, and the profits earned by the individual firms add up to the total profits in the economy as a whole.

That the quantity of a fixed factor in the economy should be the sum of the quantities in the individual firms is highly acceptable, as it is that

$$Y_t^r(\cdot) \text{ is continuous and strongly increasing, each } t, r, \tag{60}$$

as we know from (38).

It would be pleasant, too, if the quantity of a factor were to double, when that of each of the corresponding inputs did so: in general, that is, if

$$Y_t^r(\cdot) \text{ is positively homogeneous of degree one.} \tag{61}$$

It seems clear that this would happen if there were constant returns to scale, since each added consignment of fixed inputs would be combined with the same variable goods to yield the same increase in profits. We will see later in this section that this is indeed so, so that (61) holds as well as (59) and (60) if each firm works under constant returns to scale.

(59), (60), and (61) comprise between them almost everything which we might wish to require of such measures. The difficulty remains, however, that the aggregates are tied to the particular technology, as in Nataf's case, and that the quantity of the fixed factors in the economy as a whole depends on the distribution of the fixed inputs among the firms, and not just on the total quantity of each of them.[37] The discussion in Section 2 makes it clear

[37] Except in the highly restrictive case in which

$$Y_t^r = \textstyle\sum d_i^r(y_{ti}^r - b_{ti}^r)$$

in the obvious notation. In this case fixed inputs within each class are perfect substitutes for each other, the equilibrium price ratio being d_i^r/d_j^r, whatever the circumstances; so that there is 'really' only one fixed input in each class. Or, of course, in that in which each fixed input is used by just one firm, or in the obvious combination of these cases.

that this must be so: there are no market forces to ensure that each firm makes equally profitable use of the fixed inputs, because there is no arrangement for mutually profitable exchange of such inputs between the firms. Moreover, the fixed inputs really are *given* in our model, so that there is no question of having to explain them in a wider model of the economy as a whole, in which the demand for them by these firms is faced by a supply from their producers, the only meeting-point being the total quantity of each fixed input.

Note, by the way, the absence of Nataf's arbitrary weights in this case. This is due to the fact that the profits of different firms do naturally add up.

There are two natural ways in which we can think of these aggregates: as index numbers of the quantities of the corresponding inputs, or as quantities of the factors, thought of as 'intermediate goods' produced from these with production functions

$$Y_t^r(y_t^r), \qquad \text{each } t,\, r \tag{62}$$

for individual firms or for the economy as a whole

$$Y^r(y^r) = \sum_t Y_t^r(y_t^r).$$

Either interpretation is perfectly acceptable under constant returns, where (61) holds as well as (59) and (60). However, (61) does not hold in general, and the idea that an index number should double when each of its component series does, seems fundamental to me. In general, therefore, I prefer the 'intermediate good' interpretation, which has the further advantage that the fictitious industries producing these intermediate goods can be introduced into complete models, should one after all wish to determine the *given* Y_t^r.

It will be convenient to write the gross profit functions of the individual firms and the economy as a whole in terms of these fictitious intermediate goods as

$$G_t(p,\, Y_t) = \sum c^r(p)\, Y_t^r + d_t(p) \tag{63}$$

$$G(p,\, Y) = \sum c^r(p)\, Y^r + d(p) \tag{64}$$

as we can by (55) and (56), where, of course

$$Y = \sum Y_t, \quad d = \sum d_t. \tag{65}$$

I will call these *quasi-gross profit functions*, because they are defined in terms of the fictitious fixed factors instead of the genuine fixed inputs. Similarly, we have the *quasi-production possibility sets* $\tilde{S}_t(Y_t)$, $\tilde{S}(Y)$ as against the *production possibility sets* proper $S_t(y_t)$, $S(y)$ *quasi-technologies*, and, where appropriate, *quasi-production functions*.

Because of (64) and (65) the quasi-gross profits in the economy as a whole are unchanged if we shift fixed factors about among the firms, keeping the totals constant.[38] Since this quasi-gross profit function defines the quasi-production possibility set $\tilde{S}(Y)$ for the economy as a whole, this, too, is unaffected. Hence each of the firms must use the fixed *factors*—as contrasted with the fixed *inputs*—equally effectively. That is, the lack of a market for the fixed factor is not felt: in guaranteeing that the variable goods be distributed efficiently over the given fixed factors, the market for the variable goods guarantees that the fixed factors themselves be used as efficiently as possible. Indeed (32) and (55) immediately imply that the efficiency price of the rth factor

$$Q^r = c^r(p), \qquad \text{each } r. \tag{66}$$

Earlier in this section I promised to show formally that we could normalize so that

$Y_t^r(\cdot)$ is positively homogeneous of degree one, each t, r,

if each firm produced under constant returns. According to the argument leading up to ($G4$) in Section 3, constant returns implies

$$g_t(p, ky_t) = kg_t(p, y_t), \quad y_t,\, ky_t \in \Omega_t,\, k \geqslant 0. \tag{67}$$

Let us assume further that

($\Omega 5$) if $y_t \in \Omega_t$ and $k \geqslant 1$, then $ky_t \in \Omega_t$,

since it is clearly sufficient for (67) to assume it for all $k \geqslant 1$. (67) then yields

$$\sum_r c^r(p)\{Y_t^r(ky_t^r) - kY_t^r(y_t^r)\} + (1-k)d_t(p) = 0 \tag{68}$$

if $y^r \in \Omega^r$ and $k \geqslant 1$. Solving for $Y_t^r(ky_t^r) - kY_t^r(y_t^r)$ we immediately see that

$$Y_t^r(ky_t^r) - kY_t^r(y_t^r) = \alpha_t^r(k), \text{ say}, \quad k \geqslant 1,\, y_t^r \in \Omega_t^r, \tag{69}$$

since the right-hand side of the equation cited is independent of y_t^r. Now

$$\begin{aligned} \alpha_t^r(ab) &= Y_t^r(aby_t^r) - aY_t^r(bY_t^r) + a\{Y_t^r(by_t^r) - bY_t^r(y_t^r)\} \\ &= \alpha_t^r(a) - a\alpha_t^r(b), \quad a, b \geqslant 1 \\ &= \alpha_t^r(b) - b\alpha_t^r(a), \text{ by symmetry,} \end{aligned} \tag{70}$$

so that

$$\frac{\alpha_t^r(a)}{a-1} = \frac{\alpha_t^r(b)}{b-1} = \beta_t^r, \text{ say}, \quad a, b > 1. \tag{71}$$

[38] This is quite different from keeping the total quantities of the fixed *inputs* constant, of course, since different firms will, in general, not use such inputs equally efficiently.

Substituting into (69), we get

$$Y_t^{*r}(ky_t^r) = kY_t^{*r}(y_t^r) \quad \text{if} \quad y_t^r \in \Omega_t^r, \quad k \geqslant 1 \tag{72}$$

as required for (61), where

$$Y_t^{*r}(y_t^r) = Y_t^r(y_t^r) - \beta_t^r, \tag{73}$$

a trivial change of origin.[39] (68) similarly becomes

$$G_t^*(p, Y_t^*) = \sum_r c^r(p) Y_t^{*r}, \tag{74}$$

so that there are *quasi-constant returns to scale*, too, in this normalization, that is, doubling the quantities of the fixed factors available to them just permits each firm to double the net output of each variable good.

This result has an interesting corollary. Consider a vintage model in which there is only one factor, capital, only one capital good—or machine—of each vintage, and constant returns to scale. Let t stand for the vintage, so that the 'firms' are 'plants' of the different vintages. In the appropriate normalization, the gross profit functions are

$$g_t(p, y_t) = c(p) Y_t(y_t), \quad \text{each } t, \tag{75}$$

where the y_t and Y_t are scalars, representing the number of machines used by the tth firm and the amount of capital represented by them. The only positively homogeneous functions of a single variable are

$$Y_t(y_t) = e_t y_t, \quad \text{each } t.^{40} \tag{76}$$

If we normalize so that $e_1 = 1$, this comes to measuring capital in 'equivalent period-one machines'. Of course

$$Y = \sum Y_t = \sum e_t y_t \tag{77}$$

is also measured in this way. Moreover (75) implies that each of the firms, and, by (77), the economy as a whole, has the same quasi-gross profit function $c(p)Z$, where Z can be taken to represent either the quantity of capital in an individual firm t, or in the economy as a whole. In terms of equivalent machines, therefore, all the firms, and the entire economy, have the same production possibilities.

[39] If $0 \in \Omega$, it comes to taking 0 instead of b in our definition (44) of Y_t^r, which is surely necessary. In general we can extend the positively homogeneous function $Y_t^{*r}(\cdot)$ over the positive orthant. The extended function vanishes when $y_t^r = 0$.

[40] We can have different coefficients for positive and negative y_t. Formally, therefore, we have to assume $y_t \geqslant 0$ if $y_t \in \Omega_t$. This is quite acceptable.

7. INTERPRETATION OF THE GROSS PROFIT FUNCTIONS IN TERMS OF INDEPENDENT PLANTS

According to (63) and (64) we can write the quasi-gross profit functions in the form

$$G_t(p, Y_t) = \sum_r c^r(p) Y_t^r + d_t(p); \quad Y_t^r \in I_t^r = [0, a_t^r\rangle \tag{78}$$

$$G(p, Y) = \sum_r c^r(p) Y^r + d(p); \quad Y^r \in I^r = [0, a^r\rangle, \tag{79}$$

where, of course,

$$Y = \sum Y_t, \quad d = \sum d_t, \quad a^r = \sum_t a_t^r. \tag{80}$$

(78) and (79) remind one of the relationship $g(p, y) = \sum g_t(p, y_t)$ between the gross profit functions of the economy as a whole and of the individual firms which make it up.

Can, then, the components on the right-hand sides of (78) and (79) be interpreted as the quasi-gross profit functions of individual plants?

We will see below that they often can be, though, of course, the plants in question are mere theoretical constructs, which would normally have no physical existence—mere fictions, in fact. For the moment, assume that we are in such a case, and see what we can learn.

Notice first that the rth plant in both (78) and (79) has a quasi-gross profit function

$$c^r(p)Z, \tag{81}$$

where Z may be interpreted either as the quantity of the rth factor in the tth firm, or in the entire economy. All of these plants, having the same quasi-gross profit function, have the same quasi-technology. Moreover it clearly yields quasi-constant returns to scale. We may call them the *plants using the* r^{th} *factor*. Because of the quasi-constant returns, doubling the quantity of the rth fixed factor available to the tth firm doubles its net output

$$x_t^r = Y_t^r c'^r(p)^{41} \tag{82}$$

from its plant using this factor.

This helps us to understand why shunting fixed factors back and forth among the firms does not affect what happens in the economy as a whole. Because of the quasi-constant returns, the same quantities of the variable goods are associated with each unit of the rth factor, wherever it is located.

[41] The prime denotes 'grad' as in the paragraph below (26).

In addition to these *fixed factor-using* plants, each firm has in general a *basic plant* with gross profit function $d_t(p)$, which produces a net amount

$$x_t^0 = d_t'(p) \tag{83}$$

of the variable goods, say, at prices p, however much of the fixed factors are available to it. Because of (S1)–(S2) the production possibility sets of these basic plants are necessarily closed and convex. Except for this, they may be of any sort whatever: in particular, those in different firms may differ as much as we like. Since the plants using the fixed factors are the same in all the firms, any difference between their quasi-technologies appears in the basic plants. We may regard them as using fixed inputs specific to the individual firms, which are not listed in y. In that sense (Ω3) in Section 4 merely tells us that only such fixed inputs as are used in at least two firms are listed, and is not really a genuine restriction at all.

If each firm produces under quasi-constant returns, each $d_t(p) \equiv 0$, and so, too, does $d(p)$. There are therefore no specific plants, and all the firms have the same given technology. The only difference between their actual technologies therefore lies in the aggregation functions $Y_t^r(\cdot)$, or, if you like, in the efficiency of their 'fixed factor-producing plants', as defined in Section 4.

We saw in Section 6, of course, that there are quasi-constant returns, in an appropriate normalization, if there are proper constant returns. Of course this condition is far from necessary.

For the interpretation in terms of separate plants to be legitimate, each $c^r(\cdot)$ and $d_t(\cdot)$ must satisfy (G1) and (G2), that is, be positively homogeneous of degree one and closed convex. In finding whether this is so we can use the fact that each $G_t(p, Y_t)$ and $G(p, Y)$, as admissible gross profit functions, do so.

Now

$$d_t(p) = G_t(p, 0), \quad d(p) = G(p, 0), \qquad \text{by (78) and (79)}, \tag{84}$$

so that they satisfy (G1)–(G2) like the G's if $0 \in I_t$ or $0 \in I$ as the case may be. Moreoever

$$\begin{aligned} c^r(p) &= \{G_t(p, \tilde{Y}_t^1, \ldots, Y_t^r, \ldots, \tilde{Y}_t^R) - G_t(p, \tilde{Y})\}/(Y_t^r - \tilde{Y}_t^r) \\ &= \{G(p, \tilde{Y}^1, \ldots, Y^r, \ldots, \tilde{Y}^R) - G(p, \tilde{Y})\}/(Y^r - \tilde{Y}^r), \end{aligned} \tag{85}$$

so that it is certainly positively homogeneous of degree one like the G's and therefore satisfies (G1).

The question is: do the $c^r(p)$ also satisfy (G2), that is, are they closed convex?

Consider first the case in which $0 \in I_t$, each t, in the chosen normalization, at least one firm t, or the economy as a whole, produces under quasi-constant returns, and, for each r, at least one of the entities producing under quasi-constant returns permits the use of a strictly positive amount of the rth fixed factor.[42] Then (85) yields

$$c^r(p) = G_t(p, 0, \ldots, Y_t^r, \ldots, 0)/Y_t^r \quad \text{or} \quad G(p, 0, \ldots, Y^r, \ldots, 0)/Y^r \tag{86}$$

for the entity in question, with Y_t^r or $Y^r > 0$. Hence $c^r(p)$, like the G's, satisfies (G2).

In this case, therefore, the interpretation in terms of independent plants is certainly legitimate.

Next let us drop the assumption that any of the firms produces under quasi-constant returns. Having done so we are free to use the normalization (44), in which

$$I_t^r = [0, a_t^r\rangle, \quad I^r = [0, a^r\rangle, \quad a^r = \sum a_t^r, \tag{87}$$

are the domains of Y_t^r and Y^r respectively. (84) therefore implies that, like the G's,

$$\text{each } d_t(p), \text{ and } d(p), \text{ satisfies (G1)–(G2)} \tag{88}$$

Let us now assume that

$$\text{each } a_t^r = \infty. \tag{89}$$

This will only be true, of course, if each Ω_t^r is unbounded above, so that there is no upper limit to the potential supply of inputs in any class to any firm, and if having an indefinitely large supply of the inputs in any particular class permits any firm to earn indefinitely large gross profits.

When considering any particular firm t, or the economy, I may certainly require

$$p \in R_t^0 = \{p \mid d_t(p) < \infty\},$$

that is,

$$p \in R^0 = \{p \mid d(p) < \infty\} = \cap_t R_t^0 \tag{90}$$

as the case may be, since the breakdown of an infinite gross profit function into components is of little interest. I will do so.

Taking $\tilde{Y}_t = 0$ and letting $Y_t^r \to \infty$ in (85) we immediately see that each $c^r(p)$ is convex in each R_t^0, and therefore in R^0. Is it closed convex? If not, there is a *frontier point q of and in*

$$R^r = \{p \mid c^r(p) < \infty\} \tag{91}$$

[42] Because of (G2), for each r, the same limit of I_t^r must be zero for each firm producing under quasi-constant returns. All the same, this is a weak assumption. It will hold, for instance, if $0 \in \Omega_t$, each $t \in \Theta$, say, where Θ is a set of firms producing under genuine constant returns, at least one member of $\Theta \in T(r)$, each r, and, of course, you cannot have negative fixed inputs.

such that

$$\lim\inf\{c^r(p)\,|\,p \to q\} = c^r(q) - \gamma; \quad \gamma > 0. \tag{92}$$

Choose a sequence

$$p^n \to q \qquad \text{such that} \qquad c^r(p^n) \to c^r(q). \tag{93}$$

We have already seen that we may take $q \in R_t^0$ without loss of generality. Assume

$$q \in \text{Int } R_t^0, \qquad \text{some } t. \tag{94}$$

Then the sequence $\{d_t(p^n)\}$ is ultimately bounded. Hence it has a limit point

$$d_t(q) + \delta, \tag{95}$$

say. Choose a sub-sequence which converges to this limit and relabel the corresponding p^n: $p^1, p^2, \ldots$. (93) continues to hold. Moreover, since $G_t(p, Y_t) = \sum c^r Y_t^r + d_t$ is closed convex by (G1), $\lim G_t(p^n, Y_t) \geqslant G_t(q, Y_t)$. Hence

$$-\gamma Y_t^r + \delta \geqslant 0, \quad \gamma \geqslant 0. \tag{96}$$

Letting $Y^r \to \infty$ in (96), we have a contradiction. If, therefore, $c^r(p)$ is not closed convex, there is a point q in the intersection of R^r with its frontier which is also in the intersection of each R_t^0 with its frontier. If the intersection of all these intersections is empty for each r, the interpretation in terms of independent plants is legitimate, as it is if we consider only prices in a set P which does not contain any such intersections.

Since we know that the efficient output of a set of independent plants is the sum of the efficient outputs of each taken separately.

$$x_t = \sum c'^r(p)\, Y_t^r(p) + d_t'(p) \tag{97}$$

$$x = \sum c'(p)\, Y^r + d'(p) \tag{98}$$

are the production plans of the individual firms and the economy, where the primes denote gradients, as in the paragraph following (26), when the interpretation in terms of independent plants is legitimate.

Even if it is illegitimate, (97)–(98) are still true whenever all the functions of p are differentiable, as they are almost everywhere in the set where G_t, or G, is finite by (84), (85), and (20).

Since (97)–(98) are the main implications of the representation in terms of independent plants—indeed the only ones in this section—it is not seriously misleading even when illegitimate.

(97) also permits us to examine the substitution and complementarity relationships between the factors and the variable goods. Despite the interpretation of (78) in terms of independent plants for each factor, it turns

out that they may be either substitutes or complements for each other, or for the variable inputs.

Admittedly this is in terms of rather jejune, non-Hicksian, definitions of substitution and complementarity.

Because the shadow price of the rth fixed factor

$$Q^r = c^r(p) \tag{99}$$

by (66), we cannot vary it independently. Moreover it is the same however much of the fixed factors the firm has at its disposal, so that the x's and Y's cannot be written as functions of p and Q. Hicks's definitions are therefore difficult to apply and we are thrown back on the idea that two inputs should be *complements* if increasing the supply of one increases the marginal product of the other, and *substitutes* if it decreases it.[43] Of course this is immediately applicable only if there is a single output and the production function is smooth.[44] Assume this is so and that there is only one variable input. Given its price q in terms of the product as numeraire—that is its marginal product—we can divide the fixed factors into two groups, according to whether they are complementary with it or substitutes for it. I will prove

fixed factors in the same group are substitutes; in different groups, complements. (100)

The quantity of the variable input, *measured as an input*, is

$$z = -\sum \dot{c}^r(q)\, Y^r - \dot{d}(q), \tag{101}$$

where the point represents differentiation with respect to q. Now

$$\frac{\partial q}{\partial Y^r} = -\frac{\partial z}{\partial Y^r}\bigg/\frac{\partial z}{\partial q} = \dot{c}^r\frac{\partial q}{\partial z}. \tag{102}$$

Now $\partial q/\partial z \leqslant 0$ because of the declining marginal productivity of the variable input implied by (S2). Hence the variable input and the rth fixed factor are

substitutes if $\dot{c}^r \geqslant 0$[45]

complements if $\dot{c}^r \leqslant 0$. (103)

[43] If they are *neutral*, that is if the marginal product is not affected, I will say they are both substitutes and complements. i and j are complements if $\phi_{ij} \geqslant 0$, substitutes if $\phi_{ij} \leqslant 0$, where ϕ is the production function and suffixes denote differentiation, so that the definitions are symmetric, as long as there is sufficient smoothness to yield $\phi_{ij} = \phi_{ji}$, which I assume there is.

[44] We could have several products, and hold their relative prices constant in the definition; in other words the 'single' product might be a Hicksian aggregate. So, for that matter, might the single variable input be. We could talk of declining efficiency prices instead of marginal products if the production functions were not smooth, but then i might be a substitute for j, and j a complement for i.

[45] $c^r > 0$ means, of course, that the input good is an output of the rth plant. What does this matter, since it is only a fictional plant in any case? If we could have $Y^r \to \infty$, of course, it would be an actual output eventually, but even that is not very disturbing (Gorman, 1965*a*).

Moreover, by (99) and (102)

$$\frac{\partial Q^r}{\partial Y^s} = \dot{c}^r \frac{\partial q}{\partial Y^s} = \dot{c}^r \dot{c}^s \frac{\partial q}{\partial z}, \tag{104}$$

which immediately implies (100).

Since the quantity of a factor increases when the corresponding fixed inputs increase, fixed inputs corresponding to factors in the complementary group are complementary with the variable input, those corresponding to factors in the substitute group are substitutes for it. Moreover fixed inputs corresponding to different factors in the same group are substitutes, while those corresponding to factors in different groups are complements.

As Gorman (1965*a*) has shown,[46] these results hold 'on the average' when there are several variable inputs. However, the average in question is not sufficiently interesting to justify my spelling the result out here.

When discussing the 'independent plants' interpretation of (78), I pointed out that it meant that each firm would make exactly the same use of a unit of a fixed factor as any other. (97) implies that this is true in general, at least 'almost everywhere'.[47]

This is pretty damaging for aggregation. Not everyone will make equally efficient use of a lathe, for instance—indeed some firms may have no use for it at all; but any who use it at all, will produce new variable goods on it in the same proportion as anyone else—*and in the same proportion as someone who gets a new steel press instead.*

Of course firms may vary greatly in the relative efficiency with which they fabricate the different fixed factors from the corresponding inputs, and, if so, will presumably vary greatly in the proportions in which they hold these fixed factors. Or the production from their basic plants may be relatively large. Either phenomenon can lead to different firms producing, or using, the different variable goods in quite different proportions.

Wriggle as I may, however, I cannot persuade myself that this condition for aggregation is remotely likely to be met in practice in an economy as a whole, with theoretically interesting definitions of the fixed factors.

It may be more reasonable for a model of an industry, or in cases where the variable goods are themselves highly aggregated, as in vintage capital models, for instance.

It certainly does not help justify the practice of fitting aggregate production functions.[48]

[46] There are a pair of idiotic mistakes, which luckily cancel out, in this section of Gorman (1965*a*), and I rule out the possibility of a fixed factor being a substitute for the variable good for the reason given in n. 44, but the statement in the text is nevertheless true.

[47] 'In general' = 'even if the "independent plant" interpretation is not legitimate'; 'almost everywhere' = 'except on a set of Lebesgue measure zero'.

[48] This criticism holds even when the $c^r(p)$ are not closed convex and not differentiable at the given prices p. An extra unit of the rth factor changes the production possibilities, and therefore the efficient production plan, for the economy as a whole by the same amount whichever firm t gets it. But the only firm whose individual production plan changes is t. Hence the changes which are profitable are the same whatever firm gets the extra unit.

20

Some Engel Curves

Editorial Summary

The first version of this paper was presented to a workshop at LSE in January 1977. Entitled 'On Polynomial Engel Curves', it was a special case of the paper reprinted here, which appeared in the Festschrift for Sir Richard Stone. The generalization was in fact suggested by John Wise after the seminar.

The question addressed is so straightforward that its consequences are all the more surprising. What restrictions, if any, are placed on the preferences of a rational individual whose Engel curves are of the form

$$x_i = \sum_{r \in R} b^{ri}(p)\psi^r(m), \tag{0.1}$$

where R is some finite set?

It turns out that the rank of the matrix $[b^{ri}(p)]$ can be at most 3. When it is exactly 3 then either $\psi^r(m) = m(\ln m)^r$, $\psi^r(m) = m^{r+1}$, or $\psi^r(m) = m\sin(r \ln m)$ (or $m\cos(r \ln m)$). In this case, the cost function of the consumer can be written as

$$g(u, p) = \phi(\alpha(p), \beta(p), \gamma(p), u) \tag{0.2}$$

so that it is as though there are only three commodities. Because g is concave in prices, one can be certain from the construction that α, β and γ are concave; but one cannot be certain that ϕ is a concave function of α, β and γ.[1] If it is concave, however, then α, β and γ can be treated as if they are the unit cost functions which are dual to linearly homogeneous utility functions, and ϕ as dual to a utility function F. This in turn means that the utility function can be expressed as

$$u = f(x) = \max_{y, w, z} \{F(a(y), b(z), c(w)) \,|\, y + z + w = x\}, \tag{0.3}$$

where a, b and c, are all linearly homogeneous. It is as if the consumer purchases a quantity x with which he or she can produce intermediate goods a, b and c from which actual utility is derived. The optimization problem simply ensures that each of the three intermediate goods is produced efficiently.

This result is so surprising that it is worth while returning to the original question to see why it was posed in the first place. One of Gorman's suggestions is that (0.1) arises naturally in the context of an aggregation problem. To see how this happens,

[1] If it is not concave, the interpretation is rather bizarre; see the Appendix to 'More Measures for Fixed Factors'.

let the demands of consumer t for commodity i be given by a function of prices, p, and income, m_t,

$$x_i^t = f_i^t(p, m_t), \tag{0.4}$$

so that aggregate demand is

$$x_i = \sum_{t=1}^{T} x_i^t = \sum_{t=1}^{T} f_i^t(p, m_t). \tag{0.5}$$

The aggregation problem which he poses in equation (1.2) can be expressed as

$$x_i = \sum_{t=1}^{T} f_i^t(p, m_t) = f_i(p, \phi(m_1, \ldots, m_T)) \tag{0.6}$$

for all i. That is, in what circumstances can aggregate demand—which is a function of the vector of incomes $(m_1, \ldots, m_T)$—be written as a function of some scalar $\phi(m_1, \ldots, m_T)$? Multiplying (0.6) by p_i and summing over i, one obtains, using (0.4) and (0.5),

$$\sum_{t=1}^{T} m_t = \sum_i p_i f_i(p, \phi(m_1, \ldots, m_T)) =: F(p, \phi(m_1, \ldots, m_T)). \tag{0.7}$$

As the left side of (0.7) depends upon the sum of incomes, so must the right side. Hence the aggregate in (0.6) can only be the sum of incomes. However, this is the representative consumer problem which Gorman solved in 1953, so we already know the answer to that question.

He then suggests that the ϕ in (0.6) might be a vector of aggregates, for example the mean and the variance of the income distribution. To see how that might lead to (0.1), suppose that there are two aggregates and that the aggregation question can be posed as

$$x_i = \sum_{t=1}^{T} f_i^t(p, m_t) = f_i(p, \phi^1(m_1, \ldots, m_T), \phi^2(m_1, \ldots, m_T)). \tag{0.8}$$

Solve the first two of the equations in (0.8) for $\phi^1(m_1, \ldots, m_T)$ and $\phi^2(m_1, \ldots, m_T)$ to obtain

$$\phi^i(m_1, \ldots, m_T) = \Phi^i\left(p, \sum_{t=1}^{T} f_1^t(p, m_t), \sum_{t=1}^{T} f_2^t(p, m_t)\right) \tag{0.9}$$

for $i = 1, 2$. Substituting these back into all of the equations in (0.8) and normalizing, we obtain

$$x_i = \sum_{t=1}^{T} f_i^t(p, m_t) = \tilde{f}_i\left(p, \tilde{\phi}^1\left(\sum_{t=1}^{T} \psi^{t1}(m_t)\right), \tilde{\phi}^2\left(\sum_{t=1}^{T} \psi^{t2}(m_t)\right)\right); \tag{0.10}$$

that is, even if aggregate demand depends upon two aggregates, it must depend upon two additive aggregates. This linearity forces aggregate demand to have the form

(0.1) above.[2] Hence, the question is not only a natural one to ask, but is also important. Requiring that there are two or more aggregates and that the demand system satisfies the usual Slutsky symmetry conditions have stronger implications than previously imagined.

[2] For a formal argument along these lines see Sect. 1 of 'More Measures for Fixed Factors'.

Some Engel Curves

1. INTRODUCTION[1]

In this paper I investigate the conditions under which rational[2] individuals have Engel curves of the type

$$x_i = \sum_{r \in R} b^{ri}(p)\psi^r(m), \quad \text{for each good } i, \tag{1.1}$$

in the usual notation, where R is a finite set. They are of interest for three, related, uses:

(i) for fitting to surveys;

(ii) as a generalization of linear Engel curves, which have turned out to be useful in several contexts, particularly as the solution of the aggregation problem

$$x_i = f^i(p, \phi(m)), \quad \text{for each } i,\ m = (m_1, m_2, \ldots, m_T), \tag{1.2}$$

where m_t is the income of the tth household, x_i the market demand for good i, and $\phi(\cdot)$ a scalar aggregate;

(iii) as the solution of the more general version of (1.2) in which $\phi(\cdot)$ is a vector of aggregates.

Incidentally, the $\psi(\cdot)$ may contain equivalent adult and other corrections. On the other hand, they are rendered less interesting by the fact that m in (1.1), and each m_t in (1.2), stands for *money* income.

If the Engel curves in (1.1) represent well-behaved preferences, we find that

(i) The rank $R(B(p))$ of the coefficient matrix $B(p) = [b^{ri}(p)]$ is at most 3.

(ii) When $R(B(p)) = 3$,[3] either

[1] I had planned a contribution worthier of Sir Richard Stone, in which the results would have been related to more general ideas. Unfortunately, I miscalculated the time available and this paper is the rather incomplete result.

The ideas in this paper were first presented to the Quantitative Economics Workshop at the London School of Economics in January 1977 and January 1978. I am grateful to John Wise, who, for the special case of polynomial Engel curves, suggested the probable importance of the rank of the coefficient matrix. I am also grateful to John Muellbauer and my colleagues at the LSE for their comments. I thank the SSRC for its funding and the LSE for my colleagues.

[2] Having smooth strictly quasi-concave preferences, and being greedy.

[3] Of course the rank of $B(p)$ depends on p in general. It is $\leqslant 3$ everywhere. If it equals 3 at a point, it will in an open neighbourhood of it. The analysis of $R(B(p)) = 3$, which takes up most of the paper, may be thought of as carried out in such a neighbourhood. Presumably regions in which it takes lower values commonly divide those in which it takes higher. See Sect. 5.

(*a*) each $\psi^r(m) = m(\log m)^r$, and each $r \in R$ is an integer, or
(*b*) each $\psi^r(m) = m^{r+1}$, or
(*c*) each $\psi^r(m) = m \sin(r \log m)$ or $m \cos(r \log m)$, for each $r \geqslant 0$,[4]

with $0 \in R$ in each case. In Section 5, I conjecture that $R = \{-m\omega, -(m-1)\omega, \ldots, 0, \omega, \ldots, n\omega\}$ with a few gaps sometimes.

(iii) When $R(B(p)) = 3$ the cost function underlying (1.1) may be written

$$m = \phi(\alpha(p), \beta(p), \gamma(p), u), \tag{1.3}$$

where $\alpha(\cdot)$, $\beta(\cdot)$, $\gamma(\cdot)$ are unit cost functions, which may be thought of as corresponding to baskets of commodities. It is tempting to rewrite (1.3) in primal form as

$$u = f(x) = \max\{F(a(y), b(z), c(w)) \mid y + z + w \leqslant x\}, \tag{1.4}$$

where $a(\cdot)$, $b(\cdot)$, $c(\cdot)$ are the corresponding *conical*[5] production functions, in which case $\phi(\cdot, u)$ in (1.3) would be the cost function corresponding to $u = F(\cdot)$. Unfortunately $\phi(\cdot, u)$, though conical, is not necessarily concave, so that this interpretation is not strictly justified. When it is, we may say that the various goods affect our welfare through the basic wants a, b, c—an interpretation which remains enlightening even when not strictly justified.

(iv) (ii*b*) clearly includes the polynomials. When $R(B(p)) = 3$, then $\phi(\cdot, u)$ in (1.3) is additively homogeneous, as well as conical, that is, multiplicatively homogeneous. That is,

$$\phi(\lambda\theta, u) = \lambda\phi(\theta, u); \qquad \phi(\theta + \mu e, u) = \phi(\theta, u) + \mu, \tag{1.5}$$

so that

$$\phi(\lambda\theta + \mu e, u) = \lambda\phi(\theta, u) + \mu,$$
$$\phi(\alpha, \beta, \gamma, u) = \alpha + (\beta - \alpha)\psi[(\gamma - \alpha)/(\beta - \alpha), u],^{6} \text{ say}, \tag{1.6}$$

where $e = (1, 1, \ldots, 1)$, $\lambda \geqslant 0$, so that, where justified, (1.4) may be rewritten

$$u = f(x) = \max\{\bar{F}(a(y), b(z)) \mid c(x - y - z) \geqslant 1\}, \text{ say}, \tag{1.7}$$

so that $c = 1$ may be thought of as the satisfaction of a basic 'need', or, if you like, an overhead of existence. These results are extended to a wider class of Engel curves at the end of Section 4.

(v) Since $R(B) \leqslant 3$, quadratics are particularly interesting. The cost function is then

$$m = \alpha(p) + \delta(p)/(1 - u\varepsilon(p)), \tag{1.8}$$

[4] Both terms will normally occur.
[5] i.e. positively homogeneous of degree one. The term is Sydney Afriat's.
[6] $\psi(\delta, u) = \phi(0, 1, \delta, u)$.

where

$$\delta = \beta - \alpha, \qquad \varepsilon = (\gamma - \beta)/(\beta - \alpha). \tag{1.9}$$

(vi) When $R(B(p)) = 2$, the cost function may be written

$$m = \phi(\alpha(p), \beta(p), u), \tag{1.10}$$

where $\alpha(\cdot)$, $\beta(\cdot)$ are once more unit cost functions and $\phi(\cdot, u)$ is conical but not necessarily either concave or additively homogeneous.

Iff it is closed concave, the corresponding primal may be written

$$u = f(x) = \max\{F(a(y), b(z)) \mid y + z \leqslant x\}, \tag{1.11}$$

where $u = F(\cdot)$ is the dual of $\phi(\cdot, u)$, $a(\cdot)$, $b(\cdot)$ of $\alpha(\cdot)$, $\beta(\cdot)$. When $\phi(\cdot, u)$ is additively homogeneous, (1.10) may be written

$$m = \alpha(p) + u\delta(p), \qquad \delta = \beta - \alpha, \tag{1.12}$$

so that the Engel curves are straight lines, as in the standard case referred to in the opening paragraph.

(vii) When $R(B(p)) = 1$, $u = f(x)$ is homothetic, and the Engel curves straight lines radiating from the origin.

2. PRELIMINARIES

It will be convenient to write the equations of the Engel curves in terms of the budget shares $w_j = p_j x_j/m$, and accordingly to use the logarithmic cost function

$$h(q, u) = \log g(p, u) = \log m; \qquad q_j = \log p_j, \qquad \text{for each } j, \tag{2.1}$$

since

$$w_j = h_j(q, u), \qquad \text{for each } j, \tag{2.2}$$

where I use suffixes to function names to denote differentiation.

Consider complete systems of Engel curves of the type

$$h_j(q, u) = \sum_{r \in R} a(r, j; q)\phi(r; h(q, u)); \qquad \text{for each good } j, \tag{2.3}$$

where R is a finite set.

This is a curious notation. One would expect the labels r, j to appear as subscripts, as in $a_{rj}(q)$, or superscripts as in $a^{rj}(q)$, rather than as arguments, as in $a(r, j; q)$. However, I will be using subscripts to denote derivatives, and powers will come into the analysis so often that I cannot use the superscript notation either. To distinguish between the discrete labels such as r, j and the continuous variables such as q, m, I will put the labels before, and the variables after, the ';' in each case. It will frequently be convenient not to mention the latter explicitly, writing $a(r, j)$ for $a(r, j; q)$, for instance.

Assume without loss of generality that this representation is unique so that

$$\sum_{r\in R} c_r\phi(r;\cdot)=0 \quad \text{implies} \quad \text{each } c_r=0 \tag{2.4}$$

$$\sum_{r\in R} c_r a(r,\cdot;\cdot)=0 \quad \text{implies} \quad \text{each } c_r=0,$$

the former since we would otherwise have

$$\sum_{r\in R} a(r,j;q)\phi(r;h)=\sum_{r\in R}\left\{a(r,j;q)+c_r\sum_{s\in R} d_s a(s,j;q)\right\}\phi(r;h), \tag{2.5}$$

the latter since we would otherwise have

$$\sum_{r\in R} a(r,j;q)\phi(r;h)=\sum_{r\in R}\left\{a(r,j;q)+d_r\sum_{s\in R} c_s a(s,j;q)\right\}\phi(r;h) \tag{2.6}$$

for any $d_R=(d_r)_{r\in R}$, so that (2.3) would not be unique as required in either case.

What else can we say about

$$\phi(R;\cdot)=\{\phi(r;\cdot)\mid r\in R\} \tag{2.7}$$

and the space $\Phi(R)$ it spans?

In the first place

$$\sum_{r\in R}\left\{\sum_j a(r,j;q)\right\}\phi(r;h)=\sum_j h_j(q,u)=\sum w_j=1, \tag{2.8}$$

so that $1\in\Phi(R)$ and we can, and do, take

$$\phi(0;h)=1 \tag{2.9}$$

without loss of generality, so that (2.8) yields

$$\sum_j a(0,j;q)=1; \qquad \sum_j a(r,j;q)=0, \qquad r\neq 0\in R. \tag{2.10}$$

Now look at the linear space, $\mathcal{A}(q)$, spanned by the vectors

$$a(r;q)=(a(r,1;q),a(r,2;q),\ldots), \qquad \text{for each } r\in R. \tag{2.11}$$

We will see in the next section that its dimension $N(q)\leqslant 3$, for each q, so that the $a(r;q)$, $r\in R$, will typically be linearly dependent. However,

$$\sum_{r\in R} c(r;q)a(r;q)=0 \quad \text{implies} \quad c(0;q)=0 \tag{2.12}$$

because of (2.10), so that $a(0;q)$ is linearly independent of the other $a(r;q)$, $r\in R$.

So much for the condition that the budget shares add up to one. I will now turn to the more powerful Slutsky or integrability conditions $h_{jk}(q, u) = h_{kj}(q, u)$. These will allow me to specify the admissible $\phi(r; h)$ completely.

Now

$$h_{jk} = \sum_{r\in R} a_k(r, j)\phi(r) + \sum_{r\in R} a(r, j)\phi'(r)\cdot \sum_{s\in R} a(s, k)\phi(s), \quad \text{for each } j, k, \tag{2.13}$$

by (2.3), where I have dropped the explicit reference to the variables q, h, as will frequently be convenient, and where $a_k(r, j) = \partial a(r, j; q)/\partial q_k$, $\phi'(r) = \mathrm{d}\phi(r; h)/\mathrm{d}h$.

Consider any $\phi'(r)\phi(s)$, $r, s\in R$. It may or may not belong to $\Phi(R)$. If not, add it to the basis $\phi(R;\cdot)$ to get $\phi(R^*;\cdot)$, say, spanning $\Phi(R^*)$. Next take any other $\phi'(r)\phi(s)$, $r, s\in R$. It may or may not belong to $\Phi(R^*)$, . . . ; since there are only a finite number of such products, we ultimately end up with a linear space $\Phi(T) \supseteq \Phi(R)$, with a basis $\phi(T; \cdot)$, $T \supseteq R$. Clearly, then

$$\phi'(r)\phi(s) = \sum_{t\in T} c_{rst}\phi(t), \qquad \text{for each } r, s\in R, \text{ say}, \tag{2.14}$$

and, in particular,

$$\phi'(r) = \phi'(r)\phi(0) = \sum_{t\in T} c_{r0t}\phi(t), \qquad \text{for each } r\in R, \tag{2.15}$$

and

$$\text{each } c_{0st} = 0, \tag{2.16}$$

since $\sum_{t\in T} c_{0st}\phi(t) = \phi'(0)\phi(s) = 0$, and $\phi(T; \cdot)$ is linearly independent.

Substitute from (2.14) into (2.13), and use the fact that $h_{jk} = h_{kj}$, to get

$$\sum_{r\in R}\sum_{s\in R} c_{rst}\{a(r, j)a(s, k) - a(r, k)a(s, j)\}$$

$$= a_j(t, k) - a_k(t, j), \quad \text{for each } t\in T \tag{2.17}$$

$$= 0, \quad \text{for each } t\notin R, \tag{2.18}$$

since $\phi(T; \cdot)$ is linearly independent, where we define

$$a(t, j; q) = 0, \qquad t\notin R. \tag{2.19}$$

Sum (2.18) over j, and use (2.10) and (2.16) to get

$$\sum_{r\in R} c_{r0t}a(r; q) = 0, \qquad \text{for each } t\notin R, \text{ each } k, \tag{2.20}$$

since $a(r; q) = (a(r, 1; q), a(r, 2; q), \ldots)$, and hence

to get

$$h_j(q, u) = \sum_{n=1}^{N} \left\{ \sum_{r \in R} b(r, n; q)\phi(r; h(q, u)) \right\} c(n, j; q). \tag{2.37}$$

Define the gradient of $h(\cdot, u)$ by

$$h'(q, u) = (h_1(q, u), h_2(q, u), \ldots) \tag{2.38}$$

and choose $u_1 < u_2 < \ldots < u_N$ such that $h'(q, u_1), h'(q, u_2), \ldots, h'(q, u_N)$ span $\mathscr{A}(q)$. Define

$$\theta(n; q) = h(q, u_n), \quad c(n; q) = (c(n, 1; q), c(n, 2; q), \ldots), \quad n = 1, 2, \ldots, N. \tag{2.39}$$

The θ's are functionally independent and

$$\theta'(m; q) = \sum_{n=1}^{N} \left\{ \sum_{r \in R} b(r, n; q)\phi(r; \theta(m; q)) \right\} c(n; q), \quad n = 1, 2, \ldots, N. \tag{2.40}$$

Solving this for the $c(n; q)$ in terms of the $\theta'(m; q)$ and substituting into (2.37), we get

$$h_j(q, u) = \sum_{n=1}^{N} \left\{ \sum_{r \in R} \mathrm{d}(r, n; q)\theta(r; h(q, u)) \right\} \theta_j(n, q), \text{ say,} \quad \text{for each } j, \tag{2.41}$$

so that

$$h(q, u) = H(\theta(1, q), \theta(2, q), \ldots, \theta(N, q), u), \tag{2.42}$$

given the necessary smoothness and connectivity.

Now $\theta(n, q) = h(q, u_n)$ is a logarithmic cost function, for each n, and may without loss of generality be taken to be the logarithmic *unit* cost function for a fictitious intermediate good, or composite commodity, produced under constant returns, that is, they may be taken to be the logarithmic prices of those intermediate goods. Now there is no integrability problem when there are only two goods, and it is the integrability conditions which I will be examining in Section 3. Hence my concentration on the case where $N > 2$.

So far I have not used the fact that the consumer's behaviour, and hence the budget shares, are unaffected when prices and income all change in the same proportion. It is easiest to approach this matter indirectly.

Take any 'logarithmic price index' $\alpha(q)$ such that

$$\sum_j \alpha_j(q) = 1, \tag{2.43}$$

so that $\exp \alpha(q)$ is homogeneous of degree one in the prices $p_j = \exp q_j$, and write

$$k(q, u) = h(q, u) - \alpha(q), \tag{2.44}$$

which may be thought of as a 'real' logarithmic expenditure function. Clearly

$$\sum_j k_j(q, u) = 0. \tag{2.45}$$

Now substitute $h = k + \alpha$ into (2.31) to get

$$k_j = \sum_{\lambda \in L} \sum_{m=0}^{M(\lambda)} b(\lambda, m, j) k^m e^{\lambda k}, \tag{2.46}$$

where

$$b(\lambda, n, j) = e^{\lambda\alpha} \sum_{m=n}^{M(\lambda)} \binom{m}{n} \alpha^{m-n} a(\lambda, m, j), \qquad \text{unless } n = \lambda = 0, \tag{2.47}$$

$$b(0, 0, j) = \sum_{n=0}^{M(0)} \alpha^m a(0, m, j) - \alpha_j, \tag{2.48}$$

or, equivalently,[7]

$$a(\lambda, n, j) = e^{-\lambda\alpha} \sum_{m=n}^{M(\lambda)} \binom{m}{n} (-\alpha)^{m-n} b(\lambda, m, j), \qquad \text{unless } n = \lambda = 0, \tag{2.49}$$

$$a(0, 0, j) = \sum_{m=0}^{M(0)} (-\alpha)^m b(0, m, j) + \alpha_j. \tag{2.50}$$

Multiplying each price p_j and income m by θ is the same as adding $\mu = \log \theta$ to each q, h, and α. Doing this in (2.46) and equating coefficients of $k^n e^{\lambda k}$ we get

$$b(\lambda, n, j; q + \mu e) = b(\lambda, n, j; q), \qquad \text{for each } \lambda, n, j, q, \mu, \tag{2.51}$$

where

$$e = (1, 1, \ldots, 1), \tag{2.52}$$

which is clearly sufficient as well as necessary for homogeneity. That the a's should be generated by b's, satisfying (2.51)–(2.52), as in (2.49)–(2.50), is therefore both necessary and sufficient for the homogeneity of the Engel system (2.31).

Finally a little more notation. Since the λ's are the latent roots of a general square matrix C, they may be complex. If so, they come in conjugate pairs. Write

[7] Since $h = k + \alpha$ is equivalent to $k = h - \alpha$, one merely replaces α in (2.47)–(2.48) by $-\alpha$ to get (2.49)–(2.50).

$$\lambda = \sigma + i\tau = (\sigma, \tau), \qquad r = (\lambda, m) = (\sigma + i\tau, m) = (\sigma, \tau, m) \tag{2.53}$$

$$R = \{(\lambda, m) \mid \lambda \in L, m = 0, 1, \ldots, M(\lambda)\} \tag{2.54}$$

$$S = \{\sigma \mid \sigma + i\tau \in L, \text{ some } \tau\}, \qquad T = \{\tau \mid \sigma + i\tau \in L, \text{ some } \sigma\}. \tag{2.55}$$

Note by the way that

$$0 \in R, \qquad \text{and hence} \qquad 0 \in L, 0 \in S, 0 \in T, \tag{2.56}$$

because $c_{00t} = 0$ for each t, since $\phi'(0; h) = 0$ and $\phi(T; \cdot)$ is linearly independent. It would be surprising were this not so!

3. THE MAIN THEOREM

THEOREM 1(a): *If the complete Engel system* (2.3) *reflects well-behaved preferences, the rank $N(q)$ of its coefficient matrix is at most* 3.

THEOREM 1(*b*): *When* $N(q) = 3$, (2.3) *takes one of the forms*

$$h_j(q, u) = a(j; q) + b(j; q)h + c(j; q) \sum_{m=1}^{M} C(m; q)h^m \tag{3.1}$$

$$h_j(q, u) = a(j; q) + b(j; q) \sum_{\sigma \in S}^{\sigma < 0} B(\sigma; q)e^{\sigma h} + c(j; q) \sum_{\sigma \in S}^{\sigma > 0} C(\sigma; q)e^{\sigma h} \tag{3.2}$$

$$h_j(q, u) = a(j; q) + b(j; q) \sum_{\tau \in T}^{\tau > 0} B(\tau; q)\cos \tau h + c(j; q) \sum_{\tau \in T}^{\tau > 0} C(\tau; q)\sin \tau h. \tag{3.3}$$

PROOF: Equation (2.35) will be used repeatedly, so I will record it here:

$$\begin{aligned}\sum_{m > n/2} (2m - n - 1)\{&a(\lambda, m, j)a(\mu - \lambda, n - m + 1, k) \\ &- a(\lambda, m, k)a(\mu - \lambda, n - m + 1, j)\} \\ + \sum_{\lambda > \mu/2} (2\lambda - \mu)\{&a(\lambda, m, j)a(\mu - \lambda, n - m, k) \\ &- a(\lambda, m, k)a(\mu - \lambda, n - m, j)\} \\ &= 0,\end{aligned} \tag{3.4}$$

when

$$\mu \notin L \qquad \text{or} \qquad \mu \in L, \ m > M(\mu). \tag{3.5}$$

I will proceed in a series of lemmas.

LEMMA 1: *Suppose S contains a positive element. Then*

$$a(r, j) = C(r)c(j), \text{ say,} \qquad \text{when } \sigma \geqslant 0, \qquad \text{unless } r = (\sigma + i\tau, m) = 0. \tag{3.6}$$

PROOF: Set

$$\sigma^* = \max\{\sigma \in S\} > 0, \qquad \tau^* = \max\{\tau \mid (\sigma^*, \tau) \in L\} \geqslant 0 \tag{3.7}$$

$$\lambda^* = \sigma^* + i\tau^*, \qquad m^* = M(\lambda^*), \qquad r^* = (\lambda^*, m^*), \tag{3.8}$$

and define the lexicographic ordering

$$\begin{aligned} r > r' \text{ if } \quad & \sigma > \sigma', \\ \text{or } \quad & \sigma = \sigma',\ \tau > \tau', \\ \text{or } \quad & \sigma = \sigma',\ \tau = \tau',\ m > m'. \end{aligned} \tag{3.9}$$

Set

$$c(j) = a(r^*, j), \quad \text{for each } j, \tag{3.10}$$

and erect the inductive hypothesis

$$a(r, j) = C(r)c(j), \text{ say,} \qquad \text{for each } j, \tag{3.11}$$

when

$$r > \bar{r} > 0, \text{ say.} \tag{3.12}$$

I will show that this implies that (3.11) holds for $\bar{r}$ too. Since it certainly holds for r^*, it will hold for each $r > 0$.

Take then $r^* > \bar{r} > 0$.

(i) If $\bar{\lambda} = \lambda^*$, $\bar{m} < m^*$, write down (3.4) with $\mu = 2\lambda^* \in L$, $n = \bar{m} + m^* - 1$, to get

$$(m^* - \bar{m})\{c(j)a(\bar{\lambda}, \bar{m}, k) - c(k)a(\bar{\lambda}, \bar{m}, j)\} = 0, \tag{3.13}$$

all the other terms vanishing by the inductive hypothesis (3.11)–(3.12). Hence (3.11) holds for $r = \bar{r} = (\bar{\lambda}, \bar{m})$ too.

(ii) If $\bar{\lambda} \neq \lambda^*$ write down (3.4) with $\mu = \lambda^* + \bar{\lambda}$, $n = m^* + \bar{m}$, to get

$$(\lambda^* - \bar{\lambda})\{c(j)a(\bar{\lambda}, \bar{m}, k) - c(k)a(\bar{\lambda}, \bar{m}, j)\} = 0, \tag{3.14}$$

so that (3.11) holds for $r = \bar{r} = (\bar{\lambda}, \bar{m})$ too.

This leaves us with the cases where $\bar{\sigma} = 0$, $\bar{\tau} < 0$. For them we merely replace the ordering (3.9) by one in which we put τ first at the second stage when $\sigma = 0$.

This completes the proof of Lemma 1.

Remark: when $\bar{r} = 0$, $r^* + \bar{r} \in R$, so that (3.5) does not hold.

LEMMA 2: *If S has a negative element*

$$a(r, j) = B(r)b(j), \text{ say,} \qquad \text{when } \sigma \leqslant 0, \qquad \text{unless } r = (\sigma + i\tau, m) = 0. \tag{3.15}$$

COROLLARY: *If $S \neq \{0\}$ and*

$$N(q) \geqslant 3, \tag{3.16}$$

S has both positive and negative elements.

LEMMA 3: *If $T \neq \{0\}$,[8] then unless $r = (\sigma, \tau, m) = 0$,*

$$a(\sigma, \tau, m, j) = D(\sigma, \tau, m)d(j) \tag{3.17}$$

$$a(\sigma, -\tau, m, j) = \tilde{a}(\sigma, \tau, m, j) = \tilde{D}(\sigma, \tau, m)\tilde{d}(j), \tag{3.18}$$

where we take $\tau \geqslant 0$ without loss of generality and ~ denotes the complex conjugate.

PROOFS: These lemmas are proved in the same way as Lemma 1. Remember that T is symmetric about the origin.

LEMMA 4: *When $N(q) \geqslant 3$ either $S = \{0\}$ or $T = \{0\}$.*

PROOF: Suppose neither is $\{0\}$. If $\tau^* \in T$, so does $-\tau^*$, because complex latent roots come in conjugate pairs. Suppose without loss of generality that $\lambda^* = \sigma^* + i\tau^* \in L$, with $\sigma^* \geqslant 0$. Then Lemmas 1 and 3 imply that

$$D(\sigma^*, \tau^*, 0)d_j = C(\sigma^*, \tau^*, 0)c_j; \quad \tilde{D}(\sigma^*, \tau^*, 0)\tilde{d}_j = C(\sigma^*, -\tau^*, 0)c_j, \text{ for each } j, \tag{3.19}$$

so that $\tilde{d} = Ed_j$ each j, say. Hence $N \geqslant 2$ by Lemma 3, and we have a contradiction.

LEMMA 5: *When $N(q) \geqslant 3$, $M(0) = 0$ unless $S = T = \{0\}$.*

PROOF: Suppose $S \neq \{0\}$. The Corollary to Lemma 2 implies that it has both positive and negative elements, and Lemmas 1 and 2 that $B(0, 1)b_j = C(0, 1)c_j$ if $M(0) \geqslant 1$.

The proof for $T \neq \{0\}$ is similar.

LEMMA 6: *When $N(q) \geqslant 3$ and $L \neq \{0\}$, then $M(\lambda) = 0$ for each $\lambda \in L$.*

PROOF: $L \neq \{0\}$ iff either $S \neq \{0\}$ or $T \neq \{0\}$. Let $S \neq \{0\}$. According to the corollary to Lemma 2 it has both positive and negative elements. Define

[8] One can obviously apply the same arguments to T as S, remembering only that the final results have to be real, in particular T symmetric.

$$m^+ = \max\{M(\sigma) \mid \sigma > 0, \sigma \in S\}, \quad \sigma^+ = \max\{\sigma \in S \mid M(\sigma) = m^+\}$$

$$m^- = \max\{M(\sigma) \mid \sigma < 0, \sigma \in S\} \quad \sigma^- = \max\{\sigma \in S \mid \sigma < 0, M(\sigma) = m^-\}. \tag{3.20}$$

If $m^+, m^- > 0$, $m^+ + m^- > M(\sigma^+ + \sigma^-)$ when $\sigma^+ + \sigma^- \in S$. Hence we can apply (3.4) with $n = m^+ + m^-$, $\mu = \sigma^+ + \sigma^-$, to get

$$(\sigma^+ - \sigma^-)C(\sigma^+, m^+)B(\sigma^-, m^-)\{b(j)c(k) - b(k)c(j)\} = 0, \tag{3.21}$$

so that $N(q) < 3$, contradicting our assumption.

If $m^+ > 0$, $m^- = 0$, define

$$\sigma^{\pm} = \min\{\sigma \in S \mid M(\sigma) = m^+\}; \qquad \sigma^{=} = \min\{\sigma \in S\} < 0.^{9} \tag{3.22}$$

Consider $\mu = \sigma^{\pm} + \sigma^{=} < \sigma^{\pm}$, $n = m^+ > M(\sigma^{\pm} + \sigma^{=})$ when $\sigma^{\pm} + \sigma^{=} \in S$. Hence we may apply (3.4) to this (μ, n) to get:

$$(\sigma^{\pm} - \sigma^{=})C(\sigma^{\pm}, m^+)B(\sigma^{=}, 0)\{b(j)c(k) - b(k)c(j)\} = 0,^{10} \text{ say,} \tag{3.23}$$

so that $N(q) \leqslant 3$ again.

A similar proof holds for $m^+ = 0$, $m^- > 0$. Hence $m^+ = m^- = 0$, so that $M(\sigma) = 0$, for each $\sigma \in S$, as required.

A similar proof holds for $T \neq \{0\}$. It is rather simpler because $m^+ = m^-$ in that case.

LEMMA 7: *When $N(q) \geqslant 3$ and $M(0) = M \neq 0$,*

$$a(0, m, j) = A(m)c(j), \text{ say,} \qquad \text{each } j, \text{ for each } m \geqslant 2. \tag{3.24}$$

PROOF: Since $L = \{0\}$ I will drop the 0 in $a(0, m, j)$ for simplicity. Clearly $M \geqslant 2$. Define

$$a(M, j) = c(j), \qquad \text{for each } j, \tag{3.25}$$

and erect the inductive hypothesis

$$a(m, j) = A(m)c(j), \text{ say,} \qquad \text{for each } j, \tag{3.26}$$

for each $m > \bar{m} \geqslant 2$. Then $M + \bar{m} - 1 > M = M(0)$, so that we can apply (3.4) with $n = M + \bar{m} - 1$, $\mu = 0$ to get

$$(M - \bar{m} + 1)\{c(j)a(\bar{m}, k) - c(k)a(\bar{m}, j)\} = 0, \tag{3.27}$$

the other terms vanishing by the inductive hypothesis. Hence (3.26) holds for $m = \bar{m}$, too. Since it holds for $m = M$, it holds for all $m \geqslant 2$.

[9] S has both positive and negative elements by the corollary to Lemma 2.

[10] We sum over (σ, m), $(\sigma', m') \in S$ such that $\sigma + \sigma' = \mu = \sigma^{\pm} + \sigma^{=}$, $m + m' = n = m^+$. When $\sigma\sigma' \geqslant 0$ the term vanishes. When $\sigma\sigma' < 0$, take $\sigma > 0$, $\sigma' < 0$. Then $0 \leqslant m' \leqslant m^- = 0$. Hence $m' = 0$, $m = m^+$. Hence $(\sigma^{\pm}, m^+)$, $(\sigma^{=}, 0)$ are the only such pair in S.

This completes the proof of the theorem. (3.1), (3.2), and (3.3) correspond to the cases in which $M(0) \neq 0$, $S \neq \{0\}$, $T \neq \{0\}$ respectively.

COROLLARY 1: *If S has just one negative element* $-\omega$,

$$h_j = a(j) + b(j)e^{-\omega h} + c(j)\sum_{r=1}^{r^*} C(r)e^{r\omega h}, \quad say, \quad \prod C(r) \neq 0. \tag{3.28}$$

PROOF: Arrange the positive elements $\sigma_1 < \sigma_2 < \ldots < \sigma_{r*}$ in increasing sequence and define $\sigma_0 = 0$.

Erect the inductive hypothesis

$$\sigma_r = r\omega, \qquad r = 0, 1, \ldots, \bar{r} - 1. \tag{3.29}$$

It certainly holds for $r = 0$. If, therefore, (3.29) implies that it holds for $\bar{r}$, it will hold for $r = 0, 1, \ldots, r^*$. Now $\sigma_{\bar{r}} > (\bar{r} - 1)\omega$. Hence $\sigma_r > \sigma_r - \omega > (\bar{r} - 2)\omega$, so that,

$$\sigma_{\bar{r}} - \omega = (\bar{r} - 1)\omega \tag{3.30}$$

if it is in S. If it is not in S, apply (3.4) with $\mu = \sigma_r - \omega$, to get

$$(\sigma_{\bar{r}} + \omega)C(\sigma_{\bar{r}})\{c(j)b(k) - c(k)b(j)\} = 0 \tag{3.31}$$

in the notation of Lemmas 1 and 2, the other terms vanishing by Lemma 1, so that $N(q) < 3$. Hence $\sigma_{\bar{r}} - \omega = (\bar{r} - 1)\omega$, and (3.29) holds for $r = \bar{r}$, completing the proof of the lemma.

COROLLARY 2: *If S has just one positive element,*

$$h_j = a(j) + b(j)\sum_{r=1}^{r^*} B(r)e^{-r\omega h} + c(j)e^{\omega h}, \qquad \prod B(r) \neq 0 \tag{3.32}$$

by an exactly similar argument.

Remark 1: (3.32) may be written

$$k_j = b(j) + a(j)k + c(j)\sum_{r=2}^{r^*+1} C(r-1)k^r, \qquad \prod C(r-1) \neq 0, \tag{3.33}$$

with a trivial change in notation, where

$$k(q, u) = e^{\omega h} = g(p, u)^{\omega}; \qquad q_j = \log p_j, \qquad \text{for each } j, \tag{3.34}$$

$g(p, u)$ being the cost function. In particular this represents a complete system of polynomial Engel curves when $\omega = 1$. It is clearly the most general case.

Remark 2: The point to note is that none of the B's or C's vanishes.

Remark 3: Unfortunately (3.4) does not imply this in general, because of condition (2.33). Indeed,

$$h_j(q, u) = a(j; q) + b(j; q)(e^{-2h} + B(q)e^{-h}) + c(j; q)(e^{3h} - 5e^{2h}/3B(q)) \quad (3.35)$$

is a counter-example for $S \neq \{0\}$ because the coefficient of e^h vanishes,

$$h_j(q, u) = a(j; q) + d(j; q)\{e^{4ih} - A(q)e^{-iB(q)}e^{-3ih} - 1.4e^{2iB(q)}e^{-2ih}\}$$
$$+ \tilde{d}(j; q)\{e^{4ih} - A(q)e^{iB(q)}e^{3ih} - 1.4e^{-2iB(q)}e^{2ih}\} \quad (3.36)$$

a counter-example for $T \neq \{0\}$ because those of e^{ih} and e^{-ih} do. Each is the most general for the particular L used. No such gaps can occur when S has less than six elements or T less than seven.

I imagine that we can restrict ourselves to S, T of the form $\{n\omega \mid n \in N\}$, where N is a set of positive and negative integers with a few gaps permitted in general, symmetric when T is being represented. I have not seriously attempted the combinatorial feat required to settle the matter, but mention a few relevant considerations in Section 5.

THEOREM 2: *When* $N(q) = 2$,

$$h_j = a(j) + b(j)\sum_{\lambda \in L}\sum_{m=0}^{M(\lambda)} B(\lambda, m)h^m e^{\lambda h}, \text{ say,} \quad (3.37)$$

where

$$B(\tilde{\lambda}, m) = \tilde{B}(\lambda, m); \quad B(0, 0) = 0; \quad \textstyle\sum_j b(j) = 0; \quad \sum_j a(j) = 1 \quad (3.38)$$

or, to be more precise,

$$h_j(q, u) = \alpha_j(q) + \beta_j(q)\sum_{\lambda \in L}\sum_{m=0}^{M(\lambda)} D(\lambda, m; \beta(q))\{h(q, u) - \alpha(q)\}^m e^{\lambda(h(q, u) - \alpha(q))}, \quad (3.39)$$

where[11]

$$\alpha(q) = h(q, u_1); \quad \alpha(q) + \beta(q) = h(q, u_2), \text{ say,} \quad (3.40)$$

and where I have taken u_1, u_2 *such that* $u_2 > u_1$.

$$(a) \sum_{\lambda \in L}\sum_{m=0}^{M(\lambda)} D(\lambda, m; \beta)\beta^m e^{\lambda\beta} = 1;$$

$$(b) \sum_{\lambda \in L} D(\lambda, 0; \beta) = 0;$$

[11] Put $u = u_1, u_2$ in (3.39), and eliminate $a(j)$, $b(j)$ from it and the resulting equations.

(c) $D(\tilde{\lambda}, m; \beta) = \tilde{D}(\lambda, m; \beta)$;

$$(d)\ \left\{\sum_{\lambda \in L} \sum_{m=0}^{M(\lambda)} D(\lambda, m; \beta) k^m e^{\lambda k}\right\} \cdot \left\{\sum_{\lambda \in L} \sum_{m=0}^{M(\lambda)} D(\lambda, m; k) \beta^m e^{\lambda \beta}\right\} = 1. \tag{3.41}$$

PROOF: For (3.37) all we need is the fact that $a(0, 0, j; q)$ is linearly independent of the other $a(\lambda, m, j; q)$ because $\sum_j a(0, 0, j; q) = 1$, $\sum_j a(\lambda, m, j; q) = 0$ when $(\lambda, m) \neq (0, 0)$. This is repeated in the last two equations in (3.38). $B(0, 0) = 0$ is just a convenient normalization. $B(\tilde{\lambda}, m) = \tilde{B}(\lambda, m)$ is the sort of condition we always have with complex conjugates in the analysis of real systems.

To derive (3.39) we write down (3.37) with $u = u_1$, put

$$k(q, u) = h(q, u) - \alpha(q), \tag{3.42}$$

and use (3.40) to get

$$k_j = b(j) \sum_{\lambda \in L} \sum_{m=0}^{M(\lambda)} C(\lambda, m; q) k^m e^{\lambda k}, \text{ say,} \tag{3.43}$$

as in Section 2, where

$$\sum_{\lambda \in L} C(\lambda, 0; q) = 0 \tag{3.44}$$

because $k(q, u_1) = h(q, u_1) - h(q, u_1) \equiv 0$. Writing (3.43) down for $u = u_2$ and dividing into (3.43) we get

$$k_j \Big/ \sum_{\lambda \in L} \sum_{m=0}^{M(\lambda)} C(\lambda, m; q) k^m e^{\lambda k} = \beta_j \Big/ \sum_{\lambda \in L} \sum_{m=0}^{M(\lambda)} C(\lambda, m; q) \beta^m e^{\lambda \beta}, \tag{3.45}$$

so that

$$k = K(\beta, u) \tag{3.46}$$

with

$$\partial k / \partial \beta = \sum_\lambda \sum_m D(\lambda, m; \beta) k^m e^{\lambda k} \equiv \psi(k, \beta), \text{ say,} \tag{3.47}$$

with the D's satisfying (3.41). This is in principle integrable when the functions are reasonably well behaved, and leads immediately to (3.39) which is in principle always integrable, too, under similar conditions.

(3.41c) merely says that we are interested in 'real' solutions. The other three parts may be written

$$(a)\ \psi(\beta, \beta) = 1; \quad (b)\ \psi(0, \beta) = 0; \quad (d)\ \psi(k, \beta)\psi(\beta, k) = 1, \tag{3.48}$$

where $\psi(\cdot)$ is defined in (2.27).

To derive (a), put $u = u_2$ in (3.46), to get $k \equiv \beta$, so that $\partial k/\partial\beta = 1$. For ($b$), put $u = u_1$, to get $k \equiv 0$, and $\partial k/\partial\beta = 0$. ($d$) is a little more difficult. Fix u_1, but think of $v = u_2$ as potentially variable. (3.46) then becomes

$$k(q, u) = K^*(k(q, v), u, v), \text{ say,} \tag{3.49}$$

or, equivalently,

$$k(q, v) = K^*(k(q, u), v, u). \tag{3.50}$$

(d) merely states that $\partial k(q, v)/\partial k(q, u)$ is the inverse of $\partial k(q, u)/\partial k(q, v)$, u and v being held constant during both differentiations.

4. POLYNOMIAL ENGEL CURVES

As we saw at the end of the previous section,[12] complete systems of polynomial Engel curves can always be written as

$$x_j = a(j; p) + b(j; p)m + c(j; p) \sum_{r=2}^{R} A(r; p)m^r, \text{ say.} \tag{4.1}$$

In terms of the cost function

$$g(p, u) = \min\{p \cdot x \mid f(x) \geqslant u\}, \text{ say,} \tag{4.2}$$

this becomes

$$g_j(p, u) = a(j; p) + b(j; p)g(p, u) + c(j; p) \sum_{r=2}^{R} A(r; p)g(p, u)^r. \tag{4.3}$$

To proceed further, assume first that $a(p) = (a(1; p), a(2; p), \ldots)$, $b(p)$ and $c(p)$ are linearly independent, and write

$$\theta(r; p) = g(p, u_r), \quad r = 1, 2, 3; \quad u_1 < u_2 < u_3 \tag{4.4}$$

as in Section 2, and substitute into (4.3). Now write

$$\alpha(p) = \theta(1; p) \tag{4.5}$$

$$h(p, u) = g(p, u) - g(p, u_1) = g(p, u) - \alpha(p) \tag{4.6}$$

to get

$$h_j(p, u) = b(j; p)h(p, u) + c(j; p) \sum_{r=1}^{R} B(r; p)h^r(p, u), \text{ say.} \tag{4.7}$$

Set now

[12] Put $\omega = 1$ in (3.34).

$$\beta(p) = h(p, u_2) = \theta(2; p) - \theta(1; p) \tag{4.8}$$

$$k(p, u) = h(p, u)/\beta(p) = [g(p, u) - \alpha(p)]/\beta(p) \tag{4.9}$$

in (4.7) to get

$$k_j(p, u) = c(j; p) \sum_{r=1}^{R} C(r; p)k^r(p; u), \text{ say,} \tag{4.10}$$

where[13]

$$\sum_{r=1}^{R} C(r; p) = 0. \tag{4.11}$$

Finally set

$$\begin{aligned} \gamma(p) = k(p, u_3) &= h(p, u_3)/h(p, u_2) \\ &= (\theta(3; p) - \theta(1; p))/(\theta(2; p) - \theta(1; p)) \\ &= [\theta(3; p) - \alpha(p)]/\beta(p) \end{aligned} \tag{4.12}$$

to get

$$k_j(p, u) \Big/ \sum_{r=1}^{R} C(r; p)k^r = \gamma_j(p) \Big/ \sum_{r=1}^{R} C(r; p)\gamma^r, \tag{4.13}$$

so that

$$k(p, u) = K(\gamma(p), u), \text{ say,} \tag{4.14}$$

and (4.13) becomes

$$\partial k/\partial \gamma = K'(\gamma, u) = \sum_{r=1}^{R} D(r; \gamma)k^r, \text{ say,} \tag{4.15}$$

so that we have reduced the problem to the integration of an ordinary first-order differential equation which can always be done in principle for sufficiently well-behaved functions. Putting $u = u_3; u_2$ in (4.15), we have

$$\sum_{r=1}^{R} D(r; \gamma)\gamma^r = 1; \qquad \sum_{r=1}^{R} D(r; \gamma) = 0, \tag{4.16}$$

the former reflecting the fact that $\partial K(\gamma, u_3)/\partial\gamma = \partial\gamma/\partial\gamma = 1$, the latter that $\partial K(\gamma, u_2)/\partial\gamma = \partial 1/\partial\gamma = 0$. Setting $u = u_1$ confirms that $D(0; \gamma) = 0$.

Finally,

$$\left(\sum_{r=1}^{R} D(r; \gamma)k^r\right)\left(\sum_{r=1}^{R} D(r; k)\gamma^r\right) = 1 \tag{4.17}$$

as in the proof of (3.48*d*).

[13] To derive (4.11): set $u = u_2$ to get $k(p, u_2) = 1$, and $0 = \partial 1/\partial p_j = c(j; p)\sum_r C(r; p)$. Remember that $c(p) = (c(1; p), c(2; p), \ldots) \neq 0$ since $N = 3$.

According to (4.6), (4.9), and (4.14),

$$\begin{aligned} g(p, u) &= \alpha(p) + \beta(p)k(p, u) \\ &= \alpha(p) + \beta(p)K(\gamma(p), u) \\ &= G(\theta(p), u), \text{ say,} \end{aligned} \tag{4.18}$$

where

$$\theta(p) = (\theta(1; p), \theta(2; p), \theta(3; p)) \tag{4.19}$$

and

$$K(\gamma, u) = G(0, 1, \gamma, u), \tag{4.20}$$

so that

$$G(\lambda e + \mu\theta, u) = \lambda + \mu G(\theta, u); \quad \mu \geqslant 0, \ e = (1, 1, \dots, 1). \tag{4.21}$$

Differentiating (4.18) by p_j, using (4.15), and writing $g_j = x_j$, $g = m$, we have the general equation

$$x_j = \alpha_j(p) + \beta_j(p)(m - \alpha(p))/\beta(p) + \beta(p)\gamma_j(p) \sum_{r=1}^{R} D(r; \gamma)\{m - \alpha(p))/\beta(p)\}^r. \tag{4.22}$$

α, β, γ are defined in (4.5), (4.8), and (4.12) in terms of the cost functions $\theta(1; p)$, $\theta(2; p)$, $\theta(3; p)$ and the D's satisfy (4.16) and (4.17).

Let us now look at the quadratic case—in a reasonable sense the most general non-degenerate polynomial system. (4.16) implies that $D(2) = -D(1) = 1/\gamma(\gamma - 1)$, so that

$$x_j = \alpha_j(p) + \beta_j(p)(m - \alpha(p))/\beta(p) + \beta(p)\gamma_j(p)[(m - \alpha(p))/\beta(p) - \{(m - \alpha(p))/\beta(p)\}^2]/\gamma(1 - \gamma) \tag{4.23}$$

and, in (4.15),

$$\partial k/\partial\gamma = K' = k(k - 1)/\gamma(\gamma - 1). \tag{4.24}$$

Now $dz/z(z - 1) = dz/(z - 1) - dz/z = d \log\{(z - 1)/z\}$ so that (4.24) yields

$$(k - 1)/k = u(\gamma - 1)/\gamma \tag{4.25}$$

in an obvious normalization. Hence

$$\begin{aligned} g(p, u) &= \alpha(p) + \beta(p)k(p, u) \\ &= \alpha(p) + \beta(p)/(1 - u\delta(p)), \end{aligned} \tag{4.26}$$

where

$$\delta(p) = (\gamma(p) - 1)/\gamma(p) = (\theta(3; p) - \theta(2; p))/(\theta(3; p) - \theta(1; p)) \tag{4.27}$$

is the cost function corresponding to a complete quadratic system of Engel curves.

So much for the quadratic case. What made it relatively straightforward was the fact that

$$D(1;\gamma) : D(2;\gamma) = -1 : 1. \tag{4.28}$$

Consider now the more general case with $R > 2$ and

$$D(1;\gamma) : D(2;\gamma) : \ldots : D(R;\gamma) = a_1 : a_2 : \ldots : a_R, \tag{4.29}$$

where the a_r are constants and, of course,

$$\sum a_r = 0; \quad a_R = 1, \tag{4.30}$$

without loss of generality, by (4.16). (4.15) then becomes

$$\partial k/\partial\gamma = \sum a_r k^r \Big/ \sum a_r \gamma^r. \tag{4.31}$$

I will confine my attention to the case where the zeros, $b_1 = 0$, $b_2 = 1$, $b_3 \ldots b_R$ of $\sum a_r z^r$ are real and distinct, though a similar treatment works when they are not. We then have

$$1\Big/\sum_r a_r z^r = \sum_r c_r \Big/ (z - b_r), \text{ say;} \qquad c_r = 1\Big/\prod_{s\neq r} (b_r - b_s), \tag{4.32}$$

so that

$$\mathrm{d}z\Big/\sum a_r z^r = \sum c_r \mathrm{d}z/(z - b_r) = \mathrm{d}\log \prod (z - b_r)^{c_r}. \tag{4.33}$$

(31) therefore yields

$$\prod (k - b_r)^{c_r} = u \prod (\gamma - b_r)^{c_r} \tag{4.34}$$

in an appropriate normalization. Moreover

$$\sum c_r = 0, \tag{4.35}$$

as can be seen by equating coefficients of z^r in $\sum c_r \prod_{s\neq r}(z - b_s) = 1$, derived from (4.32). Since $m = g = \alpha + \beta k$ by (4.18), we may therefore rewrite (4.34) in the form

$$\begin{aligned} u &= \prod \{(m - \alpha(p) - b_r\beta(p))/(\gamma(p) - b_r)\}^{c_r}; \quad \sum c_r = 0 \\ &= \prod \{[(m-\alpha)/\beta - b_r]/(\gamma - b_r)\}^{c_r} \end{aligned} \tag{4.36}$$

or, if you prefer,

$$u = \prod \left(\frac{b_r(m - \theta(2;p)) + (1 - b_r)(m - \theta(1;p))}{b_r(\theta(3;p) - \theta(2;p)) + (1 - b_r)(\theta(3;p) - \theta(1;p))} \right)^{c_r}. \tag{4.37}$$

Drop (4.29) and turn to the *fully degenerate* case in which

$$\lambda(p)a(j; p) + \mu(p)b(j; p) + \gamma(p)c(j; p) = 0, \tag{4.38}$$

where it is not true that $\lambda(p) = \mu(p) = \gamma(p) = 0$. Since $\sum p_j x_j = m$, $\mu(p) = 0$. Hence either

$$c(j; p) = 0, \tag{4.39}$$

yielding the familiar linear Engel system with

$$g(p, u) = \alpha(p) + \beta(p)u \tag{4.40}$$

in the obvious normalization, or

$$a(j; p) = \rho(p)c(j; p), \text{ say,} \tag{4.41}$$

so that

$$x_j = b(j; p)m + c(j; p) \sum_{r \neq 1} A(r; p)m^r, \text{ say.} \tag{4.42}$$

A simplified version of the proof leading up to (4.22) yields (4.15)–(4.17), (4.22), with

$$\alpha(p) = \theta(1; p) = 0. \tag{4.43}$$

The polynomial Engel curves were generated by putting $\omega = 1$ in (3.32). According to (3.32) a similar analysis applies for g^{ω} in the general case discussed there. We can analyse it exactly as we have just done the polynomial case. The results are so similar that I will not spell them out here.

Replacing $g(\cdot)$ by $h(\cdot)$ in the discussion one can apply the same analysis to (3.1). Note that the polynomial form is guaranteed here, not a further assumption.

5. CONCLUDING REMARKS

In order to keep this article to a reasonable length, the following remarks have been kept to a perhaps undesirable brevity. The discussion in Sections 3 and 4 was entirely local, asking, if you like, when is

$$x_i \sum_{r \in R} a(r, i; p)\phi(r; m) \tag{5.1}$$

to the second order nearer $\bar{p}$, $\bar{m}$? If so, it will clearly still be so near $\lambda\bar{p}$, $\lambda\bar{m}$, and I will normalize to take $\bar{m} = 1$ for simplicity. The main condition was then that the rank $N(\bar{p})$ of $A(\bar{p}) = [a(r, i; \bar{p})]$ is at most 3.

Let us now assume that representations similar to (5.1) are possible throughout an open set Ω in p space. Then $N(\bar{p}) \leqslant 3$ throughout Ω.

Suppose that $N(\bar{p}) = 3$, some $\bar{p} \in \Omega$. Then it will be so throughout a maximal neighbourhood $\Omega(\bar{p}) \subseteq \Omega$ of $\bar{p}$. There may be many such disjoint neighbourhoods. They will commonly be divided by $\bar{n} - 1$ dimensional surfaces on which $N(p) = 2$, and these by $\bar{n} - 2$ dimensional surfaces when $N(p) = 1$, when $\bar{n}$ is the number of goods. Clearly one cannot move in just any direction and stay in one of these surfaces, as my calculus arguments require. I do not believe that this is a genuine problem, at least if there are sufficient goods, but I have not verified this. If you like, apply the arguments for $N(p) = 1, 2$, only in cases where this region is solid. $N(p) = 3$ is, of course, the important case. A similar argument may be applied when $\max\{N(p) \mid p \in \Omega\} = 2$, for instance. There the neighbourhoods $\Omega(p)$ are those in which $N(p) = 2$, rather than 3.

Look again at the main theorem as stated at the beginning of Section 3. If $N = 3$, it states, we are in one of the cases (i), (ii), and (iii). Of these, (iii) differs from (ii) only in having purely imaginary exponents, rather than purely real, while (i) is the usual logarithmic limiting case of an expression like (ii). We may therefore concentrate on (ii) as a representative case. It may be written

$$h_j(q, u) = a(j; q) + b(j; q) \sum_{b \in B} B(b; q)e^{-bh} + c(j; q) \sum_{c \in C} C(c; q)e^{ch}, \tag{5.2}$$

where $B = \{b > 0 \mid -b \in S\}$, $C = \{c > 0 \mid c \in S\}$. This equation may be treated like (4.1). We set $u = u_1, u_2, u_3$ in turn, $\theta(r; q) = h(q, u_r)$, to get

$$\begin{aligned} h(q, u) &= H(\theta(1), \theta(2), \theta(3), u) \\ &= \theta(1) + \tilde{H}(\theta(2) - \theta(1), \theta(3) - \theta(1), u) \\ &= \alpha + \tilde{H}(\beta, \varepsilon, u), \text{ say,} \end{aligned} \tag{5.3}$$

when the second representation is possible because the coefficient of $a(i)$ is 1.

The bother about this is that $\tilde{H}(\cdot, \cdot, u)$ has two arguments, and so there is an integrability problem. One can say a good deal about the nature of a complete solution, but not find it explicitly as one can in the cases discussed in Section 4.

B and C have each at least one element. What made a complete solution possible in Section 4 was the assumption that one or other had just one. Let it be B, and set $B = \{\omega\}$. Then

$$h_j(q, u) = a(j; q) + b(j; q)e^{-\omega h} + C(j; q) \sum_{m=1}^{n} c(r; q)e^{r\omega h}. \tag{5.4}$$

Because the coefficients of $a(j; q)$ and $b(j; q)$ both depend only on h, it is possible to reduce the 3 variables in (5.3) to 1, not just 2. Because they are $1, e^{\omega h}$, this takes the form

$$h(q, u) = \alpha + \beta K(\gamma, u), \quad \gamma = \varepsilon/\beta. \tag{5.5}$$

Since $K(\cdot, u)$ has only one argument, there is no integrability condition to be solved. $B = \{1\}$ is the polynomial case, $B = C = \{1\}$ the quadratic, given $\omega = 1$.

Turn now to the purely imaginary case (iii). $B = \{\omega\}$ then corresponds to $T = \{-\omega, 0, \omega\}$, so that we get a direct analogue of the quadratic of the form

$$h_j = a(j) + b(j)\cos \omega h + c(j)\sin \omega h. \tag{5.6}$$

When $B = \{\omega\}$, $C = \{\omega, 2\omega, \ldots, n\omega\}$, say, so that $S = \{-\omega, 0, \omega, 2\omega, \ldots, n\omega\}$. It is *not* true that $S = \{-m\omega, -(m-1)\omega, \ldots, 0, \omega, \ldots, n\omega\}$ in general—(3.35) and (3.36) are counter-examples. However, it can[14] be shown that this will be so in a 'generic' sense in what I think is a reasonable use of the word; and I suspect that S is always of this form, wherever $N = 3$, if we allow a few gaps.

[14] Consider this as a conjecture. I have lost my notes on the point, and do not even remember the meaning I gave to generic, let alone the proof.

21

More Measures for Fixed Factors

Editorial Remarks

This is a brilliant paper; it is in several ways the culmination of the aggregation project which began in 1953. The version presented here stems from 1978 with minor additions made ten years later when Gorman presented the paper at the Nuffield Conference on Measurement and Modelling. It was published in the proceedings of that conference. The problem is cast as a capital aggregation problem, but we shall see later how the results can be used in other contexts as well.

The paper begins by mentioning an extension of his 1968 result on capital aggregation. We have no record of this document, but it was apparently presented to the Mathematical Economics Workshop at LSE sometime in 1976. We first lay out this argument in a little more detail than Gorman does.

Editorial Summary

This time the aggregation question concerns the existence of a set of aggregates, $\phi(y) = (\phi^1(y), \ldots, \phi^r(y), \ldots, \phi^R(y))$, where each aggregate can in principle depend upon all types of capital.[1] This extends the 1968 result which asked for the existence of aggregates $\phi(y) = (\phi^1(y^1), \ldots, \phi^r(y^r), \ldots, \phi^R(y^R))$; that is, the rth aggregate depends only upon a subvector y^r of the capital stock. Formally, Gorman requires that the short-run technology set of the economy, $S(y)$, can be written as

$$S(y) = \tilde{S}(\phi^1(y), \ldots, \phi^r(y), \ldots, \phi^R(y)) = \tilde{S}(\phi(y)). \tag{0.1}$$

The gross profit function for firm t is

$$g_t(p, y_t) = \max\left\{\sum_{i=1}^{n} p_i x_{ti} \mid x_t \in S_t(y_t)\right\}; \tag{0.2}$$

[1] Of course, one might as well assume from the beginning that these aggregates are functionally independent. If not, one can always reduce the number of aggregators until one arrives at a functionally independent set.

and for the economy it is

$$g(p, y) = \max\left\{\sum_{i=1}^{n} p_i x_i \mid x \in S(y)\right\}, \tag{0.3}$$

which is also

$$g(p, y) = \sum_{t=1}^{T} g_t(p, y_t) \tag{0.4}$$

because

$$S(y) = \sum_{t=1}^{T} S_t(y_t). \tag{0.5}$$

The gross profit function dual to $\tilde{S}(\phi(y))$ is

$$G(p, \phi(y)) = \max\left\{\sum_{t=1}^{T} p_i x_{ti} \mid x_t \in \tilde{S}(\phi(y))\right\}, \tag{0.6}$$

so that the aggregation question posed in (0.1) can be written equivalently as

$$g(p, y) = G(p, \phi(y)). \tag{0.7}$$

The solution (0.7) is an obvious generalization of the 1968 result and is proved directly in Section 3 of this paper:

$$g_t(p, y_t) = \sum_{t=1}^{R} a^r(p)\phi^{rt}(y_t) + b^t(p) \tag{0.8}$$

and

$$g(p, y) = \sum_{r=1}^{R} a^r(p)\phi^r(y) + b(p), \tag{0.9}$$

where

$$\phi^r(y) = \sum_{t=1}^{T} \phi^{rt}(y_t) \tag{0.10}$$

for all aggregates $r = 1, \ldots, R$, and

$$b(p) = \sum_{t=1}^{T} b^t(p). \tag{0.11}$$

This answer is remarkably similar to the one obtained under more restrictive assumptions in Gorman (1968*a*).

In the first paragraph Gorman suggests different circumstances in which a problem like this might arise. One that he does not mention however leads nicely into his next generalization of the problem. Why would one ever want an aggregate which depended upon the entire vector of fixed factors? One reason might be that these factors, although not distributed efficiently, are none the less produced somewhere in the economy. So the quantity of one fixed factor would actually depend upon the amount (and perhaps the distribution) of the other fixed factors. Although this would reduce the number of fixed factors by one, it would also require an aggregate of all the remaining fixed factors. This, then, would generate a problem that is a special case of the one above, provided that the way in which the fixed factor depended upon all of the other is independent of prices. If not, then we would have an aggregate which would have to depend upon prices, and that leads into the next problem.

Suppose that one looks for a vector of aggregates of the form

$$\phi(p, y) = (\phi^1(p, y), \ldots, \phi^r(p, y), \ldots, \phi^R(p, y)), \tag{0.12}$$

where each aggregate depends not only upon the entire set of fixed factors but also upon prices. First note that to require the existence of these aggregates in the profit function (0.7) would not be any constraint. That is, the profit function of the economy can always be written as

$$g(p, y) = G(p, \phi(p, y)). \tag{0.13}$$

Instead he asks that the supply functions themselves depend upon the aggregates, that is, the supply function can be written as

$$x_i = g_i(p, y) = G^i(p, \phi(p, y)) \tag{0.14}$$

for all commodities $i = 1, \ldots, n$. Because the vector $\phi(p, y)$ remains the same in every equation, this is a restriction unless $R \geqslant n$. Hence the assumption throughout that $R < n$. Next, observe that the functions G^i which depend upon the aggregate are not required to be partial derivatives. If they were partial derivatives, then one would be assuming from the outset that one could ignore the dependence of the aggregates upon prices in deriving the net supplies from the profit function. That would be a rather strong assumption indeed. Nevertheless, that is exactly what happens.

The solution technique itself is ingenious. Solve any R of the equations in (0.14) for the aggregates $\phi^1(p, y), \ldots, \phi^R(p, y)$. To lighten the notation, let $R = 2$, and using

$$g(p, y) = \sum_{t=1}^{T} g^t(p, y_t), \tag{0.15}$$

solve the first two equations of

$$x_i = g_i(p, y) = G^i(p, \phi(p, y)) = \sum_{t=1}^{T} g_i^t(p, y_t) \tag{0.16}$$

to obtain

$$\phi^1(p, y) = \Phi^1\left(p, \sum_{t=1}^{T} g_1^t(p, y_t), \sum_{t=1}^{T} g_2^t(p, y_t)\right) \tag{0.17}$$

and

$$\phi^2(p, y) = \Phi^2\left(p, \sum_{t=1}^{T} g_1^t(p, y_t), \sum_{t=1}^{T} g_2^t(p, y_t)\right). \tag{0.18}$$

Substitute (0.17) and (0.18) into (0.16), so that

$$g_i(p, y) = G^i\left(p, \Phi^1\left(p, \sum_{t=1}^{T} g_1^t(p, y_t), \sum_{t=1}^{T} g_2^t(p, y_t)\right), \Phi^2\left(p, \sum_{t=1}^{T} g_1^t(p, y_t), \sum_{t=1}^{T} g_2^t(p, y_t)\right)\right)$$

$$= \bar{G}^i\left(p, \sum_{t=1}^{T} g_1^t(p, y_t), \sum_{t=1}^{T} g_2^t(p, y_t)\right). \tag{0.19}$$

That is, the first two derivatives themselves can be taken to be the required aggregates. Gorman then redefines variables and designates

$$\phi^r(p, y) = \sum_{t=1}^{T} g_r^t(p, y_t) = \sum_{t=1}^{T} \phi^{rt}(p, y_t), \tag{0.20}$$

where

$$\phi^{rt}(p, y_t) = g_r^t(p, y_t) \tag{0.21}$$

is the amount of the rth aggregate in firm t. Rewriting (0.19) using (0.20) and (0.21) yields

$$g_i(p, y) = \sum_{t=1}^{T} g_i^t(p, y_t) = \bar{G}^i\left(p, \sum_{t=1}^{T} \phi^{1t}(p, y_t), \sum_{t=1}^{T} \phi^{2t}(p, y_t)\right) \tag{0.22}$$

for $i = 1, \ldots, n$, as the system of equations which must be solved in the case $R = 2$.

Continuing with this special case, the solution is given by

$$g^t(p, y_t) = G^t(a^1(p), a^2(p), y_t) + b^t(p) \tag{0.23}$$

for each firm, so that the profit function for the economy as a whole is given by

$$g(p, y) = G(a^1(p), a^2(p), y_t) + b(p)$$

$$= \sum_{t=1}^{T} [G^t(a^1(p), a^2(p), y_t) + b^t(p)]. \tag{0.24}$$

As these are profit functions, G^t can be chosen to be linearly homogeneous in $(a^1(p), a^2(p))$ and each a^r is itself linearly homogeneous. Taking the derivative of (0.24) with respect to i yields

$$g_i^t(p, y_t) = G_1^t(a^1(p), a^2(p), y_t)a_i^1(p) + G_2^t(a^1(p), a^2(p), y_t)a_i^2(p) + b_i^t(p). \tag{0.25}$$

Multiply each equation in (0.25) by p_i and sum over i to obtain, using Euler's theorem,

$$g^t(p, y_t) = G_1^t(a^1(p), a^2(p), y_t)a^1(p) + G_2^t(a^1(p), a^2(p), y_t)a^2(p) + b^t(p). \tag{0.26}$$

Finally, setting

$$\phi^{rt}(p, y_t) = G_r^t(a^1(p), a^2(p), y_t) \tag{0.27}$$

we obtain

$$g^t(p, y_t) = a^1(p)\phi^{1t}(p, y_t) + a^2(p)\phi^{2t}(p, y_t) + b^t(p) \tag{0.28}$$

for each firm and

$$g(p, y_t) = a^1(p) \sum_{t=1}^{T} \phi^{1t}(p, y_t) + a^2(p) \sum_{t=1}^{T} \phi^{2t}(p, y_t) + \sum_{t=1}^{T} b^t(p) \tag{0.29}$$

for the economy as a whole. Sufficiency is obvious. What is surprising is that, using (0.27), the net supplies (0.25) can be written as

$$g_i(p, y_t) = a_i^1(p) \sum_{t=1}^{T} \phi^{1t}(p, y_t) + a_i^2(p) \sum_{t=1}^{T} \phi^{2t}(p, y_t) + b_i(p). \tag{0.30}$$

That is, in taking the partial derivative one can ignore the dependence of the aggregates upon prices. Furthermore, this an implication and not an assumption.

Section 2 of the paper performs the same exercise upon the relative supplies, g_i/g_1. The answer is the same except for two features: (i) that $b(p) = \sum b^t(p)$ must be equal to zero even though the individual b^t's need not be; and (ii) that only $R - 1$ aggregates are required to generate the solution (as opposed to R aggregates in the previous case). Hence, for example, asking for one aggregate in the relative supplies g_i/g_1 is sufficient to generate (0.28) and (0.29).

As already mentioned, Section 3 considers the case where the aggregates are independent of prices. Section 4 presents an alternative characterization of the solution. In general the functions which are i-dependent in the solutions are not necessarily derivatives. Section 5 presents a nice argument which permits one to convert them into partial derivatives.

There are in addition three appendices. Appendix A solves a system of partial differential equations similar to those encountered in this paper. Appendix B analyses what must be true when the marginal profit function a^r cannot be chosen to be convex. Finally Appendix C relates the results of this paper to the starting-point of 'Some Engel Curves'.

More Measures for Fixed Factors

ABSTRACT[1]

Existing 'perfect' aggregates can be considered as quantities $v = (v_m)$ of intermediate goods $m \in M$: intermediate, e.g. as between fixed inputs $u = (u_f)$, say, and current goods *measured as outputs*.

$$x_i = \sum_f x_{fi} = \sum_f \pi_i^f(p, u_f) = \sum_f \partial\pi^f/\partial p_i = \psi^i(p, v), \text{ say}, \tag{1}$$

where $v = \phi(p, u)$, in an obvious notation. Here I take (1) and its Muellbauer style analogue $x_i/x_1 = \theta^i(p, v)$ as definitions, and explore their implications informally. These are that corresponding subaggregates $v_f = (v_{fm})_{m \in M}$ exist for each firm f such that $v = \sum_f v_f$ in an appropriate normalization: that its gross profit function $\pi^f(p, u_f) = \lambda_m^f(a(p), u_f) + \mu^f(p)$, say, where $a(p) = (a^m(p))_{m \in M}$ is a vector of shadow prices for the aggregates so normalized; and that $v_{fm} = \lambda_m^f(a(p), u_f) = \partial\lambda^f/\partial a^m$, as one would like. These results clearly apply to aggregates for Labour, or Food, as well as for Capital, and to groups of households as well as firms.

Various related topics are discussed briefly in the text and in appendices.

1. INTRODUCTION

The discussion is cast in terms of fixed factors. With appropriate changes it can be applied to vector social welfare, vector income measures, equivalent adult contructions, . . . as could the earlier versions.[2]

Last year I generalized the discussion in Gorman (1968*a*) to the case where there might be a vector $\phi(y)$ of aggregates for capital, y being the extended vector of fixed inputs Y into the firms $t = 1, 2, \ldots, T$ in the community. I required that

$$g(p, y) = \sum g^t(p, y_t) = G(p, \phi(y)), \tag{2}$$

be the gross profit function for the economy as a whole. This implied the existence of subaggregates

$$\phi^t(y_t) = (\phi^{1t}(y_t), \ldots, \phi^{Rt}(y_t)), \tag{3}$$

[1] The paper is essentially that given to the Quantitative Economics Workshop at LSE in January 1978, and to Jim Mirrlees's seminar at Oxford later that year. I thank the participants, especially Jim, for their comments.

[2] In particular they can be taken as vectors of aggregates for current goods. See the text between equations (38) and (39).

such that

$$g^t(p, y_t) = \sum_r a^r(p)\phi^{rt}(y_t) + b^t(p), \tag{4}$$

$$g(p, y) = \sum_r a^r(p)\phi^r(y) + b(p), \tag{5}$$

$$g = \sum_t g^t, \quad \phi^r = \sum_t \phi^{rt}, \quad b = \sum_t b^t, \tag{6}$$

so that the apparent generalization of Gorman (1968*a*) gave no extra mileage.

In this paper I will seek capital aggregates of the form

$$\phi(p, y) = (\phi^1(p, y), \ldots, \phi^R(p, y)), \tag{7}$$

into which the prices p of the variable goods may enter. Since $g(p, y)$ is already of this type, we cannot merely require that such aggregates enter into the gross profit function. Instead I explore two related problems:

$$g_i(p, y) = \partial g/\partial p_i = G^i(p, \phi(p, y)), \tag{8}$$

$$g_i(p, y)/g_1(p, y) = H^i(p, \phi(p, y)), \tag{9}$$

each good i. That is, the net supplies of the variable goods, or the relative net supplies, only depend on these aggregates.

2. NET SUPPLY FUNCTIONS

We require

$$g_i(p, y) = \sum_t g_i^t(p, y_t) = G^i(p, \phi(p, y)), \quad \text{each } i, \tag{10}$$

and 'show' that this is so if and only if

$$g^t(p, y) = K^t(a(p), y_t) + b^t(p), \text{ say}, \tag{11}$$

$$g(p, y) = K(a(p), y) + b(p), \text{ say}, \tag{12}$$

$$\sum g^t = g, \quad \sum K^t = K, \quad \sum b^t = b; \quad a(p) = (a^1(p), \ldots, a^R(p)), \tag{13}$$

each $a^r(\cdot)$ a marginal profit function, in which case we may take

$$\phi^{rt}(p, y_t) = K_r^t(a(p), y_t) := \partial K^t/\partial a^r =: \theta^{rt}(a(p), y_t), \tag{14}$$

$$\phi^r(p, y) = K_r(a(p), y) = \sum_t \theta^{rt}(a(p), y_t) =: \theta(a(p), y). \tag{15}$$

Now

$$K^t = \sum_r K_r^t a^r; \quad K = \sum_r K_r a^r, \tag{16}$$

by homogeneity. Hence

$$g^t(p, y_t) = \sum_r a^r(p)\phi^{rt}(p, y_t) + b^t(p), \tag{17}$$

$$g(p, y) = \sum_r a^r(p)\phi^r(p, y) + b(p), \tag{18}$$

$$g = \sum_r g^t, \quad \phi^r = \sum_t \phi^{rt}, \quad b = \sum_t b^t, \tag{19}$$

which is remarkably similar to (1), (4)–(6), and the corresponding result in Gorman (1968*a*).

Note that the net supply functions

$$x_{ti} = g_i^t = \sum_r K_r^t a_i^r + b_i^t = \sum_r a_i^r \phi^{rt} + b_i^t, \tag{20}$$

$$x_i = g_i = \sum_r K_r a_i^r + b_i = \sum_r a_i^r \phi^r + b_i, \tag{21}$$

may be derived by differentiating (17) and (18) and neglecting the dependence of the aggregates on p. That is, we can treat the aggregates as pure measures of capital.

To do all this we proceed much as in Gorman (1968*a*, 1976). I eschew rigour to a remarkable degree.

Assume $R < n$ = number of goods. There is no problem otherwise. Solve (10) for $\phi(p, y)$ in terms of $g_1(p, y), \ldots, g_R(p, y)$[3] and normalize to take those as the new $\phi^1(p, y), \ldots, \phi^R(p, y)$. Then

$$\phi^r(p, y) = \sum_t \phi^{rt}(p, y_t); \qquad \phi^{rt}(p, y_t) = g_r^t(p, y_t), \tag{22}$$

and (10) becomes

$$\sum_t g_i^t(p, y_t) = G^i\left(p, \sum_t \phi^t(p, y_t)\right), \text{ say}, \qquad \text{each } i, \tag{23}$$

$$\phi^t = (\phi^{1t}, \ldots, \phi^{Rt}). \tag{24}$$

This is just the affinity[4] equation of Gorman (1968*a*, 1976) and, as shown there, in a wide class of cases its solution is (17) as required.

I will sketch the argument again here. First

$$g_i^t(p, y_t) = G^{ti}(p, \phi^t(p, y_t)), \text{ say}. \tag{25}$$

To show this, hold p, y_s, $s \neq t$ constant, and vary y_t holding $\phi^t(p, y_t)$ constant in (23). Now choose a reference vector $\bar{y}$ and define

$$b_i^t(p) = G^{ti}(p, \phi^t(p, \bar{y}_t)) = g_i^t(p, \bar{y}_t),$$

$$b_i(p) = G^i(p, \phi(p, \bar{y})) = g_i(p, \bar{y}), \tag{26}$$

[3] So that the appropriate Jacobian is of rank $R \geqslant 1$ in the neighbourhood in question, we then number the appropriate rows 1, 2, ..., R.

[4] By analogy with Cauchy's 'linearity equation'.

$$K^{ti}(p, \phi^t(p, y_t)) = G^{ti}(p, \phi^t(p, y_t)) - b_i^t(p) = g_i^t(p, y_t) - g_i^t(p, \bar{y}_t), \tag{27}$$

$$K^i(p, \phi(p, y)) = G^i(p, \phi(p, y)) - b_i(p) = g_i(p, y) - g_i(p, \bar{y}), \tag{28}$$

to get

$$K^{ti}(p, z) = K^i(p, z), \quad z = \phi(p, y) \tag{29}$$

$$\sum_t K^i(p, z_t) = K^i\left(p, \sum_t z_t\right), \quad z_t = \phi^t(p, y_t) \tag{30}$$

in (25)–(28). This is the linearity equation yielding

$$K^i(p, z) = \sum_r a^{ri}(p) z_r, \tag{31}$$

under very general conditions. (25)–(27) then yield[5]

$$g_i^t(p, y_t) = \sum_r a_i^r(p)\phi^{rt}(p, y_t) + b_i^t(p), \tag{32}$$

and (10), (28) give

$$g_i(p, y) = \sum_r a_i^r \phi^r(p, y) + b_i(p). \tag{33}$$

Now $g^t = \sum_i p_i g_i^t$, $g = \sum_i p_i g_i$, etc. Hence

$$g^t(p, y_t) = \sum_r a^r(p)\phi^{rt}(p, y_t) + b^t(p). \tag{34}$$

$$g(p, y) = \sum_r a_r(p)\phi^r(p, y) + b(p). \tag{35}$$

Alternatively, integrating (32), (33) we get

$$g^t(p, y_t) =: K^t(a(p), y_t) + b^t(p), \tag{36}$$

$$g(p, y) =: K(a(p), y) + b(p), \tag{37}$$

and differentiating with respect to p_i and identifying with (32)–(33),

$$K_r^t(a(p), y_t) = \phi^{rt}(p, y_t); \quad K_r(a(p), y) = \phi^r(p, y) \tag{38}$$

as required. This 'proves' (2)–(21).

It might not seem that this further weakening of our requirements has got us very far either. On the other hand, (36)–(37) is reasonably wide.

Some interpretation is called for. Suppose for the moment that $a^1(\cdot), \ldots, a^R(\cdot)$ are actual profit functions, not merely marginal profit

[5] The essential condition is that we should be able to manipulate enough y's while holding the others constant. To do so, we may need to group firms as in Sect. 6. If so, the appropriate Jacobian for the economy as a whole, and for each subeconomy formed by throwing out just one of the groups, must be of the same rank R. If you like, none of the 'factors' must be specific in a particular group, when the group have been appropriately assembled; for this it seems to be enough that none be specific to a single firm. The replacement of a^{ri} in (31) by a_i^r in (32) is justified in Sect. 6 below.

functions. $b^1(\cdot), \ldots, b^T(\cdot), b(\cdot)$ certainly are by (26). Then we can treat them as unit profit functions. As such they will have dual constant returns 'transformation functions' corresponding to $a(\cdot)$, $b(\cdot)$, $f(\cdot) = (f^r(\cdot))$, $h(\cdot) = (h^t(\cdot))$. These are quantities of fictitious variable goods, i.e. variable goods aggregates, and

$$z_r := f^r(x_r) = \partial K/\partial a^r = \phi^r(p, y), \tag{39}$$

$$z_{tr} := f^r(x_{tr}) = \partial K^t/\partial a^r = \phi^{rt}(p, y_t), \tag{40}$$

so that each unit of fixed aggregate r yields a unit of variable aggregate r without other inputs!—either in the economy at large or in the individual firm.

$$w_t = h^t(x_{t0}) = \partial g^t/\partial b^t = 1, \qquad \text{each } t, \tag{41}$$

is, if you like, the overhead variable good in firm t, $w = h(x_0) = 1$ for the economy as a whole.

Where the $a^r(\cdot)$ are not profit functions, it is better to interpret them as processes, and the $b^t(\cdot)$, $b(\cdot)$ still as common overheads. Then one unit of $\phi^r(p, y)$ supports process r at level one where it is available.

When process r is running at intensity z_r it yields $z_r a_i^r(p)$ units of variable good i, at prices p. When I say that $\phi^r(p, y)$ supports it, I mean that $z_r = \phi^r(p, y)$, $z_{tr} = \phi^{rt}(p, y_t)$, as in (39)–(40).

Note that the shadow price of the rth capital factor is $a^r(p)$ everywhere, without there being a market for it. This is as in Gorman (1968*a*, 1976).

3. RELATIVE SUPPLIES

I require

$$g_i(p, y)/g_1(p, y) = \sum_t g_i^t(p, y) \Big/ \sum_t g_1^t(p, y) = H^i(p, \phi(p, y)), \text{ say,} \tag{42}$$

as a further relaxation.

Solve the first R equations and normalize to get

$$\phi^r(p, y) = g_r(p, y)/g_1(p, y) = \psi^r(p, y)/\psi^1(p, y), \text{ say,} \tag{43}$$

where

$$\psi^r(p, y) := g_r(p, y) = \sum_t g_r^t(p, y_t) =: \sum_t \psi^{rt}(p, y_t), \text{ say,} \quad r = 1, \ldots, R+1. \tag{44}$$

(42) now reads

$$\sum_t g_i^t(p, y) = H^i(p, \psi/\psi^1)\psi^1 = G^i(p, \psi(p, y)) = G^i\left(p, \sum \psi^t(p, y_t)\right);$$
$$G^i(p, \cdot) \text{ conical, } \psi^t = (\psi^{1t}, \ldots, \psi^{R+1,t}). \tag{45}$$

Treating this affinity equation just like (23), we get

$$g_i^t(p, y_t) = \sum_r a_i^r(p)\psi^{rt}(p, y_t) + b_i^t(p), \tag{46}$$

$$g_i(p, y) = \sum_r a_i^r(p)\psi^r(p, y), \tag{47}$$

since

$$b(p) = \sum_t b^t(p) = 0, \tag{48}$$

because $G^i(p, \cdot)$ is conical in ψ. We also get

$$g^t(p, y_t) =: K^t(a(p), y_t) + b^t(p), \text{ say,} \tag{49}$$

$$g(p, y) =: K(a(p), y), \tag{50}$$

$$\psi^{rt}(p, y_t) = K_r^t(a(p), y_t); \quad \psi^r(p, y) = K_r(a(p), y), \tag{51}$$

$$g^t(p, y_t) = \sum_r a^r(p)\psi^{rt}(p, y_t) + b^t(p), \tag{52}$$

again, as in Section 2.

(48) may be thought rather a coincidence. In particular, we would have

$$\text{each } b^t(p) = 0, \tag{53}$$

in (49) and (52), if we required firms to be born and die.

It is easily seen that (42) is satisfied with

$$\phi^r(p, y) = K_{r+1}(a(p), y)/K_1(a(p), y) = \psi^{r+1}/\psi^1. \tag{54}$$

Compare with the results in Section 2 and notice how little extra mileage the further relaxation (42) of our requirement on the aggregates yields.

4. AGGREGATES INDEPENDENT OF PRICES

If, in Section 2,

$$g_i(p, y) = G^i(p, \phi(y)), \qquad \text{each } i, \tag{55}$$

then

$$g(p, y) = \sum p_i G^i(p, \phi(y)) = G(p, \phi(y)), \text{ say,} \tag{56}$$

and vice versa, the case discussed in Gorman (1968*a*, 1976). We are left with the case discussed in Section 3,

$$g_i(p, y)/g_1(p, y) = H^i(p, \phi(y)). \tag{57}$$

Using (48) and (50),

$$K_m(a, y)/K_1(a, y) = h^m(a, \phi(y)), \text{ say.} \tag{58}$$

Writing this down for $a = \bar{a}$, $m = 2, 3, \ldots, R+1$, say, solving for $\phi(y)$ and substituting back, we get

$$\sum_t K_m^t(a, y_t) = L^m\left(a, \sum_t \psi^t(y_t)\right)\sum_t K_1^t(a, y_t), \text{ say,} \tag{59}$$

where $\psi^t = (\psi^{1t}, \ldots, \psi^{R+1, t})$, and

$$\psi^{rt}(y_t) = K_r^t(\bar{a}, y_t), \quad r = 1, 2, \ldots, R+1, \tag{60}$$

$$L^m(a, \cdot) \text{ is positively homogeneous of degree zero.} \tag{61}$$

Hold a and each y_s constant, $s \neq t$ and vary y_t to $\tilde{y}_t$, where $\psi^t(\tilde{y}_t) = \psi^t(y_t)$. (61) then yields

$$K_m^t(a, \tilde{y}_t) - K_m^t(a, y_t) = L^m\left(a, \sum \psi^t(y_t)\right)(K_1^t(a, \tilde{y}_t) - K_1^t(a, y_t)). \tag{62}$$

Unless

$$K_1^t(a, \tilde{y}_t) - K_1^t(a, y_t) = 0, \tag{63}$$

we can divide across by it, to find

$$L^m\left(a, \sum \psi^t(y_t)\right) = \ell^m(a), \text{ say.} \tag{64}$$

Rejecting this degenerate case, we have (63), which of course implies

$$K_m^t(a, \tilde{y}_t) = K_m^t(a, y_t) = M_m^t(a, \psi^t(y_t)), \text{ say,} \tag{65}$$

in (62), so that (59) becomes

$$\sum_t M_m^t(a, \psi^t) = L^m\left(a, \sum_t \psi^t\right)\sum_t M_1^t(a, \psi^t). \tag{66}$$

Set now

$$\tilde{\psi}^t = \psi^t + \mu; \quad \tilde{\psi}^\theta = \psi^\theta - \mu; \quad \tilde{\psi}^s = \psi^s, \text{ otherwise,} \tag{67}$$

to get

$$\begin{aligned}(M_m^t(a, \psi^t + \mu) - M_m^t(a, \psi^t)) - (M_m^\theta(a, \tilde{\psi}^\theta + \mu) - M_m^\theta(a, \tilde{\psi}^\theta))\\ = L^m\left(a, \sum \psi^t\right)\{(M_1^t(a, \psi^t + \mu) - M_1^t(a, \psi^t))\\ - (M_1^\theta(a, \tilde{\psi}^\theta + \mu) - M_1^\theta(a, \tilde{\psi}^\theta))\},\end{aligned} \tag{68}$$

which once again implies (64), unless $\{\cdot\} = 0$, implying

$$M_m^t(a, \psi^t + \mu) - M_m^t(a, \psi^t) = M_m^\theta(a, \tilde{\psi}^\theta + \mu) - M_m^\theta(a, \tilde{\psi}^\theta) = \lambda_m(a, \mu), \text{ say,} \tag{69}$$

and, in turn,

$$\lambda_m(a, \mu + \nu) = \lambda_m(a, \mu) = \lambda_m(a, \nu), \tag{70}$$

so that

$$\lambda_m(a, \mu) = \sum c^r_m(a)\mu^r, \text{ say}, \tag{71}$$

and

$$K^t_m(a, y_t) = M^t_m(a, \psi^t) = d^t_m(a) + \sum\nolimits_r c^r_m(a)\psi^{rt}, \text{ say}, \tag{72}$$

where

$$d^t_m(a) = M^t_m(a, 0). \tag{73}$$

This is the same as

$$K^t(a, \psi^t) = \mathrm{d}^t(a) + \sum\nolimits_r c^r(a)\psi^{rt}, \tag{74}$$

yielding

$$K(a, \psi) = \sum\nolimits_r c^r(a)\psi^r, \tag{75}$$

where

$$\sum\nolimits_t d^t(a) = 0, \tag{76}$$

by (7).

Clearly (75)–(76) also imply (58) with

$$\phi^r(y) = \psi^{r+1}(y)/\psi^1(y), \quad r = 1, 2, \ldots, R. \tag{77}$$

(76) may seem rather a coincidence. If we require aggregation to remain possible when firms die, it implies

$$\text{each } d^t(a) = 0. \tag{78}$$

Look now at (49) and (75). Merge $d^t(a)$ into $b^t(p)$, and renormalize to call c^r, a^r. (75) then becomes

$$g^t(p, y_t) = b^t(p) + \sum\nolimits_r a^r(p)\psi^{rt}(y_t), \tag{79}$$

$$g(p, y) = \sum_{r=1}^{R+1} a^r(p)\psi^r(y); \quad \psi^r(y) = \sum\nolimits_t \psi^{rt}(y_t), \tag{80}$$

with

$$\sum b^t(p) = 0, \tag{81}$$

always, and

$$\text{each } b^t(p) = 0, \tag{82}$$

if firms may die.

The conditions (79)–(80) are clearly sufficient for (58) as well as necessary.

5. ADDITIVE HOMOGENEITY

Consider the solution

$$g(p, y) = K(a, y) + b(p) = N(a + be, b, y), \text{ say,} \qquad e = (1, \ldots, 1) \tag{83}$$

in Section 2. Clearly

$$N(a, 0, y) = K(a, y), \tag{84}$$

$$N(c, y) = N(c - c_R e, 0, y) + c_R, \text{ say,} \tag{85}$$

$$N(c + de, y) = N(c - c_R e, 0, y) + c_R + d = N(c, y) + d, \tag{86}$$

which I call *additive homogeneity*, for an obvious reason. More precisely, it is *of degree one*.

I came upon it first in this context a couple of years ago when I was discussing polynomial Engel curves, and again in a problem in social choice theory. The general condition for it is (83) with $b(\cdot)$ functionally independent of a. Note that, were it not, it could be subsumed into $K(\cdot, y)$.

Now look at (83) with this functional independence. Write

$$h(p, y) = g(p, y) - b(p) = \tilde{G}(p, \psi) - \tilde{G}(p, 0), \text{ say,} \tag{87}$$

a marginal cost function and take

$$\tilde{a}^r(p) = h(p, \tilde{y}^r), \tag{88}$$

where $\tilde{y}^r$ is a fixed y vector. Then solve the equations

$$\tilde{a}^r = \sum_s a^s \psi^s(a, \tilde{y}^r) = \sum_s a^s \psi^{sr}(a), \text{ say,} \tag{89}$$

for the a's in terms of the $\tilde{a}$'s, substitute back to get

$$\sum a^r(p)\psi^r(a, y) = \sum \tilde{a}^r(p)\tilde{\psi}^r(\tilde{a}, y), \tag{90}$$

in general, and drop the ~'s. The new $\tilde{a}$'s are now marginal profit functions and

$$c^r(p) = g(p, y^r) = b(p) + a^r(p), \qquad r = 1, 2, \ldots, R+1, \qquad b(p) = \tilde{G}(p, 0) \tag{91}$$

are ordinary profit functions. Finally

$$g(p, y) = \sum_{r=1}^{R} a^r(p)\psi^r(a, y) + b(p),$$

$$= \sum_{r=1}^{R+1} c^r(p)\psi^r(c, y); \quad \sum \psi^r(c, y) = 1,$$

$$= N(c, y), \text{ say.} \tag{92}$$

Differentiating with respect to p_i, we get

$$g_i = \sum_{r=1}^{R+1} N_r(c, y)c_i^r. \tag{93}$$

Multiply this by p_i, add, and note the fact that $g(\cdot, y)$, and each $c^r(\cdot)$, is a profit function, to get

$$g(p, y) = \sum_{r=1}^{R+1} N_r(c, y)c^r(p); \tag{94}$$

so that we may take

$$\psi^r(c, y) = N_r(c, y). \tag{95}$$

Using the solution of (88) again and substituting into (83), we see that it holds in the new normalization too, given (91). Hence (86) holds, or differentiating with respect to d, and setting $d = 0$,

$$\sum N_r(c, y) = 1, \tag{96}$$

which is what we would expect from (92) and (95).

One advantage of this form is that the $c^r(\cdot)$ are profit functions, though there seems no necessity for $N(\cdot, y)$ to be one. It is conical of course, but does not seem to need to be closed convex. If $f^r(\cdot)$ is the dual of $c^r(\cdot)$, however,

$$z_r = f^r(x_r) = N_r(c, y), \text{ say;} \quad x = \sum\nolimits_r x_r, \tag{97}$$

rather as at the end of Section 2.

A simple example is the affine cost function

$$g(p, u) = a(p)u + b(p) = (a(p) + b(p))u + b(p)(1 - u),$$

$$= c^1(p)u + c^2(p)(1 - u), \tag{98}$$

where

$$c^1(p) = g(p, 1); \quad c^2(p) = g(p, 0). \tag{99}$$

6. A HINT OF RIGOUR

The critical assumption underlying the arguments from linearity above is that the components of the ϕ^{rt} can be varied independently. There are important cases where this is not so. For example, y_t might be a scalar and $R > 1$ in Section 2, or $R > 0$ in Sections 3 and 4.

It is quite easy to rearrange[6] the argument to take account of this. Group the 'firms' into 'industries', = 1, 2, . . . , each sufficiently large for

$$\phi^{r\theta}(p, y_\theta) = \sum_{t \in \theta} \theta^{rt}(p, y_t), \tag{100}$$

to be independently variable. Then (23) becomes

$$\sum\nolimits_\theta g_i^\theta(p, y) = G^i\left(p, \sum\nolimits_\theta \phi^{r\theta}(p, y_\theta)\right), \qquad \text{each } i \tag{101}$$

where

$$g^\theta(p, y_\theta) = \sum_{t \in \theta} g^t(p, y_t), \tag{102}$$

so that the argument leading up to (31) implies

$$g_i^\theta(p, y_\theta) = \sum\nolimits_r a_i^r(p)\phi^{r\theta}(p, y_\theta) + b_i^\theta(p), \tag{103}$$

and thus

$$\sum_{t \in \theta} g_i^t(p, y_t) = \sum_{t \in \theta}\left\{\sum\nolimits_r a_i^r(p)\phi^{rt}(p, y_t)\right\} + b_i^\theta(p), \tag{104}$$

by (101) and (102). Hence

$$g_i^t(p, y_t) = \sum\nolimits_r a_i^r(p)\phi^{rt}(p, y_t) + b_i^t(p), \text{ say,} \tag{105}$$

where

$$\sum_{t \in \theta} b^t(p) = b^\theta(p). \tag{106}$$

(105) is the result from which everything else in Section 2 flows.

A precisely similar argument works in Section 3, and, with only a little, rather obvious, adaptation in Section 4.

The other difficulty lies in the normalizations used. They have functionally independent components at national level, and the equations determining them have to be invertible. For this, I presume, one might have to use different bases in different subdomains. I have not gone into this.[7]

[6] Read in conjunction with nn. 3 and 5.

[7] See Gorman (1986) for a treatment.

A further point worth taking up is this: how does

$$g_i^t(p, y_t) = b_i^t(p) + \sum_r a^{ri}(p)\phi^{rt}(p, y_t), \tag{107}$$

implied by (25), become

$$g_i^t(p, y_t) = b_i^t(p) + \sum a_i^r(p)\phi^{rt}(p, y_t), \tag{108}$$

in (31). In (107), i is only an index in a^{ri}, in (108) it denotes differentiation in a_i^r.

Here is the construction. First define

$$h^t(p, y_t) = g^t(p, y_t) - g^t(p, \bar{y}_t) = g^t(p, y_t) - b^t(p),$$

$$h(p, y) = \sum h^t(p, y_t) = g(p, y) - g(p, \bar{y}) = g(p, y) - b(p), \tag{109}$$

where $\bar{y}$ is taken from (26). Then take fixed vectors $y^1, \ldots, y^R$ and set

$$\tilde{a}^r(p) = h(p, y^r) = g(p, y^r) - b(p). \tag{110}$$

The natural version of (107) then yields

$$\tilde{a}_i^s(p) = \sum_r a^{ri}(p)\phi^r(p, y^s) = \sum_r a^{ri}(p)\psi^{rs}(p), \text{ say.} \tag{111}$$

Solve this for $a^{ri}(p)$ as

$$a^{ri}(p) = \sum_s \theta^{rs}(p)a_i^s(p), \text{ say,} \tag{112}$$

and define

$$\tilde{\phi}^{st}(p, y_t) = \sum_r \theta^{rs}(p)\phi^{rt}(p, y_t), \tag{113}$$

$$\tilde{\phi}^s(p, y) = \sum_r \theta^{rs}(p)\phi^r(p, y) = \sum_t \tilde{\phi}^{st}(p, y_t). \tag{114}$$

Substitute from (112)–(114) into (107), and drop the ~'s, to get (108).

Appendix A

Consider the differential equations[8]

$$g_i(x) = \lambda^r(x) f_i(x), \qquad \text{each } i \in r, \text{ each } r \in R, \tag{A.1}$$

where

$$x = (x_i)_{i \in I}, \tag{A.2}$$

$$R = \{r \in R\} \text{ is a partition of } I, \tag{A.3}$$

$$\text{the } \lambda(\cdot)\text{'s are distinct and } \lambda^r(x) > 0, \qquad \text{each } r \in R. \tag{A.4}$$

Given appropriate smoothness and connectivity, which I will assume throughout,

$$g(x) = \phi^r(y_r, f(x)), \text{ say}, \qquad \text{each } r \in R, \tag{A.5}$$

where

$$x_r = (x_i)_{i \in r}, \qquad y_r = (x_i)_{i \notin r}, \qquad \text{each } r \in R, \tag{A.6}$$

and

$$\phi_0^r(y_r, f(x)) := \partial\phi^r/\partial f = \lambda^r(x) > 0, \qquad \text{each } r \in R. \tag{A.7}$$

When $\# R = 1$

$$g(x) = \phi(f(x)), \text{ say}, \tag{A.8}$$

of course, given appropriate connectivity.

When $\# R = 2$, (A.5) may be written

$$g(x, y) = \phi(x, f(x, y)) = \psi(y, f(x, y)), \tag{A.9}$$

so that

$$f(x, y) = \psi^{-1}(y, \phi(x, f(x, y))) = \phi^{-1}(x, \psi(y, f(x, y))) \tag{A.10}$$

since $\psi(y, \cdot)$ and $\phi(x, \cdot)$ are strongly increasing. With luck this may be solved iteratively. Similarly

$$g(x, y) = \phi(x, \psi^{-1}(y, g(x, y))) = \psi(y, \phi^{-1}(x, g(x, y))), \tag{A.11}$$

and as we will see later

$$h(x, y) = \tilde{\phi}(y, f(x, y)) = \tilde{\psi}(x, f(x, y)), \tag{A.12}$$

[8] Equations like (A.1)–(A.4) below often turn up in the theories of aggregation and decentralization. In the past I had dealt with them on an *ad hoc* basis, with the help of whatever else I knew of the structure. Here I guess at what may be the general solution of them, or something like it.

some $\tilde{\phi}(\cdot)$, $\tilde{\psi}(\cdot)$ iff

$$h(x, y) = H(f(x, y), g(x, y)), \qquad \text{some } H(\cdot). \tag{A.13}$$

This suggests the following construction for any finite $R = \{1, 2, \ldots, n\}$, say,

$$a^r(x) = \alpha^r(x_r, \alpha^{r+1}(x_{r+1}, \alpha^{r+2}(\ldots, \alpha^{r-1}(x_{r-1}, a^r(x))\ldots))), \text{ each } r \in R, \tag{A.14}$$

where

$$\alpha^r(x_r, \cdot) \text{ is strongly increasing}, \qquad \text{each } r \in R. \tag{A.15}$$

Assuming that (A.14) converges for each $r \in R$,

$$a^r(x) = \alpha^r(x_r, \alpha^{r+1}(\ldots, \alpha^{s-1}(x_{s-1}, a^s(x))\ldots)), \qquad \text{each } r \in R, \tag{A.16}$$

where we identify α^{n+p} with α^p throughout, that is, work modulo n. Hence

$$a^r(x) = A^{rs}(x_r, \ldots, x_{s-1}, a^s(x)), \text{ say}, \quad \text{each } r, s \in R, \tag{A.17}$$

$$= A^r(x_r, \ldots, x_n, a^1(x)), \text{ say}, \quad \text{each } r \in R, \tag{A.18}$$

and equally, (A.16) yields

$$a^r(x) = B^r(x_1, x_2, \ldots, x_{r-1}, a^1(x)), \text{ say}, \quad \text{each } r \in R, \tag{A.19}$$

when we put $r = 1$, $s = r$ in (A.17) and invert.

Thus $f = a^r(x)$, $g = a^s(x)$ satisfy equations like (A.5), for each $r, s \in R$.

Now consider any well-behaved

$$f(x) = F(a^r(x) \mid r \in R) := F(a(x)), \quad a(x) = (a^r(x))_{r \in R}. \tag{A.20}$$

It yields

$$f_i = \sum_{r \in R} F^r a_i^r. \tag{A.21}$$

Now (A.18) and (A.19) imply

$$a_i^r(x) = \mu^{rt} a_i^1(x), \text{ say}, \quad \text{each } i \in t;\ r, t \in R, \tag{A.22}$$

so that

$$f_i(x) = \sum_{r \in R} F^r \mu^{rt} a_i^1 = \nu^t(x) a_i^1(x), \text{ say}, \qquad \text{each } i \in t \in T, \tag{A.23}$$

and hence

$$g_i(x) = \lambda^t(x) f_i(x), \quad \text{each } i \in t, \quad \text{by (A.1)}, \tag{A.24}$$

$$= \sigma^t(x) a_i^1(x), \text{ say}, \quad \text{each } i \in t \in R. \tag{A.25}$$

I will now show that this implies

$$g(x) = G(a^r(x) \mid r \in R), \text{ say.} \tag{A.26}$$

This will be so iff

$$g_i(x) = \sum_{r \in R} \pi^r(x) a_i^r(x), \text{ say,} \tag{A.27}$$

so we want to throw (A.25) into that form.

To do so, introduce

$$\rho^{rs}(x), \text{ each } r, s \in R, \quad \text{such that } \sum_{s \in R} \rho^{rs}(x) = 1, \text{ each } r \in R, \tag{A.28}$$

to get

$$g_i(x) = \sigma^r(x) \sum_{s \in R} \{\rho^{rs}(x) a_i^s(x)/\mu^{sr}(x)\}, \quad i \in r \in R, \tag{A.29}$$

by (A.22) and (A.25), which implies (A.27) if

$$\sigma^r \rho^{rs}/\mu^{sr} = \pi^s, \qquad \text{each } r, s \in R, \tag{A.30}$$

or, equivalently,

$$\rho^{rs} = \pi^s \mu^{sr}/\sigma^r = \pi^s \theta^{rs}, \text{ say,} \tag{A.31}$$

so that

$$\sum_{s \in R} \theta^{rs}(x) \pi^s(x) = 1, \tag{A.32}$$

by (A.28), which is always possible unless

$$\sum_{s \in R} \theta^{rs}(x) q^s(x) = 0, \qquad \text{some } q \neq 0, \tag{A.33}$$

or, equivalently,

$$\sum_{s \in R} \mu^{sr}(x) q^s(x) = 0, \tag{A.34}$$

itself equivalent to the functional dependence of the $a^r(\cdot)$. Thus (A.1) and (A.20) imply

$$g(x) = G(a(x)), \text{ say,} \quad a(x) = (a^r(x))_{r \in R} \tag{A.35}$$

when the $a^r(\cdot)$ are functionally independent. It is trivial that (A.20) and (A.33) imply (A.1).

One could begin this argument with (A.14)–(A.15) instead of (A.1)–(A.4). Because of (A.18) and (A.19), f depends only on $a^r(\cdot)$, given y_r. Because of the strict monotonicity, a knowledge of f, y_r yields a^r and hence each a^s, and thus any $G(a^r(x) \mid r \in R)$. That is at least one side of the argument.

I am now in a position to state a conjecture.

CONJECTURE: The pairs $f(\cdot)$, $g(\cdot)$ satisfying equations like (A.1) can be constructed in the following manner. Define a *structure* Ω on $R = (1, 2, \ldots, n)$. It is a set of subsets $S \subseteq R$ closed under intersection. To be precise

$$R,\ \Phi \in \Omega;\ \text{and if } S,\ T \in \Omega, \text{ then } S \cap T \in \Omega. \tag{A.36}$$

Call R, Φ the *trivial* elements of Ω, the others its *proper elements*, and the minimal proper elements, *bottom elements*. For each bottom element $S \in \Omega$ construct a vector

$$a^S(x_S) = (a^r(x_S))_{r \in S}, \qquad x_S = (x_r)_{r \in S}, \tag{A.37}$$

of independent functions of x_S, as in (A.14).

The next step is to construct similar functions on the higher elements of Ω. If a bottom element $S \subset T \in \Omega$, $a^S(x_S)$ will be among the arguments of $a^T(x^T)$. That is how the x_r, $r \in S$, enter into $a^T(\cdot)$. The simplest way to deal with this is to regard the $a^S(x_S)$ which have been constructed at any stage as parameters entering into each $a^T(\cdot)$, $S \subset T \in \Omega$, and remove the corresponding sectors $r \in S$ from the listing of each $T \in \Omega$ with $S \subset T$, including R. Call the correlates of R, Ω, $S \in \Omega$: R^*, Ω^*, $S^* \in \Omega^*$. Ω^* is clearly a structure on R^*. Take its bottom elements. Let T^* be one of them and T its correlate in Ω. Then

$$a^T(x_T) = a^{T^*}(x_{T^*}, a^S(x_S) \mid S \subseteq T \text{ and } S \in \Omega) \tag{A.38}$$

and so on up the graph of Ω.

This construction will yield just n a's, and each sector $r \in R$ will have a unique vector $a^S(\cdot)$, $S \in \Omega$, into which it first enters, and through which it enters into each $a^T(\cdot)$, $S \subset T \in \Omega$. It is this which ensures that (A.1) holds and

$$f(x) = F(a(x)), \qquad g(x) = G(a(x)). \tag{A.39}$$

Remember that (A.23) and (A.25) hold by construction for any element of $a(x)$ into which x_t first enters.

Given sufficiently good behaviour, then, this procedure does generate solutions of our problem.

What remains to be proved is that they are the only solutions. 'Proved' is far too strong a word for the arguments in this appendix. 'Argued' or 'suggested' might be better.

Note in particular that I have done nothing at all about:

(i) The possible functional dependence of the $a^r(\cdot)$ generated in this way, either on paper or in my own mind. My thoughtless guess is that this would be avoided were we to insist that each $a^r(\cdot)$ depends on both its arguments, except for single-member bottom elements. For them $a^r = a^r(x_r)$, or, for an $S^* \in \Omega^*$, $a^r(x_r;$ lower a's). If so, its dependence on x_r is probably all that is required.

(ii) The condition that the $\lambda^r(\cdot)$ be distinct; or even the precise meaning to be given to that term.

(iii) My arbitrary ordering of the elements of R as $1, 2, \ldots, n$.

Appendix B: Processes

In the text we found profit functions

$$g(p, y) = b(p) + G(a^1(p), \ldots, a^R(p); y), \tag{B.1}$$

where the $a(\cdot)$'s, though conical, were not necessarily convex. I suggested that they might be thought of as representing processes. They were in fact marginal profit functions but, if not convex, could not be profit functions, or more particularly unit profit functions. I will call them *quasi-profit functions*.

Suppose one of these were not convex. If actually concave it is just a loss function, and the observed behaviour loss minimizing. If not, the situation is a little peculiar.

For simplicity, let there be only two goods, x and y; take the latter as numeraire and let the price of the former be p. I will consider the locus of the net supplies x, y from this process as p varies.

Suppose, for definiteness, that $a''(p) > 0$ for $p < p^*$, $a''(p^*) = 0$ and $a''(p) < 0$ for $p > p^*$. The quasi-profit function is then convex—or 'normal'—for $p < p^*$, concave for $p > p^*$ and has an inflection at p^*.

Now

$$x = a'(p), \qquad y = a(p) - pa'(p), \tag{B.2}$$

here. Incidentally I have taken both x and y to be outputs in the illustration in Figure 21.1. Now let the price p increase from zero towards p^*. In this convex section of the quasi-profit function, (x, y) trace out a normal transformation locus in Figure 21.2, x increasing and y decreasing, in particular. At p^*, however, $dx/dp = dy/dp = 0$, so that it comes to a halt,

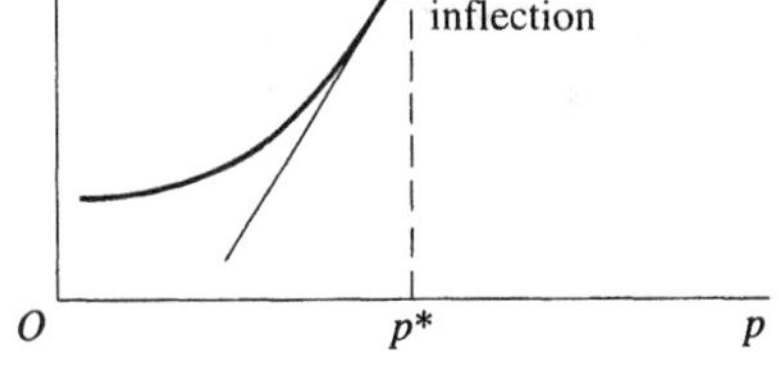

FIG. 21.1

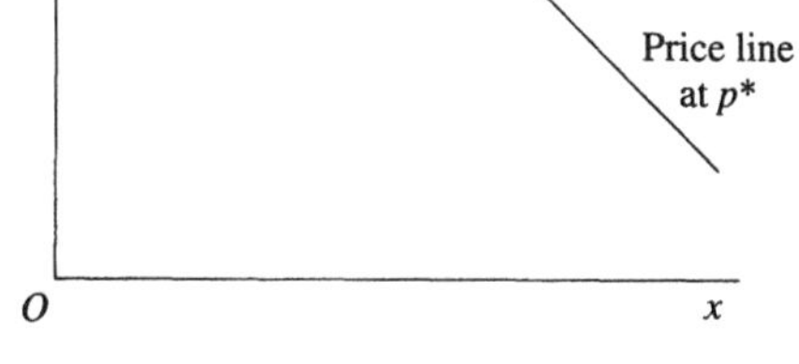

FIG. 21.2

momentarily, and then reverses direction with x increasing, y decreasing. Of course it still lies on the price line at p^* to a first approximation in x—or second in p since $a''(p^*) = 0$. Hence it goes off in a cusp as in Figure 21.2.

Had there been a higher $p^{**} > p^*$, such that $a''(p)$ became positive again after p^{**}, we would have had something like that depicted in Figures 21.3 and 21.4.

You must decide for yourself whether Figure 21.4 is acceptable as a picture of process production.

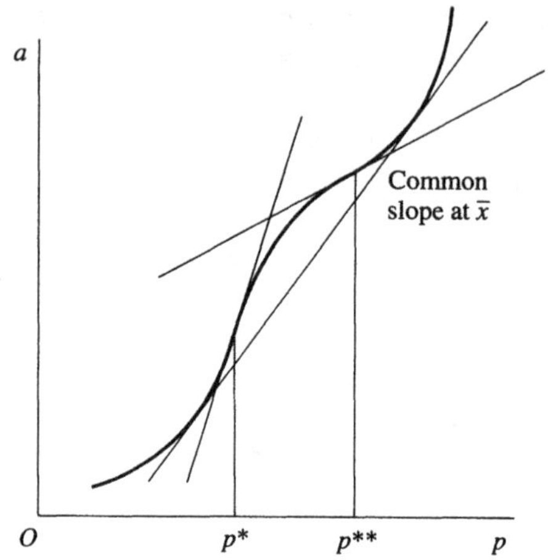

FIG. 21.3

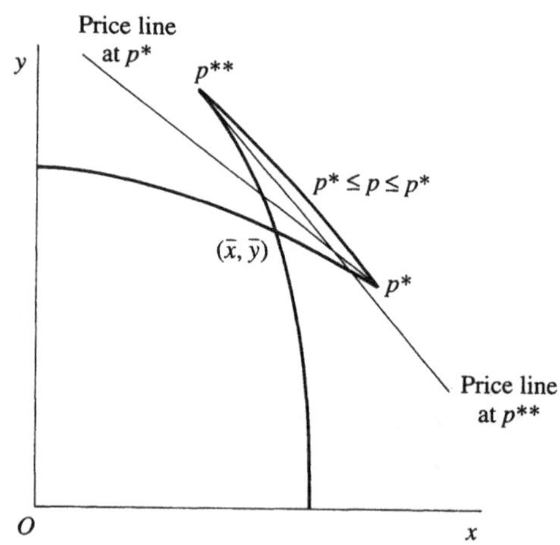

FIG. 21.4

Appendix C: Market Production

As I mentioned in discussing polynomial Engel curves, that system is not very realistic. Nevertheless it may be worth while tying the present discussion up with it.

Set then

$$\sum f^{ti}(p, y_t) = F^i(p, \phi(y)), \tag{C.1}$$

where y_t is now income. Arguments like those in Sections 2 and 6 quickly yield

$$f^{ti}(p, y_t) = b^{ti}(p) + \sum_r a^{ri}(p)\phi^{rt}(y_t) \tag{C.2}$$

which was the starting point for 'Polynomial Engel Curves'.[9]

Similarly, in the market shares version,

$$\frac{\sum_t f^{ti}(p, y_t)}{\sum_t f^{t1}(p, y_t)} = F^i(p, \phi(y_t)) \tag{C.3}$$

we first set $p = \bar{p}$ to get

$$\sum f^{ti}(p, y_t) = H^i\left(p, \sum \psi^t(y_t)\right)\sum f^{t1}(p, y_t) \tag{C.4}$$

as in Section 3, where

$$H^i(p, \cdot) \text{ is now positively homogeneous of degree 0,} \tag{C.5}$$

and then arguments like those in Section 6 quickly yield

$$f^{ti}(p, y_t) = b^{ti}(p, y_t) + \sum_{r=1}^{R+1} a^{ri}(p)\psi^{rt}(y_t) \tag{C.6}$$

$$\sum f^{ti}(p, y_t) = f^i(p, y) = \sum_{r=1}^{R+1} a^{ri}(p)\psi^r(y_t), \tag{C.7}$$

where

$$\psi^r(y) = \sum \psi^{rt}(y_t); \qquad \sum b^{ti}(p) = 0. \tag{C.8}$$

Homogeneity gives

$$\phi^{rt}(y_t) = c_{rt}y_t(\log y_t)^{\beta_{rt}}, \tag{C.9}$$

[9] [eds.] 'Polynomial Engel Curves' was an earlier, more narrowly defined, version of 'Some Engel Curves'.

without loss of generality, and then in (C.8),

$$\alpha_{rt} = \alpha_r, \qquad \beta_{rt} = \beta_r. \tag{C.10}$$

The argument for (C.9) is given in 'Polynomial Engel Curves'. As I mentioned, I think one would deflate y_t in defining Engel curves. In doing so one would lose (C.9) and (C.10).

22

Muellbauer's Representative Consumer

Editorial Remarks

The following paper has been constructed from handwritten notes which contain only an introduction, the beginning of a proof, and a conclusion; the proof of the main result is missing. Fortunately, a straightforward application of the main result of Section 2 of 'More Measures for Fixed Factors' fills this gap. The problem itself is an interesting one, posed and solved by Muellbauer (1976).

The representative consumer in the problem addressed by Gorman in 1953 can be conceived in either of two equivalent ways: either the representative consumer replicates average demand with average total income; or else it replicates total demand with total income. Muellbauer suggested looking for a representative consumer who replicates the shares demanded, but not necessarily the levels. Furthermore, he permitted the utility level of the representative agent to depend upon prices, as well as upon the incomes of all members of the society.

We present these notes because they show how Gorman began to think about a new problem, and because it is such a clean application of the previous paper. The notes probably date from 1976 but we cannot be certain. In any case they certainly precede 'More Measures for Fixed Factors'.

Editorial Summary

Suppose that there are T consumers with preferences represented by their expenditure functions $g^t(u_t, p)$, $t = 1, \ldots, T$. Using Shephard's lemma, the share of the ith commodity in the expenditure of consumer t is given by

$$\frac{p_i x_i}{\sum_j p_j x_j} = \frac{p_i g_i^t(u_t, p)}{g^t(u_t, p)}. \tag{0.1}$$

Now the expenditure-weighted average share of the ith commodity is given by

$$\sum_t \left[\frac{g^t(u_t, p)}{\sum_t g^t(u_t, p)} \times \frac{p_i g_i^t(u_t, p)}{g^t(u_t, p)} \right] = \frac{\sum_t p_i g_i^t(u_t, p)}{\sum_t g^t(u_t, p)}. \tag{0.2}$$

Muellbauer (1976) determines the conditions under which there exists a share- representative consumer such that

$$\frac{\sum_t p_i g_i^t(u_t, p)}{\sum_t g^t(u_t, p)} = \frac{p_i g_i(\bar{u}, p)}{g(\bar{u}, p)} \tag{0.3}$$

where $\bar{u} = \theta(u_1, \ldots, u_T, p)$ for some function θ. Gorman proceeds by rewriting the problem in terms of the logs of the prices, but we will not need this step in the original proof. Dividing all equations in (0.3) by the first equation yields the question posed in Section 2 of 'More Measures for Fixed Factors' for the case where $R = 1$.

Note that the Engel curves are at most rank two and satisfy the conditions set out in 'Some Engel Curves'. This is interesting in part because the representative consumer of Gorman (1953*a*) is a slightly more restrictive rank two demand system. In concluding, Gorman discusses briefly the meaning of this type of representative consumer.

Muellbauer's Representative Consumer

INTRODUCTION

Dr Muellbauer (1975, 1976) has recently discussed the conditions under which there exists a 'representative consumer', the proportional breakdown of whose consumption mirrors that of society as a whole.

In this paper I will follow the general lines of his treatment, showing that the solution he gets is not quite the general one, that this has misled him into believing that his central result is not a direct generalization of that in Gorman (1953*a*), and discussing the ideas of the 'representative consumer' underlying the two analyses.

1. TECHNICAL DISCUSSION

Let us specify the tth citizen's preferences by his cost function $g^t(u_t, p)$ in the obvious notation, and his *pseudo-cost function*

$$h^t(u_t, q) = g^t(u_t, p); \quad q_i = \log p_i, \quad \text{each } i, t. \tag{1.1}$$

Dr Muellbauer seeks the conditions under which there is a 'representative consumer', with pseudo-cost function $\bar{h}(\bar{u}, q)$ such that

$$\frac{\sum_t h_i^t(u_t, q)}{\sum_r h^t(u_t, q)} = \frac{\bar{h}_i(\bar{u}, q)}{\bar{h}(\bar{u}, q)}, \qquad \text{each } i, \tag{1.2}$$

where

$$\bar{u} = \theta(u, q), \tag{1.3}$$

in general, and suffixes denote differentiation.

Note that no problem arises when there are only two goods. Since, together, they exhaust the entire expenditure, (1.2) becomes

$$\frac{\bar{h}_1(\bar{u}, q)}{\bar{h}(\bar{u}, q)} = \frac{\sum_t h_1^t(u_t, q)}{\sum_t h^t(u_t, q)}, \tag{1.4}$$

which implicitly defines $\theta(\cdot)$ in (1.3). This is not surprising, since there is no integrablity problem in two dimensions. It suggests that the solution may in general depend on the existence of a pair of aggregate goods, as we will see it does.

Editorial note: At this point the manuscript contains the first two pages of a proof, the rest of which is lost. However from the main theorem in Sect. 2 of 'More Measures for Fixed Factors' with $R = 1$, it is immediate that the solution, written now in terms of the original cost functions, is given by

$$g^t(u_t, p) = G^t(u_t, a(p), b(p)) + c^t(p) \tag{E1}$$

for all t and

$$g(\bar{u}, p) = G(\bar{u}, a(p), b(p)) \tag{E2}$$

for the representative consumer. This then is the two-good world which Gorman refers to above.

2. INTERPRETATION

Let us first assume

$$c^t(p) = 0, \qquad \text{each } t, \tag{2.1}$$

and set

$$a^t(p) = (a_1(p), \ldots, a_n(p)), \quad b^t(p) = (b_1(p), \ldots, b_n(p)). \tag{2.2}$$

The tth consumer then combines the expenditure items

$$a'(p)/a(p), \quad b'(p)/b(p), \tag{2.3}$$

in the proportions

$$aG_a^t/G^t, \quad bG_b^t/G^t. \tag{2.4}$$

The society also combines these expenditure items, in fact in the proportions

$$a\sum_t G_a^t \Big/ \sum_t G^t, \quad b\sum_t G_b^t \Big/ \sum_t G^t. \tag{2.5}$$

All that we require of the representative consumer's cost function

$$g(\bar{u}, p) = G(\bar{u}, a(p), b(p)) \tag{2.6}$$

is that it be capable of aping these proportions in the form

$$aG_a(\bar{u}, a, b)/G(\bar{u}, a, b), \quad bG_b(\bar{u}, a, b)/G(\bar{u}, a, b) \tag{2.7}$$

for some value of $\bar{u}$. This clearly leaves a very wide class of 'representative preferences' indeed, each defining its own θ in (1.3). This is somewhat disturbing, as is the fact that a high $\bar{u}$ may go with low consumption, and a low $\bar{u}$ with high consumption.

If we deny (2.1) but remember that

$$\sum_t c^t(p) = 0 \tag{2.8}$$

we see that market demand, which is all that the 'representative consumer' is responsible for, is unchanged. Individual foibles of consumption, if you like, which cancel out over the whole society, do not matter from this point of view. This being so, I will revert to (2.1) while seeking a more detailed interpretation of (E1) and (E2) in terms of two aggregate goods.

Now $a(\cdot)$ and $b(\cdot)$ are cost functions, and may therefore be taken as unit cost functions. As such they represent constant returns technologies with homogeneous production functions

$$\alpha(\cdot),\ \beta(\cdot),\ \text{say}, \tag{2.9}$$

which yield quantities of two fictitious 'intermediate' goods, 'alpha' and 'beta' if you like.

Assume now that

$$\text{each } G^t(u_t, \cdot, \cdot),\ \ G(\bar{u}, \cdot, \cdot) \tag{2.10}$$

is also a cost function. If so they will correspond to utility functions

$$u_t = F^t(\alpha_t, \beta_t), \quad \bar{u} = F(\bar{\alpha}, \bar{\beta}), \tag{2.11}$$

where α_t, β_t and $\bar{\alpha}$, $\bar{\beta}$, represent consumption of these intermediate goods, by the tth consumer and the representative consumer, respectively. In terms of ordinary goods

$$u_t = f^t(x_t) = \sup\{F^t(\alpha(y_t), \beta(z_t)) \mid y_t + z_t \leqslant x_t\} \tag{2.12}$$

and

$$\bar{u} = f(\bar{x}) = \sup\{F(\alpha(\bar{y}), \beta(\bar{z})) \mid \bar{y} + \bar{z} \leqslant \bar{x}\}. \tag{2.13}$$

The consumer in question divides his expenditure between alpha and beta in proportions determined by their prices $a(p)$ and $b(p)$ and his income in (2.4) and (2.7). The expenditure on alpha is used to buy inputs y in the expenditure proportions a'/a and expenditure on beta is used to buy inputs z in the expenditure proportions b'/b. Unfortunately the fact that g^t and g are well-behaved cost functions does not imply that G^t and G are also, in their different arguments a, b, so that this more intuitive interpretation is not in general available.

3. CONCLUSION

As we have seen, Dr Muellbauer's representative consumer is rather an odd chap. His preferences are not all fully defined by his market choices, and, once they are arbitrarily fixed, he is as likely as not to be radiantly happy when those he represents are miserable and vice versa.

This is, of course, because it is only the proportional breakdown of expenditure which is to be predicted. Given that our index of income is to be chosen *ad hoc* this is enough to define the preference field and given the index of income defined in terms of these proportions, there is nothing in general to make it an increasing function of actual incomes. Of course, there may be canonical preference representations in certain cases which yield an income index which does increase. In particular, it is clear from Dr Muellbauer's analysis that when an index which depends only on the incomes can be found, choosing the representative preference ordering in such a way as to yield this index does yield monotonicity, and since there is a unique dual representation in shares, the imprecision about the underlying preferences disappears.

Thus the representative consumer is really a most reasonable idea in this case.

23

Assembling Efficient Organizations?

Editorial Summary

This paper appeared in a Festschrift in honour of Kenneth Arrow. The ideas contained in it clearly flow from those in 'More Measures for Fixed Factors', although the techniques used to obtain the results are different.

Gorman suggests that managers may buy and sell different firms with an eye toward efficient control within a large enterprise. This behaviour leads to an enterprise consisting of many different factories and subsidiaries chosen with this efficiency in mind. The manager of the enterprise wishes to be able to decentralize decision-making without any loss of efficiency. This paper rationalizes this procedure—a particular type of two-stage budgeting within profit-maximizing firms.

The firm uses a set of efficiency prices p and has a profit function

$$g(p, u) = \sum_{f \in F} g^f(p, u_f), \tag{0.1}$$

where each g^f is the profit of factory f given its vector of fixed inputs, u_f, and evaluated at the (possibly firm-specific) efficiency prices. He looks for a set of controls, v, which can be used to decentralize final production, x. That is,

$$x = \theta(p, v) = g'(p, u) = \sum_{f \in F} g'^f(p, u_f); \tag{0.2}$$

the primes represent the gradient with respect to prices. These controls turn out to be additive,

$$v = \sum_f v_f, \tag{0.3}$$

where

$$v_f = k'^f(a(p), u_f); \tag{0.4}$$

the prime represents a gradient with respect to the vector aggregate price indices $\{a^m(p)\}$, and k^f is given by

$$g^f(p, u_f) = k^f(a(p), u_f) - b^f(p). \tag{0.5}$$

If k^f is convex in the price indices then there is a technology set $S^f(u_f)$ such that

$$k^f(a(p), u_f) = \max\left\{\sum_m v_{fm}a^m(p) \mid v_f \in S^f(u_f)\right\}. \tag{0.6}$$

This means that the control variables v_{fm} can be chosen to ensure optimal output $v_{fm}a'^m(p)$ in each process. If a^m is convex, this can be a simple optimization problem. Of course, as a matter of choice, the firm itself looks very much like each of its component parts, given the argument above. Returning to the original question, this implies that managers in the buying and selling of component parts of an enterprise choose individual units that have a structure similar to those currently existing in the firm. If successful, the type of decentralization envisaged here would be efficient.

This paper shows another use of the reasoning behind 'More Measures for Fixed Factors' and perhaps renders more clearly the depth of that paper.

Assembling Efficient Organizations?

INTRODUCTION[1]

This chapter is a variation on a theme[2] by Arrow (1974), that the limits of organization are set by the need to economize on information flows, thought, committee meetings, and infighting. It is scored for the instruments I can play: duality, profit functions, and, above all, aggregates.

Why *aggregates*? Macroeconomics was invented by Keynes for the management of natural economies. For that, most economists agree, one would like to deal in terms of them. Is that a reasonable possibility? Aggregation theorists say no! The condition for them to work perfectly is that everyone should behave similarly at the margin. Were there to be a single aggregate for equipment, for instance, a steel firm would change its production in the same way when given a new blast furnace as a typewriting agency given enough word processors.[3] That seems altogether too unrealistic for them to work reasonably well in practice.[4]

God did not make the world, then, for the benefit of macroeconomists.

It is not God but businessmen who make our large firms, commonly by taking others over, breaking them up, and selling off the pieces they do not want. Presumably they do so for their own benefit and, in particular, with an eye to ease of control. If countries would be easier to manage through broad aggregates, were this not misleading, would not large firms be, too, and would not businessmen bear this in mind in deciding what to take over and what to sell off?

It would only be one goal, of course, to be traded off against others, and only important if realistic. Hence the '?' in the title.

Are appropriate components likely to exist?

The condition that all the firms in a country should behave similarly at the margin requires them to be too alike. Its implications for individual firms are more acceptable. They run in terms of *overheads*, *variable costs*

[1] The general ideas developed here were discussed in a number of seminars, workshops, and conferences in the 1970s, including Kenneth Arrow's on organization theory. I am grateful to him, Angus Deaton, James Mirrlees, and John Muellbauer for their comments.

[2] Of course, there are other themes. The difficulty of getting people to agree on a common aim is also important and can also be regarded as a problem in aggregation. The profit centres that emerge from the analysis may be interpreted in this light.

[3] Enough to increase its profits, at the given prices, by the same amount as the blast furnace would the steel firm's. Remember, both are gifts.

[4] i.e. assuming all the firms do not march step in step, investing and disinvesting together, for instance. Tom Stoker (1982, 1984), in particular, explored cases in which this is not so, as had Henri Theil (1954). One does not need many degrees of freedom to get the results I have quoted, and it is rather easy to see what sort of changes lead to the use of aggregates being badly misleading.

that are constant per unit over a range of output, *activities* running at levels determined by their relative profitabilities and the equipment available, and, given appropriate convexity, *profit centres*. These, moreover, are consequences of the theory, not assumptions, and the technologies in question are the only ones for which they work perfectly.[5] They are the terms that accountants, statisticians, industrial consultants, and businessmen use, presumably because they fit their experience. The chances are, then, that individual plants commonly are more or less of the appropriate type; the predatory businessman's role is to search out those that are sufficiently similar to each other or to those he already has.[6]

In what sense should the plants be 'similar'?

The activities correspond to the aggregates. The implications of similarity is that all firms use the same activities.[7] In the case of capital, the scale at which the corresponding activity runs depends only on the capital equipment it has[8]—similarly for land. In the case of consumer durables, for instance, its *only* outputs are consumer durables, although actual activities use labour and other current inputs, that is, as negative outputs. The latter, at least, is unrealistic. However, industrialists need not think in this way. If they have assembled a number of factories, each using the same activities, into a large firm, it will be quite natural for them to think in terms of the levels at which those activities run, as this theory will predict. In that case, as we will see, each activity may produce or use all the current goods and services, whereas the scale at which it operates depends on its relative profitability and the fixed inputs available. The different plants may vary markedly in their overheads and in the efficiency with which they use their machines to produce 'capacity', but given the capacity available to an activity, it operates in the same way in different plants.

Two peculiarities remain.

First, there is the asymmetry between fixed and current inputs. The former affect only the scale at which the various activities operate, not the manner. This reflects in part the history of aggregation theory, initially focused on the differences between capital and other factors. However, the arguments use fixed inputs as shift parameters, to isolate particular firms, and to compare their behaviour at the margin. This can be avoided,[9] but at the cost of returning to aggregates specific to particular classes of goods. Its disadvantage here is that the managers of individual factories presumably know the state of their equipment better than those at the centre; its

[5] Remember, however, that equipment and the like affect only the capacities at which the individual activities are run, not how they are.

[6] As it turns out, by using the same activities.

[7] At given prices, each activity produces current goods, net, in the same proportions wherever it is used—in the same amounts, indeed, per unit of capacity.

[8] Indeed, it is the most convenient measure of that firm f's *capital* or of its excess over that corresponding to a base endowment $\bar{u}_f$.

[9] See Gorman (1982*a*, 1982*b*) and the last paragraph of Sect. 1.

advantage is that the latter should presumably decide where investment should go.

Second, economists commonly believe in decentralization via prices, not target quantities. In fact, this is what happens here. The important macro-variables turn out to be the profitabilities of the different activities, price aggregates dual to the scale variables whose value central management has been assumed to set. In fact, it turns out to be more sensible for them to estimate these profitabilities, pass them on to the factory managers, and leave it to each of them to choose the levels at which the various activities should operate in his own factory.

That cancels out the first peculiarity. Note that this, too, is a conclusion, not an assumption.

Two final admissions need to be made. First, ease of control is only one goal, to be traded off against others. This really is a case for bounded rationality, not optimization. Nevertheless, conditions for optimization are what economists know about and often give useful clues for the wider problem. Here, too, one of the goals is monopoly. Now, efficient monopolies presumably do better than inefficient ones and are more likely to last. For efficiency one needs common shadow prices.[10] These replace the perfectly competitive prices of classical aggregation theory, arguably with more justification.[11]

Second, my modelling is distinctly lax. I fix the number of control variables and ask what the operating units should be like for these controls *not to reduce* their efficiency, that is, *not to cause costs to be set against the gains in the collection, dissemination, and processing of information assumed inherent in hierarchical control*, not to speak of possibly monopoly profits. I do not model the central office at all, although the analysis would hold were its costs to depend only on the values of the control variables.[12]

In particular, therefore, I seek perfect aggregates, or control variables, although I am really interested in those that perform reasonably well. The hope, as usual, is that the condition for this is that those for perfect aggregates hold approximately. Since my ultimate aim is approximate, however, I will be content with local results[13] and will feel free to use

[10] Of course, the goods have to be carefully defined; if the market for some goods is divided and some factories are only allowed to sell in one part, some in another, we would have to distinguish between those goods according to their market.

[11] However, monopolies are pretty robust even when inefficient and may even be defended against take-over bids by monopoly commissions and the like. One should remember Sir John Hicks's dictum that the prime gain from monopoly is an easy life for the managers—perhaps not the sort of easy life I have been sketching.

[12] Of the form $\psi(p, v)$ where ρ is the price vector for current goods, and that of the target set by the centre. If so, the net demand for i by the central office would be $\psi_i(p, v) = \partial\psi/\partial p_i$ under weak conditions, given v, and this can be subtracted from the right-hand side of equation (1.9).

[13] Not approximate. Aggregates that work perfectly in a neighbourhood of the point in question. The neighbourhood may cover the whole space considered.

calculus and rely on the implicit function theorem. (I have not used it since my college days, so that the argument is distinctly clumsy.)

1. HEURISTICS

Aggregation theorists have traditionally dealt with the short run,[14] in which the *endowments*,

$$u = (u_f)_{f \in F}, \tag{1.1}$$

of *fixed inputs* are taken as given, where u_f is the *fixed input*, or *endowment, vector* for the firm f; the *net production vector*,

$$x = \sum_{f \in F} x_f, \tag{1.2}$$

of *current goods* is chosen from the *short-run production possibility set*, or *technology*,

$$R(u) = \sum_{f \in F} R^f(u_f), \tag{1.3}$$

whose simple additive structure, reflecting the absence of external economies and diseconomies, is the source of all the results to date and, in particular, explains their close family resemblance. This additive structure is preserved in the *gross profit function*

$$g(p, u) = \sup\{p \cdot x \mid x \in R(u)\} = \sum_f g^f(p, u_f), \tag{1.4}$$

in an obvious notation, where p is a vector of *efficiency prices*, and in the *production plan*

$$x = g'(p, u) = \sum_f g'^f(p, u_f), \tag{1.5}$$

where the prime denotes the price gradient[15] of the convex function in question. Since we are dealing with the short run, it is reasonable to assume that the technologies are closed strictly convex bodies, which implies that the gradients in question exist.

Traditional aggregates, whether for capital, land, semi-skilled labour, or consumer durables and whether scalars or vectors, can all be presented as quantities of intermediate goods; that is

[14] Charles Blackorby, in particular, has recently published interesting papers on aggregation in intertemporal models (e.g. Blackorby and Schworm, 1982), and both he (Blackorby and Schworm, 1984*b*) and Frank Fisher (1982) on long-run aggregation. I refer to some unpublished work of my own on the latter below; however, this work does not really affect the point at issue.

[15] i.e. the vector of price derivatives $g' = (g_i) = \partial g / \partial p_i$. Under the convexity condition, they exist throughout the interior of the function's domain, which is enough for our purposes.

$$u \to v \to x, \tag{1.6}$$

so that v looks both ways, if you like, and particular structural assumptions are needed to identify particular components with one side rather than the other, assumptions that reflect the ideas of macroeconomists and are not appropriate here.

Suppose now that $h(p, v)$ is the gross profit function of the *downstream technology* $v \to x$. Then

$$h(p, v) = g(p, u) = \sum_f g^f(p, u_f), \tag{1.7}$$

and hence

$$h'(p, v) = g'(p, u) = \sum_f g'^f(p, u_f), \tag{1.8}$$

either of which may be used to discuss particular problems in aggregation. Equation (1.8) was used to discuss the general problem in the version of this paper read at Kenneth Arrow's workshop in 1980. However, there is no reason to require that control variables be interpreted as intermediate goods. I will therefore revert to an earlier treatment (Gorman, 1982*a*) and require only that, given the prices p, they determine the production plan x; that is,

$$x = \theta(p, v) = g'(p, u) = \sum_f g'^f(p, u_f), \tag{1.9}$$

where $\theta(p, v)$ is not necessarily the gradient vector of a potential function $h(p, v)$,[16] much less of an admissible profit function.

In general,

$$v = \phi(p, u), \tag{1.10}$$

so that the central management might have to know the detailed efficiency prices p before making its decisions. One hopes that it will only need to know a few price indices, as indeed it will. In fact, it is these price indices, marginal profitabilities associated with the individual control variables, that turn out to be the valuable controls, allowing the central management to decentralize even broad planning to the individual factories in the short run and confine itself to gathering and processing information and to long-run planning. In fact, (1.10) becomes

$$v = \sum_f v_f = \sum_f \phi^f(a(p), u_f), \text{ say}, \tag{1.11}$$

at least locally, given reasonable smoothness, where

[16] By a *potential function* $h(\cdot)$ I merely mean one for which $x = h'$ with no restriction as to shape.

$$a(p) = (a^m(p))_{m \in M}. \tag{1.12}$$

Here M is a minimal set of controls, none of which is specific (see the argument below justifying (2.5)) to any one factory f, and $a^m(p)$ is the marginal profitability associated with the control m in a convenient normalization. Indeed, we can go further, for there exists a potential function[17]

$$k^f(a(p), u_f), \qquad \text{for each } f \in F, \tag{1.13}$$

such that

$$v_f = k'^f(a(p), u_f), \tag{1.14}$$

where the prime represents the gradient with respect to the profitabilities a.

All these functions are conical in the prices or profitabilities, as one would like. When they are convex,[18] too, they correspond to perhaps fictitious technologies. If, for instance, $k^f(\cdot, u_f)$ is convex as well as conical, it corresponds to an *upstream technology* $S^f(u_f)$ for factory f, from which the factory's general manager chooses v_f to maximize profits $a \cdot v_f$ at the shadow prices a set by the central office. In other words, it is run as a profit centre. In general, however, $k^f(\cdot, u_f)$ is a potential function; the duty of the general manager of f is to know it and the state u_f of the factory's equipment and to calculate its gradient $k'^f(a, u_f)$ once he has been told the values of the a's.

That yields v_f. What next?

Here is another wonder. It turns out that

$$g^f(p, u_f) = k^f(a(p), u_f) - b^f(p), \qquad \text{for each } f \in F, \tag{1.15}$$

so that

$$\begin{aligned} x_f = g'^f(p, u_f) &= \textstyle\sum_m k^f_m a'^m(p) - b'^f(p) \\ &= \textstyle\sum_m v_{fm} a'^m(p) - b'^f(p), \end{aligned} \tag{1.16}$$

in an obvious notation, by (1.14), so that

$$g^f(p, u_f) = p \cdot x_f = \textstyle\sum_m v_{fm} a^m(p) - b^f(p), \tag{1.17}$$

and

$$g(p, u) = \textstyle\sum_m v_m a^m(p) - b(p), \text{ say}, \qquad v_m = \textstyle\sum_f v_{fm}. \tag{1.18}$$

See why I called the $a^m(p)$ marginal profitabilities? Note, too, that they yield net production patterns $a'^m(p)$ once the prices p are known. These net production patterns are called *activities*. They operate under constant

[17] Strictly $k^f(\cdot, u_f)$, each $u_f \in U_f$, $f \in F$.

[18] Profit functions are closed convex conical and to each such function there corresponds a convex technology for which it is indeed the profit function.

returns, where v_{fm} is the level at which activity m operates in factory f. As we have seen, this level is decided by the general management of the factory in light of the profitabilities a passed on to them by central management. The job of the specialist manager of activity m in factory f is to know $a^m(\cdot)$ and the relevant prices p, and then to calculate $a'^m(p)$ and produce $v_{fm}a'^m(p)$. If $a^m(\cdot)$ is convex as well as conical, and if we have normalized so that $v_{fm} \geqslant 0$ then there will be a technology A_m associated with $a^m(\cdot)$; the job of the specialist manager will be to choose x_{fm} from $v_{fm}A_m$ so as to maximize the profits $p \cdot x_{fm}$. Hence the specialist manager also would operate a profit centre.

Finally, the maintenance managers cover the overheads[19] as cheaply as possible.

The costs of central managers have not been explicitly modelled, so this is metatheory. At that level, their function is first to estimate the macro-prices $a(p)$ for the coming period and then to pass their values to factory management. In the longer run, their function is to direct investment, research, and development and decide what to take over and what to sell off. The latter has already been discussed. To direct the flow of investment, estimates of future profitabilities $a(p)$ and of the general technological structure of their component factories *at the macro-level*, as defined by $k^f(\cdot)$ are needed. The forms $a^m(\cdot)$ and $k^f(\cdot)$ also give a natural breakdown of research and development into *process research* (to make the individual activities more profitable) and that intended to squeeze more capacity out of existing equipment (to help different factories learn from each other by comparing their performance in that regard and to develop machines directed towards the more profitable activities).[20] Against this, the division between fixed inputs, determining, with $a(p)$, the scale at which activities operate, and the current production plans *within* these activities independent of the equipment available, seems unnatural and yet goes to the heart of the matter.

As mentioned in the Introduction, very similar results were derived by Gorman (1982*a*, 1982*b*) in the absence of fixed inputs, using appropriate prices rather than the endowments as the driving parameters, but only so far as the aggregates correspond to distinct classes of goods,[21] which I have already rejected as inappropriate in the present context.

2. THE MAIN RESULT

The interest here is in local results and so calculus methods and, in particular, the implicit function theorem will be used. That turns on the rank,

[19] $b^f(p) = -g^f(p, \bar{u}_f)$ in a convenient normalization, where $\bar{u}_f$ is a base endowment vector and, therefore, closed concave conical and hence a true cost function.

[20] Metaphoric only. Of course, one can double the profits per unit in an activity by rescaling it.

[21] I have not investigated the matter fully. It may be possible to get more general results.

$$\rho = \# M, \tag{2.1}$$

of control variables $m \in M$ needed, of the Jacobian matrix,

$$G(p, u) = [g_{is}(p, u)], \tag{2.2}$$

involved, where

$$g_{is}(p, u) = \partial^2 g/\partial p_i \partial u_s = g^f_{is}(p, u_f), \quad s \in f, \tag{2.3}$$

in an obvious notation.

First, I assume that these cross-derivatives *exist and are continuous*—broadly that the corresponding short-run technologies are closed strictly convex bodies and that a small change in the endowment of fixed inputs does not lead to a large change in output[22]—and that the rank ρ of $G(p, u)$ is *constant* throughout an open product set

$$P \times U; \quad U = \prod_f U_f, \tag{2.4}$$

in (p, u) space.

Second, I require that none of the controls be *specific to individual factories* f in the *firm* F. Even if its endowment u_f is held constant, that is, all ρ controls will be needed for the others. Hence the rank of the Jacobian matrix

$$G^{-f}(p, u_{-f}) = [g^{-f}_{is}(p, u_{-f})]_{s \notin f} \tag{2.5}$$

$$= [g_{is}(p, u)]_{s \notin f} \tag{2.6}$$

is ρ throughout $P \times U$ where

$$g^{-f}(p, u_{-f}) = \sum_{g \neq f} g^g(p, u_g) = g(p, u) - g^f(p, u_f) \tag{2.7}$$

is the gross profit function for the remaining factories.

Why is this important?

The basic argument in aggregation theory runs roughly as follows: Fix prices. Having done so, measure v_m, say, by the quasi-rents it generates.[23] Increase these by a million dollars by increasing[24] the endowments u_f of a particular *factory* f. Observe the change δx in total output, noting that $p \cdot \delta x = 1$.[25] It has all occurred in f; hence $\delta x_f = \delta x$. Now revert to the previous position and change the endowment u_g of another firm $g \neq f$

[22] Because $g_{is} = \partial x_i/\partial u_s$ is assumed to exist. Continuity goes a little further.

[23] The quasi-rents are the profits over and above those generated by a base equipment vector $\bar{u}$. Read on for some problems.

[24] The precise terms I have used are most appropriate for capital aggregation though not really misleading for other aggregates. If we are seeking to increase the amount of skilled labour used at a certain p, it may be appropriate either to increase or decrease the endowment of fixed inputs—'vary' might be a better word.

[25] The unit being a million dollars' worth at these prices.

instead, again by just enough to increase those quasi-rents by a million dollars. The change δx will be the same as before, so that $\delta x_g = \delta x = \delta x_f$. Return to the original position. Increase these quasi-rents by two million dollars by giving two successive gifts of new equipment to f, each worth a million dollars in these terms. In each case f will vary its production in the same way as g would have had it been given the million in question. But nothing has happened to g in the meanwhile: had it been given either gift, it would have raised its output by the same δx_g. Hence both δx_f's equal this δx_g, and hence each other. The relevant Engel curve in f, and hence in all the firms, is therefore a straight line; these are parallel to each other at these prices; and that is true at any prices in P. These parallel lines correspond to the activities I have talked about so much.

There are difficulties in this argument. How do we arrange, for instance, that the other aggregates v_n, $n \neq m$, are held constant or, failing that, identify the changes due to the variation in v_m? In traditional theory, where there is a single aggregate for each class of fixed input or current good, this is easily done. Here we have no such simple structure to help us, hence my reliance on calculus methods and search for merely local results.[26] The problem nevertheless remains: each control must relate to at least two factories.

Let us summarize our assumptions by saying that the *technologies are appropriately convex and smooth* and that *just* ρ *general*[27] *controls are needed* throughout $P \times U$.

That rank condition can be weakened. If you look over the argument, you will see that I moved one firm at a time, holding the others at the baseline. I threatened to move them, too, but never actually did; if I had, it would have been by one unit only. In a calculus framework, that would be an infinitessimal jump. This suggests the following weaker condition:

> There is a $\bar{u} \in U$ such that $G(p, u_f, \bar{u}_{-f})$ and $G^{-f}(p, \bar{u}_{-f})$ have the same rank $\rho = \# M$, each $p \in P$, $u_f \in U_f$, $f \in F$.

In fact, this too can be considerably weakened, as will be seen in Corollary 3, but I will nevertheless assume it at the outset, together with the existence and continuity of each $g^f_{is}(\cdot)$ in the same region, also over sufficient. Summarize this by saying that the technology is sufficiently convex and smooth and requires just ρ general controls.

I am now in a position to state the main result.

PROPOSITION: *If these conditions hold, there exist* $\rho = \# M$ *functions* $a^m(\cdot)$, $2\# F$ *functions* $k^f(\cdot, u_f)$, $b^f(\cdot)$ *about any point* $\bar{p} \in P$, *and for all* $u \in U$, *such that*

[26] The localities, i.e. neighbourhoods, may, of course, be large; the results are exact, not approximations.

[27] 'General' means not specific to any individual factory.

$$g^f(p, u_f) = k^f(a(p), u_f) - b^f(p), \qquad \textit{for each } f \in F, \tag{2.8}$$

where

$$a(p) = (a^m(p))_{m \in M}, \tag{2.9}$$

PROOF: Choose a price vector $\bar{p} \in P$ and a particular firm $h \in F$. Then $G(p, \bar{u})$ has a column basis

$$(g'_m(p, \bar{u}))_{m \in M}, \text{ say,} \tag{2.10}$$

chosen from $G^{-h}(p, \bar{u}_{-h})$ in a neighbourhood $N(\bar{p})$ of $\bar{p}$, where the prime still denotes the price gradient. Set

$$a^m(p) = g_m(p, \bar{u}), \qquad \text{for each } m \in M; \qquad a(p) = (a^m(p))_{m \in M}, \tag{2.11}$$

to get

$$g_s'^f(p, u_f) = \sum\nolimits_m \lambda^{sm} a'^m(p), \text{ say,} \qquad s \in f \in F, p \in N(\bar{p}). \tag{2.12}$$

If the level sets

$$P(\alpha) = \{p \in P \mid a(p) = \alpha\} \tag{2.13}$$

were arc connected on $N(\bar{p})$, we could integrate (2.12) to get

$$g_s^f(p, u_f) = \gamma^s(a(p)), \text{ say,} \qquad \text{for each } s \in f \in F, \tag{2.14}$$

and would be well on the way to proving the theorem. Unfortunately they need not be on $N(\bar{p})$. However, in the Appendix, I will construct a neighbourhood $N^*(\bar{p}) \subseteq N(\bar{p})$ of $\bar{p}$ on which they are arc connected, so that (2.14) holds on it.

Now choose any factory $f \in F$. $G(p, u_f, \bar{u}_{-f})$ and $G^{-f}(p, \bar{u}_{-f})$ have the same rank ρ, each $p \in P$, $u_f \in U_f$. Hence[28]

$$\begin{aligned} g_s'^f(p, u_f) &= \sum_{t \in f} \mu^{st} g_t'^{-f}(p, \bar{u}_{-f}) \\ &= \sum \nu^{sm} a'^m(p), \qquad \text{for each } s \in f, \ u_f \in U_f, p \in N^*(\bar{p}), \end{aligned} \tag{2.15}$$

by (2.12). Integrating this in the same manner, we get

$$g_s^f(p, u_f) = k_s^f(a(p), u_f), \text{ say,}^{29} \tag{2.16}$$

and thus

[28] The μ and ν below are functions, of course; hence the superscripts. It does not matter what they are functions of.

[29] It is trivial that this is a derivative. Call it k^{fs}. Then $k_t^{fs} = g_{st}^f = k_s^{ft}$.

$$g^f(p, u_f) = k^f(a(p), u_f) - b^f(p), \qquad \text{for each } u_f \in U_f,\ p \in N^*(\bar{p}), \tag{2.17}$$

because we chose any $f \in F$. That proves (2.8) and the Proposition.

COROLLARY 1: *We can replace the rank condition by*

$$R(G(p, u_f, \bar{u}_{-f})) = R(G^{-f}(p, \bar{u}_{-f})) =: \rho^f(p), \tag{2.18}$$

where R stands for 'rank of', for each $p \in P$, $u_f \in U_f$, $f \in F$, and get similar results.

Hints: Set $u_f = \bar{u}_f$ to get $\rho^f(p) = R(G(p, \bar{u})) = \rho(p)$, say. Since the ρ's are finite integers, $\bar{\rho} = \max\{\rho(p) \mid p \in P\}$ is attained at $\bar{p}$, say, and, since $G(\cdot, \bar{u})$ is continuous, in a neighbourhood $N^{**}(\bar{p})$ of $\bar{p}$. Proceed as above until $P(\bar{\rho}) = \{p \mid \rho(p) = \bar{\rho}\}$ has been exhausted. We now run into difficulty. The rank of a matrix is the order of the largest minor whose determinant does not vanish. Determinants may vanish at isolated points, for instance, or along curves. We have therefore to confine our attention at the outset to *regular points* at and about which $\rho(p)$ is constant and then extend our results to the others by continuity.

COROLLARY 2: *We can choose each $a^m(\cdot)$, $b^f(\cdot)$, $k^f(\cdot, u_f)$ to be conical.*

The functions are clearly differentiable. We may take

$$b^f(p) = -g^f(p, \bar{u}_f) \tag{2.19}$$

if we wish; it is then a loss function and hence closed concave, whereas each $a^m(\cdot)$ is then a marginal profit function.

COROLLARY 3: $g(p, u) = k(a(p), u) - b(p)$, *where*

$$k(a, u) = \sum_f k^f(a, u_f), \quad b(p) = \sum_f b^f(p). \tag{2.20}$$

COROLLARY 4: *We can take*

$$v = k'(a(p), u) = (\partial k / \partial a^m)_{m \in M}, \tag{2.21}$$

since then

$$x = g'(p, u) = \sum_m k_m a'^m(p) - b'(p) = \sum_m v_m a'^m(p) - b'(p). \tag{2.22}$$

COROLLARY 5: *If so,*

$$v = \sum v_f, \tag{2.23}$$

where

$$v_f = k'^f(a(p), u_f), \qquad \text{for each } f \in F, \tag{2.24}$$

and

$$g^f(p, u_f) = p \cdot x_f = \sum_m a^m(p) v_{mf} - b^f(p), \tag{2.25}$$

$$g(p, u) = \sum_m a^m(p) v_m - b(p). \tag{2.26}$$

The interpretation of v_{fm} as the scale at which activity m is run in factory f is now clear, as is that of $a^m(p)$ as its gross profitability, which is the same in all the factories.

The other main claim in the Introduction was that, given appropriate convexity, these results could be interpreted in the primal in terms of profit centres. I will consider one example. Suppose $k^f(\cdot, u_f)$ is closed convex as well as conical, as in the paragraph following equation (1.14). Define

$$S^f(u_f) = \{v_f \mid a \cdot v_f \leqslant k^f(a, u_f)\}; \tag{2.27}$$

then

$$v_f = k'^f(a, u_f) \tag{2.28}$$

maximizes $a \cdot v_f$ on $S^f(u_f)$ by the basic theorem of duality. Of course, this is only a local result here, too, because $k^f(\cdot)$ is defined only in a neighbourhood $N^*(\bar{p})$ or $\bar{p}$.[30]

3. SOME COMMENTS AND DISCLAIMERS

Managers probably take over other firms to increase their sense of power or security and their socially acceptable pay—buccaneers in search of immediate cash to stay in the game. Taking over and selling off are often moves that come to mind to meet immediate contingencies; and once consulted, the experts will naturally see reasons why they might work. That is not just a matter of self-interest: to a cobbler there is nothing like leather. Even under straightforward long-run profit maximization, ease of control is not the only parameter that is important. Nevertheless, ease of control is important; in that context, people often talk in terms of management by objectives and of profit centres. This essay suggests that quantitative objectives are misconceived, at least for the organization as a whole; appropriately normalized, they have shadow prices associated with them, which are better planning tools; and given appropriate convexity, they

[30] I have not extended the technologies beyond the region in question.

naturally lead to the location of appropriate profit centres and management structures.

Under imperfect competition, of course, one would have to deal with internal shadow prices instead of observed market prices and probably distinguish between physically identical products in different submarkets.[31] That does not seem to affect the argument, nor, I think, do tax-distorted transfer prices, though I have not looked into that in detail.

That the central office's function in short-run planning should largely be confined to the prediction of market conditions as shown in appropriate broad price indices seems reasonable.[32] That these should relate to the short-run profitabilities of a few basic processes would fall in very well with its long-run role, as in planning investment, where it would concentrate on the investment costs of increasing capacity in different locations and in planning future take-overs and sales.

Firms made up in this way would also accumulate expertise in selecting, appraising, and promoting their managers.

Martin Weitzman has shown how important it may be in practical programming that the right quantitites of the right goods should be available in the right place at the right time. This cannot be done by setting a few control variables or their shadow prices, and may require quite a different mode of operation.

[31] Physically identical activities in different locations might accordingly be economically different. Their physical identity might, nevertheless, make it easier to predict their distinct marginal profitabilities as well as, of course, simplifying the choice and training of factory and process managers.

[32] In the short run, most markets are pretty imperfect. I have not looked into this in any depth; doing so would turn on the extent to which a firm would wish to exploit such imperfections, given the effect on its long-run position.

Appendix

LEMMA: *Using the assumptions of the Proposition in Section 2, there is a neighbourhood* $N^*(\bar{p}) \subseteq N(\bar{p})$ *of* $\bar{p}$ *within which the level sets*

$$P(\alpha) = \{p \in P \mid a(p) = \alpha\} \tag{A.1}$$

are arc connected.

PROOF: Take a row basis I for[33]

$$A(p) = [a_i^m(p)] = [g_{mi}(p, \bar{u})]_{m \in M}, \tag{A.2}$$

and hence for $G(p, \bar{u})$ and each $G^{-f}(p, \bar{u}_{-f})$ in a neighbourhood $N^1(\bar{p}) \subseteq N(\bar{p})$, set

$$p_i = \begin{cases} q_i & \text{when } i \in I \\ r_i & \text{when } i \notin I, \end{cases} \tag{A.3}$$

and solve

$$a(q, r) = a(p) = \alpha \tag{A.4}$$

in a neighbourhood $N^2(\bar{p}) \subseteq N^1(\bar{p})$ of $\bar{p}$ to get[34]

$$q = b(\alpha, r). \tag{A.5}$$

Since $b(\cdot)$ is bicontinuous,[35] the set

$$C = \{(\alpha, r) \mid \alpha = a(q, r), \text{ for some } (q, r) \in N^2(\bar{p})\} \tag{A.6}$$

is open. It contains $(\bar{\alpha}, \bar{r})$ where

$$\bar{\alpha} = a(\bar{q}, \bar{r}) = a(\bar{p}). \tag{A.7}$$

Take a rectangular neighbourhood $D \subseteq C$ of $(\bar{\alpha}, \bar{r})$ and its image

$$N^*(\bar{p}) = \{(q, r) \mid q = b(\alpha, r) \text{ for some } (\alpha, r) \in D\} \subseteq N^2(\bar{p}) \subseteq N^1(\bar{p}). \tag{A.8}$$

Since $b(\cdot)$ is bicontinuous, $N^*(\bar{p})$ is open. Since $N^*(\bar{p})$ contains $\bar{p}$, it is a neighbourhood of $\bar{p}$.

I am now ready to show that the level sets $P(\alpha)$ are indeed arc connected by $N^*(\bar{p})$.

To do so, take any $(q^*, r^*) \in N^*(\bar{p})$. Let

$$\alpha^* = a(q^*, r^*). \tag{A.9}$$

[33] That corresponding to the original non-zero $\rho \times \rho$ determinant.
[34] By the implicit function theorem.
[35] By the implicit function theorem again.

Take any $(q^{**}, r^{**}) \in N^*(p)$ such that $a(q^{**}, r^{**}) = \alpha^*$, and construct a path

$$r(t) = (1 - t)r^* + tr^{**}; \quad q(t) = b(\alpha^*, r(t)), \quad 0 \leqslant t \leqslant 1, \tag{A.10}$$

connecting (q^*, r^*) and (q^{**}, r^{**}).

Since $(\alpha^*, r(t)) \in D$, its image $(q(t), r(t)) \in N^*(\bar{p})$. Since $b(\cdot)$ is differentiable, it traces a smooth arc. Since α^* was freely chosen,[36] it is indeed true that the $P(\alpha)$ are arc connected in $N^*(\bar{p})$.

[36] Here $\alpha^* = a(q^*, r^*)$, (q^*, r^*) freely chosen from $N^*(\bar{p})$ implies (α^*, r^*) freely chosen from D.

24

Aggregates for Variable Goods: An Application of Duality

Editorial Remarks

At the same time that Gorman was solving the problems associated with the aggregation of fixed factors, the natural extension of these arguments to variable goods—that is, commodities that are efficiently distributed throughout the economy—was clearly also on his mind. However, we have only incomplete sets of notes which address a somewhat special case. The complete solution appears in 'Aggregation in the Short and Long Run' which did not begin to appear before the early 1980s. One set of notes is an LSE draft from 1967 of which only Section 1 survives; another set was prepared for the Berkeley–Stanford Seminar in February 1967. We have chosen an extract from a set of notes presented at the University of North Carolina in 1970.

Editorial Summary

There are R firms in the economy each with variable goods $(x^r, y^r) \in S^r(z^r)$, a short-run technology set which depends upon the vector of fixed factors z^r. The total quantity of variable goods is given by $x = \sum_r x^r$, and $\sum_r y^r$. The profit function for each firm is given by $g^r(p, q, z^r)$ and their sum yields profits for the economy as a whole.

The variable goods are partitioned into M and N groups, respectively, so $x = (x_1, \ldots, x_M)$ and $y = (y_1, \ldots, y_N)$. This induces a similar partition in the variable goods of each firm. The variable goods aggregation question posed is the conditions under which there exist vectors of aggregates $X(x) = (X^1(x^1), \ldots, X^M(x^M))$ and $Y(y) = (Y^1(y^1), \ldots, Y^N(y^N))$, and a short-run macro-technology set $T(z)$, such that

$$(x, y) \in S(z) = \sum_r S^r(z^r) \leftrightarrow (X(x), Y(y)) \in T(z) \tag{0.1}$$

where the aggregates are all well-behaved.

The macro-problem is broken down into two stages. First, the cost and profit functions of the groups of variable goods are found. Let

$$h_m(X_m, p^m) = \min\{p^m x^m \mid X^m(x^m) \geqslant X_m\} \tag{0.2}$$

and

$$k_n(Y_n, q^n) = \max\{q^n y^n \mid Y^n(y^n) \leqslant Y_n\}, \tag{0.3}$$

where h_m and k_n are respectively the sector-specific cost and revenue functions. The profit function of the economy can now be written at the second stage as

$$g(p, q, z) = \max\left\{\sum_n k_n(Y_n, q^n) - \sum_m h_m(X_m, p^m) \mid (X(x), Y(y)) \in T(z)\right\}. \tag{0.4}$$

In the special case[1] which is analysed, (0.4) requires that

$$k_n(Y_n, q^n) = Q_n(q^n)\, Y_n + B_n(q^n) \tag{0.5}$$

for all n, and that

$$h_m(X_m, p^m) = P_m(p^m) X_m + A_m(p^m) \tag{0.6}$$

for all n. Hence there is a macro-profit function such that

$$g(p, q, z) = G(P, Q, z) - \sum_m A_m + \sum_n B_n, \tag{0.7}$$

where

$$G(P, Q, z) = \max\left\{\sum_n Q_n Y_n - \sum_m P_m X_m \mid (X, Y) \in T(z)\right\}. \tag{0.8}$$

Each sector has a quasi-homothetic aggregate and this can be shown to generate the same structure in each firm. In fact, for the variable aggregates X and Y to be distributed efficiently throughout the economy they have to have the same shadow prices everywhere. Hence, not only do these aggregates have to have the same structure, they must have parallel expansion paths.

The general case solved in 'Aggregation in the Short and Long Run' admits two more solutions than are found in this case. The argument there is completely different because one cannot manipulate the fixed factors in order to isolate the individual firms in the economy.

[1] Essentially, he requires that the firms cannot produce anything without a vector of fixed inputs.

Aggregates for Variable Goods: An Application of Duality

1. INTRODUCTION

My main purpose in presenting this paper is not to solve a problem in aggregation, but to illustrate a style of argument which is not yet generally used, but which is sometimes useful.

We commonly specify tastes and technologies in terms of *quantities* of goods which might be consumed or produced. Yet, when it comes to actual problems, we normally think of consumers or competitive producers as reacting to changes in *prices*; that is, prices become the independent variables and quantities the dependent ones. It is from this reversal of roles—requiring us for example to solve a set of marginal utility conditions to find the demand functions—that some of the complications of economic analysis occur. Moreover, these complications are essentially mathematical: under what conditions does a set of equations have a solution? What properties does the solution have? In discussing such points it is easy to miss the economic problems at issue. Yet they are basic. For how can one trace out the effect of economic change unless one knows how consumers and producers will react to price changes; that is, without knowing the properties of their demand and supply functions.

Might we not do better then, to set up the analysis in the beginning in terms of the 'natural' independent variables?

As it happens this can usually be done in a natural and simple manner. For a consumer, for instance, we may define the *cost*

$$m = g(p, u) = \min\{p \cdot x \mid u(x) \geqslant u) \tag{1}$$

of reaching the level u of utility at prices $p = (p_1, \ldots, p_n)$. Knowing it, we would know the position of all the budget lines touching the indifference curve $u = u(x)$ and thus, at least if it were convex, be able to reconstruct the curve. Knowledge of this function would therefore be equivalent to that of the utility function itself, under normal assumptions.

Suppose now that $\bar{x}$ is chosen at prices $\bar{p}$ as being the cheapest way of reaching the level $\bar{u}$ of utility. Then

$$m = \bar{p} \cdot \bar{x} = g(\bar{p}, \bar{u}) = \sum \bar{p}_i \bar{x}_i. \tag{2}$$

Suppose now that $\bar{p}$ were changed a little, and with it $\bar{u}$. Then

$$\bar{g}_i \mathrm{d}\bar{p}_i + \bar{g}_0 \mathrm{d}\bar{u} = \mathrm{d}\bar{g} \tag{3}$$

$$= \sum \bar{x}_i \mathrm{d}\bar{p}_i + \sum \bar{p}_i \mathrm{d}\bar{x}_i$$

$$= \sum \bar{x}_i \mathrm{d}\bar{p}_i + \lambda \sum \bar{u}_i \mathrm{d}\bar{x}_i$$

$$= \sum \bar{x}_i \mathrm{d}\bar{p}_i + \lambda \mathrm{d}\bar{u}, \tag{4}$$

where $\bar{g}_i = \partial g/\partial p_i$, $\bar{g}_0 = \partial g/\partial u$, at $(\bar{p}, \bar{u})$; $\bar{u}_i = \partial u/\partial x_i$ at $\bar{x}$; and λ is the inverse of the marginal utility of income. Hence, remembering that prices and utility can be varied independently,

$$x_i = g_i(p, u), \tag{5}$$

where I have dropped the bars for simplicity, is the compensated demand function for good i, when prices are p and 'real income' or utility is u. Differentiating with respect to p_j we have the Slutsky condition,

$$\delta x_i/\delta p_i = g_{ij} = g_{ji} = \delta x_j/\delta p_i, \tag{6}$$

where $g_{ij} = \delta^2 g/\delta p_i \delta p_j$ and the δ denotes the fact that 'real income' u, rather than money income m, is held constant.

It is easily shown that $g(\cdot, u)$ is positively homogeneous of degree one and closed concave. Given any such function, moreover, we can construct a unique concave indifference curve corresponding to it, so that tastes may equally well be specified by either the cost or utility function.[1]

Exactly the same analysis can be applied to production functions; we merely interpret u as the quantity produced, or the vector of the quantities of different goods produced, and x as the input vector. Revenue functions, in which x is given and u allowed to adjust to the market, and profit functions, where both are allowed to, have similar properties and uses.

Two special cases are of some interest and will be useful later. In the first case

$$m = g(p, u) = uP(p), \tag{7}$$

$$x_i = g_i = uP_i = mP_i/P, \tag{8}$$

so that it takes twice as much money, and twice as much of each good, to sustain twice as high a level of utility. In other words, utility is produced under 'constant returns'. For the second case

$$m = g(p, u) = uP(p) + A(p), \tag{9}$$

$$x_i = g_i = uP_i + A_i = (A_i - AP_i/P) + mP_i/P, \tag{10}$$

[1] Of course, cost function reflect market behaviour and therefore yield only the convex hull, so to speak, of the original indifference curves.

so the expansion paths are straight lines, but not necessarily through the origin. The marginal expenditure pattern is therefore independent of income.

Both of these cases are important in the theory of aggregation. One reason is obvious. If $u(x)$ is a quantity aggregate, $P(p)$ is rather an acceptable price aggregate corresponding to it in each case. Another reason will emerge from the analysis below.

The particular problem I am going to discuss is of secondary interest, but a word or more of motivation may nevertheless be in order.

Joan Robinson is not the only economist to feel that the measurement of 'capital' is likely to be particularly difficult. One reason is that capital goods tend to be thought of as fixed in the short run at least, so that there is no reason to believe that similar capital goods will have similar efficiency prices in different firms. So we cannot weight them in this obvious manner to get a total quantity of capital. A number of writers have shown that this does indeed make it difficult to measure the quantity of capital except in very special cases. The question remains: is it more commonly possible to measure, for example, the quantity of 'labour' or 'output' in a meaningful sense. This is what I discuss below, answering 'not really', though I admit that I may be thought to have laid down altogether too stringent a definition of 'meaningful'.

2. THE MODEL

An economy is composed of R firms. There are no external effects.

Goods are of two types: variable and fixed. *Variable goods* are perfectly adjusted to the market, having the same efficiency prices everywhere. For simplicity of exposition I ignore intermediate goods. The *input* and *output* vectors—both referring only to variable goods—are

$$x = \sum x^r, \quad y = \sum y^r, \tag{11}$$

where x^r, y^r, are those of the rth firm. I will sometimes call the (x, y) vectors *production plans. Fixed goods* are thought of, and measured as, *inputs*. There is no market for them, and nothing to bring the efficiency prices of physically identical fixed inputs into equality. We therefore write the fixed input vector

$$z = (z^1, \ldots, z^R), \tag{12}$$

where z^r is that for the rth firm, as an extended list, if you like, of the items of equipment available in each firm.

The production plans (x, y) which are feasible with fixed inputs z are summarized in the *short-run technology* or production possibility set $S(z)$. Because of the absence of external effects

$$S(z) = \sum S^r(z^r), \tag{13}$$

where $S^r(z^r)$ is the *short-run technology for firm r*. Since the fixed inputs are taken as given in these short run technologies, it is reasonable to assume that they are convex as well as closed. For simplicity of exposition I will go somewhat further and assume strict convexity.

3. THE PROBLEM

The variable goods fall into $M + N$ classes.

$$x = (x_1, \dots, x_M), \quad x^r = (x_1^r, \dots, x_M^r), \quad p = (p_1, \dots, p_M),$$

$$y = (y_1, \dots, y_N), \quad y^r = (y_1^r, \dots, y_N^r), \quad q = (q_1, \dots, q_M), \tag{14}$$

are the corresponding partitions of x, y, x^r, y^r and the efficiency price vectors p, q. Under what conditions do there exist continuous strictly increasing aggregates

$$(X_1(x_1)), \dots, X_M(x_M)) = X(x), \quad (Y_1(y_1), \dots, Y_N(y_N)) = Y(y), \tag{15}$$

one for each class, and a *short-run macro-technology* $T(z)$ such that

$$(x, y) \in X(z) \quad \text{iff} \quad (X(x), Y(y)) \in T(z). \tag{16}$$

Under my assumptions the aggregates are strictly quasi-convex. Since they are ordinal, convexity would be meaningless for them.

4. THE APPROACH

Since we are assuming perfect competition and the absence of external effects, the economy will act as if someone had set out to maximize $q \cdot y - p \cdot x$ given that $(x, y) \in S(z)$ or, equivalently, $(X(x), Y(y)) \in T(z)$. This can be regarded as being done in two steps. A *central controller* chooses $(X, Y) \in T(z)$ first. Then *class controllers* choose x_m to minimize the costs $p_m \cdot x_m$ subject to

$$X_m(x_m) \geqslant x_m, \quad \text{each } m; \tag{17a}$$

and y_n to maximize the receipts $q_n \cdot y_n$ subject to

$$Y_n(y_n) \leqslant Y_n, \quad \text{each } n. \tag{17b}$$

Suppose that the result of this minimization and maximization are the conditional costs

$$h_m(X_m, p_m) = \min [p_m \cdot x_m \mid X_m(x_m) \geqslant X_m], \quad \text{each } m, \tag{18a}$$

and receipts

$$k_n(Y_n, q_n) = \max\{q_n \cdot y_n \mid Y_n(y_n) \leqslant Y_n\}, \quad \text{each } n. \tag{18b}$$

Then the job of the central controller is to choose $(X, Y) \in T(z)$ such as to maximize $\sum k_n(Y_n, q_n) - \sum h_m(X_m, p_m)$. Now we will see below that

$$h_m(X_m, p_m) = P_m(p_m)X_m + A_m(p_m), \text{ say,} \qquad \text{each } m, \tag{19a}$$

$$k_n(Y_n, q_n) = Q_n(q_n)Y_n + B_n(q_n), \qquad \text{each } n, \tag{19b}$$

when $X_m(\cdot)$, $Y_n(\cdot)$ are approximately normalized. Since $\sum B_n(q_n) - \sum A_m(p_m)$ is unaffected by the choice of X, Y, the task of the central controller is to choose $(X, Y) \in T(z)$ to maximize $\sum Q_n(q_n)Y_n - \sum P_m(p_m)X_m$. Let us call the result of this maximization the gross macro-profits

$$G(P, Q, z) = \max\{Q \cdot Y - P \cdot X \mid (X, Y) \in T(z)\}. \tag{20}$$

Then the gross profits of the economy as a whole are

$$\begin{aligned} g(p, q, z) &= \max\{q \cdot y - p \cdot x \mid (x, y) \in S(z)\} \\ &= g(P(p), Q(q), z) + \sum B_n(q_n) - \sum A_m(P_m). \end{aligned} \tag{21}$$

In a moment I will discuss the implications of these results. First a pseudo-economic interpretation of the process I have been describing.

Think of X_m, each m, as an intermediate good produced from x_m with production function $X_m(\cdot)$, under the direction of the mth *input controller.* These fictitious intermediate goods $X = (X_1, \ldots, X_M)$ are then transformed into intermediate outputs $Y = (Y_1, \ldots, Y_N)$ with the aid of the fixed input z, in the macro-technology $T(z)$, under the direction of the *central controller.* Finally, Y_n is transformed into actual final goods y_n in a technology defined by the *input requirement function* $Y_n(\cdot)$ under the direction of the nth output controller. These last fictitious technologies produce many goods from a single output—about as realistic as producing a single output from many inputs!

$h_m(X_m, p_m)$, $k_n(Y_n, q_n)$, $G(P, Q, x)$, and $g(p, q, z)$ are cost, revenue, and profit functions whose advantage is that they specify technologies in terms of the prices p of variable goods and the quantities X_m, Y_n or z of those fixed from outside. For obvious reasons these are frequently the appropriate independent variables to work with. Let us take $g(p, q, z)$ as the leading example, since it does not include any fictitious elements. It can be shown to be closed convex, positively homogeneous of degree one, and differentiable, in p, q, under our assumptions. Furthermore,

$$S(z) = \{(x, y) \mid q \cdot y - p \cdot x \leqslant g(p, q, z), \qquad \text{each } p, q\} \tag{22}$$

is the set of programmes which never claim to yield more than the maximum profits attainable, so that it is a complete specification of the technology; and the profit-maximizing net output vector

$$x = -g_p(p, q, z) = \text{gradient of } g \text{ with respect to } p, \tag{23a}$$

$$y = g_q(p, q, z) = \text{gradient of } g \text{ with respect to } q, \tag{23b}$$

so that $x_i = -\partial g/\partial p_i$, $y_j = \partial g/\partial p_j$. The parallel with marginal productivity is clear.

Similar results hold for the h's, k's and G.

5. INTERPRETATION

The interpretation of the results in the previous section is easiest in two fairly general special cases: that of constant returns to scale, and that in which no production is possible without fixed inputs. For the most part, I will keep to these special cases.

Consider that in which the fixed inputs are essential, so that $S(0)$ reduces to the origin. Normalize so that $X(0) = 0$. Then the lower curve in Figure 24.1 shrinks to the origin through which all the expansion paths pass. $X_m(\cdot)$, $Y_n(\cdot)$ become homogeneous of degree one, so that the mth class's fictional technology yields constant returns, and each $A_m(p_m) = B_n(q_n) = 0$, so that

$$g(p, q, z) = G(P(p), Q(q), z). \tag{24}$$

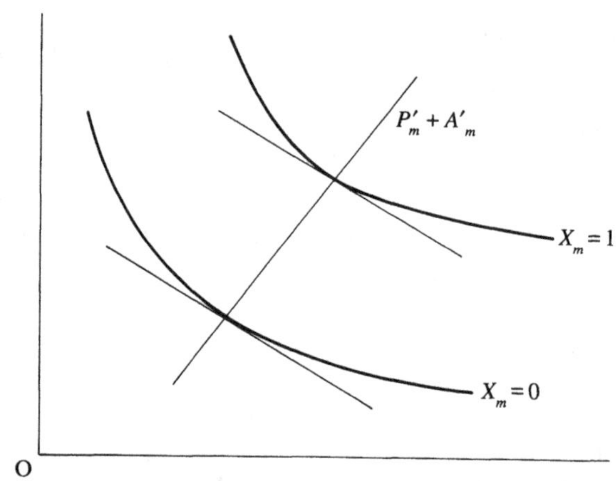

FIG. 24.1 *Linear expansion path*

Now look at the individual firms. They can neither produce, nor make a profit, without fixed inputs. By taking $y_s = 0$, $s \neq r$, we can reduce the entire economy to a single firm r, to get

$$g^r(p, q, z^r) = g(p, q, \ldots, 0, z^r, 0, \ldots, 0) = g(P(p), Q(q), \ldots, 0, z^r, 0, \ldots, 0)$$
$$= G^r(P(p), Q(q), z^r), \text{ say,} \tag{25}$$

so that

$$G(P(p), Q(q), z) = g(p, q, z) = \sum g^r(p, q, z^r) = \sum G^r(P(p), Q(q), z^r), \tag{26}$$

since the gross profits of the economy as a whole are the sum of those earned in the individual firms.

The gross profit function $G^r(P(p), Q(q), z^r)$ is of course the reflection of the macro-technology.

$$T^r(z^r) = T(0, \ldots, 0, z^r, 0, \ldots, 0) \tag{27}$$

of the rth firm as a degenerate economy. Because of this

$$(x^r, y^r) \in S^r(z^r) \quad \text{iff} \quad (X(x^r), Y(y^r)) \in T^r(z^r). \tag{28}$$

Calling $(X(x^r), Y(y^r))$, (X^r, Y^r) the macro-program of firm r, it is shown that

$$X = \sum X^r, \; Y = \sum Y^r \quad \text{so that} \quad T(z) = \sum T^r(z^r), \tag{29}$$

reflecting (26) and the common macro-prices (P, Q).

Similar results hold in the case of constant returns, basically because the X's and Y's can once again be normalized to be positively homogeneous of degree one. This is in itself a desirable property in index numbers; if we had laid it down as a requirement at the outset, we would have found the above results always holding.

Incidentally, P_m, X_m, Q_m, Y_n are Divisia indices in these cases, and these are the most general cases in which such indices are independent of the past paths of the variables.

In general, unfortunately, these simple results do not hold. However, one damning result does. If we give any firm extra equipment, and this causes it to vary its production of goods in group r, it will do so *in the same proportions* as would any other.

The basis of the argument is that it does not matter what changes in z cause a given change in X_m; the change in x_m will be the same. Suppose that we can cause this change either by varying firm r's or firm s's endowment, z^r, z^s. The variation in firm r's production plan for class m will be the same as that of firm s. Moreover this will be true *whatever its initial endowment*. Hence all firms have linear expansion paths, all in the same direction. So, therefore, does the economy as a whole.

The equation of a straight line is of the form $x = a + (b - a)t$, where a, b are points on it and t is a current parameter. Taking them as the points where the expansion path for prices p_m intersects $X_m = 0$ and $X_m = 1$ we get

$$h'_m(X_m, p_m) = A'_m + P'_m \Phi_m(X_m, p_m), \tag{30}$$

where

$$A_m = h_m(0, p_m), \qquad P_m = h_m(1, p_m) - h_m(0, p_m), \tag{31}$$

and $h_m(X_m, p_m)$ itself are all positively homogeneous of degree one in the prices, and primes denote gradients with respect to p_m. Premultiplying (19) by p_m and using homogeneity,

$$h_m(X_m, p_m) = A_m + P_m \Phi_m(X_m, p_m). \tag{32}$$

Taking the gradient yields

$$h'_m = A'_m + P'_m \Phi_m + P_m \Phi'_m, \tag{33}$$

so that $\Phi'_m = 0$ by (30) and $\Phi_m = \Phi_m(X_m)$, which is strictly increasing in X_m because X_m is in x_m. We can therefore write $\tilde{X}_m = \Phi_m(X_m)$ and drop the ~ to get $h_m = X_m P_m + A_m$ as required.

25

Aggregation in the Short and Long Run

Editorial Remarks

This paper begins with a very brief survey of known results in aggregation theory, reminding us that the basic trick in most aggregation problems is to change the endowments of firms and to see how this changes the economy overall. Section 2 starts with the long-run problem. The reason for calling this a long-run problem is that the technologies do not depend upon vectors of capital stocks or endowments which, in principle, could be used to move the firms around in the economy. The same analysis would therefore hold if firms' technologies depend on a set of endowments that could not be moved about for the analysis.

Sections 2, 3, and 4 are devoted to the case where there is only one aggregate in each firm as well as in the economy. This analysis was done in the early 1980s and presented at Mirrlees's lunch-time workshop in 1982 and at the LSE mathematical economics seminar in 1983.[1]

The rest of the paper analyses the case when there are many aggregates both in the firms and in the economy as a whole. This part existed in various handwritten forms until the present version was written for a conference at the London Business School in October 1989. The analysis here is complex and at times difficult to follow, but this seems to be inherent in the nature of the problem being analysed. Each of the aggregates can be one of three different types. Furthermore, these different types, in some circumstances, interact with one another to produce still further restrictions. At best, a notational nightmare!

Editorial Summary

There are a fixed number, F, of firms in the economy, and each firm, as well as the economy as a whole, has an aggregate over a subset of the commodities, the x's in this case.[2] That is, the technology set of each firm is given by

$$(x_f, y_f) \in T_f \leftrightarrow \Phi^f(\phi^f(x_f), y_f) \geqslant 0, \tag{0.1}$$

while that of the economy is

[1] These one-aggregate results appeared independently in Blackorby and Schworm (1988).

[2] In addition it is assumed that there is an aggregate for any subset of firms.

$$(x, y) \in T \leftrightarrow \Phi(\phi(x), y) \geq 0, \tag{0.2}$$

where

$$\sum_f T_f = T, \tag{0.3}$$

$$\sum_f x_f = x, \tag{0.4}$$

and

$$\sum_f y_f = y. \tag{0.5}$$

Using the implicit function theorem, this can easily be rewritten as

$$(x_f, y_f) \in T_f \quad \leftrightarrow \quad \phi^f(x_f) \geq u_f \geq \psi_f(y_f) \tag{0.6}$$

for all $f \in F$ and

$$(x, y) \in T \quad \leftrightarrow \quad \phi(x) \geq u \geq \psi(y). \tag{0.7}$$

That is, the assumption of an aggregate for the x's forces there to be an aggregate of the y's in each firm, as well as in the economy as a whole.

This means that the profit function for the firms and the economy can be written as

$$\pi^f(p, q) = \max_{u_f} \{\rho^f(q, u_f) - \kappa^f(p, u_f)\} \tag{0.8}$$

and

$$\pi(p, q) = \max_{u} \{\rho(q, u) - \kappa(p, u)\}, \tag{0.9}$$

respectively, where

$$\rho^f(q, u_f) = \max_{y_f} \{q \cdot y_f \mid \psi^f(y_f) \leq u_f\}, \tag{0.10}$$

$$\kappa^f(p, u_f) = \min_{x_f} \{p \cdot x_f \mid \phi^f(y_f) \geq u_f\}, \tag{0.11}$$

$$\rho(q, u) = \max_{y} \{q \cdot y \mid \psi(y) \leq u\}, \tag{0.12}$$

and

$$\kappa(p, u) = \min_{x} \{p \cdot x \mid \phi(y) \geq u\}, \tag{0.13}$$

where κ^f and κ are cost functions, and ρ^f and ρ are revenue functions.

After normalizing a few times, he shows that

$$\sum_f \kappa^f(p, u_f) = \kappa(p, u), \tag{0.14}$$

$$\sum_f \rho^f(q, u_f) = \rho(q, u), \tag{0.15}$$

for optimal values of the u_f's and u, where it is also the case that $\sum u_f = f$.

Notice here that if the u_f's could be moved independently in (0.14), then this would be a Pexider equation and would yield the same solution as before.

Section 3 of the paper focuses on an economy with only two firms and demonstrates that (i) the u_f's can be moved independently by moving q; or (ii) the u_f's can be moved independently by moving p; or (iii) all of the u_f's are ordinally equivalent in (p, q). Case (i) makes (0.14) a Pexider equation and Case (ii) renders (0.15) a Pexider equation, leaving Case (iii) to be interpreted. Section 4 extends these results to economies with a arbitrary number of firms. The three cases can be summarized as follows:

Case (i): The cost functions can be written as

$$\kappa^f(p, u_f) = a(p)u_f + c^f(p) \tag{0.16}$$

for all $f \in F$ *and*

$$\kappa(p) = a(p)u + c(p), \tag{0.17}$$

where $\sum c^f = c$ *with no additional restrictions on* ρ^f. *That is, the cost technologies are quasi-homothetic and similiar (having the same marginal cost function* $a(p)$*);*

Case (ii): The revenue functions can be written as

$$\rho^f(q, u_f) = b(q)u_f + d^f(q) \tag{0.18}$$

and

$$\rho(q, u) = b(q)u + d(q), \tag{0.19}$$

where $\sum d^f = d$ *with no additional restrictions on* κ^f. *That is, the revenue functions are quasi-homothetic and similar; and*

Case (iii): The marginal cost and marginal revenue functions can be written as

$$\kappa_0^f(p, u_f) = \lambda^f(u)\kappa_0(p, u) \tag{0.20}$$

for all $f \in F$ *and*

$$\rho_0^f(q, u_f) = \lambda^f(u)\rho_0(q, u) \tag{0.21}$$

for all $f \in F$.

In the last case the technologies are so similar that the intersector aggregators are all ordinally equivalent.

Section 5 begins the analysis of the multiple-aggregate case and serious changes in notation take place. The prices are represented by p and inputs and outputs by x. A partition M of these is formed, one aggregate for each element of the partition. Hence, for each element, m, of the partition there is an aggregate, $\phi^{fm}(x_{fm})$, in each firm and one in the economy, $\phi^m(x_m)$. This, of course, induces an aggregate of everything else which is represented by $\psi^{fm}(x_{f,-m})$ for each firm and by $\psi^m(x_{-m})$

for the economy as a whole. From this it is immediately clear that the existence of more than one aggregate forces overlapping groups of aggregates. For example, if there were three groups, group 3 would not only have an aggregate of its own, but would also be aggregated in *not one* and in *not two* as well. Furthermore, it could satisfy Case (i) on its own, Case (ii) when part of *not one*, and Case (iii) when part of *not two*. Of course, similar statements can be made for sectors one and two as well, and it is this that leads to the complexity in the remainder of the paper.

Sections 5, 6, and 7 complete the analysis of those sectors satisfying Cases (i), (ii), and (iii) respectively. Section 8 is called 'Bringing the Pieces Together', and can be read without having completely understood every step of the preceding arguments, although the main points must have been appreciated to obtain a good grasp of the central result.

Aggregation in the Short and Long Run

1. THE SHORT RUN[1]

The basic trick in aggregation theory is to vary the behaviour of one firm f while that of the others remains unchanged. We accomplish the former by changing just f's endowment x_f of fixed inputs parametrically, the latter by holding the endowments of other firms unchanged and expressing the problem in terms of these endowments and the prices q of the other, current goods. This is easiest done in terms of the *gross profit function*

$$g(x, q) = \sum_{f\in F} g^f(x_f, q), \quad x = (x_f)_{f\in F}, \tag{1.1}$$

or, better still, the *quasi-rent functions*

$$r(x, q) = g(x, q) - g(\bar{x}, q) = \sum_f (g^f(x_f, q) - g^f(\bar{x}_f, q)) = \sum_f r^f(\bar{x}_f, q), \tag{1.2}$$

where

$$\bar{x} = (\bar{x}_f)_{f\in F} \tag{1.3}$$

is a given *basic endowment vector of fixed inputs*.

Suppose first we are measuring 'Capital' by an aggregate

$$u = \phi(x), \tag{1.4}$$

where $\phi(\cdot)$ is not known, but where u stands as a perfect proxy for all the fixed inputs. Choose

$$\bar{u} = \phi(\bar{x}) = 0, \text{ by } \textit{normalization}, \tag{1.5}$$

to get equivalent quasi-rent functions

$$\rho(u, q) = \rho(\phi(x), q) = r(x, q), \tag{1.6}$$

$$\rho^f(u_f, q) = \rho(\phi(x^f), q) = r(x_f, q) = \rho(u_f, q),^2 \tag{1.7}$$

where

$$x^f = (x_f, \bar{x}_{-f}), \quad u_f = \phi(x_f, \bar{x}_{-f}) = \phi^f(x_f), \text{ say}, \tag{1.8}$$

$$\rho(u, q) = \sum_f \rho(u_f, q); \quad \rho(0, q) = \rho^f(0, q) = 0, \quad \text{each } f\in F. \tag{1.9}$$

[1] I thank the members of Jim Mirrlees's lunch-time workshop in Trinity 1982, members of the LSE mathematical economics/econometrics seminar in Autumn 1983, and most particularly Chuck Blackorby, for comments.

[2] Remember that $\phi(\bar{x}_f, \bar{x}_{-f}) = \phi(\bar{x}^f) = \phi(\bar{x}) = 0$ and that all the quasi-rents at x^f accordingly accrue to f.

Now take a given price vector $\bar{q} > 0$, note that $\rho(\cdot, \bar{q})$ is strictly increasing under minimal assumptions, and define new measures $\tilde{u}$, $\tilde{u}_f$ of capital as

$$\tilde{u} = \rho(u, \bar{q}), \quad \tilde{u}_f = \rho(u_f, \bar{q}); \quad \tilde{u} = \sum_f \tilde{u}_f, \tag{1.10}$$

to get the appropriately adjusted quasi-rent functions

$$\tilde{\rho}(\tilde{u}, q) = \sum_f \tilde{\rho}(\tilde{u}_f, q) = \rho(u, q) = \sum_f \rho^f(u_f, q). \tag{1.11}$$

In the light of (1.10), this is Cauchy's additivity equation and yields[3]

$$\rho(u, q) = a(q)u, \quad \rho(u_f, q) = a(q)u_f, \text{ say,} \tag{1.12}$$

$$g(x, q) = \gamma(u, q) = a(q)u + g(\bar{x}, q) = a(q)u + b(q), \text{ say,} \tag{1.13}$$

$$g^f(x_f, q) = \gamma^f(u, q) = a(q)u_f + b^f(q), \text{ say,} \tag{1.14}$$

where I have dropped the tildes.

Then the supplies of current goods are

$$y_i = \gamma_i(u, q) = \partial\gamma/\partial q_i = a_i(q)u + b_i(q), \tag{1.15}$$

$$y_{fi} = \gamma_i^f(u, q) = a_i(q)u + b_i^f(q),^4 \tag{1.16}$$

so that the marginal production pattern $\nabla a(q) = (a_i(q))$ is the same for each firm in the economy whether it makes tin-tacks or nuclear bombs.

Unlikely perhaps.

The argument for any aggregate v_m for a class of variable goods can be run in the same way, but I will turn to heuristics instead, still working with the *quasi-rent function*.[5]

The basic argument about the conditions for an aggregate v_m to exist for current goods Y_m is as follows: fix prices q. Having done so, measure v_m,

[3] [eds.] The Cauchy equation referred to is

$$f(x + y) = f(x) + f(y),$$

whose only continuous solution is

$$f(t) = at$$

for some real a. A slight generalization of the Cauchy equation which arises frequently in Gorman's work is the Pexider equation

$$f(x + y) = g(x) + h(y).$$

Continuous solutions of the Pexider equation are given by

$$f(t) = at + \gamma$$
$$g(t) = at + \alpha$$
$$h(t) = at + \beta,$$

where $\gamma = \alpha + \beta$.

[4] Since U is an intermediate good, u is also a measure of output capacity, so that this absurdity is equally true for aggregates for current goods.

[5] The *gross profit function* would do just as well.

say, by the quasi-rents it generates through the sales of y_m. Increase these by a million dollars by varying the endowments x_f of a particular factory f. Observe the change δy_m in output y_m, noting that $q \cdot \delta y_m = 1$. It has all occurred in f; hence $\delta y_{fm} = \delta y_m$. Now revert to the previous position and change the endowment x_g of another firm $g \neq f$ instead, again by just enough to increase those quasi-rents by a million dollars. The change δy will be the same as before, so that $\delta y_{mg} = \delta y_m = \delta y_{mf}$. Return to the original position. Increase these quasi-rents by two million dollars by giving two successive gifts of new equipment to f, each worth a million dollars in these terms. In each case f will vary its production in the same way as g would have had it been given the million in question. But nothing has happened to g in the meanwhile. Had it been given either gift, it would have raised its output by the same δy_{mg}. Hence both δy_{mf}'s equal this δy_{mg} and hence each other. The relevant Engel curve in f, and hence in all the firms, is therefore a straight line; these are parallel to each other at these prices; and that is true at any price q, as in (1.16).[6]

All firms use labour of various skills in the same proportion at the margin, too, if v_m is the labour aggregate.

Can you wonder that conventional aggregation theorists find neoclassical macroeconomics surprising, though they may, of course, argue that their aggregates exist, for example, because all firms react sufficiently similarly to the same news?

2. THE LONG RUN: A SINGLE AGGREGATE

Suppose that we are given a set F of firms, each of which has an input *aggregate*[7]

$$u_f = \phi^f(x_f), \quad f \in F, \tag{2.1}$$

and make a similar requirement for the economy as a whole, so that

$$u = \phi(x), \quad x = \textstyle\sum_f x_f. \tag{2.2}$$

The corresponding technologies T_f, each $f \in F$, and

$$T = \textstyle\sum_f T_f, \tag{2.3}$$

may be written

[6] Since Cauchy works just as well for vectors of aggregates as for scalars, this is an unnecessary variation, though, I hope, suggestive.

[7] Strong assumptions are needed for this when there are no fixed inputs to be varied parametrically e.g. those of A or B in Sect. 4. However these are overstrong and many alternatives exist, and, of course, one might explore the case where there is only a single overall aggregate vector for the economy as a whole.

$$T_f : \Phi^f(\phi^f(x_f), y_f) \geqslant 0; \quad T : \Phi(\phi(x), y) \geqslant 0, \tag{2.4}$$

where y_f, each f, and

$$y = \sum_f y_f, \tag{2.5}$$

are *output vectors.*

Of course I have called the two classes inputs and outputs respectively merely for ease of exposition. There is no reason why they might not both be mixed, or include intermediate goods. However I will measure the x's as net inputs, the y's as net outputs, even though this may lead to negative components.

Under minimal assumptions, (2.4) may be solved to yield

$$T_f : \phi^f(x_f) \geqslant \psi^f(y_f), \quad \text{each } f \in F; \quad T : \phi(x) \geqslant \psi(y), \tag{2.6}$$

or, more suggestively,

$$T_f : \phi^f(x_f) \geqslant u_f \geqslant \psi^f(y_f), \quad \text{each } f \in F; \quad T : \phi(x) \geqslant u \geqslant \psi(y), \tag{2.7}$$

with equalities on the production frontiers, to which (2.1) and (2.2) refer. The u's may equally well be interpreted, then, as *output aggregates*. Best of all, think of them as *quantities of intermediate goods*, produced by fixed inputs, and setting the *capacity* for the net production of outputs.

Assume that, given this capacity, production is strictly convex, that is, that $\phi(\cdot)$, and each $\phi^f(\cdot)$, is strictly quasi-concave, $\psi(\cdot)$, and each $\psi^f(\cdot)$, strictly quasi-convex, and furthermore that all are continuous, strictly increasing in an appropriate normalization in the interior of their domains, to which I will restrict myself; and note that this defines each u_f, and u, up to independent continuous, strictly increasing, transformations, allowing scope for convenient normalizations, which I will frequently use below.[8]

Under these assumptions the input and output technologies in (2.7) may be represented by their *cost and revenue functions.*

$$\kappa^f(p, u_f) = \min\{p \cdot x_f \mid \phi^f(x_f) \geqslant u_f\},$$

$$\rho^f(q, u_f) = \max\{q \cdot y_f \mid \psi^f(y_f) \leqslant u_f\},$$

$$\kappa(p, u) = \min\{p \cdot x \mid \phi(x) \geqslant u\} = \sum_f \kappa^f(p, u_f),$$

$$\rho(q, u) = \max\{q \cdot y \mid \kappa(y) \leqslant u\} = \sum_f \rho^f(q, u_f),^{9} \tag{2.8}$$

[8] It is sufficient for the natural technologies to be smooth and strictly convex for many normalizations of $\phi(\cdot)$, $\psi(\cdot)$, $\phi^f(\cdot)$, $\psi^f(\cdot)$ to be available.

[9] These are smooth and strictly convex, or concave, as appropriate in p and q.

with equations where the u's are optimally chosen, that is to yield the *profits*[10]

$$\pi^f(p, q) = \max_{u_f} \{\rho^f(q, u_f) - \kappa^f(p, u_f)\},$$

$$\pi(p, q) = \max_{u} \{\rho(q, u) - \kappa(p, u)\} = \sum_f \pi^f(p, q). \tag{2.9}$$

It will be very convenient to assume the profit functions differentiable *for the present*, as is implied by our strong convexity conditions. This is far from acceptable if we are considering genuine long-run aggregates, since we must surely expect increasing returns over considerable ranges in the long run. Alternatively suppose that there are absolutely fixed inputs, not even parametrically variable, which stop this, to which we do not refer explicitly.

Under it the maxima in question are attained at the unique points:

$$u_f = \theta^f(p, q), \quad u = \theta(p, q), \tag{2.10}$$

at which

$$\rho_0^f(q, u_f) := \partial\rho^f/\partial u_f = \partial\kappa^f/\partial u_f =: \kappa_0^f(p, u_f),$$

$$\rho_0(q, u) := \partial\rho/\partial u = \partial\kappa/\partial u =: \kappa_0(p, u), \tag{2.11}$$

in a notation I will use throughout the paper, a suffix zero being reserved for differentiation with respect to an odd argument out.[11] Moreover, each u_f and u, will actually increase if $q \to \lambda q$, or $p \to p/\lambda$, $\lambda > 1$, $(p, q) > 0$.

Taking the u's to be determined by (2.11), then

$$\rho(q, u) = \sum_f \rho^f(q, u_f), \quad \kappa(p, u) = \sum_f \kappa^f(p, u_f), \tag{2.12}$$

and, of course,

$$\pi(p, q) = \sum_f \pi^f(p, q), \tag{2.13}$$

in consequence, as one would scarcely have doubted. Remember now that the aggregates are defined up to continuous strictly increasing transformations and that $\rho(q, \cdot)$, $\rho^f(q, \cdot)$, $\kappa(p, \cdot)$, $\kappa^f(p, \cdot)$ all have to be appropriately redefined after such transformations, and are themselves continuous and strictly increasing when $(p, q) > 0$. Take then some[12]

[10] Some of the discussion based on the profit functions below is better carried out in terms of the cost and revenue functions—e.g. because it may avoid the use of derivatives—and hence of the smoothness postulate in the dual, implying strict convexity in the primal.

[11] Can be reduced to a special case of a class of differential equations

$$f_i(z) = \delta f/\delta z_i = \lambda^r(z) g_i(z),$$

$i \in r \in R$ a partition of the subscripts, and the $\lambda(r)$'s are distinct. Hence $\# R = 2$. See the Appendix of Gorman (1990).

[12] Note that the differentiability of these functions with respect to u_f and u is a further assumption.

$$(\bar{p}, \bar{q}) > 0, \tag{2.14}$$

and define

$$u_f^* = \kappa^f(\bar{p}, u_f), \quad u^* = \kappa(\bar{p}, u) = \sum_f u_f^*, \tag{2.15}$$

$$u_f^{**} = \rho^f(\bar{q}, u_f), \quad u^{**} = \rho(\bar{q}, u) = \sum_f u_f^{**}, \tag{2.16}$$

by (2.12) in each case. Choosing either normalization, redefining the cost and revenue functions accordingly, and dropping the asterisks we get

$$\rho\left(q, \sum_f u_f\right) = \sum_f \rho^f(q, u_f); \tag{2.17a}$$

$$\kappa\left(p, \sum_f u_f\right) = \sum_f \kappa^f(p, u_f). \tag{2.17b}$$

These are very like Cauchy's equation yielding linearity. Were the x_f parametrically variable fixed inputs, for instance, we could vary the u_f independently in (2.17*a*), and get

$$\rho^f(q, u_f) = b(q)u_f + d^f(q); \quad \rho(q, u) = b(q)u + d(q), \text{ say}, \quad d(q) = \sum_f d^f(q), \tag{2.18}$$

and similarly

$$\kappa^f(p, u_f) = a(p)u_f + c^f(p); \quad \kappa(p, u) = a(p)u + c(p), \text{ say}, \quad c(p) = \sum_f c^f(p), \tag{2.19}$$

in (2.17*b*) were the y_f parametrically variable. However they are not. Instead, they are determined endogenously by (p, q). To be precise

$$x_{fi} = -\pi_i^f(p, q) := -\partial\pi^f/\partial p_i, \quad y_{fk} = \pi_k^f(p, q) := \partial\pi^f/\partial q_k, \tag{2.20}$$

for instance. The only shift parameters at our disposal are these prices of inputs and outputs. Should we be able to move the u_f independently by adjusting the p's only, (2.17*a*) would again give (2.18); if by adjusting the q's only, (2.17*b*) yields (2.19). Call these the *p-driven* and *q-driven cases*, respectively. It is possible that neither works and the system is *undriven*. It turns out that this third case is also subject to analysis and can be interpreted in much the same way.[13]

I will consider the simplest case, where $\#F = 2$, in the next section, generalizing to larger economies in Section 4, before going on to cases in which there are many aggregates as well as many firms.

3. A SINGLE AGGREGATE: TWO FIRMS

I assume aggregates u_1, u_2 to exist for the two firms taken separately, and, u, for the pair.

[13] I will vary these terms and definitions below as the argument progresses. It will lead to greater precision.

For them to be p-driven we have to be able to vary u_1 and u_2 independently by changing p alone. This will be so iff there is no $\lambda(p, q)$ such that

$$\theta_i^2(p, q) := \partial\theta^2/\partial p_i = \lambda(p, q)\theta_i^1(p, q), \qquad \text{each input } i. \tag{3.1}$$

In this case we adopt the normalization (2.15)[14] to get

$$u = u_1 + u_2, \tag{3.2}$$

$$\rho^f(q, u_f) = b(q)y_f + d^f(q), \quad f = 1, 2; \quad \rho(q, u) = b(q)u + d(q), \tag{3.3}$$

as in (2.15) and (2.18).

Similarly they will be q-driven iff there is *no* $\mu(p, q)$ such that

$$\theta_k^2(p, q) := \partial\theta^2/\partial q_k = \mu(p, q)\theta_k^1, \qquad \text{each output } k, \tag{3.4}$$

in which case we can adopt the normalization (2.16) to get (3.2) again and

$$\kappa^f(p, u_f) = a(p)u_f + c^f(p), \quad f = 1, 2; \quad \kappa(p, u) = a(p)u + c(p). \tag{3.5}$$

In the undriven case, $\lambda(\cdot)$, $\mu(\cdot)$ exist such that (3.1) and (3.4) hold. I will now show that this can only be so if

$$\lambda(p, q) = \mu(p, q), \tag{3.6}$$

in which case

$$u_2 = \theta^2(p, q) = \chi(\theta^1(p, q)) = \chi(u_1), \text{ say}, \tag{3.7}$$

where $\chi(\cdot)$ is smooth and strictly increasing, and we can therefore normalize so that

$$u_2 = u_1 = u, \tag{3.8}$$

and we have a sort of generalized Leontief technology, at least 'between firms'.

This arises from two facts. First, $\theta^1(\cdot)$, $\theta^2(\cdot)$ are clearly positively homogeneous of degree zero, so that[15]

$$\sum_i \theta_i^1 p_i + \sum_k \theta_k^1 q_k = 0, \tag{3.9}$$

$$\lambda\sum_i \theta_i^1 p_i + \mu\sum_k \theta_k^1 q_k = \sum_i \theta_i^2 p_i + \sum_k \theta_k^2 q_k = 0, \tag{3.10}$$

and hence

$$(\mu - \lambda)\sum_i \theta_i^1 p_i = 0, \tag{3.11}$$

[14] [eds.] This is the same as assuming θ^1 and θ^2 are *not ordinally equivalent* in the p's.

[15] This is better done using the revenue and cost functions as I did at the Mirrlees lunch-time workshop in 1982.

and secondly the production, u_1, of the intermediate good in firm 1 actually falls when input prices rise in the same proportion, so that

$$\sum_i \theta_i^1 p_i < 0, \tag{3.12}$$

and we can divide across by it in (3.11) to get $\mu = \lambda$ as required, which in turn implies that

$$du_2 = \sum_i \theta_i^2 dp_i + \sum_k \theta_k^2 dq_k = \lambda\left(\sum_i \theta_i^1 dp_i + \sum_k \theta_k^1 dq_k\right) = \lambda du_1, \tag{3.13}$$

and thus

$$u_2 = \chi(u_1), \text{ say,}$$

as in (3.7), where $\chi(\cdot)$ is smooth and strictly increasing as required. We can therefore normalize to get

$$\tilde{u}_1 := \chi(u_1) = u_2, \tag{3.14}$$

and drop the tilde and get

$$u_1 = u_2. \tag{3.15}$$

Now (2.15), for instance, clearly implies that

$$\alpha(u) = \alpha^1(u_1) + \alpha^2(u_2), \text{ say,}[16] \tag{3.16}$$

in general, where $\alpha(\cdot)$, $\alpha^1(\cdot)$ and $\alpha^2(\cdot)$ are smooth and strictly increasing. Hence we can take

$$u_1 = u_2 = u, \tag{3.17}$$

here without loss of generality: and even these are only defined up to a common smooth strictly increasing transformation.

What happens here is that the scale of production varies in strict tempo, if you like, in the two firms and in the economy as a whole. In so far as this aggregate is concerned, the *interfirm behaviour is Leontief.*

Another way of looking at it is to take the common u as the quantity of a public good, entering into each firm's technology. Now (2.10)–(2.11) imply that

$$\rho_0^1(q, u) = \kappa_0^1(p, u); \quad \rho_0^2(q, u) = \kappa_0^2(p, u); \quad \rho_0(q, u) = \kappa_0(p, u), \tag{3.18}$$

are three equivalent statements. Moreover, we can change u freely, by changing q, for instance, while holding p constant. Hence,

$$\kappa_0^f(p, u) = \lambda^f(\kappa_0(p, u), u), \text{ say,} \qquad f = 1, 2. \tag{3.19}$$

[16] (3.16) is obscure: other approaches are possible and were used in the version I read to Jim Mirrlees's workshop in Nuffield in Trinity 1982.

Choose smooth, strictly increasing $\alpha^1(\cdot)$, $\alpha^2(\cdot)$, and define $\alpha(\cdot) = \alpha^1(\cdot) + \alpha^2(\cdot)$, to get (3.17).

However, both $\kappa_0^f(\cdot, u)$ and $\kappa_0(\cdot, u)$ are conical. Hence (3.19) becomes

$$\kappa_0^f(p, u) = \lambda^f(u)\kappa_0(p, u), \text{ say}, \quad f = 1, 2, \tag{3.20}$$

in a slightly changed notation. Similarly

$$\rho_0^f(q, u) = \lambda^f(u)\rho_0(q, u), \quad f = 1, 2, \tag{3.21}$$

where $\lambda^f(u) > 0$ always. Moreover,

$$\lambda^1(u) + \lambda^2(u) = 1, \tag{3.22}$$

always, as may be seen by setting $u_f = u$ in (1.11). Hence (3.18) and (3.19) tell us that the shadow, or transfer, price for the public good in the economy as a whole, is the sum of its shadow prices in the two firms, which is agreeable.

In another normalization, however, this aggregate appears as the quantity of a private good, with the same shadow price everywhere.[17]

To see this, remember that $\lambda^f(\cdot)$ is continuous and positive, and so may be taken as the derivative of a smooth strictly increasing function $\mu^f(\cdot)$. We may therefore take

$$\tilde{u}_f := \mu^f(u_f) = \mu^f(u) = \int_0^u \lambda^f(u)\mathrm{d}u = \lambda^f(u)u - \int_0^u u\, \mathrm{d}\lambda^f(u), \text{ say}, \quad f = 1, 2, \tag{3.23}$$

with

$$\tilde{u}_1 + \tilde{u}_2 = u =: \tilde{u}, \tag{3.24}$$

to get

$$\kappa^f(p, u_f) = \tilde{\kappa}^f(p, \tilde{u}_f) = \tilde{\kappa}^f(p, \mu^f(u)), \tag{3.25}$$

$$\kappa_0^f(p, u) = \tilde{\kappa}_0^f(p, \tilde{u}_f)\lambda^f(u), \tag{3.26}$$

so that

$$\tilde{\kappa}_0^f(p, \tilde{u}_f) = \kappa_0(p, u) = \tilde{\kappa}_0(p, \tilde{u}), \tag{3.27}$$

in this normalization by (3.20) and (3.24). Similarly

$$\tilde{\rho}_0^f(q, \tilde{u}_f) = \tilde{\rho}_0(q, \tilde{u}), \tag{3.28}$$

so that the quantities $\tilde{u}_1$, $\tilde{u}_2$ of the 'private' good add up to the total quantity $\tilde{u}$, as they should, by (3.24), its shadow, or transfer, price is the same in each firm as in the economy as a whole, by (3.27) and (3.23).

In this normalization, too,

$$\partial x_{fi}/\partial \tilde{u}_f = \tilde{\kappa}_{0i}^f(p, \tilde{u}_f) = \tilde{\kappa}_{0i}(p, \tilde{u}) = \partial x_i/\partial \tilde{u}, \tag{3.29}$$

[17] It can be useful to carry out parallel normalizations like this to bring out different interpretations of a common formula or theorem.

$$\partial y_{fk}/\partial \tilde{u}_f = \tilde{\rho}^f_{0k}(q, \tilde{u}_f) = \tilde{\rho}_{0k}(p, \tilde{u}) = \partial y_k/\partial \tilde{u}, \tag{3.30}$$

by (3.25) and (3.26), so that the marginal input and output patterns are both the same in each of the firms as in the economy as a whole.

So much for the moment for the undriven case. We have rather similar results in the two driven cases. In the p-driven case, (3.3) yields

$$\partial y_{fk}/\partial u_f = \rho^f_{0k} = b_k(q) = \partial y_k/\partial u, \tag{3.31}$$

and in the q-driven case, (3.5) gives

$$\partial x_{fi}/\partial u_f = \kappa^f_{0i}(p, u_f) = a_i(p) = \partial x_i/\partial u, \tag{3.32}$$

so that the marginal pattern of output is the same in each firm in the former case, and of input in the latter. Since the aggregates, or scales of production, can be varied separately in each of these cases, this yields quasi-homotheticity on the side in question, but nothing about the other side.

Say that technologies are similar if they yield the same marginal pattern. Then there are three cases:

(i) p-driven: the output technologies, defined by the revenue functions $\rho^f(q, u_f)$, are similar and quasi-homothetic,

(ii) q-driven: the input technologies, defined by the cost functions $\kappa^f(p, u_f)$, are similar and quasi-homothetic,

(iii) undriven: the input technologies as defined by the $\kappa^f(p, u_f)$ are similar and so are the output technologies defined by the $\rho^f(q, u_f)$. Neither need be quasi-homothetic.

To draw the results closer together, return to the original normalization (3.14)–(3.17) in the undriven case, set

$$\theta(\bar{p}, \bar{q}) = \bar{u} = 0, \qquad \text{at a fixed } \bar{p}, \bar{q}, \tag{3.33}$$

and define

$$\kappa^f(p, \bar{u}) =: c^f(p), \quad \rho^f(q, \bar{u}) =: d^f(q), \quad f = 1, 2,$$

$$\kappa(p, \bar{u}) = c(p) = c^1(p) + c^2(p); \quad \rho(q, \bar{u}) = d(q) = d^1(q) + d^2(q). \tag{3.34}$$

Then

$$\kappa^f(p, u) = c^f(p) + \int_0^u \lambda^f(u)\kappa_0(p, u)du, \quad f = 1, 2, \tag{3.35}$$

$$\kappa(p, u) = c(p) + \int_0^u \kappa_0(p, u)du,$$[18]

[18] Integration by parts in (3.35) yields

$$\kappa^k(p, u) = \lambda^f(u)\kappa(p, u) - \int_0^u \kappa(p, u)d\lambda^f(u) + \tilde{c}^f(p)$$

$$\rho^f(q, u) = \lambda^f(u)\rho(q, u) - \int_0^u \rho(q, u)d\lambda^f(u) + \tilde{d}^f(q).$$

since $\bar{u} = 0$ in (3.33), with exactly similar formulae on the output side. That is, we have the 'overheads' $c^f(p)$, $c(p)$, $d^f(q)$, $d(q)$ as in the quasi-homothetic case, supplemented by a list of small 'plants' yielding constant returns to du, with cost and revenue functions $\kappa_0(p, u)du$, $\rho_0(q, u)du$, each divided between the two firms in the ratio $\lambda^1(u)/\lambda^2(u)$.

Remember that $\lambda^1(u) = \lambda^2(u) = 1$ by (3.22).

These correspond to the single 'plant' yielding constant returns on one side or the other, complementing the corresponding overhead $c^f(p)$, or $d^f(q)$, and running at the efficient scale in each firm.

Of course this interpretation in the primal is valid only given appropriate convexity. It is quite suggestive, nevertheless.

4. A SINGLE AGGREGATE: MORE THAN TWO FIRMS

Here the main result is:

A. If aggregates exist for each firm $f \in F$ and each pair of firms $f, g \in F$, they do for F and each subset $G \subseteq F$. Moreover, all the aggregates are of the same type; that is, either (i) p-driven, (ii) q-driven, or (iii) undriven.

The argument turns on the notions of p-connectivity and q-connectivity. I will define p-connectivity; q-connectivity is precisely similar.[19]

Say that each $f \in F$ is *p-connected* to itself, and that a distinct pair $f, g \in F$ is *p-connected* iff there is a chain,

$$f = f_1, f_2, \ldots, f_n = g, \tag{4.1}$$

each link of which is either p-driven or undriven, and at least one link of which is p-driven.

Being p-connected is an equivalence relation. It therefore allows us to partition F into equivalence classes, each pair of elements of any of which is p-connected, while no pair in distinct classes is. Call those with two or more elements *p-components*, with only one *p-isolates*, and the set of the latter the *p-residue*.

Let $\{f_m, f_{m+1}\}$ be p-driven in the chain (4.1). We can then normalize so that

$$\rho^m(q, u_m) = b(q)u_m + d^m(q), \quad \rho^{m+1}(q, u_{m+1}) = b(q)u_{m+1} + d^{m+1}(q), \tag{4.2}$$

by (3.3), in an obvious notation. Now consider $f = m + 2$, for example. Suppose $\{m + 1, m + 2\}$ is undriven. We can then normalize u_{m+2} in such a manner that

$$\rho_0^{m+2}(q, u_{m+2}) = \rho_0^{m+1}(q, u_{m+1}) = b(q), \tag{4.3}$$

[19] The switching between p-, and q-, connectivity may make your head swim. If interested, think on, and consider the relationship with aggregates being undriven because affine on each side. Such connectivity arguments are powerful. I will use them a lot.

by setting $f = m + 2$, $m + 1$ in (3.28) with m replacing the economy, and using (4.2). Hence

$$\rho^{m+2}(q, u_{m+2}) = b(q)u_{m+2} + d^{m+2}(q), \text{ say.} \tag{4.4}$$

We can repeat this step at each undriven link in turn. The argument at p-driven links is left to you.

Hence

$$\rho^f(q, u_f) = b(q)u_f + d^f(q), \qquad \text{each } f \in P \subseteq F, \tag{4.5}$$

a p-component of F.

Suppose now that

$$P \subset F, \tag{4.6}$$

and take a p-connected pair $f, g \in P$ and an $h \notin P$.

Were $\{g, h\}$ p-driven, they would be p-connected. Were it undriven $\{f, h\}$ would be p-connected. In either case $h \in P$, which it does not. Hence $\{g, h\}$ is q-driven. So is $\{f, h\}$ by the same argument. So therefore is $\{f, g\}$ via the chain f, h, g. Hence $P \cup \{h\} \subseteq Q$, a q-component of F. But this is true of every $h \notin P$. Hence F itself is q-connected when $P \subset F$.

If it contains a p-connected pair, then, F is q-connected if $P \subset F$, and p-connected if $P = F$; *mutatis mutandis* if it contains a q-connected pair. Hence we can write either

$$\kappa^f(p, u_f) = a(p)u_f + c^f(p), \qquad \text{each } f \in F, \tag{4.7}$$

or

$$\rho^f(q, u_f) = b(q)u_f + d^f, \qquad \text{each } f \in F, \tag{4.8}$$

or

$$\text{each pair } f, g \in F \text{ is undriven.} \tag{4.9}$$

Note that these possibilities are not mutually exclusive. In particular, both (4.7) and (4.8) may hold, in which case (4.9) does too. Once more, I leave the proof to you.

It remains to prove that aggregates exist from each $G \subseteq F$.

First consider the q-driven case (4.7). The profit function for f,

$$\begin{aligned}
\pi^f(p, q) &= \max\{q \cdot y_f - p \cdot x_f \mid \phi^f(x_f) \geqslant u_f > \psi^f(y_f)\} \\
&= \max\{q \cdot y_f - \min\{p \cdot x_f \mid \phi^f(x_f) \geqslant u_f\} \mid u_f \geqslant \psi^f(y_f)\} \\
&= \max\{q \cdot y_f - a(p)u_f - c^f(p) \mid u_f \geqslant \psi^f(y_f)\} \\
&= \max\{q \cdot y_f - a(p)u_f \mid u_f \leqslant \psi^f(y_f)\} - c^f(p) \\
&= \Pi^f(a(p), q) - c^f(p), \text{ say,}
\end{aligned} \tag{4.10}$$

where

$$\Pi^f(\cdot) \text{ is smooth strictly convex concial,} \tag{4.11}$$

being the profit function for a smooth strictly convex technology. That for $G \subseteq F$ is

$$\pi^G(p, q) = \sum_{g \in G} \pi^g(p, q) = \Pi^G(a(p), q) - c^G(p), \tag{4.12}$$

where

$$\Pi^G(a, q) = \sum_{g \in G} \Pi^g(a, q), \quad c^G(p) = \sum_{g \in G} c^g(p), \tag{4.13}$$

so that $\Pi^G(\cdot)$ is also smooth strictly convex conical, and hence the profit function for a smooth strictly convex technology

$$T_G^* = \left\{(u_G, y_G) \mid q \cdot y_G - au_G \geqslant \Pi^G(a, q) \mid \text{each } (a, q) \geqslant 0\right\}.^{20} \tag{4.14}$$

I leave it to you to show $u_G = \sum_{g \in G} u_g$.
The same proof holds for (4.8).
In (4.9) consider a pair f, $g \in G$. Define

$$u = u_f, \tag{4.15}$$

without loss of generality, and choose a normalization like (3.14) to get

$$u_g = u, \tag{4.16}$$

while

$$\kappa_0^g(p, u) = \lambda^g(u)\kappa_0(p, u), \quad \rho_0^g(q, u) = \lambda^g(u)\rho_0(q, u), \text{ say,} \tag{4.17}$$

by (3.20)–(3.21), since $\{f, g\}$ is an undriven pair with aggregate u in this normalization. Hence

$$\begin{aligned}\kappa^g(p, u) &= \int_0^u \kappa_0(p, u)\lambda^g(u)\mathrm{d}u + c^g(p) \\ &= \lambda^g(u)\kappa(p, u) + \tilde{c}^g(p) - \int_0^u \kappa(p, u)\mathrm{d}\lambda^g(u),\end{aligned} \tag{4.18}$$

$$\begin{aligned}\rho^g(q, u) &= \int_0^u \rho_0(q, u)\lambda^g(u)\mathrm{d}u + d^g(q), \\ &= \lambda^g(u)\rho(q, u) + \tilde{d}^g(p) - \int_0^u \rho(q, u)\mathrm{d}\lambda^g(u),\end{aligned} \tag{4.19}$$

[20] $a = a(p)$, just like a price once overheads $cf(p)$ or $c(p)$ are met.

each $g \in G$, in a slightly changed notation, by (4.17). Define now,

$$\kappa^G(p, u) := \sum_{g \in G} \kappa^g(p, u) = \int_0^u \kappa_0(p, u)\lambda^G(u)du + c^G(p),$$

$$\rho^G(q, u) = \int_0^u \rho_0(q, u)\lambda^G(u)du + d^G(q), \tag{4.20}$$

where

$$\lambda^G(u) = \sum_{g \in G} \lambda^g(u), \quad c^G(p) = \sum_{g \in G} c^g(p), \quad d^G(q) = \sum_{g \in G} d^g(q), \tag{4.21}$$

to get

$$\pi^G(p, q) = \sum_{g \in G} \pi^g(p, q) = \sum_{g \in G} \max\{\rho^g(q, u) - \kappa^g(p, u)\}$$
$$= \max\{\rho^G(q, u) - \kappa^G(p, u)\} \tag{4.22}$$

because the u which maximizes $\rho^f(q, u) - \kappa^f(p, u)$ does so for each $g \in G$ too, by (4.17). Morever, $\rho^G(\cdot, u)$, $\kappa^G(\cdot, u)$, as the sum of smooth strictly convex revenue and concave cost functions are themselves such. Hence they define smooth strictly increasing, strictly quasi-convex/concave functions $\psi^G(\cdot)$, $\phi^G(\cdot)$, and a technology

$$T^G : \phi^G(x_g) \geqslant u \geqslant \psi^G(y_G), \qquad \text{each } G \subseteq F, \tag{4.23}$$

as required, and, in particular, for $G = F$.

That completes the proof of A.

It may sound topsy-turvy to derive the nature of the large aggregates, which is what interests us, from the assumed existence of aggregates for individual firms and pairs of firms. In the case of short-run aggregation, where shift parameters x_f exist for the individual firms, the existence of aggregates for them and for subcollections of them followed from their existence for the economy as a whole. Nothing like that holds here. However, the following is true, and goes a little of the way.

B. Suppose that aggregates exist for the economy F as a whole, for each $f \in F$ and its complement, $-f = F/f$. Then we can write just one of:

B(i) (a) $\kappa(p, u) = a(p)\alpha(u) + c(p)$; (b) $\rho(q, u) \neq b(q)\beta(u) + d(q)$, say,
B(ii) (a) $\kappa(p, u) \neq a(p)\alpha(u) + c(p)$; (b) $\rho(q, u) = b(q)\beta(u) + d(q)$;
B(iii) (a) $\kappa(p, u) \neq a(p)\alpha(u) + c(p)$; (b) $\rho(q, u) \neq b(q)\beta(u) + d(q)$,
B(iv) (a) $\kappa(p, u) = a(p)\alpha(u) + c(p)$; (b) $\rho(q, u) = b(q)\beta(u) + d(q)$,

each in an appropriate notation and with appropriate regularity conditions. In the first case each pair f, $-f$ is q-driven, in the second p-driven, and in the third undriven. Accordingly, equations corresponding to B(i), B(ii),

B(iii) respectively hold for each $f \in F$, and hence for each $G \subseteq F$, so that G has an aggregate: rather like A in fact.

B(iv) is more complicated. Some pairs f, $-f$ may be q-driven, some p-driven, and the others undriven, with equations like B(i), B(ii), or B(iv) holding in the corresponding cases. Writing $Q = \{f \in F \mid \{f, -f\}$ is q-driven$\}$, $P = \{f \in F \mid \{f, -f\}$ is p-driven$\}$ and $R = \{f \in F \mid \{f, -f\}$, is undriven$\}$, aggregates exist for each subset of $P \cup C$, $Q \cup C$, and C, satisfying relations like B(i), B(ii), and B(iv) respectively.

I leave the proof to you.

5. MORE THAN ONE AGGREGATE: PRELIMINARIES

I assume that we are given a partition M of the goods, for each element m of which an aggregate exists. For definiteness, assume that we are in A or B of Section 4.

Measure each good as an output, so that inputs appear as negative outputs. The net output vectors for f and for the economy as a whole will be written:

$$x_f = (x_{fm})_{m \in M}, \quad \text{each } f \in F, \quad x = (x_m)_{m \in M} = \sum_{f \in F} x_f, \tag{5.1}$$

while

$$x_{f,-n} = (x_{fm})_{m \in M \setminus n}, \quad \text{each } f \in F, \quad x_{-n} = (x_m)_{m \in M \setminus n}, \quad \text{each } n \in M. \tag{5.2}$$

Consider now the aggregate $u_{fm} = \phi^{fm}(x_{fm})$, each $f \in F$, $u_m = \phi_m(x_m)$, each $m \in M$. Since $x_{f,-m}$, x_{-m} are measured as outputs rather than inputs, (2.7) may be replaced by

$$\phi^{fm}(x_{fm}),\ \psi^{fm}(x_{f,-m}) \geqslant u_{fm}; \quad \phi^m(x_m),\ \psi^m(x_{-m}) \geqslant u_m, \tag{5.3}$$

with equality signs on the production frontier, and these *inner* and *outer* technologies be represented by their revenue functions:

$$\rho^{fm}(p_m, u_{fm}),\ \sigma^{fm}(p_{-m}, u_{fm}), \quad \text{each } m \in M;$$

$$\rho^m(p_m, u_m),\ \sigma^m(p_{-m}, u_m), \quad \text{each } m \in M. \tag{5.4}$$

We could call m *self-driven* when p_m-driven, *other-driven* when p_{-m}-driven, and *undriven* otherwise. Instead I will commonly use a division based on B(i)–B(iv), and say that m is *self-affine* if B(i) or B(iv) hold; *other-affine* if B(ii); and *non-affine* if B(iii). Of course B(iv) might be grouped with B(ii) instead, or kept separate, but the grouping I have given is the most convenient.

Consider first the self-affine groups $m \in I \subseteq M$, say,

$$\rho^{fm}(p_m, u_{fm}) = a^m(p_m)u_{fm} + c^{fm}(p_m); \quad \rho^m(p_m, u_m) = a^m(p_m)u_m + c^m(p_m). \tag{5.5}$$

It seems pretty obvious that $a^m(p_m)$ is the shadow price of the aggregate U_m[21] in each case with 'overheads' $c^{fm}(p_m)$, $c^m(p_m)$, so that the profit function for the economy as a whole, for instance, is of the form

$$\pi(p) = \Pi^I(a^I(p_I), p_{-I}) + \sum_{m\in I} c^m(p_m); \quad a^I(p_I) = (a^m(p_m))_{m\in I}, \tag{5.6}$$

and so it indeed is. I will give a formal proof, nevertheless, partly because it will be an easy example of a type of argument which I will frequently deploy below.

Now

$$\begin{aligned}\pi(p) &= \max\{a^n(p_n)u_n + c^n(p_n) + \rho^{-n}(u_n, p_{-n})\}\\ &= \Pi^n(a^n(p_n), p_{-n}) + c^n(p_n), \text{ say,} \qquad \text{each, } n\in M,\end{aligned} \tag{5.7}$$

by (5.5). Suppose

$$\pi(p) = \Pi^J(a^J(p_J), p_{-J}) + c^J(p_J), \qquad \text{some } J\subseteq I,\ \#J>0, \tag{5.8}$$

where

$$a^J(p_J) = (a^m(p_m))_{m\in J}, \quad c^J(p_J) = \sum_{m\in J} c^m(p_m). \tag{5.9}$$

If $J=1$, (5.6) holds. We may therefore assume $J\subset I$ without loss of generality. Take an $n\in I\backslash J$, define

$$K = J\cup\{n\}, \tag{5.10}$$

take some fixed $\bar{p}_{-K}$, and substitute into $\pi(p)$, to get

$$\bar{\pi}^K(p_K) := \pi(p_K, \bar{p}_{-K}). \tag{5.11}$$

(5.7) and (5.8) then yield

$$\begin{aligned}\hat{\pi}^K(p) &:= \pi(p) - \bar{\pi}^K(p_K),\\ &= \Pi^J(a^J(p_J), p_{-J}) - \bar{\Pi}^{Jn}(a^J(p_J), p_n) =: \hat{\Pi}^{Jn}(a^J(p_J), p_{-J}),\\ &= \Pi^n(a^n(p_n), p_{-n}) - \bar{\Pi}^{nJ}(a^n(p_n), p_J) =: \hat{\Pi}^{nJ}(a^n(p_n), p_{-n}),\end{aligned} \tag{5.12}$$

where

$$\bar{\Pi}^{Jn}(a^J, p_n) := \Pi^J(a^J, \bar{p}_{-K}, p_n); \quad \bar{\Pi}^{nJ}(a^n, p_J) := \Pi^n(a^n, p_J, \bar{p}_{-K}). \tag{5.13}$$

Changing p_n while holding $a^n(p_n)$ constant does not affect the third line of (5.12), nor changing p_J while holding $a^J(p_J)$, the second. Hence

$$\hat{\pi}^K(p) = \hat{\Pi}^{Jn}(a^J(p_J), p_{-J}) = \hat{\Pi}^{nJ}(a^n(p_n), p_{-n}) = \hat{\Pi}^K(a^K(p_K), p_{-K}), \text{ say,} \tag{5.14}$$

[21] [eds.] As elsewhere, upper-case letters refer to variables, lower-case letters to the values of these variables: hence u_m is the value of the aggregate U_m.

so that

$$\Pi^J(a^J(p_J), p_{-J}) = \hat{\Pi}^K(a^K(p_K), p_{-K}) + \bar{\Pi}^{Jn}(a^J(p_J), p_n),$$

$$\Pi^n(a^n(p_n), p_{-n}) = \hat{\Pi}^K(a^K(p_K), p_{-K}) + \bar{\Pi}^{nJ}(a^n(p_n), p_J), \tag{5.15}$$

by (5.12). Substituting into (5.7) and (5.8) and manipulating, we get

$$\bar{\Pi}^{Jn}(a^J(p_J), p_n) - c^n(p_n) = \bar{\Pi}^{nJ}(a^n(p_n), p_{-J}) - c^J(p_J)$$

$$= \tilde{\Pi}^K(a^K(p_K), p_{-K}), \text{ say,} \tag{5.16}$$

since changing $c^J(p_J)$ while holding $a^J(p_J)$ constant does not affect the left-hand side of (5.16), nor does changing $c^n(p_n)$ while holding $a^n(p_n)$ constant affect the right-hand side. Substituting from (5.15) and (5.16) into (5.7) and (5.8) then yields[22]

$$\pi(p) = \Pi^K(a^K(p_K), p_{-K}) + c^K(p_K), \qquad \text{each } K \subseteq I, \tag{5.17}$$

on dropping the tilde, where

$$a^K(p_K) = (a^m(p_m))_{m\in K}, \quad c^K(p_K) = \sum_{m\in K} c^m(p_m), \quad K \subseteq I. \tag{5.18}$$

Since (5.17) implies that (5.8) holds for $\# J = 1$, it therefore does so for each $K \subseteq I$, and hence for $K = I$ in particular, that is, (5.6).

It will sometimes be convenient to work with the *quasi-rent function*

$$Q(p) = \pi(p) - \sum_{m\in I} c^m(p_m) = \Pi^I(a^I(p_I), p_{-I}), \text{ say,} \tag{5.19}$$

where we can always normalize to get each $a^n(\cdot)$ conical, and to write[23]

$$a^m(p_m) = a_m, \quad \text{each } m\in I, \quad a^I(p_I) = a, \;\; p_{-I} = p, \;\; \Pi^I = \Pi, \tag{5.20}$$

in a modified notation,[24] to get

$$\pi = \Pi(a, p) + c(p), \text{ say.} \tag{5.21}$$

[22] The important case is $K = I = \{m \mid m \text{ self-affine}\}$

$$\Pi(p) = \Pi'(a^I(p_I), p_{-I}) + c^I(p_I)$$

$$a^I(p_I) = a^m(p_m))_{m\in I}, \quad c^I(p_I) = \sum_{m\in I} c^m(p_m)$$

[23] [eds.] Repeated application of Case B(i) has transformed the quasi-rent function from being a function of the $(\{a_m(p_m)\}_{m\in I}, p_{-I})$, where I is the subset of sectors satisfying Case B(i). He now rewrites this as a vector (a, p), so that what used to be p_{-I} is now simply p. Failure to keep this in mind makes the sequel even more difficult to understand.

[24] A self-affine aggregate with shadow price $a^m(p_m)$ can be regarded as a good with price a_m, the overheads $c^m(p_m)$ being held over.

This is a great convenience: on the other hand it stops us learning more about the structure as in the other-affine and non-affine cases.

We now consider three cases: other-driven; self-driven, and non-driven. If m is other-driven, we can write

$$\pi(p) = \Pi^m(a^m(p_m), p_{-m}) + c^m(p_m) \tag{5.22}$$

as in (5.7), where all the functions are conical, and $\Pi^m(\cdot)$, $c^m(\cdot)$ are profit functions. If (5.22) holds we can easily normalize to get all the functions conical. I will nevertheless say that m is *self-affine* iff (5.22) holds, *from now on*.

Second, if m is self-driven, we can write

$$\pi(p) = \Pi^m(b^m(p_{-m}), p_m) + d^m(p_{-m}) \tag{5.23}$$

by (3.3) and (2.9), with the same conditions.

Say that m is *other-affine* iff (5.23) holds and (5.22) does not. This allows us to get (5.19) for the set I of all self-affine groups; eliminate them via (5.20), which now yields m *other-affine* iff

$$\Pi(a, p) = \Pi^m(b^m(a, p_{-m}), p_m) + d^m(a, p_{-m}), \qquad \text{some } \Pi^m(\cdot), b^m(\cdot), d^m(\cdot),$$

$$\neq \tilde{\Pi}^m(\tilde{b}^m(p^m), a, p_{-m}) + \tilde{d}^m(p_{-m}), \quad \text{any } \tilde{\Pi}^m(\cdot), \tilde{b}^m(\cdot), \tilde{d}^m(\cdot). \tag{5.24}$$

Thirdly, the aggregate m is *non-affine* iff neither (5.22) nor (5.23) holds. Of course it has to exist and the analysis of Section 3 can therefore be applied.

It will commonly be convenient to drop the $a(\cdot)$, treating a_m as the price of a single macro-good m, which does not enter into any group to which we will not refer explicitly until it becomes necessary. M is a partition of which this m is now a singleton element, so that no aggregation problem remains for it.

That disposes of the self-affine aggregates, which are relatively easy to deal with. I will discuss other-affine, and non-affine aggregates in the next two sections, where I will unfortunately have to use calculus methods and hence draw on the strong convexity assumptions in the primal.

6. OTHER-AFFINE AGGREGATES

Let M be the set of other affine aggregates. Then $\backslash m$[25] is separable each $m \in M$ in a reasonable use of the term, and actually in the quasi-rent function. Hence each set $N \cup M^*$, $M^* \subset M$, $N = \backslash M$, is separable, giving the additive separability we find.[26]

[25] [eds.] Notice that the symbol $\backslash m$ means everything in M that is not m plus everything that is not in M.

[26] At least, that is what I very strongly suspect now [1991].

Note that N is separable, too, since $N = \cap\{\backslash m \mid m \in M\}$. However it does not overlap any other separable set, while each $\{m_1, m_2\} \cup N$ does as long as $\# M > 2$, and it is overlap that generates additivity.

Now for the technical argument. According to (5.22), we can write

$$\pi(p) = \Pi^n(b^n(p_{-n}), p_n) + \mathrm{d}^n(p_{-n}), \tag{6.1}$$

when n is other-affine. In this section I will strengthen this to show that

$$\pi(p) = \sum_{m \in K} \Pi^m(b^m(p_{-K}), p_m) + \mathrm{d}^K(p_{-K}), \tag{6.2}$$

when each sector $m \in K$ is other-affine, that is when $K \subseteq M$, *the set of other-affine sectors.*[27]

If $\# M = 1$, (6.1) is (6.2). We may therefore assume $\# M \geqslant 2$. Do so and let m, n be distinct elements of M. Write

$$p_m = r, \quad p_n = s, \quad (p_\ell)_{\ell \neq m, n} = t. \tag{6.3}$$

(6.1) then implies

$$\begin{aligned}\pi(r, s, t) &= \phi(a(s, t), r) + c(s, t),\\ &= \psi(b(r, t), s) + \mathrm{d}(r, t),\end{aligned} \tag{6.4}$$

say.[28] Hence

$$\pi_{ij} := \partial^2\pi/\partial r_i \partial s_j = \phi_{0i} a_j = \psi_{0j} b_i, \qquad \text{each } i \in m,\ j \in n, \tag{6.5}$$

given the slightly stronger assumption that those several derivatives exist throughout the domain we are employing.

Suppose first that

(A) $\pi_{i^* j^*} \neq 0, \qquad \text{some } i^* \in m,\ j^* \in n,$

so that

$$\phi_{0i^*},\ \psi_{0j^*},\ \alpha_{j^*},\ b_{i^*} \neq 0. \tag{6.6}$$

Write (6.5) down for $j = j^*$, and for $i = i^*$, $j = j^*$. Divide the former by the latter to get

$$\phi_{0i}(a(s, t), r)/\phi_{0i^*}(a(s, t), r) = b_i(r, t)/b_{i^*}(r, t), \tag{6.7}$$

each $i \in m$. Since $a_{j^*} \neq 0$, $a(s, t)$ depends on s, while nothing on the right does. Hence each side of (6.7) depends only on r. Take now a fixed $\bar{t}$ and define

[27] The important version of (6.2) is

$$\pi(p) = \textstyle\sum_{m \in M} \Pi^m(b^m(p_N), p_m) + d^N(p_N).$$

If this is so one can avoid calculus arguments again.

[28] [eds.] Notice that the functions a, b, c, and d are not the same functions as those defined previously; for example, a and b here correspond to b^m and b^n respectively, in equations (6.2) and (6.1), while ϕ and ψ correspond to $\Pi^m$and Π^n.

$$\alpha(s) := a(s, \bar{t}), \quad \beta(r) := b(r, \bar{t}), \tag{6.8}$$

to get

$$b(r, t) = B(\beta(r), t), \text{ say.} \tag{6.9}$$

Similarly,

$$a(s, t) = A(\alpha(s), t), \text{ say.} \tag{6.10}$$

Hence

$$\phi_0(a(s, t), r) = \Phi_0(A(\alpha(s), t), \beta(r)), \text{ say,} \tag{6.11}$$

and (6.4) yields

$$\begin{aligned}\pi(r, s, t) &= \Phi(B(\alpha(s), t), \beta(r)) + \delta(r) + c(s, t), \text{ say,} \\ &= \gamma(\beta(r), s, t) + \delta(r), \text{ say,}\end{aligned} \tag{6.12}$$

so that m is self-affine and hence not other-affine. (A) is therefore impossible, so that

(B) $\pi_{ij}(r, s, t) = 0, \quad$ each $i \in m, j \in n$,

and hence

$$\phi_{0i} a_j = \psi_{0j} b_i = 0, \quad \text{each } i \in m, j \in n. \tag{6.13}$$

There are now three possibilities

(i) $a_j \neq 0, \quad$ some $j \in n$,

which implies that

$$\phi_{0i}(a(s, t), r) = 0, \quad \text{each } i \in m, \tag{6.14}$$

and hence

$$\pi(r, s, t) = ka(s, t) + \beta(r) + c(s, t), \text{ say,} \tag{6.15}$$

where k is a constant,[29] so that m is self-affine, though in a degenerate form. Call it a *dummy*. Hence it is not other-affine, as it is required to be, and (i) is ruled out.

(ii) $b_i \neq 0, \quad$ some $i \in m$,

implying that n is a dummy, and hence not other-affine as required.

(iii) $a_j = b_i = 0, \quad$ each $i \in m, j \in n$,

which is therefore the only possible case.

Hence, in the original notation,

$$b_i^n(p_{-n}) = 0, \quad \text{each } i \in m \in M, \; n \in M \tag{6.16}$$

[29] [eds.] This step follows because ϕ and a have been picked to be homogeneous of degree one in their arguments.

and thus

$$b^n(p_{-n}) = b^{*n}(p_N), \text{ say,} \qquad \text{each } n \in M. \tag{6.17}$$

Now substitute this into (6.1) and drop the * to get

$$\pi(p) = \Pi^n(b^n(p_N), p_n) + d^n(p_{-n}), \qquad \text{each } n \in M, \tag{6.18}$$

and erect the inductive hypothesis

$$\pi(p) = \sum_{m \in J} \Pi^m(b^m(p_N), p_m) + d^J(p_{-J}), \text{ some } J \subset M. \tag{6.19}$$

It certainly holds for $\#J = 1$. Take $n \in M \backslash J$ and use (6.18) to get

$$\begin{aligned} \textstyle\sum_{m \in J} \Pi^m(b^m(p_N), p_m) - d^n(p_{-n}) \\ &= \Pi^n(b^n(p_N), p_n) - d^J(p_{-J}) \\ &= -d^K(p_{-K}), \text{ say,} \end{aligned} \tag{6.20}$$

where $K = J \cup \{n\}$, since the left-hand side is independent of p_n and the right of p_J. Hence

$$\pi(p) = \sum_{m \in K} \Pi^m(b^m(p_N), p_m) + d^K(p_{-K}), \qquad \text{each } K \subseteq M, \tag{6.21}$$

as required, by the obvious mathematical induction.

7. NON-AFFINE AGGREGATES

Basically these are undriven aggregates of Section 3, though I reject those which are also self-, or other-affine, calling all the former *self-affine*, restricting the latter to those which are *other-affine* in the natural sense of the word, but not self-affine, and restricting *non-affine* to those which are neither.[30]

First look at a single non-affine sector m. Write

$$p_m = r, \quad p_{-m} = s, \tag{7.1}$$

and drop the superscript m, to get

$$\rho_0^f(r, u) = \lambda^f(u)\rho_0(r, u), \quad \sigma_0^f(s, u) = \lambda^f(u)\sigma_0(r, u), \quad \lambda^f(u) > 0 \tag{7.2}$$

by analogy with (2.20)–(2.21), where we have taken the 'public good' version. u is then uniquely determined by

$$\rho_0(r, u) + \sigma_0(s, u) = 0, \tag{7.3}$$

[30] Other reorganizations which would allocate each aggregate to just one type are possible. I find this the most convenient.

given r, s. The corresponding equation for f also holds but comes to the same thing in the light of (7.2).

How does u change as r and s do?

$$\rho_{0i}(r, u) = -(\rho_{00} + \sigma_{00})u_i, \quad \sigma_{0j}(s, u) = -(\rho_{00} + \sigma_{00})u_j, \tag{7.4}$$

$$\rho^f_{0i}(r, u) = -(\rho^f_{00} + \sigma^f_{00})u_i, \quad \sigma^f_{0j}(s, u) = -(\rho^f_{00} + \sigma^f_{00})u_j, \tag{7.5}$$

where $i \in m$, $j \notin m$. Now

$$\pi(r, s) = \rho(r, u) + \sigma(s, u), \tag{7.6}$$

where u is determined by (7.3). Hence

$$\pi_i(r, s) = \rho_i + (\rho_0 + \sigma_0)u_i = \rho_i, \tag{7.7}$$

by (7.3), and

$$\pi_{ij}(r, s) = \rho_{0i}u_j = \sigma_{0j}u_i = (\rho_{00} + \sigma_{00})u_iu_j \tag{7.8}$$

$$= \alpha u_iu_j = \beta\rho_{0i}\sigma_{0j} = \gamma^f\pi^f_{ij}, \quad \text{each } i \in m, j \notin m, \tag{7.9}$$

by (7.3)–(7.5), where

$$\alpha = (\rho_{00} + \sigma_{00}), \quad \beta = 1/\alpha; \quad \gamma^f = \alpha^f/\alpha, \quad \alpha^f = -(\rho^f_{00} + \sigma^f_{00}), \tag{7.10}$$

the last because u is equally well determined by $\rho^f_0 + \sigma^f_0 = \lambda^f(u)(\rho_0 + \sigma_0) = 0$, by (7.2). However (7.2) also yields

$$\rho^f_{00} + \sigma^f_{00} = \lambda^f(u)(\rho_{00} + \sigma_{00}) + \lambda^f_0(\rho_0 + \sigma_0) = \lambda^f(u)(\rho_{00} + \sigma_{00}), \tag{7.11}$$

by (7.3), so that

$$1/\gamma^f = (\rho^f_{00} + \sigma^f_{00})/(\rho_{00} + \sigma_{00}) = \lambda^f(u), \tag{7.12}$$

by (7.10) and (7.11), and hence

$$\pi^f_{ij} = \lambda^f(u)\pi_{ij}, \quad \text{each } i \in m, \ j \notin m, \tag{7.13}$$

by (7.9) and (7.12), where u is determined by (7.3) unless

$$\rho_{00} + \sigma_{00} = 0, \tag{7.14}$$

in which case

$$\pi_{ij}(r, s) = 0, \quad \text{each } i \in m, \ j \notin m, \tag{7.15}$$

and hence

$$\pi(r, s) = \phi(r) + \psi(s), \text{ say}, \tag{7.16}$$

m is a dummy, hence self-affine, hence not non-affine as required. Hence

$$\pi_{ij} \neq 0, \quad \text{some } i \in m, j \notin m, \text{ and non-affine } m, \tag{7.17}$$

and (7.13) holds.

Suppose now that $\#N > 1$, where N is now the set of non-affine sectors, and say that any $m \in N$ is *directly connected* to itself, to an $n \in N \backslash \{m\}$ if

$$\pi_{ij} \neq 0, \quad \text{some } i \in m,\ j \in n,\ m \neq n, \tag{7.18}$$

and *connected* to n if $m = n$, or if there is a chain

$$m = m_1, m_2, \ldots, m_t = n, \tag{7.19}$$

each element of which, other than the last, is directly connected to its successor.

'Being connected to' is therefore an equivalence relationship, allowing us to partition N into equivalence classes, or *clumps*, with the property that any pair of sectors in the same clump are connected, and no pair in different clumps are.

All these clumps may be singletons, in which case

$$\sigma^n(p_{-n}, u_n) = \sigma^{*n}(p_{-N}, u_n), \quad \sigma^{fn}(p_{-n}, u_n) = \sigma^{*fn}(p_{-N}, u_n), \text{ say}, \tag{7.20}$$

each $n \in N$, $f \in F$, and

$$\pi(p) = \sum_{n \in N} \pi^n(p_n, p_{-N}) \tag{7.21}$$

$$\pi^f(p) = \sum_{n \in N} \pi^{fn}(p_n, p_{-N}); \tag{7.22}$$

each $f \in F$, $n \in N$.

In general let Θ be the set of clumps of N, and $\theta \in \Theta$ a typical element of it. Then

$$\sigma^n(p_{-n}, u_n) = \sigma^{*n}(p_{\theta-n}, p_{-N}, u_n), \quad p_{\theta-n} = (p_m)_{m \in \theta \backslash \{n\}}; \text{ say}, \tag{7.23}$$

$$\pi(p) = \sum\nolimits_\theta \pi^\theta(p_\theta, p_{-N}). \tag{7.24}$$

Suppose that at least one of these has more than one sector. Call it θ, take $m \in \theta$, and an $n \in \theta$ which is directly connected to it. Then

$$\pi^\theta_{ij}(p_\theta, p_{-N}) = \lambda^{fm}(u_m), \quad \pi^{f\theta}_{ij}(p_\theta, p_{-N}) = \lambda^{fn}(u_n), \quad \pi^{f\theta}_{ij}(p_\theta, p_{-N}) \neq 0, \tag{7.25}$$

some $i \in m$, $j \in n$. Hence

$$\lambda^{fm}(u_m) = \lambda^{fn}(u_n), \tag{7.26}$$

when m, n are directly connected. Suppose next that they are any two elements of θ, and are therefore connected. We can then construct a chain like that in (7.19), getting an equation like (7.26) at each link, to yield

$$\lambda^{fm}(u_m) = \lambda^{fn}(u_n), \quad \text{each } m, n \in \theta, \text{ each } f \in F. \tag{7.27}$$

One possibility is that these are all constants in a neighbourhood P—for we must remember that all the arguments I have used have been local. In that case

$$\pi^{f\theta}(p_\theta, p_{-N}) = k_{f\theta}\pi^\theta(p_\theta, p_{-N}) + \sum_{n\in\theta} c^{fn}(p_n) + \alpha^{f\theta}(p_{-N}), \quad \sum_f k_{f\theta} = 1, \qquad (7.28)$$

each $\theta\in\Theta$, $f\in F$.[31]

We may think of the $\pi^{f\theta}(\cdot)$, $\theta\in\Theta$, as representing independent plants in firm f, each using inputs[32] from the sectors $m\notin N$—that is, from the self- and other-affine sectors—to produce outputs from the non-affine sectors $n\in\theta$, each $\theta\in\Theta$, each f.

Call the self- and other-affine sectors and aggregates, *affine*. There is of course no reason why all the goods in such sectors should be inputs, nor those in the non-affine outputs. That was just a turn of phrase to make the $\pi^{f\theta}(p_\theta, p_{-N})$ easier to understand. Forget about it. Then the $d^f(p_{-N})$ would represent plants which dealt only with goods in the affine sectors—call them *affine goods*—whether as outputs or inputs. The $c^{fn}(p_n)$, $n\in N$ would just be specific overheads, if you like.

Otherwise the θ-plant in firm f is in effect[33] just a scale model of that in the economy as a whole. If this is true of each firm $f\in F$ we are in the degenerate case discussed at the end of Section 3[34] as far as the sectors in θ are concerned. These put no constraints on the economy-wide technology as defined by $\rho^n(p_n, u_n)$ and $\sigma^n(p_{\theta-n}, p_{-N}, u_n)$.

In what immediately follows I will dismiss this as an uninteresting special case. That is to say, I will assume that each non-affine clump $\theta\in\Theta$ contains at least one sector $n\in\theta$, such that

$$\lambda^{fn}(\cdot) \text{ is not constant, some } f\in F, \qquad (7.29)$$

or, to be more precise, let us assume we are working in a closed convex body P in p space. Then I assume that there is a neighbourhood $N(\bar{p}\mid\theta)$ of each point $\bar{p}$ within which $\lambda^{fn}(\cdot)$ is strictly monotonic, some $f(p)$, $n(p)\in\theta$. Then each $\lambda^{fm}(\cdot)$ is strictly monotonic for $f=f(p)$, $m\in\theta$, in a sub-neighbourhood

[31] Because the corresponding macro-technology, using Hicksian aggregates, for instance, is Leontief, otherwise, as noted below, it is not smooth and hence does not satisfy the assumptions on which the analysis is based. Hence (7.28) is the general solution for this case. I see I have it as such in my handout for Jim Mirrlees's lunch-time workshop in 1982.

[1989 Postscript] Not so, I now believe, since the differentiation is in the primal which is forbidden, and mine is in the dual, replacing strict convexity, etc., by convexity etc. It does lead to difficulties but of the sort that 'revealed efficiency' may deal with.

[32] Of course these are only tricks to fire our ideas. In a sense they may be validated by measuring each class of goods in the desired manner. In the last analysis self-affine inputs, other-affine outputs, and non-affine outputs and/or intermediate goods is possibly the simpler story.

[33] Except, of course, for overheads as in (7.28).

[34] This must refer to an earlier version of Sect. 3.

$N^*(\bar{p} \mid \theta)$ of $N(\bar{p} \mid \theta)$. I will confine myself to *canonical neighbourhoods* of the type[35]

$$N(\bar{p}) = \bigcap_{\theta \in \Theta} N^*(\bar{p} \mid \theta) \tag{7.30}$$

which I take to be conical without loss of generality.

In keeping with the fact that we measure all goods as outputs, inputs appearing as negative elements, it at first seems natural to measure each aggregate in such a manner that it increases when the prices within the group all increase, the others being held constant.[36] Take now a firm f for which $\lambda^{fn}(\cdot)$ is strictly monotonic, each $n \in \theta$ in a given canonical neighbourhood. We could clearly normalize to define

$$\begin{aligned} u_n^* &= \lambda^{fn}(u_n), \quad \text{each } n \in \theta \\ &= u_\theta^*, \text{ say,} \end{aligned} \tag{7.31}$$

without breaking this convention if $\lambda^{fn}(\cdot)$ were strictly increasing there, each $n \in \theta$, or

$$\begin{aligned} u_n^* &= \lambda^{fn}(u_n), \quad \text{each } n \in \theta, \\ &= u_\theta^*, \text{ say,} \end{aligned} \tag{7.32}$$

if each were strictly decreasing, in which case $u_\theta^* \leqslant 0$ in the neighbourhood, and each sector in θ may be said to be composed of inputs, not outputs.

I will compromise by using the normalization (7.31) throughout, calling n an output sector if $\lambda^{fn}(\cdot)$ is strictly increasing, and u_θ^* the level of input there. In any case it will be quite sensible to say that there is strict complementarity between the aggregates, or macro-goods, $n \in \theta$, and call the corresponding macro-technology Leontief, so that the primal is not smooth, but neither was it required to be.

Of course these terms refer only to individual canonical neighbourhoods. Note, too, that $\sum_f \lambda^{fn}(u_n) = 1$. If therefore there is a neighbourhood for which all of the $\lambda^{fn}(\cdot)$, $n \in \theta, f \in F$, are strictly monotonic, a sector which would be dubbed 'output' when one uses one f for the normalization (7.31) would be dubbed 'input' when one uses another, so that the terms must not be taken too seriously.

Dropping the *'s, in any case, we have

$$u_n = u_\theta, \quad \text{each } n \in \theta \in \Theta, \tag{7.33}$$

in this normalization, within a canonical neighbourhood. To be more precise, I will work with the clump of that neighbourhood which includes $\bar{p}$.

35 I use the old terminology in which a neighbourhood of $\bar{p}$ is an open set containing it.

36 Say, are Hicks.

Notice that

$$u_\theta = \underset{u}{\operatorname{argmax}}\{\rho^{fn}(p_n, u) + \sigma^{fn}(p_{\theta-n}, p_{-N}, u\}, \quad \text{each } f\in F,\ u\in\theta,$$

$$= \underset{u}{\operatorname{argmax}}\{\rho^{n}(p_n, u) + \sigma^{n}(p_{\theta-n}, p_{-N}, u\}, \quad \text{each } n\in\theta, \tag{7.34}$$

in this normalization, and within the appropriate neighbourhood.

8. BRINGING THE PIECES TOGETHER[37]

Let me remind you that we have three sorts of aggregates: *self-affine*; *other-affine*, defined so as to exclude the self-affine; and *non-affine* defined so as to exclude both the others, and that we call the sectors corresponding to these aggregates by the same names, with price vectors p, q, r.

(a) Self-affine sectors

Call typical self-affine sectors and aggregates

$$u_h = \phi^h(x_h), \quad \text{each } h\in H, \quad u = (u_h)_{h\in H}, \tag{8.1}$$

and the corresponding price vectors

$$p_h = (p_i)_{i\in h}; \quad p = (p_h)_{h\in H}, \tag{8.2}$$

in terms of which we were able to define marginal profitabilities

$$a_h = a^h(p_h), \quad \text{each } h\in H; \quad a = (a_h)_{h\in H} = a(p) = (a^h(p))_{h\in H}. \tag{8.3}$$

The overall profit function

$$\pi(p, q, r) = \sup\{p\cdot x + q\cdot y + r\cdot z \mid (x, y, z)\in T\}, \text{ say}, \tag{8.4}$$

$$= \Pi(a(p), q, r) + \sum_{h\in H} c^h(p_h), \text{ say}, \tag{8.5}$$

where the function

$$\Pi(a, q, r) = \sup\{a\cdot u + q\cdot y + r\cdot z \mid (u, y, z)\in T^*\}, \text{ say}, \tag{8.6}$$

has the properties of an ordinary profit function. Hence the notation. Throughout most of this section I will work with it.

[37] I use arguments based on differences rather than calculus as much as possible here in an attempt to drop strict convexity in the technology and hence allow the wider class of macro-technologies discussed at the end of Sect. 7. Of course the earlier argument would have to have been cleared of calculus, too, which seems an unlikely possibility given the role of maximization. Conceivably one might use 'revealed efficiency' in some way instead. However, it is unimportant, since it is differentiability in the primal that matters, and I have been able to drop that.

It might be thought that the separability results (6.21) ≡ (8.10) and (7.24) ≡ (8.12) would yield our results through conventional separability arguments, but only much weaker conclusions follow.

(b) Other-affine sectors

Call typical other-affine sectors, and their aggregates

$$m,\ n \in N; \quad v_n = \psi^n(y_n), \quad v = (v_n)_{n \in N}, \tag{8.7}$$

and the corresponding price vectors

$$q_m = (q_i)_{i \in m}, \quad q = (q_n)_{n \in N}. \tag{8.8}$$

We can define *marginal profitabilities*

$$b_n = b^n(a, r), \quad b = (b_n)_{n \in N} = (b_n(a, r))_{n \in N}, \tag{8.9}$$

for these, in terms of which the quasi-rent function can be written[38]

$$\Pi(a, q, r) = \sum_{n \in N} \rho^n(b^n(a, r), q_n) + d(a, r), \text{ say,} \tag{8.10}$$

by (6.21), where the ρ's denote the fact that I have not shown them to be profit functions.

(c) Non-affine sectors

These can be partitioned into clumps[39]

$$s,\ t \in T, \text{ say, with aggregates } w_t = \chi^t(z_t),\ w = (w_t)_{t \in T}, \tag{8.11}$$

in terms of which

$$\Pi(a, q, r) = \sum_{t \in T} \sigma^t(a, q, r_t), \text{ say,} \qquad \text{by (7.24),} \tag{8.12}$$

a form of additive separability. Note that there are no simple marginal profitabilities or shadow prices corresponding to these sectors, and I again use a notation which does not imply that each clump has its own profit function.

In this section we will exploit the equivalence between the two representations (8.10) and (8.12) of the gross profit function $\Pi(a, q, r)$. a's appear everywhere, so that we cannot do much about them. The price vectors q_n, r_t enter additively into (8.10) and (8.12), on the other hand, so that we may reasonably hope to get a finer, and still additive, decomposition of $\Pi(a, q, r)$, based on a partition of the set

$$\Omega = N \cup T, \tag{8.13}$$

of other-affine sectors, and non-affine clumps, into *blocks* $\omega \in \Omega$; and so we shall, at least locally, about a given

$$\bar{P} = (\bar{a}, \bar{q}, \bar{r}). \tag{8.14}$$

[38] From Sect. 5.

[39] From Sect. 7. Most of the remainder of this section exploits (8.10) and (8.12).

Moreover we will be able to do this without invoking calculus, and thus under weak regularity conditions.

Say that $f(x, y, z)$ is *additive in x and y about* $(\bar{x}, \bar{y}, \bar{z})$ if we can write

$$f(x, y, z) = g(x, z) + h(y, z), \tag{8.15}$$

in a neighbourhood of $(\bar{x}, \bar{y}, \bar{z})$; and that *x and y interact about* $(\bar{x}, \bar{y}, \bar{z})$ otherwise, in a completely general notation.[40] According to (8.10), $\Pi(a, q, r)$ is additive in any pair q_m, q_n; to (8.12), in any pair r_s, r_t about

$$\bar{P} = (\bar{a}, \bar{q}, \bar{r}), \text{ say.} \tag{8.16}$$

In a slightly different terminology then,

LEMMA 1: *No pair $m, n \in N$ of other-affine sectors, or $s, t \in T$ of non-affine clumps, interact.*

I am going to use the idea of interaction between its elements to partition $\Omega = N \cup T$ into *blocks*, in terms of which $\Pi(a, q, r)$ is additive.

Say then that $\omega, \omega' \in \Omega$ are *connected*, if they are identical, or interact, or if we can find a sequence

$$\omega = \omega_1, \omega_2, \ldots, \omega_k = \omega' \tag{8.17}$$

of distinct elements of Ω, each adjacent pair of which interact. 'Being connected to' is an equivalence relationship, and so allows us to partition Ω into equivalence classes—the *blocks* mentioned above—with the property that a pair $\omega, \omega' \in \Omega$ are connected iff they belong to the same block.

Some blocks may contain only one element. Call them singletons. They may be sectors or clumps. Write

$$M = \{m \in N \mid \{m\} \text{ is a singleton}\}, \tag{8.18}$$

$$S = \{s \in T \mid \{s\} \text{ is not a block}\}, \tag{8.19}$$

so that $T \backslash S$ is composed of the singleton clumps. Finally write

$$\omega \in \omega' \quad \text{or} \quad \omega' \in \omega \tag{8.20}$$

as is convenient when ω, ω' are connected, that is, belong to the same block. Clearly (8.20) implies $\omega' = \omega$ when $\{\omega\}$ is a singleton.

Return to the sequence (8.17); Lemma 1 implies that successive elements in it come from N and T in turn: that is, are sectors and clumps.[41]

We can go further and say

[40] i.e., where I do not specify $f(\cdot)$, etc.

[41] Where the clumps may be singletons, in which case they are non-affine sectors.

LEMMA 2: *No block contains more than one clump* $t \in T$,

which, with the remark just made, implies

LEMMA 3: $N \backslash M$ *is partitioned into sets,*

$$N(s) = \{n \in N \mid n \in s\}, \qquad \text{each } s \in S, \tag{8.21}$$

from which our main result

PROPOSITION: *We can write*

$$\Pi(a, q, r) = \sum_{m \in M} \rho^m(b^m(a), q_m) + \sum_{t \in T} \sigma^t(a, r_t) + \sum_{s \in S} \sum_{n \in s} \rho^n(b^n(a, r_s), q_n). \tag{8.22}$$

Comment: Note that, while m is confined to the singleton sectors in the first summation, t runs over all the clumps in the second. This is not surprising since (8.10) is more specific than (8.12).

It remains to prove Lemma 2. The main Proposition will appear as a by-product.

First some notation. Take any function $f(x, y)$, where x and y are vectors or scalars, but are otherwise quite general, and a value $\bar{y}$ of y. Define

$$\bar{f}(x) := f(x, \bar{y}); \quad f^*(x, y) = f(x, y) - \bar{f}(x); \tag{8.23}$$

and note that

$$f^*(x, \bar{y}) = 0. \tag{8.24}$$

Define further

$$q_A = (q_m)_{m \in A}, \quad q^A = (q_A, \bar{q}_{\backslash A}); \quad r_B = (r_t)_{t \in B}, \quad r^B = (r_B, \bar{r}_{\backslash B}), \text{ etc.} \tag{8.25}$$

Now return to Lemma 2. Suppose that $s, t \in T$ are distinct elements of the same block. They are then joined by a sequence (8.17) of which the first element is s. The second is an $n \in N$ and the third, $s' \neq s \in T$, too. Hence, for this n, at least two

$$t \; i \; n, \qquad \text{if the block contains more than one } t \in T, \tag{8.26}$$

where 'i' is read as 'interacts with'.

I will prove this impossible, and thus the Lemma by *reductio ad absurdum.*

Set $q_n = \bar{q}_n$ in the crucial equations (8.10) and (8.12), and subtract from the originals, to get

$$\Pi(a, q, r) - \Pi(a, q_{-n}, r) = \rho^{*n}(b^n(a, r), q_n) \tag{8.27}$$

$$= \sum_{t \in T} \{\sigma^t(a, q, r_t) - \sigma^t(a, q_{-n}, r_t)\} \tag{8.28}$$

$$= \sum_{t \in T} \{\sigma^t(a, q, r_t) - \sigma^t(a, \bar{q}, r_t)\} \tag{8.29}$$

$$= \sum_{t\,in} \lambda^{tn}(a, q_n, r_t), \text{ say;} \tag{8.30}$$

(8.29) because the right-hand side of (8.27) is independent of q_{-n}, so that we can get $q_{-n} = \bar{q}_{-n}$ without changing it or (8.28); (8.30) because, when t does not interact with n we can write

$$\Pi(a, q, r) = g^{nt}(a, q_{-n}, r) + h^{nt}(a, q, r_{-t}), \text{ say,} \tag{8.31}$$

about $\bar{P}$, by (8.15), so that

$$\Pi(a, q, r) - \Pi(a, q_{-n}, r) = h^{nt}(a, q, r_{-t}) - h^{nt}(a, q_{-n}, r_{-t}) \tag{8.32}$$

is independent of r_t, and we can put $r_t = \bar{r}_t$ in (8.30), each t which does not interact with n.

Since at least some t interact with n, we can find a $\bar{\bar{q}}_n$ in which

$$\rho^{*n}(b^n(a, r), \bar{\bar{q}}_n) = \sum_{t\,in} \lambda^{tn}(a, \bar{\bar{q}}_n, r_t) =: \sum_{t\,in} \mu^{tn}(a, r_t) \tag{8.33}$$

does in fact depend on $b^n(a, r)$ about $\bar{a}$, $\bar{r}$. Now suppose we have so normalized the aggregate v_n that $v_n > 0$ at $(\bar{a}, \bar{\bar{q}}_n, \bar{r})$. We can then solve (8.33) for

$$b^n(a, r) = \tau^n\left(\sum_{t\,in} \mu^{tn}(a, r_t)\right), \text{ say,} \tag{8.34}$$

and substitute into (8.27) to get

$$\Pi(a, q, r) - \Pi(a, q_{-n}, r) = \rho^{*n}(b^n(a, r), q_n) =: \theta^n\left(\sum_{t\,in} \mu^{tn}(a, r_t), q_n\right)$$

$$= \theta^n(\mu^n(a) + \sum_{t\,in} \mu^{*nt}(a, r_t), q_n) \tag{8.35}$$

using the notation defined in (8.23), where

$$\mu^n(a) = \sum_{t\,in} \mu^{-nt}(a, \bar{n}_t), \tag{8.36}$$

and hence, by (8.30),

$$\theta^n\left(\mu^n(a) + \sum_{t\,in} \mu^{*nt}(a, r_t), q_n\right) = \sum_{t\,in} \lambda^{tn}(a, q_n, r_t)$$

$$= \lambda^n(a, q_n) + \sum_{t\,in} \lambda^{*nt}(a, q_n, r_t), \tag{8.37}$$

in a similar notation, where

$$\lambda^n(a, q_n) = \sum_{t\,in} \lambda^{-nt}(a, q_n) = \theta^n(\mu^n(a), q_n). \tag{8.38}$$

Let us now define

$$\phi^n(\mu^n(a), \sum_{t\,i\,n} \mu^{*nt}(a, r_t), q_n) := \theta^n(\mu^n(a) + \sum_{t\,i\,n} \mu^{*nt}(a, r_t), q_n) - \theta^n(\mu^n(a), q_n)$$

$$= \sum_{t\,i\,n} \lambda^{*nt}(a, q_n, r_t), \tag{8.39}$$

take any $t\ i\ n$, and set $r_s = \bar{r}_s,\ s \neq t$, to get

$$\phi^n(\mu^n(a), \mu^{*nt}(a, r_t), q_n) = \lambda^{*nt}(a, q_n, r_t), \quad \text{each } t\ i\ n, \tag{8.40}$$

and hence

$$\phi^n(\mu^n(a), \sum_{t\,i\,n} \mu^{*nt}(a, r_t), q_n) = \sum_{t\,i\,n} \phi^n(\mu^n(a), \mu^{*nt}(a, r_t), q_n). \tag{8.41}$$

This is Cauchy's equation in the μ^* argument. Since we have assumed that more than one t interacts with n, it yields

$$\phi^n(x, y, z) = \alpha^n(x, z)y, \text{ say,} \tag{8.42}$$

in a general notation. Returning to the definition of $\phi(\cdot)$ in (8.39) we get

$$\alpha^n(x + y, z) = \alpha^n(x, z)y + \theta^n(x, z) \tag{8.43}$$

or, setting

$$w := x + y \tag{8.44}$$

$$\theta^n(w, z) = \alpha^n(x, z)(w - x) + \theta^n(x, z) =: \alpha^n(x, z)w + \beta^n(x, z)$$

$$= \gamma^n(x)w + \delta^n(z), \text{ say,} \tag{8.45}$$

since the left-hand side is independent of x. Hence (8.35) yields

$$\Pi(a, q, r) = \Pi(a, q_{-n}, r) + \gamma^n(q_n) \sum_{t\,i\,n} \mu^{tn}(a, r_t) + \delta^n(q_n), \tag{8.46}$$

implying that n is self-affine, which it is not since it is other-affine and we used exclusive definitions. Hence there is no $n \in N$ which interacts with more than one $t \in T$. However we saw in Lemma 2 that such an n would exist if any block contained more than one $t \in T$. Hence none does.

Take now any $n \in t$. Hence $n\ i\ t$, since there would otherwise be another $s \in T$ in the sequence (8.17) connecting n and t; s and t would then belong to the same block; and that we have just proved impossible. In particular this is the only $t\ i\ n$, and (8.34) and (8.35) yield

$$b^n(a, r) = \beta^n(a, r_t), \text{ say,} \tag{8.47}$$

$$\rho^{*n}(b^n(a, r), q_n) = \theta^n(\beta^n(a, r_t), q_n), \text{ say,} \tag{8.48}$$

in turn when $n\ i\ t$. Remembering that we have been using the notation introduced in (8.23), we see

$$\rho^n(b^n(a, r), q_n) = \theta^n(\beta^n(a, r_t), q_n) + \bar{\rho}^n(\beta^n(a, r_t)), \text{ say,}$$
$$= R^n(\beta^n(a, r_t), q_n), \text{ say, when } n\,i\,t. \tag{8.49}$$

A similar argument yields

$$\rho^m(b^m(a, r), q_m) = R^m(\beta^m(a), q_m), \quad \text{when } m \in M, \tag{8.50}$$

that is to say, when no $t\ i\ m$.

Setting

$$\beta^n(a, r_t) = \tilde{b}^n(a, r_t), \quad \beta^m(a) = \tilde{b}^m(a); \tag{8.51}$$

in these two cases, and $R^n(\cdot) = \tilde{\rho}^n(\cdot)$ in general, and dropping the tildes as seems reasonable in the light of (8.47),

$$\Pi(a, q, r) = \sum_{m \in M} \rho^m(b^m(a), q_m) + \sum_{s \in S} \sum_{n \in s} \rho^n(b^n(a, r_s), q_n) + d(a, r) \tag{8.52}$$

where S is defined in (8.19)

Setting $q = \bar{q}$ say, in (8.12) and (8.52) and solving for $d(a, r)$, we get

$$d(a, r) = \sum_{t \in T} \sigma^t(a, \bar{q}, r_t) - \sum_{m \in M} \rho^m(b^m(a), \bar{q}_m) - \sum_{s \in S} \sum_{n\,i\,s} \rho^n(b^n(a, r_s), \bar{q}_n)$$
$$=: \sum_{t \in T} \sigma^t(a, r_t), \tag{8.53}$$

in a slightly different notation. This yields (8.22) and proves the Proposition asserting it.

Write

$$r_s = (r_u)_{u \delta s}, \tag{8.54}$$

where u is a non-affine sector in the clump s. Normalize non-affine aggregates to be private goods with shadow prices $\nu^k(r_u)$, each $u\,\delta\,s \in T \supseteq S$. We would then expect

$$b^n(a, r_s) = \beta^n(\nu^s(a, r_s), a), \quad \nu^s(a, r_s) = (\nu^u(a, r_u))_{u \delta s}, \text{ say.} \tag{8.55}$$

I will now prove that there exist functions $\gamma^u(a, r_u)$, each $u\,\delta\,s$ when $\#\{n\,i\,s\} > 1$, such that

$$b^n(a, r_s) = \beta^n(\gamma^s(a, r_s), a), \quad \gamma^s(a, r_s) = (\gamma^u(a, r_u))_{u \delta s}, \text{ say.} \tag{8.56}$$

I cannot prove this for s such that $\#\{n\,i\,s\} = 1$. However one can define

$$\gamma^s(a, r_s) := b^n(a, r_s) \quad \text{when } \#\{n\,i\,s\} = 1 \tag{8.57}$$

to prove

COROLLARY:

$$\Pi(a, q, r) = \sum_{s \in S} \sum_{n i s} \rho^n(\beta^n(\gamma^s(a, r_s), a), q_n) - \sum_{m \in M} \rho^m(\beta^m(a), q_m) + \sum_{t \in T} \sigma^t(a, r_t), \text{ say,} \tag{8.58}$$

where $\gamma^s(\cdot)$ has the two distinct definitions given above according to whether $\#\{n i s\} > 1$, or $= 1$.

The temptation to regard $\gamma^u(a, r_u)$, properly normalized,[42] to be the shadow price $\nu^u(a, r_u)$ of u in the appropriate normalization is somewhat clouded by what happens when $\#\{n i s\} = 1$. Perhaps one could argue that the $u \delta s$ for such s do not have to be allocated over different $n \in s$, though it does sound somewhat slim when we remember that they do have to be deployed efficiently in producing the other-affine aggregate n.

Perhaps, after all, the result is true for such cases and I just have not found a proof. It is certainly true that the condition (8.58) holds much more widely, so that I have not proved sufficient conditions for non-affine aggregates. The other variants are more difficult to apply, partly because they involve $d^s(a, r_s)$ which disappears under differentiation with respect to q_n, for instance, below, but partly for other reasons too.

PROOF OF COROLLARY: Since u is a non-affine sector[43]

$$\pi_{hi}\pi_{kj} = \pi_{hj}\pi_{ki}, \tag{8.59}$$

where

$$h \in \ell i s \quad k \in n i s, \quad i, j \in u \delta s. \tag{8.60}$$

Hence

$$\rho_0^\ell \rho_h^\ell b_i^\ell \rho_0^n \rho_k^n b_j^n = \rho_0^\ell \rho_h^\ell b_j^\ell \rho_0^n \rho_k^n b_i^n. \tag{8.61}$$

[42] Note that we can replace $\gamma^u(a, r_a)$ by $\tilde{\gamma}^u(a, r_a) = \delta^u(\gamma^u(a, r_a), a)$ to get $\tilde{\gamma}^u(\cdot)$ conical as required, as long as convexity holds.

[43] Let

$$u = \theta(q, r);\ h, k \text{ be subscripts in } q;\ i, j \text{ in } r, \tag{i}$$

and maximize

$$\rho(r, u) - \kappa(q, u) \tag{ii}$$

where u is an aggregate. Then

$$\pi(q, r) = \rho(r, \theta(q, r) - \kappa(q, \theta(q, e)) \tag{iii}$$

$$\rho_0(r, \theta(q, r)) = \kappa_0(q, \theta(q, r)). \tag{iv}$$

Verify (8.59), using (iii) and (iv). Note that this proves (8.59) for affine sectors too, for which it is in any case trivial.

Now it is clear that

$$\rho_0^{\ell}, \rho_h^{n} \neq 0, \tag{8.62}$$

since otherwise m would be a dummy, and that there exist $h \in \ell$, $k \in n$ such that

$$\rho_h^{\ell}, \rho_k^{n} \neq 0, \quad \ell\, i\, s, \ n\, i\, s. \tag{8.63}$$

Hence (8.61) implies

$$b_i^{\ell} b_j^{n} = b_j^{\ell} b_j^{n}. \tag{8.64}$$

Let us say that ℓ, $n\ i\ s$ are connected in u when there is a good $j \in u$ such that

$$b_j^{\ell},\ b_j^{n} \neq 0, \tag{8.65}$$

so that

$$b_i^{\ell}/b_j^{\ell} = b_i^{n}/b_j^{n}, \qquad \text{each } i \in u, \tag{8.66}$$

or if there exists a chain

$$\ell = n_0, n_1, \ldots, n_k = n, \tag{8.67}$$

each successive link in which is connected in u. Being an equivalence relation this partitions $\{n\ i\ s\}$ into equivalence classes $N(u) \in \mathcal{N}(u)$ such that elements of the same class are connected with u, in different $n\ i\ u$, together with a compatible[44] partition of the goods in u into equivalence classes $V(u) \in \mathcal{V}(u)$. Then $r_u = (r_V)_{V = V(u) \in \mathcal{V}(u)}$ and

$$b^n(a, r_s) = \beta^n(\gamma^V(a, r_V, r_{s-u}), r_{s-u}, a) \tag{8.68}$$

when $n \in N(u)$, which incidentally proves that the elements of $N(u)$ are directly connected, and the chains (8.67) are superfluous in this case. Now apply the variants of (8.59) described above to V. They imply that it is a non-affine sector. If we therefore require that we have already listed all the sectors yielding aggregates, then $V = u$ so that the partition $\mathcal{N}(u)$ is degenerate having only one element.

Applying this argument to each $u\,\delta\, s$ in turn one gets

$$b^n(a, r_s) = \beta^n(\gamma^r(a, r_s)), \qquad \text{where } \gamma^s(a, r_s) = (\gamma^u(a, r_u))_{u\,\delta\,s}, \tag{8.69}$$

as required when $\#\{n\,i\,s\} > 1$. Substituting into (8.22), we get (8.58) with the trick definition (8.57) when $\#\{n\,i\,s\} = 1$.

Call the goods in u, Z_u, their quantities z_u. Rebundle them to get a square proper transformation

[44] Some prices in the sector n may not appear in $b^n(a, r, s)$.

$$z_u^* = A_u^T z_u, \tag{8.70}$$

so that

$$r_u = A_u r_u^*, \tag{8.71}$$

and

$$r_u^T z_u = r_u^{*T} A_u^T z_u = r_u^{*T} z_u^*, \tag{8.72}$$

as we would wish.

Now consider the last column of A_u, corresponding to $r_{\hat{u}}^*$. (8.71) yields $r_j = \ldots + a_{j\hat{u}}^* r_{\hat{u}}^*$. Set $a_{j\hat{u}}^* = 1$ for the j's appearing in (8.65) and its analogues for the various elements in the partition $V(u)$, and zero otherwise. Then

$$\partial b^\ell / \partial r_{\hat{u}}^* = b_j^\ell \neq 0, \tag{8.73}$$

for the appropriate j in each $V(u)$, and $r_{\hat{u}}^*$ gives the appropriate connectivity to yield

$$b^n(a, r_s) = \beta^{*n}(\gamma^{*u}(a, r_u^*), a)$$
$$= \beta^{*n}(\gamma^{*u}(a, A^{-1} r_u), a) = \beta^n(\gamma^u(a, r_u), a), \text{ each } nis, \ \#\{nis\} > 1 \tag{8.74}$$

as in (8.69), and with the trick definition (8.57) when $\#\{nis\} = 1$, for the Corollary.

26

Long-Run Aggregates under Constant Returns

Editorial Remarks

A weakness of the previous paper, 'Aggregation in the Short and Long Run', is the use of strong convexity assumptions. Such assumptions seem easier to justify in the short run, rather than the long run. In this paper all firms, actual and potential, have constant-returns-to-scale technologies. Hence, those firms that actually exist in any particular equilibrium are determined endogenously, but their outputs are of course undetermined. This is consistent with the structure of many general equilibrium models; for example, in trade models, an economy is often endowed with a set of firms that have linear homogeneous production functions. One can find the equilibrium price vector, and those industries that produce positive output at those prices, without actually establishing the levels of their individual outputs.

Gorman begins by assuming that there is an input aggregate in each firm as well as in the economy as a whole. As in the previous paper, this implies the existence of an output aggregate in each firm and in the economy. Equilibrium is characterized by zero profits and a finite production plan for every firm. This in turn determines those firms that exist in the equilibrium. The main result is one that we have seen in the previous aggregation papers; an aggregate exists if and only if it is deployed efficiently among those firms producing positive outputs. The paper finishes with an extended set of examples to demonstrate which firms can exist at a particular set of price vectors.

Long-Run Aggregates under Constant Returns

INTRODUCTION

Though fixed inputs were originally distinguished in aggregation theory because of the presumed difficulty of measuring capital, they have continued to be distinguished because of their value as shift parameters. Aggregates are commonly required for an industry as a whole: changing a firm's endowment of fixed inputs allows us to observe its marginal behaviour through that of the industry. In the long run, the distinction disappears, and with it the possibility of using endowments in this way. Last year I suggested how appropriate prices might be used instead.[1] The argument turned on the use of profit functions—which are identically zero or $+\infty$ under constant returns—and more particularly on their differentiability, equivalent to profit-maximizing plans being unique and to strict convexity. This was needed only locally: nevertheless it did not sit well in a long-run analysis.

In this paper I consider the case of constant returns interesting because the firms in production are endogenously determined, and the levels at which they operate are not determined at all.

1. TWO GROUPS

Consider an *industry* F composed of technologically independent firms $f \in F$. Firm f produces a *vector* y_f *of outputs* Y, using a *vector* x_f *of inputs* X at *prices* q, p, using a *technology* T_f defined by

$$y_f T_f x_f : \theta^f(x_f, y_f) \geqslant 1, \tag{1}$$

where

$$\theta^f(\cdot, y_f) \text{ is strictly increasing, } \theta^f(x_f, \cdot) \text{ is strictly decreasing.} \tag{2}$$

The *technology*

$$T = \sum_{f \in F} T_f \tag{3}$$

is similarly defined by

$$T : \theta(x, y) \geqslant 1, \tag{4}$$

where

$$\theta(\cdot, y) \text{ is strictly increasing, } \theta(x, \cdot) \text{ is strictly decreasing; } x = \sum x_f,\ y = \sum y_f. \tag{5}$$

[1] [eds.] This refers to 'Aggregation in the Short and Long Run'.

Require now that there exist *continuous input aggregates*

$$u_f = \phi^f(x_f), \quad v = \phi(x), \tag{6}$$

for each firm $f \in F$, and industry F as a whole, such that

$$\theta^f(x_f, y_f) \equiv \tilde{\theta}^f(\phi^f(x_f), y_f); \quad \theta(x, y) = \tilde{\theta}(\phi(x), y), \tag{7}$$

say. Because of (2) and (5) we may assume

$$\phi^f(\cdot), \phi(\cdot) \text{ are strictly increasing,} \tag{8}$$

without loss of generality, in which case

$$\tilde{\theta}^f(\cdot; y_f), \ \tilde{\theta}(\cdot, y) \text{ are strictly increasing,} \tag{9}$$

too, so that we may solve for

$$u_f = \phi^f(x_f) \geqslant \psi^f(y_f); \quad v = \phi(x) \geqslant \psi(y), \text{ say,} \tag{10}$$

where

$$\psi^f(\cdot), \psi(\cdot) \text{ are strictly increasing,} \tag{11}$$

and where the inequalities become equations when production is efficient, so that the *output aggregates* $\psi^f(y_f)$, $\psi(y)$ exist iff the input aggregates do.

For symmetry I will change my terms slightly and write

$$\phi^f(x_f) \geqslant u_f \geqslant \psi^f(y_f); \quad \phi(x) \geqslant v \geqslant \psi(y), \tag{12}$$

where the inequalities are replaced by equations

$$\phi^f(x_f) = u_f = \psi^f(y_f); \quad \phi(x) = v = \psi(y), \tag{13}$$

when production is efficient. We may, and do, normalize to get

$$\phi^f(\cdot), \ \psi^f(\cdot), \ \phi(\cdot), \ \psi(\cdot) \text{ conical} \tag{14}$$

iff production takes place under *constant returns*, in which case they may be represented by their *unit cost* and *revenue functions*

$$\begin{aligned} a^f(p) &= \min\{p \cdot x_f \mid \phi^f(x_f) \geqslant 1\}; \quad a(p) = \min\{p \cdot x \mid \phi(x) \geqslant 1\}; \\ b^f(q) &= \max\{q \cdot y_f \mid \psi^f(y_f) \leqslant 1\}; \quad b(q) = \max\{q \cdot y \mid \psi(y) \leqslant 1\}. \end{aligned} \tag{15}$$

We may also require that

$$a^f(p) \geqslant b^f(q), \qquad \text{each } f \in F, \tag{16}$$

to rule out infinite plans, while

$$\max\{b^f(q)/a^f(p) \mid f \in F\} = 1 = b(q)/a(p), \tag{17}$$

at competitive prices, the maximum being attained on the set

$$G(p, q) = \{g \in F \mid b^g(q)/a^g(p) \geqslant b^f(q)/a^f(p), \text{ each } f \in F\} \tag{18}$$

of firms competitive at (p, q). We then have

$$a(p)v = \sum_g a^g(p)u_g = \sum_g b^g(q)u_g = b(q)v, \tag{19}$$

where (p, q) are competitive prices, and the summation is over $G(p, q)$. Hence

$$v = \sum_{g \in G} \alpha^g(p)u_g = \sum_{g \in G} \beta^g(q)u_g, \tag{20}$$

where

$$\alpha^g(p) = a^g(p)/a(p) = \beta^g(q) = b^g(q)/b(q) \tag{21}$$

when (p, q) are competitive prices and firm g is competitive at those prices. Note, moreover, that $\alpha^g(\cdot)$, $\beta^g(\cdot)$ are homogeneous of degree zero. Given any $p, q > 0$, one can find the set $G(p, q)$ of potentially competitive firms, which become actually competitive on our normalizing p, or q, to get (17). (20) and (21) then hold for all prices $p, q > 0$ and each potentially competitive firm g, while

$$b^f(q)/a^f(p) \leqslant b(q)/a(p) \tag{22}$$

in general, and

$$b^g(q)/a^g(p) = b(q)/a(p) \tag{23}$$

iff $g \in G(p, q)$ according to (17), appropriately adjusted.

Unsurprisingly this implies that

$$\alpha^g(p) = \beta^g(q) = \gamma_g, \text{ say,} \qquad \text{each } g \in G(p, q). \tag{24}$$

To prove this, let $g \in G(\bar{p}, \bar{q})$, too. Then

$$b^g(\bar{q})/a^g(\bar{p}) = b(\bar{q})/a(\bar{p}), \tag{25}$$

as in (23), while

$$b^g(\bar{q})/a^g(p) \leqslant b(\bar{q})/a(p); \quad b^g(q)/a^g(\bar{p}) \leqslant b(q)/a(\bar{p}), \tag{26}$$

implying

$$\alpha^g(p) = \beta^g(q) \leqslant \alpha^g(\bar{p}) = \beta^g(\bar{q}) \leqslant \alpha^g(p), \tag{27}$$

so that the inequalities are equations and (24) holds.

We may now normalize to get

$$\gamma_g = 1, \qquad \text{each } g \in G(\bar{p}, \bar{q}), \tag{28}$$

and hence

$$v = \sum_{g \in G} u_g, \tag{29}$$

given that the firms in G are competitive at some common price vectors $(\bar{p}, \bar{q})$. Moreover

$$a(p) = \min\{a^f(p) \mid f \in F\}; \quad b(q) = \max\{b^f(q) \mid f \in F\}, \tag{30}$$

by (21)–(24) and (28). Say that g is *efficient, at p, on the input side* if

$$a^g(p) = a(p) \leqslant a^f(p), \qquad \text{each } f \in F, \tag{31}$$

efficient, at q, on the output side if

$$b^g(q) = b(q) \geqslant b^f(q), \qquad \text{each } f \in F, \tag{32}$$

and *efficient at* (p, q) iff efficient on both sides. g is efficient at (p, q), then, iff it is potentially competitive there, that is iff

$$g \in G(p, q) = \{g \in F \mid b^g(q)/a^g(p) \geqslant b^f(q)/a^f(p), \text{ each } f \in F\}, \tag{33}$$

which is very agreeable.

Look at (12) again, in the light of (15), (29), (31), and (32). It is natural to think of u_f and v as quantities of a fictitious intermediate good U, 'produced' from the original inputs X with the conical *production functions*

$$\phi^f(\cdot), \; \phi(\cdot) \tag{34}$$

in firm f, and in industry F as a whole, and then used as the sole input in the production of Y with the conical *input functions*

$$\psi^f(\cdot), \; \psi(\cdot), \tag{35}$$

respectively. Because of (31) and (32), each firm $g \in G(p, q)$ produces just the amount u_g of U which it uses, so that U is efficiently deployed without the need for a market: a common result in aggregation theory.

Suppose that we are given the cones

$$P_g = \{p \mid a^g(p) \leqslant a^f(p), \text{ each } f \in F\},$$

$$Q_g = \{q \mid b^g(q) \geqslant b^f(q), \text{ each } f \in F\},$$

$$R_g = P_g \times Q_g, \tag{36}$$

in which g is input, output, and overall efficient. We may then neglect the absolutely inefficient firms for which R_g—equivalently P_g and Q_g—is empty. More importantly, define the sets

$$A(p) = \{g \in F \mid a^g(p) \leqslant a^f(p), \text{ each } f \in F\}, \tag{37}$$

$$B(q) = \{g \in F \mid b^g(q) \geqslant b^f(q), \text{ each } f \in F\}, \tag{38}$$

of firms efficient on the input and output sides respectively. Then

$$G(p, q) = A(p) \cap B(q) \tag{39}$$

should never be empty.

This is the key requirement, to be used in checking whether aggregates exist in particular cases, as in the examples in the next section.

2. EXAMPLES[2]

Example A: $\# F = 2$

Define

$$\lambda(p) = a^2(p)/a^1(p); \quad \mu(q) = b^2(q)/b^1(q). \tag{40}$$

$\lambda(\cdot)$ and $\mu(\cdot)$ are continuous on the open unit simplices, which will do as domains since both functions are homogeneous of degree zero. Their ranges are therefore intervals. If these intervals do not intersect, then one of the firms is absolutely inefficient, by (18). Assume, therefore, that the ranges overlap. Then $\lambda(\bar{p}) = \mu(\bar{q})$, say, and since both firms are competitive at $(\bar{p}, \bar{q})$, we have $G(\bar{p}, \bar{q}) = \{1, 2\}$. Moreover, the normalization (28) ensures

$$a^1(\bar{p}) = a(\bar{p}) = a^2(\bar{p}); \quad b^1(\bar{q}) = b(\bar{q}) = b^2(\bar{q}), \tag{41}$$

and hence $\lambda(\bar{p}) = \mu(\bar{q}) = 1$ whenever both firms are competitive at prices $(\bar{p}, \bar{q})$. It follows that the ranges of $\lambda(\cdot)$ and $\mu(\cdot)$ intersect at the single point $\lambda = \mu = 1$, which can happen iff either one of the ranges is degenerate

$$\mu(q) \equiv 1 \quad \text{or} \quad \lambda(p) \equiv 1, \tag{42}$$

or one of the firms is always efficient

$$\begin{aligned} &\mu(q) \geqslant 1 \geqslant \lambda(p) \quad \text{for all } (p, q) \text{ or} \\ &\lambda(p) \geqslant 1 \geqslant \mu(q) \quad \text{for all } (p, q). \end{aligned} \tag{43}$$

These yield the four cases

$$\text{(i) } b^1(q) \equiv b^2(q). \tag{44}$$

$$\text{(ii) } a^1(p) \equiv a^2(p). \tag{45}$$

$$\text{(iii) } b^2(q) \geqslant b^1(q) \text{ for all } q; \quad a^1(p) \geqslant a^2(p) \text{ for all } p. \tag{46}$$

$$\text{(iv) } b^1(q) \geqslant b^2(q) \text{ for all } q; \quad a^2(p) \geqslant a^1(p) \text{ for all } p. \tag{47}$$

If (i) or (ii) occurs, but not (iii) or (iv), then each firm is uniquely competitive at appropriate prices; if (iii) occurs, firm 2 is always efficient, firm 1 only when prices are right.

[2] [eds.] This section has been slightly redrafted to clarify the argument.

Here is another approach, generally useful.

What we really need are the lists

$$\mathscr{A} = \{A \mid A = A(p), \text{ some } p\},$$

$$\mathscr{B} = \{B \mid B = B(q), \text{ some } q\},$$

$$\mathscr{G} = \{A \cap B \mid \text{some } A \in \mathscr{A},\ B \in \mathscr{B}\}, \tag{48}$$

of input, output, and overall efficient collections of firms. The critical point is that

$$G = A \cap B \neq \emptyset, \qquad \text{any } A \in \mathscr{A},\ B \in \mathscr{B}, \tag{49}$$

by (39). Now $\{1, 2\} \in \mathscr{G}$ by the argument above. Hence $\{1, 2\} \in \mathscr{A}, \mathscr{B}$. In the table I consider all the possibilities:

$\mathscr{G}$				$\mathscr{B}$
	$\{1\}$	$\emptyset$	$\{1\}$	$\{1\}$
	$\emptyset$	$\{2\}$	$\{2\}$	$\{2\}$
	$\{1\}$	$\{2\}$	$\{1,2\}$	$\{1,2\}$
$\mathscr{A}$	$\{1\}$	$\{2\}$	$\{1,2\}$	

The possible elements of $\mathscr{A}$ and $\mathscr{B}$ are listed along the edges. The corresponding possible elements for $\mathscr{G}$ occur at the intersections of the rows and columns. Thus $A = \{1\}$, $B = \{1\}$ gives $G = \{1\}$, as does $A = \{1, 2\}$, $B = \{1\}$, for instance. $A = \{1\}$, $B = \{2\}$, or $A = \{2\}$, $B = \{1\}$, both yield $G = A \cap B = \emptyset$. *Hence both have to be ruled out.* This can be done by deleting rows 1 and 2, *or* columns 1 and 2, or row 1 and column 1, or row 2 and column 2, only thus. In the first case $b^1(q) \equiv b^2(q)$; in the second $a^1(p) \equiv a^2(q)$; in the third $b^2(q) \geqslant b^1(q)$ and $a^2(p) \leqslant a^1(p)$ everywhere, so that firm 2 is always efficient; in the fourth $b^2(q) \leqslant b^1(q)$ and $a^2(p) \geqslant a^1(p)$ everywhere, so that firm 1 is always efficient.

These are the cases already noted in (44)–(47).

Example B: $\# F = 3$

$\mathscr{G}$								$\mathscr{B}$
	$\{1\}$	$\emptyset$	$\emptyset$	$\{1\}$	$\{1\}$	$\emptyset$	$\{1\}$	$\{1\}$
	$\emptyset$	$\{2\}$	$\emptyset$	$\{2\}$	$\emptyset$	$\{2\}$	$\{2\}$	$\{2\}$
	$\emptyset$	$\emptyset$	$\{3\}$	$\emptyset$	$\{3\}$	$\{3\}$	$\{3\}$	$\{3\}$
	$\{1\}$	$\{2\}$	$\emptyset$	$\{1,2\}$	$\{1\}$	$\{2\}$	$\{1,2\}$	$\{1,2\}$
	$\{1\}$	$\emptyset$	$\{3\}$	$\{1\}$	$\{1,3\}$	$\{3\}$	$\{1,3\}$	$\{1,3\}$
	$\emptyset$	$\{2\}$	$\{3\}$	$\{2\}$	$\{3\}$	$\{2,3\}$	$\{2,3\}$	$\{2,3\}$
	$\{1\}$	$\{2\}$	$\{3\}$	$\{1,2\}$	$\{1,3\}$	$\{2,3\}$	$\{1,2,3\}$	$\{1,2,3\}$
$\mathscr{A}$	$\{1\}$	$\{2\}$	$\{3\}$	$\{1,2\}$	$\{1,3\}$	$\{2,3\}$	$\{1,2,3\}$	

Ø's are not allowed and have to be removed by deleting rows and/or columns. This leaves maximal sets of the following types:

Type I:

$\mathcal{A} = \{\{1,2,3\}, \{1,2\}, \{2,3\}, \{1,3\}\}$ all 'large' sets,

$\mathcal{B} = \{\{1,2,3\}, \{1,2\}, \{2,3\}, \{1,3\}\}$ all 'large' sets.

Type II: (example)

$\mathcal{A} = \{\{1,2,3\}, \{1,2\}, \{1,3\}, \{1\}\}$ all sets containing 1,

$\mathcal{B} = \{\{1,2,3\}, \{1,2\}, \{1,3\}, \{1\}\}$ all sets containing 1.

Type III: (example)

$\mathcal{A} = \{\{1,2,3\}, \{1,2\}, \{2,3\}, \{1,3\}, \{1\}, \{2\}\}$ all sets containing 1 *or* 2,

$\mathcal{B} = \{\{1,2,3\}, \{1,2\}\}$ all sets containing 1 *and* 2.

It may be confirmed that these are possible with continuous cost and revenue functions.

REFERENCES

Aczel, J. (1966): *Lectures on Functional Equations and Their Applications* (New York: Academic Press).

Allen, R. G. D., and Bowley, A. L. (1935): *Family Expenditures* (London: P. S. King & Sons Ltd.).

Arrow, K. J. (1974): *The Limits of Organization*, Fels Lectures (New York: Norton).

—— Barankin, E., and Shephard, R. (1951): 'A Note on the Problem of Aggregation', Research Memorandum 674, Rand Corporation, Calif.

Bernouilli, D. (1738): 'Exposition of a New Theory on the Measurement of Risk' (trans. by L. Sommer), *Econometrica*, 22 (1954): 23–36.

Blackorby, C., Davidson, R., and Donaldson, D. (1977): 'A Homiletic Exposition of the Expected Utility Hypothesis', *Economica*, 44: 351–8.

—— Donaldson, D., and Auersperg, M. (1981): 'A New Procedure for the Measurement of Inequality within and among Population Subgroups', *Canadian Journal of Economics*, 14: 665–85.

—— Primont, D., and Russell, R. R. (1978*a*): *Duality, Separability, and Functional Structure* (Amsterdam: North-Holland).

———— (1978*b*): 'An Extension and Alternative Proof of Gorman's Theorem on Perfect Price Aggregation', in W. Eichhorn (ed.), *The Theory of Economic Index Numbers* (Wurzburg: Physica): 109–41.

—— and Schworm, W. (1982): 'Aggregate Investment and Consistent Intertemporal Technologies', *Review of Economic Studies*, 49: 595–614.

———— (1984*a*): 'The Structure of Economies with Aggregate Measures of Capital: A Complete Characterization', *Review of Economic Studies*, 51: 633–50.

———— (1984*b*): 'Consistent Aggregation in Competitive Economies', CORE Discussion Paper 8446, Louvain.

———— (1988): 'The Existence of Input and Output Aggregates in Aggregate Production Functions', *Econometrica*, 56: 613–43.

Bliss, C. J. (1975): *Capital Theory and the Distribution of Income* (Amsterdam: North-Holland).

Deaton, A. (1974): 'A Reconsideration of the Empirical Implications of Additive Preferences', *Economic Journal*, 84: 338–48.

—— and Muellbauer, J. (1980*a*): *Economics and Consumer Behaviour* (Cambridge: Cambridge University Press).

———— (1980*b*): 'An Almost Ideal Demand System', *American Economic Review*, 70: 312–26.

Debreu, G. (1951): 'The Coefficient of Resource Allocation', *Econometrica*, 19: 273–92.

—— (1954): 'Representation of a Preference Ordering by a Numerical Function', in R. Thrall, C. Coombs, and R. Davis (eds.): *Decision Processes* (New York: Wiley), 159–65.

—— (1960): 'Topological Methods in Cardinal Utility Theory', in K. Arrow, S. Karlin, and P. Suppes (eds.), *Mathematical Methods in the Social Sciences* (Stanford, Calif.: Stanford University Press).

Divisia, F. (1928): *Economique Rationelle* (Paris: G. Doin).

Dresch, F. W. (1938): 'Index Numbers and General Economic Equilibrium', *Bulletin of the American Mathematical Society*, 44: 134–40.

—— (1949): 'Continuous Index Numbers and Quantitative Study of the General Economy', *Proceedings of the Berkeley Symposium on Mathematical Statistics and Probability, 1945, 1946* (Los Angeles: University of California Press).

Drèze, J. (1960): 'The Permanent Income Hypothesis: A Methodological Survey'. Paper read at the Naples Meeting of the Econometric Society, 1960.

Eggleston, H. G. (1958): *Convexity* (Cambridge: Cambridge University Press).

Fisher, F. M. (1965): 'Embodied Technical Change and the Existence of an Aggregate Capital Stock', *Review of Economic Studies*, 32: 263–88.

—— (1968*a*): 'Embodied Technology and the Existence of Labour and Output Aggregates', *Review of Economic Studies*, 35: 391–412.

—— (1968*b*): 'Embodied Technology and the Aggregation of Fixed and Movable Capital Goods', *Review of Economic Studies*, 35: 417–28.

—— (1969): 'The Existence of Aggregate Production Functions', *Econometrica*, 37: 553–77.

—— (1982): 'Aggregate Production Functions Revisited: The Mobility of Capital and the Rigidity of Thought', *Review of Economic Studies*, 49: 615–26.

—— (1983): 'On the Simultaneous Existence of Full and Partial Capital Aggregates', *Review of Economic Studies*, 50: 197–208.

Fourgéaud, C., and Nataf, A. (1959): 'Consommation en Prix et Revenu Réels et Théorie des Choix', *Econometrica*, 27: 329–54.

Friedman, M. (1957): *A Theory of the Consumption Function* (Princeton, NJ: Princeton University Press).

Frisch, R. (1959): 'A Complete System of Computing All Direct and Gross Demand Elasticities in a Model with Many Sectors', *Econometrica*, 27: 177–96.

Geary, R. C. (1951): 'A Note on "A Constant Utility Index of the Cost of Living"', *Review of Economic Studies*, 18: 65–6.

Goldman, S. M., and Uzawa, H. (1964): 'A Note on Separability and Demand Analysis', *Econometrica*, 32: 387–98.

Gorman, W. M. (1953*a*): 'Community Preference Fields', *Econometrica*, 21: 63–80. Repr. as Ch. 15 of this volume.

—— (1953*b*): 'Klein Aggregates and Conventional Index Numbers', unpublished paper presented to the Innsbruck Meeting of the Econometric Society, Sept. 1953. Repr. as Ch. 16 of this volume.

—— (1959): 'Separable Utility and Aggregation', *Econometrica*, 27: 469–81. Repr. as Ch. 3 of this volume.

—— (1961): 'On a Class of Preference Fields', *Metroeconomica*, 13: 53–6. Repr. as Ch. 17 of this volume.

—— (1965*a*): 'Capital Aggregation in Vintage Models', unpublished paper presented to the First World Congress of the Econometric Society, Rome, Sept. 1965. Repr. as Ch. 18 of this volume.

—— (1965*b*): 'Consumer Budgets and Price Indices', unpublished typescript. Repr. as Ch. 5 of this volume.

—— (1967*a*): 'Aggregates for Variable Goods', unpublished typescript, London School of Economics, Aug. 1967. Repr. as Ch. 24 of this volume.

—— (1967*b*): 'The Structure of Utility Functions', Technical Report no. 151, Institute for Mathematical Studies in the Social Sciences, Stanford University, Stanford, Calif.

—— (1968*a*): 'Measuring the Quantities of Fixed Factors', in J. N. Wolfe (ed.), *Value, Capital and Growth: Essays in Honour of Sir John Hicks* (Edinburgh: Edinburgh University Press), 141–72. Repr. as Ch. 19 of this volume.

—— (1968*b*): 'Conditions for Additive Separability', *Econometrica*, 36: 605–9. Repr. as Ch. 11 of this volume.

—— (1968*c*): 'The Structure of Utility Functions', *Review of Economic Studies*, 35: 367–90. Repr. as Ch. 12 of this volume.

—— (1970): 'The Concavity of Additive Utility Functions', unpublished typescript, University of North Carolina, Oct. 1970. Repr. as Ch. 9 of this volume.

—— (1971): 'Preference, Revealed Preference and Indifference' in J. S. Chipman *et al.* (eds.), *Preferences, Utility and Demand* (New York: Harcourt Brace Jovanovich Inc.).

—— (1976): 'More About Fixed Factors', unpublished paper presented to the Mathematical Economics Study Group of the SSRC.

—— (1982*a*): 'Aggregation in the Short and Long Run', unpublished typescript, Oxford, Oct. 1982. Repr. as Ch. 25 of this volume.

—— (1982*b*): 'Long-Run Aggregates under Constant Returns', unpublished typescript, Oxford, Oct. 1982. Repr. as Ch. 26 of this volume.

—— (1986): 'Assembling Efficient Organisations?' in W. P. Heller, R. M. Starr, and D. A. Starrett (eds.), *Uncertainty, Information and Communication. Essays in Honor of Kenneth J. Arrow*, iii (Cambridge: Cambridge University Press), 213–28. Repr. as Ch. 23 of this volume.

—— (1990): 'More Measures for Fixed Factors' in G. D. Myles (ed.), *Measurement and Modelling in Economics* (Amsterdam: North-Holland). Repr. as Ch. 21 of this volume.

Green, H. A. J. (1961): 'Direct Additivity and Consumer's Behaviour', *Oxford Economic Papers*, 13: 132–6.

Griliches, Z. (1963): 'The Sources of Measured Productivity Growth: United States Agriculture, 1940–60', *Journal of Political Economy*, 71: 331–46.

Haavelmo, T. (1944): 'Probability Approach in Econometrics', Supplement to *Econometrica.*

Houthakker, H. S. (1952): 'Econometrics of Family Budgets', *Journal of the Royal Statistical Society*, Series A, 115, Pt I: 1–21.

Hurwicz, L. (1952): 'Aggregation in Macro-Economic Models'. Report of Boston meeting of the Econometric Society, *Econometrica*, 20: 489–91.

Jorgenson, D. W., and Griliches, Z. (1967): 'The Explanation of Productivity Change', *Review of Economic Studies*, 34: 249–83.

Kaldor, N. (1939): 'Welfare Propositions of Economics and Interpersonal Comparisons of Utility', *Economic Journal*, 49: 549–52.

Karlin, S. (1959): *Mathematical Methods and Theory in Games, Programming and Economics* (Reading, Mass.: Addison-Wesley).

Klein, L. R. (1946*a*): 'Macroeconomics and the Theory of Rational Behaviour', *Econometrica*, 14: 93–108.

—— (1946*b*): 'Remarks on the Theory of Aggregation', *Econometrica*, 14: 303–12.

Koopmans, T. C. (1960): 'Stationary Ordinal Utility and Impatience', *Econometrica*, 28: 287–309.

Koopmans, T. C. (1966): 'The Structure of Preferences over Time', Cowles Foundation Discussion Paper no. 206, Yale University, Apr.

—— Diamond, P. A., and Williamson, R. E. (1964): 'Stationary Utility and Time Perspective', *Econometrica*, 32: 82–100.

Leontief, W. W. (1947*a*): 'A Note on the Interrelation of Subsets of Independent Variables of a Continuous Function with Continuous First Derivatives', *Bulletin of the American Mathematical Society*, 53: 343–56.

—— (1947*b*): 'Introduction to a Theory of the Internal Structure of Functional Relationships', *Econometrica*, 15: 361–73.

Mak, K-T. (1984): 'Notes on Separable Preferences', *Journal of Economic Theory*, 33: 309–21.

Malinvaud, E. (1956): 'L'Agrégation dans les Modèles Economiques', *Cahiers du Seminare d'Econométrie*, 5: 69–146.

Malmquist, S. (1953): 'Index Numbers and Indifference Surfaces', *Trabajos de Estadistica*, 4: 209–41.

May, K. (1946): 'The Aggregation Problem for a One-Industry Model', *Econometrica*, 14: 285–98.

Muellbauer, J. (1975): 'Aggregation, Income Distribution and Consumer Demand', *Review of Economic Studies*, 42: 525–43.

—— (1976): 'Community Preferences and the Representative Consumer', *Econometrica*, 44: 979–99.

Nataf, A. (1948): 'Sur la Possibilité de la Construction de Certains Macromodeles', *Econometrica*, 16: 232–44.

—— (1967): 'Possibilités d'Agrégation de Fonctions de Production à Variables Capital et Main d'Oeuvre', *Review of Economic Studies*, 34: 219–26.

Pearce, I. F. (1961): 'An Exact Method of Consumer Demand Analysis', *Econometrica*, 29: 499–516.

Pigou, A. C. (1910): 'A Method of Determining the Numerical Value of Elasticities of Demand', *Economic Journal*, 21: 636–40.

Pollak, R. A. (1971): 'Additive Utility Functions and Linear Engel Curves', *Review of Economic Studies*, 38: 401–14.

—— (1972): 'Generalized Separability', *Econometrica*, 40: 431–53.

Pu, S. S. (1946): 'A Note on Macroeconomics', *Econometrica*, 14: 299–302.

Ramsey, F. P. (1931): 'Truth and Probability' in *The Foundations of Mathematics and Other Logical Essays* (London: Paul, Trench & Trubner).

Richter, M. K. (1966): 'Invariance Axioms and Economic Indexes', *Econometrica*, 34: 739–55.

Samuelson, P. A. (1952), 'Probability, Utility, and the Independence Axiom', *Econometrica*, 20: 670–8.

—— (1956): 'Social Indifference Curves', *Quarterly Journal of Economics*, 70: 1–22.

—— (1965), 'A Theory of Induced Innovation along Kennedy–Weisäcker Lines', *Review of Economics and Statistics*, 47: 343–56.

Sargan, J. D. (1957): 'The Danger of Oversimplification', *Bulletin of the Oxford University Institute of Statistics*, 19: 171–8.

Savage, L. J. (1954): *The Foundations of Statistics* (New York: Wiley).

Shephard, R. W. (1953): *Cost and Production Functions* (Princeton, NJ: Princeton University Press).

—— (1970): *Theory of Cost and Production Function* (Princeton, NJ: Princeton University Press).

Simmons, P. (1978): 'A Note on Budgeting, Separability, and Generalized Separability', *Econometrica*, 46: 455–8.

Solow, R. M. (1957): 'Technical Change and the Aggregate Production Function', *Review of Economics and Statistics*, 39: 312–20.

—— (1964): 'Capital, Labor, and Income in Manufacturing', in *The Behavior of Income Shares.* Studies in Income and Wealth, National Bureau of Economic Research, 27 (Princeton, NJ: Princeton University Press), 101–28.

Sono, M. (1971): 'The Effect of Price Changes on the Demand and Supply of Separable Goods', *International Economic Review*, 2: 239–71.

Stigum, B. P. (1967): 'On Certain Problems of Aggregation', *International Economic Review*, 8: 349–67.

Stoker, T. M. (1982): 'The Use of Cross Section Data to Characterize Macro Functions', *Journal of the American Statistical Association*, 77: 369–80.

—— (1984): 'Completeness, Distribution Restrictions and the Form of Aggregate Functions', *Econometrica*, 52: 887–907.

Stone, J. R. N. (1954): 'Linear Expenditure Systems and Demand Analysis: An Application to the Pattern of British Demand', *Economic Journal*, 64: 511–27.

Strotz, R. H. (1957): 'The Empirical Implications of a Utility Tree', *Econometrica*, 25: 269–80.

—— (1959): 'The Utility Tree: A Correction and Further Appraisal', *Econometrica*, 27: 482–8.

Theil, H., (1953): 'A Statistical Approach to the Problem of Aggregation'. Report of Cambridge meeting of the Econometric Society, *Econometrica*, Jan. 1953.

—— (1954): *Linear Aggregation of Economic Relations* (Amsterdam: North-Holland).

—— (1975): *Theory and Measurement of Consumer Demand*, i (Amsterdam: North-Holland).

—— (1976): *Theory and Measurement of Consumer Demand*, ii (Amsterdam: North-Holland).

Von Neuman, J., and Morgenstern, O. (1944): *Theory of Games and Economic Behavior* (Princeton, NJ: Princeton University Press).

Wald, A. (1947): *Sequential Analysis* (New York: John Wiley & Sons).

—— (1950): *Statistical Decision Functions* (New York: John Wiley & Sons).

Whitaker, J. K. (1966): 'Vintage Capital Models and Econometric Production Functions', *Review of Economic Studies*, 33: 1–18.

The manufacturer's authorised representative in the EU for product safety is Oxford University Press España S.A. of el Parque Empresarial San Fernando de Henares, Avenida de Castilla, 2 – 28830 Madrid (www.oup.es/en or product.safety@oup.com). OUP España S.A. also acts as importer into Spain of products made by the manufacturer.

www.ingramcontent.com/pod-product-compliance
Lightning Source LLC
LaVergne TN
LVHW011858200926
848484LV00002B/480

* 9 7 8 0 1 9 8 2 8 5 2 1 2 *